JOHN

Also by James Buchan

FICTION

A Parish of Rich Women
Davy Chadwick
Slide
Heart's Journey in Winter
High Latitudes: A Romance
A Good Place to Die
The Gate of Air

NON-FICTION

Jeddah: Old and New
Frozen Desire: An Enquiry into the Meaning of Money
Capital of the Mind: How Edinburgh Changed the World
Adam Smith and the Pursuit of Perfect Liberty
Days of God: The Revolution in Iran and Its Consequences

James Buchan

JOHN LAW

A Scottish Adventurer of the Eighteenth Century

MACLEHOSE PRESS
QUERCUS · LONDON

First published in Great Britain in 2018 by MacLehose Press
This paperback edition published in 2019 by

MacLehose Press
An imprint of Quercus Editions Ltd
Carmelite House
50 Victoria Embankment
London EC4Y 0DZ

An Hachette UK company

Maps by William Donohue

A CIP catalogue record for this book is available
from the British Library

ISBN (MMP) 978 1 84866 608 5
ISBN (Ebook) 978 1 84866 607 8

10 9 8 7 6 5 4 3

Designed and typeset in Cycles by Libanus Press, Marlborough
Printed and bound in Great Britain by Clays Ltd, Elcograf S.p.A.

FSC www.fsc.org MIX Paper from responsible sources FSC® C104740

Papers used by Quercus are from well-managed forests and other responsible sources

CONTENTS

PARIS
c. 1720
Drawn from the maps of
Jaillot (1713)
and
Delagrive (1728)
To Chaillot
1
2
3
4
5
6
7
8
9
10
11
12
13
14
15
16
24
26
27
28
29
30
31

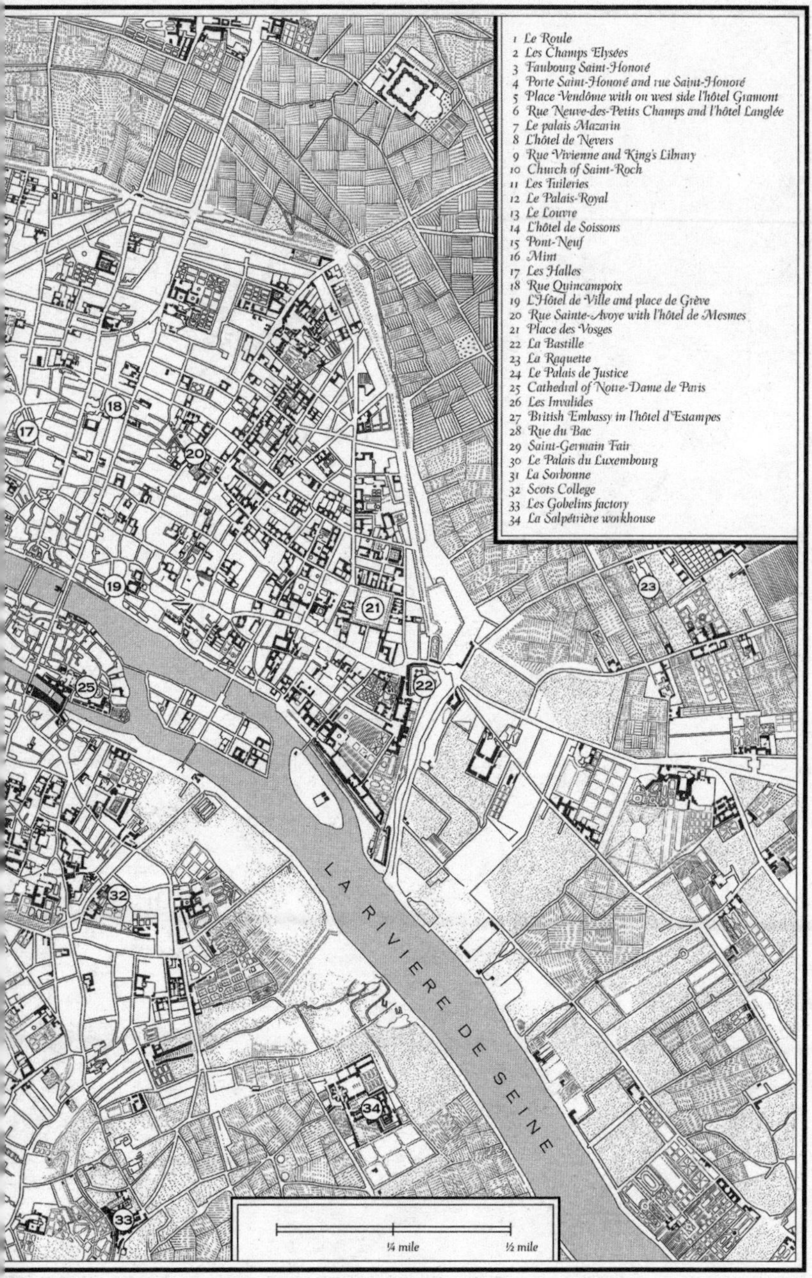
1 Le Roule
2 Les Champs Elysées
3 Faubourg Saint-Honoré
4 Porte Saint-Honoré and rue Saint-Honoré
5 Place Vendôme with on west side l'hôtel Gramont
6 Rue Neuve-des-Petits Champs and l'hôtel Langlée
7 Le palais Mazarin
8 L'hôtel de Nevers
9 Rue Vivienne and King's Library
10 Church of Saint-Roch
11 Les Tuileries
12 Le Palais-Royal
13 Le Louvre
14 L'hôtel de Soissons
15 Pont-Neuf
16 Mint
17 Les Halles
18 Rue Quincampoix
19 L'Hôtel de Ville and place de Grève
20 Rue Sainte-Avoye with l'hôtel de Mesmes
21 Place des Vosges
22 La Bastille
23 La Raquette
24 Le Palais de Justice
25 Cathedral of Notre-Dame de Paris
26 Les Invalides
27 British Embassy in l'hôtel d'Estampes
28 Rue du Bac
29 Saint-Germain Fair
30 Le Palais du Luxembourg
31 La Sorbonne
32 Scots College
33 Les Gobelins factory
34 La Salpêtrière workhouse
18
17
20
19
21
23
22
25
32
34
33
LA RIVIERE DE SEINE
¼ mile
½ mile

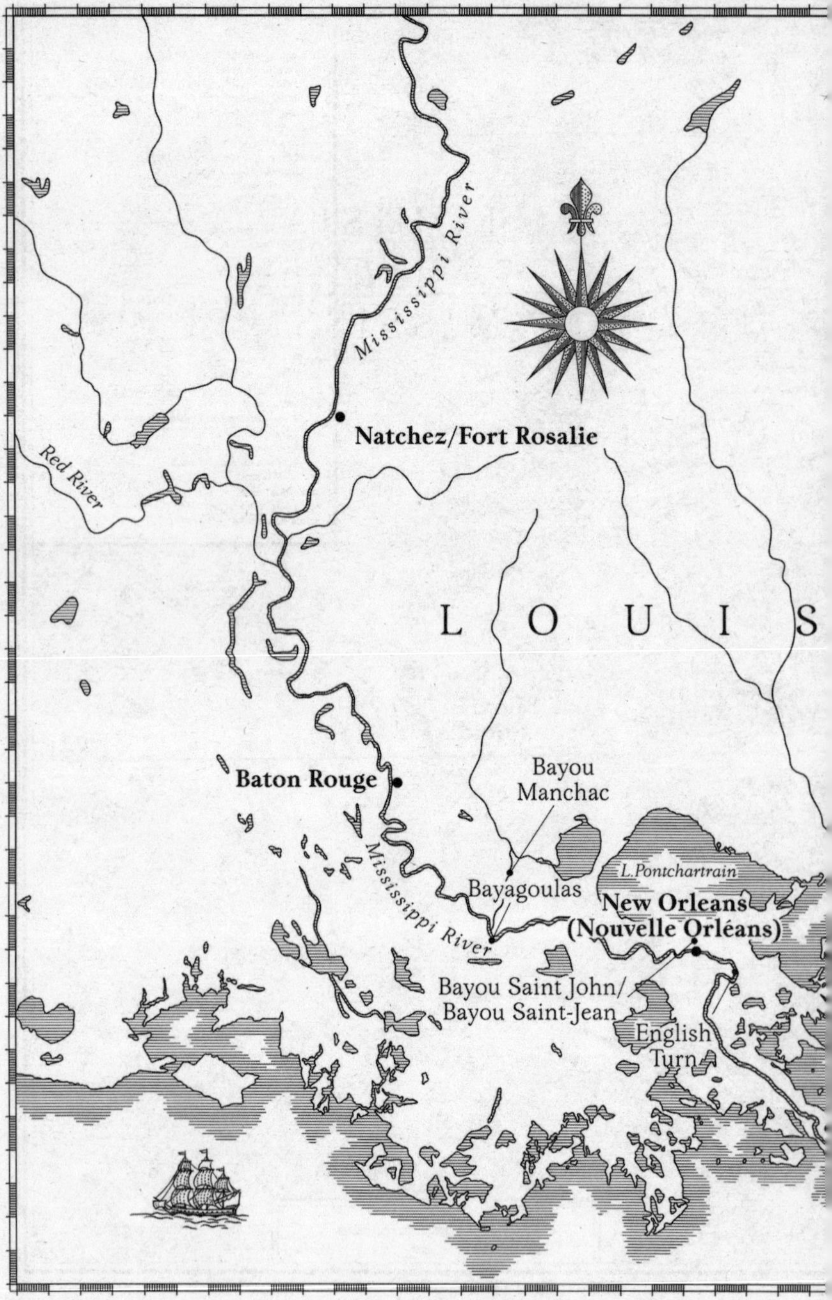
Mississippi River
Natchez/Fort Rosalie
Red River
L O U I S
Baton Rouge
Bayou
Manchac
L.Pontchartrain
Bayagoulas
New Orleans
(Nouvelle Orléans)
Mississippi River
Bayou Saint John/
Bayou Saint-Jean
English
Turn

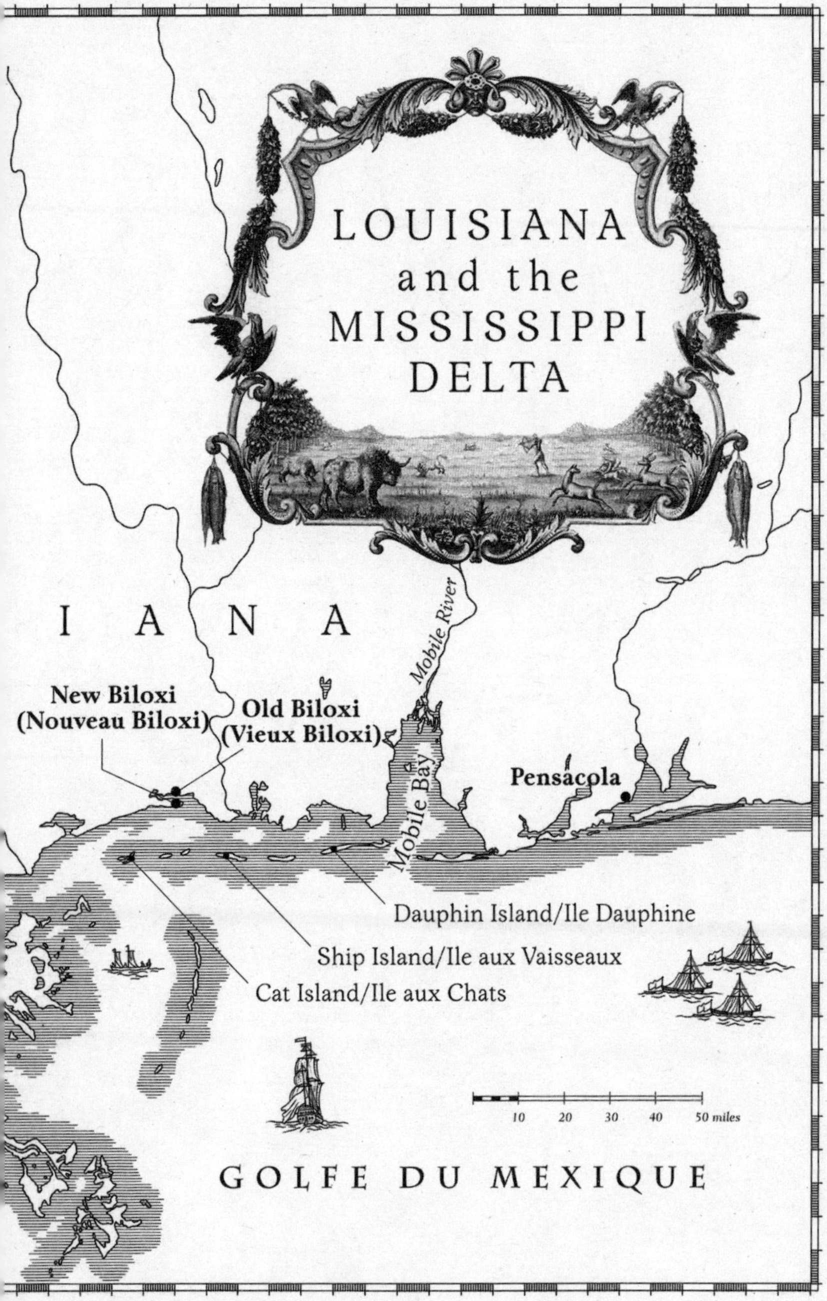

LOUISIANA
and the
MISSISSIPPI
DELTA
I A N A
Mobile River
New Biloxi
(Nouveau Biloxi)
Old Biloxi
(Vieux Biloxi)
Mobile Bay
Pensacola
Dauphin Island/Ile Dauphine
Ship Island/Ile aux Vaisseaux
Cat Island/Ile aux Chats
10 20 30 40 50 miles
GOLFE DU MEXIQUE

AUTHOR'S NOTE

In John Law's lifetime, two principal calendars were in use in western Europe. The Roman Catholic countries as well as the Netherlands, Denmark, the German states and Switzerland used the Gregorian or New-Style calendar, while England, Ireland and Scotland persisted with the Julian or Old-Style calendar, which was eleven days in retard. Colonies used the calendar of the metropolis.

The date given in the text is always the date current at the place in which the incident occurs or the letter is written. Where there may be confusion, as in correspondence between Paris and London, or on shipboard, two dates are shown in this form: October 11/22, 1720. The Gregorian is always the later of the two dates.

In Great Britain and Ireland, the new year began on March 25. In the text, it is assumed the year began on January 1. In the notes, letters dated from those countries in the winter months are shown thus: A to B, January 1, 1720 [i.e. 1721].

C'est bien domage quil nest pas que bornee letandue enfinie de son imaginations car il a de grande calitee il est perdue par un trop grand hidee de luymemes.

(It's a shame really that he did not once place limits on his boundless imagination for he has something great about him. He has perished for too grand a conception of himself.)

ELEANOR DE MÉZIÈRES

CHAPTER ONE

Lotteries and Other Games

Nota: seijds een Schotsman van Edenburg te wesen.
(Note: Is said to be a Scotsman from Edinburgh.)

BURGOMASTERS OF THE HAGUE

The marquis d'Effiat, Charleval and Toucy, comte de Tancarville and Valençay, chamberlain and hereditary constable of Normandy, baron de La Rivière, seigneur de Gerponville, Saint-Suplix, Roissy, Orcher and Guermantes and proprietor of Arkansas in the New World, also de Ferry, Dujardin, Annington, Wilmot, Hamilton, Gardiner, Hamden and, in the Jacobite cipher, 888.75.1804, was born in the year 1671 in the Parliament Close of Edinburgh, capital of the Kingdom of Scotland.

He was baptised John in the church of St Giles, a few feet from his cradle, on April 21 of that year.[1]

His father was William Law, master goldsmith. His mother was Jean Campbell. John was their first son to survive. In all, William Law and Jean Campbell had twelve children, of whom four died in childhood and were buried in Greyfriars churchyard in an angle of the city walls to the south.[2]

In the year of John Law's birth, Edinburgh was a crowded stone town of some 30,000 inhabitants. Described in a debate in the

Parliament at that time as "the most unwholesome and unpleasant town in Scotland",[3] Edinburgh clung within its defensive walls to the debris of an extinct volcano. A broad street ran down a mile from the castle in the west to the palace of Holyroodhouse in the east and the aristocratic suburbs of the Canongate. To the north and south, the town halted at precipices. About halfway down the High Street on the south side stood the gothic High Church of St Giles, and behind it a square or close in front of the Parliament House of Scotland. It was against the south wall of the church that William Law probably had his workshop, and there, above the shop or in a tenement nearby, John Law was born.[4]

The Scotland of that time was in ferment. In the sixteenth century, the Roman Catholic Church in western Europe disintegrated, and reformed or Protestant faiths became established in Switzerland and Bohemia, the Baltic territories, parts of Germany and France, the Netherlands, Denmark, Sweden, England and Scotland.

Though united under a single crown since 1603, when James VI of the Scottish ruling house of Stuart succeeded Elizabeth on the thrones of England and Ireland, those countries were at odds over religious practice and how their Churches should be governed. The Church of Scotland, which was Presbyterian in character and drew its inspiration from John Calvin's Geneva, rejected the Anglican institution of bishops. On such matters hung the salvation of the whole world.

In the course of the 1630s, the animosity of the two Protestant Churches broke out into warfare. The Presbyterians objected to the wish of King Charles I and Archbishop William Laud of Canterbury to impose on Scottish congregations the English prayer book. In 1638, an open-air meeting in Greyfriars Churchyard launched a National Covenant to protect the Presbyterian Church. The consequence was a war that engulfed England, Scotland and Ireland, and in 1649 cost King Charles his head.

The regicides, under Lord Protector Oliver Cromwell, established a republic or Commonwealth in which Scotland lost its independent Church, its laws and parliament. After Cromwell's death, the triple monarchy was restored in 1660 under Charles's son, Charles II, and Scotland recovered its institutions, but that brought no peace to the Church. Many Presbyterian ministers, particularly in the south-west of Scotland, rejected the authority of bishops over parish elders or kirk sessions and took their flock into the fields. One of the witnesses at John Law's baptism, his grandfather Mr John Law, who succeeded his own father as minister at Neilston, near Paisley in the west of Scotland, was turned out of his parish in 1649 and may have decided that the reformed Church was too precarious a living for his sons and grandsons.[5]

Goldsmithing in Edinburgh was a profession protected by craft exclusions and the patronage of the town, Church and Parliament. To align the practice of the Protestant Churches in his kingdoms, King James I/VI sponsored an Act of the Scots Parliament in May, 1617 to oblige Scottish parish churches to use "bassines" "lavoiris" (jugs) and "coupes" for the two sacraments, Baptism and Holy Communion, in the manner of English parishes.[6] That law made the fortunes of several master goldsmiths in Edinburgh.

William was apprenticed goldsmith just after his brother John in 1650,[7] and received the right or freedom to practise the craft in March 1662. William Law's "assay" or masterpiece consisted of "ane silver coupe with ane cover graven and ane voupe": that is, an engraved silver cup and cover and a wedding ring.[8] About that time, William set up shop, at a rent paid to the town of £40 Scots per year or about three pounds and six shillings sterling.[9]

He had married, on the day after Christmas of 1661, Violet or Violat, the nineteen-year-old daughter of a brother-goldsmith, George Cleghorne, and Helen Wilson.[10] The marriage did not long last. Violet died in giving birth to a son, named after her father, and was buried in Greyfriars on October 18, 1662.[11]

William mourned his wife for a year and then, on October 22, 1663, at St Cuthbert's Church under the castle, married for a second time.[12] No doubt he needed a mother for the infant George. His second wife was Jean Campbell. Jean or Jeane, who was baptised on August 13, 1639, was one of four daughters of James Campbell, a merchant of Edinburgh, and his wife Isobell Orr. All four girls made good marriages in or around the Parliament Close. Agnes, the oldest, married Andrew or Andro Anderson, appointed in 1671 the King's printer in Scotland; Jean married William Law, master goldsmith; Isobell the merchant John Melvill; and Beatrix Archibald Hislope, bookseller in the Close.

They were forceful women in the old Scots style. As widows, Agnes, Jean and Beatrix managed their husbands' businesses. Agnes became notorious for her ruthlessness. After her husband's death in 1676, to all intents insolvent, she enforced his monopoly of printing Bibles, New Testaments, Acts of Parliament and other authorised texts and defended it in the Scottish courts for nearly forty years, though her productions were riddled with blasphemous misprints.

Since every literate family in Scotland had been required since 1581 by Act of Parliament to possess a Bible and psalter, hers was a rewarding business and she died in 1716 as Lady Roseburn with a fortune of £78,197 Scots or about £6,500 sterling.[13] Her principal rival, James Watson, wrote of her printing works in the College Yards: "In fine, nothing was study'd but gaining of Money by printing Bibles at any rate, which she knew none other durst do, and that no Body could want [was permitted to be without] them."[14] She is said single-handed to have postponed the Scottish Enlightenment fifty years.

Those four women and their husbands hung together. Archibald Hislope and John Melvill stood witness at John Law's baptism. If they had a recreation, it was a cause at law.

At his first wife's death in 1662, William had silver and gold stock in the shop of 700 merks or £466 Scots, and an estate net of debt of £260 Scots or £22 sterling.[15] With Jean Campbell's help, he prospered. He took his first apprentice, John Calquhoun, in 1666,[16] and in 1670 rented a second shop from the town to accommodate his expanding trade.[17] In 1675 and 1676, he served as deacon of the Incorporation of Goldsmiths or leader of the craft.

There is a picture of an Edinburgh goldsmith's shop of the seventeenth century. In 1624, George Heriot, the third of his line to be admitted to the Incorporation in 1588, left some £24,000 sterling to endow a charitable orphanage just outside the city walls which exists as George Heriot's School to this day. A sandstone frieze of about 1630 above the north door of the school shows the interior of a goldsmith's shop from the generation before William Law.

Heriot is shown working his bellows before a furnace. Beside it is an anvil. To the right is a work bench, with two scalloped work positions with leather bags beneath to catch the silver scrapings, and above it a tool bar of hammers, pincers and dies. To stand before this antiquated frieze, and then think of John Law's plans for the Paris stock exchange and his colony of Louisiana is to feel the horizons recede and a new world open up to view. In no other life of the time, except that of Captain James Cook in his dormitory in Whitby, does a small beginning become so enlarged.

There survive from William Law's shop communion cups and baptismal basins at the kirks or churches of North Leith, Aberlady, Ballingry, Culross, Gamrie, Glencorse, Kilwilling, Kinglassie, Lauder, Midcalder, Stirling St Ninians, Salton and Yester.[18] His finest sacred work is the Murray Cup, presented by Anne Murray, Lady Halkett, to the College of St Leonards at St Andrews University in 1681 in gratitude for her son's good report from the regents or professors. It is eight inches tall, eight inches across the bowl and five inches across the foot. This communion cup, made by William and his apprentices between 1679 and 1681, John Law would have seen and handled.

William's profane pieces pass at high prices through the saleroom. In the course of the wars of mid-century, Covenanting committees had power to gather in "all siler worke and gold worke in Scotland" outside the churches and turn it into coin to pay soldiers and munitioners. As John Law was to write in the only one of his works printed in his lifetime, *Money and Trade Considered*, "The plate at the restauration [1660] was inconsiderable, having been called in a little time before."[19]

The plate melted down had to be replaced. William's hallmark, which consists of a crown and the initials "WL", can be found on table pieces such as the stemmed shallow dishes known as tazzas, the bowls called porringers, two-handled cups (quaitches) and the little silver spoons with their pairs of initials that bridal couples liked to order on a trip to town. There is also an invoice, to one David Pringill in 1679, where in return for 37 ounces of "broken silver" and £25 14s. Scots in cash, William and his apprentices made a watch-key, a ring setting, a plain ring, a dozen flowered spoons and a "Shewgar Castor".[20] By 1705, Scotland's treasure of profane silver was estimated at £150,000 sterling.[21]

At some date no later than 1674, William followed George Heriot into the business of banking. Just downhill from the lock-up goldsmiths' workshops or "buithes" against the walls of St Giles, the town's trade was conducted at the Mercat or Market Cross. The goldsmiths were needed to assay or verify the muddle of Scots, English, Dutch and other foreign coins that turned up in trade, to provide safe deposit for coins, jewellery or bullion, and to lend their own money or clients' deposits at interest to finance agriculture, commerce or simple expenditure.

Lending, even for the small sums involved, was more remunerative than smithing. According to John Law himself, the "fashion" or what the goldsmith charged as his fee over and above the precious metal in a piece amounted to a sixth, or a 20 per cent premium.[22] William Law lent money at between 6 and 8 per cent per year. He was also engaged, from at least 1676, in victualling drovers to take Highland black cattle to England for the London beef market. In an inventory of assets later drawn up for John Law, there is a debt remaining from that year from two Highlanders, Alexander McMilland and Donald McNeill, "drobers", of £1,000 Scots.[23]

By 1681, William had outgrown his shops. On May 26 of that year, he signed a contract with Robert Mylne or Milne, the Master Mason to King Charles II, and Andrew Patersone, former deacon of the Incorporation of Wrights in Edinburgh, to build a "tenement and fabric" (workshop) on the "east side of the entry to the Parliament House". In the ashlar building, with six storeys and a basement on the Close side and two basements on the slope, William was to have two shops, with iron-bound doors and windows of Newcastle glass, well-seasoned wainscoting, seasoned deals for flooring, chimneys and cellars. As his share of the enterprise, William was to pay £334 and twelve shillings sterling in four instalments.[24]

Mylne was the principal developer in Edinburgh of that period. The "great stone tenement and land" was damaged on February 3, 1700, when fire broke out in the closet window of a certain John Buchan at the top of the Meal Market, and fanned by a wind from the south-west, engulfed the east side of Parliament Close. The high-flying kirk ministers saw that as judgment on the wicked men who dared to raise such "Babels".[25] The building was destroyed by a second fire in 1824, but one of Mylne and Patersone's schemes from 1690, known as Milne's Court, a small open square of six- and seven-storey tenements on the north side of the Lawnmarket above St Giles, exists to this day. Those apartments, now fit only for college students, were none the less an advance on their predecessors and commemorate both the prosperity and overcrowding of Edinburgh at this time.

As William's business grew, so did his family. His first child with Jean, Isobell, died in 1664 and was followed to Greyfriars burying yard the next year by his son by Violet Cleghorne, George. Of the surviving children, Agnes was born in 1666, Jean in 1669, John (1671), Andrew (1673), William (1675), Robert (1678), Lilias (1680) and Hugh (1682).

John Law's childhood passed under a pall of religious anxiety. On May 3, 1679, a band of Covenanters waylaid the coach of James Sharp, Archbishop of St Andrews, on the road from Edinburgh and assassinated him. Rebellion spread across lowland Scotland. King Charles II sent north his illegitimate son, the Duke of Monmouth, who defeated the Covenanters in a pitched battle at Bothwell Bridge in Lanarkshire in June. To enforce royal and bishops' rule in Scotland, Charles in October despatched his brother and heir, James, Duke of York, to Edinburgh as Lord High Commissioner.

James had converted to the Roman Catholic faith and that May a bill was introduced in the English parliament to exclude him for that reason from succession to the throne. The crisis gave rise to the aboriginal division in British politics between the exclusionist Whigs and loyalist Tories, which survived, in ever-changing complexion, for two centuries. King Charles dissolved Parliament and sent his troublesome brother north, but James was no more welcome among the Presbyterians.

Robert Law, a kinsman of William's and minister at Easter Kirkpatrick in Dunbarton, reported that on Christmas Day, 1680, the College boys at Edinburgh made an effigy of the Pope, his belly stuffed with gunpowder, carried it in procession up Blackfriars'

Wynd and burned it in the high town, which "the Duke of York took ill, being then in Abbay of Halyrudhous".[26] The appearance of two blazing comets over the town, Kirch's or C/1680V1 that December, 1680 and Halley's in August, 1682, compounded the anxiety as being, in Mr Robert's words, "prodigious of great alterations, and of great judgements on these lands and nations for our sins".[27]

James did succeed on his brother's death in 1685 to the throne as James II of England and VII of Scotland, but that provoked a rebellion in Scotland by the Earl of Argyll, which was suppressed. James was ejected three years later by a conspiracy of English parliamentarians and the Dutch stadtholder or chief magistrate, William of Orange-Nassau, who was married to James's Protestant daughter Mary. James's adherents, who followed him into exile in France or lay low in their shops or on their estates, became known as "Jacobites" after the Latin for James, Iacobus. Many families hedged their bets, with one branch opting for James and another for William.

Some authors say that John Law attended the Edinburgh High School. This claim appears in a nineteenth-century history of the school[28] and cannot be true. In the two hundred or so of John Law's letters seen by this author, as well as his manuscript memorials to princes and parliaments, there is not one word of Latin or scripture. In his writings in French, Law makes small mistakes that he would not have made had he known the Latin grammar underlying that language. John Law could not have attended the best grammar school in the British Isles without learning something of the humanities.

On September 9, 1679, at the age of eight, he was apprenticed to his father.[29] Unlike his younger brothers Andrew, apprenticed in 1694, and William (1703), John never passed master or received a hallmark. It was not until October, 1719 that the Town Council granted its prodigal son the freedom of Edinburgh, together with a Burgess Ticket in a gold box costing £127 16s. 3d. sterling and a giddy letter.[30] At some time in his childhood and youth, John Law contracted smallpox, which was by no means unusual.

In the summer of 1683, William bought the estate of Lauriston and Randleston on the estuary or firth of the River Forth just to the north of Edinburgh. The seller was Margaret Dalgliesh, daughter of Robert Dalgliesh, a lawyer who had served both King and Commonwealth, and Jean Douglas. In the deeds, which were confirmed by King Charles II and registered on August 10, 1683, William provided that after his death and that of Jean, who would enjoy the rents during her lifetime, the estate was to go to his eldest surviving son, John Law. There is no mention of the sum paid.

The estate consisted of an oblong stone tower house, built at the end of the sixteenth century by Sir Archibald Napier of Murchieston or Merchiston and by then inconvenient and old-fashioned, and fields and pasture stretching down to the shore of the Firth. The house, which was given to the city of Edinburgh in 1926, has been much altered over the years. To see it as William Law and Jean Campbell saw it in June 1683 it is necessary to screen out a nineteenth-century wing and garden, and some municipal paraphernalia, while preserving the cattle in the pasture and the redshanks whistling from the Firth. The ghost of Scots wizardry haunts the stone, composed of a Napier horoscope on the south front, an anagram Dalglish and Douglas over the south door, and a secret chamber reached by a tiny stair.

In a survey of the parish of Cramond conducted in 1630, the fields of Lauriston were valued at 142 bolls of bear and 50 bolls of oats and oatmeal or about 20 to 25 tons of grain.[31] (Bear is an ancient variety of low-yielding barley still grown by crofters in the Highlands and Western Isles of Scotland.)

In buying the estate, William did not abandon business. The

castle bears no trace of William or John Law or Jean Campbell, and there is no record that any of them lived there. William had few months to live anywhere. On July 25, 1683, "being necessarly called to goe furth of this kingdom", William drew up his will and set off from Edinburgh.

John Fairley, who was commissioned by the owners of Lauriston Castle in the early twentieth century to collect materials on the Laws, surmised that William travelled to Paris for surgery to remove kidney stones, a disease that by reason of the high-protein and low-fibre diet of the age was prevalent. A dynasty of barber-surgeons in Paris, the Colot or Collot family, had for a century specialised in an operation to cut out calculi from the urinary tract, and surgery was also offered at the poor hospitals of the hôtel Dieu and Charité. The fame of the Collots drew patients from all over Europe, including Scotland. In the Gordon Papers in the Register House in Edinburgh, there is a letter of 1709 in which one Robert Colinson asks Father Lewis Inese or Innes, the superior of the Scots College, the old Roman Catholic seminary at the university of the Sorbonne in Paris, to give the bearer Lord Huntly "that rare and wonderfull gravell stone left by me at your Colledge tuentie years agoe".[32]

If Fairley's is a true conjecture, the operation was a failure. In the register of William's testament, made on August 15, 1684, William is described as "deceast in the moneth of [blank] 1683 years in the Kingdome of ffrance". Though a Protestant, he was still a Scot and was buried at the Scots College. There are impulses to action that never reach the conscious mind, and it may be that John Law was drawn to Paris by his father's tomb. He later made a donation to the College of fifty of his company shares, worth at their peak more than £30,000 sterling or many millions today.[33]

In his will before leaving Edinburgh, William charged Jean as principal guardian (*tutrix sine qua non*) "during her widowitie" and six tutors "to uplift the soumes and @rents* [capital and interest] due to my said eldest sone John, and to educat him and the remanent [remaining] children at schools and trades as they shall think most convenient." The tutors comprised William's brother John, goldsmith; Isobel's husband Melvill; Beatrix's second husband Robert Currie, stationer; Jean's cousin Robert Campbell; and the attorney Hugh Maxwell of Dalswintoun.[34]

The property included the insight and plenishing (furniture and stock) of the shop and house, valued at £3,333 Scots, and bonds, mortgages and invoices, including arrears of interest, of £25,832 Scots, making a total of £29,165 or about £2,500 in the sterling of the period. The loans, at annual rates of from 6 to 7.5 per cent, were to the best-known families and most solid risks in Scotland, including the Duchess of Hamilton, the Marquesses of Douglas and Huntly, the Earls of Argyll, Annandale, Atholl, Balcarres, Breadalbane, Dundonald, Forfar, Kintore, Roxburgh and Seaforth, the Goldsmiths' Incorporation (1000 merks) and the towns of Jedburgh and Cupar. The principal debtor was Charles, Earl of Mar, owing 7,000 merks principal or about £390 sterling. William had become a substantial banker, among the most substantial in town outside the high nobility, and a prosperous man. John Law was served heir to his father on September 25, 1684.[35]

Jean did not marry again. A new husband would gain rights over her property and might interfere with the children's estate. Her widowed sister Agnes, who remarried in 1681, obliged her new husband, Patrick Tailfer, to forgo his husband's right or *ius mariti* over "the printing irons, and other estate" in return for a dowry of £10,000 Scots, and still had to go to court against his creditors.[36] After Beatrix died in 1687, her children's tutors sued her second husband, Robert Currie, for mismanaging their inheritance.[37]

* "@rents" is an old-fashioned Scottish Secretary abbreviation for "annual rents" or what we call interest.

William Law's goldsmithing fell to his second son Andrew, then apprenticed to his uncle John Law. In 1687, a contract with Mylne and Patersone provided Andrew with the south half of the fourth storey of the "new great stone tenement", with five rooms and a cellar below the scale stairs.[38] As for the banking business, Jean was not above having a debtor consigned to the Old Tolbooth prison beside St Giles's kirk.[39] In the nine years after her husband's death, she doubled the loan book, both in her own name[40] and that of her eldest son John.[41]

That son was proving a handful. The historian Robert Wodrow, who wrote an account of the persecution of the Presbyterians under the Stuarts, came across the young John Law at school in the west of Scotland in 1683 or 1684. After Bothwell Bridge in 1679, Wodrow's father James, a candidate for the ministry and a strong Presbyterian, had taken refuge in his native village of Eaglesham, about ten miles south of Glasgow, "a very retired corner", where his family joined him in 1680. The minister of the village, James Hamilton, who was permitted to preach under the so-called Act of Indulgence of 1669, managed a small grammar school.

"I mind [remember]," Robert Wodrow wrote in a life of his father, "among the scholars at that school, there was one about the 1683 or 4, John Law, son to a goldsmith at Edinburgh, whom his father sent to Eglishame, both to be removed from the temptations of Edinburgh, and to be under the care of Mr Hamilton, who was nearly related to him, and to be under my father's inspection who was pretty nearly related to him."[42]

Though Wodrow was a small child in 1683, there is reason to trust his recollection. On April 4, 1684, John Law's elder sister, Agnes, married Hamilton's only son, John, who had just been admitted as a Writer to the Signet or attorney at law in Edinburgh.[43] John Law was by then about thirteen years old, an age at which in the next generation the philosopher David Hume was leaving

Edinburgh University. It is strange to think of this hulking youth in the manse schoolroom with the five-year-old Robert Wodrow. William Law, or Jean Campbell, must have been desperate.

John Law's mental ornaments as a man, his grasp of mathematics, music and painting, his fluent French and Italian, and his good manners, were not to be acquired in the Scotland of the late seventeenth century. He did learn to write. As an adult, John Law wrote in the modern Italic script, but his writing, though legible, retains some peculiarities of the Scottish Secretary hand taught in the previous century: an *e* that resembles the Greek theta, and a superscript mark like a first-quarter moon or reversed *c* to distinguish a *u* from an *n*.

In 1686, back in Edinburgh, John reached his legal puberty and agreed to accept Jean as his curatrix or guardian. Then, at the end of 1687 or the beginning of 1688, mother and son quarrelled so comprehensively that the sixteen-year-old John left home or Jean turned him out of doors. John refused to sign receipts for payments of interest on the loans and mortgages Jean had out in his name. He also sued her under a so-called Writ of Aliment, that then and now in Scotland requires a parent or guardian to support a child. So much can be deduced from Jean's rejoinder or protest to the Court of Council and Session, the highest civil court in Scotland.[44] This is the voice of Jean Campbell:

> Jean Campbell, relict of the deceast William Law Goldsmith burgess of Edinburgh and curatrix [guardian] to his children and whith whom they are appointed by the father to remayne in famillie with me ther mother during their minoritie to be educat and alliemented [supported]: that where John Law my eldest sone without any offence or provocatione has laitely deserted my famlily, contrair to the will of his father and as I am informed has given in ane petitione to your

Lordships craving ane aliement to be modified by your Lordships to be payed to him by me

Against which it is humbly represented that therecan be no aliement modified or payed to him by me

1mo/ because I am willing to aliement him my selfe in my familly with the rest of his brethrene and sisters as I have done hitherto since the father deceise [father's decease] and which is appoynted by his fathers last will

2o/ it is most just that he should returne to my familly, not only, because of his said father's will but also that I may have the better opportunitie to oversee his behaviour night and day, that it be blameless and deceint. which is my great designe according to the trust repoised in and by his father And the trew cause of his deserting of my familly, was because of my motherlly reprehending him for bydeing late out at night and goeing to the Lotterie and other Ghames And

3o/ ther can be no aliement allowed by the mother to him because he being yet minor and not yett seventeen years and she his Curatrix and he reffuses to subscrybe recepts with me aither for @rents or stock so that I cannot lift money to pay aither aliement to him or the rest of the childrene as instruments taken upon his said reffusal produced heare. Theirefore I humbly beseech your Lordships to take the premises to your serious consideratione and to reffuse the said John Law his said petitions and to ordaine him to returne home againe to my familly where it shall not be questioned but that he shall be alimented and cloathed as becomes

> his fathers son And in the meantyme that your Lordships will be pleased to ordaine him to subscrybe recepts and discharges for money as occasion affords and your Lordships please.[45]

There was no licensed lottery in Edinburgh until 1694 but that does not mean there were not unlicensed lotteries. As for the "other ghames", it was said Law was an expert player of the sport then known in Scotland as catch or cache, and today as real or court tennis. William Tytler of Woodhouselee, a lawyer-antiquary, told an Edinburgh audience just before his death in 1792: "I have heard that the famous John Law of Laurieston . . . and James Hepburn, Esq. of Keith, were most remarkable players of tennis."[46] Another lawyer, Sir David Dalrymple, raised to the Court of Session as Lord Hailes, reported that Law "addicted himself to the practice of all games of skill, chance, and dexterity and was noted as a capital player at tennis, an exercise much in vogue in Scotland towards the close of the seventeenth century."[47]

Those witnesses may be quoting the same source, but may also convey the ruins of a fact. Tennis had been brought over to Scotland from France in the sixteenth century. A court built for James V in 1539 at Falkland Palace in Fife is in use today. There was also at least one tennis court in Edinburgh, just outside the Water Gate and opposite the main front of Holyroodhouse. A warrant, signed by King Charles I at Windsor on July 15, 1625, instructed John Erskine, 2nd Earl of Mar and Lord High Treasurer of Scotland to pay £50 to the mason, Alexander Peeres, as the price of the court.[48] It is shown and labelled "31" on Gordon of Rothiemay's map of 1647. Tennis was scarcely likely to please the Presbyterians, but between 1679 and 1682, James, Duke of York and his daughter Anne had revived a number of aristocratic pastimes, including tennis and drama, in the Scottish capital. The court was in use as both a tennis-play and a theatre till at least 1710, after which at some point it became a linen works.

Like other sports at that time and in the eighteenth century, such as horse racing, prize fighting and cricket, tennis was principally an occasion for wagering. Today, real-tennis players are handicapped like race horses so that the outcome is uncertain and a skilful player may still be beaten by a novice. There is another small piece of evidence. In 1728, in Venice, the French legal philosopher Charles-Louis de Montesquieu interviewed Law. He wrote up longhand notes of the conversation, during which Law used a term from real tennis to describe the treachery of a man he trusted: *faux-bond* or "false bounce", where the ball comes off the court walls or penthouses at an unexpected speed or angle.[49]

On February 16, 1688, the justices of the Court of Session referred both John Law's petition and his mother's response to one of their number, Lord Harcarse, "with power to him to determine them as he finds just & in case of difficulties to report".[50] That was Sir Roger Hog of Harcarse, who passed advocate 1661 and joined the bench as Court of Session Justice or Senator in 1677. In fact, Harcarse was ousted from Court of Session a month after Jean's petition by King James II and VII, in one of the King's last acts before he himself was chased from his three kingdoms by Dutch William and Mary Stuart in what became known as the Revolution.

The case never proceeded to full court, and was settled, but it took several years. There is evidence that John Law was planning to leave Scotland in 1690, and on April 22 of that year appointed a factor or agent, the writer or attorney James Marshall, to manage his affairs and collect rents while he was abroad.[51] On July 1, Marshall and Jean Campbell recovered an old debt of John, Lord Bargany of £1 in money.[52] John Law did not go abroad, for he was still in Edinburgh on his twenty-first birthday two years later.

At issue was not the estate at Lauriston, of which Jean had the liferent or use and profit during her lifetime,[53] or the shops in the Close, but how the bonds or loans should be divided between John, on the one hand, and on the other Andrew, William, Robert, Hugh and Lilias. (Agnes and young Jean had received their inheritances of respectively 10,000 merks and 8,000 merks at their marriages in 1684 and 1688).[54]

On July 27, 1689, John Law obtained a so-called Decreet of Compt and Reckoning at the Burgh Court of Edinburgh which required his executors to account for and pay out the money due to him. Jean transferred to him bonds valued at £31,759 18s. 4d. Scots. After more to-ing and fro-ing by the lawyers, Jean handed over the writs for bonds totalling a further £25,600 Scots. Those included the £1,000 Scots borrowed in 1676 by the Highland cattle drovers.

Finally, on April 16, 1692, on or soon after his twenty-first birthday, in the presence of John Hamilton, WS, husband of sister Agnes, Hamilton's servant George Carson, and John Murray, writer in Edinburgh, "me John Law of Louristoun" pronounced himself "fullie satisfied" with his tutors and mother in the administration and care of his estate, and discharged them.[55] Then, with his boats damaged but not entirely burned, and furnished with securities offering an uncertain income of £200–£300 sterling a year, John Law set off for London.

In those days, people did not like to travel far alone. A kinsman of Law's on his mother's side, John Campbell, who had been apprenticed in Edinburgh (to the master goldsmith John Threipland) in the same year as Law,[56] had a design to set up in London as a goldsmith-cum-banker to the London Scots. His business was to have much to do with John Law and eventually became the long-lived bank, Coutts & Co.

John Campbell is first listed in London as paying contributions to the poor or "rates" in the parish of St-Martin-in-the-Fields for a property on the south-east side of the Strand between the modern Craven and Hungerford Streets, on June 20, 1692.[57] It is likely the two young men and brother apprentices sailed south from the Port of Leith in each other's company.

CHAPTER TWO

A Money Business

In englandt soll es nicht so schimpfflich sein gehengt zu werden als In franckreich undt teutschlandt.
(In England to be hanged is apparently not the disgrace it is in France and Germany.)

ELIZABETH CHARLOTTE D'ORLÉANS[1]

London dominated Great Britain at the end of the seventeenth century more than today, for there were then no manufacturing cities in the Midlands and North. With 600,000 persons, London was twenty times the size of Edinburgh. Scots were bewildered and intimidated, as King James I and VI in 1616: "All the countrey is gotten into London; so as with time England will onely be London, and the whole countrey be left waste."[2]

The capital of England had three parts. Between the court city of Westminster in the west, with the royal palaces of St James's and Whitehall and the Parliament, and the commercial city in the east with its port and dockyards, the intervening fields of Middlesex were being built over. Noblemen's houses were thrown up, and just as soon torn down and replaced by tenements for merchants and gentry, in the manner of a modern city that is simultaneously built and destroyed.

The town was at war. The snag or drawback in inviting Dutch William in 1688 to occupy with Queen Mary the thrones of England, Scotland and Ireland was war with the Jacobites. That consisted, in its first episode, of uprisings in support of King James in both Ireland and the Scottish Highlands, which ended with the massacre of the Macdonalds at Glencoe in February, 1692. It was also a share in William's quarrel with Louis XIV of France, the richest and most powerful ruler in Europe. The phase in that conflict known as the Nine Years War, or in North America as King William's War, began in 1688 and deployed English forces not only on the sea, where they felt at home, but on continental soil in the southern or Spanish Netherlands.

One consequence was to draw enlisted men and officers into the capital, where they camped in Hyde Park, on Blackheath or on Hounslow Heath, and gamed and brawled in the streets and taverns of Covent Garden in Middlesex. The practice of duelling, which had arrived from Italy in the sixteenth century, had been suppressed under the Puritan Oliver Cromwell but had broken out again at the restoration of the Stuart kings in 1660. For the diarist Samuel Pepys, writing in 1667, duelling on petty quarrels had become "a kind of emblem of the general complexion of this whole kingdom".[3]

In a comedy by Thomas Shadwell presented at the Theatre Royal at the time of John Law's arrival in London in 1692, *The Volunteers, or the Stock-Jobbers,* a beau or man-about-town, up to then a poltroon, discovers in himself a taste for duelling, and picks a quarrel with every man he meets. "It's an admirable exercise! I intend to use it a mornings instead of tennis."[4]

Duels then were not the tournaments of the Middle Ages or the affairs of honour of later years, governed by written codes of conduct and discharged at dawn with pistols in some snowy forest clearing. They were melees with rapiers or short swords in hot or barely cooling blood, sometimes with seconds drawn and fighting, and shading away into assassination and armed robbery. Gentlemen wore swords in public. That showed they were gentlemen. Duels with pistols, which were less lethal, did not come into fashion until the second half of the eighteenth century.

For the common law, the Church of England and civilian London, duels were crimes and gentlemen needed to take themselves to corners of Barnes Common, Barn Elms and Hyde Park or defend their honour amid the rubbish dumps, stables, market gardens and wastes north of Great Russell Street behind the palaces of Montagu House and Southampton House. King William showed no inclination to abate the belligerence of his officers, but rather tolerated it, and duellists condemned to death by the courts received a royal pardon.

Among John Law's certain acquaintance at this time were two men who fought duels. Richard Steele wounded a brother officer in Hyde Park and later campaigned against duelling in the journals he founded, *The Tatler* and *The Spectator*.[5]

Elizeus Burges, later British Resident in Venice but then an officer of the Horse Guards, in the space of five weeks killed a gentleman of the King's bodyguard in Leicester Fields (now Leicester Square) and a stage actor in the Rose Tavern in Russell Street, Covent Garden (now occupied by the Drury Lane Theatre).

To take those men out of the taverns and into the siege trenches in Flanders required money. To protect the land of his birth from French expansion, and pay subsidies to his allies, William needed in the region of six million pounds sterling a year at a time when ordinary taxes and excises produced just two millions.

Unlike the Stuart Kings, who came to grief over money, William had the support of Parliament and the commercial district of London, known then and now as the City. In the course of the 1690s, William's ministers erected a system of public borrowing which allowed Great Britain to spend far more on the war than it could raise in taxes, and meet France, during a hundred and twenty-five years of intermittent conflict, on equal and then superior terms. Louis XIV did not help his fiscal cause by persecuting the French Protestants or Huguenots, who were active in trade and financial markets. With his revocation of the act of toleration known as the Edict of Nantes in 1685, some two hundred thousand Huguenot craftsmen, merchants and financiers left France for England, Ireland, the United Provinces of the Netherlands, Prussia, Geneva and Switzerland.

In conditions of war, English merchants could not insure their cargoes and, cut off from their European and American markets, and suppliers, found working capital lying idle in their shops. They put it into speculation, or "stock-jobbing" as it was known. That might be in a flurry of joint-stock companies floated to buy some commercial privilege or monopoly from the Crown, or in simple wagers. Daniel Defoe, a good financial mind but always and ever for hire, estimated that "there was not less gaged [wagered] on one side and other, upon the second siege of Limerick [August–October 1691] than two hundred thousand pound."[6] The coffee houses in Exchange Alley in the City, which served as stock exchanges, dealt in rumour, libel and military intelligence.

William's ministers sought to capture this spirit of speculation for the war effort.

In those days, English government departments consisted merely of the Secretaries of State and a few clerks. For ideas and policies, particularly in the revenue, they depended on private men or what were called "Projectors", always, as Defoe wrote, "their mouths full of Millions".[7] Among their number was Thomas Neale (1641–1699), an industrialist and property developer, who in 1678 bought for £6,000 the court position of King's Groom Porter.[8] Along with such duties such as having kindling and coal carried to the King's chamber and privy lodgings, the Groom Porter supervised play at court and resolved disputes at the tables. He also had the power to license all billiard tables, bowling alleys, dicing and gaming houses and tennis courts, from which he profited. Neale was the spit of James II.[9]

In 1693, Neale received the right to offer a lottery, comprising 50,000 tickets at ten shillings each, with 250 winning tickets offering prizes from £20 to £3,000. It was copied from a Venetian lottery of the previous year, and caught the imagination of the town.[10] "Now soe it is," Samuel Pepys wrote to the mathematician Sir Isaac Newton on November 22, 1693, "that the late Project (of which you cannot but have heard) of Mr Neale the Groom-Porter his Lottery, has almost extinguish'd for some time at all places of publick Conversation in this Towne, especially among Men of Numbers, every other Talk but what relates to the Doctrine of determining between the true proportions of the Hazards [probability] incident to this or that given Chance or Lot."[11]

So successful was his own lottery, that Neale persuaded William's ministers to allow him to raise one million pounds for the war, the so-called Million Adventure. This time it was a lottery loan, somewhat like modern Premium Bonds, in which the money staked is not at risk. The lottery consisted of 100,000 tickets at £10 each, each with the right to an annual payment or annuity of £1 for sixteen years. Of those tickets, 2,500 would offer further annuities for sixteen years, ranging from £10 a year to £1,000 a year. The subscription opened on March 16, 1694 and began to fill.

The lottery tickets, because they carried no person's name, were commodities and were bought and sold in the Alley and elsewhere long before the draw set for the autumn of 1694. As if the lottery were not risk enough, by at least midsummer people were trading rights to buy or sell the tickets at a certain price.[12] Such contracts are now known as "options". There is no evidence that John Law was trading in lottery tickets, except that he did so in 1688 and again in 1712, and it is hard to imagine he abstained in the interim, like a smoker in mid-career.

Meanwhile, William's ministers had become intrigued by a cant phrase in the City, "a fund of Credit". All that meant was that a secure and reliable revenue from a parliamentary tax or excise over a number of years could be used to pay the annual interest on a loan to the King or, as the term now is, capitalised. On January 12, 1692, the House of Commons appointed a committee of ten men to "receive proposals for raising a Sum of Money towards the carrying on the War against *France*, upon a Fund of perpetual Interest".[13]

Among the proposals studied by the committee was one from William Paterson (1658–1719), of farming stock in Dumfries, who had traded in the West Indies and the Netherlands. After debate in the committee, and refinement by the Treasury Commissioner Charles Montagu, Parliament in April, 1694 granted the King duties on ships' cargoes ("tunnage") and beer and spirits up to £100,000 a year that was sufficient (after management expenses) to pay an 8 per cent interest on a loan of £1.2 million to prosecute the war. (£1.2m × 8 per cent = £96,000 plus £4,000 for management = £100,000.)[14]

In return for their money, the subscribers to the loan were allowed to incorporate themselves, in the fashion of the public creditors of the Commune of Genoa, who three centuries before had banded together as the Casa di San Giorgio, or House of St George. Since that name was taken, the London adventurers were to be known as "the Governor and Company of the Banke of England". They at once solicited deposits from the public, for which the bank issued receipts or "Bank notes" which were used as money alongside coins from the royal mints. The public deposits were then put out in further advances to the King. As Law later wrote, the Bank of England not only helped finance a war but lowered the rate of interest and provided a convenient currency for business.[15]

It is frustrating that for Law's first eighteen months in London, which formed him at a time of life when he was impressionable, there is small information. Certain features of his personality took shape, such as his habit of expressing his opinions as wagers or the fashion in which he tied his tie. In that period, John Law was exposed in the English capital to new ideas about the nature and creation of money, which gave him his occupation in life and which he elevated to a level unimaginable in his father's shop in Edinburgh.

At that time and for years afterwards, the London Scots kept their own company. At the heart of the Scots colony in London, was the "Scots Box", a society for mutual aid founded in the reign of James I/VI to assist those countrymen who had come up to London and fallen on hard times, and to give the better-off occasions for good cheer. It survives to this day as ScotsCare.

Granted a royal charter in 1665 as "the Scottish Hospital of the Foundation of Charles II", the box at once expended all its funds in burying three hundred Scottish paupers in the bubonic plague of that year. By the time of Law's arrival, the society managed a workhouse or hospital in Blackfriars and included "almost all Scotishmen that frequent London", with some two hundred and fifty members paying a penny sterling each a week towards the hospital.[16]

The members met at Covent Garden taverns, with a quarterly dinner at five shillings and an annual dinner on St Andrew's Day, November 30. Most of the corporation's records were burned in a fire at its Covent Garden offices in 1877, but there survives a list made in the 1730s of all contributors up to then. The list includes amid Williamites and Jacobites all mingled together – "tis impossible for this Charity to be of any Party"[17] – John Law with a contribution of fifteen guineas, or £15 15s.[18]

Among those Scots, Law would have known his father's debtors, or their sons, such as John, Earl of Mar (Box donation: £20). He also had an introduction to a merchant at St Catherine Coleman in the City, William Stonehewer (£5), who boasted an estate of some £600 and was to leave his son and daughter at his death in 1698 "moneys bills bonds and parts of shipps and accounts with my household goods rings and apparell diamonds and pearles to be equally divided".[19]

Whatever John Law was doing, it was not enough to cover his expenses. On February 6, 1693, he travelled to the City and signed over the fee or freehold of Lauriston and Randleston to his mother, together with "my seat in the Kirk of Cramond", in recognition that Jean "hath advanced, paid and delivered to me certain soumes of money as the full availl pryce". The deed, which was described by Fairley but not found by this author, was witnessed by the merchant Stonehewer and his servant Peter Johnston.[20] By April of that year, John Law had also disposed of the late Lord Mar's debts to his father.[21]

On April 9, 1694, John Law ceased to be obscure. About one hour after noon that Monday, he killed a man in Southampton Square (now Bloomsbury Square), probably at the north-east corner. He was arrested and confined to Newgate, the prison built into the western wall of the City.

Newgate was a fearsome place, violent, dirty and overcrowded, but Law had money or friends enough to secure the best billet.[22] That was in the Press-Yard, a stone-paved open space some fifty-four feet by seven feet, on the east side of the prison abutting the College of Physicians. It formed part of Keeper James Fell's lodgings and was let out by him for profit. Here a dozen or two dozen prisoners who could pay a "praemium" of at least £20, and a rent of 11s. 6d. a week, were housed in "divers large spacious rooms, which in general have very good air and light, free from all ill smells", as a later account described them.[23] Law was given the best of them, the "parlor" on the ground floor, "towards the Colledge", where he had a bed to himself.[24]

The next day, April 10, George Rivers, Esq., Middlesex coroner, empanelled twenty jurors to inspect the dead body and determine the cause of death. The inquest identified the body as that of one Edward Wilson. He was a younger son of Thomas Wilson, a London merchant who had bought Keythorpe Hall, near Tugby in Leicestershire, and Anne Packe, daughter of Sir Christopher Packe, who had been Lord Mayor of London under the Commonwealth. Edward Wilson is listed on the monument to the family erected by his elder brother Robert at a cost of £100 in the church of St Thomas à Becket at Tugby. Like his adversary, he was dusty enough from the shop to be playing with swords.

Edward had been an elegant young man, first among the beaux and "mirrour" of the town. London wondered how the younger son of a £200-a-year Leicestershire gentleman had lived for the past five years at a rate of £4,000 or £5,000 a year.[25] As the diarist John Evelyn wrote, Edward Wilson lived "in the garb and equipage of the richest nobleman, for house, furniture, coaches, saddle-horses, and kept a table, and all things accordingly, redeemed his father's estate, and gave portions [dowries] to his sisters."[26] Richard Lapthorne, the London newswriter for the Coffin family at Portledge in Devon, wrote to the family on the 14th: "Wilson is the subject of the general chatt of the towne. Hee [was] no Gamster nether was hee known to keepe women company & it canot bee yet discovered how he came to live at so prodigious an extravagancy."[27]

Nobody appears to have remarked on the place of assignation. On the street known as Great Russell Street, Thomas Wriothesley, 4th Earl of Southampton, Lord Treasurer, had built on the north side a wide, low house, designed by Inigo Jones, with two wings, a garden behind with views of Hampstead and Highgate hills[28] and a broad square in front. The square, which became known as Southampton Square, was divided into parterres with speculative houses and tenements on the east and west sides and to the south a market, commemorated in the modern Barter Street. Evelyn wrote in his diary on February 9, 1665: "Dined at my Lord Treasurer's, the Earle of Southampton, in Blomesbury, where he was building a noble square or piazza, a little toune." By 1694, Southampton Square was a fashionable address. There was no cover of trees or thickets. It was not one of the places listed by *The Spectator* as "fit for a Gentleman to die in".[29]

The coroner's jury resolved that a certain John Law lately of the Parish of St Giles-in-the-Fields and the County of Middlesex:

> . . . moved and seduced by the devil's instigation on the 9th day of April in the sixth year of the reign of the King and Queen, by force of arms and in the said parish a certain Edward Wilson, Gent . . . feloniously, of his own free will and malice aforethought made attack and the said John Law with a sword made of iron and steel of a value of five shillings, the same John Law, in his right hand drawn and held and was holding, struck and hit the same Edward Wilson in the lower part of the stomach a mortal wound of two inches breadth from which the said Edward Wilson instantly died.[30]

On the following Tuesday, April 17, Law was brought at 7 a.m. to the Middlesex Quarter Sessions at Hicks Hall in St John Street, where he was committed to trial at the main criminal court, next to his prison, the Justice-Hall at the Old Bailey.[31] This was a three-storey building, built in brick in the Italian style to replace the old courthouse destroyed in the Fire of London in 1666, set back from the street behind a yard where witnesses and lawyers liked to congregate. The ground-floor courtroom was open at the front to allow air to circulate and dispel the infections and gaol fevers brought up from Newgate by the prisoners.

The next day, April 18, Law was brought in. The Crown, to make a case against Law of premeditation or "Propense Malice", read out some letters which had passed between Wilson and the accused about a lady, Mrs Lawrence, "who was acquainted with Mr Lawe".[32] Law's letters, which were unsigned (which was not unusual for the period) were "very full of Invectives, and Cautions to Mr Wilson to beware, for there was a design of Evil against him". There were also two letters from Wilson, one to Law and one to Mrs Lawrence. The court reporter wrote: "Mr. Wilson's man, one Mr. Smith, swore that Mr. Lawe came to his Master's house a little before the Fact was done, and drank a Pint of Sack [sherry] in the Parlor; after which, he heard his Master say, That he was much surprized with somewhat that Mr. Lawe had told him."

A witness was called, a Captain Wightman, "a person of good Reputation". He testified that he had been a "familiar friend" of Wilson. The three men had been together that morning at the Fountain Tavern. That was an inn on the south side of the Strand, in the place now occupied by the restaurant Simpson's-in-the-Strand. It was well-known for its kitchen and cellar[33] and was used by the Leicestershire men for their weekly Box dinners. "After they had staid a little while there," the reporter continued, "Mr Lawe went away, after which Mr Wilson and Captain Wightman took Coach, and were drove towards Bloomsbury; whereupon Mr Wilson stept out of the Coach into the Square, where Mr Lawe met him." The journey by coach was approximately half-a-mile. Law evidently did not possess a coach, or even the hire of one.

"Before they came near together, Mr Wilson drew his sword and stood upon his Guard. Upon which Mr Lawe immediately drew his Sword, and they both pass'd together, making but one pass, by which Mr Wilson received a mortal Wound upon the lower part of the Stomach, of the depth of two Inches, of which he instantly died.

"This was the Sum [total] of the Evidence for the King."[34] Other witnesses supported Wightman's account.

Who was this Captain Wightman, of good reputation? By far the best candidate is Joseph Wightman, who went on to be one of the great soldiers of his age. He rose through the ranks in the Duke of Marlborough's wars, commanded a division of the Royal Army at Sherrifmuir during the Jacobite rising of 1715 and beat an invasion by Spanish forces in support of Highland Jacobites at Glen Shiel in western Scotland in 1719. A painting of that action by the Dutchman Peter Tillemans, now in the Scottish National Portrait Gallery, shows Wightman on a prancing black horse amid the smoke and shot. He was much liked in Scotland for his decency. He died a major general, of apoplexy, at Bath in October, 1722.[35] An early life of John Law, a bookseller's cuttings-job called *The Memoirs, Life and Character of the Great Mr Law*, described Wilson's second in the duel as one "who is since a greater Man".[36]

That spring day of 1694, this Joseph Wightman was lieutenant and brevet-captain in the 1st Regiment of Foot Guards, the Grenadier Guards.[37] It is possible that he was of the Wightman family of Burbage, half a day's ride from Edward Wilson's Keythorpe, and that he had been a friend of Wilson's since their childhoods in the county.

John Law then took the stand and said that "Mr Wilson and he had been together several times before the Duel was fought and never no Quarrel was betwixt them, till they met at the Fountain Tavern, which was occasioned about the Letters; and that his meeting with Mr Wilson in Bloomsbury was meerly an accidental thing, Mr Wilson drawing his Sword upon him first, upon which he was forced to stand in his own defence. That the misfortune did arise only from a sudden heat of Passion, and not from any Propense Malice."

The judge instructed the jury that if they found the two young men

> did make an Agreement to fight, though Wilson drew first, and Mr Lawe killed him, he was (by the construction of the law) guilty of murder: For if two men suddenly quarrel, and one kill the other, this would be but Manslaughter [punishable by a brand on the thumb]; but this case seemed to be otherwise, for this was a continual Quarrel, carried on betwixt them for some time before, therefore must be accounted a malicious Quarrel, and a design of murder in the person that killed the other.[38]

Despite character witnesses "of good Quality" for Law, the jury followed the judge's instruction and found him guilty of murder. He was condemned to hang along with a rapist/murderer and three counterfeiters, making three men and two women in all, after the close of the court session on April 20. (Transcript in Appendix I.)

Some thought Wilson's family had bribed the jury.[39] In reality, the judge's instructions were clear. The question which exercised London was not whether the killing was unlawful, but whether it was unfair. What mattered was not the law of the land but that of good society.[40]

An examination of the scene and the Old Bailey Sessions Papers or court reports, though cold for three hundred years, is in Law's favour. Law–Wilson was the only duel to come before the Old Bailey in the 1690s that took place in Southampton Square, while there were four in that decade in the fields behind Southampton House.[41] That was for good reason. The principal obstacle to duelling was the common public, and Southampton Square at 1 p.m. on a Monday would have been crowded, "a little toune".[42] No doubt, the two young men agreed to meet at the top of the square for Wilson to leave his coach, whence they would proceed on foot into the wastes to the north. Yet, as Wightman testified, and the Judge accepted, Wilson instead got down and drew on Law. Law defended himself. There was just a single pass.

King William, impatient to leave on campaign in the Low Countries and occupied with reviewing troops in Hyde Park, reprieved Law. Law later wrote that that was through "the intercession of severall noblemen of Scotland".[43] The Wilson family, led by the eldest brother Robert, Edward's heir, believing the reprieve was prelude to a royal pardon, moved to organise their interest.[44] On April 22, a note was written into the Cabinet records: "Caveat that nothing pass relating to a pardon for John Laws . . . till notice first be given to Mr Robert Wilson, brother of the deceased, at his house in Stratton Street, Berkeley Square."[45] (In English law, a caveat is an order filed with a court or minister to suspend a proceeding until opposition can be heard.)

Exploiting the mystery over Edward's fortune and, perhaps, the below-the-belt wound, Robert set about convincing London and the King that death occurred not from his brother's discourtesy to Mrs Lawrence, but from an armed robbery gone awry, "a Money business". Wightman was probably by then out of the country on campaign and not around to deny it. Robert Wilson would hang Law by way of a civil prosecution, where the King and Queen had no power to pardon. On or about May 5, Wilson submitted an appeal of murder to the Sheriff of Middlesex, who had Law in custody at Newgate. The same day, after two false starts, King William left London and sailed from Margate on May 6.

Robert Wilson's last will and testament, written at the end of 1726 and full of precise little legacies, reveals a man purse-proud, churchy and officious. He left a substantial property to his two surviving brothers, William and James, including estates at Keythorpe and Goadby in Leicestershire, at least £2,000 in securities, the building known as the Plough on the corner of Lombard Street and Change Alley in the City of London (which later housed Martin's and then Williams and Glyn's Banks), and two houses in Paternoster Row near St Paul's Cathedral. To his brother-in-law, Charles Parker, he left "one shilling and no more".[46]

Robert Wilson was not without allies. His aunt, Mary Wilson, had married a leading West Country industrialist, Sir Joseph Ashe, and now a widow was living in state on the Thames at Twickenham. Their daughters had married into two rising Norfolk families, who were to be active in politics throughout the eighteenth century. Katherine Ashe in 1669 married William Windham of Felbrigg, and her dowry built the west front of the house and the orangery and planted the wood which is today at or some little past its prime.[47] Mary Ashe four years later married Horatio, Baron Townshend of Raynham, and their son Charles or 'Turnip' Townshend, part statesman, part improving farmer, was master of an unencumbered 20,000-acre estate yielding £5,000–£6,000 a year.

The appeal was set for May 9 at the Court of King's Bench, an appeal court that had sat since the Middle Ages under the angel roof of Westminster Hall. For the hearing of the appeal, there are accounts from both sides. Thomas Carthew, acting for Law, left a report which was printed by his son.[48] William Cowper, later Lord Chancellor, who attended from beginning to end as a junior for Wilson, left a manuscript account now in the Hertford record office.[49] Law himself, in a letter to Queen Anne, said that Robert Wilson prosecuted the appeal "with great violence".[50] From the surviving papers, that is the opposite of the truth.

On May 9, a Wednesday, Law was brought by the Sheriff of

Middlesex from Newgate before the Lord Chief Justice, Sir John Holt, and two fellow judges, Samuel Eyres and Giles Eyres. Representing him were Serjeants William Thomson and Clement Levinz and Carthew. In the first of many attempts at delay, Law's counsel asked for extra time to prepare a plea to the writ. Throughout the case, at a time when jurists were still feeling their way in the common law, Holt wanted to ensure that both parties to the appeal should accept the judgment and went to great lengths to indulge the defence or appellee. "At last," Cowper wrote, "upon much importunity & that the Appellee might have no colour of exception to the justice of the Court, the Appellee had two days time (viz.) till fryday next following given time to plead, so as he would stand by it."[51] Law was taken away to the King's Bench Prison, which occupied two houses on the east side of Borough High Street which ran down into Surrey from the only bridge over the Thames, London Bridge.[52]

Like Newgate and, indeed, all prisons in England before the reforms of the nineteenth century, the Marshalsea of the Court of King's Bench was a private enterprise. Granted as a freehold with its fees, profits and perquisites by James I in 1617, it had come into the possession of the Lenthall family of Oxfordshire. In 1682, William Lenthall mortgaged the office of marshal and some other assets to the merchant Sir John Cutler for £10,000 at a rate of interest of 5½ per cent per year. At some point, the debt increased to £18,000.[53]

The consequence of this arrangement was that the Lenthalls had to squeeze out of the debtors and other prisoners and their families sufficient income to cover the interest on the mortgage and make a profit. This they did by selling the office of acting marshal to a succession of other men who, in turn, delegated the administration to favoured prisoners. A sort of caricature of the society outside its walls, the King's Bench prison was divided into unequal sections: the Master's Side, where prisoners with money might share rooms in a minimum of comfort and safety, and the Common Side, which does not bear thinking about. Those with money were fleeced for accommodation ("chamber rent"), discharge fees, beer, wine, food, bedding and exeats to the surrounding streets to ply their trades in the so-called Liberties of the King's Bench. As Jonathan Swift wrote in "A Description of the Morning":

> The Turn-key now his flock returning sees
> Duly let out a-Nights to steal for Fees.

The keepers solicited bribes to permit debtors to escape, which infuriated the creditors who had put them there.[54]

For Lenthall and his servants, there was no incentive to maintain the buildings or keep the several hundred prisoners in health and, by 1754, the prison was so ruinous that it could no longer support either prisoners or mortgage, which had risen to £30,397 3s. 3d. The ministry decided to buy out the creditors and rebuild it. The lenders accepted 6s. 9d. on the pound from the Crown, or a loss to the face value of slightly under two-thirds.[55] It is just that a debtors' prison should be bankrupt.

On the evening of May 9, when Law was admitted, the acting marshal was William Briggs, who had bought the post for life from Lenthall for £1,500 at Easter, 1690. He delegated his duties to John Farrington, a broken Haymarket victualler and prisoner for debt since at least 1677. Not much is known of those men, all of it bad. In November, 1690, the poor debtors had revolted against the Briggs-Farrington regime and petitioned Parliament, alleging that Farrington "doth barbarously oppress and extort upon the Petitioners, and causeth them to be put in lousy and stinking Rooms, except [unless] they sign a Book to pay extravagant Fees and Demands".[56]

When the House of Commons set up a committee of inquiry under Sir Jonathan Jennings, Briggs and Farrington beat up the witnesses. John Mallett, Esq.was dragged out from the Master's Side and, "after several oaths, sworn by Mr Briggs, against this House, he was thrown into the common Ward, so dark and dank a Hole, that his Life, if not suddenly retrieved, is in Danger."[57] Briggs was heard to say "they would do what they pleased with ther prisoners; for the Parliament had nothing to do with them" and, as for Jennings, "God damn Sir Jonathan Jennings, he did not care a fart for him."[58] For that sally, Briggs was arrested by the serjeant-at-arms and forced to make "an humble Acknowledgement" of the offence to the House.[59]

On Friday May 11, the court reconvened with Robert Wilson present. Law's counsel again asked for time to plead, which Holt refused. Word of the duel had by now reached Scotland and the Lord Advocate, or attorney general, Sir James Steuart of Goodtrees, wrote for information to one of the Secretaries of State for Scotland in London, James Johnston of Warristoun.

On May 15, Johnston replied: "Mr Law's Case is very doubtfull, all indifferent [impartial] Men are ag't him, & I never had so many Reproaches for any Business since I knew England, as for concerning my Self for him: My Ld Ch Just [Sir John Holt,] is earnest to have his Life; the Archbp [John Tillotson, Archbishop of Canterbury] owns to me that he himself press'd the King not to pardon him, as being a Thing of an odious Nature, & which would give great Offence." King William, before his departure, still favoured pardon. "The King said none had dy'd for Duells these many years, & the Law should be first reviv'd." Johnston added: "He [Law] is in the King's bench, & a Blockhead, if he make not his Escape, which he may easily do, considering the nature of that Prisson."[60]

On the 19th, for some reason Law was not in court, and Thomson raised an objection. Holt again permitted the objection, and the court rose until the following Monday, May 21, which happened to be the last day of the Easter term. That day, the court told Wilson's counsel to prepare for a trial of murder "some time the beginning of the next Term" in the event that their appeal might be successful.[61]

Fashionable London began to disperse. The duchesse de Mazarin, Charles II's mistress, who was now living in retirement in Chelsea, wrote on May 31 to her young protégé, the Earl of Aran. "The fine youth have left on campaign, some at Windsor, and the others in Flanders."[62]

On June 9, the court returned and Law's lawyers began to split hairs. On that day, and on June 22, they challenged the Latin writ, and every procedure in Law's judicial treatment since the Old Bailey trial, on points of law and even Latin grammar and syntax. On each point, recorded by Cowper and Carthew in detail, the court responded that the defects did not obscure the common-sense meaning.

None the less, Holt was determined to be fair and, in recognition that Law's life was in jeopardy (*in favorem vitae*), gave the defence until the next term for further preparation, while again inviting Wilson's team to make ready for the trial for murder.[63] Meanwhile the subscription books for the Bank of England were opened at the Mercers Chapel in Cheapside and, in twelve days of glorious sunshine, were filled.[64]

There was that Trinity Term before the King's Bench Court one Charles Knollys, a name inscribed in the annals of English justice for a lawsuit, beside which *Jarndyce v Jarndyce* of Charles Dickens' *Bleak House* is an instance of judicial panic. The Banbury Peerage case, which was first heard before the House of Lords in 1661 and for the last time in 1813, flared up in 1883 and may not even now be extinguished, has made much law in matters of adulterine bastardy, the rights of the English Peerage and the relation of the House of Lords to the courts.

Knollys was an unruly man whose once substantial family property consisted of "a bowling-green at Henley" in Oxfordshire.[65] He had married his wife in the Nag's Head coffee house in James Street, Covent Garden and then wandered off with another lady to the continent.[66]

In December, 1692, Knollys, then aged thirty, fought and killed his brother-in-law, Captain Philip Lawson and when arraigned at the Old Bailey on Saturday, December 10, pleaded misnomer. He was not Charles Knollys, Esq, but the 4th Earl of Banbury with a right to be tried by his peers in the House of Lords.[67]

Flummoxed, the bench postponed the case to the next sessions. On January 17, 1693 the House of Lords rejected his petition for trial by his peers on evidence that his father was illegitimate. His case was transferred to the Court of King's Bench where, in the spring of 1693, Holt granted him bail. There is no particular reason to believe that when Law arrived at the prison gate on May 9, 1694, he met his fellow duellist and gentleman, except this coincidence: Banbury's sister, Lady Katherine Knowles (as she spelled her name) was the love of John Law's life.

Lady Katherine was then about twenty-one years of age.[68] Those of a romantic turn may compose a love story in the manner of Dickens's *Little Dorrit* (set in the Marshalsea Prison in the same street). Years later, in Paris, Lady Katherine was accused by Law's enemies of acting the queen. The following pedigree does not excuse, but may explain such conduct:

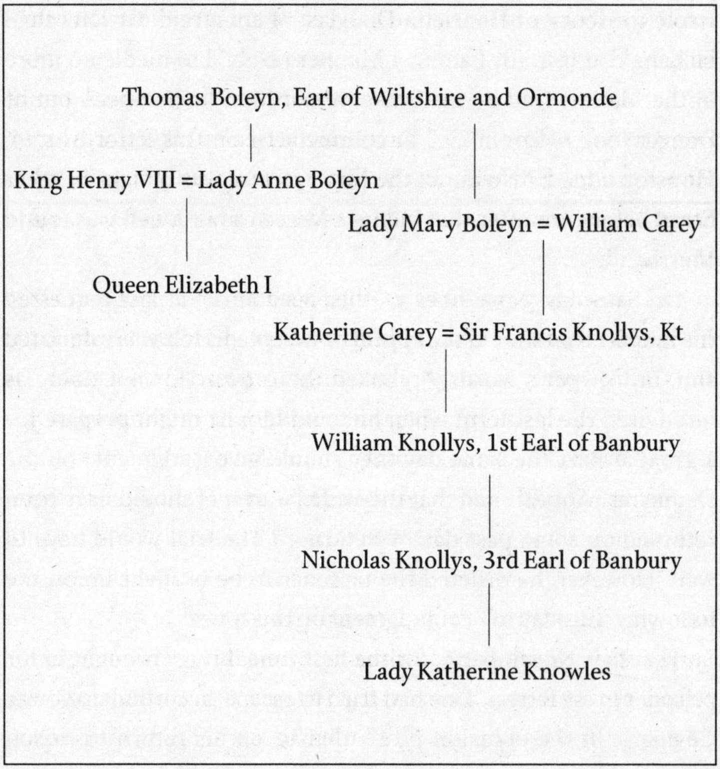

As it turned out, Holt in that summer of 1694 took issue with the Lords, saying that that house had no more right to take away a peerage than it had to make one, and quashed the indictment. Amid such high reasonings, the bloody corpse of Captain Lawson was forgotten. Banbury walked free. What is probable is that Law's acquaintance with Lady Katherine, first recorded on a French passport in 1702, must be brought forward some years. The Knollys family was in luck, for the daughter Lady Katherine bore to John Law stabilised their fortunes and preserved them to the present day.

By the end of October, Secretary Johnston was disgusted with both the case and Law's languor and passivity. On the 30th, he wrote to Henry or Henrietta Douglas: "I am afraid Mr Law shall be hang'd at last, for I am in a Manner resolv'd to medle no more in the Matter: Had he his Senses about him, he had been out of Danger long before now." In commenting on this letter in 1719, Johnston added: "No doubt the Jury agt' him was bought I nether heard before nor after that killing a Man in a fair Duell was found Murther."[69]

On Saturday, November 3, Wilson's counsel at last requested the murder trial should the appeal be accepted. Holt was infuriated and, in Cowper's words, "rebuked the Attorny for not doing as he advised the last term when he tould him he might prepare for a Tryal at Barr the same day they should give j[udgment] on the Demurrer [Appeal] and that the Ve:fa [warrant] should have been returned on some past day of Return".[70] The trial would have to wait. However, he ordered the prisoner to be brought up on the following Tuesday to hear judgment on the appeal.

That day, November 6, for the first time, Briggs brought in his prisoner in leg fetters. Law had tried to escape, according to young Cowper, "in the occasion past", that is, on his return to prison from his last appearance on November 3.[71] The three judges unanimously dismissed all the defence's objections. Holt said: "Appeal is the just right of a Subject not to be overthrown on too nice [hair-splitting] Exceptions." The appeal was upheld and Law now faced the rope in the new year.[72] The tale of Johnnie Law, a Scotchman, who defied his wise mother and frittered away his inheritance, was coming to an end.

None the less, for all their pettifoggery, such a delight to critics of the common law, Law's counsel had earned their fees. Three days later, November 9, after a frustrating campaign, King William landed at Margate and was at Kensington after dinner on November 10.[73]

In 1719, by then in retirement and with Law famous, Secretary

Johnston wrote down his recollections of the case for the British ministry. Those are of much less value than his copy-letters. As often happens so late after the event, his recollections compress the time elapsed, so that it is not at all clear when he is speaking of the spring of 1694 and when of the autumn: that is, before the King went on campaign in April or after he returned in November. A complication is that the diarist Narcissus Luttrell reports that the Duke of Shrewsbury was from at least November 20 "ill of a feavour".[74]

Johnston's notes say that Law's life had become a stumbling block in the fraught relations of Scotland and England or, as he called it, a "national Business". He wrote that King William "had no quiet from the Townsend, and Ash, and the Windham's Interest who were all cousin germains [first cousins] to Willson, who strangely prepossessed K Wm. When I reasoned the matter with the King, I was more rudely treated by him and the Nation [i.e. Scotland] too, than we had ever been on any Occasion."

At the morning reception, known as the Levee, badgered by Johnston and one of the Scottish courtiers, Charles Douglas, Earl of Selkirk,[75] William made a false step. "It's well known," Johnston continued,

> that talking to him at his Levy amongst other things I told him that it was hard to make Mr Laws suffer for his Ingenuity [honesty]; that without Mr Laws confession the ffact could not have been prov'd, for those that saw it being strangers to him when brought to Prison to see him, could only Swear that it was one like him. What [!,] said the K: Scotchmen suffer for their Ingenuity. Was ever such a thing known, added he, turning to My Ld Selkirk, who to do him Justice, was at the same time, seconding me in ffavour of Mr Law. Two or three more that stood next [near] heard it, and the

Thing took Wind [got about] but with some pains I got the story suppress'd then. The next day being upon the same Subject, I told the K: the Scotch would not forget such an Expression. He said that I & Selkirk provok'd him to use it; but he wish'd he had not done it, and added cann't you & he keep your own Secrets . . .

But that which stood most with him, & which he told me he could not but believe, was that Mr Laws want'd [was short of] Money, & that he had quarrell'd with Willson, who, he said, was a known Coward; in order to make him give him Money; All I could say to take of this signifi'd nothing.

At a loss, Johnston sought the aid of the first minister and Secretary of State, Charles Talbot, who had in April been elevated to the Dukedom of Shrewsbury and "had more Power then with the King, than any man alive". Shrewsbury was doubtful, said King William was "mightily possess'd" against Law, but promised to keep the matter out of Cabinet for a week until Johnston could gain some proofs that it was not a "Money business". Johnston sent to the City, to a Scots banker whose name he did not recollect, who offered to tell Shrewsbury that Law had just received from Scotland a bill or credit of £400. The Duke was satisfied but reported that the King would not pardon Law "without the friend's [Robert Wilson's] consent; tho' added he, I think the K: is willing he should be saved, provided it can be done in such a Manner as that his Majtie did not appear in it, nor must I said the Duke of himself."[76]

From traces in the papers of the Stuart court in exile, it seems that Law owed his escape to William's pet favourite at that time, James Butler, second Duke of Ormonde. The premier Irish nobleman and a man of princely habits, as an undergraduate at Christ Church, Oxford, aged fourteen, Butler had kept a valet, a page, two footmen and a groom. A gentleman of the bedchamber since 1689, Ormonde had delighted the King on campaign with his bravery and that summer of 1694 in the Low Countries travelled in William's coach.

A "good natured, profuse, innocent man", as the Scotsman Sir John Clerk described him,[77] Ormonde in 1715 embraced the cause of the exiled Stuart King James III and became his resident at the court of Spain. At the summit of his power, in 1720, John Law told James III's resident in Paris "that he had former obligations to 1102 [cipher for Ormonde] and would send him 150,000*l* [French livres] to sustain his caracter" at the court in Madrid.[78] In a letter to the Regent of France at the end of 1720, answering charges that he had consorted too much with the Jacobites, Law wrote: "the Duke of O saved my life."[79] It is no surprise that Secretary Johnston in his 1719 memorial made no mention of the man who was by then the principal Jacobite general.

A little later, Shrewsbury came up to Johnston and "whisper'd to me in a Crowd that my ffr:d [friend] was at Liberty, but had been ver slow to understand Matters, & pray'd me to keep the Secret, which I did till K: Wms Death [in 1702], or at least that the D: [Duke of Shrewsbury] was out of all Business [retired from office]." Wilson's party were convinced that Briggs had connived in the escape. "However," Cowper wrote, "the manner of escape was so contrived that the Marshal was never indicted nor any way punished for the same."[80] They sought a writ of exigent against the fugitive, declaring him an outlaw.[81]

Johnston himself retired in 1702 to Twickenham, a village on the Thames west of London, where he bought an estate on the north bank that abutted Cambridge House, where Robert and Edward Wilson's aunt, Lady Ashe, who had £9,000 in the East India Company and a further £1,000 in trust, lived as a widow. Johnston wrote in 1719: "How my old Lady Ash, my neighbr at Twittenham smoak'd this [learned of his role in Law's escape], I know not; but tho' we liv'd as good Neighbrs, she allways said that she had a great Quarrell in her heart with me."[82]

On December 28, Queen Mary died of smallpox at Kensington Palace and nobody had any thought for John Law. With his ordinary insolence, Briggs inserted a Wanted notice in the *London Gazette*, which gives some information about Law's appearance at this time.

> Captain John Lawe, a Scotchman, lately a Prisoner in the Kings-Bench for Murther, aged 26 [23], a very tall black [dark-haired] lean man, well shaped, above Six foot high, large Pockholes in his face, big high Nosed, speaks broad and loud, made his escape from the said Prison. Whoever secures him, so he may be delivered at the said Prison, shall have 50 l. paid immediately by the Marshal of the Kings Bench.[83]

The captaincy is honorific. Duellists were presumed to be military men.

For all that, the King's Bench Prison had become too hot for Briggs. The next year he sold on the office of Acting Marshal for £2,000.[84] Farrington continued to run the prison. In 1697, Parliament passed an Act stating that any marshal or acting marshal who took payment to procure an escape from the King's Bench would be liable to a fine of £500 and the forfeit of the office for all time.[85] It had no effect.

The duel in Southampton Square was the capital event of John Law's life. Without intending it, he had shown himself to be a rough customer. There is no evidence of his having ever to fight again. In the words of *The Spectator*, he had joined the 'Club of Duellists' with the right to sit at the high table, reserved for those who had slain their Man.[86]

Had he stayed in London, Law might have been just another financial pamphleteer or Lower Alley projector. History concerns itself with what was, not what might have been. An outlaw, John Law was driven into the world, to live on his wits and his engaging manners, without allegiance, except to his family and his ideas. As he wrote years later, "I should never have engadged in the service of france, if my pardon had not been refused me."[87]

CHAPTER THREE

Gibberish Language

Le vieux Lasse parlant de tant de genies beaus qui sont perdus dans le nombre innombrable des hommes disoit come des marchands, ils sont mort sans deplier.

(Law in old age, in speaking of so many fine spirits lost in the numberless mass of humanity, used a phrase from commerce: They died before they could unfurl their merchandise.)

MONTESQUIEU, *PENSÉES*[1]

The winter of 1694–5 was one of the coldest ever in England and Scotland. As Queen Mary lay in state in the Banqueting House of the palace of Whitehall, snow began to fall and it snowed without interruption for nearly two months. On January 13, the Thames froze over at Southwark.[2] The smallpox was everywhere. People kept to their houses. It was a good time to be on the run.

Twice in his life, between 1695 and 1701, and again in the early 1720s, John Law vanished. In the second period, he used false names, and it is fair to presume that he did so in the earlier. It helped that his surname had many natural variants: Lawe, Laws and Lawes in England, Las, Lass, Lasse and Lavv in France, Laur in the United Provinces, Lau and Laus in Italy, Lauu and Labuu in Spain. There were other John Laws of note, such as Mr John of Campsie, the kirk minister, or the British resident in Brussels, a war profiteer, to draw the curious up blind alleys.

Where did John Law go? By his own account, Law did not see Italy before 1706 and never was in Austria. He could not travel to France in wartime without forfeiting any chance of pardon for the killing of Wilson. That left Holland, long the resort of Scotsmen for religious asylum, trade and study, Scotland, Ireland and the Americas.

Travel to Holland was either 'down the river' to a merchant ship at Gravesend, or by coach to Harwich and by packet boat in a minimum of twelve hours to Rotterdam.[3] John Mackye, the surveyor of coasts at Harwich and a Scotsman, "stops whom he will at Harwich, and whom he pleases he lets go," as one of the Secretaries of State grumbled at the time. "It has been an old complaint on this side and that against yachts, merchant-men and convoys that they smuggle passengers."[4]

In wartime, it was high treason to travel abroad without a passport signed by the Secretary of State.[5] Among the Dutch seamen, soldiers' wives, subjects of the kings of Denmark and Sweden, German tailors, poor Jews, poor Palatines, oculists, buttonmakers, shoemakers, gingerbread makers, barbers and dancing masters issued with passes by the Duke of Shrewsbury to make the crossing into Holland and Flanders, there may have been a disguised John Law.[6]

Yet there is no trace of him in the Low Countries. Since the Middle Ages, and even more since Scottish Covenanters had taken refuge in Holland from Stuart persecution, there had been Scots colonies in the United Provinces. In Rotterdam alone, there were five hundred Scots with their own church then a-building on the Schiedamse Dijk or, as it was nicknamed, the Schotse Dijk.

Scottish boys reported home on their countrymen studying

medicine or Roman law at Utrecht, Groningen and Leiden, apprenticed to Dutch merchant houses at Rotterdam or Amsterdam, serving in the Scots regiments in Dutch service or passing through on tour to Italy. They would have known John Law even *incognito*, but in the letters home that survive in the Scottish archives, there is no mention of him. Nor does Law appear in the despatches of Matthew Prior, the English resident at The Hague. Law did make friends with officers serving in the Dutch Scots Brigade, but that may have been after 1705.

It is conceivable that Ormonde spirited him away to his estates in Ireland. Years later, in 1724, and under pressure from his creditors, Law spent "several months in Ireland".[7] More likely, Law returned to Scotland, though it must have gone hard with him to appear before his family in pieces. Robert Wilson's lawyers were convinced he had gone to Scotland. "The Def[endan]t made his Escape, as was said, into Scotland," Cowper wrote at the close of his trial report.[8]

Another possibility is that Law crossed the Atlantic. The projecting fever in London had spread to the Scots. In June and July, 1695, the Scottish Parliament passed acts for two joint-stock or shareholder-owned enterprises, the first for a long-haul Scottish trading company on the pattern of the English East India and the Dutch Vereenigde Oost-Indische Compagnie (VOC) and the second for a "Bank in Scotland".[9]

The more modest of the two, the Bank of Scotland, raised £100,000 sterling in capital in London and Scotland and, after many vicissitudes, survives to this day. The trading company, the Company of Scotland Trading to Africa and the Indies, ran into opposition from the English East India, which mobilised support in the English Parliament and at King William's court, causing the English investors to withdraw their subscriptions.

William Paterson and the other projectors travelled to Scotland in early 1696 and, in a sort of patriotic euphoria, collected £400,000 sterling from the nobility, lairds, merchants, burghs and towns, guilds and incorporations. Nearly half of the shareholders put in the minimum of £100. Law's younger brother Andrew ventured £200 and his aunt Agnes Campbell £100. In return, she received £50 as an advance on a "bargan [bargain] of Bibles and Catechisms" for the use of mariners and colonists.[10] There is no trace of Jean having invested.

Beset at every turn by English and Dutch obstruction, the Company of Scotland adopted Paterson's idea to plant a colony on land claimed by the King of Spain on the Atlantic coast of the isthmus of Darien or Panama. The plan was to offer trade to all nations with the East Indies by way of a portage across the isthmus, a sort of dry Panama Canal. It would spare shippers the stormy and pirate-ridden passage round the Cape of Good Hope. Without making a reconnaissance, the company despatched two flotillas from Scotland in 1698 and 1699, but provisions were inadequate, there was no support from Jamaica and the English plantations, colonists succumbed to fever and a Spanish attack, and New Caledonia, as it was called, collapsed. Some two thousand people lost their lives and Scotland its investment capital.

There is no record that John Law volunteered for Darien, though his younger brother did so. Andrew, who was Deacon of the Incorporation of Goldsmiths while still in his twenties, had been imprisoned for a debt of £300 Scots. He petitioned his fellow goldsmiths to bail him out, which they did taking his £50 down payment on his Company of Scotland shares and a charge on his shop rent as security.[11] His share subscription was raffled to the members of the incorporation at £1 sterling per ticket. On June 30, 1699, the company's Court of Directors in Milne's Square recommended Andrew be examined for his "merit and behaviour . . . to go to Caledonia with the Company's first intended equipage".[12] By October 1700,

Andrew was known or presumed in Edinburgh to have perished.[13]

Exhausted after the inconclusive war, the belligerents signed a peace at King William's country house at Rijswijk or Ryswick, outside The Hague, in September, 1697. With the peace, Law probably travelled to Paris. In later life, he spoke and wrote French with such fluency that he must have lived for some long time in France. His manners could only have been acquired in Paris. He was also in later life acquainted with certain English officers and noblemen who came to Paris in 1698 as part of the Earl of Portland's embassy: Captain James Stanhope (later Secretary of State and Prime Minister), Thomas Wentworth, later Earl of Strafford, and the Earl of Orrery. Was Law the 'Scotch gentleman' who took part with Stanhope in Brussels in an all-night drinking bout, that culminated in rousing a "Chocolat house" and draining it of rum?[14]

There is another source that places him in Paris at about this time, but it is not of the best. Attributed to Barthélemy Marmont du Hautchamp, an author whose relics include a couple of novels in eastern settings, a six-volume history of Law's financial innovations in France appeared in 1739.[15] Jules Michelet, the nineteenth-century historian, used this work but with the utmost reluctance.

This author writes that, after the duel with Wilson, Law "came to Paris, where he cut quite a figure, sustained by a faro bank. He used to keep the bank at the house of a well-known actress [glossed as Marie-Anne Duclos], where the stakes were high [*un très-gros jeu*]." Du Hautchamp continues:

> He was as much in demand among princes and noblemen of the first rank as in the most famous gaming-clubs [*Académies*], where his refined manners and even temper distinguished him from the other gamesters. He played at Poisson's house, in the rue Dauphine, where he never had less than two bags of gold worth one hundred thousand livres. It was the

same story at the hôtel de Gêvres, in the rue des Poulies. The gold was too difficult to carry in the hand, and so he had chips [*jettons*] made for eighteen [gold] Louis apiece. For all his sweet manners, he made enemies who rendered him suspect to the government, and particularly Mr d'Argenson, lieutenant general of police. That magistrate ordered him to leave Paris on the pretext that he was too expert in the game he had introduced into the capital. On leaving France, Law was in Genoa.[16]

The author, who was probably a child in the 1690s, has compressed a number of different periods. Faro or pharaon, the game of Pushkin's *Queen of Spades*, of Dolokhov in Tolstoy's *War and Peace* and of the nineteenth-century American West, did not become fashionable in Paris until the new century.[17] Law did not go to Genoa until, at the earliest, 1706. Nothing elsewhere suggests that Law had in the 1690s one hundred thousand livres in play-money. In gold louis, that sum would have weighed more than a bale of straw. There is no other report of play at this period at the hotel des Gesvres, though there was licensed play there in the 1730s.[18]

On the other hand, Duclos, who made her debut at the Comédie française in 1693, was the leading tragic heroine from May, 1696 until the grand style went out of fashion at the death of Louis XIV. Paul Poisson (1658–1735) succeeded his father in the stock role of Crispin in 1686 and continued till he retired in 1711. Marc-René de Voyer, marquis d'Argenson, was appointed lieutenant general of police of Paris in 1697. Somewhere, in all this muddle, there is the debris of a fact.

On April 7, 1701, a "Mr Law" was arrested in Paris. A record survives of the imprisonment of a "Sr. Las"* by the Marshals of

* There was then no *w* in French and the sound "aw" was often represented by "as", hence Arkansas.

France "at this place" (*esté ammené ez prisons de Ceans*). He was released on the order of the maréchal de Choiseul six days later.[19] In those days, the Marshals of France had jurisdiction over military police and the duty to prevent affairs of honour ending in the duels that had decimated the young nobility at the beginning of the seventeenth century.[20] Louis XIV issued repeated decrees against duelling, and in the allegorical paintings of his exploits on the ceiling of the Gallery of Mirrors at the Palace of Versailles, there is a panel entitled "The Fury of Single Combats Arrested". The record of "Mr Law's" short imprisonment may be the trace of a duel that was not fought.

Lady Katherine has left more of a trail. On Saturday July 27, 1695, George Seignior "of the parish of St Andrew Holborn, London, Gent" swore before Sir Charles Hedges, master of the faculties of the ecclesiastical province of Canterbury, that he intended to marry "the Honoble the Ladye Katherine Knowles maiden aged about 22 years whose parents are dead" and there was no impediment to the match. He requested a licence to marry at St Clement Danes Church in the Strand, near the lawyers' district known as the Inns of Court, or some other place left blank. Seignior was, like John Law, "aged about 24 years".[21] (See Appendix II.)

Such an oath, known as a marriage allegation, was demanded by the Church of England from couples who were unable or unwilling to have marriage banns read in their parish churches on three successive Sundays. The bride might be with child or the couple might otherwise wish for privacy or haste. Generally, the groom posted a bond that would be forfeit should he have concealed an impediment, but there is no record of such in this case.

Like Law, George Seignior is hard to pursue amid the various spellings of the name: Signor, Segnor, Seiginor, Sennior, Seignieur. The best candidate is the George Seignior who was baptised at

St Mary Woolnoth in the City on January 4, 1671, bred to the Bar, and admitted to the Inner Temple on November 28, 1685 and the Middle Temple on June 19, 1689.[22] His father was Robert Seignior (1645–1686), master clockmaker at the sign of "The Dyall" in Exchange Alley, who employed three apprentices in the 1670s, and was with Thomas Tompion the principal London master of the craft. Robert's will, dated September 19, 1685, appointed his "sonne, George Seigniour" as principal beneficiary and executor.[23]

At least eight of Robert's clock movements, and a few watches, survive and are valued, but he was in continuous dispute with the clockmakers' guild or company and accused of stealing others' improvements. Robert Hooke, the natural scientist who followed advances in timekeeping, recorded in his diary in 1675: "To Garaways Signor and Tompion cheats grand."[24] (Garraways was one of the Alley coffee-houses.) Robert died before May 4, 1687.[25]

This George Seignior was no catch. On October 12, 1692, he wagered with Charles Davenant, a financial pamphleteer and intermittent Tory MP, a diamond ring worth £30–£40 against 100 guineas that he would not be "fluxed" (that is, treated with mercury for venereal disease) within the next seven years.[26]

Lady Katherine's marriage settlement, which was supposed to maintain her in a respectable condition should her husband die, consisted of an annuity of £120 granted her by Lord Halifax on certain properties in London and Northamptonshire, and miscellaneous assets from the Seigniors, including gambling and other debts of £400 due her new husband from a Cambridge undergraduate named Paul Powney. The lad, whose father John had made a fortune supplying hay and livestock to Windsor Castle and been an MP for the town,[27] "did not well understand play" and had since died. His debts had been endorsed by his sister's husband, Henry Trinder, but that man had absconded and "gone into remote parts".

The trustees appointed for the marriage settlement included

Sir John Brownlow, the Lincolnshire gentleman who built the famous house called Belton Hall. They refused to stand surety for such assets.[28] As late as February, 1715, Lady Katherine was litigating for her money.[29]

The couple did not marry. There is no record of their marriage in the parish registers of St Clement's Church in the Strand or any London church, or in the lists of clandestine marriages. Was George Seignior John Law under an assumed name? That theory removes the two problems of John Law's biography: where he was between 1695 and 1702; and why George Seignior disappears so utterly from the record.[30] It also explains why the Seignior-Knowles marriage did not take place at St Clement's. Law would not want to appear at the altar of a church teeming with Seignior's fellow barristers.[31] However far fetched, it is the best conjecture.

At the Peace of Ryswick of 1697, travel to France became both possible and easy. It was reported that the pair attended the court of the exiled James II at Saint-Germain-en-Laye, just downstream from Paris.[32] That was a common enough Whig slur, and there is no record of them in the Jacobite papers of the period, which are now owned by the British Crown.

None the less, in the sunshine of her husband's success between 1718 and 1720, Lady Katherine chose to spend her time with women who had lived at the Stuart court in France. Those included Eleanor and Charlotte Frances ("Fanny") Oglethorpe, both known for their high spirits and charm, who invested by her influence in John Law's company stock. Then again, that may be coincidence. There were more Jacobites than Whigs in the British colony in Paris.

John Law could hope, in the end, for pardon of his crimes against the statutes. For her crimes against custom Lady Katherine could not. Alone, he might return to his native land. Together, they were bound to exile.

*

By 1702, the European powers were ready to go back to fighting. On March 8 by the Julian calendar in use in England, King William died after a fall from his horse. He was succeeded on the throne by his late queen's younger sister, Anne, and as commander of the English and Dutch forces by John Churchill, Earl of Marlborough, whose wife Sarah was Anne's beloved friend. On May 15, the Allies declared war on France and soon after, on June 19, Lady Katherine was granted a passport to leave France as "Catherine Sennior", travelling with her valet Guillaume Atkinson. Also issued a passport that day was "Mr Laws, Scottish gentleman" and his two Scottish servants, Henlay and Murray.[33] It is likely they were all travelling together. That is the first record of the lovers together.

On October 6 of that year, John Law was granted the freedom of the city of The Hague in Holland. The entry in the citizens' book or *Burgerboek* reads: "October 1702: Jean Law [has] become a citizen and has taken the oath. Note: is said to be a Scotsman from Edinburgh."[34]

It is plain to see why Law settled in The Hague. Chosen by the Earl of Marlborough for his headquarters, the little court town had for years been the centre of European diplomacy and intelligence, the "whispering gallery" of Europe. The princes of Austria, Russia, Poland, Portugal, Denmark, Sweden, Savoy, Lorraine and the German states maintained envoys or residents in the town.[35] There were not only officers to relieve of their cash at play, but ministers to interest in schemes and projects. What is hard to see is why Law thought he needed to take the oath. To live in The Hague did not require citizenship or *burgerschap*, which was a condition only of the right to ply certain regulated trades. Those did not include gambling, dealing in lottery tickets or promoting financial innovations. If Law did have in mind to set up in a corporate trade as, say, a jeweller, there is no evidence to hand.

It was probably in Holland that John Law became familiar with certain business practices of which the most important was the options trade or, in Dutch, *premienegotie*. The trade began as a form of insurance for merchants against movement in the price of long-haul merchandise, such as pepper, coffee, whale oil or borax. At the cost of a fee or premium (*premie* in Dutch, *prime* in French), a trader could strike a bargain with another person (of a contrary opinion) to fix the price at which he sold or bought an incoming cargo.

In the course of the later sixteenth and the seventeenth century, these premiums took on a life of their own, separated from the palpable merchandise and became instruments of speculation in their own right. Men and women who could not be doing with ships in the Texel roads or warehouses on the Verversgracht still wished to bet on the future price of commodities or securities. A commercial writer in 1722 described how, in Amsterdam, "one very often trades several sorts of merchandise in the air, whether by selling what one does not possess, or buying what one has no intention to accept."[36] Stationers in the town sold blank forms which had only to be filled in with the date, the names of the parties to the contract, the commodity or security, the price and the premium paid. When writing in French, Law uses the word *prime* to describe both options of this sort and simple bets or wagers.

Another Amsterdam practice was the short sale or, in Dutch, *baissetransactie* in which, instead of buying a commodity or security in the hope of a rise, the speculator sells it for the fall. In other words, he sells merchandise or shares that he does not own in the belief that, when the time comes to deliver them, he can buy them cheaper in the market that day and enjoy a gain. In practice, as in the options trade, the underlying goods or securities rarely changed hands, and only the gain or loss was paid. Such is the ingenuity of human beings and the Dutch.

By 1704, Law was back in Scotland. The year before, his mother had reinstated him in the succession to Lauriston Castle. On April 3, 1703, Jean Campbell established an entail or multi-generational settlement for the estate of Lauriston in favour of John Law, her eldest son, and the heirs male of his body, the which failing to William Law and his sons, the which failing to Robert Law and sons and so on to Hugh Law.[37] Andrew was presumed dead in the West Indies.[38] In a later "Ratification and Obligation" of July 18, 1707, Jean admitted the heirs female of John Law to the entail, the which failing she asked that the lands be sold for the benefit of the children of "the deceased Andrew Law" along with her other surviving grandchildren. She had continued to lend, at least until 1701, for a record survives of March 7 of that year for a loan of £63 14s. sterling to the Jacobite William Keith, Earl Marischal of Scotland.[39]

John Law had also reached an understanding with Robert Wilson. In the late summer of 1704, Law petitioned Queen Anne for pardon both for "the death of the said John [*sic*] Willson" and for breaking from prison. He wrote that he was "now recideing in Scotland, and by the intercession of friends have prevailed with the said Appellant [Robert Wilson] to annull his Appeale. Yet your Petitioner is debarred from serving your Majestie (as he is most desirous) in the just Warr wherein your Majesty is now engadged." Law prayed therefore for pardon of both offences that he "may be at Liberty to employ the Remainder of his Life owing to your Majestie's Goodness in your Majestie's Service". In the left margin, Robert Harley, Secretary of State for the Northern Department (which at that time included Scotland), or his clerk wrote: "September 5, 1704. Rejected".[40]

At the best of times, Queen Anne detested duelling, but Law could not have chosen a worse time for his petition. Relations between Scotland and England had deteriorated. Scotland, distressed by the failure of the Darien expeditions, which it blamed on the English ministry, and sceptical of Queen Anne's war, was no longer in a mood to accept a subordinate role.

All the Queen's children had died. In 1701, by the Act of Settlement, the English Parliament had named a Protestant princess, the dowager Electress Sophia of Hanover, granddaughter of James I/VI, and her heirs, as successors to Anne, should she have no more children. In 1703, the Queen's High Commissioner, the Duke of Queensberry, lost control of the Scottish Parliament which passed an Act of Security that stated that should the Queen remain childless, Scotland would choose her own Protestant prince "always of the Royal Line of Scotland" as ruler. There would be no joint sovereign unless Scotland was granted "limitations" on the power of the Crown and unrestricted access to the English colonial trade. For good measure, the Scottish Parliament made funds for the war contingent on royal assent to the Act of Security. Finally, on August 5, 1704, the Queen through her new Commissioner, the Marquess of Tweeddale, was obliged to assent.[41]

In reopening the question of succession, which had troubled the British Isles for thirty years, the Act of Security was received in England, as Defoe wrote, "as in Effect, a Declaration of War".[42] Engaged against Louis XIV on the continent, England could not afford to leave a postern gate open at its back. The old idea of a full or incorporating union, with a single parliament and a free trade area, such as Cromwell had imposed by force of arms, was resurrected in London.

Shortly before Law's petition, on Saturday, August 12, 1704, in the harbour of Leith on the Firth just north of Edinburgh, "between 30 and 40 Scots persons" boarded an English merchantman with cargo from the East Indies, the *Worcester*, which had taken shelter there.[43] They drew their swords and took possession of ship and cargo, in recompense for the impounding by the English

East India Company of one of the Company of Scotland's ships, the *Annandale*, in the Downs (that is, off the Kent coast).

It made no difference that the *Worcester* was owned by four East London merchants trading on their own capital not that of the East India. Investigators then claimed to have found evidence that the *Worcester*'s commander, Captain Thomas Green, who was then sick on shore, and some of his crew had in the first part of 1703 pillaged another Scottish ship, the *Speedy Return*, off the coast of Malabar, by Calicut, murdered the sailors and thrown their bodies overboard.[44] All the crew was arrested.

Westminster retaliated in December with an Aliens Bill which even Defoe, no friend of the Scots, called "the most impolitic, I had almost said Unjust, that ever past that great Assembly".[45] Unless Scotland accepted the Hanoverian succession and agreed terms for a full union by Christmas Day, 1705, Scots would lose their privileges under English law and be treated as foreigners, and imports from Scotland would be banned.[46] Those Scots with property in England, principally the nobility, which was the dominant estate in the Scots Parliament, would face difficulty in passing it on to their heirs.

In addition, the Scots would lose some £80,000 sterling a year in the sale of Highland black cattle, handloom linen and coal to England. Poor harvests throughout the 1690s had cost lives, ruined indebted landowners and forced Parliament to send money to England for victual. Payments of wages and pensions were many years in arrears. With Scotland importing more than she exported, the difference had to be made up by sending out money with the result that there was a shortage or dearth of coin. In December, 1704, the Bank of Scotland ran out of cash to honour its banknotes and stopped lending for five months.[47]

On March 14, 1705, the High Court of Admiralty in Edinburgh found Captain Green and thirteen others of his crew guilty of piracy, robbery and murder.[48] The vessel pirated was not named, and the crew of the *Worcester*, as a Scottish Lord Advocate put it thirty years later, "seemed to me to have no other crime but that of being Englishmen".[49] Against the express request of the Queen, Captain Green, First Mate John Madder and Gunner James Simpson were hanged on April 11 above the flood mark on Leith Sands. Men and women from across the Scottish Lowlands converged on the sands to applaud the execution. The *Worcester* was transferred to the Company of Scotland. "This bussines of Green, &c. is the devil and all," the former Secretary Johnston wrote from London. "It has spoilled all bussines."[50]

In the insurrectionary atmosphere, Agnes Campbell printed an essay by her nephew entitled *Money and Trade Considered; with a Proposal for Supplying the Nation with Money*. It made a change from quarto Bibles by the hundred dozen and *Durham on Death*. It is a clean production. Law may have supervised her apprentices in the College Yards, as later Robert Burns the compositors of the Edinburgh edition of his poems.

While timed to coincide with the coming session of the Scottish Parliament, due to open after some delay on June 28, the essay was not addressed to the Scottish estates and was not signed. Its author was a fugitive from English justice and did not want his notoriety to stand in the way of his ideas. In this short work, which has been admired by economic writers in recent years, Law asks what money is and then suggests how to create it for the exigencies of the Kingdom of Scotland in 1705. He proposes an issue of paper money, secured not on deposits of silver (as at the Bank of Scotland) or the promises-to-pay of the King (as at the Bank of England) but the direct and indirect source of all wealth at that time, which was land.

The idea of a money backed by mortgages, always attractive to families with fields but without cash, was not new. It was first mooted under the Commonwealth, was the talk of London in the mid-1690s and surfaced in the English colonies of North America, where many financial innovations of that era had a sort of afterlife.

To finance King William's War, the English Parliament in 1696 approved a scheme in which adventurers, in return for lending the King £2.5 million, might incorporate as the "Governor and Company of the National Land Bank of England" and lend on mortgage to landed men up to that sum. No doubt, the National Land Bank would have issued banknotes against those mortgages but the flotation was too much even for the London capital market, which was anyway short of cash because of a recoinage. There was a run on the Bank of England, and by the closing date only £7,100 had been subscribed to the Land Bank.[51] Though the fiasco discredited land banks in England, and disrupted the financing of the war, the projector Hugh Chamberlen presented similar schemes to the Parliaments of Ireland and Scotland.

By his own account, Law had been mulling his land bank or mint for "several years before I had seen any of his [Chamberlen's] papers".[52] An unsigned manuscript, published as *Essay on a Land Bank* in 1994 by the Irish scholar Antoin Murphy and ascribed by him to Law, may be an early draft. French historians have thought to see the hand of Law in a set of memoirs from 1701 and 1702 in Paris for a paper money based on land.[53] It is certain that Law sent memorials on finance to the English ministers including Sidney Godolphin, the Lord High Treasurer and a member, with the Marlboroughs (since 1702, Duke and Duchess), of the Queen's inner court.[54]

Law later said that *Money and Trade* was "badly enough written", and when it was translated into French and printed in Holland in 1720, he had the French foreign service buy up and destroy all the copies it could find. He was, no doubt, embarrassed to be associated with an antiquated doctrine. As he wrote in 1722, he had come to see "great difficulties in the idea of a money from immovable property".[55] Whatever its virtues or defects, Law's land-mint scheme was engulfed in the partisan animosities of the Scottish nobility and gentry of that time and was never enacted.

In those days, thought about money was, as so often with human beings, both obstinate and confused. Though men and women used ledger entries, paper bonds, banknotes and bills of exchange to settle debts, those must (it was thought) be converted in the end into gold and silver coins, which alone were money in its timeless or universal essence. The Roman Empire lived on in its currency, though the Roman *libra* that had become the English and Scottish pound, the French *livre* and the *lira* of Italy was no longer a pound weight in silver or even any tangible thing, but an imaginary value against which the palpable guineas, crowns, florins or pistoles varied.

The working of mines of silver in the New World in the sixteenth century, and the ships unloading treasure in the Spanish ports, had augmented the metal money, but not so far as to match the expansion in trade, which was discharged on credit. Anyway, much of the New World silver passed straight through Europe to pay for cloths and spices from India and the East, and did not return.

If a merchant had money due him at some distant city or foreign port, he might bring it home through an instrument called a bill of exchange, or sell the bill and credit in the market to a merchant, tourist or state envoy who needed funds at that place. Credit was a sort of merry-go-round which worked until a mishap or accident caused merchants to lose faith in one another and demand "ringing coin" of which there was not remotely enough. The merry-go-round halted, merchants went out of business and trade was disrupted for months or years. In wartime, the system was yet more unstable because soldiers of every nation, not knowing whether they would be alive the next day, would accept only coin else they would not fight.

What John Law saw as well as anybody of his age was the double duty of the precious metals. He had watched in his father's shop in the Parliament Close of Edinburgh a handful of "broken silver" become both a drinking bowl and the security for a loan. He had been told how, in the disturbed conditions of the seventeenth century, silver plate had been melted down to make coins to pay soldiers and then, in better times, shaped again into a porringer. Yet though the two uses of the metals met and overlapped in the imagination, and gold and silver brought prestige to ornaments from their use as money, those uses were in reality distinct. If there was any interior value to a silver coin, it was its beauty in ornament which could only be revealed by the destruction of the coin. As Law wrote: "Silver while money is of no other use."[56]

Law knew no more than his generation about the origin of money. He thought it had been invented to remedy the inconveniences of barter. Aristotle had surmised that money was created as a sort of "middle term" to allow A to have what he wanted from B when B did not want anything A had to offer. A gave silver for B's object or service, and B used the silver to buy from C something he did want.[57] (In reality, credit long pre-dated money, for what else are the gift exchanges of *The Odyssey* but forms of credit?)

For Law, what gave silver its value in trade (as opposed to the imagination) was precisely its use in trade, a sort of premium for convenience, which varied according to the demands of commerce and the supply of silver. Silver was a chip or token, and not a very good one, for the profusion of American silver had caused the metal to fall in value against almost everything. Law seems to have been rummaging in the old Scots records, for he gives the price in silver of wheat in 1495, claret in 1520, malt in 1532 and mutton in 1551.[58] He ends with a sentence that shows that his English style, though lean, is not without pith: "Money is not the value for which goods are exchanged, but the value by which they are exchanged; the use of money is to buy goods, and silver while money is of no other use."[59]

At this point, John Law seems ready to present the modern argument that anything can serve as money. Instead, Law moves on to examine what he calls "trade", which means for him all the things bartered or sold in a country or what is nowadays called "the economy". With its greater natural advantages, Scotland could be more prosperous than Holland but men and women, "arts-men" (craftsmen), lands, buildings and vessels lay idle for want of a money to set them in motion or use.

The wealth of a nation did not consist, as almost everybody thought at the time, of holdings of the rare and beautiful metals, but of the labour of its people and the fruits of the earth. "National power and wealth," Law wrote, "consists in numbers of people, and magazines of home and forreign goods. These depend on trade, and trade depends on money. So to be powerful and wealthy in proportion to other nations, we should have money in proportion with them; for the best laws without money cannot employ the people, improve the product, or advance manufacture and trade."[60] In other words, money must be turned to the service of trade, and lie at the discretion of the prince or parliament to vary according to the needs of trade. Such an idea, orthodox and even tedious for the past fifty years, was thought in the seventeenth century to be diabolical.

An objection, a commonplace since antiquity, was that creating money without a corresponding increase in things to buy with the new money merely causes those things to rise in price. Abroad, foreigners will have no occasion for the new money and its rate of exchange into foreign moneys will fall. Law counters by saying that the men and women put to work by the inflated money will both make and consume more thus absorbing the new-minted or -printed money and increasing the volume and sophistication of goods for export.

Law conjures up an island, a theoretical territory first cultivated in modern times by Sir Thomas More in his *Utopia* and soon to become famous in Jonathan Swift's *Gulliver's Travels* and Defoe's *Robinson Crusoe*. Law's island is a place more rudimentary even than Scotland, in which under a single proprietor one thousand persons live by bartering the produce of their farms, but have nothing to do in the winter while another three hundred are "poor or idle [unemployed], who live by charity".[61] Any surplus is exchanged for "cloaths" and other goods from the continent across the water.[62]

The proprietor introduces money. In place of the crop he receives from each tenant in rent, the owner proposes to take a certain number of paper notes. Since he is always ready to take the notes, the islanders have confidence in them and begin to use them in trading with one another. The consequence, Law writes, is that the three hundred unemployed and poor now have some spur to finish and improve those agricultural goods that were hitherto exported to the continent in a raw state. The thousand tenant farmers will be tempted to work through their winters, which would "lessen their import . . . from the continent and raise their export to 3 or 4 times the value it had".[63]

If the proprietor then issues paper beyond the old annual equivalent in corn, meat and milk, he will attract "the poor and idle" from the continent who will produce and consume yet more. In other words, Law says that an increase in money within reason will increase the product and thus not cause price rises or an adverse balance in foreign payments. Fifteen years later, in an experiment covering all of France and its overseas territories, Law put his theory to the test.

Having accustomed his readers to his island economy, Law takes a further step. He supposes that the proprietor issues paper not just for the rent of land but for the land itself, which then as now was valued as a multiple of its annual rent. In creating money from land, the proprietor in no way impairs the primary use of land (as occurs with silver) or needs rely on a foreign source (such as the mines of Spanish America). Moreover, since land is the distant origin of all things bought and sold, paper issued against productive land will stand in a relation to both what is produced and what is required.

After all this reasoning, the proposal when it comes is perfunctory. Law suggests that the Parliament of Scotland appoint forty commissioners with the authority "to coin notes" up to £50,000 in the first instance: "which notes to be received in payments, where offer'd" or as the modern phrase is, legal tender. Law suggests three ways in which that might be done, from which Parliament "in their wisdom may determine which will be the most safe". The commissioners could issue notes to the landed men for a portion of the value of their lands, one half or two-thirds; as a mortgage on the whole value for a fixed term; or through buying the lands outright. Those wishing to redeem their notes would receive the lands or mortgages on the lands but not the equivalent in silver.[64] If that sounds cumbersome, at least they might redeem their banknotes, which is not the case today. If you present at the Bank of England one of its £5 notes, the cashier will give you a duplicate or its sum in alloy coins or a flea in your ear. In addition, Law recommended that the Scots pound and shilling be reformed to the English standard.

The Queen's Commissioner to the 1705 session of the Scots Parliament was the young John Campbell, 2nd Duke of Argyll (1680–1743), a professional soldier who arrived from England towards the end of April. His instructions from the Queen were to seek approval of the Hanoverian succession and only failing that to open negotiations or "treaty" for a full or "incorporating" union of the two kingdoms.

With him was his younger brother, Lord Archibald Campbell (1682–1761) who had been named Lord High Treasurer of Scotland. It is probable that Law was known at least to Lord Archie, who the next year was made Earl of Ilay. They were later friends. As leaders of the Campbell clan (which included Law's mother), they were the dominant force in north and western Scotland, but without any particular allegiance except to themselves. "We always judge for ourselves without any prejudice of any side farther than honour and interest joined oblige us," Ilay later wrote.[65] On June 7, Law was summoned to the Palace of Holyrood to explain his plan to the brothers.[66]

Law's was not the only proposal to tackle the financial crisis in Scotland that summer. William Greg, a Scottish clerk in the office of Robert Harley, English Secretary of State, was sent up by his master at the beginning of June to report on the session of the Scots Parliament. (Greg was to be hanged three years later for passing Harley's papers for money to the French war minister and controller general of finances, Michel Chamillart.) Greg wrote to Harley that June 7: "The poverty this country labours under at present is so great, that any project for remedying such an epidemical distemper, must needs find an easy impression here."[67]

Despite the failure at Darien, the Company of Scotland was in talks with two delegates purporting to come from pirates established on the island of Madagascar, who in return for Scottish protection, pardon and nationality, were offering to open a trade in African slaves to Brazil. The senior of the two, Captain John Bryholt, "a notable talking man", and presumably a Dane, offered fifty sail and five millions in money, later reduced to ten sail and no money.[68] (He proposed a similar plan to the English ministry, with equal success.)[69] Greg then passed on to a man well known, at least in the Secretary of State's office, as an airy visionary.

"But lest a project so far fetched should not succeed," Greg wrote to London of the Bryholt plan on June 9, "so speedily as they could wish, a homespun one is set afoot here by a gentleman who of all men living once was thought to have the worst turned head that way. Mr Law, who killed Beau Wilson in England is the man and so fond is the Commissioner [Argyll] of this project for a Land Bank (since money fails) that the day before yesterday his Grace sent for the quondam [former] Rake in order to discourse him fully upon this important point, so very necessary at this time. He [Law] proposes the striking tallies for [raising] 50,000l sterling at first and then proceeding according as issues are made."[70]

It was decided to hear again Dr Chamberlen's proposal for a land bank from 1704. There survives also in the parliamentary record for that year a pamphlet, printed by George Mosman in the Parliament Close for the sitting, entitled: "Money encreased and Credit Raisd". Attributed to James Donaldson, editor of the *Edinburgh Gazette*, it recommended buying in about a third of the silver plate in Scotland to the tune of £50,000 sterling, minting debased coins with a face value of £75,000 and using the £25,000 left over to capitalise a national bank which would lend four times its capital at 4 per cent. The author reckoned on a £3,000 net profit in the first year, which would be added to the bank's capital, further expanding its capacity to lend.[71]

On Tuesday, July 10, George Baillie of Jerviswood presented Law's proposal or, as it was reported, "a proposal for remeid of the coin given in by Jerviswood, in four articles, taken out of Mr Law's book".[72] At that time, the Scots nobility was in love with all things Italian, and Baillie of Jerviswood belonged to a new party in Parliament nicknamed the *squadrone volante* after a grouping of Cardinals at the Papal election of 1655. The *squadrone* saw themselves as independent of both the court in London, represented by

Argyll and other office-holders and -seekers, and the nationalists and Jacobites of the Country Party.

At the next sitting, on July 12, Andrew Fletcher of Saltoun, a patriot and bully-boy who had led the agitation against the royal prerogative in the 1703 Parliament, demanded that Law and Chamberlen be called to the bar to explain their proposals in person. The Duke of Montrose's clansman and chamberlain, Mungo Graham of Gorthie, in a letter to his chief of July 13, 1705, set the scene.

> Salton . . . said [the proposals] were shoals and shams to ruine the country, and to enslave the nation. Jerviswood said that Salton's saying so of them did not make them such, and that he believed they deserved the parliament's consideration; and that the subject being yet new to a great many of the members, it would be inconvenient to have any discoursing upon it so soon.
>
> Salton's next effort was to have a day appointed for hearing of them, and that Mr Law and Doctor Chamberlain might be ordered to attend the house; and says he when these two are confronted together, perhaps they might explain their gibberish language so to the house, as would make them understand it.
>
> Upon this my lord Roxburgh [another *squadrone* member] said that Mr Law having out of designs to serve his country written his thoughts in that matter without proposing any reward for himself, might at least expect a civill treatment from the parliament, and he thought it good manners the P[arliament]. would not oblidge him to answer for his opinions, unless he desired it himself. Upon which Salton said he knew very well what good manners was, and it was ill manners in my lord Roxburgh to tax him of being unmannerly.[73]

Greg, who was also in the chamber, wrote that "had he [Fletcher] been near Roxburgh they would have gone together by the ears."[74]

It was clear to all that Fletcher and the Earl of Roxburghe would fight. Fletcher had already killed at least one man, in the English West Country, in 1685, over a horse.[75] Argyll ordered both men not to stir from their lodgings, but next morning, the 13th, they slipped out and met on Leith Sands. Roxburgh was so crippled in his legs,[76] that Saltoun offered to fight with pistols, something of a novelty for that period. Baillie of Jerviswood acted as second for the Earl of Roxburgh, and Lord Charles Kerr for Fletcher.

Argyll sent out a detachment of guards which could not find the duellists. As it turned out, both seconds were keen there be no blood shed. "Lord Charles is on the tope [point] of his mariage," John Erskine, Earl of Mar, wrote to his wife at Alloa on the 16th. "If they had fought it had been unluckie for him."[77] Baillie of Jerviswood concurred and the duellists fired in the air.[78] (Pushkin wrote *The Shot*, one of the very best of all short stories, on the theme of wedding-morning duels.)

Many members of Parliament thought Law's scheme was a distraction from the main question: was there to be a treaty of union? "We have trifled all this time," Mar continued to his countess. "There's one Act past against importing Irish or English butter or chise for useing in the country, but alowed for export. This Act will probablie be keept as the rest of our Acts are [that is, not at all]. Laws paper project was spoke of in Parl., and some words past between Roxbrough and Salton."[79]

Law reworked his project as a joint-stock company. There is a draft prospectus in the Scottish parliamentary records, with corrections in what may or may not be Law's handwriting, entitled "Act for a Land Mint". It proposed a "free incorporation by the name of the Land Mint of Scotland", with £100,000 sterling in capital consisting of one thousand shares, issued each for "good land security to the value of 100 lib sterling per share". Once the incorporation had 200 subscriptions it would begin to "coin notes upon land or a land money".[80]

It was not adopted. In retrospect, it is hard to imagine a quarrelsome Scottish Parliament ever consenting to give the Duke of Argyll and his supporters control over the supply of credit in Scotland. It was not until 1727 that Ilay, and some of Law's associates but not Law himself, were to found a bank in the Campbell interest, the Royal Bank of Scotland.

On July 27, Parliament considered the "proposal for supplying the nation with money by a paper credit. After reasoning and debate thereon, it was agreed that the forceing any paper credit by an act of parliament was unfit for this nation."[81] After heated exchanges through the course of August, the house resolved to enter into negotiations with England for a union. The articles, which were signed in London in July, 1706 enshrined the Hanoverian succession, a single Parliament in London, a common currency and an equal free trade. Without admitting any fault in her ministers, the Queen paid £398,085 and 10s. to make whole the shareholders of the Company of Scotland, which was liquidated, and to discharge arrears of offices and pensions. The Kingdom of Great Britain came into existence on May 1, 1707. The Union was unloved by many Scots and remained so for fifty years, providing a rich ground for the Jacobites to hoe.

John Law drew conclusions from his failure. He seems to have resolved to have no more to do with factional politics and parliaments, but to win over some prince inclined to seek glory not in war or building but in the prosperity of his subjects. At some point in 1705 or early 1706, John Law left his homeland. There is no evidence he ever returned.

CHAPTER FOUR

Plum Man

Si j'etois mon maitre je prefererois l'Italie a l'allemagne a la danemark, meme a la France.
(If I were my own master, I would choose Italy over Germany and Denmark and even France.)

JOHN LAW[1]

The War of the Spanish Succession (1701–14), or Queen Anne's War as it is known in North America, was fought not only in Flanders, but on the upper Rhine and Danube, in Piedmont and Milan, on the Mediterranean, in Spain, Portugal and Catalonia, and in North America. Armies of 100,000 men were put into the field, and their maintenance strained European treasuries and private credit to the limit.

At issue in the fight was, once again, the power of France. The accession in 1700 to the throne of Spain of Louis XIV's grandson, Philippe, duc d'Anjou, threatened Europe with a joint monarchy of the Bourbon family and a single empire controlling the Atlantic trade. England and Holland, the so-called maritime powers, and Austria and its German allies combined to support a rival candidate for the Spanish throne, the son of the Habsburg Emperor, Archduke Charles. He was crowned Charles III of Spain in Vienna in 1703.

Under the pressure of a war on several fronts, Michel Chamillart, the controller general of the French finances, sought to monopolise the coin in France to pay her soldiers and sailors. In 1701, he began offering those bringing silver and gold to the mints not coin but paper receipts, known as *billets de monnoye* or mint bills, in the hope that those would supply the shortage of coin in commerce.

A series of French defeats at the hands of the Duke of Marlborough and the Imperial commander, Prince Eugene of Savoy, shook confidence in the mint bills. By 1707, they were changing hands at under half their face value. Merchants took to writing contracts that specified payment in cash "without any mint bills at all".[2] The exercise defeated itself and France resumed her descent towards bankruptcy.

For a part of the war, Law and Lady Katherine were at The Hague, where their son William was born, probably in 1706. The baptismal registers of the city's churches, and of the Scottish church in Rotterdam, have no record for William under any plausible surname, and it is possible that William was not baptised as a child.[3] That says something about the religious sentiments of his parents.

John Law was certainly in The Hague in the middle of 1706.[4] Later that year or during the next, John Law went to Genoa and was to remain there, off and on, for the next six years.[5] In that city he made a fortune. It was not a rich fortune by the standards of the Duke of Marlborough or the Hon. James Brydges, paymaster of the British forces in Flanders, or of the financiers Samuel Bernard and Antoine Crozat in France, but adequate to establish his small family and to maintain appearances amid princes and statesmen. There, on April 21, 1710, his daughter Mary Catherine was born and survived.[6] She was known as Kate to her father and Kitty to her mother and was the darling of both.

On the way to Genoa, John Law passed through Paris. If he had not been under sentence of death in England, this journey would have earned him one, for high treason.

Two letters in the archives of the controllers general of finances in Paris, printed by the Walloon historian Paul Harsin in 1928, were written by Law from Paris.[7] The first, dated June 15, 1707 asks for passports to leave France. It appears to be addressed to a colleague of the marquis de Torcy, the King's secretary for foreign affairs.[8] Law requests an allowance of six weeks for his journey out of France, "because it is hot, and I would like to have the time to travel in comfort". That suggests Law was heading southward.

"It appears, Sir," Law wrote, "that the scheme I have in mind is not deemed worthy of a hearing in the Council. I cannot say I am surprised. A new species of money more suitable than silver sounds rather impracticable. All the same, I have put forward nothing on that subject that I cannot substantiate."

A month later, John Law was still amusing himself in antechambers. On July 18, he wrote to the same official, reminding him about his passports. He also asked leave to take out of the country plate weighing sixty marks or 490 ounces. Since the French would not have allowed him to take so much precious metal out in wartime, he presumably had brought the plate with him from Holland to cover his expenses. Law added, with a hint of weariness: "I await the audience that the abbé de Thesu has given me hope of receiving, having no other business to keep me here." Jean de Thesut was the secretary of the King's nephew, the duc d'Orléans, who was to have much to do with John Law.

Law left behind in Paris at least one memorial or essay. A manuscript in the Arsenal Library in Paris has for its first sentence: "I propose to prove that a new species of money can be established and be more suitable than gold or silver." In it, Law provides the same high-flown arguments for a land money as in *Money and Trade*, though he draws his examples from France rather than

Scotland.[9] There is nothing in it that addresses the King of France's pressing need for cash.

While Law was still in Paris, or on his way south, on July 21/ August 1, 1707, Jean Campbell died in Edinburgh at the age of sixty-seven. "Lady Lauriestoun" was buried in Greyfriars churchyard on the 23rd, on the south side of the church.[10] She had brought up eight children, improved their estate, married the daughters. There is no monument to her, which is small credit to her eldest son and principal heir. With her death, John Law came into the rents of Lauriston, assessed in the Land Tax of 1708 at £566 Scots, which he placed under the administration of his brother William.[11] A couple of years later, William saw off an encroaching neighbour.[12]

Genoa was then a beautiful town. Lady Mary Wortley Montagu, who stopped there a few years later on her way back from her husband's embassy in Constantinople, described the town thus: "Genoa is situate in a very fine bay; and being built on a rising hill, intermixed with gardens, and beautified with the most excellent architecture, gives a very fine prospect off at sea." She was impressed by the furniture and pictures in the houses on the Strada Nuova (now Via Garibaldi) which she thought "perhaps the most beautiful line of building in the world".[13]

A maritime republic, Genoa had in time lost her possessions in the eastern Mediterranean to Venice and the Ottoman Empire, but her merchants lent their accumulated capital to the Crown of Spain which lorded it over the Italian peninsula. In settlement, they took cargoes of bullion from the American mines. In the sixteenth century, the Castilian poet Francisco de Quevedo wrote of Don Dinero or "My lord Money", born to high estate in the Indies:

Viene a morir en España
Y es en Génova enterrado
(He cometh then to Spain to die
And now in Genoa doth lie.)[14]

In 1705, the Allies captured Barcelona and began using Genoa, in preference to Lisbon, as the base for their supply to the English, Dutch and Imperial forces in Catalonia.

Even by the measure of the age, Genoa was a town devoted to games of chance. The five-number lotto, which has colonised the world, originated in a gamble on the biannual election by lot of five new members of the two principal magistracies, the Senate or *Governatori* and the House or *Procuratori*. After several attempts to ban a game so little suitable to the dignity of the Most Serene Republic, the magistrates in 1644 decided to profit from it and sold the lotto to a consortium of forty investors who, in return for a monopoly on gambling, furnished the Republic with 36,000 lire per year.

By the time of Law's arrival, the concession-holder, Gian Luca Pinelli, was paying the Republic 320,000 lire a year for his privilege. Even so, anonymous denunciations placed in the "urns" of the *Inquisitori di Stato,* the intelligence service set up in 1628 on the Venetian model to monitor seditious or immoral conduct among the citizenry, told of clandestine gambling in "inns, taverns, hostelries and other places out of public view, and places where wine, bread and other comestibles are sold".[15] In December 1710, the Senate issued new laws against these "and other prohibited games".[16]

It is unlikely the Genoese lotto, with its mathematics refined over more than a century, would much have attracted Law who preferred large wagers on favourable odds. No doubt he saw from Holland that the port offered him a living from idle officers waiting to embark for the Allied camp at Barcelona, and the supply of coin, rations, fodder, beasts and munitions to the armies in the Iberian Peninsula. There is a hint in later sources that Paymaster Brydges had done Law a bad turn: so bad, that when John Law was powerful, and Brydges, now the Duke of Chandos, wrote him caressing letters for stock-market intelligence, Law did not reply.[17] Away from the heavy guns of Brydges and the Duke of Marlborough in the Low Countries, Law had a better chance of feeding his family. He came to prefer Italy above all countries.[18]

In addition, Genoa was home to the greatest financial institution to have emerged from the Middle Ages, the Bank of St George. Named after the patron saint of Genoa, the bank was founded at a period of crisis in Genoese affairs at the dawn of the Renaissance in 1407. Known as the Casa delle compere di San Giorgio, it was an institution with a legal existence distinct from its members, a forerunner of the modern company.

For years, the Commune of Genoa had given its lenders the rights to lay customs duties or excises on such staples as grain, wine and salt as the security for their loans. Those rights were known as *compere*, from Latin *comparare* "to buy". They were a form of loan interest, but since the yield from the excises would vary from year to year according to harvests, the weather and other uncertainties, they did not provoke the Church's ban on lending at fixed rates of interest or usury.

In 1407, crippled by its wars with Venice, the Commune was all but bankrupt. As part of the reforms of that year, the existing *compere* were consolidated and the lenders were permitted to incorporate. To accommodate the changing fortunes of its proprietors, each of the *compere* was broken into shares of 100 lire face value, known as *luoghi*, which could be bought and sold, mortgaged, inherited or otherwise transferred through the bank's ledgers.

Law thought the Bank of St George "the best-governed in Italy", which had so monopolised the revenue of the state that it was "a sort of separate republic".[19] He was attracted to the dispersion of risk. Any shortfall in the yield from taxes, by reason of war, a business slump, a poor harvest or act of God, fell not on the state, with all its military and other obligations, or on the poor, but on the several thousand *luogatori*, possessors of surplus capital and thus the people and institutions best able to suffer loss. If they thought the *luoghi* poor investments, they could sell them. The public creditors were therefore not parasites on the state and the pennies of the poor but investors at risk or, as we might say, shareholders in the nation. This notion, advanced even for today, Law tried to realise in France.[20]

In addition, the Casa di San Giorgio operated a banking business. Two benches or *banchi* were established at the Palazzo San Giorgio on the sea-front to take deposits from individuals and pious institutions. Those could then settle debts with one another without resort to cash but simply through movements in the ledgers. Those benches were later supplemented by others dealing in specific Italian and Spanish coins. From those *banchi* come our banks.

During this time, Law sent proposals to the French ministers. One of them must have been well-circulated, for it survives in six handwritten copies in Paris (and another in the British Library). It describes how at Genoa the rate of interest falls on the sight of a bullion ship from Spain, and rises if there is adverse news.[21] Law was also in discreet correspondence with John Campbell's bank at the sign of the Three Crowns in London's Strand, for his address has been scrawled by a clerk on the waste front endpaper of the 1709 outletter book: "Mr Lawe att Mr Chetwines in Genova undr his Cover".[22]

William Chetwynd (known as Chettvoynd in the Genoese

confidential reports) was the British resident in Genoa. From an age-old family long settled at Ingestre (pronounced Ingustray) in Staffordshire in the English Midlands, William had entered the English foreign service as secretary to his brother, John, envoy in Turin to the Duke of Savoy, Victor Amadeus II. In 1708, William was appointed resident at Genoa, where he remained until 1712. As well as acting as postbox for Law, William was also his friend, and there is a sort of snapshot of their pleasant life in the spring of 1709 in the memoirs of a German soldier of fortune, Casimir, Count von Schlippenbach (1682–1753). Those memoirs, written in French and entitled *Journal de ma Vie*, are in the Dutch archives.[23] They are as reliable as eighteenth-century memoirs generally are, which is not very reliable.

Born in the Kurland, a German-ruled enclave west of Riga in what is now Latvia, the Protestant Schlippenbach had entered the Dutch service and travelled to Genoa in March 1709 seeking passage to Barcelona. Once arrived, he found there were no Dutch ships of war in the Mediterranean and English skippers would carry him only on a written order from the Duke of Marlborough or a large sum of money. Frustrated, Schlippenbach resolved to seek help from the "the English gentlemen" in Genoa.

"I had been well acquainted at The Hague," he wrote, "with that famous Law, who was then at Genoa where he made a rich living from play and other business dealings [*autres negociations*]."[24] Both Law and Chetwynd promised to help Schlippenbach aboard the first English warship to sail, and that duly arrived, three weeks later, towing a rich prize. The captain, a gruff, salty, weather-beaten nautical tyrant, sold return passages to Barcelona to civilians for 150–300 gold louis but refused to take Schlippenbach without the Duke of Marlborough's order.

At a splendid supper in his honour, Law and Chetwynd plied the sea-dog with wine and punch, which he drank to the point of stupor (*jusqu'à se saouler*), while muttering in English: "I know what you are about but, God damn, I tell you I'll have none of it."[25] On the morrow, Schlippenbach went to the merchants' exchange, the Loggia dei mercanti, and booked a berth on a vessel shipping gunpowder. Meeting his English friends nearby at a café (*limonadier*), he told them of his good fortune but Law and the others were aghast and refused to hear of it. Finally, to cut short this shaggy-dog story, the Englishmen smuggled Schlippenbach on board the warship in the garb and wig of a servant and, once she had sailed, the captain relented and admitted him to his table. Schlippenbach was years later kind to Law's daughter.

A month later, the storm lowering over the French finances burst and engulfed Genoa. Louis XIV's principal banker, the converted Protestant Samuel Bernard (1651–1739) had for some time been unable to repay in cash his foreign lenders. Instead, Bernard and his Swiss partner Jean Nicolas (a Huguenot refugee from the Languedoc) postponed or rolled over settlement at the quarterly fairs at Lyons, then the prime French money market and door or gateway to the Huguenot financiers of Geneva.

In the month following each fair, that is in March (*Roys*), June (*Pâques*), September (*Août*) and December (*Saints*), accounts between merchants were cast up and netted off, postponed or settled in cash in an antiquated procedure known as the Paiements de Lyon. In a last-ditch attempt to stave off disaster, Bernard and other investors pressed in 1708 to float a national bank or *banque royale*, on the pattern of the Bank of England, to buy out the mint bills with banknotes and meet some 40 million livres in payments at Lyons. The effect was to add yet more uncertainty and the bank project was dropped in February, 1709.

The winter of 1709 had been severe. On the day of Epiphany, a freeze began that lasted a month, ruining vines, figs, chestnuts and fruit trees even in the south of France, destroying the winter-sown wheat, and killing beasts in the fields. Through the spring it rained without ceasing. The price of bread more than doubled and there were riots in Paris, Bordeaux, Lyons, Rouen and elsewhere. Poor people starved or froze to death. At the delayed *Paiement des Roys* in April, Bernard's Lyonnais and Swiss lenders refused to let him postpone payment, and demanded cash. On the 8th his correspondent in the city, Bertrand Castan, refused to honour bills on him and set off a chain-reaction of bankruptcies and failures. Chamillart's successor as controller general, Nicolas Desmaretz, rescued Bernard but the capital markets of Lyons, Geneva, Turin and Genoa dried up.

Bankers in Italy were afraid to honour bills on the pay contractor in London, Sir Henry Furnese, for the British army in Spain. John Chetwynd wrote to Brydges from Turin: "The want of money is so general or the apprehension of severall Bankrupts [bankruptcies] so great, upon suspicion of Bernard & Nicolas's failing, that all the purses in these p[ar]ts are shut."[26] William Chetwynd in Genoa told Law's acquaintance, General James Stanhope in Spain on May 9: "For above these six weeks, nobody has dared to offer a bill upon the Exchange here for fear of it being refused nor advance a farthing of money."[27]

The Chetwynds, who like most of the Queen's servants abroad had an eye for their own affairs, took their chance. That day, May 9, 1709, they foregathered at the town of Alessandria, halfway between Turin and Genoa, and resolved to use their own commercial credit to supply Stanhope with the £20,000–£30,000 a month he needed to keep his men from mutiny. In the evening at the inn in Alessandria, they wrote circular letters to Stanhope and Brydges; the Earl of Godolphin, Lord Treasurer; Sir Henry Furnese and the British admiral commanding in the Mediterranean, Sir George Byng. Furnese was displeased at so being pushed aside, but Stanhope supported the brothers and the business was theirs.

There is no evidence, either in the brothers' letters in the record offices of Stafford and Maidstone in England, or in the acts of the notaries of Genoa that Law was involved in this operation. It carries his imprint only in its audacity, which is uncharacteristic of the Chetwynds. The ledgers of the Bank of St George, swaddled in calfskin and deer-sinew against the sea air at an industrial estate on the outskirts of Genoa, offer a hint. On October 1, 1709, Giovanni Lau deposited with one of the banks the cash equivalent of 25,378 lire and four denari or pennies.[28] That was about £1,270 sterling, perhaps £100,000 today, which he withdrew a fortnight later. John Law becomes easier to follow. It is a fact of modern history that the more money a man has, the greater his imprint on the record.

In the spring of 1710, General Stanhope passed through Genoa on his way back from London to Spain. James Stanhope, who was two years younger than Law, was one of those soldier-statesmen that England in those days raised in abundance. Born in Paris, he had returned as a young officer in the embassy of the Earl of Portland in 1698, and made friends with the tutor or governor of the young duc d'Orléans, the abbé Guillaume Dubois, and with the duke himself, who dearly loved him.[29] This triangle, with the addition for a while of a fourth point in John Law, was to transform European politics. Too impetuous to be a soldier of the first rank, Stanhope devised a new style of diplomacy, conducted in rapid journeys and face-to-face negotiation, visionary, careless of procedure, forceful to the point of roughness.

Queen Anne's instructions to Stanhope, when he took over command in Spain in 1708, empowered him to buy corn in Genoa and also "take up such Sum or Sums of Money as you shall need for the carrying on these services . . . and to draw Bills for the same on our High Treasurer, or the Paymaster General of our Forces, at the most moderate and easy Rates of Exchange".[30] It is unthinkable that he did not pass some time with Law at the *limonadier* by the Loggia dei mercanti. Seven years later, when he became Chancellor of the Exchequer, Stanhope told King George I that England had lost in the person of John Law more than the fifty millions she had borrowed for her wars.[31]

Law's fortune at the Casa di San Giorgio crept up. At the end of August, 1710, when the subsidiary banks cast up their half-yearly accounts, Law had a credit balance of 64,831 lire, 7 soldi and 2 denari at one of the banks and 1,297 lire and 10 soldi at another. At that time, a labourer in Genoa earned one or two lire per day. His depositors included army contractors such as Joseph Bouer, the British consul in Turin; John Scudamore, who was in partnership with George Henshaw, British consul in Genoa; Guillaume Boissier, a Huguenot merchant in Genoa originally from the Cévennes; and members of the Cambiasso and Frugoni families of Genoa.[32]

Stanhope arrived in Barcelona to find the campaign progressing towards stalemate. Charles III had little support outside Catalonia and Aragon and he, and his principal captain, Guido, Count Starhemberg, were inclined to the defensive. Stanhope won them over for an aggressive policy and after scattering Philip's army in Aragon, the Allied advance guard under Stanhope entered Madrid on September 21. Much of the citizenry had abandoned the town and when Charles III arrived in his capital on the 28th, he found the streets empty and houses shut up. Meanwhile, Louis XIV had despatched reinforcements from Bayonne under Louis Joseph, duc de Vendôme.

Unwilling to risk a winter in hostile Castile, the Allies set off for the coast in December, short of food and even money and, as Stanhope wrote on December 2 to the new admiral of the Mediterranean fleet, Sir John Norris, "with the country about us all up in arms".[33] To make foraging easier, the army divided into three columns marching in parallel. On December 8, Vendôme overtook Stanhope's column of some 4,500 men in the little town of Brihuega, in Guadalajara. His gunners shattered the northern gates, breached the Moorish walls with a mine, and enfiladed the narrow streets with canister. By evening on the 9th, Stanhope had lost six hundred men and, despairing of aid from Starhemberg, surrendered and took his surviving men into Spanish captivity.

That battle marked the end of Stanhope's military career, of the Pensinsular campaign and, at least for the British, of the war itself. After his Pyrrhic victory at Malplaquet on the French frontier in 1709, the Duke of Marlborough was stalled. In a country tired of fighting, the new Tory ministry under Robert Harley was content to hold on to British gains in North America and the Mediterranean (Gibraltar and Minorca) and let Prince Eugene, the Dutch and the Catalonians shift for themselves. Negotiations began in London for the preliminaries of a separate peace with France.

Early in 1711, Sarah, Duchess of Marlborough, was dismissed from her offices at Queen Anne's court. Her husband was relieved of his command in December, 1711 and replaced by Law's old benefactor, the Duke of Ormonde, who received "restraining orders" the following May not to engage the French in battle. The Tory press and majority in Parliament hounded Marlborough for profiteering while a House of Commons committee of inquiry under the Jacobite Tory William Shippen appointed commissioners to examine the accounts of the Spanish campaign.

The commissioners travelled to Genoa, Barcelona, Port Mahon in Minorca, Gibraltar and Lisbon; they found nothing to implicate John Law in any loss to the Queen. Stanhope did admit to the committee that he had, by an oversight, over-invoiced the cost of some fireworks in Tarragona to celebrate the Queen's birthday in 1709 by some 266 pieces of eight or £60, but insists elsewhere that he made money for her account. The inquiry petered out in a thicket of mules, bullocks, remounts, forage and wagon money, abandoned anchors and knapsacks, fortifications, moidores and crozados.[34]

With the war winding down, and the prospect of peace negotiations in the Netherlands, Law thought of returning to The Hague. He remained throughout 1711. Mary Catherine, who was scarcely a year old, was probably too young to travel. Law was also doing well in business and, had he stayed in Genoa, might have made a handy fortune. The Duke of Argyll, who succeeded Stanhope as commander in Spain, was well disposed towards him. Law's balance at the bank, which was 48,290 lire, 9 soldi and 5 denari at the end of August, increased with several large transfers in the autumn and, at the end of December, 1711, stood at 138,116 lire, 13 soldi and 2 denari.[35] The depositors included, alongside the business houses already mentioned, Thomas Langhorne, a merchant of Genoa involved with the British Treasury in supplying the troops in Catalonia.

The last transfer in the ledgers, of just 380 lire on November 9, 1711, came from one Ippolito De Mari, a young nobleman for whom Law lost quite a lot of money, but nevertheless was to be his most devoted friend. Ten years younger than Law, grandson and nephew of Doges of the Republic, Ippolito went on to carry out diplomatic errands for the Republic in the 1720s and 1730s. His house, a stone's throw from the Bank of St George at Via San Luca, 5, survives.

Law was also pressing a banking scheme on the Duke of Savoy, Victor Amadeus II (1666–1732). The duke was a man of wide horizons, little education or culture, violent, bigoted, and economical. John Chetwynd's predecessor as British envoy, the Revd Richard Hill, described him as "very vigorous, active and laborious [industrious], and able to undergo any fatigues of mind and body: loving business more than pleasures, or ease".[36] Looking past Mont Blanc at Louis XIV's France, he was determined to imitate the great king and strengthen the state at the expense of the nobility and the clergy. Law later wrote that what attracted him to the duke's service over that of other princes was the pleasure of dealing directly with him "without being obliged to deal with Your Majesty's ministers".[37] Law later said that Victor Amadeus was one of only two men – the other being Philippe, duc d'Orléans – who understood what he was talking about.[38]

In the long years of warfare, by playing off France against the Empire and changing sides at approximately the right moments (1696 and 1703), Victor Amadeus achieved gains out of proportion to the mediocrity of his title and estate. He had come through the war thanks to the brilliance of his cousin Prince Eugene, whose relief of Turin in 1706 is one of the greatest of all military exploits, and also subsidies from the allies, amounting to 8.6 million lire from the States General and no less than 28.6 million from the Treasury in London.[39] The prospect of receiving an increase in territory from his British allies may have turned the duke, and his advisers, to the thought of a bank to finance it. No doubt John Chetwynd helped introduce Law to the Savoyard ministers, but the duke was always likely to listen to a citizen (even if an outlaw) of the land of fog and money.

Law's proposals for a bank survive in the Turin archives. They were printed by the Savoyard scholars, Antonio Perrero in 1874 and Giuseppe Prato in 1914, and by the Irish economist Antoin Murphy in the 1990s. They are part of a correspondence between Law and Victor Amadeus and his ministers that lasted until January, 1716. Written in fluent and inaccurate French, the bank proposals are undated, except for a specimen banknote which carries the sample date of March 1, 1712.[40]

Breaking with *Money and Trade* and the memorials to the French statesmen, Law now had no thought for a money based on land security.

In one memorial, he describes how the multiplicity of credit in England, from Bank of England notes to Exchequer tallies, goldsmiths' notes and the shares of the Bank and East India Company, had doubled the capital available to trade and industry, furnished merchants with a convenient method of payment, allowed the King to borrow large sums and reduced the rate of interest for private men from 8 per cent to 5 per cent.[41] (If the rate of interest on money falls, merchants and landowners can live with a lower rate of profit, and hence are more ready to invest and to take on workers.)

Possibly in response to a query from one of Victor Amadeus's ministers, Law contrasts the success of the Bank of England notes and the failure of the mint bills in France. In the first case, private investors reinforced King William's credit whereas the mint bills were too obviously a measure of war finance. There were too many of them, in too high denominations and insufficient effort was made to give them currency in trade. The decision in 1711 to try to retire the discredited mint bills by allowing holders to convert them into state annuities or *rentes*, turned a productive merchant into a state pensioner: "instead of being useful to the state, he will become a charge on it".[42]

As for his concrete proposals, Law offers Victor Amadeus and his ministers a choice: a private or "general" bank (like the Bank of Scotland), with a capital of 100,000 pistoles (about £85,000), a twenty-one-year monopoly, and the right to make loans and issue banknotes; or a ducal or state-owned bank or *caisse générale*, which would receive the state revenues, issue banknotes, make loans and cash bills of exchange. No shareholder might own more than ten shares except the "projector", who might have one hundred or 10 per cent of the company.

On October 9, 1711, Law signed in person in the day-book or *giornale* of the bank for a withdrawal of 57,000 lire.[43] On November 15, he was in Milan with Ippolito De Mari and his brother, Giovanni Battista (b.1686), staying in the parish of San Giorgio al Pozzo

Bianco near the Porta Orientale.[44] They may have been on a jaunt to Venice for the opera season, which in those days began on St Martin's Day (November 11) and lasted, with an interval for Advent and Christmas, until Lent. In Venice over the winter, there were opportunities not just for music but for cards.

The peace conference opened at the Town Hall in Utrecht on January 29, 1712. On his way back through Milan, on March 7, 1712, Law was summoned to meet an envoy of Victor Amadeus who was in the town and said he had letters from the duke. The envoy was Giangiacomo Fontana, since 1709 *contadore generale* or auditor general of the military, and one of Victor Amadeus's closest advisers. Fontana, a year younger than Law, born into a modest family in Mondovi, had risen in the duke's service and as quartermaster general (*intendente generale dell'esercito*) been praised by Prince Eugene for managing transport and supply in the relief of Turin.

Law's reply to the duke the next day showed that Victor Amadeus was considering his proposals: "Sire, I thank Your Royal Highness for your great bounty in honouring me with your letter and in approving my proposals for your service and giving me the opportunity to confer with Auditor General Fontana over the means to make possible the execution of the project."[45]

In a second letter of the same day, probably to the Duke's controller general of finances, Giambattista Groppello, conte di Borgone, Law wrote: "Sir, Since I believed that His Royal Highness would not have the leisure at the moment to consider the project in question, I had planned to leave for Holland to see to my private affairs. But having received the honour of your letter and the packet that it has pleased His Royal Highness to send me, I have changed my resolution, and I will return to Genoa only to make certain remittances which I need in Holland." He would delay his departure till after a meeting with Fontana on the morrow, but "since

I foresee that more than one conference will be necessary, I will use all despatch to return here before the Contador General leaves, or myself come to Turin to carry the matter to its conclusion." For some reason, he counselled secrecy on the ministers, "but since I have reason to believe His Royal Highness will have expressed his will on that subject, I imagine that it will not be necessary."[46]

If Law took the post coach, which needed two days for the journey, he would have been back in Genoa by the 11th. Certainly between that day and March 23, 1712, Law drew out from his accounts at the Bank of St George 118,116 lire, 13 soldi and 2 denari in nine separate transactions, closing out the account on March 23 with a withdrawal of 6,216 lire 13 soldi and 2 denari.[47] While that may not have been his sole fortune, for he may have had jewels and stock-in-trade, it was a substantial one. At the same time, he remitted £100 to John Campbell's bank in London.[48]

Law probably left Genoa a day or two later. If he travelled by Turin, he has left no trace, and something caused him to give up on Victor Amadeus and continue to Holland. No doubt, Victor Amadeus wished to wait on the peace conference. It is possible Law went by way of Venice for the Ascension opera season, for on May 6 he transferred money from there to Amsterdam.[49]

Re-established in The Hague, on July 21, Law bought a town house for the sum of 4,000 guilders or the equivalent of about £400 sterling.[50] That was a pretty price at a time when a good house could be had for 1,000 guilders. The house stood in a new development, on the northern tip of The Hague, facing north-west to the sea, with to the east the Haagse Bos, the remnant of the wood that once covered Holland. The scheme, by the master carpenter Jacob van Dijk, was the most substantial in Holland since the outbreak of war twenty-five years before and was known as the "new extension" or Nieuwe Uitlegging, or today Nieuwe Uitleg.[51] The house was in the middle of the street, beside a wine merchant,[52] at the modern Nos 34 and 35, now covered by a nineteenth-century façade.

It was a splashy buy, designed not only to give Lady Katherine and the children the first respectable accommodation in their vagabondage but also to show Europe that John Law had made his fortune. He now proceeded to augment it.

He opened an account at the Amsterdam Exchange Bank, or Amsterdamsche Wisselbank, founded on the Italian model by the city fathers in 1609 to allow merchants to settle their business without resort to coin. He also established, jointly with his friend Archibald, Lord Ilay, an account at John Campbell's bank in London to invest in the British and Dutch lotteries and the shares of the South East and East India Companies.[53]

John Campbell had died in November, 1712, leaving two dwelling-houses, plate, jewels, cargo and securities net of debts of some £8,539 to his four children "share and share alike". The business was to be managed during his son's minority by "my faithfull and honest partner George Middleton".[54] Son of the principal of King's College, Aberdeen, who was later turned out for supposed Jacobite sympathies, Middleton had been apprenticed as a goldsmith, joined Campbell in The Strand in 1703 and become his partner in 1708. He later married Campbell's daughter, Mary. Law was to both make Middleton's fortune and destroy it.

Betrayed by its British allies, the Netherlands had run through its formidable credit, and could finance the war only by offering ever more generous terms to the families and charitable institutions and guilds that supported it. According to two modern historians, by 1713 the richest province of Holland and West Friesland was in debt to the tune of 310 million guilders, and the States General, which administered the "Generality" lands in the south of the country, by 68 millions.[55] The Generality was paying 10 per cent for its loans.[56]

To raise additional funds to finance mercenary armies without British help, and compete with the British lotteries and securities of the Bank of England and the East India and South Sea Companies, Dutch public borrowers had to offer a little fantasy. They found it in the Neale's English lottery loans of the 1690s where lenders gave up some percentage points of interest in return for the chance of a great prize.

In July 1712, the Council of State of the United Provinces announced a Generality lottery loan of 17,500 tickets at 200 guilders each (3.5 million guilders in total) with a prize fund, payable over thirty years, of 1.46 million guilders and interest on the losing tickets or blanks of 4 per cent until redemption. Misled by the reception from the investing public, the Council early in August almost doubled the loan to 6 million guilders.[57]

Throughout the late summer and autumn the take-up was slow and then dried up entirely. Antonie Heinsius, the Grand Pensionary of Holland and the leading Dutch official, wrote on October 26: "Regarding the lottery, I fear that the Generality's credit is so decried that the augmentation will not help."[58] On December 2, the Council of State was obliged to split the loan in two and improve the terms. With the first 3 million guilders, to be drawn on December 12 and the days following, the prize fund was increased in a leap to 1.83 million guilders, and the ratio of large prizes to blanks fixed at one to seven.

The lottery, already "more advantageous than its predecessors",[59] had become very much more so. On Tuesday, December 6, Law took out an advertisement in the *Gazette d'Amsterdam* offering to insure investors in the lottery against drawing a blank. It was his first appearance in the public prints since the 'Wanted' notice in the *London Gazette* of January 3, 1695.

The advertisement, which is in French, reads:

> Mr John Law offers to insure prizes for those who have tickets in the Lottery of the Generality to be drawn on the 12th of this month. For a premium of 100 florins [guilders], he will pay out 300 if in a batch of ten tickets (whose numbers must be supplied him) there is no prize. In the case of 15 tickets, the premium is 100 and the payout 500; and so on in proportion. He also offers to buy the prize chances on each ticket for an immediate 20 per cent or 40 florins per ticket. Alternatively, he will guarantee a 25 per cent gain in cash on each batch of 100 tickets, on condition that should the gain be more than 25 per cent he will take half of the surplus, also in cash. He can be reached in Amsterdam at the house of Mr Isaac Abrabanel, who will answer for payments.[60]

The notice was repeated the following Friday, December 9, 1712 and Tuesday, December 13, 1712, with the addition of Law's new address in The Hague.

Lottery insurance was not new. The diarist Samuel Pepys attended Sir Arthur Slingsby's lottery at the Banqueting House in Whitehall on July 20, 1664, which was licensed by the King, but the real winner was "Mr Cholmley" (Sir Hugh Cholmley of Whitby, Yorkshire), who had no licence, but took in £10 in premiums to insure against the single blank and did not have to pay out at all. Law, who was doing the same with blanks in the Generality Lottery, was, in effect, running an unlicensed secondary lottery, which will not not have endeared him to the receiver general of the States, Gijsbert van Hogendorp.

The puzzle is that in the country of Christiaan Huygens and other pioneers of probability, the Dutch would think Law's scheme attractive. There were 15,000 tickets to be drawn on December 12 and the days after, with 1,922 prizes and 13,078 blanks. If Law insured the entire lottery, he would receive 150,000 guilders in insurance premiums and pay, for all the possible groups of ten blanks, 116,100 guilders. That was a gross profit to Law on each contract of 22.6 per cent. It was precisely the sort of wager he liked.

The most important part of the notice was its last phrase. Isaac Abarbanel de Souza, merchant on the Verversgracht, born in 1661 and buried at the Beth Haim Portuguese-Israelite cemetery on January 16, 1733,[61] was descended from one of the most distinguished families of Jewish Spain and Portugal, leading financiers until the expulsion of the Jews in 1492. Dispersed throughout Europe, the family had been drawn like many Iberian Jews to the Dutch Republic by the promise of religious freedom. They formed a close-knit community in the long-distance trade, foreign exchange and securities markets of Amsterdam. It is a tribute to Law's charm and address that this man was willing to lend a Gentile his credit.

Whether it was Law's public intervention, the much improved terms or intelligence coming out of the peace conference at Utrecht, the Generality lottery started, as the eighteenth century liked to say, "to go". The States General, who seem to have misjudged the market, announced the second slice of 3 million guilders in the gazettes on December 27, with yet more opulent terms. Law responded in the *Gazette* of January 6, and then again on February 10 and 14, offering to insure tickets in the second drawing and proposing various other side-bets. The tickets went to a premium: that is, changed hands above their issue price. When Law called at van Hogendorp's office in The Hague on February 6, "tickets . . . were not to be had, they being all engadged to the magistracy and people of interest here".[62] Punters had to pay up to 206 guilders per ticket from brokers' offices in Amsterdam and on the street.

Four letters from Law to his friends in Genoa, which survive in the Staffordshire county records, throw a sidelight on his activity at this time. They show him gambling to the hilt in the Generality lotteries and shuttling between the brokers in Amsterdam, his new house and family in The Hague and the peace conference in the Town Hall of Utrecht. They also reveal a certain inattention or haste in his office work, and a short-handedness, which are ominous.

On January 24, 1713, Law wrote to William Chetwynd, sending him the numbers of one hundred tickets he had bought for him in the Generality lottery, and adding that he was himself resolved "to employ 10,000 pounds in this lottery, which is by much the most advantageous [that] has yet been proposed in this country".[63] Law then discovered he had sent the wrong numbers, and wrote in a fluster to William in Genoa (February 3) and at Turin (February 9), and to John Chetwynd in Turin (March 21), giving the correct series. "I have above a thousand numbers in this lottery of the generality which has occasioned this mistake," he wrote to John Chetwynd on March 21. He had also bought 300 tickets in a new six-million-guilder lottery of the State of Holland, announced on March 10. He ended: "Excuse this scral for I have little time, the brokers swarm about me."[64]

Thus Law had approximately 260,000 guilders or nearly £25,000 sterling at risk in the Dutch lotteries, including more than 3 per cent of the two Generality loans. The ledgers or *Grootboeken* of the Bank of Amsterdam show for the first half of 1713 transfers and payments on Law's current account of some 99,000 guilders (about £10,000). The counterparties include some French Huguenots but are primarily men with Sephardic Jewish names, and no doubt covered transactions in the tickets.[65] Of the Scots or thirteenth tribe of Israel, there is just one representative, Andrew Henderson. Henderson had a house behind the Stadhuys or Town Hall of Amsterdam, home of the Bank, and it seems Law lodged with him when he stayed the night in Amsterdam.[66]

Many of the tickets Law bought with borrowed money. The

Bank of Amsterdam did not lend to individuals. In those days, in Holland, as in Italy and France, it was the notaries that matched those of their clients who had cash with those that needed it. In the records of the Amsterdam notary Dirk van der Groe, Law borrowed 3,000 guilders on January 6, 1713 from Wolfert van Aferen (secured on 20 lots of the Generality lottery)[67] and 6,000 against 45 tickets on January 21, 1713 from the widow Christina de Flines.[68] (She was now old and rich, but at her marriage at eighteen to the merchant Jacob Leeuw in 1666, her great-uncle Joost van den Vondel wrote for her two wedding songs of which Shakespeare would not have been ashamed.) Law won at least one large prize, for ticket No. 16141, of 25,000 guilders.[69] Some of his debts to Abarbanel were settled through his joint account in London with Archibald Ilay.

In his letter to William Chetwynd of February 3, Law wrote: "If the peace be made soon I may have the pleasure to meet you in Paris this spring."[70] The main treaties were signed in April and July, but before setting off for France, Law sought to win over the new Tory administration in London, offering his services to the British revenue in return for his pardon.

There was at that time in Amsterdam a Scottish merchant banker named John Drummond of Quarrel, who was not much of a businessman but was a capable secret agent for the Tory ministry, and a kind man. Born in Perthshire in 1676, he was sent to Holland at the age of fifteen with a letter to Andrew Henderson, who specialised in finding places for Scottish boys in Dutch business houses. After the Peace of Ryswick in 1697, Drummond set up in partnership with a Dutchman, Jan van der Heiden, investing his small inheritance and his Dutch wife's dowry in the business.

For a while their trade in fine stuffs, coffee, tea, chocolate and wine prospered. With the outbreak of Queen Anne's war in 1702, Drummond plunged into the business of supplying cash to the

British army in the Low Countries, and providing stock-market intelligence to Brydges. At the formation of the Tory ministry in London in 1710, he became the principal Dutch intelligencer for Robert Harley, who was made Earl of Oxford, and Henry St John, Viscount Bolingbroke, who used him to go behind the Duke of Marlborough's back to the *primus inter pares* of the Dutch government, the pensionary of Holland, Anthonie Heinsius.

Meanwhile, and without informing his Dutch partner, Drummond had withdrawn £5,000 from the business with a view to buying a seat in the British Parliament. Even before that, the partnership had nowhere near enough of its own money to support its borrowings in the Amsterdam money market for the regimental paymasters. On May 9, 1712, van der Heiden and Drummond defaulted on 100,000 guilders in debts, including a bill of exchange of 453 bank ducats drawn by Law on May 6 on the merchants Thomas Williams and Joseph Smith in Venice for payment in two months by Drummond at Amsterdam.[71] Drummond owed Law both money and a favour.

On May 8, 1713, Drummond wrote to Harley at Law's dictation. The letter is better written than Drummond's other surviving letters and contains information only Law could have given. Drummond wrote:

> There is a famous man also in this country, one Mr John Law, who had the misfortune a great many years ago to kill one Willson. This Mr Law has picked up in Italy a great estate, some say by army undertakings at Genoa, and some say partly by gaming. When the States General lottery was at a stand, as they were obliged to divide it, this gentleman, by the power of his ready money and by a calculation of setting a price and buying in of chances in the said lottery, made it take so favourable a turn in a few days, that it did not only

run full, but was at three per cent. above par. The Savoy ministers commend him much for some project of credit, and easier and better management of finance than they had before, and he has a good deal of money in the funds in England, I believe in Lord Ilay's name, or under his direction. I should be sorry to see him settle at The Hague, where he has bought a fine house, seeing he is rich, and can be very useful, and unless his crime be very black, the service he may be able to do his country really deserves his pardon, and he has often, and now especially since the peace has been signed, said if my Lord Treasurer would get him his pardon which was once granted by the King [William III], but the friends of the person killed entered an appeal but are now willing to take a small sum, he would make himself very useful.

Characteristically, both for himself and his age, Law then offered Harley a wager. Drummond continued:

I told him that his friends the Duke of Argyll and Lord Ilay were able to do him the best service, but now he only desires a reprieve for twelve months, to have a warning to retire again of three months, if he does not do something for the nation's service in money matters to your Lordship's satisfaction, and which you may think deserves the Queen's pardon or long reprieve. He is betwixt fifty and sixty years of age [he was forty-two], and is really admired by all who know him here. I take the freedom to give your Lordship this account of him, knowing that he is soliciting to have a pardon or reprieve, and that I should always wish the Queen's subjects of such good estates and sense established at home.[72]

The letter had no effect. Law remained an outlaw.

He continued his self-promotion. Nicolaas Struyck (1686–1769), son of an Amsterdam goldsmith, was then at work on a treatise on probability whose Dutch title translates as "Analysis of the Probabilities in Games of Chance, Employing Arithmetic and Algebra, Together with a Discussion of Lotteries and Interest". This work, which has suffered in reputation from being written in Dutch rather than Latin, was not published until 1716 but contains no material from later than October, 1713.

Struyck provided solutions to five problems set by Christiaan Huygens in his *De ratiociniis in ludo aleae* ('On Computations in Games of Chance', 1657) and also two others from the wagers of a certain "Hr. JAN LAW". Law is the only contemporary gambler mentioned in the treatise, and surely paid for that privilege.

In the first problem, Struyck records that Law used to offer a thousand gold pistoles to any punter who could throw six sixes at dice, but if the throw was four or five sixes, he or she must pay Law two pistoles. As Struyck calculated, there are with six dice 375 chances of throwing four sixes, 30 of throwing five sixes, and one of six sixes, which multiplied by the six dice makes 2,436 chances. Out of those 2,436 throws, 2,435 casts win Law two pistoles but only one cast wins the punter one thousand "so that Mr Law would have a marked advantage [*merkelijk vordeel*]".[73] In probability, he would earn 4,870 pistoles before he paid out 1,000.

The second concerned the insurance on the Six Million Generality Lottery of 1712–13. Struyck computed that if Law had insured the entire lottery in both halves of 30,000 tickets, he would receive 300,000 in premiums and pay out only 232,200 guilders on the blanks, giving him a gain of 67,800 guilders or 22 guilders and 12 stuivers per 100-guilder contract. In other words, his premiums were excessive and in a competitive insurance market would have been undersold.[74]

On June 10, 1713, John Law squared his accounts at the Bank of

Amsterdam with Abarbanel (who transferred 18,696 guilders to his account) and cashed out, leaving just 217 guilders and 17 stuivers.[75] In the course of July, Law paid off the loans from van Aferen and the widow de Flines and, no doubt, some others.[76]

Years later, Law claimed to have carried into France variously 1.6 million guilders,[77] £100,000 sterling[78] and 500,000 French crowns.[79] Men and women exaggerate both their wealth and their poverty, and Law was no exception. Even with about £8,000 remitted from the London account, which was closed the following year,[80] it is hard to reach such sums. In those days in the City of London, the pinnacle of success was an unencumbered estate of £100,000, which was known as a "plum". No doubt, Law thought he had made his plum. By fishing in the troubled waters of war finance, he had earned a competency and, as they used to say in Scotland, could "make rich".

At that time, Lady Katherine was furnishing the house in The Hague. Among the men she employed was a locksmith or ironworker (*serrurier*) named Berdin, a Protestant refugee from France, who had a son and daughter of the same ages as William and Mary Catherine.

Lady Katherine was happy for Berdin to bring his son with him. Yet those children, playing in the garden in the Dutch sunshine, were subject to sensations that, ripening over time and turning bitter and corrupt, were to bring catastrophe on the Laws and leave a blizzard of paper to make possible this book.[81]

CHAPTER FIVE

Law and Company

J'avois formé le dessein de rétablir la France.
(I had conceived the project of putting France back on her feet.)

JOHN LAW[1]

The place de Vendôme, now in the heart of Paris, in 1714 stood on the western edge of the city amid convents, market gardens and vacant lots. In 1685, Louis XIV had bought the house, park and riding school of the duc de Vendôme and a Capuchin cloister to make an open space, the place de Nos Conquêtes, to match and outshine in the west of town the place Royale or des Vosges made by Henry IV in the east.

Behind façades designed by the architect Jules Hardouin-Mansart, the King wished to assemble public offices scattered in old-fashioned buildings about the city, including the royal library, the Paris mint, learned academies and an hôtel for the reception of foreign ambassadors. An equestrian statue of himself in Roman dress was cast in bronze as a centrepiece.

By 1699, the project had cost the King more than 2 million livres. Chastened by nine years of warfare, Louis XIV abandoned the square and ceded the land to the city of Paris. Hardouin-Mansart designed new, arcaded façades, canted at the corners to make the irregular octagon of today. The square was renamed place Louis-le-Grand, which name did not stick. The city sold off building lots behind the arcades to the nobility and the financiers who had profited from the war.

In the spring of 1714, John Law rented for 6,000 livres a year a house in the middle of the north-western side from Anne Baillet, second duchesse de Gramont, described with his usual charity by the duc de Saint-Simon as "a beggar-woman . . . old, ugly and one-eyed".[2] The house, which received some improvements from Lady Katherine, is now the southern part of the Ritz Hotel (No. 15).[3]

Law had been in Paris since before Christmas, living at the hôtel d'Entragues, rue Tournon on the south or left bank of the Seine, seeking a private meeting with Nicolas Desmaretz, controller general of the King's finances.[4] At some point in the spring, Lady Katherine and the two children joined him. On May 6, 1714, Law wrote to Desmaretz from the place Vendôme, asking that his furniture and baggage, arriving by boat from Holland at Rouen, be given free passage to Paris, for "among them is some plate and other things that might go astray if opened on the road".[5] Since such a privilege was denied even ambassadors, Desmaretz refused but offered to order the boxes sealed as far as the Paris customs house, where Law could supervise their opening.[6]

The hôtel Gramont was a conspicuous address, and caught the eye of the marquis d'Argenson, the lieutenant general of police and a man notorious for knowing every cobble and brick in the city. Argenson wrote on July 22 to the foreign secretary, the marquis de Torcy, that Law had bought the house (which was not true) and was living in "high style [*en grand équipage*] . . . even though nobody believes he has any property but what he gains from play". Torcy minuted the letter: "He [Law] is not a suspect. He may be left in peace."[7]

Even so, the Laws were not so well off as to forgo £100 a year from Lady Katherine's marriage settlement, which now consisted only of the mortgage on some property at Fotheringhay in Northamptonshire in the English Midlands. Pressed on the matter that March, George Middleton or his clerk in the Strand muddled her name as "Lady Katherine Sorquier".[8] Middleton filed suit in Chancery (before Lord Chancellor Cowper, who last appeared in this story as a junior in *Wilson* vs *Law*).[9] In March 1716, Lady Katherine received £200 for two years' arrears.[10]

As he waited on Desmaretz, Law attended to his other customers. With the death of Queen Anne, Law wrote a set of letters to Scottish noblemen to lobby the new king for his pardon. One of those letters, to the Duke of Montrose, survives. It is dated September 29, 1714, the day (September 18 in the English calendar) George I landed at Greenwich. Law wrote: "The assurances which the Duke of Argyle, the Marquess of Annandale and the Earle of Ilay are pleased to give that they will intercede with the King for my pardon encourages me to ask the same favor of your Grace. I have writte to the Duke of Roxburgh and the Earle of Stairs who I hope will [illegible] doe me the honor to appear for me. I wish your grace happiness."[11]

Law followed up the letters by calling on the Earl of Stair, the new British envoy, on Stair's first evening in Paris, January 23, 1715. They were acquainted from Holland.

John Dalrymple, 2nd Earl of Stair embodied to perfection the virtues and vices of the Scots nobility of that period. He was, in the words of his first biographer, Andrew Henderson (who had worked in his household), "a Man about six Feet high, exceeding Streight, and genteel in his Body, which inclined to an agreeable Slenderness; he was, perhaps, one of the handsomest Men of his Time."[12] He had blue eyes.

Stair was a gallant soldier, who had fought in each of

Marlborough's four pitched battles and several of his sieges. He was also arrogant beyond measure, overbearing, avaricious, rough, an uncontrollable gambler, a Protestant bigot and false as a jetton. Stair's flaw was not that he disliked his host country (though he did) or indeed any failing of character, but one of circumstance. The Earl of Stair was not rich enough to be Britain's senior foreign envoy. On a salary or "ordinary" of £100 a week,[13] Stair could not hope to maintain the character of Envoy and then Ambassador Extraordinary to the Most Christian King without ruining himself. He thought that he could gamble his way to an estate, as Law had done, but he was deceived. His expense sheets for his network of secret agents among the Jacobites, in both France and Spain, which include such items as "for secret services 950 louis d'or" or £1,266, certainly concealed table debts.[14]

Two years younger than Law, John Dalrymple at eight years old, at the house of Carsecreugh in Wigtownshire, playing with a pistol left on a hall table, shot his elder brother and killed him. John's parents, who could not look at him, sent him away first to a clergyman neighbour and later to his grandfather, an inflexible Presbyterian in exile from Stuart persecution in the Netherlands. Dalrymple studied at Leiden, volunteered as a soldier in 1692 and rose like a rocket in the wars. By the time of his appointment to Paris, Stair was a major general and Knight of the Thistle, the principal Scottish order of chivalry, and owned the colonelcy of a regiment. He believed his principal tasks in Paris were to keep France weak and to disrupt attempts by the Jacobites in exile there to exploit George I's unpopularity.

Britain's foreign relations were in those days assigned to two Secretaries of State. The Southern Department was responsible for France, the Latin countries, and the Ottoman Empire, while the rest of Europe came under the Northern Department. At that time, the Northern Secretary was Charles Townshend, while, since

September, 1714, Law's old acquaintance James Stanhope headed the Southern Department.

King George had little interest in the domestic life of his new kingdom but insisted on being master of her foreign relations, which proliferated into the north and east of his electorate in Hanover. Because the King knew little English, all foreign despatches of any weight, both out and in, had to be written in French. It became the habit of British diplomats to write to one another in French, or varieties of franglais, frécossais or frirlandais, out of the conceit that their letters must always be shown to the King. English was not then much spoken in the world, except in England, lowland Scotland, parts of Wales and Ireland, the east coast of North America, Jamaica and Barbados, and pockets of Bengal and the Carnatic.

Because of an insularity among Englishmen, the country had been much represented abroad by foreigners. Under William III, those were Dutchmen, French Huguenots and Swiss and, in the later years of Anne's reign, by Scots now citizens of Great Britain.[15] Stair's household at the hôtel Tarane, in the faubourg Saint-Germain on the right bank, was staffed by Scots.

The embassy secretary was Thomas Crawford. From a family in Renfrewshire in western Scotland, Crawford was perpetually on the make. While forever expressing a public spirit, and devotion to his sovereign, he was often acting for City men and always, and above all, for Tam Crawford. He was soon in debt to Law.[16]

The third Scot was Captain James Gardiner, who as Master of Horse was assembling the beasts and equipages with which Stair intended to dazzle Paris and the court. In the summer of 1719, and somewhat against the grain of events, Gardiner passed through a religious crisis and departed this story. (He was killed in the last Jacobite rebellion of 1745, cut down by a Highlander against the wall of his house in the fight known as Prestonpans. His death cast a pall of gloom over Edinburgh, Whig and Jacobite. His black horse, the best in Scotland, was given to Prince Charles Edward Stuart.) A fourth was Timothy Aird, Stair's groom and messenger.

To complete the household, Stair employed a Church of England chaplain, William Beauvoir, from a Guernsey family, whose French was good enough for intelligence missions against the Jacobites and his Latin for ecclesiastical intrigue at the Sorbonne. They were later joined by Daniel Pulteney, an official of the Board of Trade, whose mission relating to borders in North America, and claims for compensation from the Hudson's Bay Company, did not much interest the French court and ministers. Instead and short of money, Pulteney sent to London hearsay reports on Law of great acuity and greater venom.

That winter of 1715, Stair did as he was asked, writing on February 12 to both Secretary of State Stanhope and Charles Montagu, Earl of Halifax, first Lord of the Treasury. To Stanhope he wrote that Law "is a man of very good sense, and who has a head fit for calculations of all kinds to an extent beyond anybody . . . Could not such a man be useful in devising some plan for paying off the national debts?"[17]

The answers were discouraging. Halifax replied: "I had the honour to know Mr Law a little at the Hague, and have by me some papers of his sent to Lord Godolphin out of Scotland, by which I have a great esteem for his abilities and am extreme fond of having his assistance in the Revenue. I have spoke to the King and some of his Ministers about him, but there appears some difficulty in his case, and in the way of having him brought over."[18] Stanhope also recommended Law to King George. He wrote: "I find a disposition to comply with what your Lordship proposes, though at the same time it has met, and does meet, with opposition, and I believe it will be no hard matter for him [i.e. Stair] to guess from whence it proceeds."[19]

On May 7, Law had his meeting with Desmaretz. Both that day, and at a second meeting on May 11, Law presented a programme to establish a bank, to reduce over time France's unsecured or floating debts and make Paris the financial capital of the world.[20] As earnest money, he offered to deposit 500,000 livres which, if he failed, might be distributed among the poor of France.[21] The breakthrough alarmed the Earl of Stair.

Stair put no faith in the peace with France and thought it best she remain "humbled".[22] Throughout his five years in Paris, he never ceased to warn London that if France discharged her war debts and Great Britain did not follow suit, Britain would lose all she had gained from the long war. On May 20, 1715, he wrote privately to Montrose:

> At my first coming over I was very pressing to have had Laws pardon because I thought he might have been usefull to us in Brittain, and I saw he would be very serviceable to the French, which made me very fixed of having him out of this country.
>
> That matter was neglected when it might have been done, and now 'tis too late. I'm afraid he's imbarked with them, or upon the point of imbarking but this only to yourself, only I think at this time the government should not find means [?] of having him, or forwardnesse in granting his pardon, which is only to raise his price here. I shall be very glad his negociation wth this Court miscarrys, it would doe so any time but this, his demands are so very high.
>
> Ile putt a spoke in his wheell, if I can.[23]

Law knew nothing of Stair's treachery or this letter. He was fortunate in that Jacobites in Scotland under the Earl of Mar had raised the standard of revolt, and Stair was preoccupied in preventing

James III and the Duke of Ormonde crossing France and sailing to reinforce the rebellion.

In the papers of the French controllers general, Law's proposals now come thick and fast. At midsummer or soon after, he sent to Desmaretz a memorial on his scheme which survives in ten copies. Though lucid, and self-assured without arrogance, it is overlong: John Law was not yet quite a Frenchman. It is also a little mysterious, as if Law did not trust Desmaretz. (Stair wrote in June that the controller general was attempting "to get his [Law's] secret without ingaging to employ Law".)[24] After a survey of the public banks in Amsterdam, Genoa, London and Edinburgh, Law asked for a twenty-year concession for a bank, initially confined to Paris and jointly owned with the King. Though Law would bear the costs of establishment, and manage the enterprise, three-quarters of the profit would accrue to the King and a quarter to Law. (Law said the King had already agreed to that division.)[25] The King's profit share would allow him not only to pay interest on his obligations but eventually redeem up to 100 million livres in debt.

The bank would be housed at first in the place Vendôme, but would then buy the hôtel de Soissons, an old-fashioned palace and garden in the Les Halles district owned by Victor Amadeus's spendthrift son-in-law, the prince de Carignan. It would serve as seat of both the bank and a *bourse* or stock exchange where the King's debt and other securities could be traded.

Like the Bank of England, the new bank would issue banknotes as receipts for deposits of coin.[26] The banknotes would be good for taxes and other public payments, but not compulsory in commerce. More convenient and much easier to transport than wagonloads of coin, Law believed that they would be preferred. Law then had a bout of illness but by July 31, he was writing to Desmaretz that should he receive royal approval, his bank would be ready to open its doors by August 10.[27] Stair thought otherwise, having supped that very July 31 with the banker Samuel Bernard. Stair wrote in his journal: "He [Bernard] told me, the Council would refuse Law's project, there being no foundation for the Bank he proposes, in a country where every thing depends on the King's pleasure."[28]

On August 10, King Louis XIV of France felt a pain in his right leg. His physicians diagnosed sciatica, which it was not. The pain became agony, and by the third week of the month the King could not attend to business.

In all this time, Law had kept alive his Savoyard scheme. On October 3, 1713, Victor Amadeus had sailed with a British squadron and thirty transports from Nice to take over the kingdom granted him at Utrecht at Spanish expense, the island of Sicily. With him was his queen and a complement of ministers. After a week's plain sailing, the squadron anchored off Palermo on October 10 and Victor Amadeus was crowned King of Sicily in the Duomo or cathedral of that city on Christmas Eve, 1713. Sicily was a rich land, producing surpluses of grain, oil and wine, but it was bedevilled by a refractory nobility, much of it loyal to Spain, a riven Church and a brigand countryside. Fontana, Law's old acquaintance from Milan, had been charged with reforming the finances of the island.

Victor Amadeus had written to Law in the course of 1714, inviting him to Sicily. Law had taken care to advertise that he had other customers, showing the letters to Stair and, one imagines, to Desmaretz.[29] On August 15, 1715, with the onset of Louis XIV's illness, he wrote back to Victor Amadeus. A generation later, on his first day in Paris, the Venetian libertine Giacomo Casanova was told: "There is no such word in French as No."[30] Law does not say No. Always a valetudinarian, Law pleads not so much illness as imminent extinction. He had reached both the age and the city at which his father had died.

On my arrival here, and on receiving the letters Your Majesty had the grace to write me that I should attend him in Sicily, I would have had nothing more to desire and my ambition would have been fully satisfied, if only my health had permitted me to make the journey. Since that time, I have never been in a condition to make a journey of ten leagues [thirty miles] by road, and the doctors and surgeons warn me that I am too weak to undergo surgery. Since my illness is worsening, I fear that I will soon have no choice.

Law then explains that he had invested his property in annuities on the City of Paris, and in securities and obligations of the French King, which because of the disorders in the coinage and the collapse of credit and trade had fallen to a quarter of their value. He had thus thought to offer advice to the minister (Desmaretz) with whom he was acquainted from previous visits, and who was inundated with ill-founded proposals that threatened to bankrupt the French Crown.

Then comes this: "If the King [of France] approves my project, I will do France a signal service, but I do not expect long to enjoy the honours that attend success. Rather I seek to furnish some protection for two small children, whom I will leave in this foreign land and to whom I pass without regret the fruits of my labours."[31]

Victor Amadeus replied on August 29, and also instructed his resident in Paris, Filippo Nicola Donaudi, to call on Law. (Donaudi had been Savoyard envoy in The Hague and knew and liked Law.) Before those letters could be delivered there occurred an event which cast everything into the air. Early on September 1, 1715, after three weeks of torment, and seventy-two years and one hundred and ten days on the throne, Louis XIV died of senile gangrene. Stair wrote that morning to the Duke of Montrose with no affectation of grief: "Old Lewis has expir'd but this morning at half an hour past 8."[32] Paris, which had seen the great King perhaps four times since the turn of the century, went about what little business it had.

When Donaudi called on Law, he found the Scotsman disappointed but not in despair. Donaudi wrote to his master on September 6th: "He told me that if the King had lived another fifteen days, he would have had his project in execution . . . but he is now in direct negotiations with the Duke of Orléans, whom he had kept well informed of all the progress of the scheme even when the late King was alive."[33]

Law explained his banking scheme, and showed Donaudi sample banknotes. Donaudi reported: "Once this bank is established, he will extend his project into something yet more vast, and as he is a man with a rare talent for business, it may be as well founded. He assumes that the whole general revenue [national product] of this kingdom is about 1,200 millions [livres]. He believes that he can establish means by way of commerce and putting money into circulation to improve agriculture and manufacture in every part of the kingdom and raise the revenue by a quarter, or from 1,200 millions to 1,600 millions."[34]

The duc d'Orléans, universally expected to be appointed Regent in the minority of Louis XV, faced challenges that would have felled a man less intelligent and good-natured. The most urgent was to keep the little King alive, no easy matter in the state of European medical science. In the space of four weeks in 1712, measles (or its treatment) had carried off the lad's mother, father and older brother. He had survived only because his nanny or *gouvernante*, the duchesse de Ventadour, had carried him to her apartments and barred entry to the royal physicians. Should Louis XV follow them into the royal mortuary at the basilica of Saint-Denis, the duc d'Orléans's own claim to the throne of France might be disputed by King Philip of Spain and a war of French succession ensue.

Second, he needed to establish his authority as Regent against competing claims from King Philip and from Louis XIV's favourite son, the out-of-wedlock duc du Maine. Third, he must bring peace to a French Church torn apart by a reforming doctrine known as Jansenism. Above all, he had to clear the burden of war debts that were eating up the King's revenue and suffocating trade and agriculture. He was ready to try anything short of bankruptcy, including an alliance with the ancient enemy, England, and the financial experiments of John Law.

Philippe II d'Orléans was born in the palace of Saint-Cloud west of Paris in 1674. His father, Philippe I, was the younger brother of Louis XIV, a capable soldier and the most perfect fop that ever lived. His mother was Elisabeth Charlotte, nicknamed Liselotte, daughter of Karl Ludwig, ruler of the territory round Heidelberg and Mannheim known as the Palatine Electorate or Palatinate. A Protestant, she had converted at her marriage in 1671.

As a child and young man, the duc de Chartres (as he was known until his father's death in 1701) showed a bent for work, an enquiring mind, a talent for natural science, chemistry and optics, and taste in painting and literature. His tutor, the abbé Guillaume Dubois, taught him no religion. He was married by order in 1692 to one of the King's legitimised daughters, mademoiselle de Blois, full sister to the duc du Maine, who brought a dowry of two million livres but was no sort of companion.

His military career showed flashes of brilliance, especially in Spain in 1707, but those were tarnished by an indiscreet correspondence (through third parties) with his friend Stanhope in Barcelona that veered towards treason. Distrusted by the King his uncle, impatient with the forms and piety of Versailles, brave, shy, proud and rich beyond computation, the duc d'Orléans became restless and dissipated. "He was born bored [*il étoit né ennuyé*]," his friend and schoolmate, the duc de Saint-Simon, wrote in his memoirs. "He could not live except in a sort of torrent of business, at the head of an army, or in managing its supply, or in the blare and sparkle of a debauch."[35] The ignorant of all classes, suspicious of his chemical experiments, accused him of having poisoned the Dauphin and the other princes.

The late King's will was a blow to the duc d'Orléans. Far from being named Regent during Louis XV's minority, he was to be chief only of a Regency Council. The boy King's education and his household guard were put under the duc du Maine. On September 2, the duc d'Orléans convened the principal law court in the land, the Parlement de Paris, which overturned both provisions. The price for the support of the nobility and robe to this *coup d'état* was a promise to rule through a series of councils, which for some time the Regent honoured, and restore the Parlement's right to protest or remonstrate against decrees, which likewise.

On September 9, the young King was brought from Versailles, first to Vincennes, where the air was thought good for him, and then in the new year to the palace of the Tuileries. Through all the tumult of the next eight years, the duc d'Orléans never for an instant forgot this pretty child in leading-strings, but found him playfellows and devised him games.

The seat of government was now not Versailles but a house in the middle of Paris given to the Regent's father by Louis XIV and known as the Palais-Royal. This place, scene of the triumphs and disasters of Law's moment in France, had been built for Cardinal Richelieu in the previous century in phases according to his fortune.

The oldest part, in the form of a capital H with its feet on the rue Saint-Honoré, consisted of a two-storey range running west to east, and four perpendicular wings.[36] Within the arms of the H were two grand courtyards, the *avant-cour* on the rue Saint-Honoré, and the *cour royale* leading into a garden to the north. A double stairway led from the Royal Courtyard up to the first floor of the main range, where Richelieu had had his apartments. To the west of those, the Regent and his father had created an enfilade of public rooms, culminating in the *grand cabinet* or *grand salon* overlooking the rue de Richelieu. Turning north again, along the rue de Richelieu, was a gallery in which the painter Antoine Coypel was at work depicting scenes from the life of Virgil's Aeneas. The gallery enclosed to the west a private garden, onto which, on the ground floor, opened the apartments of the duchesse d'Orléans.

Through the pages of Saint-Simon, the Regent paces up and down these rooms, shuts or opens doors, bends down close to read a document, catching his pen in his wig. The duc d'Orléans disliked ceremonial, refused to dine in public but took a cup of chocolate at two p.m., allowed carriages of all sorts into the Royal Courtyard, did not attend mass even at Easter. What fretted Saint-Simon was a suite of rooms just off the west end of the enfilade, connected by a stair to a ground-floor door onto rue Richelieu. Here the Regent liked to sup late, incommunicado, amid a circle of men friends he called *roués* (gallows-fodder) and ladies unpresentable at court. Those "little suppers" became in later years notorious for debauchery, but that is to mistake the duc de Saint-Simon. Saint-Simon had no business with sexual morality. What frightened him was the destruction of social form.

In the front courtyard, on the east side, was a theatre with an entrance on the rue Saint-Honoré. On the first floor, the Regent's mother, Elisabeth Charlotte, established herself that September 9 precisely so she could be as far away as possible from her daughter-in-law whom she detested for her bastardy and idleness,[37] and as near as possible to the stage and footlights that she loved. Here her son visited her at least once a day. The rest of her time she spent writing letters, of which some six thousand survive in German and French, showing off her collection of coins and medals, and worrying about her son. The summer months she spent at the palace of Saint-Cloud, to the west of Paris.

In her own words, as unsparing of herself as of others, Elisabeth Charlotte had always been plain, and now she was fat, "cuboid as a die", red-faced, pockmarked, white-haired, double-chinned, gap-toothed, swollen-legged.[38] Born in 1652, she had passed a tomboy childhood at her father's palace in Heidelberg and at Hanover, caressed by pet animals, doing somersaults, shinning up trees, collecting wild strawberries, stealing grapes. That changed in 1671, when she abjured the Protestant faith and was betrothed at Metz to the widower Philippe I, duc d'Orléans, Louis XIV's younger brother, known at the French court as Monsieur. Elisabeth Charlotte was referred to as Madame.

At first, her high spirits and fearless riding to hounds made her popular at the French court. The King liked her and she adored him. She bore Monsieur three children of which two, the duc de Chartres and Mlle de Chartres, later duchesse de Lorraine, survived infancy. That done, her husband neglected his wife for a troop of young men, known as his *mignons*, who ate his fortune and treated Elisabeth Charlotte with insolence. Her stock declined.

In 1688, Elisabeth Charlotte was forced to watch her brother-in-law invade the Palatinate, on the pretext of securing her dowry. When the campaign went awry, the French armies laid waste the countryside and burned Heidelberg and Mannheim. She was incensed when her son in 1692 agreed to marry Louis XIV's bastard daughter by Mme de Montespan. She blamed the King's morganatic wife, Mme de Maintenon, for whom she devised a repertory of insults including "*die alte Zott* [the old cunt]", well knowing that her letters were opened by the postal service.

At her husband's death in 1701, threatened with the convent, Elisabeth Charlotte was forced to make peace with Mme de

Maintenon, and withdrew into widowhood and her letters. She remained a stickler for correct form and dress and marital legitimacy.

On September 24, 1715, the Earl of Stair called on Elisabeth Charlotte and browbeat her (*mit aller Gewalt*) to write to Caroline of Ansbach, Princess of Wales, whom she had not met.[39] No doubt Stair believed the British postal spies could extract some intelligence about both courts. Elisabeth Charlotte later wrote to one of the Princess's ladies-in-waiting, Countess Johanna Sophie von Schaumburg-Lippe, also a stranger. The two sets of letters have perhaps fifty references to John Law which in any other woman would be symptoms of a wounded heart. In reality, though Elisabeth Charlotte became curious about Law, she probably met him no more than once. She prided herself on not meddling in her son's policy.

Desmaretz was dismissed. The new Council of Finances met for the first time on September 10, under Adrien Maurice, duc de Noailles, a capable soldier with no particular fiscal expertise. "The Treasury is absolutely empty," Noailles told the council that Tuesday. There was nothing for the King's household or to pay troops and mariners. The Council decided, unanimously, "that it is absolutely necessary that the King return within his revenues".[40] The Regent himself later wrote to the comte de Luc, ambassador in Vienna, who was grumbling at having nothing to live on: "You cannot be unaware of the catastrophe in which I found the finances of the kingdom and the difficulty I have had in meeting the most urgent needs."[41]

That year of 1715, the King of France or, as we would say, the French state, could expect income from taxes and excises of some 165 million livres. Spending on the army, the palaces and court and the public administration left just 48 million livres to meet interest payments on the debts accumulated by the illustrious kings who had gone before.[42]

Those debts were of two kinds. The first consisted of annuities (*rentes constituées*) and the emoluments of public offices which had assigned to them particular taxes or excises and were, in the English term of the time, "funded". Those obligations of the King (which originated in the 1520s) and the paraphernalia of taxation to pay them, were the warp and weft of the old regime in France. The income from annuities and the wages of office allowed the nobility and bourgeois to live away from their estates whether at Versailles or in Paris and other large cities. Despite a default of two-thirds of face value in the Revolution of 1789, annuities survived to give the French nineteenth and early twentieth centuries (and the novels of Balzac, Victor Hugo and Proust) a particular financial texture.

The *rentes constituées* of the Old Regime functioned thus. In return for a loan to the King, the annuitant received the right to an income either for life or perpetually. Since it was beneath the dignity of the King himself to dole out funds, his Treasury diverted a part of its revenue to the town-halls of Paris and other places, where the annuitant appeared in person twice a year to collect his or her income. Private citizens also constituted similar annuities for dowries or legacies.

Because of the Church ban on usury, the lender could not demand repayment of his or her capital, which was immobilised unless the King volunteered to repay it, rather as a pig might fly. The annuities were expensive to the Crown. "Nothing," Law wrote later, "was more ruinous than those contracts of constitution. In a single life [of, say, 60 years], the borrower at 5 per cent re-imbursed the principal three times over while leaving it to burden his posterity."[43]

In the same class as the annuities were the wages or *gages* of some fifty thousand public servants. Because it was and is hard to tax the French public, and particularly the richer part of it, the French Crown had since the sixteenth century sold for ready cash judgeships or posts in the public administration. All the judges of the royal courts or *parlements*, most of the lawyers, the royal households, the officer corps, municipal functionaries, market inspectors, notaries, auctioneers and wigmakers bought or inherited their employments and could not be dismissed unless the King bought them out.

In return for their payment for the office, the office-holders received a wage or *gage* calculated according to the prevailing rate of interest on money. They also gained the right to collect fees and enjoy certain honours, including patents of nobility, always the most solid currency of royal government. Louis XIV's minister Jean-Baptiste Colbert, controller general of the finances from 1665 to his death in 1683, fixed the price of judicial offices as a prelude to redeeming them. The demands of war then caused him and his successors, especially Michel Chamillart, to create new offices of every species, including entire new courts of justice. They extracted from office-holders forced loans known, with that talent of the old regime for euphemism, as "increases in wages" (*augmentations des gages*). In the crisis year of 1709, when the banker Samuel Bernard failed at the Paiements de Lyon and the King melted down his gold plate, payments of *gages* were suspended.

Taken together, the annuities and wages of office were a charge on the King's revenue of approximately 90 million livres per year.

In addition, the almost unremitting warfare since 1688 had left a second class of royal IOUs to which no revenue could be assigned because there was none. By the time of the death of the great King, there were believed to be more than 900 million livres in promissory notes issued to the private financiers and munitioners that had kept France intact, fed and capable of fighting on despite her many defeats in the field. To raise any more money, the King would have to pay interest on those notes which, at 5 per cent, would add another 50 million livres in annual charges. Worse, the King's unpaid bills infected the entire merchant class and paralysed trade, for if the King were bankrupt so were his creditors. The exceptions were such men as John Law who had never done business with the King of France.

There was small possibility that the Regent, through taxes or economies, could make the King's debt manageable before his majority. There was nothing adventurous or light-headed in his listening to John Law.

Law's scheme for a bank "in the name of and for the account of the King" was presented to the Council of Finances at a special session at the château de Vincennes on October 24, 1715. Both the Regent and Noailles were present. After hearing a presentation on Law's project, which stressed that the bank would issue notes only in proportion to its deposits of coin, the Council heard evidence from Law and also thirteen bankers and men of business, including Samuel Bernard. As expected, the businessmen argued against the scheme, but by an unexpectedly large majority of nine to four.

After they had left the room, the Council members rallied behind Noailles who said he "is persuaded of the utility of the bank, but the time is not right; business confidence has entirely vanished; and, further, the opposition of the merchants whose support is essential for the credit of the bank would cause it to fail." It was first necessary to cut state expenditure to restore business confidence, he said. The only firm support for Law came from Argenson, who saw the bank as a "blameless way of recapturing confidence".

Disappointed, the Regent said that "though he had been persuaded that the bank should come about, after what he had just heard he was fully of the opinion of the duc de Noailles, and there should be an announcement that day that the bank had been found wanting."[44] To soften the blow, he ordered Noailles to call on Law the next day, October 25. According to Law, writing many years later, Noailles brought a message from the Regent that "he hoped the rejection would not cause me to leave France" (that is, for Palermo) and "that he wished to make my stay agreeable and show me favour." The Council, too, believed that "I could be useful for my expert knowledge."[45]

Law wrote more in sorrow than in anger to Victor Amadeus, sending him some of the memorials he had written for Desmaretz by way of a Piedmontese officer, the marchese di Rivarolo, and a French connoisseur, the comte de Caylus. He also seems to have given Caylus a letter of introduction to Ippolito De Mari in Genoa. "I must do justice to His Royal Highness [the duc d'Orléans]," he wrote to the King of Sicily. "That prince has worked hard to bring about this project, but I see that it is sometimes as hard to bring about a good affair as a bad one. None the less, I am of opinion that this Kingdom will be obliged to make use of my project, or lose the rank it must maintain among the Powers, because a well-founded and -managed bank is worth more than the trade of the Indies."[46] He followed it up with a more detailed letter to Groppello on January 16, 1716.

Having disposed of Law, Noailles had no choice but to open up the armoury of French royal finance, and wheel out its artillery of default, devaluation and coercion. He was in favour of convoking the Estates General, the consultative assembly which had not met since 1614, to legitimate a partial default. The Regent was not persuaded and the Estates were not called until 1789, when they set in train the revolution that suspended royal rule in France.

Instead, rates of interest on both annuities and offices were cut by a percentage point. Some four thousand offices were suppressed. The currency was devalued. On December 7, 1715, a declaration from the King was issued at Vincennes, calling on the wartime financiers and contractors to present their claims to a general audit, which became known as the "Visa of 1716". More than half the claims were annulled, while the remaining 250 millions were converted into standard notes, or *billets d'état*, payable not to any named individual but to the bearer, and carrying a uniform interest rate of 4 per cent.

The notes were now a commodity and could be traded in inns and cafés and in the open-air debt market that had become established in a sunless kennel of a street (which survives, much improved, just west of the modern Pompidou Centre) called the rue Quincampoix.[47] Since Noailles had fixed no date to redeem the notes and assigned no revenue to pay the 4 per cent coupon, the *billets* changed hands at less than half their face value.

Even before the audit commissioners had finished their work, in March, 1716, the Regency announced in the name of the King a judicial inquiry into "the contractors and business people, their clerks and employees, who in the late two wars by their exactions forced the public to pay much more than was required by the exigencies of the time". All those involved in the King's affairs since January 1, 1689, from military butchers to tax collectors and traders in the King's debts, were commanded to appear before a court of senior magistrates called the *chambre de justice*, meeting in the convent of the Grands Augustins on the left bank of the Seine.[48]

The *partisans*, as the royal contractors were known from their contract or *partie* with the King, had long been a royal scapegoat. The most severe precedent was Louis XIV's court of justice between 1661 and 1665 celebrated in the depiction of his exploits in the ceiling of the Gallery of Mirrors at Versailles. There the King, with the assistance of the goddess Minerva, chases away the financiers in the guise of harpies, voracious monsters of antiquity. As new rich, they were lampooned on the licensed stage in such plays as Alain-René LeSage's *Turcaret*, performed in the darkest year of the war, 1709.

The decree of March, 1716 left little discretion to the Chamber of Justice. "The vast and sudden fortunes of those who have prospered from these criminal acts, the excess of their luxury and display which seems to insult the misery of our other subjects, are already a glaring proof of their malversations," it read.[49] For just over a year, both morning and afternoon, some thirty judges heard evidence while eighty assistants sifted invoices and accounts. Three death sentences were handed down, though only one was carried out. Men were sent to man the galleys in Marseilles, or pilloried amid the derision of the market-wives in Les Halles.[50] In the end, the need for revenue pushed aside the pleasures of justice and spectacle, and the principal financiers were either left alone or pardoned on payment of a penalty.[51] Antoine Crozat, a leading tax collector and proprietor of the French colony of Louisiana, was assessed for a payment of 6.6 million livres and Samuel Bernard for 6 million livres.

Law opposed the Chamber of Justice as "directly contrary to public credit and the commerce of the kingdom" and later offered to reimburse from his own funds the penalised financiers.[52] Trade was crippled. "The misery caused by the famine of money does not let up," Stair's chaplain, William Beauvoir, wrote in French to his wife in England that March, 1716.[53] As it turned out, many of the moneyed men settled their fines with the same decried bills with which they had been paid in the first place, and Noailles reckoned in April, 1717 that the yield in cash had been less than fifty millions.[54]

The principal consequence of the Chamber of Justice was that the established bankers to the Crown of France kept to their houses. The field was open to John Law.

Back in 1712, Law had offered Victor Amadeus of Savoy a choice of a public bank, handling the revenues of his duchy, and a smaller private bank. The Regent pressed Law to attempt the second and more modest scheme.[55] On May 2, Noailles presented to the Regency Council a motion to "give Mr Law", according to the minutes of the meeting, "the power to establish a bank different from that first proposed, purely voluntary and in no way affecting the ordinary collection of the King's revenues".[56] It was approved. Letters patent were issued in the King's name giving "Mr Law and his Company" a licence for twenty years for a "general bank" with the right to issue banknotes under the name of "bank crowns" (écus de banque). The Parlement of Paris registered the letters on the 4th.[57]

On the 20th, a more detailed set of letters allowed the bank to issue 1,200 shares each of 1,000 "bank crowns" which, at 5 livres per crown, made 6 million livres (Article I) or about £230,000 sterling. The bank would do business each day from nine to noon, and three to six in the afternoon, except Sundays, feast days and a week each in June and December to allow the directors to strike a balance sheet (Articles IV and VII). In an instance of democracy unusual in old-regime France, general meetings in June and December would choose directors and approve any division of profits between the shareholders or dividend (Article VIII). So as not to prejudice other merchants, the bank was forbidden to engage in physical trade or marine insurance (Article XVIII) or to borrow, but might cash bills of exchange and commercial debts at a discount (Article XVII). On ledger transfers between current accounts the bank would charge a convenience premium of five bank sols per thousand crowns, or 0.025 per cent (Article XVI).[58] On May 26, the Parlement of Paris registered letters of naturalisation for "sieur Jean Law de Laurestenne".[59]

Subscriptions for the shares opened at the hôtel Gramont on June 1 and by June 12, as the *Gazette d'Amsterdam* reported that day in a letter from Paris, "all the subscriptions for the new bank have for some days been filled."[60] It helped that shareholders were permitted to subscribe not just in cash but in *billets d'état*, by now at a 60 per cent discount, for which they were credited full or face value.

Using discredited state debt as capital was an English tactic, pioneered by the Bank of England in 1697 and by the South Sea Company at its stock-market flotation in 1711–12. The General Bank exercise made a small dent in the King's debt, which would have pleased Noailles, at the cost of little hard cash in the vault to meet withdrawals. Law may have reckoned that the financiers were too intimidated by the Chamber of Justice to buy up the banknotes, present them all at once and break the bank. (Such "banknote wars" became a feature of Scottish banking in the eighteenth century and of the small-town United States in the nineteenth.)

Law himself put up 1.5 million livres or a quarter of the capital. Even if his agents had made a sweep of rue Quincampoix for cheap *billets d'état*, that was probably his entire fortune. John Law was, as card players say, "all-in". How much the Regent invested, and how much the King (in the form of new *billets d'état*), this author has been unable to establish.

Leading courtiers, and some of the terrorised bankers, bought shares to gain favour with the Palais-Royal. For example, the Pâris brothers invested 45,000 livres. The brothers – Antoine, Claude, Joseph and Jean-Baptiste – were the four sons of the proprietor of an inn, La Montagne de Saint-François, at Moirans in the Dauphiné, at the foot of the Alps north of Grenoble. Their father, Jean, had come to prominence as a haulier and contractor, ferrying supplies by fair means and foul up the Isère river to the French armies in Savoy in the Nine Years War. The brothers had continued in the business, on a much expanded capital, and made themselves indispensable in providing bread and forage in the hard fighting in Flanders in the Spanish Succession War. As often with business people, as their fortune improved so did their honesty and their self-regard.

Claude, the second brother, known as "La Montagne", wrote in a testament for his children: "The duke of Orléans, who wanted to give some credit to that establishment [Law and Company], was of the wish that we should take part and allocated us a certain number of shares. We obeyed, and that caused us to attend two general meetings of the bank, with that prince in the chair, and to enter into some relation with Mr Law."[61]

The letters patent of May 20 gave the seat of the bank as Law's house in the place Louis-le-Grand, until such time "as it can be placed at a greater convenience to the public". (Article IV). The place Vendôme was too far from the business districts around Les Halles, and at some point in the summer, Law rented from the president of the Parlement de Paris the hôtel de Mesmes, a palace built by the Montmorency family in the rue Sainte-Avoye (now rue du Temple) of which little remains.

Because the French had small experience of banking, journalists were baffled and hostile. "Almost nobody knows the real purpose of that establishment or how it will develop," wrote the author of a newsletter now in the Royal Library in The Hague, the *Gazette de la Régence*, in June.[62] On July 19, he wrote "His [Law's] bank will not succeed." and, on the 31st, "Almost everybody is making fun of the bank."

In the course of the summer of 1716, sentiment changed. The historian and memoirist, Charles Hénault, president of one of the subsidiary courts of Paris, visited the bank as a novelty, and took away an impression of solidity and opulence, always the banker's favoured decor.

"You entered an immense hall," he wrote, "divided up into I don't know how many counters, heaving with gold and silver. If you presented yourself with a bank-note in hand, there was a choice of gold or silver. If on the other hand, you preferred a note, you went to other offices where they gave you notes for your cash, with the difference that you paid a 5 per cent premium for the convenience in commerce."[63] Another customer, needing 1,800 livres transferred from Marseilles, was admitted by a Swiss guardsman "in magnificent green livery" and told that for transactions "of that character", the bank made no charge.[64]

By September 18, the *Gazette de la Régence* was grumbling that the bank was too successful, "monopolising what little business there is".[65] In a private letter to an English investor, Stair's secretary Thomas Crawford wrote: "Law's bank . . . has ruined all the banquiers here for it discounts bills and gives and takes bills upon every foreign place at one per cent cheaper than any of them."[66] On November 18, Philippe de Courcillon, marquis de Dangeau wrote in his diary: "There is scarcely a day when the bank does not take in a million."[67]

Denominated in values of ten, 100 and 1,000 silver crowns "of the weight and fineness of this day", the banknotes were claims on silver coins of a fixed weight and quality. They were thus safe from any further manoeuvre by Noailles to reduce the King's liabilities by a devaluation or recoinage. On October 7, and then on December 26, Noailles instructed tax collectors to cash the notes on demand and use them as much as possible to remit payments to the treasury.[68] The banknotes rose to par with silver and then to a small premium.[69]

At least four of the General Bank's notes survive. Engraved from copper plates on laid, watermarked paper, each is signed in ink by Law and numbered by hand. An embossed stamp or *cachet à sec* shows a seated figure of the goddess Fortune, holding compasses, above a cornucopia and the legend "Establishment of Credit." Each note was cut with scissors from a book, across an arabesque and the monogram JL. Presumably, a clerk matched the note against the other halves of the arabesque and monogram on the stub.[70] No stub survives.

At the first shareholders' meeting on December 22, with the Regent in attendance, Law announced a dividend of 8 per cent of the issue price of the shares. "That will seem a lot," Law wrote to the bank's correspondent in Genoa, Marcello Durazzo, "but considering the economy with which the Bank is serving the King and the public, the profit will in time increase."[71]

That sentence is from a run of some thirty letters from Law to Durazzo, conserved in the Durazzo family's archive in Genoa. Originally from Albania, the family became established in Genoa in the fourteenth century and supplied their first Doge in the sixteenth. Marcello Durazzo I, marchese di Gabiano (1634–1717) was one of the principal merchant bankers of the peninsula. Law inundated him with business, as no doubt he did his correspondents in London, Hamburg, Geneva and Amsterdam, where his business letters have not survived. The letters to Durazzo are in Italian, in a secretary's hand, with a formal closing scrawled by Law in French.

Having shipped funds by way of Ippolito De Mari's account at the Bank of St George, Law informed Durazzo that the Bank had taken over for the comte de Toulouse, head of the Navy Council, a contract to buy 800,000 feet a year of Italian oak timbers for shipyards at Toulon and Marseilles. A Pisan merchant named Diego Vercassoni had the privilege of cutting timber in the woods of Cisterna in the Papal States, and Durazzo acted as his banker. As Durazzo wrote to Vercassoni on March 20, "Mr Law is really the only minister of France active in this business, as in so many others."[72] John Law was not, in fact, a minister of France.

On April 10, Law told the marchese that he had reached agreement with the prince de Carignan to buy the hôtel de Soissons for the sum of one million lire of Piedmont, and asked him to make the payment at Genoa. "Business will recover in this Kingdom, God willing, in a short time," Law wrote on the 13th. "I am working tirelessly, and with all the more spirit for the encouragement I receive from the Prince who governs the Kingdom and has made [the recovery of trade] the principal object of his activity." On the 27th, Law sent Durazzo 50,000 livres in banknotes, "not doubting for a moment, that also in your market [*anco su la vostra piazza*] they have begun to be recognised and valued for their solidity and for their convenience in remittances to every part of France".[73] (The marchese died on May 21. Vercassoni failed in his navy contracts and absconded, and Law's relations with Marcello's sons, Giacomo Filippo and Giuseppe Maria, became strained.)[74]

The bank's balance sheet expanded in the end to about 40 million livres. That was no great thing in French commerce that was surely more extensive than Law's estimate of 1.2 billion livres a year, but had its effect within Paris. Working people, fortunate to earn fifteen sols a day or less than one livre, saw nothing of the General Bank's notes.

The bank was but one aspect of Law's activity. Scraps of paper show him buying prints of Old Masters in the palais Luxembourg for a Scottish gentleman and supplying cash to English tourists in Paris, including £1,000 for the young James Craggs, son of the Postmaster General and a rising MP, who was later to become Secretary of State for the Southern Department.[75] The duc d'Orléans, too, was coming to rely on Law not only for the King's navy but for every sort of personal exigency and to finance his diplomacy.[76] For the revolution in France's foreign relations that the Regent had in mind, he needed new men without allegiance to Louis XIV's policies, such as John Law and the abbé Dubois.

Guillaume Dubois (1656–1723), son of a physician of the

Limousin, sometime tutor of the Regent and his life-long confidant, was a clever and merry man, fond of women and good cheer, cunning in an anxious sort of way, and thirsty for power, rank and honours. Elisabeth Charlotte, who detested him for persuading her son to marry Mlle de Blois, allowed him some intelligence "if only he had not reduced life to a matter of position and hadn't played the matchmaker [*zu keiner heüraht geholffen*]".[77] Unlike the duc de Saint-Simon, Dubois never fussed or scolded the Regent but sought to amuse him. Wary of Law, he bided his time.

Even before the great King's death, the Regent had seen in an alliance with Great Britain a counterweight to the power of the old court and a guarantee of his rights in the French succession. With the collapse of the Jacobite rebellion in Scotland, he sought in March, 1716 to pick up the threads of his friendship with Stanhope. Stanhope, not at all impressed that James III had managed to cross France the previous autumn and join the rebellion, was cool. Dubois, who loved all things vivid and clandestine, took matters in hand.[78]

Furnished with letters of credit on Law's correspondent in Amsterdam, Pierre Testas,[79] Dubois arrived in The Hague on July 5, 1716. He lodged under the name Saint-Albin in a boarding-house frequented by Germans, and put it about that he was looking to buy old books and pictures. On the 20th, as Stanhope landed at Hellevoetsluis en route for the summer court at Hanover, a note from Dubois was pressed into his hand. Stanhope was intrigued. The two men met in secret the following day at the house of the British envoy, Horatio Walpole. Stanhope then continued his journey, while Dubois, after reporting back to the Regent, waited at the post-house in Osnabrück on August 10 for Stanhope's directions. Stanhope smuggled him into the house he was occupying in Hanover, in rooms communicating with his own, and for six weeks they re-arranged Europe, "sometimes in dressing-gowns and night-caps".[80] Dubois knew he was no match for Stanhope by day. After dinner, it was another matter.

At first, Stanhope cared only for having James III expelled across the Alps, and dismantling fortifications at the French channel ports. He came to see that Great Britain, now enmeshed in continental politics by George I's possessions in Hanover, might stand in need of French friendship. He conceived the alliance with France as the first block of a European system that would make good the defects of the Utrecht treaties and preserve the peace for a generation. Dubois pressed him, "seven or eight times", to accept a gift from the Regent in the form of a draft on Law of 600,000 livres, or more than £35,000 and enough to buy a country estate.[81] In the course of just one summer, Law's credit had become established.

Stanhope, who knew the power of parliamentary committees of inquiry, and anyway was not grasping, declined with grace.[82] (Later on, Dubois asked the Regent to have Stanhope sent thirty *pièces* of champagne and burgundy, at twenty-four dozen per *pièce* or 8,640 bottles in all.)[83]

The two men signed a draft treaty on October 9. Dubois emerged from his priest's hole and was presented to George I. The United Provinces were invited to accede to what became known as the Triple Alliance but, troubled by Britain's defection in the war and uncertain of their future course, delayed signing. Meanwhile, Law was able, through his correspondent Alexandre Bruguier in Hamburg, to start paying on October 18 the arrears of a subsidy of 150,000 Hamburg rixdalers a quarter (more than £30,000) promised by Louis XIV to King Charles XII of Sweden.[84] Law was also ordered to provide funds to the Navy Department to replace the makeshift currency of Canada, which for want of silver (and even paper) consisted of cut-up playing-cards.

*

John Law cultivated the French court. He waited on the two young princes of the blood, the duc de Bourbon and the prince de Conti, the men of the highest rank outside the royal family itself. Both were to invest in Law's companies and are memorialised by street names in New Orleans. Louis-Henri, duc de Bourbon, known as "monsieur le Duc", was in 1716 twenty-four years old. He was a polished young man, as Elisabeth Charlotte wrote, but could not attend to business for he lacked knowledge, application and patience. He had lost an eye in a hunting accident, "otherwise he would have been quite handsome". He was governed by his mistress, Mme de Prie.[85] His mother, Louise-Françoise, a legitimated daughter of Louis XIV known as "madame la duchesse", also invested in the company and was to be the Law family's steadiest friend at the French court for twenty-five years. Lively and independent, and enjoying precedence, she could do what she wished.

Louis-Armand, prince de Conti, who was rising twenty-one, inspired Elisabeth Charlotte to her most barbarous character: "It is not his face that is ugly, but his whole posture is small, crooked and repulsive, and he is so distracted, that he often seems wild or as if he had never submitted to discipline; when one least expects it, he falls over his cane like a toad."[86] His marriage was stormy.

Law took to calling, every Tuesday morning at eleven, on the duc de Saint-Simon. One day early in 1717, he waited on the duke in a state of dismay (*consterné*). He had brought with him a crystal or paste model of a large and flawless diamond. Law told the duke that he had tried to persuade the Regent to buy the jewel for the young King's coronation regalia but the price demanded had "alarmed" that prince.

Law knew his Saint-Simon. "I felt as he did," Saint-Simon wrote later, "that it ill became the majesty of a King of France to quail at the price of a unique and inestimable jewel, and the more that other princes hankered after it, the less should we allow it to slip our hands."[87] Law begged him to speak to the duc d'Orléans.

The "Regent diamond", which can be seen in the Louvre museum in Paris, was brought to the earth's surface in India, probably at Golconda near Hyderabad, at some time towards the end of the seventeenth century. In December, 1701, a merchant known as Samchund or Jamchund showed the raw stone, weighing 303 mangelins or 426 carats of the time and the size of a bitter orange, to an Englishman, Thomas Pitt.

"Diamond" Pitt (1653–1726), from a family long established at Blandford in Dorset in the English West Country, had made a career in India trading as an "interloper", that is independent of the English East India Company. In 1698, Pitt made his peace with the company, and though described by one of the directors as "that roughling, immoral man",[88] was appointed president of the company's factory on the east coast at Fort St George, later Madras, later still Chennai. In March, 1702, Pitt bought the diamond for 48,000 pagodas or just over £20,000. He believed he could sell it to a European prince at £1,500 per carat, which would make him the richest subject in England. He later called God to witness that he had used no violence or intimidation with Samchund.[89]

By now, war had broken out over the Spanish succession. Pitt's partner in London, the royal jeweller Sir Stephen Evance, was aghast when he received a model of the stone. "We are now gott in a Warr," he wrote from London on August 1, 1702, "the French King has his hands and heart full, soe he cant buy such a Stone, There is noe prince in Europe can buy itt, soe would advise You not to meddle in itt."[90] His letter crossed at sea with the stone, brought back for cutting in London by Pitt's eldest son, Robert, in his shoe. For eight years, in distant Fort St George, Pitt thought of little else but his "great affair" and "great concerne".

The cutting, entrusted to Joseph Cope, a specialist polisher in the City of London, was slow, expensive and fraught.[91] Pitt had hoped for a clean stone of 300 carats, but Cope had to cut away two-thirds of the stone to remove the flaws. It was now the size of a greengage. According to Robert, writing to his father, "the stone was entirely perfect in the middle, and of the best water in the world, but the flaws in the outside went so deep that it was necessary to saw off all those pieces, one of the last of which was so rotten that it crumbled into dirt."[92]

The clips were unsaleable. Governor Pitt was beside himself, writing to Robert and Evance: "You write that the Peices Saw'd off will yeild about 1500*l*, which I hope was a mistake, and that there was a Cypher [zero] wanting to make it thousands."[93] Evance fell bankrupt and the stone had to be spirited out of his shop to the country. What emerged, in the end, was a table-cut brilliant, all but flawless, of 140.5 carats, which some judges think the finest jewel in existence. Pitt insisted on his £1,500 a carat, "which I am sure is as cheap as Neck beef, and let any Potentate buy it, the next day 'tis worth a Million of pounds Sterling."[94]

No potentate would buy it. Returning to England in 1710, Governor Pitt offered the diamond to Queen Anne. Her court hoped the City might present it to her, but the City had no ready cash. A month after George I's arrival in his new kingdom, Pitt showed the King and the Prince of Wales the jewel but again there was no public subscription. In October 1714, according to the *Gazette d'Amsterdam*, one of Pitt's sons brought the diamond to Louis XIV of France at Fontainebleau, but the price demanded "disgusted" the King's advisers.[95] Paste models were sent out to the courts of Europe and returned.

Exhausted by his shop-worn mineral, which over fifteen years had immobilised his capital and ruined his relations with his eldest son, Pitt decided in 1716 to repair his fortunes as Governor of Jamaica. He placed the "great stone" in the care of his second son Thomas, a colonel of horse, instructing him to accept no less than £100,000.[96]

Thomas Pitt had served in Spain, had corresponded with Stanhope in his captivity after Brihuega and then, at the general's release, introduced him into his family. In 1713, Stanhope married Pitt's sister Lucy. Either Stanhope or Thomas Crawford, Stair's secretary, or both, suggested Law. Colonel Pitt crossed over to France in late April or May, 1717, and the two men soon came to terms. The duc de Saint-Simon, by his own account, had overcome the Regent's scruples.[97] On June 6, the duc d'Orléans informed the Regency Council "that he had decided to acquire for the King the great diamond of England belonging to Colonel Pitt for the sum of two millions . . . which was approved."[98] In twelve months, Law had become the greatest banker in Europe.

Law agreed to pay the two million livres in instalments, with interest on the declining balance, beginning with 720,000 livres on June 1; and then in four payments of 320,000 livres at six-monthly intervals ending on June 1, 1719. Noailles's devaluation of December 23, 1715 had brought down the exchange rate of the French livre to about sixteen to the pound sterling. That still yielded Governor Pitt some £125,000. He never sailed for Jamaica.

Law seems not to have talked of his role in acquiring the diamond, but Lady Katherine kept as a memento the paste model. It is listed in an inventory of her property in 1734: "To Madame: the model of the King of France's diamond."[99] That June of 1717, Law's attention was elsewhere.

CHAPTER SIX

The Island of Mississippi

Pourquoi les François sont ils venus dans notre Terre?
(Why did the Frenchmen come into our country?)

TATTOOED SERPENT, NATCHEZ[1]

At about the time of John Law's birth in Edinburgh, Jesuit missionaries and fur traders from the French settlements of Montreal and Quebec were pushing into the western Great Lakes. There, on the southern shore of Lake Superior, they heard from the Algonquin-speaking people of a broad river flowing to the south-east, whose name they turned into French as Mechesipi or Messipi.

In 1673, Louis de Buade, comte de Frontenac, governor of New France, and Jean Talon, the King's Intendant, sent Father Jacques Marquette, SJ, and Louis Jolliet, once a priest in minor orders and now a fur trader, to explore the river and determine if it might offer a northern route to China and the East Indies. Setting off from Green Bay on Lake Michigan, then known as *la baye des puants* (Bay of the Stinkers), in two bark canoes with five men, Marquette and Jolliet ascended the rapids of the Fox River, crossed Lake Winnebago, portaged the canoes across the prairie and marsh to the River Wisconsin and descended to a braided river flowing south, which they reached at the place called Prairie du Chien on June 17, 1673.

Riding the flood, they floated to the mouth of the Arkansas River at latitude 34 degrees north. Certain that the river emptied into the Gulf of Mexico, rather than the Gulf of California or the Atlantic, and not wishing to tangle with the Spanish in Mexico, they turned their canoes north on July 17. The going upstream was hard and Father Marquette fell ill, but at the end of September they reached Green Bay after a voyage of two and a half thousand miles.[2]

In early 1682, Robert Cavelier, generally known as the sieur de La Salle, a Jesuit novice who had abandoned his vows to trade in furs on behalf of his family in Rouen and in restless and frustrating explorations, set off from the fort he had built on the Illinois, Fort Crèvecoeur or Broken-Heart, to navigate the whole length of the Mississippi. He had with him his chief lieutenant, Henri de Tonty and twenty-two other Frenchmen and eighteen native Canadian men, ten women and three children.

On April 9, 1682, at the mouth of the river La Salle named Colbert, after Louis XIV's chief minister, near what is now Venice, Louisiana, on a piece of dry ground he took a reading at noon of latitude 27 degrees north, which was incorrect by two degrees too far to the south.

La Salle attached a cross to a tree and erected a column, painted with the arms of France and the name of Louis the Great, King of France and Navarre, and the date. Then, amid volleys of musketry and shouts of "Long Live the King", La Salle proclaimed that in virtue of the commission in his hand, he had taken and now took in the name of His Majesty and his successors to the Crown:

> this country of Louisiana, the seas, harbours, ports, bays, adjacent straits, and all the nations, peoples, provinces, cities, towns, markets, villages, mines, mine workings,

> fisheries, streams and rivers comprised within its extent from the mouth of the great river St Louis, otherwise called the Ohio, Olighin Sipou and Chukagoua, from the east . . . as also along the river Colbert, or Missisippi, and the rivers which discharge into it from its source beyond the country of the Scious or Nadouessious . . . as far as its mouth in the sea or Gulf of Mexico.

He demanded that a notary take down his words, and it was done.[3]

With that proclamation ("inaudible at half a mile," as a nineteenth-century United States author complained),[4] France gained an increase in her territory of one million square miles, or four times the size of her European homeland, stretching from the Rocky Mountains to the Alleghenies and taking in some 40 per cent of the modern United States (excluding Alaska) and part of two Canadian provinces. For the next five years, La Salle lobbied Louis XIV's court for a string of forts along the Colbert to confine the English to the eastern seaboard of the continent. He was exploring the Gulf coast for the mouth of the river when his men mutinied and he was killed near the Trinity River in Texas on March 19, 1687.

Despite fears of incursions into the territory by the English trading from Carolina, and the Spanish from Texas and Florida, La Salle's colonial plan hung fire in a France distracted by European war. In 1697, the year of the Peace of Ryswick, there was an unsuccessful attempt to float a joint-stock company of 500,000 livres on the English or Dutch model to develop the colony.[5] That year, the minister of the navy, Louis Phélypeaux, comte de Maurepas and Pontchartrain, ordered Pierre Le Moyne, sieur d'Iberville, member of one of the principal families of Canada, who had distinguished himself in the late war, to search out the mouth of the river and defend it. In a letter to the minister of June 18, 1698,

Iberville asked for three armed vessels of different draught, and a merchant ship, with eight months of provisions for sailors and marines, *filibustiers* or irregular fighting men, and artisans.[6]

In February, 1699, Iberville and his younger brother, Jean-Baptiste, sieur de Bienville, anchored in the Mississippi Sound opposite the place now called Biloxi, Mississippi. They surprised a hunting party in canoes, who fled leaving a sick old man on the beach. The Canadians gave him food and tobacco, made him a shelter and fire and left presents nearby. The next day, the natives appeared and, over the next few days, smoked the pipe with the brothers, asking if they were people from the head of the great river, which they called Malybanchia. Bienville said they were.

The brothers then found and with difficulty ascended the main channel of the Mississippi. On March 9, their native guide told them of a route that was commonly used from the river to the Biloxi country, by way of a portage to a creek now known as the Bayou Saint-Jean and the brackish estuary called Lake Pontchartrain, that avoided the bewildering Mississippi delta. Iberville wrote in his journal: "They are in the habit of dragging their canoes by a serviceable path where we found much baggage of folk who were either coming or going. He insisted to me that the distance from one place to the other was inconsiderable."[7]

Returning to the Gulf, short of provisions, they established camp at a place they named Fort Maurepas, on the north-east shore of Biloxi Bay on a bluff above what is now Ocean Springs, Mississippi. Early the next year, the brothers explored the new route to the river by way of Lake Pontchartrain, and found the portage just three miles in extent, half of it knee-deep in water and mud, half of it covered in timber and canes.[8] It is now the street called Bayou Road in New Orleans.

Fort Maurepas, in the section of Ocean Springs known as Lovers Lane, had advantages. The woods were full of deer and the water of redfish[9] but the place was unhealthy, vulnerable to hurricanes, lacked drinking water and the soil all around was poor, "a fine sand," as one of the colonists wrote, "as white and shining as snow, on which no vegetable can be raised".[10] There was an anchorage on the land side of a barrier island Iberville had named île aux Vaisseaux or Ship Island, but that was twelve miles offshore and sea-going vessels had to transfer men and goods into lighters of progressively shallower draught.[11]

All the while, the Mississippi was undefended. The nineteen-year-old Bienville was surprised in September, 1699 when, sounding the river with five men in two bark canoes at a meander just south of the Bayou Saint-Jean portage, he came on a vessel from Charles Town (Charleston) in Carolina prospecting a settlement. Bienville persuaded Captain William Lewis Bond that he was trespassing on the property of the King of France. (The place is still called "English Turn".)[12]

At the end of 1701, Iberville abandoned Fort Maurepas and moved the capital to a site on the Mobile River to the east, now known as Twenty-Seven Mile Bluff, which itself proved unsatisfactory and the capital was moved three times more before settling at New Orleans. In truth, the French never found a harbour with the advantages of Havana or Charleston, because there was none.

The next year, Iberville departed the colony never to return, but left behind a cohort of brothers and nephews. Bienville became commandant of the colony's forces at the age of twenty-one. He had mastered or invented – the scholars disagree – a pidgin language for use among the patchwork of nations, known as the *jargon mobilien* or Mobilian Jargon, and managed to preserve the French foothold through the metropolitan neglect and famine of the Spanish Succession War. Just one ship with supplies from France arrived at île Dauphine, at the mouth of Mobile Bay, between April, 1708 and the peace treaties of 1713.

By 1712, crippled by the expense of the European war, Pontchartrain sought to offload the starveling colony. He enlisted the help of Antoine Laumet, who called himself de Lamothe Cadillac, founder of Detroit and eponym of a posthumous automobile. A wit, braggart and bootlegger, Lamothe Cadillac had made himself obnoxious to both the French and the natives in Canada and been sent away as governor of Louisiana. Though Lamothe Cadillac had yet to visit the place, in Paris he persuaded Antoine Crozat, marquis du Chastel, that there were valuable mines in the territory and the potential to trade with the Spanish in Old and New Mexico.[13]

Son of a leading merchant of Toulouse, Crozat had made a fortune in tax collection in France and in slaving and trading ventures overseas, bought his marquisate and owned two large houses in the place Vendôme, the present Nos. 17 and 19. Known as "Crozat the Rich", he formed with two associates a Company of Louisiana to develop the colony, which then consisted of some twenty-seven families in Mobile, two companies of unpaid infantry and a few backwoodsmen or *coureurs de bois.*[14]

On September 14, 1712, the King at Fontainebleau granted the Crozat company a fifteen-year commercial monopoly on the whole territory from New Mexico to the "English in Carolina" and from the Gulf to the Illinois River. Crozat's sole obligation was to send two ships a year with twenty-five tons of victual and munitions for the King's garrisons, and as colonists ten boys or girls, as he pleased (Article VIII). He was also permitted to bring one ship of African slaves from the coast of Guinea to sell in the territory (Article XIV).[15]

Lamothe Cadillac arrived on June 5, 1713 at Dauphine Island on the *Baron de La Fauche,* which ran aground. His first impressions were unfavourable. "According to the proverb, 'Bad country, bad people,' one can say that they are a heap of the dregs of Canada, good only for the gallows or the plank, without subordination to religion and government, addicted to vice principally with the Indian women whom they prefer to French women."[16]

Lamothe Cadillac quarrelled with the Canadians, and demolished Bienville's native diplomacy. Crozat sent only five vessels to the colony of which one, *La Justice* in 1714, was lost off Cuba and the colony had to send for supplies to Vera Cruz in Mexico.

Though French posts were founded at Natchitoches on the Red River and at Natchez on the Mississippi, on a bluff on the outside of a bend commanding the river in both directions, and with meadowlands suitable for tobacco, Cadillac lost the confidence of the proprietors and of the comte de Toulouse, head of the Navy Council. He was recalled to France by an order dated March 3, 1716. Outraged by the demand of the Chamber of Justice for 6.6 million livres in taxes, Crozat offered his ships, sunk costs and the unexpired portion of his concession, and withdrew.

Thus thirty-five years after La Salle had claimed the territory for France, the French population of Louisiana consisted of a couple of hundred persons, eking out a living from gift exchanges with the Biloxi and Natchez, and selling skins and timber to the islands, and eggs and vegetables to the Spanish presidio at Pensacola. Canada, though far better populated, had yet to earn its bread. Ships returned empty to France or carried beaver skins to the glutted hatters of Paris, Lyons and Rouen. The young men took to the woods, living as the natives showed them, as *coureurs de bois*. The notion that the French were entranced by the prospects of John Law's Mississippi, still current even among the well-informed, is incorrect. The French were weary of North America.

In part to justify a large compensation, Crozat now talked up the colony and peppered ministers with proposals to develop it. He suggested a joint enterprise, of the King and a public company with a capital of some 1.5 million livres. Since even so modest a sum would be hard to raise in cash, Crozat took a leaf out of Law's scheme for the General Bank and suggested the funds be subscribed in the depreciated government IOUs or *billets d'état*.[17]

In discussions in the Navy Council through the spring and summer, Crozat's little scheme took shape and John Law was drawn in. For the president of the council of finance, the duc de Noailles, what mattered was less to populate a new colony than to discharge the King's war debts and make France once again creditworthy. Law's contribution was to raise the scale of the project and thus the volume of state debt absorbed. Law's bank was the only bright spot on the horizon. As Saint-Simon wrote to the Regent in May, 1717: "The only relief to the finances in remedying the chaos in foreign and domestic payments is the establishment of Mr Law's bank to which I confess I had been very opposed and whose success I regard with a joy as sincere as if I had been in favour."[18]

The enterprise was christened the Compagnie d'Occident, or Company of the West, to veil from English and Spanish eyes and ears the more narrow field of activity, which was Louisiana. In addition, the company was to have sources of revenue other than the uncleared swamps and prairies, including the monopoly of importing Canadian beaver furs (which was due to expire that year) and the right to bring African slaves from the coast of Guinea. More important than either of those, a portion of the King's excise revenue would pass to the company to pay its shareholders' dividends.

On August 21, Noailles presented to the Regency Council his proposal, which was approved with some alterations, and letters patent issued by the King and printed the following week.

Under the letters patent, the King of France and Navarre on the advice of his very dear and beloved uncle, the duc d'Orléans, and other princes, peers of France and notable personages, granted to a company of commerce "under the name of the *Company of the*

West" the sole right of trade and mining in the province and government of Louisiana including the Illinois for a period of twenty-five years, and the import of beaver skins, coat and parchment, from Canada for the same period (Article II). The King also granted to the company all the fortifications and vessels, including the hollow cypress trunks known as pirogues used on the bayous, then lying in the territory (Article L).

Louisiana was constituted a fief of the Crown in perpetuity in return only for an act of homage at the commencement of each reign and the present of a gold crown weighing thirty marcs or fifteen pounds (Article V). It might display on its buildings, vessels and cannon arms of a shield Vert, with a pile wavy Argent on which is resting a river proper, leaning on a cornucopia Or, having two savages as supporters and a flowered crown (Article LIV).

The company might raise troops, build warships, dig mines, dispose of land in freehold, appoint judges and civil officers, enter treaties with the American nations, and call on the help of the French Crown in case of interference or insult by other powers (Articles VI–XVIII). Provided that the company used French vessels, equipped and armed on French territory, it would be exempt from import and export taxes (Article XXV). It could grant rights to other merchants to trade in the concession territory (Article XXX). At the expiry of the concession, the company would continue to own the land of Louisiana but must sell the fortifications and military assets to the King at a fair price (Article LII). In return for those privileges, the company was required to transport to the territory "six thousand whites and at least three thousand blacks" and build churches of the Roman Catholic faith in all its settlements, and furnish them with clergy subject to the Bishop of Quebec (Articles LI and LIII).

As to the company's funds, the King stipulated only that to encourage as many of his subjects as possible to participate, the shares should be in denominations of 500 livres payable entirely in the depreciated state IOUs or *billets d'état.* The final capital of the company was left vague, as well it must, the King stating only that the books would be closed once "a sufficient capital" was at hand (Article XXXII). The IOUs subscribed would be transported to the town hall of "our fine city of Paris" and, in the presence of named civic officials, burned to ashes (Article XLV). In their place, the company would receive perpetual annuities from the King at the 25th penny or 4 per cent per year, payable from the revenue of a stamp duty on notarial acts, known as the *Controlle des Actes des Notaires* (Article XXXVIII).

Members of the nobility might invest without forfeiting their titles to that estate (Article I) but they enjoyed no privileges at the company's general assembly. Each lot of fifty shares carried a single vote, whatever the status or condition of its owner (Article XXXVII). Foreigners were invited to invest and would be exempt from the old feudal right of confiscation known as the *droit d'aubaine*, where the property of deceased aliens in France reverted to the Crown of France (Article XXXV).[19]

The financing of the company was ingenious. A subscriber to a share of the Company of the West exchanged a government IOU with an uncertain interest of 4 per cent for the same thing constituted as a share, paying a 4 per cent dividend, plus a claim on Louisiana and the Canada fur trade. In other words, the central territory of the United States that today produces trillions of dollars of value each year stood in the balance sheet of the Company of the West at zero. As for the beaver trade, it was to be a source of steady if unspectacular profit to the company until the cession of New France to Britain in 1763.[20]

It seemed the shareholder could only gain. He or she replaced a bad borrower (the King of France) with a better (John Law of Lauriston) and had the potential of Louisiana and the beaver trade for nothing. Admittedly, both Canada and Louisiana had proved up to then a burden to the King of France, but it is strange that Noailles and the King's advisers were giving them away. It may be that Law promised that, at some point in the future, the returns from North America would pay the share dividends unaided, the annuities could be wiped from the slate and with them a royal debt of one hundred million livres, and the tax revenues appropriated to pay the annuity interest become free for other royal purposes. If that were the intention, the letters patent make no mention of it.

There were two refinements. While the Company would receive its 4 per cent annuities on the stamp duty back-dated to the first day of 1717, it was not required to pay a dividend till July 1, 1718 (Article XL). The company would thus have money from the King for almost a year before anything was due to shareholders. That money could go towards the cost of establishing the company in Paris, rigging out ships in the French Atlantic ports, erecting warehouses and collecting recruits for Louisiana. To encourage people to invest in the shares, the *billets d'état* were to cease to pay interest from January 1, 1718.

The proposal was put to the Paris Parlement in a bundle of other measures to reduce the King's debts, including a lottery (which was a failure). The Parlement members, the *parlementaires*, suspicious of Law and anxious about their own emoluments amid the mass of unfunded debts, demanded an exact state of the royal finances.

On Sunday, September 5, 1717, the Regent summoned a deputation from the Parlement to the Palais-Royal and treated them with the utmost courtesy. He seated them at a table in the Great Gallery, himself at the head, the magistrates ranged on each side, and at the foot Noailles, beside a mountain of account books, portfolios and memoranda.[21] Over four hours, Noailles gave the deputies all the information they wanted and a great deal more. At some point, as the *Gazette d'Amsterdam* reported in a letter from Paris on the 10th, "Mr Law entered to give a detailed account of the advantages that would arise from the Company of the Mississippi."[22] The duc de Saint Simon, who affected an ignorance of commerce, wrote "advantages to the Company" which Law certainly did not emphasise.[23]

The magistrates, "infinitely pleased" with their reception at the Palais-Royal, reported favourably to their colleagues the next day. They were unhappy that the proposed stop in interest payments would, in effect, force holders of the King's obligations to convert their *billets d'état* into shares in an unknown and risky corporation. That Monday night, in her regular intelligence to King James's Secretary of State, the Earl of Mar, Fanny Oglethorpe gave a muddled account of proceedings, possibly from Lady Katherine: "Mr Laws is going to make a lottery of the *billets d'état,* offers to take for 50,000,000 and take the island of 'Mesisipy' for him. The *Parlement* wont agree to it, saying he's an adventurer, not fit for the nation to trust."[24] Ever flexible, the Regent reinstated the interest on the *billets d'état.* The edict, including the formation of the company, was registered in the Parlement on the 10th. On the 12th, the King named seven directors of the company, headed by "Mr Law, director general of the Bank".[25]

The subscription opened on September 14, 1717, and at first went well. Etienne Bourgeois, the company's cashier, reported that in the first fortnight, he had subscriptions for 28 million livres, or 56,000 shares.[26] Of those, Law as senior director bought for himself 12,000 shares for six million livres, which he later increased.[27] It was expected that the Regent would buy a large block of shares for himself and the King.

The principal subscribers were those with government IOUs lying on their hands, that is, the suppliers of food, cloth, forage and munitions to the army and navy in the late war. The "Mississippian" entered the French imagination, provincial and vulgar, embodied in the figure of Marie-Catherine Barré (1,700 shares), known to the Daughters of the American Revolution Chapter in Pascagoula, Mississippi, but to nobody else, as the "Duchess de Chaumont". Though she later termed herself "lady banker at Namur",[28] she and her husband, Antoine Chaumont, were shopkeepers in that town and branched out into supplying the French armies in Flanders during the war.

Others investors were the munitioners François-Marie Fargès for 2,000 shares, one of the Pâris brothers (600 shares), Huguenot bankers in Holland and Geneva, manufacturers, and merchants and shippers from the Atlantic ports of La Rochelle, Nantes, Le Havre, Saint-Malo and Bordeaux.[29] The *Gazette d'Amsterdam*, briefed or bought by Law or the other directors, was bullish. In a letter from Paris on December 17, its correspondent reported that the "Company of the West continues to have such success that it already has subscriptions for 70 millions."[30]

That was false. Law was not able to constitute any of the 4 per cent annuities for the company until the following February, and then for only 24 millions in subscriptions.[31] In other words, even some of the original investors mentioned by Etienne Bourgeois had had second thoughts.

French families with surplus money, inured for a century and a half to buying annuities or sinecures from the King, had little experience of investment at risk. In all that period, Canada and North America had not earned their keep. Law had also set no figure on the company's capital, for the good reason that he did not know how much the untried French stock market could provide. Shareholders thus had no idea of the size of the enterprise of which they were buying a share. Worse, there were grounds to doubt the fund allocated to pay the dividend until the Louisiana trade was on its feet. The stamp duties earmarked for the company had either already been diverted to other purposes or spent in advance. Investors suspected that the Company of the West could either pay their dividends or equip its convoys to Louisiana, but not both.

The Company took to publicity.

The monthly literary journal *Le Nouveau Mercure* had just been launched by François Buchet, a priest "but only in name", who sought to champion modernity both in literature and in public life. (He died in 1721, evidently done to death by some men about town (*petits-maîtres*) who objected to aspersions in the journal.)[32]

In its edition of September, Buchet published an account of the colony, evidently brought back by the frigate *Paon*, which had just docked at La Rochelle. It said the soil of Louisiana was fertile, game abounded in the woods and bison on the plains, wild vines and indigo grew in profusion, there was plentiful timber for masts and hulls, and the natives were well disposed, all of which was true. The only flights of fancy were marsupial rats "the size of cats",[33] and tasting like sucking-pig – raccoons – and a crag in the west from which the Americans detached with their arrow-points stones "similar to emeralds" to decorate their upper lips.[34] The article had little effect on the share subscription. Law tried to interest investors in England without great success.[35]

On September 27, 1717, Lamothe Cadillac and his son Antoine were arrested under so-called "secret letters" or *lettres de cachet* and jailed in the Bastille prison on the eastern edge of town.[36] While that was the Navy Council's doing, the Company seems to have made no objection.

Though he had been relieved of his post in Louisiana in March 1716, Lamothe Cadillac did not sail from Mobile on the *Paon* till the summer of 1717, and only escaped with difficulty when a storm on May 3 piled a sandbank across the mouth of the harbour and blocked the entrance channel.[37] Landing at La Rochelle on

September 1, 1717, he made his way with his son to Paris where they poked fun at the territory and the Company's project. The charge sheet at the Bastille recorded that father and son were "suspected of having made speeches against the government and the colonies".[38] The prisoners were not questioned and were released the following February 8. (The least vindictive of men, the Regent paid Lamothe Cadillac arrears in salary and expenses. He became mayor of the town of Castelsarrasin, near Montauban, where he died in 1730.)

A song of this time, entitled "The Company of the West", shows that Paris knew all it needed to know of Law's past:

Pour lui donner plus de crédit
On met à la tête un proscrit
Qu'on vouloit pendre en son pays.
(And since solidity's the word,
They've put in charge a gallows-bird
Who dodged the rope abroad.)

The poet recommended sending to the Mississippi the Parlement, the Regent, the duc de Bourbon and his mother, Noailles, the Jesuits, the senior prelates, and various dukes and peers.[39] On October 22, the *Gazette de la Régence*, which had been sceptical also about Law's bank, reported: "It is said the business of Mississippi will fail."

None the less, on October 25, the first Company convoy set sail from La Rochelle. It consisted of the *Dauphine*, a 250-ton fluyt or flûte, the square-rigged and broad-bottomed merchantman that was the workhorse of the Dutch long-haul trade, which Crozat had bought in 1715 in Holland, and two of his 60-ton brigantines, the *Neptune* and the *Vigilante*, to serve as lighters and navigate the Mississippi. In addition to flour, clothing and back pay for the mutinous garrison, medicine and brandy for the sick, and wax candles for the cabin churches, the *Dauphine* carried artisans such as carpenters, tailors, cobblers and bakers, of which the colony stood in need, and salt-smugglers from the prisons to serve as labourers.[40] The smaller vessels shipped ten flat boats (*chaloupes*) and ten canoes (*pirogues*) to negotiate the swamps and bayous.[41]

Law appears to have paid for the rigging and victualling of those vessels out of his own pocket.[42] He certainly imported 111 bales, or about six tons, of Canadian beaver pelts that autumn at his own expense.[43] The notion, still widespread in the United States, that Law's Louisiana was a land-jobbing scam, a sort of 1920s south Florida before its time is not so much false as the opposite of the truth. Law's was the most determined French colonial enterprise until the capture of Algiers in 1830.

The *Dauphine*'s captain, Pierre Arnaudin, carried letters from the company to Bienville, appointing him commandant general of the colony's armed forces and a local director and bringing the brevet of the Order of Saint-Louis, a decoration for officers created by the old King in 1693. The directors approved Bienville's plan for a company trading post on the river. The directors resolved to place "at thirty leagues from the mouth of the river, a market town [*bourg*] which should be called New Orleans [*la Nouvelle-Orléans*], where landing would be possible from either the river or Lake Pontchartrain".[44]

Bienville had decided on the Bayou Saint-Jean portage, where some fifty men, consisting of woodsmen, convicts and indentured workers, began clearing the site of swamp cypresses and canes in the spring of 1718.[45] The company later specified a site further upstream, at the Bayou Manchac, but Bienville was having nothing of it and awarded himself in March, 1719 two extensive riverfront tracts upstream and across the river from the Bayou Saint-Jean site.[46]

The name of New Orleans, to us so familiar, was a triumph for Bienville and Law. It showed investors and emigrants that the Regent's support for the company extended to the gift of his name. As for the site selected by Bienville, argument has rumbled for and against it for three centuries and, ever more so, every time a hurricane blows through the city or the great river overflows its billion-dollar embankments. The fact is that the capital of Louisiana was built at the Bayou Saint-Jean portage, and not at the Bayou Manchac, Biloxi, Mobile, Pensacola, Natchez or English Turn, and each generation defends the city against nature because the alternative appears so very much worse. If John Law had no other claim to fame, his part in the founding of New Orleans would earn him a line in the annals of North America.

In Paris, Law blamed Noailles for starving the company of working capital. "The disagreements of Mr Law and M. le duc de Noailles continue and pain His Royal Highness," the marquis de Nancré wrote to the abbé Dubois in London on November 2. "Nothing gets done and the projects on which we rely go backwards rather than advance." Louis-Jacques de Dreux, marquis de Nancré (1660–1719), was friendly with Law and an investor for 100,000 livres in the company. "M. de Noailles refuses to understand that the government must not meddle with a company formed for commerce. Ministers should never stick their noses into businesses which the fact of their intervention merely discredits."[47]

Law was gaining ground. On December 2, the Regent gave a long audience to the directors. Purblind and racked by headaches from a tennis-court injury eighteen months earlier, he had been persuaded to try a powder devised by the village priest at Rueil (now Rueil-Malmaison) to the west of Paris, and was wearing an eye-patch of green taffeta.[48] The *Gazette d'Amsterdam* reported that "Mr Law, who is the chief director, appeared to come away highly satisfied with the audience."[49] On December 8, Thomas Crawford reported to London that "there's a very great party form'd against the D. de Noailles."[50] On the 14th, Fanny Oglethorpe wrote to Mar: "Laws is fallen out with the duc de Noailles and pretends he can stand on his own legs."[51]

In fact, the Chancellor or senior law officer, Henri d'Aguesseau, was working to reconcile the two men. Nancré wrote to Dubois on January 2, 1718: "The Chancellor has managed to convince the duc de Noailles that Law is a good man to have on side [*à mettre dans leur manche*]."[52] To advertise the new amity, a working afternoon and supper was planned for Epiphany (January 6, 1718) at a house belonging to the financier Nicolas du Noyer in the fields to the east of the Bastille known as La Raquette or Roquette, which the Regent, Noailles and Law would all attend.

As part of the reconciliation, Law received additional funds. In a letter from Paris dated December 10, the *Gazette d'Amsterdam* reported that the Regency Council was diverting to the company revenues from the monopoly of tobacco. It also said that the capital of the company would be no less than 100 million livres.[53] On the 19th, Noailles presented to the Parlement an edict limiting the company's capital to 100 million livres, and adding to the clogged stamp duty a further one million livres each from the company farming the postal service and the general tobacco farm, a monopoly on the sale of tobacco in France managed by a syndicate led by Samuel Bernard and Antoine Crozat, and including the third Pâris brother, Joseph Pâris Duverney. The Parlement duly registered the edict on December 31.[54]

The edict had its effect on sentiment. The *Gazette de la Régence*, which in October had been inclined to bury the scheme, reported early in the new year that the "Company of the Mississippi is under weigh and its credit increases along with the share subscription."[55] None the less, there was still no cash. According to Marcel Giraud, the historian of French Louisiana, the company in this period received only 250,000 livres from the stamp duty "on the order of the Regent" and between four and seven monthly payments of 83,333 livres (beginning in January, 1718) from the tobacco farm.

Giraud surmised that the Regent ordered the 250,000-livre payment to reimburse Law for equipping the vessels.[56] Some time that month, the company sent out to Louisiana a second merchant ship, the 130-ton corvette the *Paix*, Captain Voyer commanding, carrying victuals for the colony and twenty-nine settlers for the concession of the Pâris brothers at the site of an old village of the Bayagoulas people on the west bank of the Mississippi, about 120 miles north of the future capital.

The brothers found Law's proliferating projects "suspect", but everything they did they did with care and their expedition to Louisiana, though its capital at first may not have exceeded 20,000 livres, was well led and faced no competition for boats or victual.[57] The second brother, Claude La Montagne, later wrote for his children, "As one should not judge for or against anything without a profound examination, we resolved to make an experimental participation with Mr Law in his schemes."[58]

In fixing the company's capital at 100 millions, Law must have had some assurance from the Regent that he would be investing in the new company. In the end, the Regent took 76,748 shares for 38,374,000 livres at the issue price and more than a third of the capital for the King, himself and four favoured servants (including Nancré).[59] Law, by his own account, later increased his own shareholding from 12,000 to 20,000 shares or 10 million livres and 10 per cent of the company.[60]

The most penetrating witness of Law's ascent, the envoy of the United Provinces, Cornelis Hop, believed that Law controlled thirteen millions of the company's capital, and the Regent "between thirty and forty millions".[61] The consequence, as Hop later wrote to Pensionary Heinsius, was that the free float of the company's shares was quite small and a few buyers and sellers could move the price.[62] Early in the new year, Law committed to deliver in six months 900 shares with a nominal value of 450,000 livres to the young duc de Bourbon, but it is not clear from the scrawled receipts what value Law had received in payment.[63]

Meanwhile, across the Channel in England, at the old palace of Hampton Court on the Thames, Dubois and Stanhope were working to bring Austria and the Holy Roman Empire into the Triple Alliance, or rather Quadruple Alliance. The abbé Dubois was much impressed by English prosperity and by the low rate of interest but astonished by the deep drinking. He was drawing heavily on William Law, who had come south from Edinburgh to handle his brother's business in London, at one point of more than 60,000 livres.[64] He could also see that John Law was the rising man and could be of service to his new diplomatic system.

The Regent had instructed the abbé to support Law's petition for a pardon for the killing of Wilson and breaking jail.[65] Stanhope, now Chancellor of the Exchequer and effective prime minister, almost certainly pleaded his case.[66] On December 13, the Duke of Kingston-upon-Hull, Lord Privy Seal, signed on behalf of King George and his heirs a Latin pardon for "Johannes Law".[67] Colonel Pitt despatched the document to Paris. It is a mark of Law's all-or-nothing cast of mind that having achieved the principal goal of his adulthood, he handed the pardon to the Regent and asked him to keep it, "as I had no thought of ever making use of it". The Regent at first demurred but then received the parchment.[68]

Diplomat that he was, Dubois also took care to flatter Lady Katherine. While held up at Dover on December 30, he had time to write, asking her to choose out some rich French stuffs and Indian chintzes to make dresses for George I's favourite, Melusine von der Schulenburg, Duchess of Munster, who was a champion of

Stanhope's policies; her "niece", or rather her daughter by the King; and other court ladies. The Duchess "is a very tall and large woman with black hair and eyebrows and very white complexion," Dubois wrote. Mlle Fillion or Arnauld, dressmaker in the rue Saint-Honoré, would call at the place Vendôme with samples, but Mme Law should follow her own taste "which I believe to be superior to that of any other".[69]

With that proper ecclesiastical appreciation of women's fashions, the abbé asked Lady Katherine to select at least twenty *aunes* or yards of cloth, since "here the skirts are three and three-quarter yards in the round".[70]A receipt survives, signed by Mlle Fillion, for 232 livres and 10 sols as part of the cost.[71]

CHAPTER SEVEN

The Bed of Justice

J'ai toujours hai le travail.
(I have always hated work.)

JOHN LAW[1]

On Christmas Day of 1717, John Law invited his friends to dine with him at his house in the place Vendôme. Among the guests was a Scottish soldier of fortune he had known in Holland, George Hamilton of Reidhouse, who had risen to a general's rank in the Dutch service, been wounded at Malplaquet in 1709, and for a time held a seat at Westminster for a burgh in Fifeshire.

At the death of Queen Anne in 1714, Hamilton refused to accept George of Hanover but joined the Jacobite rebellion in Scotland, travelling from London with the Earl of Mar. Hamilton commanded the rebel centre at the battle of Sheriffmuir in 1715, and took the blame for the Jacobite failure. He was now living under a cloud in Paris, amid indigent Scottish refugees from the rebellion.

There had been Jacobites in Paris for nearly thirty years. After his defeat on the River Boyne in eastern Ireland in 1690, James II left his kingdoms for ever. He was housed with his court by Louis

XIV at the old palace of Saint-Germain-en-Laye fifteen miles to the west of Paris, where Louis himself had been born. James died in 1701, but his son, James III, and his widow, Mary of Modena, continued to feed and clothe a colony of supporters on a pension from the French crown. In time, they introduced the French to freemasonry and, from the 1720s, established lodges of the Scottish and English crafts.

Louis XIV was devoted to the Stuarts. He saw them as martyrs of the Roman Catholic faith, as did most or all of France. As for the British in France, Whigs and Jacobites slid by one another in the streets of Paris or on the staircases of the palace of Versailles, constrained by French manners and the authority of the great king. When on the night of July 12, 1717, all the windows of Stair's hôtel were smashed, he went in fury to the duc d'Orléans and vowed revenge on the Jacobites. The Jacks countered that the vandals were "some French young fellows after a long and merry supper".[2] Law and Lady Katherine had friends in both camps.

Having arrived in Scotland too late to support Mar's rebellion, James III received asylum in 1716 in the papal enclave of Avignon. As the price of alliance with Great Britain, the duc d'Orléans asked James III in late 1716 to leave France's borders for Italy, where he lived first at Pesaro, then at Urbino and then in Rome. Queen Mary's pension from the French crown, already in arrears at Louis XIV's death in 1715, vanished amid the Regent's other liabilities. England, and then Great Britain, refused to pay (or made it impossible for Queen Mary to accept) her jointure or widow's dowry of £50,000 a year. The poor Irish at Saint-Germain-en-Laye who lived on the Queen's charity were swelled in 1716 by five hundred or more Scottish Jacobites from the failed rebellion, many or most of them Protestants.

John Erskine (1675–1732), James III's Secretary of State, was known as the "Duke of Mar" to the Jacobites and, to the Whigs, as "the late Earl of Mar". He treated John Law partly as his man of business,[3] as his father had treated William Law the goldsmith, and partly as a kindred spirit who shared his passion for "improvement". In Mar's case, improvement embraced scientific agriculture, mining, manufacturing, landscape, architecture, forestry and town planning.

By the spring of 1717, Mar was tiring of King James's service and did not wish to settle in Italy. That April, he asked Law to find him for sale "a little neat house and gardens somewhere in the environs of Paris". He feared the French might find him "a very dull fellow for such a gusto [taste]," but he wished to live with his wife. His first wife had died and he had remarried, in 1714, Lady Frances Pierrepont, daughter of the Duke of Kingston.

He fell into exile reverie: "The gardens I am more concerned about. Some high wood in them for shade I would wish mightily, and also water, but above all things is the situation, which I would like on a dry rising ground with a prospect rather than a flat, and near some river and a village." He thought "a little relaxation and the country air" would do Law good but begged him, when he visited, "to come with but one footman for fear of discovering me [betraying his whereabouts to the Earl of Stair]".[4]

Nothing came of the neat house or high wood but, passing again through Paris incognito in October, 1717, Mar proposed to Law that he do something for the Scottish refugees.[5] General Hamilton volunteered to pursue the matter and received Queen Mary's permission.

Neither by birth nor temperament was John Law a Jacobite. As an outlaw and continental exile, he was doomed to mess more with Jacobites than Whigs, and (as he later said) he could not be indifferent to the plight of his friends. He promised Hamilton that, provided the Regent gave him a verbal order, he would advance Queen Mary 100,000 livres and "draw out a scheme" not only to clear the arrears within three months, but to pay the pension monthly "preferable to any other".[6]

When he put the matter to the duc d'Orléans on December 26, Law had a taste of Jacobite incompetence. The Regent informed him that Queen Mary had "received several sums". As Law himself told General Hamilton the next day, "he was sorry that I [Hamilton] had not told him." None the less, Law agreed to lend the Queen 50,000 livres, or one month's pension, and on December 31 he paid the money out to her treasurer, a Catholic gentleman from Lancashire named William Dicconson. Though Law asked that Hamilton not mention it to James III, nothing was a secret in Jacobite circles, and King James wrote from Urbino on February 17, 1718 to thank Law "for his great zeal and attachment for our service".[7] Mar toyed with the fancy that Law might one day serve as the Stuart envoy to the Regent.[8] First, however, Law must be detached from the Earl of Stair.

Month by month, Law was drawn into the Jacobite web. Over one hundred years, the cause of the Stuart family ruined better men than John Law of Lauriston, but it ruined him, too.

The Stuarts were the least of John Law's entanglements in 1718. As winter gave way to a sparkling spring, and spring to a hot summer, Law found himself gathered up in a struggle for power within the French Regency. It arose in opposition to the new alliance with Hanoverian Great Britain and regret for the old friendship with Spain and the Stuarts, and fears among office-holders and state creditors that their livelihood would vanish in the Regent's financial reforms. They did not want reform. They wanted the old system, a little less corrupt and arbitrary, but the old system all the same. As a Protestant and Englishman, or rather a Scot, Law embodied in a sort of nightmare all that was going awry with the legacy of the great King.

One focus of disaffection was Louis XIV's legitimated son, the duc du Maine, brother of the Regent's wife. He and his duchess resented their demotion and loss of access to the young King. Another was the Spanish Embassy under Antonio del Giudice, prince of Cellamare. A third was the Parlement of Paris, who saw themselves as champions of legality against despotism – liberty did not then exist in France as a political purpose – and guardians of the King's creditors, not excluding themselves.

A royal law court, that judged civil and criminal cases at first instance and on appeal and promulgated decrees, the Parlement of Paris emerged from the ambulatory judicature of France's medieval kings in the thirteenth century and was settled in the royal palace on the île de la Cité at the site of the present law courts, the Palais de Justice. In time, the kings of France established provincial parlements, first in Toulouse for the Languedoc, then Grenoble, Bordeaux, Dijon, Rouen, Aix-en-Provence, Rennes, Pau, Metz, Besançon and Douai. Paris, with its array of courts beneath the senior chamber or Grand'Chambre, was always by far the most influential.

The King, as the source in France of all sovereignty, sent new laws to the parlements to be registered and enforced within their jurisdictions. The question, which was never answered during the old regime, was whether the parlements merely published the King's laws and decrees or added an element of legality, in which case the King's sovereignty was not absolute.

When the Paris Parlement was slow to register new laws, especially relating to revenue, or made remonstrances (*remontrances*), or tried to excise or amend legislation, the kings of France took to attending sessions in person, a ceremony that was refined under Charles IX in the sixteenth century under the name of a *lit de justice* or "bed of justice".

Louis XIV, who as a boy under his mother's regency in the 1640s had watched the parlements obstruct fiscal laws in the period of insurrection known as the Fronde, broke the power and even the will of the magistrates in a succession of *lits de justice*, the last in 1673. By the 1670s, when Louis XIV was engaged in the first of his Dutch wars, he and his chief minister, Jean-Baptiste Colbert, had stripped the parlements of their ability to impede or delay fiscal laws. In a century where control of the King's revenue brought new powers and consciousness to the parliaments of England and Scotland, the Parlement of Paris remained arrested.

Louis XIV's fiscal policies touched the magistrates in their private interest, which was their investment in their offices. In the first years of the War of the Spanish Succession, either from forced loans or the sale of new offices, Michel Chamillart extracted fifteen millions from the judiciary.[9] With more and more judges competing for litigants' fees (known as *épices*, "spices"), offices paid less and their prices began to fall. In his will, begun in 1711, Joachim Descartes, councillor in the Parlement of Rennes, told his heirs that the office bought for him by his father for 95,000 livres in 1659 was now worth 45,000 livres, and even that price was based on "the hope that times will not always be so bad". (They were. The charge was sold in 1721 for 38,000 livres.)[10] Louis XIV had killed the golden goose.

Like the annuities on the Paris Town Hall or Hôtel de Ville, the wages of office-holders were paid by taxes on working people in the countryside. Rising families invested in titles and sinecures their surplus funds that might otherwise have gone to agricultural improvement or manufacturing. The Scottish philosopher Adam Smith, who spent nearly three years in France in the 1760s, noted the absence of trade and industry in French parliamentary towns (apart from Rouen and Bordeaux).[11] John Law disapproved of hereditable offices as he disapproved of perpetual annuities and the parlements were right to fear him. (Law did, in June, 1720, buy the office of "Secretary to the King", which after time conferred nobility and was valued in his estate in 1722 at its cost of 140,000 livres.)[12]

For the Regent in his triple task of passing to the young King a solvent treasury, a European peace and a united Church, the parlements were good friends and bad enemies. In 1787, the Parlement of Paris refused to register new taxes and set in train the revolution that destroyed the old regime.

The Epiphany supper at La Raquette failed to clear the air. On January 21, Law told the Earl of Stair that if Noailles stayed in power, he would resign.[13] The quarrel between Law and Noailles then became submerged in a greater peril to the Regent's authority.

Between January 14 and 19, the Parlement of Paris devoted four sessions to the finances of the country. Though they did not mention Law by name, speakers warned against the diversion of royal (that is, public) revenues "from the responsible officials into the hands of persons who have no authority to receive them".[14] Some in Paris thought that Noailles and Aguesseau had merely delegated, as the marquis de Nancré reported to Dubois in London, "much of the dirty work to the Parlement".[15] Yet the Parlement's objections went beyond Law, and even Noailles, to the duc d'Orléans himself. The assault on his financial management wounded the Regent. The duc de Saint-Simon describes him walking the length of the Coypel gallery and the Grand Salon in the Palais-Royal, head bowed, furious, tense and perplexed.[16] In Brittany, the local nobility and the Parlement of Rennes so obstructed the tax collectors that Noailles sent several battalions of infantry, cavalry and dragoons to protect them.

On January 26, a deputation from the Parlement of Paris was received at the Tuileries by the King, in the presence of the Regent. The first president, Jean-Antoine de Mesmes, read at the top of his voice a remonstrance which, beneath a veneer of obeisance, accused the Regency of ruining the King's credit and pauperising his subjects.[17]

The Regent was stung. On the 28th, to the astonishment of both court and robe, he summoned Chancellor Aguesseau, demanded from him the seals of France and rusticated him to his country estate. Noailles was permitted to resign as president of the Council of Finances. In the place of both men, he appointed Marc-René de Voyer, marquis d'Argenson, lieutenant general of police in Paris. Argenson had no particular leaning towards finance and the Earl of Stair, for one, believed the intention was to have at the council of finances a man who could be "led by Law [*être conduit par Law*]".[18] The marquis d'Argenson was led by nobody.

Born in 1652 in Venice where his father was French Ambassador, Argenson was bred to the law, was taken up and promoted by Pontchartrain and, in 1697, was appointed lieutenant general of police for Paris. Police at that time embraced not only law enforcement, but all that pertained to order and security in the capital, from the price of bread to the disposal of refuse. For the old King, the lieutenant general of police was, in Saint-Simon's description, "a sort of secret and confidential minister or inquisitor".[19]

Argenson knew everybody's secrets, attended fires and riots in person and, in the words of the eulogist of the Académie royale des sciences, "devoted himself to the most sordid affairs, which were gilded in his eyes by their necessary connection with the public good".[20] He worked at night and expected others to do so, dictated to four secretaries at once, dined in his coach, slept in an apartment against the outer wall of a convent in the faubourg Saint-Antoine, to whose prioress, Mme de Veyny, he was devoted.[21] He was in unremitting dispute over jurisdiction with the magistrates, who sought to try him for embezzlement in office at the Chamber of Justice in 1716, but failed.

His appointment infuriated the *parlementaires* but brought a truce. In the lull, Law registered on February 18 the first 22 million livres in subscriptions for the Company of the West, with a further 2 million on February 24.[22]

As if to celebrate the improvement in French fortunes, the Regent's pet daughter, the duchesse de Berry, four days later gave a ball for her aunt and uncle, the duc and duchesse de Lorraine who were visiting Paris.[23] It was the most sumptuous feast since the war. The palais du Luxembourg on the left bank was illuminated outside and in. One hundred and twenty-five ladies were served at supper, and as many or more gentlemen. There was one waiting servant for each guest.[24] Unusually for the period, only those invited were served and a gate crasher was rewarded with two nights in the château de la Bastille. Afterwards, masked guests arrived for the ball in the gallery painted by Rubens. The diplomat Michel Amelot, marquis de Gournay, wrote to a correspondent in Rome: "If foreign spectators are not convinced that there is spare change in France, they will be making a great mistake."[25]

The launch of the Company of the West in the autumn of 1717 and the despatch of the first flotilla had stirred an interest in Louisiana among the adventurous and the desperate. "A quantity of people are preparing to make the voyage" to Louisiana, the *Gazette de la Régence* reported on January 9, 1718.[26] To transport them, Law had bought two new frigates of 300 and 350 tons, renamed the *Duchesse-de-Noailles* and the *Victoire*, to escort another of Crozat's Dutch merchantmen, the *Marie* (300 tons). Those vessels were now being fitted out at Saint-Malo and La Rochelle.

The three hundred or so emigrants were of all conditions. Jean-Baptiste Bénard de La Harpe, from a family of seafarers of Saint-Malo in Brittany, had led an adventurous life. In Peru, he had married a rich widow older than himself, quarrelled with her and fallen on hard times. Now in his mid-thirties, he set off on board the *Victoire* on April 10 from Saint-Malo with forty-six volunteers to take over a concession of four leagues square or 144 square miles granted by the company on the Red River, which rises in the Texas Panhandle and flows into the swamplands of the Mississippi and Atchafalaya north of the modern city of Baton Rouge.

Held up by contrary winds, the *Victoire* put in at Falmouth on the coast of Cornwall, and then turned back to La Rochelle to join the other vessels. In a journal he made of his voyage, La Harpe says the company officers loaded short rations and then allocated places indiscriminately, so that "one found oneself messing with ex-footmen and -grooms, a matter most disagreeable to the officers and other people of condition reduced to that extremity."[27]

Another emigrant was Antoine-Simon Le Page du Pratz, who was to write a history of the colony, leading a party of ten settlers. Others were on their own or in groups of three or four: a merchant from Rouen, a wigmaker, a surgeon, who could not hope to clear anything larger than a market garden round the future town of New Orleans. Even the three joint-stock companies – the Scourion brothers, Messrs Delaire-Demeuves and the Brossard brothers – had small capital for the task ahead. The two Scourion brothers, gentlemen from Picardy, had raised only 16,000 livres in cash and 3,000 in merchandise from the sale of shares in their concession. Etienne Demeuves had put up 20,000 livres and a letter of credit on the company payable in Louisiana of 25,000 livres. The Brossards appear to have had less at their disposal.[28] In truth, nobody knew what capital would be required. The second convoy sailed at last from La Rochelle on May 25. The company also despatched two frigates from Saint-Malo, the *Aurore* and the *Grand-duc-du-Maine*, to Benin in West Africa to buy slaves to sell to the concessionaires.

Law tried to drum up interest in the shares. He turned once again to the gazettes to challenge sceptics and short-sellers of his company, just starting to be known in stock markets as "bears".[29]

He proposed what are now known as call options, offering a 2 per cent premium or 10 livres per share to anybody ready to sell him the shares at 70 per cent of their issue price or 350 livres at any time of his (Law's) choosing within the next year.[30] If the bears were mistaken and the shares rose above 360 livres (350 for the share and 10 for the *prime*), Law was in the money. More to the point, the bears would have to go into the Quincampoix to buy stock to fill their bargains with Law, thus further raising the price. Receipts and records survive for at least four option trades between May 5 and May 17 over a total of 440 shares.[31]

Law was also parading his credit in other ways.

On April 30, 1718, he bought the estate of La Marche, the sort of jewel-like rural box, in reach of town, that rich citizens in all countries and ages like to sell to one another. With its ballroom and wainscoted billiard room, water garden, woods and twenty-acre lake, La Marche stood a couple of hours by coach to the west of Paris, on the road between the royal palaces of Saint-Cloud and Marly. It survives only in a street name in the town of Marnes-la-Coquette beside the Normandy motorway. Two controllers general of finance, Chamillart and Desmaretz, had owned the house and Desmaretz sold it to Law for 80,000 livres.[32]

More substantial was the château de Tancarville, which Law bought from the comte d'Evreux, son of the marquis d'Effiat and son-in-law to Antoine Crozat, on June 30.

The ancient castle still guards the mouth of the Seine a little upstream of Harfleur in Normandy. Evreux had just built a modern dwelling within the walls, known today as the Château neuf, but he was in debt to Law and preferred to sell the entire property to Law and Lady Katherine for 650,000 livres, of which under half was in cash, and the remainder to be paid as a dowry for his daughter when she came of age.[33] It was a complicated transaction, that sprang in some way from Law acting for Evreux to buy the plot of land in the faubourg Saint-Honoré that became the Elysée, the residence of the Presidents of the French Republic.[34]

The lordship of Tancarville conveyed a title of nobility. It is possible that the Regent, who approved the sale on behalf of the King, may have wanted his servant ennobled. Law is called comte de Tancarville in notarial documents, but there is no evidence that he ever used the title in society and his contemporaries all called him Monsieur Law. Lady Katherine was in Paris always Madame Law. There was no more talk of Seignior.

Over two years, Law bought twenty-one country estates in France, including some of the fairest in that country (Appendix III). He owned the Renaissance château de Valençay on the Loire, where Napoleon's foreign minister, the prince de Talleyrand, was to live; Toucy in Burgundy; Effiat in Auvergne; many places in Normandy; the estate of Roissy now part-covered by Charles de Gaulle Airport; and Guermantes, east of Paris, whose name haunted the writer Marcel Proust. There is no record that Law visited any but those nearest Paris, La Marche and Guermantes.[35]

Those country estates brought rents from tenants of at least 120,000 livres a year,[36] but that was not their principal benefit. Law bought the properties at high prices to show his financial solidity, rather as in England the Hoare family, bankers in Fleet Street, had the year before bought Stourton manor in Wiltshire and begun digging the famous garden of Stourhead. In those days before limited liability, woods and lakes and grottoes and hermitages could serve as banking capital because they could be sold to repay depositors should the banking business go awry. (The Hoares have only ever lent out a portion of their deposits and have survived in profound security the wars and panics of three centuries.)

Law had plans for the Normandy properties. Once he had acquired Tancarville, he bought a contiguous estate and other lands in Normandy as sites for factories and mills in reach of two river ports, Harfleur and Rouen. Law's industrial ambitions escaped many of his contemporaries in France, but frightened the British across the Channel.

On that same June 30, Law also bought from the financier Claude Le Bas de Montargis a property in Paris.[37] That was the hôtel Langlée, No. 19, rue Neuve-des-Petits-Champs, with a carriage gateway and garden, described in a guide to Paris of 1706 as "without contradiction, one of the most proper and regular [residences] that one could wish".[38] He also began on July 21 buying up building lots behind the façades of the place Vendôme and, in time, owned most of the square.[39]

By midsummer, it was a question whether Law would live to enjoy those houses. At the end of May, during the Pentecost recess, Argenson published a set of monetary measures complex even by the standards of the French monarchy.[40] At their heart was a devaluation of about a third in the value of the livre in terms of gold and silver. The public was ordered to bring its coin and plate to the mints to be recast into lighter pieces with a higher face value in livres.

The French had long been used to the King in difficulties writing up his stock of gold and silver, paying bills to his suppliers and creditors in devalued money, and collecting the mint fee known as seignorage. The exercise was known, in the usual old-regime euphemism, as an "augmentation". The duc de Noailles had effected a less drastic devaluation in December, 1715. The exchange rate of French money into sterling, which had been at 40 or 41 pence per écu or crown of three livres during the war and had risen to around 48 pence as the British required French currency for wines and luxuries after the peace, fell with the two devaluations. On June 12, Law's correspondent in London, George Middleton, was applying a rate of 33 pence per crown to bills drawn by Law on his brother William (and vice-versa) and 32 pence in July.[41] The exchange then remained steady at 29–30d. per crown until November, 1719.

Tacked on to the devaluation was another measure to reduce the King's unfunded debts. Along with coins and bullion, the public might bring to the mints a proportion of the state IOUs known as *billets d'état* and receive their face value in the new lighter coins. Holders hurried to make the best of a bad deal. The numismatic scholar Jérôme Jambu, in a study of the mint at Caen in Normandy, found that the value of *billets* exchanged there in July amounted to more than 140,000 livres, or ten times the sum of May.[42] France's unfunded debt was diminishing.

Argenson had a powerful mind and was a quick learner, but it is hard to believe that he had progressed to the frontiers of eighteenth-century monetary theory in four months. The Parlement of Paris saw the hand of John Law.[43] The memoirist Dangeau reported that Law had on May 18 walked for a long time with the Regent in the garden of La Meutte or Muette, the duchesse de Berry's country house in what is now Neuilly-sur-Seine.[44]

Argenson took the precaution of sending the decree for registration not to the Parlement, but to a subsidiary court, the cour des monnaies, which had jurisdiction over currency matters. The *parlementaires* were incensed not only at the devaluation but the breach of constitutional practice, and on June 20 forbade any person within their jurisdiction to use the new coins and any notary from writing contracts on the basis of the new value of the livre. On the 27th, the magistrates again processed to the Tuileries where First President Mesmes read a long remonstrance.[45] There was agitation against the recoinage in provincial towns, notably Lyons.

The Regency Council was divided. The duc du Maine, his younger brother the comte de Toulouse and representatives of the "Old Court" opposed to the British alliance and financial innovation, were for abandoning the recoinage. Argenson was implacable. On July 2, the magistrates returned to the Tuileries to hear him brush aside their financial arguments, saying only that the magistrates were intent on protecting their own privileges. He all but accused them of sedition in that they had quoted a law of 1652, during a period (the Fronde) "whose memory should be utterly abolished". He then recast the whole dispute as an insult to the King's authority, and laid out a doctrine of royal government of a terrible purity. The law of France, he said, "derives exclusively from the sovereign's will and requires only that will to be law". The registration of laws in the courts which will execute them was nothing but an act of "indispensable obeisance".[46]

Such an insult could not go unanswered, and the magistrates retired to the île de la Cité to prepare a reply. Meanwhile, the Regent's rough British allies were making demands on him that would have troubled a French king let alone a regent, and were a provocation to the old court and the public.

The treaties of Utrecht, and subsequent treaties at Rastatt and Baden, had failed to reconcile two of the belligerents in the War of the Spanish Succession, the Austrian Emperor Charles and King Philip of Spain. Each sought a field for his dynastic ambitions in Italy, where they were bound to come into conflict and ignite another European war. That would be disaster for the duc d'Orléans. As Stair had written to Stanhope the previous October, "The great object of the Regent, which is to assure his succession to the crown of France should the young King die, must engage him to prevent the outbreak of a foreign war, which given the present condition of France and the strength of the Spanish Party, would not fail to produce here quickly a civil [war]. So long as peace endures, the Regent, equipped as he is and master of the finances of the Kingdom, can hardly fail."[47] Austria was on the point of signing the Quadruple Alliance. Somehow, Spain had to be bullied into it.

In the summer of 1717, Sardinia, which had been granted to Austria at Rastatt, fell to a Spanish fleet under the marquis de Lede. Now King Philip and his chief adviser, Cardinal Giulio Alberoni, had their eyes on Victor Amadeus's kingdom of Sicily. On June 8/19, 1718, an armada of over four hundred sail, consisting of twelve ships of the line, fire-ships, bomb vessels, frigates, merchantmen and troop transports, some 22,000 infantry, 7,000 horse and a hundred siege guns, put out from Barcelona for Sardinia under sealed orders.[48] On the same day, a British fleet comprising twenty-two ships of the line under Sir George Byng, was off Cape St Vincent on the coast of Portugal with instructions to prevent a Spanish landing in Italy.

From his flagship, the ninety-gun *Barfleur*, off Cadiz, Byng on June 20 despatched his secretary with letters to Philip by way of James Stanhope's cousin, Colonel William Stanhope, envoy to Madrid. Byng informed the Spanish Court that he had orders from King George "to maintain, as far as I may be able, the neutrality of Italy and to defend the territories of the Emperor in opposing any Power that seeks to attack the states of which he is master".[49] Byng's messenger did not arrive in Madrid until July 10 and received a dusty answer. On the 15th, at the Escorial Palace, Alberoni minuted Byng's letter: "His Catholic Majesty has honoured me with the instruction that the Chevalier Byng may execute whatever orders he has from the King his Master."[50] When Colonel Stanhope tried to show him Byng's order of battle, Alberoni threw the paper on the ground.[51]

On June 28,[52] James Stanhope, Secretary of State and newly granted an earldom, arrived in Paris with the text of a secret convention that bound each country to defend the other in the event of attack. At a private meeting the next day, the Regent assented but then found no minister ready to sign such a document. In the end, the clause about mutual help in the event of attack had to be dropped.

On Friday, July 15, Law gave a "great dinner" for Stanhope,[53] probably at La Marche, for Stair's coach with his guest passed under the windows of Saint-Cloud both on the way out and on the way back, and Elisabeth Charlotte was hurt that he had not brought Lord Stanhope to call on her. When they did call, on July 20, she was setting off for a drive, and said: "What you have to say to me cannot be so very urgent, for it is not a week that you passed and repassed Saint-Cloud without coming in. I know perfectly well that you were on your way to Mr Law at La Marche."[54] No doubt, Stanhope questioned Law as to whether France was in a financial condition to wage war.

That Wednesday, July 20, as the Regent was taking his midday chocolate, the Ambassador of Savoy, Giuseppe, conte di Provana, asked for a private audience and handed him a letter from Victor Amadeus. The letter informed him that the Spanish fleet had landed its force in Sicily and Palermo had surrendered to the marquis de Lede.[55] The next day, Earls Stanhope and Stair wrote jointly to Admiral Byng instructing him "strictly and vigorously" to carry out his orders.[56] The letter was shown to the Regent on the 23rd.[57] Then, with that mixture of guts and perfidy so characteristic of the British of that era, Stanhope set off for Madrid to try one last time to bring the Spanish Court to hand, offering among other inducements the return of Gibraltar, captured by English and Dutch marines in 1704. On August 2, the Empire signed the Quadruple Alliance.

Back at the Palais de Justice, on August 12, the Parlement ordered Law's General Bank to be reduced to the private institution of its Letters Patent and to return to the regular fiscal officials the King's tax revenues. It also banned all foreigners "even if naturalised" from direct or indirect involvement in the King's finances on pain of punishment.[58] President Henri Feydeau proposed the decree and cited Law by name. It passed by a majority of 130 to 29. On the 18th, the decree was read in full court with the doors open and sent to be printed. "The decree caused a great stir. People were reading it everywhere," the lawyer Edmond Barbier wrote in his journal and added: "Nobody was in any doubt that if Law had been taken at that time, he would have been tried quickly and hanged in the courtyard of the Palais."[59]

The August 12 decree was the most assertive action by the Parlement since the Fronde. For the duc de Saint-Simon and other traditionalists, it was an assault on the King's authority which threatened the sort of breach in the royal prerogative achieved by the parliaments in England and Scotland. The Regent, who was often careless of his own dignity (much to Saint-Simon's disgust), was alert to any abridgement of that of the young King. The diplomatic edifice, constructed with such pain by Stanhope and Dubois, was threatened with collapse. In a sort of panic, Dubois hurried back from London, arriving just after midnight on the 17th.[60]

For Law, who depended for his vision for France on the absolute authority of the Regent, it was frustrating. On May 16 and June 11, he had bought annuities for another six million livres in subscriptions, taking the company's capital up to 30 millions. To hurry the subscribers along, he had then proposed an option: an immediate down-payment of one-fifth of the price or 100 livres per share with the remainder payable in five months (that is, by October 31) on pain of forfeiting the down-payment.

To give the Company of the West a more reliable source of working capital than the monthly charge on the tobacco monopoly, Law resolved to cut the Gordian Knot and take the entire tobacco trade in hand. This audacity had its effect and by July 15, the marquis de Dangeau was writing that the share subscription was "entirely filled".[61] On August 1, the Council of State awarded to Jean Ladmiral (or Lamiral or Lamirail), a straw-man for the Company of the West, the exclusive right for six years to import and sell tobacco at fixed prices in most of French territory, starting on October 1, 1718.

There was competition from the syndicate that had held the monopoly since 1697 and other financiers, and Law had to promise the King twice the incumbents' price, or 4,020,000 livres per year. Law also had to commit to supply the entire French market from Louisiana within three years. The Parlement now threatened to put that in reverse and take Law's life into the bargain. For the speculators in Paris, London, Lyons and Geneva, the company shares were just *billets d'état* plus or minus John Law. They bought one or the other according to their views of Law's life-expectancy.[62]

At a meeting at the duc de Saint-Simon's house on the afternoon of Friday, August 19, Law "hitherto so brave and firm, was shaken to the point of tears".[63] By his own account, which is minute, Saint-Simon advised Law to go to the Palais-Royal and Law did so, lodging that evening in the apartment of his friend the marquis de Nancré, who had been sent as envoy to Spain, where he was cooperating with the Stanhopes.

Saint-Simon and others resolved that day to advise the Regent to suppress the magistrates in a *lit de justice*, the first for nearly fifty years, but foresaw difficulties. In the Regency Council, the duc du Maine, under the old King's will in charge of the King's education, might accuse them of risking the boy's health by asking him to travel to the île de la Cité in the crushing heat. Maine might also forearm the magistrates. Again by his own account, Saint-Simon hit on the expedient of holding the *lit de justice* in the Tuileries itself, and keeping it secret until the very day of the ceremony, which was set for August 26.

Over the weekend, Saint-Simon called on Law in Nancré's apartments, and found Lady Katherine there. She at once left the room, but not before Saint-Simon thought to have glimpsed a birthmark (*tache de vin*) on her cheek, which is mentioned by no other witness.[64] He found that Law had won over the young duc de Bourbon. What reservations the Regent might have had diminished on the Monday, August 22, when the Parlement on its high horse demanded that he open up his treasury accounts to ensure that the *billets d'état* submitted as part of Argenson's recoinage on May 27 had been destroyed and not turned to other purposes. He turned his back on the delegation.[65]

Over the next three days, Saint-Simon busied himself with the staging of the *lit de justice*, and such details as seating and draperies. (In a republic, he might have been a decorator or a stage designer.) As rumours of a *lit de justice* percolated into the streets, some of the magistrates had second thoughts and on the morning of the 24th called on Law, who had regained his firmness and returned home, to apologise.[66]

Friday, August 26, 1718, dawned hot and bright. Towards 5 a.m., drums sounded across town, mustering dragoons, guards and musketeers to key positions, such as the Tuileries and the markets. At six, members of the Regency Council were called to a meeting in two hours' time, while the King's master of ceremonies, Michel Desgranges, arrived at the Palais de Justice with a sealed letter summoning the magistrates, who were just beginning to assemble, to a *lit de justice* at ten.

At the Tuileries, the council was to meet in a large chamber that, because of the heat, the King was using as a bedroom. Saint-Simon found the duc d'Orléans looking untroubled. The Regent took the comte de Toulouse to one side and suggested that he take his elder brother, the duc du Maine, looking "pale as death", away from the meeting.

The Regent informed the Council that he had called a *lit de justice* so as to annul the Parlement's decree against the bank

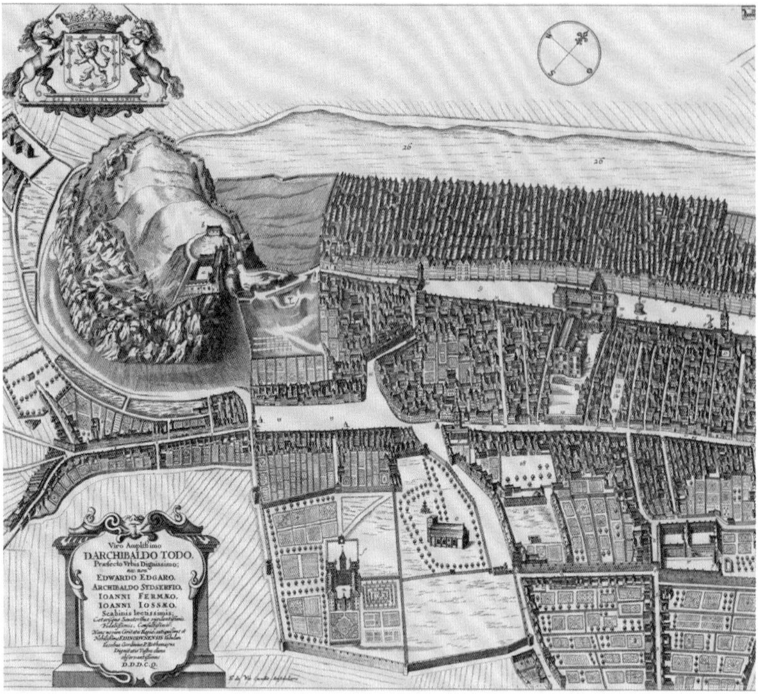

Gordon of Rothiemay's bird's-eye view of Edinburgh (1647), showing (clockwise from top left) the Castle, the High Kirk of St Giles, the Parliament Close, Greyfriars Kirk and George Heriot's Hospital.

Lauriston Castle from the south-east. Only the tower house to the left existed in the time of John Law's ownership, and it has since been much altered.

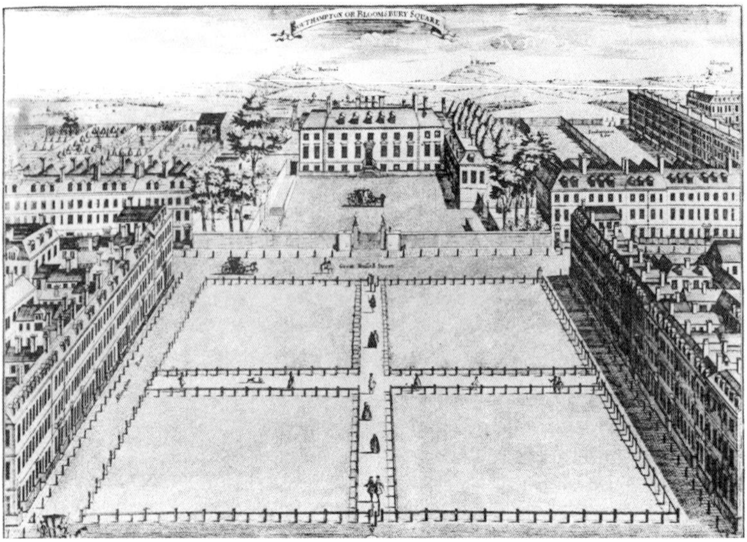

Southampton or Bloomsbury Square about thirty years after the Law–Wilson duel, by which time it was complete. Southampton House is in the background. Beyond are the fields and wastes leading to Hampstead and Highgate Hills.

The Bank of St George, still standing on the seafront in Genoa. The bank, which operated from 1407 to 1805, more than any other institution formed John Law's ideas on the financing of the state.

Portrait of a gentleman believed to be John Law, by Alexis-Simon Belle, from around 1716. Belle was the principal painter at the Jacobite court at Saint-Germain-en-Laye until its expulsion from France, and portrayed several Scottish exiles.

Philippe II, duc d'Orléans and Regent during Louis XV's minority. He saw John Law as the best hope of restoring France to solvency.

John Dalrymple, 2nd Earl of Stair, British Ambassador in Paris, who did everything he could to obstruct Law, short of fighting him.

Etching by Adam Pérelle of the Palais-Royal from the rue Saint-Honoré, residence of the ducs d'Orléans, seat of government under the Regency, and scene of Law's triumph and disgrace.

Louis XV, aged ten, drawn in pastels in June 1720 at the Tuileries by Rosalba Carriera, who was invited to Paris by Law and the connoisseur Pierre Crozat. This pastel ignited a Rosalbamania in Paris.

Elisabeth Charlotte, dowager duchesse d'Orléans, by Hyacinthe Rigaud. Her letters, of which thousands survive, are a brilliant and scurrilous commentary on Regency France. Having thought the world of Law, she turned against him.

The open-air stock exchange in the garden of the hôtel de Soissons, done in ink and wash by Antoine Humblot in August, 1720. Note the numbered booths to the right and the dog escaping with a stockbroker's notecase.

Attempting to cash Law's banknotes at the Mint in Rennes, Brittany, July 1720. Watercolour painted from memory by Jean-François Huguet. Note the musketeers, just a single open cashier's window, and the dying man receiving the sacraments in the centre.

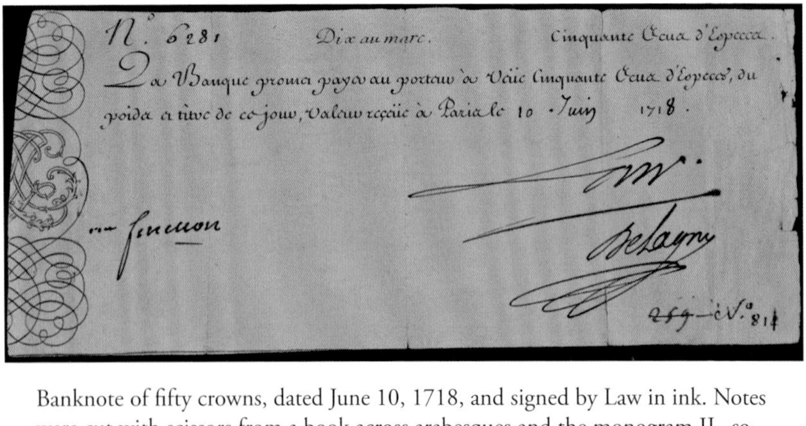

Banknote of fifty crowns, dated June 10, 1718, and signed by Law in ink. Notes were cut with scissors from a book across arabesques and the monogram JL, so that each note could be matched with its stub.

of August 12. Argenson then read the annulment, and set out a new code for parliamentary remonstrances, which would exclude the magistrates from all matters of finance and government. The Regent called for votes. "There was a silence in which you might have heard a cheese-mite creep," Saint-Simon wrote.[67] All voted in favour, though the duc de Noailles "could scarcely contain himself".[68]

The Regent then said he had "another, and far more important motion to propose". He intended to strip the legitimated princes, the duc du Maine and comte de Toulouse, of their rank as princes of the blood and reduce them to peers. As a consequence, Maine could no longer fulfil the role of superintendent of the King's education, which was offered to the duc de Bourbon, and accepted. When their allies protested, the Regent replied: "Sir, Monsieur du Maine is my brother-in-law but I prefer an open to a hidden enemy."[69] The session broke up into uncomfortable little groups, till word came that the magistrates were approaching on foot. "Like children, we crowded the windows to watch them," Saint-Simon wrote.[70]

The magistrates had set off from the Palais de Justice at 9.30 a.m.; one hundred and fifty-three of them in their heavy red robes made their way along the quai des Orfèvres, crossed the Pont-Neuf and passed in the heat up the rue Saint-Honoré towards the Tuileries. They filed into the antechamber on the first floor of the Tuileries, done up by Saint-Simon to resemble their own great chamber at the Palais de Justice, except that their eyes were level with the feet of the peers. The young King entered, and sat on a throne on a platform. Beneath him, Argenson, the royal seals on a desk before him, accused the magistrates of usurping royal authority, and claiming a say over issues of finance that lay outside their jurisdiction. First President Mesmes asked for time for the Parlement to deliberate on the laws requiring registration, but

Argenson took no notice, approached the boy King, knelt on one knee, turned about, replaced his hat and said: "The King wishes to be obeyed and obeyed this instant!"[71] Then using the seals, wax and burner at his desk, Argenson registered the new laws. In the rue Quincampoix, speculators bought the shares and sold the *billets*.[72]

Stunned by the theatre of the event, the magistrates trooped out but First President Mesmes was summoned back to the Tuileries by the duchesse du Maine, and subjected to an hour of abuse: "like the lowest underservant," as Saint-Simon wrote, "caught on the take".[73] Determined to respond, the magistrates set up a commission to examine the legality of the *lit de justice* and proposed to investigate Argenson and summon Law for questioning. During the night of August 28–9, Argenson sent armed musketeers to arrest three of the most outspoken deputies. They were carried off under escort to island fortresses. One of them, President Nicolas-Remy Frizon de Blamont, was not released from the île Sainte-Marguerite off the Mediterranean town of Cannes until the following May. That made the magistrates careful and, for the next eighteen months, the Parlement adopted a martyred air but ceased to pursue John Law or obstruct his projects.

Amid rumour and counter-rumour, Paris waited in the heat. Elisabeth Charlotte, writing from Saint-Cloud on August 30, was convinced that the duc du Maine, and far more the duchess "who is much more diabolical than her husband", intended to depose her son. She was "in deathly fright" that he would be assassinated.[74]

On Sunday, September 7, in the afternoon, a young man, dishevelled from the road, burst into Stair's house in the faubourg Saint-Germain. It was Admiral Byng's nineteen-year-old son Pattee, who had travelled post (that is, with relays of fresh horses every twenty or so miles) in eleven days from Naples, never once sleeping in a bed or taking off his boots.

Pattee Byng told Stair that his father, without waiting for

orders from Lord Stanhope or Alberoni's reply to his own letter from sea, had engaged the Spanish fleet under Vice-Admiral Antonio de Castañeta off the south-eastern tip of Sicily, Cape Passaro or Capo di Passero. In running fights, the British men-of-war captured seven of the Spanish capital ships including the commander's flagship and ran ashore or burned many of the transports.[75] Anxious at how his action would be received in London and Paris, and trusting only his son, Byng had sent the young man with despatches saying that a Spanish vessel, the *Santa Rosa,* had fired first. News of some great battle had been percolating into Paris for a week.[76] Stair received the confirmation "with the greatest expression of joy" and whisked the young man off to Saint-Cloud.

Mindful of his wigging back in June, Stair presented Pattee to Elisabeth Charlotte but could not anywhere find the duc d'Orléans. That excited ribald comment when the young man arrived at Hampton Court on the 11th before he passed out and was laid on the junior Secretary of State's bed. Even King George, otherwise so heavy, the next day "laughed very heartily" at the Regent's gallantry and gave Pattee £1,000.[77]

In Madrid, Alberoni was not hopeful of peace. Unless Stanhope could produce better offers, Alberoni wrote to his friend, the conte di Rocca, in Parma on September 5, "There will be a good war next spring."[78] When news of the loss of the fleet reached him a week later, he was livid with rage at Stanhope (now safely out of Spain) and "black English infamy".[79]

The question was whether there would be civil war in France. Though the heat broke in the second half of the month, the tension did not dissipate. On the 22nd, Elisabeth Charlotte wrote to her half-sister, Luise: "My son is not completely sure of his life, which often keeps me awake at night. On my life, I have not enjoyed a moment of his Regency."[80] She claimed that the duchesse du Maine had been heard to say that, like Jael in the Bible, she would drive a tent-spike through the Regent's temples.[81]

There was news from Louisiana. On September 16th, the *Dauphine* and the *Vigilante* anchored in the harbour at La Rochelle, having left Dauphine Island on July 12. The correspondent of the *Nouveau Mercure*, writing from the port on September 20, claimed to have interviewed one of the captains. "It is an enchanted land, with an excellent soil that will produce anything one would want. Wheat grows to perfection, and one could even make wine if one wanted to. Everything one sows comes up a hundredfold. It is only necessary to send some industrious and hard-working people to make it the most flourishing colony in the world . . ." He named some people of condition planning to go, "so that soon there will be some good society. There is also an order to send forty young girls on the next vessels to leave. At this very moment, their trousseaux are being assembled."[82]

On that September 20, the Malouin Bénard de La Harpe and his colonists were broiling on the sands of île Dauphine. After a crossing of fifty-four days in the *Victoire*, they anchored on July 18 at Cap Français, on the north coast of Saint-Domingue (now Cap-Haïtien), to take on supplies. They lost nine deserters and the fiancée of an officer at Mobile (which gentleman proved, when the convoy at last brought the news, "not hard to console"). A company engineer perished of "pestilential fever".[83]

They spent days searching for Mobile Bay, mistaking the barrier islands for the continent and sailing too far to the west, until they sighted the brigantine *Neptune* on its way to the site of New Orleans and gave chase. On August 23, a cask of brandy caught fire in the hold of the *Victoire*. The fire threatened to engulf the powder magazine at the base of the main mast, but was extinguished. Arriving at île Dauphine on August 25, 1718, one of La Harpe's indentured servants, along with his smith, a soldier and several others, deserted, taking provisions worth 600 livres and one of Bienville's pirogues. They were found on September 14th by one of the chiefs of the Natchez nation, near the île aux Chats (Cat Island), west of Biloxi, lost and half-dead with hunger and misery.[84]

La Harpe set his carpenter to building a seven-ton launch for the voyage to Natchitoches on the Red River, where he intended to open trade with the Spanish of León and New Mexico, but not before giving Bienville and the civilian administrator, Marc-Antoine Hubert, a piece of his mind. He told them that the "newly arrived concessionaires would use up all their supplies before the company management was in a state to convey them to their destinations."[85] La Harpe finally set off for the site of New Orleans, with fifteen men, in the boat he named the *Malouin*, on November 7.

In France, there was little interest in Louisiana, except among the British and Irish Jacobites, who would try anything. Even before the return of the *Dauphine* and *Vigilante*, on September 7, the marquis de Mézières, husband of Eleanor Oglethorpe, along with the "dlle Charlotte Ogletorphe" (Frances Charlotte Oglethorpe) formed a partnership to develop a plantation in Louisiana.[86]

The Oglethorpe sisters were friends of Lady Katherine, and that they had persuaded Eleanor's husband, a capable and distinguished soldier, to add his name was a coup for her. The sisters were to provide for the concession in Louisiana letters of credit or rights to draw on the Company for 30,000 livres at Cap-Français and 100,000 livres in the colony itself. "Never did a plantation carry with it such considerable funds," the man Fanny was to marry, the marquis des Marches, later wrote.[87]

Eleanor, born about 1684, and Fanny, who was much younger, were daughters of Sir Theophilus Oglethorpe, from an antique Yorkshire family, and Eleanor or Ellen Wall, a Roman Catholic from

Tipperary who held the post of Head Laundress and Seamstress to Charles II at Whitehall on a salary of £2,000 a year.

The parents were devoted to the exiled Stuarts but, like many British families of that age, hedged their bets. In 1696, Sir Theophilus swore allegiance to William III while his wife sent young Eleanor and her elder sister Anne to be bred as Roman Catholics at Saint-Germain. Their younger brother, born that year, was christened James Edward after the Stuart Prince of Wales but later founded the colony of Georgia in North America in the Hanoverian interest.

Eleanor married Mézières in 1707. Fanny followed her to France and, in 1713, became a Roman Catholic. Two years later through the influence of Mézières and François Fénelon, author of *Les aventures de Télémaque* and Archbishop of Cambrai, she received a pension of 2,000 livres a year from a fund provided by Louis XIV for converted Protestants.[88] The sisters were now living at the hôtel de Mézières, rue du Bac, which with the death of Queen Mary of Modena in May, 1718 became the focus of Jacobite society in the new aristocratic district of faubourg Saint-Germain. Because Eleanor had forgotten or never learned how to write English,[89] and Mar did not well read French, Fanny handled most of the Jacobite correspondence. The Earl of Stair had by now rented, for 10,000 livres a year, the hôtel d'Estampes,[90] rue de Varenne, not two hundred yards away, so each side could spy on the other.

A little later, Law entered a partnership with Richard Cantillon, an Irishman who had taken over his cousin's banking business with the Jacobite court, and Joseph Gage to establish "a settlement in the Mississippi colony".[91] Cantillon (?–1734) went on to write a work of political economy. Gage (*c.*1689–1768), son of a Roman Catholic landowner near Watlington in Oxfordshire, was at that time living from play.[92] He had been schooled at the Jesuit college of La Flèche, between Le Mans and Angers along with his brother,

Thomas, and other sons of the British recusant nobility.[93] Thomas Gage gave up his faith to return to England (and later received an Irish peerage), but Joseph remained in France.

At La Flèche, Joseph became friendly with Lords William and Edward Herbert, sons of the leading Jacobite family of Wales, the Marquesses of Powys, and in about 1717 became hopelessly attached to their sister, Lady Mary Herbert, then living in Paris with her aunt Ann, Lady Carrington.[94] Though they never married, Gage and Lady Mary went into business together, first as speculators in financial securities and then as miners in Andalusia. In February, 1719, Gage paid 20,000 livres for two-fifths of the Louisiana partnership, which suggests a total capital (not necessarily in cash) of 50,000 livres.[95] Cantillon's brother, Bernard, was recruiting colonists for the plantation.

At this time, Law was erecting a third leg to his business, besides bank and colony. One of the reasons La Harpe and his companions became lost in their search for île Dauphine was their ignorance, off an uncharted coast, of the *Victoire*'s east–west position or longitude. Mariners could measure their north–south position or latitude by taking the angle of the sun or stars. For longitude, they needed to measure the local noon and subtract (in the west) or add (in the east) the time at Greenwich or Paris from an accurate shipboard clock, and multiply by 15. (One hour of time difference corresponds to 15 degrees of longitude.)

The motion of a vessel at sea made pendulum clocks useless. In 1714, the British Parliament passed the Longitude Act offering a scale of rewards for solving the longitude problem. In France, where the persecution of the Huguenots had all but destroyed advanced watch-making, the Regent, in March, 1716, promised a bounty of 100,000 livres to whoever "of whatever nation, will have been fortunate enough to find this admirable secret".[96]

In May, 1716, Henry Sully, an Englishman probably of Huguenot provenance, presented to the Académie royale des sciences in Paris "a watch of a new construction".[97] An examining committee that included Pierre Varignon and Jacques Cassini II dismantled the watch and found in the movement "an exactitude full of dexterity".[98] The Regent instructed Law to give Sully a prize of fifteen hundred livres.[99]

Sully returned in secret to London to recruit workers and, in the first months of 1718, Law set him up with sixty craftsmen in three grace-and-favour houses in the ghost town of Versailles, the modern Nos 14, 16 and 18, rue de l'Orangerie.[100] (Law later found Sully extravagant, and replaced him with his deputy, James Reith, and William Blakey.)

On October 3, 1718 Law bought from his own purse for 125,000 livres, in the town of Harfleur, a watermill on the banks of the Lézarde stream, near the present rue de la République, and a house and garden, as the site for a works to supply high-quality steel for the watches' springs, balance-wheels and pinion wire, and glass for the cases.[101] Again, English men and boys were to provide the workforce (which is, in part, why Law sited the factory so close to English shores). According to Blakey's son, the factory expanded into making "locks, blades, files, steel etc. and was of the first importance for French metallurgy".[102] Early in the new year, Law presented to Louis XV at the Tuileries Messrs Sully and Reith and a miniature watch on a gold chain from the Versailles factory, with which last the boy King was delighted (*très-contente*).[103]

The Law brothers' best-known English recruit was the larger-than-life cannon-founder and engineer Richard Jones, known as "Gun Jones". Jones, who operated the foundry at the Falcon Inn in Southwark, received in 1710 the contract to supply cast-iron gates and railings to enclose the churchyard of the new Saint Paul's Cathedral.[104] A fragment of one bay, strong enough to keep out elephants, survives in the Victoria & Albert Museum in South Kensington.

The contract, let against the wishes of the architect, Sir Christopher Wren, was dogged by scandal and cost the public £11,704 8s.[105] In the pamphlet war that erupted, Jones was said to have been found guilty in 1700 of the manslaughter in Bishopsgate in the City of London of Robert Newey at an anti-Popery demonstration, and narrowly acquitted in 1711 of forging a £250 payment order or *debentur* from the Board of Ordnance for a hundred Coehorn mortars and selling it for cash.[106]

In 1716, Jones failed to fulfil artillery contracts with the Board and lost his main British customer.[107] On October 14, 1718 a correspondent of the Whig *Flying Post* wrote from Calais about "the English Jacobites, who swarm here. Gun Jones is one of them, but he talks of staying some time in Paris."[108] In the new year, Law contracted Jones to set up an iron foundry at Chaillot, across the river from where the Eiffel Tower now stands.

The British ministry was exasperated.[109] In those days, people thought one country's gain must inevitably be another's loss. It was only in the next two generations that David Hume and Adam Smith showed that competition for labour does not injure a craft but, on the contrary, by raising wages attracts to the craft recruits from less favoured branches of industry.

Parliament in London drafted a law forbidding any "artificer of or in wooll, iron, steel, brass or any other metal, clock-maker, watch-maker, or any other artificer or manufacturer" of Great Britain to ply his trade abroad on pain of confiscation of his property; and for anyone contracting such an artificer to leave His Majesty's dominions a fine or imprisonment.[110] It was enacted in the new year. This cross-Channel "jealousy of trade", as Hume was to call it, was to become a fever in 1720.

*

Lady Mary Wortley Montagu, who was returning from her husband's embassy in Constantinople, arrived in Paris that October where she ran into her sister Frances, Mar's second wife, on her way to join the Stuart Court in Urbino. Lady Mary wrote to a friend in England on October 27: "I must say I saw nothing in France that delighted me so much as to see an Englishman (at least a Briton) absolute at Paris. I mean Mr. L–, who treates their dukes and peers extremely *de haut en bas* [with condescension] and is treated by them with the utmost submission and respect. Poor souls!"[111]

A little later, the Paris banker William Gordon wrote to John Drummond of Quarrel: "Our friend Mr Law is above anything you can imagine, and I wish he were as much my friend as I would be his tho I can't say but he is civile to me." Gordon then expressed a reservation that appears in many of the English and Scottish letters of that period: "At same time you think aright that he is nowayes acceptable to the generality of the people and I suppose he is indifferent to that."[112]

With the British pressing for a declaration of war on Spain, the Regent of France needed some provocation to make war less unpalatable to French opinion, and money to pay for it.

The abbé Dubois provided the first. It was clear in the summer, after the fiasco over the mutual-help treaty with Britain, that the Regent could no longer rely on the late King's foreign service. On Stanhope's return from Spain, and probably at his request, on September 24 the duc d'Orléans appointed his old tutor Secretary of State for Foreign Affairs. For Dubois, it was a matter of linking the indiscretions of the duchesse du Maine at her house at Sceaux, south of Paris, with Cardinal Alberoni and the Court of Madrid. That did not prove difficult.

Two young Spanish gentlemen, one the son of the ambassador to London, the other the nephew of the cardinal-archbishop of

Toledo, set off for home from Paris in their own carriage with a false bottom (*à double fond*) in the first week of December. Changing horses at Poitiers on December 8, they fell in with a City of London bankrupt, Sir Joseph Hodges,[113] who was seeking to start anew in Spain. Hodges sounds like a single-use agent of the Earl of Stair.[114]

There was a warrant out for Hodges. A magistrate and archers surprised the three men at dinner at the inn, arrested Hodges and searched the Spaniards' baggage. They found letters in Italian from Prince Cellamare, the Spanish ambassador in Paris, to Cardinal Alberoni. The magistrate sent the letters to Dubois and the following day, Friday, December 9, Cellamare was arrested.

Over the next week, fact and rumour fluttered about Paris. It seemed the duchesse du Maine's circle at Sceaux planned uprisings in Brittany and elsewhere, a Spanish military intervention, the calling of the Estates General and the replacement of the duc d'Orléans as Regent by Philip V of Spain. The copy of Niccolò Machiavelli's *Discorsi* in the duchess's bedroom, open at Book 3, Chapter 6, "On Conspiracies", was squirrelled out of sight.[115]

Several leading men of the old court were taken to the Bastille. The duc du Maine found himself in the citadel of Doullens in Picardie and the duchess, a more delicate object "by reason of her birth and sex, her unflinching courage and terrible rages" (Saint-Simon) in strict confinement at the château de Dijon.[116] (The Regent rewarded the officer attending her with shares in Law's company.)[117] None of the conspirators was brought to trial or held beyond 1720.

As an exercise in manipulating opinion, the "Affair of the duc and duchesse du Maine", now known as the "Cellamare Conspiracy", was a success. "On the first day," the *Gazette de la Régence* wrote on the 12th, "people were shocked and only spoke of the thing in whispers, but once the conspiracy became a certainty, people were relieved that it had been uncovered, for fear of a civil war."[118] Cellamare was declared *persona non grata* and crossed with the French ambassador to Madrid at the border. War was now a formality.

John Law saw to the money. Law had always thought the General Bank just a precursor of a state bank where he might control the supply of money. According to one account, the matter had been discussed at the Epiphany supper at La Raquette.[119] With the old Court scattered and the Parlement of Paris in sulks, and needing to finance some sort of military display, the duc d'Orléans agreed. On December 4, an edict in the King's name announced the conversion of the General Bank into the Royal Bank, of which the King would be sole proprietor.[120]

Law bought out the other shareholders and was reimbursed by the King at the face value of the shares, that is at 5,000 livres per share.[121] The original six millions in *billets d'état* had, it was now revealed, gone into the subscription for the Company of the West, and the King was content to leave them there (Article II) Since the original investors had put in *billets* worth less than half face value, and then received half-yearly dividends and 5,000 livres, all in cash, they had more than doubled their money in two and a half years. It was worth investing in the Scotsman's companies.

The King, too, had done well. An audit for the Crown of the balance sheet of the General Bank in the new year found 39.5 million livres in banknotes in circulation, and a reserve in silver against them at the rue Sainte-Avoye of 9.2 million livres, or about a quarter.[122]

The following is conjecture. Law lent out the other thirty and a bit millions at interest rates no lower than 4 per cent per year. For all the Swiss guardsman's green livery, costs of management and direction were probably in proportion to those of the Bank of England, bad debts were not abnormal and there were no taxes to pay.

If that were the case, Law's bank was earning in clear profit more than a million livres a year. The King would have his money back in six years. Profitable banks nowadays are valued at a minimum of twelve years' profits. It was an instance of Law's generosity to the King of France that was to punish him.

A second decree on December 27 stipulated that in Paris, and in those towns which were to have a branch of the bank (Lyons, La Rochelle, Tours, Orléans and Amiens) all transactions over 600 livres were to be paid in banknotes.[123]

In the midst of the bank nationalisation, Law had time to buy a fleet of merchant ships. On December 15, the Company of the West took over the Compagnie royale du Sénégal, founded in 1696 and now under the control of interests in Rouen. Its trade was in gum arabic, used in drugs and fine textiles, and slave labour for the American plantations. Its assets, valued at Rouen on October 1 at 1,917,600 livres, consisted of merchandise, forts, dwelling houses, privileges and seventeen ocean-going vessels not in the best of condition. (Only five were put by Law to service.) Yet Law was still short of hard cash, for he insisted on writing down the stocks of gum by 317,600 livres, and paying over only 400,000 livres at once, only half in cash, and the remainder in equal payments in three trimesters.[124] The Rouennais were left in place to manage the business.

On January 17, 1719, Master Paul Ballin, notary at the Châtelet, rue des Déchargeurs, received into his hands the last twenty-five million livres in subscriptions for shares in the Company of the West, and constituted the remaining twenty-five annuity contracts.[125] To conduct a trade that Antoine Crozat thought could be done with 1.5 million livres, the Scotsman had one hundred millions. The two men could not both be right.

CHAPTER EIGHT

Mills of Paper

Hercule est sous la tombe et les monstres renaissent.
(Hercules is dead and the monsters revive.)

VOLTAIRE[1]

On Sunday, February 5, 1719, a procession of coaches, horses, riders and footmen set off from La Raquette out in the fields to the east of Paris, entered the Marais, made a circuit of the place des Vosges, passed by the hôtel de la Ville, crossed over the Pont-Neuf and followed the rue Tournon to the house known then as the hôtel des Ambassadeurs extraordinaires (now hôtel de Nivernais).

Riding in the King of France's coach, preceded by thirty-six valets wearing his livery, six grooms and twelve mounted pages likewise attired, was John Dalrymple, Earl of Stair, Ambassador Plenipotentiary of His Britannic Majesty to the Most Christian King. He was followed by the coaches of "M. de Cracofurd [Crawford], secretary of the Embassy of His Majesty the King of Great Britain" and "several English lords and gentlemen attending His Excellency the Ambassador".[2] Among them was John Law of Lauriston, either in person or represented by his coach.[3]

Stair's "public entry" was the most sumptuous diplomatic show in Paris since the embassy of the Earl of Portland in 1698.[4] William Beauvoir, the embassy chaplain, who "was very very sick & in violent pain" during the procession, none the less called it "the most magnificent entry that ever was seen here".[5] It was a sort of Triumph, in the old Roman meaning of the word, a parade of British self-assertion, the humiliation of Spain, the glory of old Scotland and the pride of the second Earl of Stair.

The public entry of foreign ambassadors and princes, a favourite spectacle of European and eastern capitals since the Middle Ages, was often long delayed. Craftsmen had been working on the coaches and liveries since Stair's arrival in 1715. His Master of Horse, James Gardiner, cleared the paddocks of Europe for teams of eight horses powerful and well-enough matched to pull coaches weighing a ton or more: grey and black Friesians, Spanish and Danish bays and dun (*poil de souris*) Neapolitans.

On October 7/18, 1718 Beauvoir visited the coachworks and told his wife in England that the main coach was larger than that used by the Imperial Ambassador. Harnessed for eight horses, it was lined outside and in with Iranian velvet brocade of crimson and gold, which also covered the cushions, coachman's box, reins, harness and plumes. The panels and doors were embossed with the arms of the King of Great Britain and the corners with the devices of the principal British orders of chivalry, the Garter and the Thistle. Curtains of Genoa damask hung in the eight glass windows.[6]

For at least eighteen months, Stair had been pressing the Regent for a day to present his credentials to the King.[7] The duc d'Orléans put him off for fear of irritating an anti-British public. Stair's preferred date of November 30, Saint Andrew's Day, patron saint of Scotland and the Order of the Thistle, of which he was a knight, came and went.[8] It was only with the Maine Affair and the French declaration of war on Spain on January 9 that the Regent felt he could go ahead.[9]

Stair's profligacy and arrogance turned everything to ash. The Paris Jacobites were not inclined to let his parade go by without a splash of rain and at least one of them, Charles Ratcliff, later Earl of Derwentwater, then aged twenty-five, made fun of it. He had been "out" in the 1715 rebellion, captured at Preston and condemned to death but had bought or broken his way out from the Press-Yard at Newgate and got over to France.

Stair had him arrested and confined under so-called *lettres de cachet* or sealed orders in the For-l'Evêque prison. Fanny Oglethorpe stormed at Stair in full company, saying he was "worse than the Grand Inquisitor".[10] Fearing ridicule, which is said to be fatal in an absolute monarchy, Stair allowed the young man to be released into the custody of the marquis de Mézières. (Charles Ratcliff went on to be Grand Master of the Paris freemasons, was out again in 1745, and captured. Since, this time, he had a French military commission, he was executed on the original charge.)

To present his Letters of Credence to the King on February 7, Stair demanded that he bring coaches-and-six into the courtyard of the Tuileries.[11] That was without precedent and the Master of Ceremonies ordered him to unharness two pairs. The coaches were too heavy to be drawn by a single pair. Stair made a scene. At his audience, Stair spoke to the boy King in English, then had to translate his address into French for his despatch to King George.[12]

On the 26th, as the prince de Conti was returning his ceremonial visit, Stair refused to descend the outside staircase or *perron* at the hôtel d'Estampes to receive him, at which point the "introducer" of foreign envoys, the chevalier de Sainctot, called off the visit. Conti was a booby, which was why Stair picked on him.

Stair insisted an ambassador had equality with a prince of the blood, and demanded that the rest of the diplomatic corps support him.[13] He pestered Dubois to dig out the journals of the Masters of Ceremonies going back to Portland's embassy of 1698, and caused the cheerful abbot to lose his temper.[14] The court sided with Conti while the Regent, who never could be bothered with this sort of thing, was annoyed. "The impertinence of that English Ambassador had disgusted all France," wrote the duc de Saint-Simon.[15]

Stair was also fishing in troubled ecclesiastical waters. During the seventeenth century, clergy and laity in France had been drawn to a form of romanised Calvinism known, after the Dutch theologian and bishop of Ypres, Cornelius Jansen, as Jansenism. Pope Clement's Bull of 1713 against the Jansenists, called from its opening word *Unigenitus*, was taken by even the orthodox in France as an assault on the "Gallican Liberties", or independence of the ancient French Church.

Stair had authorised Beauvoir to hold secret talks with two doctors at the Sorbonne towards a union of the English and French Churches. Beauvoir was reporting back to the Archbishop of Canterbury, William Wake. As the *Gazette de la Régence* boiled down the Anglican argument, "the main thing is not to recognise the Pope, and the other stuff can be sorted out [*l'on peut s'ajuster sur le reste*]."[16] Stair tried to persuade the Regent to throw in his lot with the Jansenists and create his own party.[17]

In a sort of ecclesiastical civil war, papal supporters arrested Protestants attending Sunday service at Stair's chapel in the faubourg Saint-Germain and that of the Dutch Ambassador, Cornelis Hop, in the faubourg Saint-Honoré, rue d'Anjou.[18]

Stair's dispute with the prince de Conti went on for two months and overshadows, in the British correspondence, Alberoni's preparations to unleash a Spanish-Jacobite force on Scotland and the West of England. On March 9 by the British calendar, and then again on March 24, King George sent orders by way of Secretary Craggs that Stair was to follow the precedent set by the Imperial Ambassador.[19] Conti was talking of going to Stair's house to demand satisfaction.[20]

On April 29, the Regent summoned both men to his private office and commanded them to make up.[21] Stair said he was sorry for the incident and bowed to the prince. The return visit went ahead. As Cornelis Hop reported, the Earl of Stair descended to the lowest of the five treads of his staircase and placed one foot – it is not recorded which one – on the ground (*met de eene voet op de plaats ende de andere voet op de laatste drempel*).[22]

Amid those commotions, nobody asked how Lord Stair had paid for his great day. Stair was not the Earl of Portland, favourite of King William III, but a Scottish soldier of moderate estate. Back in March, 1718, he had asked Stanhope to give him the gold and silver "perquisite" plate supplied to the Paris embassy from the Jewel House in the Tower of London. "Upon my word I am very poor," he wrote on March 6.[23] No doubt he had borrowed against the plate.

By October, 1718, Secretary Craggs (who was his friend) was exhausted by Stair's demands and scolded him for his gambling and "exorbitant" expense sheets, adding "I do not see how they will be made up to you."[24] Fanny Oglethorpe put about that Stair's absences in the country, ostensibly for his health, were designed to save money lost at play.[25]

London suspected Stair had frittered away the funds sent for the entry ceremony. Stair's response was not straightforward. "I have laid out, and with economy – that I don't take to my praise – all the money the King was pleased to give me for my equipage and entry," he wrote to Craggs on January 14, 1719. "These things, being true, as they are, I cannot have taken the King's money to squander away."[26] None the less, Stair promised to "give over every sort of play".

Craggs asked the Lords of Treasury to approve an extraordinary payment to Stair of £5,000 (enough to buy a fine London house) which they did, with sinister grace.[27] Alas, five thousand pounds would scarcely have built even one of the coaches.

The British Gold State Coach, which can be harnessed for a team of eight and is still in use, cost £7,562 to make in 1762. The Earl of Cadogan, who as the Duke of Marlborough's quartermaster general had done well enough from the war of the Spanish Succession to make a show as ambassador to the United Provinces, spent £3,000 on the state coach for his entry at The Hague on June 8, 1718. The Earl of Stair, no doubt, was somewhere between the two. Then there were the liveries which cost Cadogan £35 for each footman, uniform and harness for the Master of Horse (£100) and the mounted pages, and £50 for each carriage horse, and that in the parsimonious Low Countries.[28]

As Stair's biographer wrote in 1748, "So many grand Occasions and honourable Appearances proved a mean of incumbering his personal Estate, which, with the Debts he had contracted in Gaming, . . . "[29] How much Stair borrowed from John Law this author cannot determine, but a proud Scot who needed money, and another who had it in profusion, were bound to come to blows.

War with Spain did not diminish the traffic to Louisiana. Three frigates, the *Comte-de-Toulouse*, the *Philippe* and the *Maréchal-de-Villars* sailed in the winter to aid in the defence of the colony. The *Maréchal-de-Villars*, which left La Rochelle at the end of January and arrived at île Dauphine on April 19, carried the declaration of war and orders for an immediate attack on the Spanish presidio at Pensacola.[30]

There was surprise at île Dauphine that the directors of the Company of the West had become of a sudden expert in colonial warfare. Still, Bienville had for years been eyeing the harbour at Pensacola, and set off at once for Mobile to assemble his Canadians and native allies.[31] As three to four hundred men marched along the coast, the frigates under his brother Joseph Le Moyne de

Sérigny on May 14 besieged the two Spanish stockades at the mouth of Pensacola harbour, which surrendered.

Having no means to feed the Spanish prisoners, the *Comte-de-Toulouse* and the *Maréchal-de-Villars* conveyed the Pensacola garrison to Havana. The Spanish governor seized the vessels and reflagged them for a counter-attack. (Such was the parsimony of European war in North America.)

On June 28, the 250-ton *Saint-Louis* and the *Dauphine,* on her third Louisiana campaign, arrived at Pensacola with supplies and merchandise. They were surprised by the Spanish expedition from Havana, which in August recaptured the forts, burned the *Dauphine* in the harbour, then sailed west, pillaged Mobile Bay and besieged the French garrison at île Dauphine. The Spanish could make no headway against Sérigny's batteries on the island and the *Philippe,* made fast in a protected bay on the south, and all her twenty guns shipped over to the seaward side.[32]

France knew nothing of any of that, but Law and the directors feared the worst. Two vessels, the flûte *Marie* and the 600-ton *Union* carrying 193 passengers sailed from La Rochelle on May 28 with orders to wait at Cap-Français for an escort of warships.

All the time, with that restlessness that was both his strength and his fault in business, Law was seeking to expand his trading horizons.

The first annual general meeting of the Company of the West, held at the bank in the rue Sainte-Avoye at 7 a.m. on Monday, March 27, was a success. The Regent was in the chair. Bourbon and Conti were present, as well as many of the three hundred shareholders, and Thomas Crawford of the British Embassy.

Crawford reported to London that the Company of the West had seven million livres in working capital, while another source gave these figures: 3.57 million livres in cash, 548,000 livres in merchandise in France and 220,000 livres in beaver pelts.[33] As for its profitability, that now depended entirely on the tobacco monopoly. On the basis of its first quarter in Company control, Crawford wrote, the tobacco trade would bring in 6 millions a year or 2 millions in profit after the rental payment to the King.[34] The shares, which had for eighteen months languished under their issue price of 500 livres, were finding buyers.

That was wishful thinking. Were the old tobacco proprietors, who paid just 2 million livres of rent for their privilege, cheating the King of France of 4 millions every year? Except in the Atlantic ports, the use of tobacco was not widespread in France. There was no smoking at court. Snuff was only just coming into use, though the many snuff-boxes in Lady Katherine's inventory of 1734 hint that she was trying to make it fashionable. Smuggling was rife and the exchange rate into sterling, at which the company bought Virginia tobacco from English and Scottish merchants, had turned against France.

Ships returning in ballast from Louisiana, or carrying Cuban tobacco, would in time destroy confidence in the Company of the West.[35] No doubt that is why Law decided to double up or, as it was known at the faro table, make *paroli* (or "parlay"), where the punter bends a corner of a winning card to bet his or her winnings on the next draw.

From his foothold in the white sand of île Dauphine, Law would make a world-wide company, trading to North America, the South Seas (Latin America), the Far East and India, to match and overtop the British East India and South Sea Companies and the Dutch VOC. It would be the Company of Scotland, translated into France and all its errors made good.

On March 15, Law wagered that the shares of the Company of the West would rise at least 1 per cent above those of the British South Sea Company.[36] By the summer, Law was betting that his company shares would, in a year, be higher than those of the century-old VOC.[37]

Law had long wished for the hôtel de Soissons as his company headquarters, but the place was mortgaged to the hilt, and the prince de Carignan's creditors had blocked the sale in 1717.[38] Instead, for a headquarters for the new company, Law fixed on the brick-and-stone palais Mazarin, a suite of houses and gardens assembled by the chief minister of France in the 1640s, Cardinal Mazarin, across the rue Neuve-des-Petits-Champs from the garden of the Palais-Royal.[39] Since the Cardinal's death, the property had been broken up among his heirs but on May 10, Law bought for 400,000 livres the western block, known as the hôtel de Nevers, complete in the north-west corner with a sitting tenant famed for her immobility and literary salon, the marquise de Lambert.[40]

By his own account, written after the Regency in a memorial to the duc de Bourbon, Law argued that spring over several meetings of the Council of Regency that the Company of the West take over and recapitalise two decayed trading enterprises. Those were the Compagnie des Indes orientales, founded by Colbert in 1664 to trade east of the Cape of Good Hope and the Compagnie de Chine, relaunched in 1712.

The first was indebted to merchants in France and Surat, a port on the west coast of India, and had subcontracted its privileges to a group of Saint-Malo merchants associated with Antoine Crozat. Capable and clannish, the "gentlemen of Saint-Malo" had few friends in the other Atlantic ports or at Paris. Law told Crawford the company's debts were ten times its shareholders' funds.[41] He proposed to the Council that the Company of the West take on the debts and provide fresh capital. He wanted to sell 50,000 new shares at 500 livres to raise 25 million livres to build two long-haul fleets, each of twelve 500-ton vessels. The subscribers would have to pay cash for the new shares.

Argenson objected. He pointed out that:

> I [Law] had difficulty in filling the first subscription [for the Company of the West], even though it was in state paper worth only 32 per cent of face value and I would not have succeeded if HRH [the Regent] had not taken such a large block of shares for the account of the King. He [Argenson] conceded that the shares were now only 10 per cent below par, but he suspected that it would not be easy to hold them at that high level and they would surely fall if fifty thousand more shares were offered. Even if my plan was feasible, he was inclined to give the [East] Indies trade to a new company, and not put all his eggs in one basket.[42]

The duc d'Orléans doubted whether the market could absorb the new shares and did not wish to put at risk the Company of the West "which then appeared to him to be very sound".[43]

What neither appreciated was the effect of the new money Law was creating at the Banque royale. On the strength of edicts in Council, in four issues of January 10, February 15, April 1 and April 28, the Bank cashiers engraved, cut and signed some 110 million livres in banknotes. Those were no longer denominated in silver crowns but in units of 10, 100 and 1,000 livres. They were not signed by Law. A devaluation of the gold louis on May 7 caused a rush to swap metal for banknotes at the Bank, prompting Cornelis Hop to write to Pensionary Heinsius on May 12 that even one hundred million in notes might not be adequate to the demand.[44] The new money needed something to buy.

Since the old shares had risen to 98 per cent of the par or issue price (490 livres), Law suggested the new shares be priced at a 10 per cent premium over par, or 550 livres, only the premium or 50 livres payable at once and the rest at 25 livres per month for twenty months.

Law made a gamble. He offered to buy, or as we would say underwrite, the entire issue. Though that only required him and certain noble "associates" to put up 2.5 million livres (for the 10 per cent premium), they would forfeit that if he missed any of the later payments.[45] The Regent consented and, on Sunday, May 21, issued in the name of the King an edict creating a merged company to be called the Compagnie des Indes (Article XII) or Company of the Indies. The edict, which may have been written by Law, was contemptuous of the management of both companies being taken over.[46]

The edict reached the Quincampoix the next day, Monday, May 22. The shares in the Company of the West rocketed to 600 livres. Law and his associates had booked a gain of 2.5 million livres. It was a good day's wage for a mere subject.

That night, Law did not sleep. "I feared," he wrote later, "that by the trade I had done, I would lose the great confidence I had acquired with the public."[47] He decided to forgo the gain, or rather share it with the other shareholders through what is now called a rights issue ("rights offering" in North America). Under the scheme, existing shareholders who had four shares in the old company gained the right to buy one new. The advantage for Law was that they could not sell the old to buy the new. The disadvantage was that the Regent would have to find another 9 million livres to maintain the King's share of the company's assets and profits at 38 per cent.

At seven that Tuesday morning, Law presented himself at the Palais-Royal. The duc d'Orléans was already in conference, but Law had permission to enter his cabinet at any time. The Regent agreed to release him from the underwriting.[48] By the morrow, Wednesday, May 24, the old shares (dubbed "mothers" with the new shares "daughters") were at 650 livres, giving every subscriber for the daughters a profit of 100 livres per share. "Mr Law insists," the marquis de Dangeau wrote that day in his journal, "that the gain will be much greater still by the end of the year."[49] John Law's starring hour had begun.

At some point over the next ten days, probably on June 1, Law gave an interview to Crawford.[50] Ever alert to an opportunity, Crawford wrote up the interview and sent it to Secretary Craggs, who was an active investor in securities.

In the letter, and subsequent letters over the summer, Crawford made these points. "Mr Law's great and fundamental scheme appears to be the establishing in this Countrey Companys of trade and Corporations which like ours [like ours, which] may be able to help the Most Christian King with money in his exigencys, att an easir rate than his predecessors have been in use to be furnished by the *gens d'affaires* [old-guard financiers]."[51] Law had promised "to pay the expence of the war with Spain out of the profits of the banque and the Company".[52]

Law was more capable "perhaps than any other body" but depended on absolute government: "his proceedings would stop in any other Countrey of the world but this". His position was perilous. "As his credit . . . increases among the lower sort, the spirit of wrath and envy increases likewise among the great." The ministry in London should beware of the Company of the West and the Company of the Indies. "This last may be of bad consequence for our East India Company and the first for our West India plantations, if the Regent and he live . . . for it is most certain that the Regent will sooner forsake any person or thing than Law and his projects."[53]

To modern sentiments, that is baffling. There was trade enough in the world in 1719 for several Indies companies, and, in Europe, capital for a dozen. The men of the early eighteenth century, Law included, did not think so. They saw commerce as something fixed and limited in quantity. The notion that Law's gain must be Exchange Alley's loss, and vice versa, is a theme of the next eighteen months.

On June 4, the merged company took over the trade in wax, grain and coral granted by the Ottoman regents of Algiers and Tunis to Marseillais merchants of the Compagnie d'Afrique and the Compagnie de Cap-Nègre. The Marseillais were demanding a subsidy from the French Crown to continue trading. Law promised the duc d'Orléans that he could operate without subsidy, later paying 68,679 livres for the old companies' vessels, stock and factories.[54] As well as extending the company's reach, Law gained quantities of coral, used as currency in the trade in west African slaves for the Americas. He was on the way to monopolising France's foreign commerce.

On June 17, the Parlement of Paris objected to the original merger on behalf of the Malouin merchants but on the same day was overruled. The subscription opened and on June 23 the Regent took up the King's rights (but not those of his own four favourites) by paying 951,300 livres for the first call on the new shares.[55] That day, Cornelis Hop reported the shares at 750 livres.[56]

Law's company, which already had privileged access to the royal shipyards and ironworks at Bayonne, equal rights with the navy to the draft of sailors in the ports, and oak from the woods of Béarn and Lower Navarre, and a supply of forced labour from the Paris workhouses, now gained its own harbour, shipyard, ropewalk, powder works and arsenal. At the end of June, the navy withdrew from Lorient or l'Orient in Brittany, first developed by Colbert for the Indies but since fallen idle, "leaving the entire port to the Compagnie des Indes".[57]

On July 1, Law appointed Edouard de Rigby to head the company's operations at Lorient. That man was Captain Edward Rigby (1659–1723), from a Royalist family of Layton in Lancashire, who had served with distinction in the Royal Navy.[58] As commander of the forty-gun *Dragon* in the Mediterranean in 1695, he took two valuable ships as prizes. His portrait was done by the Scots painter Thomas Murray and engraved. The engraving shows a man in a curled wig and an embroidered waistcoat, with rings on his fingers and, in the background, men in boats escaping a vessel under fire.[59]

A conviction for buggery in 1698 put a close to Rigby's English naval career. He was pilloried in Pall Mall and at Charing Cross and Temple Bar, where he "appeared very gay" in the sense of good-humoured.[60] He went to France, volunteered at Toulon and was soon serving in French vessels of war. In the Spanish Succession War, on October 21, 1711, as second captain of the sixty-two-gun *Toulouse*, Rigby was captured by the British vessel *Hampton Court* and taken to Port Mahon in Minorca. Matters might have gone ill for him, had he not convinced Admiral Sir John Jennings that King William's Secretary of State Lord Nottingham, had given him "leave . . . to gett his bread in any countrey he pleased".[61] Rigby escaped or was allowed onto a vessel bound for Genoa and almost certainly met Law in that city.

Returned to Toulon, Rigby reported on the English shipping for the Earl of Mar. In the summer of 1718, he came to Paris to be accepted into the Order of Saint Louis, a decoration for officers inaugurated by the old King in 1693 and the first to admit non-nobles, and to lobby for his back pay. (He was either born or had become a Roman Catholic.) Law promised to help him with his pay, while Stair dangled a pardon which Rigby refused, saying he was now "a Frenchman and never thought of returning to England till my master [James III] went".[62]

That was not imminent. The Spanish-Jacobite invasion in the spring of 1719 was a fiasco. The main invasion force of twenty-nine sail, carrying five thousand men under the Duke of Ormonde and arms for thirty thousand Englishmen, was scattered by storms off Cape Finisterre on March 29–30.[63] Three hundred Spanish marines and Jacobites under George Keith, Earl Marischal landed on the west coast of Scotland but were defeated, with their Highland allies, on June 10/21 in Glen Shiel by Law's old duelling acquaintance, General Wightman. James III, who had managed to slip out of Italy, came no nearer his kingdoms than Corunna. Mar was arrested in Geneva, and was now in negotiation with Stair for his pardon.[64]

Even so, the appointment of the Jacobite Rigby to command a private port on the South-West Approaches to Britain was perilous for the Hanoverians. There is no trace of a protest to the Regent by Lord Stair. Perhaps he had turned Rigby. Of Rigby's vigour and courage there was no doubt, but he was vain, tyrannical, extravagant and grasping.[65] His office work was chaotic and his French not of the best. Law hated to delegate and then, when he did so, employed desperadoes.

Law himself was recruiting indentured workers for his "property [*habitation*] in Louisiana", presumably his venture with Cantillon and Gage. There survives a list of payments that summer of 1719 by his cashier in the place Vendôme of 12 livres and 15 livres per man as journey-money from Paris to La Rochelle, and also payments of 3,000 livres "for merchandise for Louisiana" and 15,000 livres for an unspecified purpose. The dozen men engaged from June 10 were labourers, carpenters, locksmiths, masons, a toolmaker and an almoner. None of the names appears on the passenger lists to Louisiana in 1719, and it is possible that none embarked.[66]

To set an example,[67] to raise the scale of settlement, and to expand the colony upstream, Law on July 5 took for himself a concession of sixteen leagues square or 2,300 square miles, along the Arkansas River.[68] In 1682, La Salle had granted his lieutenant Henri Tonty the lower Arkansas as a manor or *seigneurie*, and for a time Tonty established a settlement about thirty miles upstream from the Mississippi confluence to trade furs with a small nation called the Quapaws.[69] There is no evidence that Law's concession conveyed a title of nobility. None the less, some United States authors delight to call John Law the "Duke of Arkansas".

By the beginning of July, the boom in the shares had passed out of Paris into the trading towns. There survives a correspondence between two men of Lyons, Laurent Dugas, president of the cour des monnaies, and his younger cousin, François Bottu de Saint-Fonds. Both were scholars, but were otherwise dissimilar. Dugas was sober, precise and analytical while his younger friend, who had abandoned the seminary to marry, was impulsive, given to fancy, a poet.

At the beginning of July, Saint-Fonds was wondering if he should invest in the Company of the Indies. Dugas consulted the Lyons merchant banker, Melchior Philibert. "You could do worse than risk a thousand or so crowns in the new company," Dugas wrote on July 4. He then listed some objections.

> M. Philibert made the point that whatever Mr Law's genius, it was impossible for a single intellect to be strong enough to conduct a trade that embraces both East and West where every part requires infinite pains and limitless foresight . . .
>
> My view (which M. Philibert endorsed) is that for the project to succeed, its author would have to be immortal and for ever sure of enjoying the same confidence of his prince, the same credit and the same authority. He must sow and sow broadcast. The preparatory expenses of all these enterprises will be prodigious, and the harvest a long way off. The Mississippi is a new colony which is not yet established and will not be sending France much by way of merchandise for a long time. The vessels to be despatched to China will

not return for three years. What assurance do we have that future ministers will have the same views as Mr Law today?[70]

On July 21, on the stroke of midnight, the Regent's eldest surviving daughter, the duchesse de Berry, died in agony at her house in the Bois de Boulogne, the château de la Muette. Spoiled since her infancy, promiscuous and a compulsive eater, drinker and gambler, Louise-Elisabeth was an object of pity and revulsion. Only the duc d'Orléans mourned her. Saint-Simon drew the Regent away from his daughter's pillow, and led him into a neighbouring room where the windows were open on the hot evening. "He stood," Saint-Simon wrote, "leaning on the iron balustrade, in such a flood of tears that I feared he would choke. When the storm had abated a little, he began to talk of the misfortunes of this world and the brief term of all that is most sweet."[71] The duc d'Orléans regained his self-control, but his Regency takes on a reckless, even frantic, character.

That day, the mother shares were bid at over 1,000 livres.[72] With an annual dividend of 20 livres per share, or 2 per cent per year, Law could raise capital more cheaply than anybody in Europe and there was not a business on the continent that he could not buy for a profit.

Law had always intended, in the fashion of all modern states but the United Kingdom, to have sole charge of the issue of currency.[73] On the 25th, the Company of the Indies received the monopoly of minting coin, for nine years at the first instance, at a price of 50 million livres payable over 15 months. To raise the 50 million, the company two days later announced a rights issue of 50,000 shares at a price of 1,000 livres, 50 livres down and the rest over nineteen months. From 1720, both new and old shares would pay a dividend of 60 livres.

The Quincampoix, which could not be bothered with Louisiana

or Africa, knew about beating out gold and silver coin at the cramped and dilapidated hôtel de la Monnoye near the Pont-Neuf and at a sort of overflow mint established during the war at the Louvre. For centuries, the coinage had been a reliable source of profit to the King of France.

To gain a right to one new share or "granddaughter", investors needed four mothers and one daughter, which were in tight supply. Half of the mothers were controlled by the Regent and Law, and the remainder by about seven hundred holders.[74] There was a panic to buy. On the 28th, the mothers were at 1,750 livres; at 2,300 livres on July 31; at 2,325 on August 2 and 3; and, on August 4, 2,500.[75] There, having risen five-fold in ten weeks, they halted for breath.

Alone among the surviving witnesses, Cornelis Hop linked the success of "the fifty million" to the banknotes pouring out of the royal printing works. Just thirty-four years old, Cornelis Hop came from a family at the heart of the Dutch administration. His father, Jacob, was treasurer general of the Netherlands and built a house on the Amsterdam Herrengracht, No. 605, which is nowadays open to the public. On the 24th, young Hop had presented his credentials to Louis XV at the Louvre as the first-ever Ambassador Plenipotentiary of the States General. It was pleasing enough to Dutch self-esteem to merit commemoration in a painting now in the Amsterdam Rijksmuseum.

On August 4, Hop reported to Pensionary Heinsius that the Banque Royale's balance sheet had increased from 100 million to 400 million livres.[76] (On June 10, the Banque Royale received authority to issue 50 million livres in banknotes, and 240 million on July 25.) Hop reckoned the gold and silver coinage in France amounted to only 500 million livres.[77] That was an underestimate but gives some idea of Law's inflation of the supply of money in France or, in the phrase of today, "quantitative easing".

In the second week of August, the heat abated a little. Voltaire's patron, the marquis de Saint-Ange, wrote on the 11th from the Quincampoix to his sister, the marquise de Balleroy, in the Norman countryside: "His shareholders greet you, saying, 'Good news, it is a little cooler. That is of the first importance for the health of Mr Law. Now, if perhaps a drop or two of rain etc.'"[78]

Voltaire himself was not pleased. Having been the sensation of the winter with his tragedy *Œdipe,* performed at the Comédie française on November 18, 1718, François-Marie Arouet (as he was still known) was not ready for a new celebrity. Feeling that Sophocles' tragedy needed improvement, he had added a love story, coded digs at the Regent and the duchesse de Berry, and regret for the great King:

> *Hercule est sous la tombe et les monstres renaissent.*
> (Hercules is dead and the monsters revive.)

The Regent gave him a medal.

Loitering that scorching summer of 1719 in country houses in the val de Loire, and then at Vaux-le-Vicomte, Voltaire was for ever meeting the Scotsman, introduced into the orangeries by visitors and newsletters from Paris. In his bread-and-butter verses, Voltaire adopts the posture of the antique poet Horace fleeing Imperial Rome for literature, wine and good company at his country villa.

"It is a fine thing," he wrote to the lawyer Nicolas de La Faluère de Génonville in August,

> . . . to come to the country while Plutus [Greek God of wealth] is turning every head in town. Have you all truly lost your heads in Paris? Nobody talks of anything but *millions.* They say that everybody who was well off is now destitute, and beggars are swimming in opulence. Is that really so? Or is it a fantasy [*chimère*]? Has half the country found the

philosopher's stone in the mills of paper? Is Lass [Law] a God, a crook or a charlatan who has taken too much of the medicine he is handing out? Are people happy in their imaginary riches? I can't make head or tail of it, and don't imagine you can. For myself, the only fantasy to which I submit is that of poetry:

> *Avec l'abbé Courtin*[79] *je vis ici tranquille,*
> *Sans aucun regret pour la ville*
> *Où certain Ecossais malin,*
> *Comme la vieille Sibylle*
> *Dont parle le bon Virgile,*
> *Sur des feuillets volants écrit notre destin.*
> *Venez nous voir un beau matin,*
> *Venez, aimable Génonville . . .*[80]
>
> (With Courtin I have settled down
> And have no hankering for Town,
> Where a certain crafty Scot,
> Like the ancient Sybil
> You find in worthy Virgil,
> Writes on scuttering leaves our lot.
> Come and see us one fine day,
> Come, dear Génonville, away . . .)

Behind the shop-worn pose is a strong mind in the process of reconsideration. Though he never lost his dislike of Law, which he took out on Lady Katherine, Voltaire came in the end to see the Scot as a forerunner or Baptist of his own mission to lift France from its mental torpor.[81]

In the third week of August, the shares revived. On the 17th, the mothers were quoted at 3,000 livres, before slipping back.

"Missisipi begins to stagger," Stair wrote in a private letter to Craggs on the 20th, "which has happened by Law's imprudence, and boundless desire of gain." He blamed the Regent for not selling out the King's shares at 2,000 livres at the end of July, when he "might have got two hundred millions".[82] Stair added: "Law risks to have the whole fabric tumble to the ground."

Stair was behind the times.

On August 22, at the Palais-Royal, the duc d'Orléans "expounded a new project of finance" in which the Company of the Indies would lend the King of France 1,200 million livres to buy out all his creditors, that is the whole national debt of France.

The King was within his rights. In Roman Catholic theory, a borrower could at any time elect to repay his creditors or, as it was said, "buy back" (*racheter*) the annuities he had granted. Law's project, a novelty for its age and even for ours, knocked out the main props of the French way of life. The King's creditors, consisting of the office-holders, the nobility and the Church with all its parishes, convents and charitable institutions would lose the income that made their existence possible. Jules Michelet, in his *History of France*, called the Regency "our greatest economic and social revolution before [17]89".[83]

More questionably, the King would also unilaterally revoke the contract, granted in 1718 to a syndicate led by the Pâris brothers, to collect the consumption or excise duties on salt, wine, paper and suchlike and bestow that privilege on Law's company. Those excises, particularly that on salt, were unpopular, inefficient and tyrannical and made criminals of the poor. The council approved a draft edict.[84]

On August 27, the edict was published, transferring to the Company of the Indies the *Fermes générales* or General Farms which collected the excises for the King. The company would pay 52 million livres a year for the privilege, as against the 48.5 million promised by the Pâris. The brothers were in the process of selling shares in the Farms to the public in imitation of Law, and those shareholders would be compensated.

At the same time, the Company of the Indies would lend the King 1.2 billion livres at the rate of 3 per cent per year, deducting the 36 million livres he would pay in annual interest from its 52 million livre rental payment for the General Farms. With the proceeds of the loan, the King would redeem the Town Hall annuities and public offices charged against the excise, the remaining *billets d'état* and the shares issued by the Pâris. The Company of the Indies' charter and all its privileges were extended to January 1, 1770.[85]

To finance the loan to the King, the Company was authorised to issue its own annuities at 3 per cent. The Company of the Indies would become the French King's sole creditor. Law's years in Genoa yielded their late harvest. Law had his Bank of St George, not a "separate republic" (as he had called it) but as a sort of parallel and constitutional monarchy.

The French were not ready for such a revolution. Hop wrote the next morning, August 28, to Pensionary Heinsius that the reduction in annuity interest from 4 to 3 per cent, "however favourable to the King, discomposes some of the most respectable folk [*voornaamste luyden*] here who ever regarded the Town Hall as the safest investment and placed most of their funds there".[86]

Mme de Balleroy's elder brother, Caumartin de Boissy, wrote to her in a sort of despair: "We are no longer certain of anything in our world."[87] Thanks to Law's money-printing, land and houses were expensive. Where could they invest in safety?

A second edict on August 31, announcing the suppression of the annuities and certain offices from January 1, 1720, gave one answer in its Article XI: "all persons are free, at their own choice, to acquire shares or annuities of the said Company of the Indies."[88]

The shares in the said company soared. According to price sheets later compiled by "Giraudeau the Nephew, merchant at Paris", and surviving in at least three manuscript copies, the mothers sold at 700 per cent or 3,500 livres on August 28; 3,550 livres on the 29th, and 3,600 on the 30th. On September 7, they were over 4,500, and on the 12th over 5,000 livres. In just over a month, the shares of the Company of the Indies had doubled in price.[89]

Stair and Dubois feared for their livelihoods. The abbé was thinking of resigning. Stair wrote in a private letter to Craggs on September 1:

> You must henceforth look upon Law as the first minister, whose daily discourse is, that he will raise France to a greater height than ever she was, upon the ruin of England and Holland. You may easily imagine that I shall not be a Minister [Ambassador] for his purpose.
>
> He is very much displeased with me already, because I did not flatter his vanity by putting into Mississippi. I have been in the wrong to myself, to the value of thirty or forty thousand pounds, which I might very easily have gained if I had put myself, as others did, into Mr Law's hands; but I thought it was my duty, considering my station, not to do so.[90]

If the last sentence was true, it would soon cease to be.[91]

In Genoa, the Durazzo brothers now regretted falling out with Law. They wrote to him on the 19th a letter so courteous it might have been addressed to a prince. The brothers complained that the adverse exchange rate would cause them "a very considerable loss" if they repatriated the 237,135 livres in capital they had invested at the Paris Town Hall. That was in addition to losses on a loan made in 1690 to the city of Lyons. They asked for advice as to how to deploy their funds to best effect. "In the multiplicity of your affairs," they wrote, "the inconvenience we impose on you is by no means trivial. None the less, we remain hopeful that you will not withhold from us your assistance."[92] There is no trace of a reply.

Among the City of London investors to cross the Channel and make their way to Paris were the Earl of Ilay and Colonel Pitt, now Lord Londonderry in the Irish peerage.[93] They arrived, probably together, on September 5.[94]

Ilay and his brother, the Duke of Argyll, were out of favour with King George. At some point in the spring of 1717, Ilay met Fanny Oglethorpe, and both brothers received a pardon from James III, which was lodged with Mézières in the rue du Bac.[95] (In the Jacobite code, Ilay was known as "the Doctor".) The brothers were now leading figures at the court of George, Prince of Wales, who had quarrelled with his father in late 1717 and been expelled with the Princess of Wales from St James's Palace.

At a rival court in Leicester Fields (now Leicester Square), the Campbell brothers enjoyed the protection of the Prince's mistress, Henrietta Howard. Born at Blickling Hall in Norfolk, and orphaned young, Henrietta had married the younger son of the Earl of Suffolk, who bullied her. Henrietta Howard was handsome, kind, a peacemaker, poor and, as Alexander Pope reminded the world in his "On a Certain Lady at Court", deaf. Everybody felt sorry for her, and Ilay a bit more than that.

Ilay bought for Mrs Howard a hundred shares in the mint issue or "Fifty Million", paying 5,000 livres for the first call. He wrote to her:

> I have laid out the money you bid me . . . It is true it is now very late, & yet by what I am informed by him who knows

all & does all here [Law], I am of opinion that whatever sum you remit here may be turned to great profit. The stocks are now at 950 [4,750 livres] & if no accidents happen of mortality, it's probable they will be 1500 [7,500 livres] in a short time . . . The subscription was full but Mr Law was so kind as to allow it me.

If Mrs Howard had further orders, she might remit by Middleton in The Strand.

Law was no doubt happy to help his friend's friend, but he had a larger beast in view. Ilay continued: "You will think that the levity of this country has turned my head when I tell you that your master [Prince of Wales] might within these [illegible] months have made himself richer than his father."[96] The Prince of Wales rose to the fly and later despatched his own emissary to Law, the Scotsman John, Lord Belhaven.[97] At about this time, probably at the Princess Caroline's request,[98] Elisabeth Charlotte started sending news of John Law.

Lord Londonderry had at first relied on a stock-jobbing arrangement with Crawford, he supplying the cash and Crawford privileged information in the diplomatic bag. That went awry in 1718 when Tim Aird, the Earl of Stair's courier, who no doubt had his own clients, took Crawford's despatch on the Cape Passaro battle to Exchange Alley.[99] Crawford was reprimanded and Stair appears to have stopped giving him certain letters to copy.

Londonderry had a commission from his father, Diamond Pitt, to collect a debt from Law in Paris. On June 1, Law had made the final payment of 320,000 livres on the great diamond. The stone was almost certainly already in Paris, in the hands of the jeweller setting the coronation regalia. In the English way, Pitt Sr needed a great deal of wine and endorsed Law's bills (drawn on Hamburg) to an English-speaking merchant in Bordeaux, Pierre de Kater.

De Kater refused to accept the bills on the grounds that the livre had been devalued (by Argenson in May, 1718).[100] That was an embarrassment to Law.

Soon after their arrival, probably the next afternoon, September 6,[101] Londonderry and Ilay dined with Law and Stair. Stair says the dinner was at Law's "own table" (that is, in the place Vendôme). That may not be true. It is unlikely that Stair would permit Law to entertain such visitors before King George's Ambassador did so.[102] Also invited was Joseph Gage, the Jacobite speculator. There is no report of women being present, and matters got out of hand.

Law and Londonderry made a wager. Law promised to deliver to Londonderry, in twelve months' time or August 25, 1720 by the English calendar, £100,000 sterling in stock of the British East India Company at 180 per cent of par or £180,000.[103] That September afternoon, East India, the most widely traded of the London joint-stock companies, was around £190 and had been so all that summer of 1719.

Law was gambling that his Company of the Indies over the next year would so succeed as to drive down the value of its British rival. If East India fell to £170, Law would buy the stock in the Alley for £170,000, sell it to Londonderry for the £180,000 agreed, and book a £10,000 gain; or Londonderry would simply pay him the £10,000. Each gambler put up £40,000 as premium or earnest money, and promised to deposit a further £10,000 each time the stock moved £10 against him. It was a typical eighteenth-century bet, unremarkable except in its scale: a "plum" or not less than £10 million in the money of today. Ilay was out of his depth, but both Stair (on Londonderry's side) and Gage (with Law) took side bets. Stair borrowed from Londonderry shares in Law's company as surety.

In his private letter to Secretary Craggs on the 9th, Stair reported the wager, but did not mention his own part in it or the presence of the Roman Catholic Gage. He wrote that Law boasted "that he can break our bank [Bank of England], whenever he has a mind; and our East India company. You may imagine what we have to apprehend from a man of this temper, who will have all the power and all the credit at this court."[104] Stair warned that Great Britain must pay off its own war debt or risk being overwhelmed by John Law's France. He took to repeating that warning in and out of season, like the older Cato calling to destroy Carthage.[105]

Stair's letter was soon in the Alley coffee houses, and found its way in various forms into the press.[106] Craggs sought to calm his ambassador: "[Law] may chance to find that in attempting to undersell our stock so publicly he has united several considerable rich bodies of men here against him."[107]

CHAPTER NINE

Atlas in the Quincampoix

Le banquier est un être impassible: toujours tranquille, toujours de sang-froid, il ne péchera jamais par défaut de conduite; il ne peut perdre la tête, et c'est ce que les pontes peuvent faire et font souvent.
(The bank is impassive, calm and cold. He never fails in the smallest article of conduct. He may not lose his head, while the punters are free to do so and often do so.)

FORTIA DE PILES[1]

The Louisiana relief convoy, comprising the warships *Hercule*, mounting sixty guns, *Mars*, fifty-four, and *Triton*, fifty, and the two company ships, *Union* and *Marie*, arrived off île Dauphine on September 1, 1719, expecting to find the French colony obliterated. In command was Gilles-Charles des Nos, comte de Champmeslin, who was taking no chances. Four of the vessels were under Spanish colours, while the *Marie* flew the French royal ensign at half-mast, as if she were their prize.

Champmeslin surprised a Spanish coaster which fled through the shallows. Leaving the *Marie* behind, for she was a bad sailer, he sailed eastwards with the King's three warships, the *Union* and the *Philippe*.

On the 9th, one of the Canadians piloted the *Hercule*, which drew twenty-two feet, over the sandbar at the mouth of Pensacola Bay and soon all five vessels were cannonading the main fort and the Spanish shipping. Besieged on the land side by a force of Canadians and Americans under Bienville and his cousin by marriage, Louis Duchereau de Saint-Denis, the Spanish commander surrendered, though the battery on Santa Rosa Island fought on till its powder was exhausted.[2]

Champmeslin took 1,200 prisoners, including some forty French deserters. Twenty of those he hanged from the *Hercule*'s mizzen yardarm, and the remainder he put to forced labour for the Company of the Indies. The Spanish prisoners were also divided, over half exchanged for the French held in Cuba, and the remainder sent to Saint-Domingue and France. To celebrate the victory, the officers at île Dauphine invited Champmeslin to dinner, serving a dog pie. The admiral pronounced it finer than French venison.[3]

The French kept Pensacola until the peace. A Spanish counter-armament from Vera Cruz in Mexico was dispersed by a storm. In Europe, the War of the Quadruple Alliance, remarkable among eighteenth-century wars for France and Great Britain fighting on the same side, was winding down.

With his main army imprisoned by the British fleet in Sicily, Philip of Spain could do little to repel the French actions in the Basque country and Catalonia, and British ravages on the Galician coast. By the autumn, it was expected that Philip would dismiss Alberoni and accede to the Quadruple Alliance. Both John Law and the City of London were looking forward with the peace to commercial opportunities in Spain.

Law had lost a whole season. The chance of extracting a profit from Louisiana for his shareholders receded another year. The only company vessels to reach the colony that autumn were the frigate the *Duchesse-de-Noailles,* which brought provisions for Champmeslin's squadron, and the pinnace the *Deux-Frères,* which carried small concessionaires, private passengers, convicted salt and tobacco smugglers, younger sons and black sheep (*enfants de famille*) and "vagabonds".[4]

Louisiana had become the dumping ground for vagrants from the Paris workhouses, known as the Hôpital général, and the provincial towns, and for deserters from the Spanish war.[5] This penal policy, which had begun under Crozat, demolished the image of the colony in metropolitan France.

Of the four hundred or so men and boys embarked by force for Louisiana that year, several were sent at the request of their families or neighbours. Louis Le Conte, master wheelwright of Paris, asked that his son Pierre, aged twenty-four, locked up for the last eighteen months in the Bicêtre workhouse in the fields south of the town, be transported to "the islands of Mississippi with the other Frenchmen". An unsigned note requested that Vincent Girard, aged thirty, shut up at his widowed mother's request in the Bicêtre, be "sent to Misipipy, for his extremely dissipated conduct will only bring him to the most dreadful end in this city". Argenson's successor as lieutenant general of police, Louis-Charles de Machault, in a briefing note for the Regent of July 25, 1719, endorsed the older Le Conte's petition and said Girard would be "an ideal subject for that colony".[6] Bienville became exasperated by such recruits.[7]

The *Deux-Frères,* which sailed from La Rochelle on August 19, 1719 and anchored off île Dauphine on October 17 or 18, carried among its two hundred passengers sixteen "seditious" women and girls from the women's penitentiary on the Left Bank of the Seine known as the Salpêtrière. Because of "rebellion", they were originally destined under *lettres de cachet* for transportation to the Caribbean islands of Saint-Domingue and Martinique or Cayenne in Guiana.[8] Conveyed in carts to the naval base of Rochefort, the women were held in unspeakable conditions and then, for want of shipping to the islands, transferred under the Regent's order to the Company of the West, and then to the Company of the Indies.

Marguerite Pataclin, the Sister Superior of the Hôpital général, saw an opportunity to clear out more of her bad subjects and invited Law to dinner on or just before September 1, 1719. The Scotsman gave her 50,000 livres to improve conditions for her inmates and the promise of the same each New Year's Day for the rest of his life.[9] A further ninety-six women and girls from the Salpêtrière sailed in December, 1719 on the frigate *Mutine*. On arrival the following February, the survivors were at once all married.[10]

The toughest of the women on the *Deux-Frères*, Marie-Anne Fontaine, aged thirty-eight, Parisian, and Marie-Anne Porcher or Chevalier, thirty, of Orléans, were both nicknamed Manon.[11] The historian Marcel Giraud thought to see in their name the germ of the abbé Prévost's novel *Manon Lescaut* (1731) and the operas by Puccini and Massenet that arose from it.[12] The novel left to this day an image of Law's Louisiana as a place of melancholy, separation and death.

To refund the King's debts, Law had been authorised to issue perpetual annuities at an interest of 3 per cent. Such was the clamour for the shares in the Quincampoix, and in the private houses where they were traded, Law changed his mind. Paying a dividend of sixty livres, each share issued at 5,000 livres cost the Company of the Indies just over 1 per cent while it was lending to the King at 3 per cent. That was an immediate profit.

On September 11, Law received permission from the Regent to issue another hundred thousand shares at 5,000 livres each, payable in instalments, to raise a further 500 million livres.[13] For good measure, a decree the next day allowed the bank to print 120 million livres in banknotes of 10,000 livres face value.[14] The new shares were five times oversubscribed on the first day of issue.

Thomas Crawford, who had spent much of August at Stair's rented country house to recover from a fever, returned to find Paris in a delirium. Attempting to call on Law in the third week of September, he found the house under siege from men and women demanding to be admitted to the share issue.

"For the past five or six days," he wrote to London on September 23, 1719, "he [Law] has been obliged to have his outer gate shut while he is within and one may see still every day 3 or 4 hundred people of fashion among whom are very often Dukes and Peers and others of the greatest quality waiting at his outer door a foot [on foot] to catch the opportunity of the Porter's letting somebody come out that they endeavour by threats & bribes to get in."[15]

Law was driving out to La Marche in the evening, as the marquis de Dangeau reported, "to have some respite to breathe".[16] Lady Katherine and the children were presumably there to escape the heat. Overworked to the point of prostration, some time before September 20, John Law persuaded his brother William to move from London to help him.[17] William and his wife of three years, Rebecca Dewes, who was eight months pregnant, were given a house in the place Vendôme, probably the hôtel Gramont.[18]

Crawford squeezed in to see Law in the last week of September. Law explained that on September 25, in the duc d'Orléans's box at the Comédie italienne, the Italian players' company at the hôtel Bourbon, for fear of "disobligeing a vast number of people", the Regent had consented to another issue of 500 million livres. Decrees to that end were published on September 26 and 28. The new shares would be payable not in cash but in drafts issued by the Treasury to annuitants and other state creditors.[19]

Those shares too were snapped up, and a third issue of 500

million livres was made on October 2, which the Regent announced would be the last.[20] The company's loan to the King now stood at 1.6 billion livres and paid an annual interest of 48 million livres. Once fully paid up, the 600,000 shares in issue would make the Company of the Indies by far the most valuable corporation in the world. By one measure, it is still so. No joint-stock company anywhere has ever been priced in the market at more than twice the annual product of France.

Still the clamour for the "Mississippi" persisted and the shares rose in price. There exists a letter of this time to William Law from Margaret, Lady Panmure. James, Earl of Panmure had been out with the Jacobite rebels in the 'Fifteen, been captured at Sheriff-muir, escaped to France, and forfeited estates in Angus worth £60,000 sterling that were on the point of being auctioned off. The Earl and Countess were living in Paris on her jointure. Somehow, Lady Panmure (who was daughter to the Duke of Hamilton) had scraped or borrowed 50,000 livres for a down-payment on the Mississippi shares but missed the deadline.

She had no interest, she wrote to William, in "heaping up treasures". Had she been a single woman, she might have lived on her jointure, but she felt it her "duty to do all that's possible for preserving all I can a Memorie of My Lord's famillie which is as dear to me as my life and even to endeavour to provide a subsistence to him in case I should happen to dye before him. This is so tender a theme to me . . . for I cannot allwayes master a weakness that our sex is lyable to for a flood of tears sometimes overwhelms me."[21]

The pressure from women to buy shares – *de drift van de dames* in Cornelis Hop's frollandais[22]– gave new life to the speculation. Elisabeth Charlotte was astonished by tales of a duchess kissing Law's hand. "When Duchesses are kissing his hands," she wrote to the Princess of Wales on October 4, 1719, "what other part do the other ladies have to kiss!"[23] She later added: "If Mr Law so desired, the French ladies would be happy to kiss – pardon my French – his arse."[24]

Her former lady-in-waiting, Marie-Thérèse de Chausserais, "who had been rather poor", had put her mite into the Mississippi and made a million.[25] Elisabeth Charlotte loved Mlle de Chausserais and liked to break her journey from the Palais-Royal to Saint-Cloud at her cottage, which stood halfway in the park of the old château de Madrid between the bois de Boulogne and the Seine.

As it turned out, Mlle de Chausserais could not bear to leave her "cows, calves, hens, doves, bees, canary birds, dogs and cats"[26] and used her million to buy the hôtel d'Armenonville from a financier and lease it back to him for 20,000 livres a year for two lives.[27] The rental yield, of just 2 per cent or "the fiftieth penny", shows how far the price of houses in Paris had risen in response to Law's money-printing.

Elisabeth Charlotte must have seen that the 150,000-livre increase in pension that her son had given her in September had something to do with Law. She appears to have asked her son to present him. For all her prejudices against the barbarous English (and *a fortiori* Scots), she was charmed. On October 24, 1719, she wrote to Caroline of Wales: "Mr Law is an honourable and intelligent man, exceedingly polite and courteous to everybody, and knows how to live. Unlike Englishmen in general, he speaks really quite good French."[28] To please her, and other ladies, Law paid to replace the stinking and smoky tallow lights (*chandelles*) at the theatre of the Palais-Royal with candles of North African wax (*bougies*).[29]

The Lyonnais doctor and erudite Charles Cheinet spent an hour in the Quincampoix in mid-October. He wrote to his friends at home: "One could scarcely fit one's nose between two persons. It is a mania, a vertigo beyond description, and yet the person who has set in train such violent transports is the coldest man in the world, who takes no part and speaks only in equations."[30] On October 26, the royal household ordered a guard to be mounted in the street of three officers and twelve men to ensure "the freedom & security of the traders".[31]

Amid those tumults, on September 17, 1719, at the convent church of the Récollets in Melun, thirty miles to the south-east of Paris, John Law of Lauriston abjured the Presbyterian faith of his fathers and was received into the Roman Catholic Church. The ceremony was not reported in the gazettes or newsletters. The Town Council of Edinburgh, which was at that moment preparing to give Law the freedom of the city, might otherwise have changed its mind.

Law was not a religious man. He may have recognised that the duc d'Orléans would not live for ever or indeed, with his regime of concentrated work and pleasure, very long. Law must make his peace with what was called the "old Court", the devout, anti-British and pro-Spanish administration left behind by Louis XIV. That year had brought him a warning. When Charles XII of Sweden was killed by a stray bullet on campaign in Norway, his German financial adviser, Georg-Heinrich, Baron Görtz, was arrested, tried and beheaded (February 19/March 2, 1719).

For at least two weeks, there had been rumours that Argenson would be relieved of the finances and replaced by someone more amenable to the Scotsman.[32] It now appeared that either Law wanted to be controller general of the finances, or the Regent wanted him so. Since Law controlled much of the King's revenue, and would soon be in charge of 90 per cent of it, Argenson's position could not have been easy.

It mattered less that Law had been born abroad than that he was Protestant. Religion sat as lightly on the duc d'Orléans as on his Scottish servant, but the Regent was not the man to trouble the shade of the old King or set a confessional precedent for the new.

The problem was Lady Katherine. To have married so late in the day would have caused scandal. Law needed a confessor and catechist who knew better than to probe. Pierre Guérin de Tencin (1679–1758), vicar general of the diocese of Sens, was the man for the task.

Though he was to rise to the cardinalate, serve as French Ambassador to the Holy See and act as confidant to both Pope Benedict XIV and King James III, the abbé Tencin at that time had few admirers. Matthew Prior, Stair's predecessor as British envoy in Paris, thought him "not worth hanging".[33] Supple and ambitious, he was reinforced by his sister, Claudine-Alexandrine. Both had come into the orbit of the abbé Dubois.

Alexandrine was born three years after her brother. To spare his estate the expense of her dowry, their father, a magistrate at the Parlement of Grenoble, confined Alexandrine to the convent of Montfleury that overlooks the town. At his death, she pleaded ill health, left the convent and eventually made her way to Paris to her elder sister, Angélique de Ferriol. After several years' bombardment, the Pope in November, 1712 annulled her vows. To redeem her years as a bride of Christ, Alexandrine plunged into the world. Her boundless ambition fixed on her brother.

Lady Katherine was later a friend of Mme de Ferriol, and it is possible that in 1719 she already knew the Tencins.[34] According to the duc de Saint-Simon, who detested the Tencins, Alexandrine had her brother "crammed [with banknotes] by Law".[35] What is clear is that Mlle de Tencin founded a stock-jobbing partnership in the Quincampoix with a capital of 3.4 million livres in banknotes, providing the largest share herself or just under 700,000 livres. It was quite a fortune for a younger daughter and an "eloped nun" (Bolingbroke).[36]

Among the twelve partners were her sister, Mme de Ferriol, her eldest brother François, a magistrate in Grenoble, and her lover, the artillery officer Major General Louis Camus-Destouches. The abbé de Tencin is not named in the deed but may have had a separate partnership with Alexandrine.

To manage the investments in "current market securities [*effets courans de la place*]", Alexandrine appointed François Duché de La Motte, whose cousin, Jean-Baptiste, was a director of the Company of the Indies. The cashier, Jean-Baptiste de Chabert, was to sleep on the premises beside a safe with a double lock, and admit nobody "whoever he or she might be" after 7 p.m. The partnership was for three months only and would liquidate on February 28, 1720.[37]

Law attended Roman Catholic Mass at least once in his life, on December 10, 1719, at the parish church of Saint-Roch in the rue Saint-Honoré.[38] There, six weeks earlier, Rebecca and William's newborn son John or Jean had been baptised a Catholic.[39] Most histories of the church report that John Law provided money to replace the wooden roof of the nave and choir with the present vault of stone.[40] That was but one instance of Law's philanthropy, both from his own pocket and from the bank and company.

As Law said later, he instructed Tencin to write to all the archdioceses and dioceses in France, to inquire about the condition of convents that were struggling because of the reduction of annuity interest. He provided the abbé with 600,000 livres to discharge poor debtors from the Paris prisons.[41] He persuaded the Regent a week later to abolish sales taxes on fish, cooking oil (olive, rapeseed, almond and walnut), suet, soap and playing cards and to buy out the small officials collecting them.[42] At the same time, Law bought out functionaries at Les Halles and other Paris markets and quays levying tariffs and fees on everything from firewood to poultry. Those offices, created during the war, included wine inspectors, beer tasters, cloth measurers, cart certifiers and barrel gaugers.[43] Such were John Law's first fiscal reforms to benefit the ordinary French public.

As for the indigent Jacobites, Law had in the summer paid the 400,000 livres in arrears of pension that had been owing to Queen Mary of Modena at her death on May 7, 1718. James III, who had left Spain after the failure of Ormonde's expedition and the defeat at Glen Shiel when "all I had in the world was 4,000 pistoles",[44] wrote to his late mother's treasurer, William Dicconson: "Had you not got the supply you mention, it had been intirely out of my power to have assisted you."[45] He instructed Dicconson to use Law's money to pay salaries and pensions, discharge tradesmen's bills and keep the Jacobite colony from starving.

Not wishing to embarrass Law by thanking him from enemy territory in Spain, James III waited until he was back in Italy. "You have sav'd the lives of many deserving countrymen of ours," James wrote in English on September 24. "By this last great and good deed of yours you have lay'd up store of merit both with God and man, it cannot fail of receiving its reward and you may be sure I shall be ever ready and desirous to give you proofs of my gratitude."[46] Law also lent his countrymen money to buy shares in the Company of the Indies.[47]

Nor were the rich forgotten. Law provided the Regent with 900,000 livres to buy for his heir, the duc de Chartres, the office of Governor of the Dauphiné.[48]

For the Regent's illegitimate son, Jean-Philippe, chevalier d'Orléans, Law bought the office of Grand Prior of the Knights of Malta.[49] (The Regent destined his out-of-wedlock sons for rich benefices in the Church or the celibate orders where they were not permitted to marry and encumber his legitimate estate.) The middle daughter, Louise-Adélaïde, installed that September 14 as abbess of the convent of Chelles east of the capital, subscribed for the convent in the share issues and ended up with at least 256 shares of the Company of the Indies.[50] For her younger sister, Charlotte-Aglaé, Mlle de Valois, at her marriage to the Prince of Modena the following February, Law was required to find a dowry of 1.3 million livres in French silver or piastres to be delivered to Genoa.[51] (She also was given or acquired herself five hundred shares in the company.)[52] In addition, this author has found traces of a speculation in lead and tin, involving the company, Law, the duc d'Orléans (both for himself and the King), the abbesse de Chelles, Prince Charles of Lorraine and the duc de Bourbon.[53]

The duc de Saint-Simon had some time earlier persuaded Law to provide 40,000 crowns for the restoration of the abbey of La Trappe, fifteen miles from the duke's estate at La Ferté-Vidame.[54] (The greatest gossip of all time, Saint-Simon treasured the abbey's rule of silence.) He now thought of himself. For all his scorn for the conduct of the Tencins, Saint-Simon submitted that autumn to the duc d'Orléans a bill of 500,000 livres for his father's expenses in fortifying and defending the citadel of Blaye on the Gironde during the Fronde which, with interest over nearly seventy years (*les intérêts tous les ans depuis*), could not have been less than a million. The Regent instructed Law to pay.[55]

This windfall allowed the duke not only to do some building at La Ferté-Vidame, which included the stables and offices that survive today (in poor repair) as the "little château".[56] On October 19, 1719, Saint-Simon bought a house with a porte-cochère leading to a front courtyard, rue Saint-Dominique in the faubourg Saint-Germain (for 100,395 livres) and, on November 11, for 54,766 livres extended the property north as far as rue de l'Université.[57]

Without Law's payment, Saint-Simon could not have undertaken for the Regent in 1721 an embassy to Spain that Dubois had devised (or so thought Saint-Simon) to ruin him. The duc de Saint-Simon could be forgiving of people who gave him large sums of money. His kindness to Law and Lady Katherine would otherwise be remarkable.

To bring some order to his empire, Law published a management plan for the Company of the Indies. He divided the business into two departments. "Commerce" comprised the mints, the commissioning and decommissioning of ships, merchandise, Louisiana, the East, the beaver trade, Guinea, Senegal and North Africa. The "Farms" handled the indirect taxes and excises. A schedule of work (*journal du travail*), also printed, established management committees for each sub-department and set the responsibilities of the different directors. Those men were expected to work from 8 a.m. to 8 p.m. each day but Sunday, with a break for a general meeting at noon and then dinner. Law himself chaired many of the committees.

As often with such things, neither scheme lasted long and both were revised at the meeting of the directors on October 2.[58] Ten days later, the business was transformed once again when the Regent handed the company responsibility for collecting the main direct taxes. The chief of those was the *taille*, a land and wealth tax, paid largely by the peasantry since clergy and nobility were exempt, which Law thought inefficient and unfair.[59] Hop reported on the 20th that the old tax collectors had been wont to pay themselves well, and Law would bring better management, or *meer menage*.[60]

Law somehow found time for several other projects. They included a fishing fleet and a scheme for the city of Rouen, two hundred miles downriver from Paris and the limit of navigation for ocean-going ships. Law intended, according to the British and Dutch press, to "make Rouen the greatest Staple [commercial port] in the Universe", by deepening and embanking the river up- and downstream of the town, and creating an industrial zone or suburbs on the left bank joined by a bridge.[61] His agent in the town was the Aberdeenshire banker Robert Arbuthnot, who was two years his senior, had fought on the Jacobite side at Killiecrankie in 1689, and then set up as a wholesaler (*marchand en gros*) in Rouen.[62]

In Paris, Law's agents were buying properties in the faubourg Saint-Honoré, the extension of the rue Saint-Honoré west of the place Vendôme and the old city walls, now planted with trees as boulevards. On September 16, they bought for 15,000 livres from a market-gardener named Guillaume Maugis a piece of ground of five *arpents* (acres), backing onto the Champs-Elysées, most of it damp meadow, with a livery stable, some thatched cottages and the main drain or sewer of the faubourg. Later that year, Law laid out 115,000 livres for two rows of shops and inns near the city gate or porte Saint-Honoré and was to acquire in 1720 at least eleven more parcels in the faubourg at a total cost of nearly 900,000 livres. What he planned for the site is not clear. One source speaks only of "a great building he intend[s] to have erected at the porte Saint-Honoré".[63]

Law commissioned from Nicolas Dulin, the architect of the Paris mint who was also buying up parcels of land in the faubourg, a plan for a 25-acre industrial estate, including a modern mint, foundries, forges, workshops, gardens and a chapel on a site then occupied by the royal tree nursery at Le Roule. There was to be a channel from the river and a grand entrance on the Champs-Elysées.[64] "All his plans are magnificent," wrote the Lyonnais Saint-Fonds, "yet he absolutely refuses to play the lord [*il ne veut point de monseigneur*]."[65]

His main project was to reassemble the palais Mazarin as a seat for the company and the bank. Paul-Jules, duc de Mazarin, was demanding the hôtel Langlée and a million livres for the eastern block and also that Law lodge him in luxury at the hôtel Gramont until he could build himself a replacement. While the negotiations dragged on, on September 24, Law bought six houses along the west side of the rue Vivienne, and began demolishing them to create an arcaded stock exchange to replace the Quincampoix.[66] In the end, Law was to buy with his own fortune the entire city block made by the rue Neuve-des-Petits-Champs, rue Vivienne, rue Colbert and rue de Richelieu. As he later told the duc de Bourbon, "I kept no account of the expenses I incurred in these building works since I had no intention of keeping these acquisitions, but rather designed to make a present of them to the Company of the Indies."[67]

He began rearranging the old-fashioned, even "gothic" palace.[68] He demolished the main entrance to make it larger. He ordered pictures from Italy and, in November, bought a library of some 35,000 volumes collected by the abbé Jean-Paul Bignon, the most powerful literary man in Paris and secretary of the Académie royale des sciences.

Bignon had on September 15 acquired the office of King's librarian (which his father had once held) for 126,000 livres.[69] To finance the purchase and to remove any suspicion of a conflict of interest, Bignon sold most of his own library to Law for between 200,000 and 250,000 livres.[70] The library included among its rarities first printed editions of Homer, Aristophanes and Pliny [71]

In November, the Venetian painter, Giovanni Antonio Pellegrini, passed through Paris on his way home. Sir Christopher Wren had wanted Pellegrini to paint the cupola of St Paul's Cathedral but was overruled by the church's trustees. The Venetian worked at houses in England, in Germany, at Antwerp and at The Hague, where he had just completed a series of ceiling and wall paintings for the Golden Room at the Mauritshuis. It is likely that the virtuoso Pierre Crozat, who had known Pellegrini at Venice, introduced him to Law. (Because he was not quite as rich as his brother Antoine, Pierre Crozat was known as "Crozat the Poor".)

Law commissioned Pellegrini to return after Easter to paint the ceiling of a first-floor gallery along the rue Richelieu that Mazarin had used to house his library. Law wanted the gallery for the shareholders' meetings of the company. Pellegrini asked for 100,000 livres.[72]

As always, Law was in a hurry and made the mistake of not staging a competition, or inviting any French artist to submit a sketch. In addition, probably again at Pierre Crozat's suggestion, Law asked Pellegrini's sister-in-law, Rosalba Carriera, to do portraits in pastels of Lady Katherine and their two children.[73] Rosalba was at least as good an artist as her brother-in-law, but each influenced the other, and it is hard to see which is the stronger of two great talents.

Also at this time, Law commissioned a rococo iron-and-brass balustrade for the main staircase from the rue de Richelieu. Beneath interlaced "JL" monograms, based on the engraved banknotes, cornucopias spill grains and fruits or coins and paper securities.[74] The balustrade was bought in the 1870s by Sir Richard Wallace, altered and enlarged to fit his house in Manchester Square, London and then given by his widow to the British public as part of the Wallace Collection. Possibly the work of the master ironsmith Guillaume Cressart in the nearby rue Sainte-Anne, it is the finest metalwork to survive from the Regency of the duc d'Orléans.[75]

One other transaction stands out. Law on October 31, 1719 bought the lot next door to the west of Stair's embassy in rue de Varenne, extending to 4,042 toises or over three acres, for 282,940 livres.[76] Simultaneously, Eleanor, marquise de Mézières acquired the embassy building. The Earl of Stair thus had his enemy over the wall and the chief Jacobite in Paris for landlady. He must have thought his wounds in his country's service counted for nothing.

Among Stair's heaviest debts was the security, originally £25,000, pledged to Lord Londonderry as his share in the East

India wagers. On November 4 he asked for grace to pay until the next Lady Day, that is March 25, 1720.[77] To Lord Stanhope he wrote on November 7, asking for home leave to sort out his affairs, sell part of his estate in Ayrshire and, as he told the chief minister, "prepare the rest to secure enough bread for my old age".[78]

King George refused. Instead, that autumn of 1719, the mission was expanded with the arrival of commissioners from the Board of Trade and Plantations, responsible for Britain's colonies, to resolve disputes with France over the borders of their respective plantations in North America left open at Utrecht. Meetings with French officials came to nothing and the commissioners, first Martin Bladen, MP for Stockbridge in Hampshire and then Daniel Pulteney, former envoy to Copenhagen, had little to do.

Bladen did not stay long but Pulteney, who arrived on November 25 and had just a single meeting with Law, lingered on, sending stock-market despatches back with the twice-weekly post to both the Board and the Secretary of State in London. (No doubt he had verbal instructions to do so.) He could do little on three pounds a day[79] but stalk the Quincampoix and an inn called the Ville de Londres, generally known as the "English ale house" or "English coffee house", whose Jacobite clientele was now swamped by Whig stockbrokers.

Pulteney is a familiar eighteenth-century British character type, expert in the arcana of finance and the regulation of trade. Arthur Onslow, a long-serving Speaker of the House of Commons, called him "a man of strong but not lively parts . . . but with all this, of most implacable hatred where he did hate".[80] Like almost everybody in this history, Pulteney intended to make a fortune from Law.

Others to come from London were Sir John Lambert, a Huguenot refugee who was a director of the South Sea Company, and John Drummond of Quarrel. Drummond told his brother on the eve of setting off from London that he had "some recommendations to Lord Stairs and Mr Law aboute an affair of some consequence to some gentlemen who are gainers by the Misizippi stock".[81] Those gentlemen, who were paying his expenses, included Sir Matthew Decker, reputed the richest citizen in England after the Duke and Duchess of Marlborough, and James Brydges, now Duke of Chandos. Chandos had bought twenty-one shares in the Company of the Indies through the Jacobite banker, Robert Arbuthnot, in Rouen but, in truth, he only liked to trade on privileged or inside information, which he expected Drummond to extract from Law.

Pulteney thought as many as 200,000 people had come into Paris. The British gazettes spoke of a quarter-million since October 13.[82] The hire of carriages had doubled and lodging was almost unobtainable. The *Daily Courant* reported from Paris on November 22: "All the stage coaches and other settled [regular] carriages from Lyons, Bourdeaux, and the several Provinces are Stock-jobbed and Passengers are made to pay treble the usual fare."[83] Over the weekend of November 18–19, the shares were bid up to 8,475 livres. Crawford surmised that that was because a great number of people from the provinces "arrived all att once in the rue Quincampoix on Saturday last [November 18]".[84]

On the following Saturday, November 25, John Law paid a visit in company to that street. According to Cornelis Hop, writing on November 27, he was recognised through an upper window and greeted by the speculators with cries of "Vive Laws!" Hop added: "Not without reason for no monarch up to now, however powerful, has brought the public such immense riches and in so short a time."[85]

The French newsletters and British gazettes embellished the story. The *Post-Boy* reported that Law "threw some handfuls of Guineas out of the window . . . to see how dirty People made themselves in scrambling for [them]".[86] That was certainly untrue. The shares, according to Giraudeau's quotations, rose to 9,325 livres on the Tuesday following and 9,375 on the Wednesday. It was reported that Law had sold 30 million livres in shares in a week to keep the price down.[87]

For all the foreigners converging on Paris, the French currency began to fall in November on the London and Amsterdam exchanges. Some investors were calling the top. Sir Matthew Decker wrote to John Drummond to sell, though Chandos resolved to stay in up to 11,000 livres.[88]

The duc de Bourbon was also cashing out. He had long been dissatisfied with the stable range for his horses and carriages at his estate of Chantilly, north-west of Paris. He could now afford to replace it. He broke ground in the summer of 1719 and paid the first mason's invoice (for 50,000 livres) on December 6.[89]

The Great Stables at Chantilly, which housed at one time more than two hundred hunters, saddle and carriage horses and twenty-three coaches, are the chief architectural relic of Law's moment in France. John Law had dreamed of a well-nourished working population and magazines of home and foreign goods. His monument is a cathedral to the horse.

For some time, James III had been urged to marry and find an heir for the royal house of Stuart. In the winter of 1717–18, he despatched from his exile at Urbino in Italy a young Irish officer in his service, Captain Charles Wogan, to investigate the courts of Europe for a bride.

Captain Wogan proposed Maria Clementina Sobieska, about to turn sixteen, the youngest daughter of Prince James Sobieski of Poland. Prince James as a young man in 1683 had fought beside his father, King John III, in the victory over the Turks before Vienna, but had been passed over for the throne of his country, which was subject to election.

Prince James was allied by blood and marriage to the ruling houses of Europe, was rich beyond calculation and was in favour of the match. In the marriage contract, signed at his dukedom of Ohlau/Oława in Silesia on July 22, 1718, the Prince granted the bridal couple an estate at Szawle/Šiauliai in what is now Lithuania and 600,000 livres invested in annuities of the French Crown, payable at the Paris Town Hall.

The match and dowry alarmed ministers in Britain, who persuaded their Habsburg allies in the Quadruple Alliance to obstruct the marriage. On her way to Italy, Clementina was arrested on imperial order and imprisoned in the castle of Innsbruck.

In the most gallant of all Jacobite exploits, Captain Wogan and three other Irish officers rescued her and brought her to Italy. James III was by then in Spain, hoping to join the rebellion in Britain, so the couple married first by proxy, at Bologna on May 9, 1719 and then, after the return of King James, at the episcopal palace of Montefiascone, near Viterbo, on September 3. Pope Clement XI had leased for them a house in the Piazza dei Santi Apostoli in Rome and given them a pension (of 10,000 scudi or £2,500) much smaller than once Louis XIV. Such open dependence on the papacy was unpopular with the Protestant Jacobites and grist to the anti-Catholic pamphleteers in England and Scotland.

With his letter to Law from Montefiascone of September 24, James III wrote a covering note to General Arthur Dillon, Wogan's commanding officer who had come to France with the Jacobite regiments (or "Wild Geese") in 1690 and was now James's resident representative to the Regent. (He got on badly with the Mézières, disapproving of Eleanor's "curiosity" or inquisitiveness.)[90]

"As from yourself," James wrote, "you may att the same time ask his [Law's] opinion as to the best way of my deploying those rents [annuities] on the hotel de ville. For the yearly rent [interest] of that part of the Queen's portion [dowry] is but a small matter and if possible I would be glad to turn it to the best advantage for her and join with it what little I have there [at the Paris Town Hall] my self." In other words, he wondered if he should convert Clementina's annuities into shares of the Company of the Indies.

James enjoined secrecy on Dillon, and stressed that "though I am in reallity master of [the 600,000 livres], I should make a very great scrupule of applying it to any other use but the Queen's att a time I can settle no jointur upon her."[91] On the same day, he wrote to his father-in-law to ask him to draw up a power of attorney not "in my name, which is by no means appropriate at this time" but in that of his late mother's treasurer, William Dicconson.

James urged haste because of the revolution in the French finances and lest he "lose a good opportunity to draw more profit from my money".[92] From his house arrest in Geneva, the Earl of Mar, who knew Law as well as anybody, was cautious: "He [Law] looks on himself now, as he well may, to be a ffrenchman, but he has a warme side I am sure to yr Maj: & yr cause & will I doubt not be glade to find a time wherein he could serve you, consistant with what is thought the interest of ffrance."[93]

It was not easy to deal with Prince James Sobieski, or his man of business in Paris, Jean-Marie de Pelucki. Naturally tedious, Pelucki was under subsidy or threat from Vienna and, ultimately, from London.[94] The Prince suggested sending Dicconson to Poland, to take his instructions in person, which exasperated James III. The Mississippi had penetrated the château de Saint-Germain. James's courtiers were weary to death of being poor and far from home and were keen to piggy-back their savings onto their master's investment. They comprised General Dillon; Dicconson; Father Lewis Innes or Inese, head of the Scots College at the Sorbonne; Dr John Ingleton, the King's confessor; Sir William Ellis, the controller of his household; and Sir David Nairne, his former secretary. The sum in question swelled towards one million livres.

At a meeting in Paris with Dicconson and Dillon in the first ten days of November, Law pointed out that the last subscription was full and that the Regent had announced there would be no more. None the less, Law promised to do what he could, while his brother William asked for the names of those exiles who had no pension or support.[95]

The King, writing back to Dicconson on December 4, approved of his servants' conduct but added: "After all this the lord knows when we shall get the Queen's 600m [600,000] livres. Peluchi is an odd sort of a gentleman, and my poor father in law is I believe the worst served prince in the world."[96] At the suggestion that Law be asked to issue shares on the security of Clementina's dowry, James on December 11 recoiled at the risk: "Tho' . . . I have had sufficient proofs of my father in laws honesty probity and generosity, yet the poor man affairs are so confused and intricat that I know not when he will be able to comply with what he stands engaged for."[97]

Once Pelucki had been cornered, and Clementina signed a back-dated power of attorney, a new obstacle appeared. Prince James's mother, the late Queen Marie Casimire of Poland, had granted her physician a pension of 4,000 livres per year, which Pelucki had constituted at the twentieth penny or 5 per cent on 80,000 livres of the Prince's fund at the Paris Hôtel de Ville. The physician's lawyers argued that the liquidation of Clementina's annuities at a time of falling interest rates would imperil the man's pension and secured a *saisie*, or attachment, on the entire fund. That was far fetched. Interest would have to fall to two-thirds of 1 per cent for the doctor's pension to be at risk ($600{,}000 \times 0.0066 = 3{,}960$).[98]

In vain did Dicconson, with his old bones and less than perfect French, make eight journeys from Saint-Germain to Paris.[99] Among others, Cardinal Filippo Antonio Gualterio, the protector of Scotland and then England at the Holy See in Rome, was ready to join his 80,000-livre holding in the French annuities to James's investment.[100] The Jacobite fund was approaching two million livres, which was hanging in the air because of a life annuity of four thousand.[101] The prospect of transforming the Jacobite court's finances, providing for Clementina and freeing James from dependence on the Pope, was slipping away.

At the same time, William Law's donation for the poor Jacobites of 124,000 livres was in the new 10,000-livre banknotes, and Dicconson needed to "get them cut into small ones before I can make my payments, & there is such a press at the banck on that account, that it will be some time ere I can get it done."[102] The 150-odd beneficiaries, ranging from Lord and Lady Dunkeld to "Tho: Butler the blind groome", were given beween 50 and 3,000 livres each.[103] These Jacobite comings and goings were noted by Stair's agents.

As the case wound on and Pelucki suffered a fire in his chimney, this happened. On or just before December 19, 1719, Dillon called on 888.75.1804 the 456.889.370.456.1430. Nobody else was present. The chains above read "Law" and "elder".

John Law gave Dillon 300,000 livres in banknotes "for 778 [James III] use". Dillon reported: "This present is from himself without 1371 [the duc d'Orléans] knowledge and he enjoyned me under the fastest tyes [strongest bonds] that none whosoever should know any thing of this matter except my cossen paul [James III]."[104] Law later asked Dillon not to call on him but on William, "where less notice would be taken".[105] Dillon, as was his habit, leapt to conclusions. He wrote to James, "On the whole you may I think be prettty sure that the person in question is willing to serve you . . . " while William Law "has been a declar'd well wisher for many years past".[106]

Law had crossed the Rubicon. This was not mere charity to destitute exiles or investing the dowry of a young girl. Nor was it a hedging of dynastic bets in the manner of Ilay and Argyll and many other British families. John Law had gone behind the back of the prince he admired and loved beyond all. He had placed his fate in the hands of an exiled court riddled with spies and double agents. What had caused the change?

Law had been showing signs of strain. At a meeting with Tam Crawford on the evening of November 28, he lost his temper, raging at an article in a gazette that called the Company of the Indies a "chimera" or illusion. (It was probably a taster for Defoe's pamphlet, *The Chimera; or the French Way of Paying National Debts Laid Open,* which appeared in the new year.)

"He was very angry," Crawford wrote on the 29th, and "spoke a little freely of our East India Company and of what it would suffer when its situation came to be made publick." Crawford advised Law against "beginning a paper war".[107] Law had broken the gambler's rule and shown feeling.

The next day, a Thursday, there was a concerted run on the bank.[108] It continued on Friday, December 1. Law regained his calm, issuing in the King's name a decree stating that all public payments must be made in banknotes. On the Saturday, he was elected honorary member of the Académie royale des sciences "by a plurality of votes".[109] (The honour was reserved for French subjects "expert in mathematics or physics".) The next day, Sunday, he and Lady Katherine acted as witnesses at the marriage of Fanny Oglethorpe to a Savoyard nobleman, Joseph-François Noyel de Bellegarde, marquis des Marches. She brought to the marriage a dowry of 800,000 livres and "the fruits that Louisiana brings", that is the produce of her share of the Mézières plantation.[110] For all her adventurous life, Fanny Oglethorpe yearned for the fathomless security of the married state. She passes out of the Jacobite correspondence, which loses some of its interest and all its charm.

On the Monday, Law set about squeezing the bears, devaluing the gold louis and silver crown and upvaluing the banknotes.

Those who had cashed banknotes into silver at the bank on the Thursday and Friday faced an immediate loss. Law scheduled two further devaluations to deter more redemptions. "Paper is today worth much more than silver," the diplomat Michel Amelot wrote that December 4 to Cardinal Gualterio.[111]

Cornelis Hop's sources told him that the bank had "begun to totter [*wagelen*]" and, but for Law's actions on the Friday, "the whole machine of the new arrangements would have crashed to earth and brought the ruin of the entire kingdom."[112] The shares slid, falling a quarter from their peak to 7,430 on December 14. The Quincampoix was awash with rumours that Stair, who had once promised to put a spoke in Law's wheel, was behind the run.

An unsigned letter of December 17 to Mar in Geneva from one of his Paris agents, almost certainly General Hamilton, reports Law's fury:

> The two Mr L--s were convinc'd . . . that England had a main hand in it, and even that Ld. S---rs had concurr'd a good deal in it, which you may believe could not fail to enrage these two gentlemen a good dale against him. The eldest complain'd warmly they say to the R[egen]t who sent for Lord S---rs and accus'd him very warmly; as he was going out from the R---t, Mr L--s was going in, but did not speak to him as he entr'd, he stay'd till Mr L--s came out, but he passed him again and avoided speaking to him.

If that was not enough, "the same gentleman told me a much odder story that there were several letters intercepted by which it appears there was some designe against Mr L--s life and that of his Brother too, the R--t has actually sent a guard of 12 Swiss to the house of the eldest."[113] (The French were convinced that Stair had sent assassins to waylay James III when he crossed France to take ship for Scotland in 1715, and were inclined to believe anything of him.)[114]

Stair's account of his audience with the Regent, in a letter to Craggs on December 11 in French (that is, to be shown to King George), began with a boast. He said he told the duc d'Orléans: "It is true that the subjects of the King my master have a very great weight of money here in this country, and it would have been simplicity itself for me to have it carried against the Bank."

Stair was constrained by the duelling code. He could not directly call Law a liar without provoking a challenge which, one way or another, would have ended his career. He employed the conditional, or what Touchstone in *As You Like It* calls the "only peacemaker", If.[115]

If it is true, Stair told the duc d'Orléans, that neither he nor any of King George's subjects had taken quantities of notes to be cashed at the bank, nor sold short the company's shares in the market, nor had he any communication with those who had organised the run, then Law's claims were "not only false, but the most atrocious and despicable calumny in the world" designed not only to mislead His Royal Highness in regard to himself but to bring the two courts to blows.[116]

As in his dispute with the prince de Conti, Stair sought to enlist his colleagues, succeeding with the Imperial Ambassador, Christof, Baron von Pentenrieder (or Penterriedter), but not with Hop.[117] He made an official protest to Dubois, and then the duc d'Orléans, about the procession of Jacobites through Law's house and the allegations of an assassination plot.[118] There is no report that he sent Law a challenge but he put about to the Regent and others that Law was a coward.[119]

On December 18, 1719, the Regent of France could bear the feuding Scotsmen no longer. That day, the abbé Dubois wrote to Lord Stanhope, complaining that their animosity was threatening the union of their two countries, and begging him and Mr Craggs to put it to rest. He said that the Regent was pained by the quarrel. Dubois knew which way the wind was blowing.[120]

Stanhope wrote back at once (the draft letter with his corrections survives in his papers now in Maidstone, Kent). He had little choice but to drop Stair. Had the Regent wanted to preserve Stair in his post, he would have reprimanded Law. Stanhope knew nothing of Law's present to James III or his commercial ambitions in Spain.

"Nothing," the Englishman wrote in French, "could be more troublesome to us than this wretched quarrel that has arisen between Lord Stair and Mr Law." While stating that King George was happy to leave the matter to Dubois's discretion, he gave a strong hint that there would be no objection to recalling the Earl of Stair.

Stanhope did not accept Stair's claim that Law was trying to break British credit. He believed that Law saw Anglo-French amity as the key to the success of his financial reforms. He wrote: "I know how far he has involved himself in the Treaty which was necessary to consolidate our union, and has regarded the union of the two crowns as the very foundation of his projects." As for Law's boasts, they were designed surely just to tease the Ambassador (*'pour picquer Mylord Stair personnellement'*).[121] With his characteristic vigour, Stanhope resolved to travel to Paris in the new year to find the root of the problem.

Law had other headaches. With the annual meeting of the Company of the Indies due on December 30, he needed to justify to the shareholders the high prices they had paid. To attract the annuitants to convert into the shares of the company, Law needed to offer, at the minimum, a dividend comparable to the 2 per cent return from land and houses. To maintain the shares at or near 10,000 livres, Law therefore had to offer for 1720 a dividend of not 60 livres but 200 livres.

In the week of Christmas, word spread that Law had some new magic up his sleeve. The mother shares climbed back over 9,000 livres. It did no harm at all that the bank was lending speculators cash to buy more shares, offering 2,500 livres at 2 per cent a year against the security of each share deposited.[122] The news reached Paris that, on December 5, King Philip V had given Alberoni three weeks to leave his kingdom. The war, which had been forgotten in the stock frenzy, would soon be over.

To reinforce the paper-money system, Law had an edict issued on the 21st to ban the use of silver for transactions over 10 livres and gold over 300 lives. "If Law has no courage of the heart," Stair wrote on the 23rd, "one must allow him courage of the imagination."[123]

On the 29th, a second edict annulled the tobacco monopoly and introduced in its place a free trade in tobacco products, such as existed then in Britain, which would be taxed at the port of entry. The growing of tobacco in most of France was outlawed. The import duties, at least on Virginia and Brazilian tobacco, were high.[124] It seems Law was more interested in immediate revenue than expanding the use of tobacco and its cultivation in the French colonies. The edict at least freed him from his impossible promise to supply the entire French market from Louisiana.

The second general assembly of the Company of the Indies took place at the bank headquarters in the rue Sainte-Avoye on the morning of Saturday, December 30, 1719. According to Duché de La Motte, who managed Mme de Tencin's syndicate in the rue Quincampoix, some twelve hundred shareholders attended and were given seats. At the head of the room, Law faced the Regent the length of a table seating seventy people, including the Regent's eldest son, the duc de Chartres, the duc de Bourbon, marshals of France, dukes and peers.

Among the thirty-one agenda items discussed and approved

was a dividend for 1720 of 200 livres per share.[125] If Law did present a profit and loss account, it was not reported at the time. (Later accounts forecast a profit for 1720 of between 80 and 100 million livres, just enough to pay the dividend on the shares held by the public, but not to invest in the business.) What was reported was agenda item 31 where, "to prevent abuses that may occur in the trading of company shares", the directors proposed opening offices to buy and sell shares at the bank.[126] (The first quotations at the bank windows in the new year were 9,700 livres (sell) and 9,650 (buy).)[127]

Law made a "pretty speech" and the Regent replied. "Then we clapped our hands," the chevalier de La Motte wrote to his friends, "just like at the theatre [*comme à la comédie*]."[128]

CHAPTER TEN

The Golden Fleece

What is it that a man cannot do, who hath all the wealth of France at his command?

CHANDOS[1]

John Law now found himself at the summit of power. In a little over twelve months, he had transformed the France of kings and convents into a corporation of his own devising, answerable to a board of directors and an assembly of shareholders.

The King's creditors, who for two centuries had lived from the taxation of the poor, were willy-nilly to risk their sons' expectations and their daughters' portions in domestic manufacture and far-flung colonial ventures. The silver money they had used since the Roman Empire (and in Provence, for some time before that) Law was about to abolish and replace with paper banknotes. It is unlikely that Law always had this scheme in mind. Under the pressure of events, it is what happened.

On January 4, 1720, the Regent appointed Law controller general of the King's finances, a position that in the previous reign Jean-Baptiste Colbert had turned into the greatest fief in the administration, managing not just the state's revenues and expenses, but also commerce, agriculture, industry and navigation. The salary was 36,000 livres. Argenson remained as chancellor, and was consoled with rich offices for his sons, including the lieutenant generalcy of police of Paris. "There was something of a murmur to see a foreigner as controller general," the duc de Saint-Simon wrote, "and all France given over to a project people were beginning greatly to mistrust. But the French will get used to anything [*les François s'accoutument à tout*]."[2]

On Saturday, January 6, the duc d'Orléans presented Law to the King at the Tuileries. Law's royal commission praised him "as much for the establishment of our Royal Bank . . . as . . . for the payment of our public debts, the increase in our State revenues and the relief of our people."[3] According to one report, the shares were posted that day at the bank window at 10,000 livres apiece. Saint-Fonds, who had given in to curiosity and travelled to Paris in December, wrote back that day to Lyons: "All the Mississippians are over the moon [*dans la joie de leur coeur*]."[4]

On January 8, the Earl of Stanhope arrived in Paris after a stormy crossing of the Channel in which his vessel lost two masts. He was preceded by news of the recapture of Pensacola, brought by Champmeslin's squadron and the *Duchesse-de-Noailles* conveying the Spanish prisoners of war.[5] Stanhope concluded that, if Law were a danger to Great Britain, to demand the duc d'Orléans dismiss his nearest adviser was a greater; and that the Earl of Stair had become a liability.

Stanhope called first on Law, rather than his ambassador.[6] Stair was mortified at the breach of protocol.[7] He raged to Craggs about both Law and Stanhope. To fight with one chief minister might be unfortunate, but with two it was careless. If Stair had had any chance of continuing in public service, he had now lost it.

Craggs replied to Stair, mixing rebuke and flattery in unequal portions. "I vow to God," he wrote from London on January 25/February 5,

> you put me in mind of what I have so often seen you do at play, that when once you began to lose, you would, though it was against all the sharpers and swordsmen in the den, play on for all you was worth. If a friend spoke or pulled you by the sleeve, nay, had a lady required your attendance, 'twas all one to the Earl of Stair – mistress, friend, estate, *tout au diable* [to hell with all of them!] rather than yield! And then one heard and agreed – This man has vast qualifications, he is a good soldier, an able statesman, a fine gentleman, an excellent scholar, an agreeable companion, *mais voicy qui gâte tout* [but that is what ruins everything].[8]

The Earl of Stair had offended so many people in France that few regretted him. To save his face, he was permitted to request his recall as soon as Spain acceded to the alliance.[9]

Though he no longer had the ear of the Regent, Stair continued to send hearsay despatches to London warning that Law was a "dangerous enemy" determined to break British prosperity. On February 14, he claimed to Craggs that Stanhope had promised Law to bring Lady Katherine's brother Banbury into the House of Lords, and give his son, Lord Wallingford (a more polished article), command of a regiment.[10] (That was untrue. Had Law asked for those things, King George would have granted them.) Stair's successor, Sir Robert Sutton, quibbled over salary and appointments, and Stair lingered in Paris till midsummer. Without money to pay his agents in France and Spain, his intelligence service decayed and the Jacobites found their way into the Palais-Royal.

Law and Lady Katherine now received a favour. Their son William, aged either thirteen or fourteen, was invited with other young gentlemen to dance in a ballet with the King in a theatre set up in his apartments at the Tuileries. The King's tutor, the maréchal de Villeroy, yearned to re-create the Versailles of his youth, where

Louis XIV had first danced a court ballet at the age of thirteen. Others, including the duc de Saint-Simon, thought Louis XV at ten too young to be exposed in such fashion.

Young William rehearsed the ballet, designed as a set of intermezzi in a revival of Thomas Corneille's *L'Inconnu* ("The Unknown"). Michel de Lalande supplied music and Claude Balon showed the boys the steps. Mary Catherine Law then fell ill with measles. That was the terror of the French court for it brought to mind the evil spring of 1712, when the disease killed the Dauphin and Dauphine and their elder son, the duc de Bretagne. William was sent home and the ballet was performed without him before the court and diplomatic corps on February 7 and on a further four days.[11] Ten of the boys dancing came down with measles, but not the King.[12]

The Laws had fallen into a palace trap. Enemies wanted to portray them as social climbers. A little later, but before February 21, the prince de Conti ordered young William out of the balcony of the Opéra. He proclaimed that he himself had little fear of the disease, but if the contagious boy did not leave, how could the prince de Conti go into the presence of the King?[13]

A word from Law did the rounds: "Those who arrive too late for a banquet are still offered a glass of Champagne."[14] It sounds a little French for John Law but no doubt he did nothing to discourage it.

Mary Drummond, Duchess of Perth in the Jacobite peerage, and a former waiting-woman of Queen Mary of Modena, wrote to her nephew Alexander, Duke of Gordon on January 9, 1720, urging him to come to Paris. (There were no grammar schools for girls in those days in Scotland, or indeed anywhere else, and women spelled as they pleased.) "Thogh the time of making great profiet by the missipie be over," she wrote, "I am told 40 per cent can still be made which is a great gaine which may encres the provisions of yr litle ladyes & leave the mor to Lord Huntly who I hope is a coming since I hear your Dutches leys in in may." (Cosmo Gordon, Marquess of Huntly, was born on April 27/May 8, 1720.)

She added: "If you resolve to come to paries order lodgings for a certain time a coache both being harde to be hade."[15] In Caen in Normandy, a correspondent wrote, "all our ladies are eager to see the rue Quincampoix. Their husbands are already there."[16]

Law needed to keep the shares high, so as to convert the King's annuities and sinecures as cheaply as possible.[17] He was writing options over the shares at 10,000 livres to maintain the ferment in the Quincampoix. Yet the surplus value or "goodwill" in the shares he had issued in such profusion hung over his head like a nightmare.

According to Nicolas Du Tot, who was taken on by the bank as an under-cashier that January of 1720, the shares in the Company of the Indies were worth about 4.55 billion livres more than the cash subscribed for them, or at least twice the annual product of France.[18] Should the company fall from favour, and investors cash in their shares, the banknotes issued would inundate the country. The bank had just received authority to issue new notes of 10, 100, 1,000 and 10,000 livres up to some 350 million livres. Half of the notes, dated January 1, were not engraved but printed, and the 10-livre notes have printed signatures. On January 28, the banknotes became legal tender throughout France.

The prices of meat and hay, under pressure from two hot and dry years, were rising. What alarmed foreign investors, and must have troubled Law, was the falling rate of exchange for French money. That was not supposed to happen on the paper-money island of *Money and Trade* back in 1705. According to George Middleton, who after William Law's move to Paris handled the Law brothers' business in London, the exchange rate of French bills into sterling was 24 at sight on January 7 by the English calendar, 23⅛ on January 14, and 22¼ on the 18th.[19] (The values are British pence per French écu or crown.)

Law needed to find new wealth to make real the goodwill in the shares and before the Quincampoix woke from its riot. As early as September 1719, at the time of the share issues, he had told Secretary Crawford he was thinking of amalgamating bank and company and taking over the colony of Saint-Domingue in the Caribbean.[20]

The Company of the Indies was gaining scale. It was buying or laying down merchant ships at Bayonne, Brest, Le Havre, Saint-Malo, Nantes and Marseilles and also Hamburg, Amsterdam, Bristol, Deptford and London. The company fleet, which ran to about thirty-eight vessels (excluding brigantines and lighters) at the end of 1719, was about to double.

The new vessels, predominantly Dutch-style flûtes of between 300 and 500 tons burthen, were named or renamed after rivers (the *Seine, Loire, Gironde . . .*); exotic animals (*Eléphant, Chameau, Dromadaire . . .*); and figures of classical myth (*Apollon, Minerve, Junon . . .*). The shipyards demanded high prices and, it was said, scrimped at their carpentry. Of the *Diane*, 330 tons, built for Law at Deptford for a campaign to take possession as a victualling station of the island of Mauritius in the Indian Ocean that had been abandoned by the Dutch in 1710, one of her captains wrote that she was "top-heavy and absolutely impossible to steer".[21] Her British-built companion on the voyage, the *Atalante*, 500 tons, rolled and shipped water.[22]

Those ships, once equipped in the Atlantic ports of France, would not be short of passengers and cargo. The boom in the shares in the autumn of 1719 had set off a flurry of new companies and partnerships to establish plantations in Louisiana, and on a larger scale. The investors included, alongside financiers and "Mississippians" such as Antoine Chaumont and his wife, Catherine Barré, such noblemen as the ducs de Guiche and de La Force. The first entered a partnership with Law for a tobacco plantation, while the second, with associates including Law, planned to invest 1.2 million livres to develop a concession of twelve leagues square or 1,300 square miles.

Alert to charges that he was depopulating France, Law in the new year sent agents to Switzerland and the Palatinate to recruit settlers and artisans for his spread on the Arkansas.[23]

Law had other schemes afoot, including a bank in Pensacola, where transactions in the transatlantic world might be settled with American silver without recourse to Cadiz.[24] Another was in Iran, where an embassy from the hard-pressed Shah Sultan Hussein had fascinated and diverted Paris in the last year of the old King's life. A treaty, favourable to French trade, was signed at Versailles on August 13, 1715. The Iranian envoy, Mehmet Riza Beg, who was nothing more than mayor of Erivan in the southern Caucasus, had overstepped his instructions and then sold or lost Louis XIV's presents. Reaching Erivan, and rather than face the music at the court in Isfahan, he killed himself.

None the less, Shah Sultan Hussein, who possessed no navy, was eager that France despatch a flotilla of ships to dislodge his enemy, the Sultan of Muscat, from the mouth of the Persian Gulf, and was said to be ready to pay for eight to ten vessels to be built in France. In Paris, the matter was taken up by the Navy Council under the comte de Toulouse, and then by Dubois and Law.

After many adventures, two French missions arrived in Iran in 1717 and 1720. Ange Gardane, seigneur de Sainte-Croix, had an audience with Shah Sultan Hussein at Qazvin on May 26, 1718. The Shah told him that he wished to "honour France above all the other nations" and gave him as consulate a palace in Isfahan that could house two hundred men and two or three ships' cargoes. Gardane also received the right to make wine and brandy for export from the famous vines of Shiraz.[25] In March, 1720, a 280-ton Malouin vessel, the *Indien*, docked at Bandar Abbas, the port for Isfahan, with a company cargo of European metal, rice, sugar, cardamom and baled goods from Bengal.[26] In May, Law despatched a new-built frigate, the *Sirène*, with orders to call at Bandar Abbas.

A second mission, under Etienne Padéry, a Greek who had been interpreter for Mehmet Riza, arrived in Iran in August with powers to negotiate over the Muscat expedition. Padéry carried plans, provided by Law, for the proposed warships.[27]

Back on December 9, the *Dauphin* set sail from Lorient to establish a lodge or factory at Beit al-Faqih, north of the port of Mocha on the Red Sea coast of Yemen, to buy coffee. With the *Solide*, which sailed for India on December 14, Law sent more than four million livres in silver bullion to clear the company's debts at Surat and on the Malabar Coast, principal source of pepper, to re-establish the factory at Masulipatam, on the Coromandel Coast, famous for its woodblock-printed chintzes, and buy cargoes in Bengal.[28] (When the vessel anchored at Pondicherry on July 2, 1720, she brought pay for the soldiers who drank themselves senseless for months on Colombo and Goa arrack.)[29] The directors also ordered Pondicherry to open trade with Manila in the Philippine Islands, and promised a second victualling station on the island of Poulo-Condore (modern Côn Son) off the coast of Vietnam, to be called île d'Orléans.

Two days before the departure of the *Solide*, a convoy of the *Diligent*, *Joseph-Royal* and the *Neptune* sailed from Saint-Malo to deal in contraband with Peru, a Spanish possession. That was a dangerous but lucrative trade that the Malouins had made a speciality. The purpose was in part to acquire American silver to buy cargoes in India, where the company's factories found it hard to sell French goods other than light cloths and metal. What the Indian merchants wanted was silver, either in ingots or minted into Spanish piastres or rupees.

Those ships would not return for three years[30] and the other plans would be just as slow to bear fruit. Law was working on an instant enterprise. It was kept secret at the time, and would have remained so, but for scraps of evidence scattered about Europe that make sense when put together. Those are: a printed account of a lawsuit in the library of the University of Seville in which Law appears in the guise of "Monsiur Lauu" and "Monsiur Labuu"; a copy of a letter in Provence from Law to an Irish merchant banker in Madrid, Edward Crean or O'Crean; a company prospectus in the British diplomatic archives; and a remark by the Regent at the company meeting of February 22 that was recorded (but not understood) by both Pulteney and Cornelis Hop. It concerned one of the most valuable businesses in the world but risked dynamiting the post-war settlement.

John Law was not an operations man. He had but one system, at cards and in business, which was to bet his winnings: *paroli*, *sept-et-le-va*, *quinze-et-le-va* and, now, *trente-et-le-va*.*

The fine-woolled sheep known as the merino, whose origins are lost but may one day be unearthed in Syria or North Africa, was as important to the wealth of Spain as her American territories. In the Middle Ages, as the Christian kingdoms gained the upper hand over the Muslim civilisation of Andalusia, they opened up new pasturelands south of the Tagus in the dry provinces of Extremadura and La Mancha. Favoured by the Crown, the ecclesiastical and lay flock owners of a guild known as the Mesta de los Pastores de Castilla grazed their flocks in the hot lowlands over the winter and then drove them north along royal rights-of-way to summer pasture in the mountains of León, Segovia and Rioja. On the drive north, the sheep were sheared and the fleeces washed once in running water.

* That is, paying *trente-et-une fois et le vade*, "thirty-one times plus the stake" or thirty-two times.

The meagre grazing and hard drift, the skill of the Spanish shepherds and the bravery of their dogs combined to make wool that was fine, lustrous and strong. By the turn of the sixteenth century, Spanish wool was displacing English in the weaving towns of the Low Countries. After disruptions in the seventeenth century, the Spanish merino flock expanded again to supply fine-textile looms in France, Holland and England. By 1720, Spain was exporting in the region of 6 million pounds of washed wool a year which was taxed at the ports at a rate of roughly 10 per cent of value.

Those taxes were collected by private collectors or "tax farmers" under a lease or *arrendamiento* in the period 1700–13, and again after 1730, but between those dates were under the direct operation of the Royal Domain or Real Hacienda. The tax take was rising.[31] Miguel de Arizcun (1691–1741), who received the lease in 1731 as a way to discharge debts to him as the principal naval munitioner, made himself a great nobleman and left his heirs a flock of 29,000 head, which would not shame a sheep station in Australia.

In 1741, José del Campillo, newly appointed by Philip V as finance minister and determined to end the tax farms, wrote: "The wool farm is a scandal, allowed to decay over successive five-year periods. It is worth at least 11 million reals, but Don Miguel de Arizcun has it for five and a half. He well knows that he has an outrageous deal [*reconoció bien esta enormidad*], since voluntarily and without anybody pressing him he paid another three million at the last renewal, which should have opened the eyes of people at the Ministry had not every one of them been fast asleep."[32]

Unlike Louisiana, the Spanish wool-tax farm was a going concern with strong markets. There was no need to clear cypress swamps, attract, press or enslave labour, or ship supplies and produce across an ocean. Once established in Spain, the Company of the Indies could seek out other opportunities in the Atlantic ports and Spanish America.

There were obstacles. To gain a share of the tax farm, Law would need Spanish allies and patrons and must outbid Spanish interests. He must exploit the influence of the Jacobites at the Spanish court and run the risk of embarrassing the Regent. Above all, he needed amity between the Bourbon crowns that a war had been fought to forestall. He risked conflict with the promoters of the English alliance: the abbé Dubois, who was looking for a chance to undermine him, and his chief protector, the Earl of Stanhope. Even by John Law's standards, the project was perilous.

Edward Crean, from a family in the west of Ireland, had come to Madrid with the Wild Geese. Together with another Irish exile, Francis Arthur, he set up in business, dealing in this and that, and advancing money to the Irish officers in Spanish service. A leading figure in the Jacobite society of Madrid, he was banker to the Duke of Ormonde, James III's resident at the court of Philip V and Elizabeth Farnese.[33] Business being business, Crean had been invaluable to Stanhope in clothing and feeding the British prisoners of war after the surrender at Brihuega in 1710.[34]

Crean's nephews, John and Rémy Carroll (Carryl, O'Carroll), acted for their uncle in Paris. It is they who seemed to have brought the wool-farm scheme to Law.[35] Law authorised Crean to draw on him to buy influence at the court of Madrid.

To make the payments in Spanish currency, Crean offered bills on Law to the financier Don Simón de Cancela. On January 8 and 27, 1720, Crean gave Cancela letters on Paris for 42,206½ pesos or pieces-of-eight, payable in gold and silver in sixty days from date plus fourteen days' grace and fifteen for transit to Paris.[36] That was about £10,000 sterling. Some time later, Law told James III's resident in Paris, Arthur Dillon, that he had "former obligations" to the Duke of Ormonde and would send him 150,000 livres "to sustain his character [at the Spanish court] and ease peter's [James III's] burden".[37]

The British South Sea Company was also founded to trade in the Spanish Empire. Back in 1711, the British wartime administration of Robert Harley, unable to pay some £9 millions in bills from naval, transport and munitions contractors, and the City merchants who had bought the invoices at a discount, allowed those creditors to incorporate under the catch-all name of "The Governor and Company of the Merchants of Great Britain Trading to the South Seas and other Parts of America and for encouraging the Fishery". The company was granted a British monopoly of trade along the coasts of South America; the right to issue shares up to the face value of the money owed them; and some £550,000 a year in interest plus £8,000 for management expenses.

Law imitated this scheme in the financing of the Company of the West in 1717, with this difference. The King of France was in possession of Louisiana, while the Spanish in America did their utmost to exclude British vessels. It was not clear how the South Sea Company would carry on its trade. The books did not close on the share issue until Christmas, 1713. The discount on the IOUs passed to the shares which remained below their issue price of £100 until late 1716.[38]

By one of the Treaties of Utrecht in 1713, Philip V granted the British Crown the so-called *Asiento*, the "privilege" or contract to supply the Spanish American colonies with African slaves. Up to then, the contract had been in the hands of the French Company of Guinea, which included Antoine Crozat and Samuel Bernard, who had made a good trade stocking the slave ships with contraband goods and bringing back American silver. Queen Anne transferred the *Asiento* to the South Sea.

Between 1714 and 1719, the South Sea Company transported

from West Africa more than twelve thousand men, women and children to Buenos Aires, Caracas, Cartagena, Portobello on the Isthmus, Vera Cruz in Mexico and Havana and Santiago de Cuba, paying a duty of 33⅓ pesos per "piece" to the Spanish Crown. In addition, the company sent three merchantmen under licence to trade duty-free at the fairs of Cartagena, Portobello and Vera Cruz.

Two of the merchant ships, the *Royal Prince* and the *Elizabeth*, made profits for the South Sea shareholders. The third, the *Bedford*, a heavy warship on loan from the Royal Navy, came into Cartagena roads in early 1716 with pipes of *aguardiente* (rum) lashed to her decks. The harbour inspectors smelled a rat, measured the cargo, found it four times larger than permitted under the treaty, and impounded the surplus. After the battle of Cape Passaro in August, 1718, Spanish colonial officials seized all the South Sea Company's warehouses or "factories", account books, vessels, cargoes, unsold slaves, weapons, ammunition and cash in Spanish America.[39] The South Sea Company lost its commerce.

In business, it is generally a good idea to follow fashion and, even where it is not, business people will still do so. According to evidence to Parliament, John Blunt, son of a Baptist shoemaker from Rochester and one of the founding directors of the South Sea, presented to Lord Stanhope in late 1719 a plan to take over all of the British National Debt.[40] A pamphlet entitled *The Secret History of the South Sea Scheme*, printed in 1723, reported that the success of the Mississippi in Paris in 1719 so "inflamed" Blunt's mind that he was often heard to say: "That as Mr LAW had taken his pattern from him . . . he would now improve on what was done in France and out-do Mr LAW."[41]

There was a difference. Law had full powers, with only the Regent, his many enemies and popular insurrection to restrain him. Blunt needed the approval of both Houses of the British Parliament, populated by landed men with no love of the City of

London, and the blessing of the King's Court. Law could make gifts and loans as he pleased. Blunt had to bribe. For that reason, the South Sea scheme has come down to us a "meer fraud" (Adam Smith) and was later in the century called the "South Sea Bubble", in the old figurative meaning of "swindle".[42]

On January 22, 1720, the Chancellor of the Exchequer, John Aislabie, presented the debt-conversion plan to the House of Commons. Secretary Craggs spoke in support. The House refused to be hurried and resolved that the other moneyed companies should be invited to better the offer. "Our great men lookt as if thunderstruck," one witness reported, "and one of them in particular, turned as pale as my cravate."[43] East India demurred but the Bank of England entered the auction. (That is not something the Old Lady likes to recollect.)

After two rounds of bidding, the Commons on February 2 chose the South Sea and authorised the company to issue shares to buy out £31.5 million in war debts, and pay £7.5 million for the privilege. The company's cashier, Robert Knight, secretly issued free options over £574,500 face value in South Sea shares to MPs, peers and the King's favourites.[44] After such an outlay, South Sea needed a boom in its stock to make the conversion of the debts profitable for the company.

The company and its supporters appealed to love of country. Defoe, whose pamphlet *The Chimera: or, the French Way of Paying National Debts* appeared at the turn of the year,[45] warned that the slow pace of Parliamentary proceedings would leave Britain indebted long after John Law had used "air and shadow" to disencumber France. "Tyranny," he wrote, "has the whip hand of Liberty."[46] To placate Spain, the duc d'Orléans and Dubois were pressing Stanhope to make good his old offer to return Gibraltar. There was uproar in Parliament and among the public. Pulteney reported that Law was hoping to retain Pensacola, and that he intended to drive the British out of the sugar trade in the West Indies.[47]

Law's friends in London responded by re-publishing his *Money and Trade*. An elegant production, it carried a tag from Cicero's speech in 52 BC in defence of T. Annius Milo: "Happy the land that welcomes this hero if we are so ungrateful as to banish him and so wretched as to lose him!"* It is unlikely that Law, who was trying to suppress a French translation of the essay in preparation in Holland, approved the publication.

The shares of South Sea began to climb. The Duke of Chandos, forever chasing some financial novelty, wrote to John Drummond in Paris on February 8/19: "The South Sea Comp . . . is rose from about 120 to 160; & in all probability will come up to 200." He thought it could "become one of the best funds in Europe to lay one's money out in".[48] (Law had not replied to any of his letters.) South Sea was pulling East India in its slipstream, up to £216 by February 16/27, which would oblige Law to make supplementary payments (or "margin calls" as they are now known) on his wager with Londonderry. At that price, Law was facing a loss of £36,000.

France and England could not shake off their habit of rivalry, but it must now be discharged not with cannon and blood but in Exchange Alley and the Quincampoix, and in the dockyards. That February, the directors of the Company of the Indies instructed George Middleton to order two colossal armed merchantmen from the Thames yards, as heavy as any sailed by the English East India and in view of the City.

Middleton, who had already ordered four vessels for the company and sent them (and their surly crews) down the river, began negotiating with Thomas Brinsden or Bronsdon at Deptford for a vessel of 1,075 tons' burthen and with William Hoare, "a very

* *O terram illam beatam, quae hunc virum exceperit: hanc ingratam, si eiecerit: miseram, si amiserit*. M. Tullius Cicero, *Pro Milone*, 105.

clever understanding fellow", at Limehouse Hole for a ship of 970 tons (later 860 tons).

Those giants, 120 and 115 feet long in the keel and 40 in the beam, would mount from sixty-six to seventy guns. Middleton feared the British ministry "will perhaps not allow ships of that force to be built for any foreign Prince",[49] but that proved not to be the case. The tenders came back at around £10,000 each with copper sheathing and masts, and they would take six months to build. Middleton asked William to order no more, for "if more are talk'd of it will raise [the] price upon us".[50] These vessels, christened the *Lys* and the *Bourbon*, were among the largest ever commissioned by the Company of the Indies. Both made three voyages to India before the *Lys* was wrecked and the *Bourbon* scrapped in 1732.

Middleton's letters show a man clinging to a native caution as to a spar in a heaving sea. George Middleton was not a man of wide experience, had not travelled, did not well read or write French. Under the influence of Ilay and Arbuthnot, he had sold South Sea and East India short and lost, and was now resolved not to risk more.[51] As January gave way to February, he fell prey to foreboding at the scale of his advances to the Laws. In early January, William Law's factor in Edinburgh, Andrew Barclay, had bought for him the estate of Errol in Perthshire from David Carnegie, Earl of Northesk, for the sum of £15,500. Even before sending the money north, Middleton was "in advance" with William alone "very near seventy thousand pounds", which was eight times the partnership capital he inherited at John Campbell's death.[52]

The exchange continued against France, falling to 20⅞ pence per crown on January 28 by the English calendar and 19½ on February 11. The payment by Law of £30,000 in sterling as his security for the East India wager with Londonderry did not help. "I am doubtfull [afraid] he'll be a loser on that bargain," Middleton wrote to William on February 15/26.[53]

The French minister in Geneva, Pierre Cadiot de La Closure, reported on January 30 that the town's merchants were withdrawing their funds from France. He feared that panic might spread to France itself. "This is how armies break," he wrote.[54] On February 3, Sir John Lambert, the South Sea director who was selling the Mississippi shares short in the Quincampoix, was given three days to leave Paris.

Since the Middle Ages, the abbey of Saint-Germain-des-Prés on the left bank of the Seine enjoyed the right to hold an annual fair to its profit on a piece of low ground to the south of the church. There, to the west of the modern marché Saint-Germain, booths were arranged under a roof in criss-cross rows. As in all medieval fairs, commerce mingled with spectacle, and auctioneers and hucksters competed with jugglers, acrobats, clowns, tightrope walkers and dancers, animal shows, confectioners, stage performances and gaming. The fair began in early February, continued through Lent and ended on the Sunday before Easter, Palm Sunday.

In 1697, Louis XIV expelled from Paris the troupe of Italian comedians when he was told their piece called *La fausse prude* insulted Mme de Maintenon. The Parisian public was not to be deprived of Harlequin and Scaramouche, and Frenchified versions of the Italian comedy took root at the fairs of Saint-Germain and, in the summer, Saint-Laurent. (The Regent had since allowed the Italians to return.)

That year of 1720, the fair of Saint-Germain began on February 5 and "Monsieur Francisque" (the Flemish acrobat François Moylin or Molin) hired Alain-René LeSage, Jacques-Philippe d'Orneval and Louis Fuzelier to write Italian-style comedies.[55]

In one of them, *Arlequin, roi des Ogres,* Harlequin is rounded up by the police with two hundred other young men and women and sent from La Rochelle "to found honest families in the Mississippi".

He is shipwrecked and washed up on an island populated by giants. In a prologue entitled *Le diable d'Argent*, the Devil of Money praises his favourite, Folly, for her "marvellous discernment" in distributing his largesse. Her predecessor, Sense, selected for the Devil's bounty people he did not care for at all.[56]

After the shows, there was play which that year ran heavy.[57] The principal high rollers were Londonderry, back in town, and Joseph Gage, renewing their rivalry. On the first evening, the stakes were set at 120,000 livres at a time.[58]

John Pye, who witnessed the game, was a Jacobite exile. Back in the autumn of 1716, while standing guard at the Tower of London, he had proposed inviting like-minded men to dinner, overpowering the loyalist garrison and turning the Tower's ordnance on the Bank of England.[59] King James and the Earl of Mar killed the scheme and Pye took himself to Paris the following year.[60] He was acting, as both stockbroker and secret agent, for Thomas Wentworth, Earl of Strafford, who like many Tories had fallen into disgrace in Hanoverian Britain and had drifted over to the Stuarts.

Pye had little to do but haunt the Quincampoix, "so faint without eating that I have been ready to drop, and what is worse with all the ill success imaginable", or "saunter round the fair which cost nothing for my Primes [wagers and option trades] have quite stript me".[61] The slush penetrated his boots. He begged Lady Strafford in London to "send Irish John" to the Quaker shoemaker at St Martin's [-in-the-Fields] church for two pairs of shoes with leather heels (for the court) and two with wooden (for the Quincampoix) "soon as possible, for I am dead for want of them[62] .... Everything is so cursed deer I cannot live."[63]

In his letters to the Straffords, Pye describes English noblemen bunking down in bath-houses, and paying 100 sols for the "bear ordinary" (fixed-price dinner) at the Ville de Londres and 60–70 pistoles a month for a coach and "they'l not keep them 3 hour for anybody, no more than the Baingo [bath-houses], who are always full."[64] The streets were jammed with coaches. "Paris is full of an unheard-of mass of people," Elisabeth Charlotte wrote to her half-sister, Luise, in Germany on February 20. "It is astonishing that the streets don't run with piss."[65]

Lord Strafford, who thought Law the "greatest subject in Europe", wanted to come to Paris and be taken in to see the Regent on Jacobite business. Pye saw Law on February 23 and asked if he had answered the earl. Law was civil, but as always at this time he was "in great hast . . . and answered in walking, No, I have not had time."[66]

Law's liabilities, the shares and the banknotes, were destroying each other and him. The more shares the bank bought to support the price, the more banknotes passed into circulation, amounting to an extra 800 million livres by the third week of February.[67]

Law could no longer hold to the belief, as in *Money and Trade* back in 1705, that paper money would from its greater convenience displace gold and silver coin in trade and investment. On the contrary, Paris was losing its taste for banknotes and was hoarding gold and silver coin. Pulteney reported on January 27 that the graziers at Poissy, the livestock market on the western outskirts of Paris, were refusing to accept banknotes and would not drive the cattle to market unless the city butchers paid in coin.[68]

Like all modern politicians (most recently, the United States Administration of Richard M. Nixon in 1971), Law resolved that paper would have to be imposed and the precious metals stripped of their use as money. He needed the French to bring their gold and silver out of hiding and deposit it at the bank, where it would provide a measure of backing to the banknotes and buy foreign currencies for trade. To that end, he was ready to use every measure of the absolute government established by Louis XIV.

In a flurry of decrees, the coinage was devalued and the mint fee altered. The Company of the Indies was given the right to search houses for hoarded coin. "People are fearful of receiving a visit and are carrying their money to the bank," Caumartin de Boissy wrote to his sister in the country.[69]

Investors were selling the shares and banknotes for any kind of portable asset that could be concealed or sent abroad. On February 4, a royal edict banned the import and wearing of diamonds, pearls and other precious stones from March 1 by all but the bishops of the Church. It was presented as a sumptuary measure of the sort that had been all too common during Louis XIV's wars. William Beauvoir wrote to his wife in England that the decree was designed to prevent "the wives of stockjobbers and other common little things [*petites roturières*] outshining the ladies of the Court".[70] A raid the following year on the convent of the Grands-Augustins revealed that a syndicate that included the duc de La Force had bought up large volumes of tea, loaf sugar, blue ginger, china root and other valuable metals, drugs and spices.[71]

One of the drawbacks of the precious metals for the statesman, as Law had written years before in *Money and Trade*, was that they migrate between money and ornament. On February 18, a second decree, also presented as a measure against ostentation, proscribed the making of gold and silver plate above a certain weight except for the churches or orders of chivalry.[72] There must have been a rage for patens and chalices, for a third decree on February 27 applied the ban to the churches and religious communities. The decree of February 27 also forbade all holdings of gold and silver over 500 livres in value, and payments in precious metal above 100 livres.[73] Du Tot, who was loyal to Law, wrote in regret: "One sees nothing of Mr Law's principles in these operations. He is just doing what he can to attract precious metal cash, but he has to contend with fear. People sense that he wants cash and for that reason they hoard it."[74]

Acting at the limit of fiscal experience, without precedent or guide, Law made mistakes, contradicted himself, reversed course. He became prickly and short-tempered (Saint-Simon) and quarrelled with Cornelis Hop over an article in the *Haarlemsche Courant*, that used the bugbear word "chimera". The Regent reassured the Dutchman with a laugh, but it is an odd state of affairs when a prince must clear up after his servant.[75]

Still the annuitants were refusing to convert into shares. On February 6, Law had set a deadline of July 1 for them to convert or face a reduction of their interest coupon to 2 per cent (the same as the dividend return on the shares at 10,000). On the 21st, Law issued a pamphlet that set out to demolish the old system of public credit and justify his financial scheme. It was also printed in the February issue of the *Nouveau Mercure* at the beginning of March.

The pamphlet was written by the abbé Jean Terrasson, a learned Lyonnais and colleague of Law in the Académie royale des sciences, but dictated and corrected by Law.[76] It is Law's most eloquent denunciation of French annuity finance and the class that depended on it.

"One of the principal laws of Government," the author wrote, "is not to allow capital . . . to become a bolt-hole or port in a storm but to function as one of the springs of commerce."[77] Lazy, timid and lacking in public spirit, the annuitants discouraged others from investing in commerce. The irony was that the "new System of Finance" (that is, John Law) had restored the annuities to solvency and made them pay but only to extinguish them in favour of "a new species of property, where your capital is of use to the entire body of the nation and your returns will grow".[78]

The letter uses the philosophic term "System" (spelled *Systême*) to describe Law's financial regime.[79] The word, which is Greek, had come with René Descartes and others in the seventeenth century to denote a doctrine or theory that can reconcile disparate or jarring moral, astronomical or physical phenomena.

Law's scheme was no mere better way of managing payments and receipts, such as able statesmen in the past had achieved, but "a suite of ideas that reinforce one another, and make more and more evident the principle from which they originate".[80] Like many scientific words put to new service, System when applied to finance gave off an air of charlatanry. Law's reforms became a System at the precise moment when they ceased to be systematic.

At the same time, the directors of the Company of the West summoned shareholders to an extraordinary general meeting. "They are promising us miracles," Saint-Fonds wrote home to Lyons on February 19. "They had better be, because confidence is dreadfully shaken. The System, and in consequence the entire kingdom, is in danger."[81]

The meeting was held on Thursday, February 22 and was packed. Though Law had at last gained vacant possession of the remainder of the palais Mazarin (by a contract dated February 12),[82] the meeting seems to have been held at the rue Sainte-Avoye.

The miracles consisted in merging bank and company, which were anyway by now indistinguishable, limiting further issues of banknotes and placing the King of France or state at arm's length. The company bought out the King's 100,000 shares at 9,000 livres each, a third payable in 1720 and the rest in monthly payments of five million livres over ten years. The company/bank was forbidden to lend to the King. In addition, the bank would cease to support the shares which would be allowed to find their own level.

In a speech that Cornelis Hop called "very vigorous and clear", the Regent said the peace treaty with Spain would be followed by a congress. He said he would ensure the company enjoyed as much advantage in Spanish commerce as any other nation, adding that he would stand firm on that (*qu'il tiendra bon là-dessus*), at which he was applauded.[83]

The effect soon dissipated. Chandos, writing from London on February 18/29, wondered "whether the Comp. could hope for the same protection & support, when the King was not a partner with them". Still, the King would do his best to keep the company in health till he was paid off. He cursed himself for sending his money to France. With the fall in the exchange rate, even if Mississippi went to 12,500 livres he would still be a "considerable loser" on his 110 shares.[84] Meanwhile, South Sea had climbed to £187. In the way of these things, Chandos blamed John Drummond.

The shares were not going to 12,500. The closing of the bank window showed there were few buyers other than John Law. The shares fell over the next eight days from the support price of 9,925 livres to 8,500 livres on March 1.[85] Whether under pressure from shareholders, or because he could not afford the loss of prestige, Law altered course. On March 5, he announced that a new office would convert shares into banknotes at 9,000 livres (and vice versa) from March 20.[86]

A week later, on March 11, he declared a devaluation for the gold and silver coinage against banknotes. After May 1, nobody but the regulated goldsmiths might own gold in coin or bullion and, after January 1, 1721, silver except in coins worth less than a crown.[87] Law thus condemned himself to issuing more and more banknotes to acquire France's treasure of gold and silver. On the 26th, the bank received permission to print another 320 million livres in 1,000-livre and 10,000-livre notes.

To some, it seemed Paris was disintegrating. Beside the foreigners and provincials crowding the rue Quincampoix were absconded apprentices and runaway footmen and scullions. On March 10, a royal ordinance stated that beggars, vagabonds and masterless people found in the capital (and elsewhere) after eight days would be arrested and those of suitable age transported to the colonies, including Louisiana.[88] The latest in a series of repressive measures against beggary going back to the 1650s, this policy would be disastrous for Law and the colony.

Jean Buvat, a copyist at the King's library across the rue Vivienne from the palais Mazarin, recorded in his journal that spring a spate of violent crimes. In an entry for March 14, he reported that a servant of a certain General de Busca, sent from the faubourg Saint-Germain across the river to the Quincampoix with 100,000 livres in shares, had been found below the pont Royal, cut into pieces.[89]

On the 19th, Elisabeth Charlotte wrote to London: "Theft and murder are horribly in vogue here."[90] John Drummond reassured Chandos that his shares (worth a million livres) were "in a strong box within a large iron chest and next my bed".[91] By the time the Quincampoix was closed by a royal ordinance of March 22, according to Buvat, there had been eleven murders for shares or bank bills.[92]

The Saint-Germain Fair was coming to an end and those who had lost money at play had run out of time to recover it. One loser was a young man from a great family of the Low Countries, related to the Habsburg Emperor and Elisabeth Charlotte among others. He was Antoine-Joseph, comte de Horn, aged twenty-one or twenty-two, a cavalry captain reduced to half-pay, not so much by reason of his youth, as the duc de Saint-Simon wrote, "but for his exceptionally bad character".[93]

On Friday, March 22, Horn and two accomplices, a Piedmontese officer also on half-pay known in French as Laurent de Mille, and one other, made an appointment with a broker early in the morning at an inn named the l'Epée de Bois ("the Wooden Sword"), in a narrow and dark ragpickers' lane called rue de Venise between rue Quincampoix and rue Saint-Martin.

Retiring to an upstairs room, Horn and Mille stabbed the broker with a dagger, bought for eighteen sols the night before, and took his bloody notecase containing more than 150,000 livres in banknotes and securities.[94] In the tumult, the third man who was on the stairs escaped, but Horn and Mille were caught and condemned to be broken alive on the wheel in the place de Grève in front of the Paris Town Hall. At the trial, it transpired that during the Saint-Germain Fair (which ended on the 24th) Horn had attempted to rob a banker's clerk at sword-point.

Horn's relations pleaded for his life and then, when that proved too much, to spare him the torture and spectacle of a commoner's death. They may have felt a premonition of the republican guillotine of 1793–4. The duc de Saint-Simon argued that were this worthless young man to die like a commoner, his relations would not be accepted into convents for five generations, which was both ludicrous and untrue.[95]

The nobility blamed Law, yet Elisabeth Charlotte did not intervene and her son was "inflexible" (Cornelis Hop).[96] When somebody reminded the Regent that he, too, was the count's relation, he replied: "Well then, gentlemen, we shall share the disgrace."[97] The poor, or what Elisabeth Charlotte called the *pöbel* or mob, wanted the assassins' blood.[98]

At 4 p.m. on Tuesday, March 26, the sentence was carried out. Each man was lashed to a St Andrew's cross and his limbs and chest smashed with a hammer. He was then exposed on a wheel set horizontally on an upright post. Mille died quickly, but Horn survived for a little under an hour. The unknown third man was broken in effigy. The boy King was out that day paying visits and in the crowd some hoped and some feared he would stop in the place de Grève and pardon the comte de Horn.[99]

The Quincampoix was closed down on the day of the murder. To the blare of a trumpet, the King's sworn crier, Marc-Antoine

Pasquier, read out the King's ordinance banning any trade in securities in the street. Guards took up station at each end. The stockbrokers dispersed into the neighbouring alleys. A Scottish newsletter-writer in Paris, who went by the pen name "Gyllé", wrote to Giles's Coffee House in Pall Mall, London: "I know the wise fools on your syde when they hear this [will say] that all here is ruined, but they are much mistaken. It was a nest of kneaves [or "theaves"] and rogues who cheated and tricked one another every day; and it will be soon on a regular, and better foot than ever."[100]

When Lord Stanhope returned to Paris on March 26, to discourage the Regent of France from offering King Philip Gibraltar, he does not appear to have called on Law. Both Stair and the Austrian Minister, Baron Christoph Pentenrieder, badgered him that Law's System was upsetting the balance of forces in Europe. (Stair was working on his own plan for a Law-style national bank in Britain.) Stanhope was less agitated but wrote to Vienna on April 1: "I am reluctant to make a firm prediction of the outcome of this System but, if it does become established and take root, as Mr de Pentenridter appears to believe, I make the bold prediction that even the Emperor, England and Holland combined will not be in state to oppose France, not even if we have the King of Prussia with us."[101] To reinforce Dubois, Stanhope and King George seconded an Austrian suggestion that the abbé be given the rich archbishopric of Cambrai. Dubois asked Law to provide a letter for 50,000 scudi at Rome, "to the order of someone I shall name to you".[102]

Law was offering wagers that the exchange rate would spring back in France's favour.[103] Pulteney was of the same opinion and took charge of 68,000 livres of Stanhope's money to hold for the rise. Lucy, Lady Stanhope sent John Drummond a "diamond necklace and a pair of pear-shaped ear-rings" to sell at the high prices for jewels in Paris.[104]

*

Law's second letter in defence of the System, dated March 11, appeared in the March issue of the *Nouveau Mercure* in early April. Here, Law/Terrasson moved on from the annuitants or *rentiers* to the nature of credit itself.

If a private merchant could borrow money to increase his stock in trade, and hence his profit, how much more so the King in the absolute government of France? Yet rather than deploy this credit in war, or in disrupting the ordinary commerce of private individuals, the King had, in conformity with the principles of the new "System", conferred his credit on a corporation in which "the whole nation becomes a body of traders, for whom the Royal Bank is the till [*caisse*]".[105] Unlike the *rentier*, who could prosper even when the state did not, the new investor could profit only from "the wealth and happiness of the whole kingdom".[106] It was this congruence of interest between the Sovereign and public that was the distinguishing feature of the new System.[107]

As to the unpopular measures of the last month, the author made no apologies. The liberal ideas of *Money and Trade* were now in the service of absolute government. Hoarding was a sort of treason. The purpose of money was not to immobilise but to circulate wealth, and "you are not permitted to use it for another purpose".[108] The sovereign knew better than the people: "The law is needed to save people from themselves."[109]

For a time, silver poured into the bank. Cornelis Hop predicted on March 29 that soon the Company of the Indies would be "master of all the coin and bullion" in France.[110] Yet the reckoning could not be long delayed. In London, the South Sea Company or what Chandos called "our growing Mississippi here" was attracting Europe's footloose money.[111] Beau Wilson's cousin Katherine Windham wrote from her house in Essex to her son, Ashe, at Felbrigg in Norfolk on April 4, 1720 (April 15 in Paris): "Sou Sea is all the talke, & fashion, the Ladys sell their jewells to bye & happy are they that are in." She was buying options on the stock at £500. "I [shall] be a rich widow at last. Never was such a time to get mony as now."[112]

The South Sea public share offering, or "first money subscription," on April 14/25, was filled by about 1,500 buyers "in an Hour's Time".[113] The company offered for sale 22,500 shares at £300 apiece to raise £6.75 million. Taking their cue from Law, the directors asked for only £60 down and the rest in eight instalments every two months.

Gamblers could sell the partly paid share at a profit without ever having to find cash for the remaining instalments. Even Law's Jacobite investors, such as the Oglethorpe sisters and Lady Mary Herbert, turned their attention to London.

The Parlement de Paris, alarmed at Law's decree to reduce the interest on all annuities, public and private, to 2 per cent broke what it called a "respectful silence" and issued on April 17 a remonstrance, the first since the Bed of Justice in 1718.[114] Reports that Law was talking of bringing interest down to 1 per cent added to the urgency.[115] The Parlements of Besançon, Dijon, Rouen and Toulouse also remonstrated.

The Paris Parlement argued that the edict reducing interest would ruin persons and institutions that depended on fixed incomes and were suffering from the rise in prices caused by the flood of paper money. Those included religious communities, domestic servants in retirement, men of letters, fathers of large families, minors and, above all, the authors of the remonstrance: "We cannot dissimulate, Sire, that this edict will be the complete ruin of all the magistrates of the kingdom."[116] Marriage would soon go out of style, the workhouses be overrun and schools and colleges close for want of pupils.

Pulteney thought it a foolish performance and sent to London the remonstrance from Dijon, where the *procureur général* or attorney general advised his colleagues to "plead the cause less of the rich than of the poor".[117] None of the remonstrances had any effect. Citing the Bed of Justice of August, 1718, Argenson as chancellor obtained letters patent on the 24th to enforce the interest-rate edict.

The magistrates had their revenge. On or just before April 22,[118] a special corps of constables known in the files of the lieutenant generalcy of police as "the new brigades", "the archers of Mississippi" or "the archers of the Company of the Indies" began enforcing the edict of March 10 and sweeping up beggars and vagrants in the poor districts of Paris. Hop reported that young Marc-Pierre Argenson, the lieutenant general of police, offered a pistole or ten livres for every person brought to the police headquarters at the Châtelet. Buvat says the bounty was paid by the Company of the Indies.[119]

The Bastille files tell of some of the people picked up: a seventy-year-old man, begging with the permission of the churchwardens at Saint-Germain l'Auxerrois, a crossing-sweeper in rue du Crucifix Saint-Jacques, two young sisters from Pontarlier in Franche-Comté who had come to Paris to witness the execution of their father's murderers, the widow of a button-maker who seemed to the constables "badly dressed".[120]

Jean Le Fevre, a musician and composer formerly in the service of the Archbishop of Embrun, returned from business in Rennes to find that his wife, Jeanne Joüe, out shopping with her two small children near Saint-Nicolas-des-Champs at 1 p.m. on April 25 had been dragged off to the Salpêtrière.[121] Witnesses in Orléans testified that a certain Lecompte and his accomplices, without the authority of any but the local director of the Company of the Indies, were kidnapping people "of all ages and sexes" for transportation to Louisiana. Antoine Rousseau, an usher, said that in the rue de l'Oye, he saw the accused and two other men of large build, all in woollen hats, dragging off two young persons of about fifteen years of age. A troop of women set upon them and freed the young people. (Lecompte was arrested and condemned to the pillory.)[122]

On Monday, April 29, Paris had had enough. According to Jean Gilbert Delisle, a clerk at the Palais de Justice who kept both minutes of proceedings and a journal, riots broke out in the rue Saint-Antoine in the east of Paris, and near the pont Notre-Dame. Men and women armed with swords, staves, billets of wood and paving stones fell on the archers, pursued them into private houses, or clubbed them to death in the gutters. One wounded man, carried to the ancient hospital of the Hôtel-Dieu by the cathedral, was killed by the inmates. The battles continued in the rue du Roi-de-Sicile the next morning, April 30.[123]

The Parlement convened that afternoon, and was able to set terms for the Argensons. In a royal ordinance, issued on May 3, the King accepted that certain of the archers "might abuse their authority". The constables must henceforth only carry out their duty in their units, wearing uniform and a shoulder-belt (*bandoulière*) and under their appointed officers. They would also be paid each week in advance.[124]

Late as it was, Law tried to mitigate the damage done to the company. On May 9, the Regency Council announced that "vagabonds, vagrants, smugglers and criminals would no longer be sent to Louisiana" but to the other French colonies.

The decree said that the Company of the Indies had informed the King that there were blacks enough in the territory for the work of clearing and cultivation, while the concession-holders refused to engage "the vagabonds and criminals, condemned to serve in the colony, idle people of bad character, less fitted to labour than to corrupt the other colonists and even the natives of the country, who are a mild and biddable nation, industrious, hard-working and devoted to the French".[125] In May 1720 there were approximately 450 Africans in Louisiana.[126] Bienville, himself a slaveholder, later blamed the colony's stagnation on the company's failure to furnish black slaves in number but it is impossible that more Africans could have been fed, let alone sold and put to work.[127]

Law's credit was vanishing. The darling of the Quincampoix and the saviour of France of the winter was with the spring one of the most hated men in the country.

For all the aspersions on his nerve and firmness, John Law did not give up. On May 19, he issued another letter explaining the System, the third, the longest and the last.[128]

In it, Law gave short shrift to the remonstrances of the Parlement de Paris and other towns, but instead set out, as well as he had ever done, his belief in the purely instrumental character of money. Coins and banknotes were alike mere tokens for the transfer of title to property – *signes de transmission* – which belonged to the King rather like the highways of the realm, not because the King wanted to possess them but to prevent another from doing so.[129]

Both in that argument, and in his belief that the wealth of France lay in its labourers and traders, Law foreshadows Adam Smith. What Smith would have opposed was Law's belief that the royal monopoly he had created was superior to competing private companies.[130] Anyway, Law and Terrasson continued, "the System has been established . . . I dare say that neither King nor Public is able to destroy it. It has so engulfed all the components of the state, that it is impossible that they can be disentangled."[131]

On that May 19, Pentecost or Whit Sunday, the Parlement de Paris went into recess. In the course of the day, the marquis de Dangeau heard that Law had been working with the Regent on a "decree of great importance".[132] The decree, with a long preamble drafted by Law, was approved on May 21.

Law argued that the devaluation of the coin on March 11 meant that it was necessary also to devalue the shares and banknotes "to sustain a just proportion with the coins and other assets of the Kingdom".[133] The shares would at once be reduced from 9,000 livres to 8,000 livres and then in stages to 5,000 livres by December 1; and the banknotes by 20 per cent at once and then in stages to half their face value by that day.

Though his reasoning is far from clear, Law probably wished to bring the speculation down to earth, stabilise the exchange rate of his new money into foreign currencies and prevent the rise in prices spreading from luxuries to provisions. According to Du Tot, there were some 2.1 billion livres in banknotes in circulation on the day of the edict, or roughly twice Law's estimate for the metal money earlier in the spring.[134] Those would now come roughly into parity.

Some merchant writers and professional investors thought it perfectly logical. Chandos, who had all but lost interest in the Mississippi, thought the edict "will in the end (if I judge aright . . .) prove not amiss for France in general".[135] As Law argued, nobody was poorer by the reduction in the shares, since the dividends would be paid at the same rate, while the holder of banknotes would have the same quantity of precious metal.

France thought otherwise. With the publication of the decree the next day, Wednesday, May 22, men and women converged on the bank, which opened in the afternoon to cash banknotes at the new parity, that is, at 20 per cent below face value.[136]

According to Dangeau, there was no other conversation but the edict. "Highly seditious" leaflets and scurrilous verses were thrown into shops and houses.[137] A printed broadside by Law had no effect.[138] At the notaries, there was at least one dispute over which rate to use for the banknotes.[139] The duc de Saint-Simon thought the bank "could not cover its arse".[140] When it was slow to open on the morning of Saturday, May 25, a crowd threw stones through the windows.[141] What shares were traded changed hands at half the support-price or between 4,000 livres and 5,000 livres apiece.[142]

The English in Paris took the decree as an affront. Pulteney was beside himself with rage and grief. "It is in every one's mouth that they are robbed of half they are worth, that it is the most notorious cheat that ever was committed, & that it is very plain now that Mr Law has as little capacity as integrity," he wrote to Craggs in London on the 24th. He was convinced that Law's "chief design . . . was against the English", both as investors in the company and holders of the banknotes "besides very considerable remittances have lately been made from England hither for the benefit of the expected rise in the Exchange." By a stroke of John Law's pen, Pulteney had lost 10,000 livres borrowed on his own account and 13,600 livres belonging to Lord Stanhope.[143] To lose the chief minister money is never a helpful stage in a British public career.

That Saturday evening, Law attended the Italian Comedy at the Palais-Royal theatre in the Regent's box "and appeared to the spectators entirely calm".[144] The following day, Sunday, Crean's bill on him for 40,000 piastres was protested.[145]

Early on Monday the 27th, the Parlement de Paris, recalled early from vacation, convened at the Palais de Justice. They sent delegates to the Louvre to seek the King's permission to "throw themselves at his feet", that is, remonstrate against the May 21 edict. The lawyer Edmond Barbier said the intention was to parade on foot to an audience with the King. Unlike at the Bed of Justice in 1718, the people of Paris would now march with them.[146]

At the Palais-Royal, Law found the duc d'Orléans "in a dreadful state".[147] The Regent hated every sort of unpleasantness. The Regency Council was in a recess and he sought advice from one of his courtiers, Louis Antoine de Pardaillan de Gondrin, duc d'Antin (1665–1736). The duc d'Antin was the legitimate son of one of the great King's mistresses, Mme de Montespan, and had never lived it down. Well-educated, conventional and reserved, he had a precocious sense of his own superfluousness and that of the nobility in general. The Regency Council, on which he served, was, he wrote, "like reading the gazette a few days early".[148] He thought the world of Law and had done well by him.

According to his own account, partly verified by Law's later recollection, Antin accused Law of breaking faith with the public in devaluing the banknotes which, he reminded the Scotsman, "the King had declared invariable whatever the mutations in gold and silver". He said Law had redeemed the King's debts only to default on half of them, "which has caused many to despair and ruined business confidence".[149] Antin was upset while Law was stunned by his friend's desertion, which he compared to a tennis ball coming at an unexpected angle. The duc de Bourbon, who had been in the country at the time of the May 21 edict, sided with his fellow peer. The Regent agreed to annul the edict and despatched the Secretary of State, the marquis de La Vrillière, to inform the Parlement. It was now about noon.

To halt the run on the bank, and to absorb the surplus banknotes, Law agreed to sell a billion livres in Town Hall annuities at 2 per cent per annum and thus restore a part of the financial regime that he despised. The bank would be closed so that inspectors could strike a balance sheet. The meeting then broke for dinner. In the afternoon, five delegates arrived from the Parlement and haggled with the Regent about the rate on the new annuities. They demanded the pre-war rate of 5 per cent. The Regent conceded 2.5 per cent.[150] An edict stating that the banknotes would revert to their face value went out to the printers and was known that evening all over town.[151]

Law continued to work as if he had nothing to fear, but his opponents, and particularly the marquis d'Argenson, were gathering against him. On the 29th, the inspectors went into the bank. That evening, after one hundred and forty-five days in office, Law was dismissed as controller general. A major of the Swiss Guards, Jean-Victor de Besenval, and sixteen men were quartered at the hôtel Langlée "to prevent any mishap occurring to him". Law later said that he believed "he would lose his head".[152] The control general of finances was split into five departments under different officials, chief among them the marquis d'Argenson. The shares fell to below 3,000 livres.[153]

Since the bank had doubled its balance sheet in three months, it surely did not have assets enough to withstand a run. Yet the inspectors proved diffident in their work. Contradictory reports seeped out from the hôtel de Nevers. The inspectors had found thirteen hundred millions in cash (Barbier) or, more likely, forty-nine millions in cash and bullion (Buvat).[154] A document in the Law papers at Maastricht, dated that May 29 and presumably presented to the inspectors, shows Law had transferred to the Royal Treasury (and the treasury of the Estates of Brittany) 841 million livres, with funds at the bank to cover payments of a further 110 million. It gives an impression of good order but is little use on its own.[155]

Law's rivals were unable to organise. According to his elder son, René-Louis, Argenson had authority to send Law to the Bastille but hesitated.[156] The Regent summoned Antoine Pâris. According to his younger brother La Montagne, Antoine feared retaliation from Law and his friends and confined himself to generalities.[157] As Law later told Montesquieu, "people were pressing schemes on the duc d'Orléans that did not convince him."[158] Law's supporters gathered. Matthieu Marais, an advocate at the Parlement, wrote in his journal: "All the great lords, who have done so well from him, are protecting him. M. le Duc [de Bourbon] has been often to see him. Today he is triumphant, tomorrow cast down."[159]

Sensing that the tide had turned, on the 30th the duc de La Force accompanied Law to the Palais-Royal. The Regent refused to receive them.

On Friday the 31st, Dangeau reported that it was being said "that the bank is in much better state than was claimed and there is plenty of money."[160] At some point during the day, the Regent authorised one of his gentlemen, the comte de Sassenage, to bring Law to him by way of a back stairs. They were together half an hour. The duc d'Orléans was cold, but permitted Law to present himself at court the next day, June 1, where the Regent said to the assembled courtiers: "You are to leave me alone with Mr Law."[161] An edict was issued permitting the French to possess as much gold and silver as they wished. That evening, worn out after ten days of anxiety, the Regent suffered a fit of vomiting.[162]

On June 2, Law was named director general of the bank and the company, and "*superintendant* of the commerce of France". The Swiss Guards were withdrawn from the hôtel Langlée.

The Venetian party, consisting of Antonio Pellegrini, his wife Angela, her sister Rosalba Carriera, and their mother Alba Foresti, had arrived in Paris with their friends and servants in four coaches by way of Lyons in April. The ladies stayed with Pierre Crozat at his house at the end of rue Richelieu by the boulevard or rampart, while Pellegrini was given rooms at the hôtel de Nevers. He worked up an oil sketch for the ceiling, called a *modello*, and showed it to Law, on or before June 10.[163] Pellegrini began work at once, and worked for eighty days (*ottanta mattine*).[164]

The ceiling or rather soffit, which was 130 feet long, 27 feet wide and 4 feet in depth from the cornice to the top of the vault,[165] was the greatest artistic commission of the French Regency.

The work, sometimes called *La Félicité de La France* ("Prosperity of France"), is lost, but not completely. The connoisseur, Anne-

Claude, comte de Caylus, whom Law had helped on his tour of Italy in 1715, published the written programme or scheme for the ceiling. (He said he found it in the Royal Library but he may, in reality, have been its author.)[166] The young French artist François Le Moyne, working from the programme but not to the correct scale, did his own sketch and had it engraved. He wanted to show his ambition and ability and, as Caylus put it, "to hint at the injustice of giving foreigners commissions that nationals could just as well carry out".[167]

In addition, at least three scenes of Pellegrini's *modello* have survived. One of the pieces, an oil sketch of 25 by 14 inches on canvas that had belonged to Queen Victoria's eldest daughter, the Princess Royal, was attributed to Pellegrini in 2014. It is now in the Musée du Petit Palais in Paris, Room 10.

On the left, the naked figures of the Seine and Mississippi embrace beneath the figure of Friendship, while between them a cornucopia spills its plenty. In the centre, as Caylus's programme states, "On the banks of the Seine, one sees a cart harnessed for two horses, on which men are loading merchandise discharged from ships arriving from Louisiana."

Somewhere, perhaps, in a family collection in Venice or in the bachelors' passage of some English country house is Pellegrini's sketch for the scene above the entrance door to the gallery. There "the Stock Exchange is represented by a portico about which diverse races in their national costumes [*avec leur habillemens*] do business one with another."[168]

CHAPTER ELEVEN

888

He that put the calf in the weall, is the fittest person to take her out again.

"GYLLÉ"[1]

That summer in Marseilles, a week's journey by post coach from Paris, there occurred a catastrophe that has become bound up with the story of John Law. On June 20, 1720, in the rue Belle-Table, in the parish of Saint-Martin, Marie Dauplan, laundress, aged about fifty-eight, died with an ulcer on her lip.

She was followed to the grave on June 28, by Michel Cresp, tailor, place du Palais, parish of Les Accoules, at the age of forty-five, and the next day by his wife, Anne Durand, who had gone to her parents at la Trinité.[2]

In those days, Marseilles was the second or third city of France, where some 75,000 people crowded into narrow streets to the north and east sides of an ancient harbour. With pretensions to republican independence, the town was subjugated by Louis XIV in 1660 and then won over with privileges. A new town was created to the east, with an esplanade then known as the Cours, lined with fountains and private houses, and an arsenal along the south side of the harbour to serve as base for the fleet of galleys and the convicts and prisoners of war who were impressed to crew them.

In 1669, Marseilles was made a free port and the only town in France permitted to trade directly with certain treaty ports of the Ottoman Empire, known as the Echelles du Levant, for the Indian painted or printed chintzes, Iranian silks and raw and spun cotton which the men and women of Europe required.

In those ports of the Levant or "East" – Istanbul, Smyrna, Alexandretta, Tripoli, Beirut, Sidon and Alexandria – and in their hinterlands, bubonic plague was endemic.

People knew nothing of the disease, its causes, treatment or carriers, nor suspected that the fleas that carried the plague bacillus thrived in the damp warmth of baled cotton and silk. They had learned through centuries of experience that isolation worked to restrict it.

At the eastern ports where the French had trading rights, merchants acting as French consuls issued each skipper with a bill of health without which he could not enter home port. A quarantine station, known as the Nouvelles Infirmeries, on the model of those at Venice, Genoa, Livorno and La Spezia, was completed in 1668. By 1720, practices had become slack. A memoir of July, 1721 speaks of quarantines handing over dirty linen to their wives at the gates, and taking food and drink and returning the napkins, cups and dishes.[3] Stock in trade carried by passengers, called *pacotille*, passed through the grille of the parlour. According to the memoir, the station was a place of pleasure parties and assignations,

The government of Provence had been for some time in the hands of Voltaire's patron, Claude-Hector-Louis, duc de Villars and marshal of France. As a soldier, Villars had given the Duke of Marlborough a bloody nose at Malplaquet in 1709 and defeated Prince Eugene at Denain in 1712. He had come to loll on his laurels. He did not think it his duty to visit even Aix-en-Provence, capital of his province, complaining that the Regent would not give him leave to travel except, it seems, to his estate south of Paris, famous today as Vaux-le-Vicomte.

From there, as late as July 28, he was writing to Cardin Lebret, the Intendant of Provence, of his harvest of apricots, figs and melons.[4] Likewise Debret, the power in the province who was also first president of the Parlement of Aix, preferred after June to direct movements from Aix and then Saint-Rémy-de-Provence and Barbentane.

The weight of town government thus fell on the *viguier* or chief magistrate, Alphonse de Fortia, marquis de Pilles and four aldermen known as *échevins*, elected from among the merchants and each serving two years in rotation. Those were Jean-Baptiste Estelle, who had served as a merchant and consul at Sidon; Jean-Pierre Moustier, whose father had served as alderman before him; Balthazar Dieudé and Jean-Baptiste Audimar. They were supported by the royal prosecutor and "orator" of the town hall, N. N. Pichatty de Croissante, who left a journal that was printed the following year. In charge of the clergy was the bishop of Marseilles, Henri-François-Xavier de Belsunce, scourge of the Jansenists.

The Town Hall had three concerns in the never-to-be-forgotten summer of 1720. The first was Law's financial policy. The aldermen were used to paper instruments for settling long-distance mercantile invoices but distrusted the banknotes that had begun to circulate in the town in March. On March 14, they complained to the duc d'Orléans that grain ships from the Levant were diverting to Malta and Messina for fear "of being paid in banknotes if they come to France".[5]

What troubled them also was Law's taste for monopoly and the threat to their darling Levant trade. Back in 1719, their commercial representative in Paris, Alexandre Grégoire, wrote that with the merger of the eastern trading companies with the Company of the West, "lo!, trade will be in single hand."[6] An edict of March 30,

1720 to protect domestic weavers permitted Marseilles to continue to import silk and cotton stuffs but only for re-export. At the request of the Company of the Indies, the use in the town of such fine fabrics to make clothes or furniture and their sale in France was forbidden.[7] This edict (repealed on September 20) was later used to blame Law, for in some way having caused the smuggling into Marseilles of infected textiles. In 1726, Lebret was still claiming that plague broke out "just as soon as Mr Law, who thought he knew everything [*qui ne doutait de rien*], outlawed chintzes [*indiennes*] in the town of Marseilles".[8]

The third concern, which had nothing to do with John Law but much to do with the commercial interests of the aldermen, was a Dutch-built 250-ton flûte named the *Grand-Saint-Antoine.* She had anchored on Saturday, May 25 after a voyage of ten months at the island of Pomègues in the road, and was seeking permission to unload a cargo of raw and spun cotton, silk, fabrics, goat- and camel-hair, leather, wax and tapestry, insured for 400,000 livres.[9]

The vessel was owned in quarters by the skipper, Jean-Baptiste Chataud, the Sidon firm of Guilhermy, Chaud & Co. (whose partners were his brothers-in-law), Antoine Bourguet, and Alderman Estelle and these had a share in the cargo. It was already known in Marseilles that, in the words of Pichatty de Croissante, "since the beginning of March the plague was present in most of the maritime ports or Echelles of Palestine and Syria."[10]

Chataud, aged thirty-nine, was an experienced skipper and had made at least ten voyages to the Levant. The *Grand-Saint-Antoine* had sailed from Marseilles on July 22, 1719 for Smyrna, sold her cargo there, picked up a shipment of wheat for Cyprus, then put in at Sidon where she took on five hundred sacks of cinders as ballast. Having received a clean bill of health (*patente nette*) from the French Consul, she coasted twenty miles to the south to Tyre to take on further cargo. At Tripoli (in what is now Lebanon) she boarded several passengers for Cyprus: five Turks, a Greek, two Armenians and some Frenchmen. Provided with a second clean bill, dated March 25, she set off on April 3, 1720 for Cyprus. On April 5, one of the Turks died and was buried at sea. Arrived at Cyprus on April 7, Chataud put his Greek and Turkish passengers ashore, took on more cargo and a third clean bill of health and sailed for France on the 18th.

On the return voyage, two sailors died and then the surgeon and two further sailors. Beset by bad weather, Chataud put in at Livorno, south of Genoa, where the bodies were examined by the surgeon of the health office, Marcellino Ittieri, who diagnosed a "malignant pestilential fever" caused by poor diet, which reassured Chataud and the crew.[11] None the less, the port authorities refused permission for the vessel to enter, buried the bodies at the quarantine station and burned their clothes on the shore. On May 19, Chataud sailed for Marseilles but anchored off Brusc, near Toulon, apparently to consult his fellow owners. Whatever passed between them, he put in at Pomègues on the 25th.

On May 29 and June 3, the inspectorate of health of the port (comprising merchants) permitted the fine cargo and bulk cotton to be transferred to the Infirmeries to be purged in the sunshine and open air, and set a quarantine of forty days from the time the last bale was landed. The cargoes of four other vessels that arrived with a plague warning (*patente brutte*) were also admitted. On June 14, the passengers of the *Grand-Saint-Antoine* were allowed to leave quarantine.

In the course of the next two weeks at the Infirmeries, a cabin boy from the *Grand-Saint-Antoine* and three porters working with the textiles died.[12] Meanwhile, according to the memorial on the Infirmeries of 1721, stuffs began to leak into town. The Marseillais doctor Jean-Baptiste Bertrand remarked how many of the first victims in the town were tailors, dressmakers, pedlars of second-hand clothes, or dealers in contraband cloth clustered in a street known as the rue de l'Escale or l'Echelle (now covered by rue de la République).[13] On July 2, two women died in that street, one of them with the rounded swellings known as buboes. The victims had a particular glance or stare, described thus by Dr Bertrand: "The sickest have eyes that are bright and sparkling, even at the greatest extremity of weakness. It is no doubt by this symptom that certain surgeons who have knocked about the Levant claim to identify a man stricken with the plague at thirty paces."[14]

On the 9th, two physicians, Charles Peyssonel and his son, Jean-André, were called to the bed of a young man named Issalene or Eissalene in the rue Jean-Galant, near the place de Lenche. Dr Peysonnel Sr, who had spent many years in practice in Cairo and Tunis having been banished for his Jansenist beliefs,[15] went straight to the Town Hall to inform the magistrates. Issalene died the next day, July 10, and his sister fell ill. In the middle of the night, the aldermen had the dead youth, his sister and the other occupants removed to the Infirmeries and sealed the house with sand and lime. The next day, in the same street, a certain Boyal or Bayol, just returned from the Levant and come from quarantine, died with a bubo in the armpit. The body was taken to the Infirmeries and buried in quicklime.

The magistrates were reluctant to recognise the disease and wished to preserve the commerce of the port. In a circular letter to health authorities at other ports in Provence and the Mediterranean on July 15, the aldermen wrote that there was, indeed, "contagion at the Infirmeries, but those are separated from the town and have no communication with it under the strictest orders that are rigorously enforced".[16] Writing to the duc d'Orléans on July 19, and then again on the 21st, the magistrates struck a confident note: "We have reason to believe there is nothing to fear."[17] Villars told the Regent that the activities of Law's Company of the Indies in the town had disrupted the conscientious precautions of the magistrates and health officers of Marseilles.[18]

Then, on the 23rd, fourteen persons fell ill in the rue de l'Escale.[19] Though the doctors despatched there disagreed in their diagnoses, the magistrates (in the words of Pichatty de Croissante) "decided as a precaution to treat these patients as if they were truly struck by the Plague, despatching them discreetly to the Infirmeries." On the night of the 27th July, Alderman Moustier and a squad of porters from the Infirmeries entered the street, carrying away the dead (sometimes using force on the survivors) and marching the sick out of town.[20]

The nightly convoys continued for ten days, the aldermen, though falling with fatigue, staying at their duties. Those struck down, knowing that the Infirmeries meant certain death, absconded to other parts of town carrying the bacillus with them. The richer families began to migrate to their *bastides* or country houses outside town. To protect the Arsenal and galleys from the contagion, a boom was run across the south-eastern edge of the harbour.

On the 28th, the Regent ordered the *Grand-Saint-Antoine* and its cargo to be burned, though his order was not carried out for six weeks. On receipt of the aldermen's letters of July 15, the authorities in such places as Arles, Antibes, Monaco, Genoa and even Venice closed their ports to traffic from Marseilles. In the United Provinces, the *Lamoignon* that had sailed from Marseilles on July 7 was refused leave to quarantine at the Texel and eventually burned with its cargo on the order of Their High Mightinesses.[21]

On the 31st, the Parlement of Aix forbade any Marseillais to leave the town or its dependent country, or any communication with the city from the rest of the province.[22] Troops and militia were despatched on orders from Paris to establish and guard a sanitary cordon. Fearing famine, and short of silver money, the

Town Hall tried to raise a loan on August 2 at 5 per cent but found the better citizens had gone, and taken their money chests with them.[23]

On August 6, the *Gazette d'Amsterdam* went on sale in Paris with a detailed report of the plague, dated from the city on July 17. The city of Marseilles descended into hell.

Restored to the Regent's good graces, John Law set to work saving from his scheme what could be saved. He needed to reduce the banknotes in circulation, to keep the bank and company solvent and meet the King's bills for his court, armed forces and other obligations. In the ports of the Atlantic coast, merchant vessels were hoisting sail for Louisiana in numbers never seen before. John Law believed he could rescue his enterprise.

To mop up the large bills of 10,000 livres and 1,000 livres, which made up 90 per cent of the notes in the hands of the public, Law proposed to tempt holders with new securities that, unlike the banknotes, paid interest or dividends but did not need to be cashed on demand. (Such instruments are known to bankers as "non-demand liabilities".) In the course of June, 1720 and the beginning of July, Law offered perpetual and life annuities, new shares in the Company of the Indies and special bank accounts, modelled on those of the Bank of Amsterdam, to a face value in banknotes of 2.2 billion livres.

To pay the interest on the Town Hall annuities, the company pledged to return to the royal treasury 25 million livres of the King's annual payment. That put in reverse Law's scheme of 1719, burdened the French state with 1,000 millions of debt at 2.5 per cent per annum and reinforced the class of public creditors. "This is undoing," Daniel Pulteney wrote to Craggs on June 11, "a great part of what Mr Law has done or rather restoring what he had undone."[24]

During his house arrest, Law had been reminded of his mortality and decided to provide for his family. He bought 4 per cent life annuities from the company of 40,000 livres a year for Lady Katherine,[25] and 50,000 livres a year each for William and Mary Catherine.[26] He also bought for 140,000 livres a noble sinecure, that of Secretary to the King, presumably to pass on to young William. At the same time William Dicconson, who had received Queen Clementina's 600,000 livres from Pelucky in April in banknotes, proposed to James III that he convert the notes into a 4 per cent life annuity from the company for her also.[27]

Because of the bank's operations to buy the company shares, the number in the hands of the public had halved and the Regent agreed to cancel the King's holding of 100,000 shares. That left just under 200,000 valid shares, which had recovered in price with Law's return to favour, trading as high as 6,350 livres in the first week of June at an open-air stock market that had sprung up in the place Vendôme, now largely owned by Law, to replace the rue Quincampoix.[28] "The place looks more like an army camp than a stock exchange," Cornelis Hop wrote after a visit.[29]

On June 3, the company offered rights to the same number of new shares at 3,000 livres, with a view to soaking up some 600 million livres in the large bills. The stockjobbers in their tent city in the half-built square doubted the company now had an income sufficient to pay the dividend, and the take-up was slow.

The third element in Law's rescue was "bank accounts" or *comptes en banque*, announced on July 13. In use at the Banks of Amsterdam and Hamburg since the early seventeenth century, they required merchants to settle large transactions not in cash but through transfers between deposit accounts that might not be overdrawn. The July 13 edict made such transfers compulsory in both Paris and the chief commercial towns of France in the wholesale merchandise trade and for the settlement of bills of exchange over 500 livres. Only the large bills would be accepted as deposits.[30] It was late in the day for such an innovation, and barely 200 million of the intended 600 million livres in banknotes was subscribed.

After being cancelled in ink (*batonnés*) and, in the presence of Chief Cashier Bourgeois and witnesses from the Treasury and the Town Hall, cut in two, the large bills were transported under guard to the place de Grève. There, in front of the Town Hall, they were burned in iron braziers as if pieces of paper, not John Law of Lauriston, had outraged the King's peace. The first bonfires took place on June 28 and July 1 and removed 273 millions in 1,000- and 10,000-livre bills from circulation.[31] The cancelled shares, including those belonging to the King, were also burned.

Despite the threat of punishment, people refused banknotes and hoarded what silver they had. Law, too, was rationing silver to pay contractors to the company and the King's troops and to satisfy the duc d'Orléans. When the Regent's daughter, the newly wed Princess of Modena, arrived at Genoa on June 3, she found her dowry had not been delivered to the city as promised in her marriage contract. Seeking any pretext to escape a marriage she dreaded, Charlotte-Aglaé threatened to return to the royal galley that had brought her from Antibes, rather than "proceed to Modena with the mortification that a promised dowry had not been discharged".[32] The duc d'Orléans was furious (*très en colère*).[33]

The Duke of Modena was desperate for the money to pay off his bankers in Genoa. Those had had enough of bills of exchange on Paris and Lyons. Law sent piastres in coin to Marseilles, which were then immobilised behind the sanitary cordon. Soon, the Italian states refused passage to carts even from Lyons. In the correspondence, Dubois displays a certain insouciance over the damage to the Regent's personal credit. No doubt, he was happy to see John Law hauled over the coals in the Palais-Royal. In contrast, his envoy at Genoa, Théodore de Chavigny, who was both capable and unscrupulous, found 160,000 piastres from his own funds and persuaded the crew of a Marseillais felucca to run the blockade to Leghorn/Livorno with a further 80,000. That still left more than 130,000 piastres for Law to find.[34]

In Paris, tradespeople were still willing to give credit to respectable customers,[35] but money for the ordinary business of life was in short supply. Pulteney reported that theatres and coffee houses were giving change for 10-livre notes in paper tokens "of their own fabric".[36] Rosalba Carriera, who was about to begin the portrait of the young King that now hangs in Dresden, had to ask little Mary Catherine Law to change her notes.[37] In the market in the place Vendôme, banknotes bought only 80 per cent of their face value in silver, and then 70 per cent and then 60 per cent.

Law saw opponents everywhere. The Regent, who had decided to conciliate the Parlement of Paris, needed little persuasion to dismiss Argenson as Keeper of the Seals. As a sop to the magistrates, the duc d'Orléans agreed to invite Aguesseau to take up the Seals again and Law himself drove out to the ex-chancellor's rural exile at Fresnes in the Marne valley south of Paris on June 5.[38] Argenson retired to his apartment by the convent of the Madeleine du Traisnel in the faubourg Saint-Antoine and passed the year of life that remained to him in charitable and religious exercises.[39]

At the end of June, his son Marc-Pierre was dismissed as lieutenant general of police of Paris. The three commissioners sent in to examine the bank were also relieved of their posts as was Charles Trudaine, merchant-provost and effective mayor of the city, "a hard, exact, charmless man, not especially well-informed, unpolitical, but universally known as a stickler for honour and justice" (Saint-Simon).[40] Trudaine had been Intendant of Lyons at the time of the payments crisis in 1709. The Regent is said to have told him that his only fault was lack of sympathy for the "System".[41]

On June 28, the four brothers Pâris, who were alone capable of replacing Law in the management of the French public finances, received sealed letters to disperse to "Normandy, Flanders, Brittany and the Dauphiné". On the intercession of their friends, the Regent permitted them to foregather in their native country and then, as the plague began to threaten the Dauphiné, to move north.

Law's principal enemy, the Earl of Stair, had set off for home on June 23, having taken leave of nobody but the King of France. Eleanor, Lady Stair stayed on a fortnight to hand over the hôtel d'Estampes to its new owner, the marquis de Mézières. The Oglethorpe sisters at once moved in "notwithstanding they are pulling down all the furniture", as their brother James Edward wrote to Lord Strafford. "Lady Catherine Law was yesterday to see them in all their dirt, as she told me."[42]

As for friends, Law was sliding into the arms of James III. He arranged for Lord Strafford to have two interviews with the duc d'Orléans in June, where the Englishman argued that the British ministry, in alliance with Law's enemies in France, was determined to prevent the restoration of French prosperity.[43] At the beginning of July, Law allowed Dillon to concoct a letter to the Duke of Ormonde in Madrid, who would then show it to Philip of Spain. Law insisted it be in French, rather than English, so that there be no need to translate it for King Philip or bring any of the Spanish ministry into the secret. "He [Law] gives all for lost if the matter takes wind," Dillon wrote to James III on July 2.[44]

In the letter, Dillon told Ormonde that "888 [Law] is sincerely and truly disposed to serve mr knight [James III]. His system is to dispose the spirit of 1370 [the duc d'Orléans] with whom he has a great deal of credit to associate himself with 780 [Philip V] in such a solid manner that it will be in the power neither of 387 [the Habsburg emperor] nor 672 [Hanover] to shake their union." He "assumes that the consequences of that will oblige 780 and 1371 [the King of Spain and the Regent] to invite our friend [James III] to their side for their mutual security."[45]

James was exhilarated and touched to the heart. "God grant he may keep his ground," he wrote to Ormonde from Rome. He was thinking of granting Law an honour (probably a Scottish dukedom and the Thistle), but Dillon thought the time not right.[46] Instead, James was working to put Law's chief rival, the abbé Dubois, in debt to himself and also to Law. Since being appointed to the archbishopric of Cambrai, the richest in France (which he never visited), the abbé had set his sights on the cardinalate. James had the privilege of nominating cardinals at the Holy See. He believed that a grateful Dubois would not only reinforce Law but also help persuade the duc d'Orléans to restore his own French pension.

"I continue soliciting the cap for Abbé Dubois," James wrote, "and I have within these few days gained my point so far that I am morally sure he will be declared Cardinal as soon as there happens one vacancy more."[47] There is a sheet in the Jacobite papers with a list in James's hand of the cardinals he was lobbying.

In Paris, the bank was open once again (and had been since June 5) but was paying out very little silver. Instead, cashiers were ready only to "cut" the large banknotes into smaller denominations for use in retail trade. In a professionally written letter dated July 6 that survives in the Law papers in Maastricht, a domestic of the marquis de Lillers claimed a note of 1,000 livres (which was all the property he possessed) had slipped from his hand at the bank. Being almost suffocated in the press, he could retrieve only a square fragment from the lower-left corner, showing the ignature of Inspector Rolland, which he pinned to his letter. He begged Law to replace it.[48] He did not say how a house servant came to have a note for a thousand livres or two or three years' wages.

The bank cashiers supplied the commissioners of the Châtelet with silver for the Wednesday and Saturday markets, for the "master roasters" or cookshops to buy poultry and game and for the livestock markets at Poissy. "It was carnage on Wednesdays and Saturdays," wrote the lawyer Edmond Barbier.[49] On that same July 6, claiming their lives and property were at risk, the commissioners refused to distribute more coin.[50]

On the 9th, the bank cashiers again began paying out silver but only at a rate of ten livres per person. According to Cornelis Hop, the crush at the bank was so intense that people had taken to employing absconded apprentices who, by muscling their way to the front and trading between coin and banknotes, could "earn four times their daily wage".[51]

On July 10, a market Wednesday, matters turned ugly. At 8 a.m., people were admitted through the entrance to the palais Mazarin on the rue Vivienne, but as the courtyard became crowded the guards, consisting of seven old soldiers from the Invalides, Louis XIV's veterans' hospital on the left bank, closed the outer gate. Those shut out tried to break down the gate and rained stones on the courtyard so that people had to flatten themselves against the walls. From beyond the gate, a man "of medium height" shouted, "Once we're in, we'll butcher them!" As the gate began to give, Corporal Jean-Antoine Dutailly fired once through the opening and hit a coachman named Lacroix, who was carried to a surgeon in the rue Neuve-des-Petits-Champs but died of the wound.[52]

The following Wednesday, July 17, the storm burst. According to Jean Buvat, by three in the morning the rue Vivienne was full from end to end with people intent on being at the front of the line when the gates opened at eight or nine. From his perch across the street in the King's Library, Buvat saw people clambering over the ruins of the houses Law had demolished, inching along the wall of the palais Mazarin garden "as if on horseback", and by means of the overhanging sweet-chestnut trees, swinging down into the garden beside the courtyard. Those who managed to reach the counters and cash a ten-livre note were saturated in sweat as if they "had stepped out of the river".

In front of the main building of the palais Mazarin was a wooden screen or *barricade en charpente* some fifteen yards long, put up either as part of the improvement works at the bank or as a way to funnel the crowd towards the banking hall.[53] Pulteney reported that this time the guards had fixed bayonets.[54] There was a stampede and several people were crushed or stifled: twelve by Buvat's account, four (Cornelis Hop),[55] five or six (*Gazette d'Amsterdam*).[56]

The crowd took up the bodies of one woman and three men, and carried them "*op een seditieuse manier*" (Hop) down to the rue Saint-Honoré and laid them out in the outer court of the Palais-Royal. It was now about ten o'clock in the morning. Law was already with the Regent and made the error of sending his coach back to the hôtel Langlée. His coachman bandied words with the crowd and, according to Buvat, was pulled down from his box and suffered a broken leg.

At the session of the Parlement, First President de Mesmes entered the chamber to say that Law's coach had been smashed to pieces which, according to the journal of one of the clerks, "gave the whole company a secret delight".[57] Emboldened, the magistrates decided to petition the King to withdraw the edict to create the bank accounts and the new company shares. That vexed the duc d'Orléans.

A portion of the crowd then moved on to the hôtel Langlée, where they smashed windows from the street. Mounted police and Swiss Guards were despatched to both the house and the bank.

Elisabeth Charlotte, who had come from Saint-Cloud that morning, was visiting the Carmelite sisters in the rue de Grenelle on the left bank. She was given the news by her lady-in-waiting,

Anne de Châteautiers, pale as death. Alarmed about her son, she went on to the Tuileries to call on the King and then drove into the tumult in the rue Saint-Honoré. Motionless in the traffic for half an hour, she heard people denouncing Law but not the duc d'Orléans. The crowd cheered her.[58] For some time, she had been anxious that Law might be a risk to her son and from now on she refused to have anything to do with him (except pass on derogatory hearsay).

Law remained at the Palais-Royal. Ever the optimist, General Dillon wrote to James III: "Still it is a comfort that he is near Seymour [the Regent] who in all appearance intends to support him."[59] The duc de Bourbon took Lady Katherine and the two children for an excursion to Saint-Maur, a Renaissance house belonging to his family in a bend of the Marne about ten miles to the south-east, and lodged them there till calm should be restored.[60]

In an edict of that evening, the King, being informed of the "disorder in the payment of notes at the Bank", suspended such payments until further notice and banned any public assembly "for any cause whatsoever".[61] The Royal Bank of France was bankrupt. With the camp at the place Vendôme outlawed, the banknotes would be left to find their price in cabarets and on street corners. An imitation banknote did the rounds with the signed legend: "I promise to suffocate at sight the bearer of this bill."[62]

The next day, at four in the afternoon, at a spontaneous meeting where the Regent sat among his advisers on stools before the windows of the Great Salon and Law was not present,[63] it was resolved to exile the Parlement to Pontoise, a small town about twenty miles north-east of Paris. There was precedent in that, in 1652, during the civil wars known as the Fronde, Louis XIV had summoned a rump Parlement to the town. This time, the decision was kept secret so that regiments could be moved into camp at Charenton and Saint-Denis, apparently to be reviewed by the young King but also, as Cornelis Hop wrote, “to keep the peace”. Market day, on Saturday, July 20, passed quietly but for a demonstration outside Law’s house.[64]

On Sunday morning, July 21, between 3 and 4 a.m., musketeers of the King’s Guard delivered sealed letters to the magistrates and staff of the Parlement, ordering them to repair to Pontoise within forty-eight hours. An hour later, guards took over the Palais de Justice and posted sentries at the main doors.[65] If there was any public protest, it is not reported in the many surviving accounts.

Most of the leading magistrates set off the next morning, Monday, July 22. First President de Mesmes was lodged in the abbaye de Saint-Martin, house of the duc d’Albret, while others bunked down where they could. Mme Charlet spent the night with her councillor-husband at the *Grand Cerf* inn on the edge of town, in a room with three other beds in each of which several gentlemen were sleeping.[66]

The magistrates were determined to make the best of their country jaunt and, with his usual clemency, the Regent ensured that Mesmes had enough money for an open table. As a sign of how they intended to proceed, on July 24 court officers waylaid a cart carrying butter for Paris and commandeered it for “the provision of the town” of Pontoise.[67] In their first full session on the 27th, in the refectory of the Franciscan convent done up with tapestries brought from Paris, they registered the edict that banished them.

Back at the Palais de Justice, the musketeers “greatly amused themselves” in torturing the concierge’s dog, which they named “Law”. They arraigned him in the Great Chamber, heard pleas from both sides, put him to the rack to explain his financial policies (*pour sçavoir le Sistème*). The answers being unsatisfactory, they condemned him to be broken alive on the wheel, but commuted the sentence, and hanged the harmless creature until dead.[68]

*

Across the Channel, matters looked happier. The principal threat to the Hanoverian peace in Britain, which was the quarrel between the King and the Prince of Wales, had ended on St George's Day, April 23, 1720, with a display of contrition by the prince on his knees. Moved despite himself, George I could only mutter over and over in French: "Your conduct, your conduct . . ."[69] Law's friend or "senior clerk", as the wits called him, the duc de La Force, volunteered to lead a mission to London to congratulate the King and Prince on their reconciliation. Young William Law was to be of the party. The abbé Dubois put paid to that exercise in tactlessness.

In a discussion with some courtiers at St James's Palace on May 29/June 9, King George said he did not believe in Law's return to favour. Quoting from one of Stair's last despatches, the King said that "the affairs of France were in the utmost confusion". Law was forced now to work with his enemies, hence the contradictory edicts.

Former Secretary Johnston, who had helped break Law from jail a quarter-century earlier, spoke up for his countryman, saying the Regent recognised Law's value and was too sensible "ever to dispense with him". Another courtier said that assuredly Law was not born for mediocrity, for his fate was to be either very great or very unfortunate. Pulteney's cousin, William, former secretary of war, quoted a letter saying that the Company of the Indies, so feared by the English and Dutch East India, "would soon go up in smoke".

The reporter continued: "It is certain that this conversation has had its effect because yesterday our South Sea shares rose [illegible] and I saw myself today that the shares were at 560 per cent. The world is become madder at this time here for our shares than they ever were in France for the Mississippi."[70] In contrast, at the court of the Prince and Princess of Wales, always more sympathetic to Law, the gossip two days later was that the Regent had given Dubois "two or three good kicks" for making representations against Law.[71]

Nowadays, where money has no nationality and puts a girdle about the earth more nimbly than Shakespeare's Puck, a fall in industrial shares on Wall Street is matched, in an instant, in Europe and the Far East. It was not so in 1720. Despite the rout in the stock of the Company of the Indies, and the check to Law's plan to channel the French national debt into commerce and industry, the South Sea project continued to attract money in both Britain and Holland. Men and women thought that Law's difficulties were due to the peculiar fragilities of French government, which were remedied in the lands of liberty and the reformed religion. In the second half of May, while Law's edifice was falling apart, South Sea shares rose by nearly three-quarters.

In reality, the directors of the South Sea copied Law's methods of 1719 to ramp up the shares, but on a much greater scale. In the colossal third money subscription, of £50 million at £1,000 per share of June 17, the down payment was only £100 per share and the rest due in nine six-monthly calls, the last on January 1, 1725. In other words, investors could buy for the rise with a small cash outlay and sell out before the other calls became due. In addition, the directors were lending against the company's shares, and probably also buying them for cash in the Alley.

In the west of town, the South Sea's friends in Parliament granted the company a corporate monopoly through a bill outlawing the copycat joint-stock companies springing up like weeds in the lower Alley. "The South Sea managers," a witness wrote, "were resolved to have the whole Game of Bubbles (so exceeding profitable) to themselves only."[72] As it happened, projectors of two insurance companies had each offered £300,000 towards the King's household or "civil list" debts and those companies were licensed and are still in business.

The so-called "Bubble Act" received royal assent on June 11/22 after which the King left for Hanover.[73] The consequence was that by June 22 by the English calendar, when the company's transfer books were closed so as to identify the investors due the £10 midsummer dividend, South Sea shares were being quoted at or near £1,000 "for the opening".

The Duke of Chandos, who in April had ridden the rising tide in the City to refloat a decayed slaving company, the Royal African, condoled with Drummond for his losses in Paris. "I wish you had been here in the [midst?] of our Mississippi, being perswaded you could not have fail'd to have a made a very advantageous hand of it."

In a letter of June 12/23, he suggested the Scotsman bear his losses with patience.[74] The Law brothers were incomparably worse off. Their bets against South Sea were under water. At the end of April and beginning of May, Middleton had to spend £33,420 to buy shares they had sold short so as to deliver them to British and Dutch stockbrokers.[75] The costs were debited to an account held in William Law's name.

The fever in the City had caused the rate of interest to soar, and Middleton's letters to William that are conserved at the successor bank Coutts & Co. are a wail for cash. Despite the ban on the export of gold and silver from France, William sent over a shipment of gold louis and also allowed Middleton to draw on an account with the company's representative in Holland, Abraham Mouchard.

The South Sea contracts were small change in comparison with the bets against the English East India. One of those, with William Lock and James Colebrook, English jobbers who had come over to Paris, concerned 950 shares.[76] As for the wagers with Londonderry, John Law had taken over Gage's contract, and he was now committed to deliver 1,500 shares by August 25 by the English calendar and a further 250 by November 25. That was about a tenth of East

India's shares in issue. While East India was the most widely traded of the London moneyed companies, large blocks were in the hands of City grandees such as Sir Matthew Decker, the leading director, who were all too aware of Middleton's embarrassment.

On May 5/16, Middleton wrote to William that Lock had told him in private that day that "there's a design amongst some people in Change Alley to play upon your Brother's India affair and am doubtful [fear] 'tis too true the price is got up to 242 and am very apprehensive they will carry it further."[77] In what is now known as a "bear squeeze", and the most brutal there ever was, Middleton could not step into the Alley without driving the price of East India higher. His own fate was now tied up with that of the Law brothers. "For God's sake remitt me," Middleton wrote to William on May 23/June 3.[78]

Middleton's only ally was Londonderry. A more prudent man than John Law, he had sold or "laid off" most or even all of the contracts to men such as William Lock, his father "Diamond" Pitt and the Duke of Chandos, either for one-off premiums or prices over the £180 per share that he had promised to pay Law. He had guaranteed himself a gain. He now needed to ensure that Law was in a condition to deliver the shares to him and his clients. On June 20 by the English calendar, when Middleton needed to buy five hundred East India shares to meet the Lock and Colebrooke contract, Londonderry "was very active in betting down the price" to 332½. "Had it not been for his assistance, 'tis very probable they might have carryed it above 40 [i.e. 340]," Middleton wrote.[79]

Londonderry was a sceptic of South Sea but gave in to the importunities of his family. He bought subscriptions for his father and his father's friends and forty-four shares for his sister Lucy, Lady Stanhope. With the closing of the transfer books on June 22, Londonderry again chose caution and sold most of the South Sea subscriptions to a partnership in Exchange Alley, Mitford and

Merttins, for delivery in three months' time. He accepted less than half the £1,000 per share being quoted for the opening.[80] Then all London waited, through a hot summer, as Matthew Prior wrote on July 2, "the Town . . . a desert and the world . . . crammed into Change Alley".[81] On July 4, as discreetly as he could, Middleton (with Londonderry's backing) began buying East India for the August 25 deadline on the main wager.

With South Sea suspended and Law at bay, the speculative tide lapped at more distant shores. The English and Dutch newspapers spoke of new joint-stock companies in Hamburg, Hanover, Vienna, the Austrian Netherlands, Lorraine, Brunswick, Lisbon, Venice, St Petersburg and Constantinople.[82] In Madrid, King Philip set up a *junta* or committee of ministers to study a sheaf of corporate projects, including a colonial company and the wool scheme.[83] Londonderry, who had no doubt heard of the projects through Law or the Carroll brothers, sent Crean £30,000 to invest in the Spanish "India Company".[84] Law himself said he was offered for sale the principality of Massa, between Genoa and Pisa, and the island fortress of Tabarqa in the territory of the Bey of Tunis, where Genoese interests fished for coral.[85]

Yet it was the Netherlands, a rich republic with savings built up from over a hundred years of successful trade and industry, that took up the mantle fallen from London and Paris. The Dutch had been drawn into South Sea in the late-May boom. Now the coffee houses in Dam Square and the Kalverstraat bid up the two Dutch chartered trading companies in tandem with the London stocks. Dutch East India or VOC rose from 800 per cent of par at the start of the year to over 1,200 per cent. West India, despite losing money in every year since the peace, as a sort of Dutch Mississippi or South Sea, rose more than sevenfold.

With its republican balances and jealousies, there was no enthusiasm in the United Provinces for national monopolies. Instead, between June and October prospectuses for some forty companies were issued to raise about 800 million guilders, or forty times the capital employed in trade by the VOC and WIC.[86]

When the city of Amsterdam, under pressure from its marine underwriters, refused in June to charter a new insurance company on the model of those founded in London and planned in Hamburg, other trading cities stepped in in an attempt to regain markets lost to the metropolis. On June 21, the city of Rotterdam floated an insurance company with a capital of 12 million guilders (about £1,000,000), with a first payment of just ten guilders. The shares almost doubled on the first day of trading. (Bailed out by the town at the end of that year, in 1874 and in the 1920s, and by the Dutch state in 2008, the company lives on as ASR Nederland.) Two other companies were floated in Middelburg.

Those were followed in July by a cluster of corporations in south Holland, in places such as Delft, Schiedam and Gouda, and then, in August and September, as a contemporary author put it, "every little town of northern Holland",[87] including Hoorn, Purmerend and Edam, and finally the Gelderland, Zwolle and East Frisia. Those companies, backed by the town halls, intended to engage in everything from insurance to shipping, canal-digging, lending, rope-making and sawmilling. Their bucolic business plans, opulent capital and penny down-payments drew the scorn of Amsterdam as recorded in the great literary production of that year, *Het Groote Tafereel der Dwaasheid*, "The Great Mirror of Folly".

What, asked the writer AZ, would the little brewing and distilling town of Weesp do with 10 million guilders except buy in more weaners to fatten on beer draff or corner the market for juniper berries for its "idiot-juice [gin]"?[88] In the euphoria, the Hague stockbroker Gabriel de Souza Britto proposed a 100-million-guilder company on the model of the Mississippi or South Sea which, in return for privileges, would take over a portion of the debts of the province of Holland. It was late for all that.

None the less, for those who had missed out on the booms in Paris and London, there seemed to be another chance. The Scots were to the fore. On June 18/29, the Edinburgh merchant James Wauchope (pronounced "walk-up"), a Roman Catholic, gave his friend Alexander Shairp, who was planning to travel to Rotterdam, "full power to dipp me for five thousand guilders". A week later, the sum had risen to "ten thousand guilders".[89]

The Duke of Gordon, who seems to have come too late to Paris and London, wrote to his clansman, John Gordon, at Rotterdam for information about the Dutch projects. John Gordon replied to his chief with circumspection: "As to the Dutch project of Stock jobbing wherein your Grace desires to be informed, I know severalls of our Countrymen that have given considerable orders to buyers of these actions [shares] & may have already made mony by them but to incourage your Grace much to be concerned is what I can't do."[90]

In Edinburgh itself, for all its sufferings from the Company of Scotland and the expeditions to Darien, subscriptions opened on August 8 to raise £1.5 millions for a fishery company, with 15,000 shares on offer at £100 each, £1 down. "You cannot imagine how eager people were upon't," Wauchope wrote to Shairp on August 13/24. That was despite the continuous drain of money to London and Amsterdam, so that "there's not a louse to be borrowed". The Co-Partnery of Freemen Burgesses of the Royal Burrows of Scotland for carrying on a Fishing Trade was to be politically neutral, its directors and officers selected with "no distinction of Faces, only with regard to capable men whither whigg or Tory, Argathelian or Squadron (Black Peas excepted)."[91] The Argathelians were adherents of the Dukes of Argyll. Black Peas were, presumably, Roman Catholics.

As August came on, Middleton added East India for John Law's account: sixty-five shares on August 2 at 362, ninety-five on the 4th at 350, ten more on the 9th at 390. On Tuesday, August 16, Middleton bought 290 shares at 370 to make up the entire 1,000 shares of the main wager. As he wrote to William Law, Londonderry had been "very obliging & civil" in advancing him money to buy the shares and other ways. The total outlay for the one thousand shares, cast up in an account sent by Middleton to William Law by the next post, was £372,762 10s.[92] Fulfilling the Gage contracts (which Law had taken over) cost an additional £168, 280 16s.[93]

Back in 1705, Queen Anne had given her beloved Duke and Duchess of Marlborough the royal hunting forest at Woodstock in Oxfordshire. During her lifetime, she allowed them at least £220,000 in cash to build, furnish and empark the house known as Blenheim Palace.[94] The Marlboroughs spent at least £60,000 of their own money. In the second half of 1720, John Law owed George Middleton and the Londonderry syndicate two Blenheim Palaces. They needed him to remain in health.

With the rustication of the magistrates to Pontoise, Law returned home to the rue Neuve-des-Petits-Champs.[95] There he was beset with visitors, including an emissary from Lord Londonderry. Colonel James Otway (1672–1725) was a gouty old soldier who had served under Stanhope in Spain during the war and been captured with him at Brihuega. He owned a small property in the Kentish Weald, Romden Castle, some twenty-five miles as the crow flies from Stanhope's estate at Chevening, where he was taken on to oversee improvement works and kept an apartment. He was devoted to his captain's family, who called him "JO", and especially to Lucy, Countess Stanhope, Londonderry's sister. Wishing to return to active service, through Stanhope's influence that June he had been appointed governor of St Philip's Castle in

Minorca. Paris was on his way. No doubt, Londonderry dared not go himself to see Law in Paris lest the Alley become suspicious of his own solvency.

Otway, who arrived on July 26, was overwhelmed with hospitality. He dined twice and supped once with John Law, "whose greatness has not in the least alter'd his affability", as he wrote to Londonderry on July 31. He was not the most observant of men. "Everything seems to me to be in a good way," he added.

With the exchange rate on France so unfavourable, Law said that he had authorised Middleton to draw on his correspondents in Hamburg and Genoa. Carried away, Otway drew for himself £1,000 on his patron and gave it to William to invest "with an assurance that I shall loose nothing".[96] Every speculation has its final buyer, after whom there are only sellers. In the Mississippi boom of 1719–20, Colonel James Otway of Romden Castle, Kent, was the final buyer.

With a ferocious devaluation of the silver currency on July 30, Law tried to rescue the banknotes. In a showy transaction, he bought the building lots behind thirty-two of the arcades of the place Vendôme for the sum of 600,000 livres in notes payable over six years at 2 per cent interest.[97] Neither ploy succeeded. The notes rose back up to par with silver, then fell back and continued falling. Silver was hidden. To the delight of the Jacobites, Clementina Sobieska was pregnant, but three gentlewomen come from London to attend her were marooned in Paris and Saint-Germain at the end of July while General Dillon scrambled to find "a little species [silver] to pay their expense on the rode".[98]

The banknotes were now being traded, along with the company shares and all manner of financial bric-à-brac, in the garden of the hôtel de Soissons.

One of the great houses of old Paris, the hôtel de Soissons occupied an irregular pentagon of streets pinned at the north-east by the church of Saint-Eustache. Built in the sixteenth century by Catherine de Médicis, widow of King Henri II of France, on the site of a much older palace, the house and garden had passed by descent to the spendthrift Prince Victor-Amadeus de Savoie-Carignan (1690–1741), cousin to Law's old patron, Victor-Amadeus II, and husband of his out-of-wedlock daughter. Law seems to have had the place in mind for a stock exchange since at least 1715 and probably earlier.[99] In one of the many traces left by John Law in his comet-like passage through Paris, the garden was later developed into a corn market and then the Paris commodities exchange.

In 1717, an exasperated Victor-Amadeus deprived Carignan of his pension. Carignan left Turin for Paris to realise his valuable property. He evicted his cousin's ambassador but was prevented by his mortgagees from selling the place to Law.

Instead, he let the garden to an entrepreneur to establish an open-air stock market, to replace the chaotic place Vendôme. It was licensed by a royal edict published on July 31. Swiss Guards in the King's livery barred entry at the two gates to carriages and to working people, servants in uniform, and the poor unemployed. An officer and eight archers kept order within the garden.[100]

Inside, some one hundred and thirty-seven numbered wooden booths were erected on a platform against the garden wall, for each of which a broker paid five hundred livres a month. A plan survives showing the booths and, in the eastern corner, latrines (*commodités*).[101] It was one of the sights of Paris. Rosalba Carriera, though greatly in demand for her portrait pastels, visited the garden in August.[102]

In the French trade in coins and medals, there appear every now and then admission tokens to the garden which may date from that summer of 1720 or are modern counterfeits. One face bears the legend HÔTEL DE SOISSONS and the cross of Savoy between three fleurs-de-lys, and the other a dismasted ship and the Latin motto INCERTUM QUO FATA FERUNT: 'Who knows where the fates will lead [us]'. Pulteney reported that Carignan was expected to clear 150,000 livres a year from this flea market.[103] A place where Blanche of Castille had lived, and Blind King John of Bohemia, who fell at Crécy, became for a while a nest of stockbrokers.

With his family out of town, Law was given an apartment at the Palais-Royal that had been occupied by the captain of the Regent's lifeguard, the comte d'Estampes.[104] The duc d'Antin wrote that Law did not feel safe at the hôtel Langlée.[105] Elisabeth Charlotte said that he was too nervous to drive out to Saint-Cloud on the 11th or 12th. "People are saying that he cannot recover from his recent scares."[106]

Law later gave a picture of his frame of mind that August. It is unique in his surviving papers. "It was the time I was staying in the apartment of Mr d'Estampes," he wrote in 1721 to the abbé Tencin. "The Regent had gone to spend the night at St. Cloud. Madame his mother, the duchesse d'Orléans, the duc de Chartres and the princesses were all in the country. I had given orders to say that I was not at home. That whole day there was nobody to be seen at the Palais-Royal. The idea came on me that one would be less wretched shut up in a plague town like Marseilles than to be overwhelmed by the world as I was always in Paris."[107]

He pulled himself together. On August 15, he sounded the death-knell of the banknotes. By an edict of that day, the large bills of 10,000 and 1,000 livres would cease to be legal tender on October 1, while the notes of 100 and 10 livres would enjoy a stay of execution until May 1, 1721.[108] Instead, Law hoped to retain a part of his System with his Dutch-style bank accounts. Large contracts could be made in gold and silver.

There was a rush to discharge debts in the moribund notes. Pulteney wrote to London that day: "He who receives what was owing to him reckons himself undone; he who pays his debts is thought unjust."[109] Montesquieu commemorated this moment in his *Persian Letters*. Rica, the Isfahanian nobleman, overhears in a Paris café someone say: "There was a man I thought so much my friend that I lent him my money and the rat paid it back! What abominable perfidy!"[110]

All over France, excepting only Marseilles behind its sanitary cordon, people streamed to the notaries to repay their debts with the decried paper. In the town of Cany in Upper Normandy, which had little to do with Rouen let alone Paris, 320,000 livres in annuities were bought back in 1720, more than twelve times the value of the year following.[111] At the other end of the kingdom, in Perpignan in the Roussillon, that August, debtors redeemed four hundred and eight annuity contracts against two the previous August. It appears that the various houses of the Church, as the principal creditor of French provincial society, suffered most from the liquidation.[112] According to the researches of Gilbert Larguier in Perpignan, the nuns of the Poor Clares saw their revenues cut in half.

In the midst of this scramble, Law lost his principal advocate. On or just before September 8, in Hanover, the Earl of Stanhope held a meeting with Philippe Destouches, the French ambassador to the Court of St James. Stanhope had come to regret his own treatment of the Earl of Stair, and had admitted as much to Stair by way of the Duke of Montrose.[113] He had little confidence in Sir Robert Sutton, who had arrived in Paris in June. He now dictated to Destouches a piece of advice for the Regent of France. The duc d'Orléans should abandon Law's System, restore the old financial arrangements (*l'ancien ordre*) and recall the Parlement de Paris.

Just visible through Stanhope's French is the ghost of a rebuke. As long as King George and his ministers "were bothered only by such views as Mr Law might have to the prejudice of England, they were quite calm and made no attempt to have him removed, trusting that HRH himself would keep matters under control and prevent any harm to their interests". Now Law had become a threat to the safety of the Regent himself, they could no longer forbear to offer their counsel.

Dubois should consult the leading bankers of Paris to devise a new plan of financial reconstruction, and then introduce it to a few selected magistrates for presentation as "an expedient that the company [i.e. Parlement] had dreamed up for the relief of the public to which it begged the Regent to give his approval". Such a ploy would not only soothe the magistrates' wounded feelings but so charm the public as to restore confidence in His Royal Highness "so he would be more beloved, trusted and secure as he ever was". As to Law, he should be banished from France but "permitted none the less to take with him a sufficiency so as to enjoy an agreable retirement".[114]

In Pontoise, the magistrates were enjoying themselves. "Play, concerts, walks," wrote the clerk Jean Gilbert Delisle, "the ladies making up parties and going everywhere, and the gentlemen the same, and all in a spirit of union and fraternity such as perhaps has never been seen. President de Lubert played the violin to perfection . . ."[115] There were jaunts out of town, including to the Cistercian abbey of Maubuisson, where François Couperin's daughter Marie Madeleine was a novice, and the master himself sat down at the organ for them.[116] It was decided to put a limit on table stakes, after Madame Président d'Aligre won more than 2,000 crowns at a single hand of lansquenet.[117]

As the courts rose for vacation that Sunday, September 8, there occurred an incident that found its way into *A Tale of Two Cities.* Setting out in late afternoon, the coach carrying President Nicolas Lambert de Thorigny struck a man and broke his leg. President Lambert tossed through the window a gold louis, but it was lost in the scramble and though the people ran after his coach, it continued on its way.[118]

CHAPTER TWELVE

Fall from Grace

La confiance ne se conqueste pas.
(Confidence cannot be forced.)

JOHN LAW[1]

Jean-François-Benjamin Dumont de Montigny, a young officer sent home from Louisiana after quarrelling with Bienville, arrived on the *Mutine* at the island of Groix off Lorient and Port Louis in Brittany in the last week of June, 1720. The next day, M. de Saint-Martin, an under-director of the Company of the Indies, came on board and demanded in the King's name that passengers, officers and crew hand over for inspection any letters they were carrying from the colony. "The whole thing was to see if anyone was denigrating the country," Dumont wrote in a memoir of his adventurous and unsuccessful career.[2]

While John Law fought to save his scheme in the Palais-Royal, so too did his minions in the Atlantic ports of France and on the barrier islands and beaches of Louisiana. Merchantmen held up in the French ports by the war with Spain could now put to sea to convey workers and settlers and their supplies for the large absentee concessionaires, including Law himself.

Beginning with the *Dryade* or *Driade*, a 350-ton frigate that sailed from Lorient in March, at least seventeen vessels that year transported about two thousand men, women and children to the territory.[3] Five frigates, the *Africain*, *Duc-d'Orléans*, *Grand-duc-du-Maine*, *Néréide* and *Fortuné* set sail for Senegal, Gambia, Guinea, Benin and Angola to barter for slaves to do the heavy work of clearing and burning.

Lorient and Port Louis were overrun. Charles-Joseph Franquet de Chaville, one of a team of four engineers contracted by the directors of the company to survey and improve its installations in Louisiana,[4] arrived in Port Louis in the summer to find "numerous tribes of colonists [*nombreuses peuplades*] assembled from different parts of France to settle this new world".

Crossing over to Lorient the next day, Franquet was startled by Edward Rigby's vice-regal pretensions. The Englishman "was so intoxicated with the honours that a mob of flatterers competed to heap on him that he barely deigned to speak except to his favourites."[5] Another witness said Rigby travelled in a launch rowed by twelve sailors in liveries of frilled green cloth, with gold braid and buttons and velvet bonnets that cost in all 13,500 livres.[6]

Among the tribes arriving in Lorient were a couple of hundred Swiss soldiers and settlers and Germans from the Rhine valley, who had been leaving home (for England, Ireland, New York and Pennsylvania) since their fields and farms were laid waste in Louis XIV's wars.

Recruited for the Arkansas by agents sent by Jean-François Melon, one of Law's secretaries who went on to make a name as a writer on trade, German families began arriving on French soil at the end of May. Elisabeth Charlotte heard from her daughter, duchesse de Lorraine, on May 29 that seventy-five families from their native Palatinate had just passed through on their way to Orléans, as a stage for Lorient and Louisiana.[7] She blamed Protestant ministers for persuading them to go. "God punish their damned parsons

[*Pfaffen*]," she wrote. In all, according to figures compiled by Marcel Giraud, 3,991 German recruits arrived at Lorient in two orderly columns in July and were handed over to Rigby.[8]

The port was not equipped to feed and shelter them. The great majority were lodged in a tent encampment according to their native parishes in Ploemeur outside the walls to the west, where a fresh-water spring was known until the nineteenth century as "the fountain of the Germans". There, exposed to the summer's heat and poorly nourished, the German immigrants fell prey to illness including "uninterrupted fevers spreading to the brain, and many instances of worms".[9] Among the children, according to the Roman Catholic registers, sixteen died in July, eighteen in August, and fourteen in September. The first German families were not embarked until November, on the pinnace the *Deux-Frères* and the flûte the *Garonne*, and they carried their infections with them.

Franquet and his colleagues, under their chief Louis-Pierre Leblond de La Tour, found berths on the 300-ton *Dromadaire*, which had on board two companies of infantry and settlers for the concessions of a well-financed syndicate that included Claude Le Blanc, the Secretary of State for War. The engineers had to buy provisions for themselves and their eight servants since Rigby said he could not supply them. They set sail from the île de Groix at 5 a.m. on August 23 in convoy with a larger vessel, the *Gironde*.

The *Dromadaire* had a slow but uneventful crossing, except that Leblond de La Tour felt slighted by the young Irish-Malouin captain, Richard Butler de Saint-Marc. They lost just one sailor "who would have died on land". The *Gironde*, meanwhile, carrying three hundred farmers and labourers for the Chaumont and the Mézières-des Marches (Oglethorpe) prospects, became a "floating hospital", with one man buried at sea and scarcely ten persons, passengers and crew, in a state fit to manoeuvre the vessel.[10] Captain Butler restricted contact between the ships to a loud-hailer (*porte-voix*).

Reaching Cap Français on October 25, the engineers rioted on salad. Leaving the *Gironde*, they sailed on in convoy with the *Eléphant*, and dropped anchor in the lee of Ship Island on December 14, amidst the *Marie*, the *Loire*, the *Profond*, the *Alexandre* and other company ships. Across the Mississippi Sound twelve miles away, at the place now occupied by the lighthouse and casinos of the city of Biloxi, Bienville and the company had allocated ground for camps or staging-posts for the large concessions.

There four days earlier, a young man named Jean-Baptiste Michel Le Bouteux moored a barge to the pilings of a jetty in the shallows and took out his pen and ink and watercolour. He had been asked by his superior, Louis-Elias Stutheus, a Breton ship's captain who was due to come out to manage Law's properties in Louisiana, to portray the concession camp. Though his purpose was only to be accurate, something unusual occurred in the sunshine, and Le Bouteux made one of the great pictures of colonial North America: *View of the Camp of Mr Law's Concession at New Biloxi.*

It is a scene both orderly and industrious. Beneath the trees, loggers, carpenters, boat builders, roofers, barrel makers and gardeners are at work. A broad road leads to an eighty-foot-long warehouse with a hipped roof in the process of being laid. The building rests on a sill like an old Norman barn. Beside it are thatched cabins for the workers and the tents of the tobacco-grader and the managers, where a sentry stands guard. To the right or east is the house of the chaplain, Father Maximin, the shops of the butcher, armourer and cutler, and the forges and bakers' oven. Beside the shore are thatched huts for the apothecary and surgeons and the hospital, where an invalid takes the air and watches a broth pot on a sunken hearth. Also marked is a sweet-water spring which flows today. At the extreme left or west is the camp of the duc de Guiche's concession.

For all the ravages of time and wind, the place is easily found

French warships and merchantmen off Cap-Français (now Cap-Haïtien) on the north coast of Saint-Domingue. That was the last anchorage for French shipping destined for Louisiana.

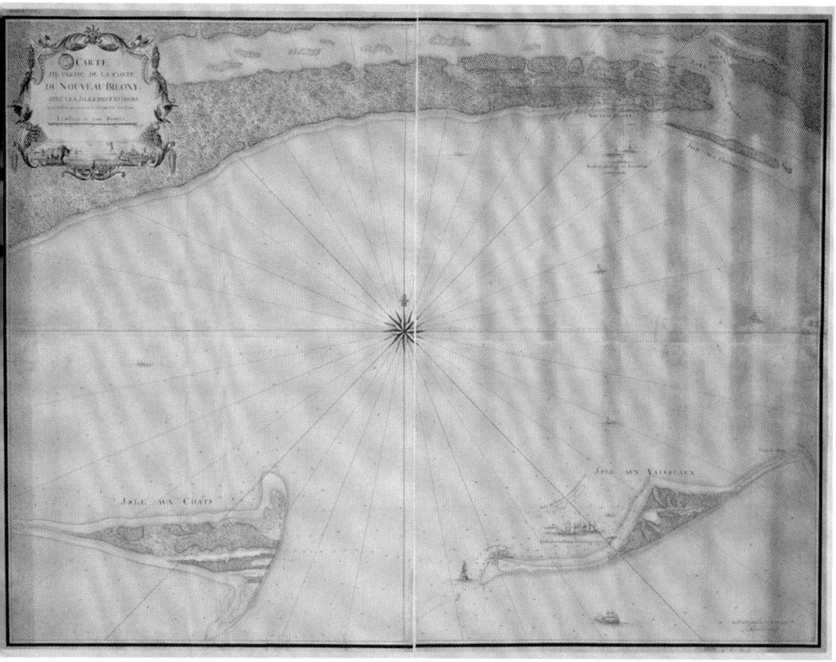

The approaches to New Biloxi, drawn by the engineer Louis-Pierre Leblond de La Tour, showing the anchorages in the lee of Ship Island and the soundings in feet.

Echelle de deux Cens Toises
Echelle de soixantedix Toises Pour

Watercolour view of New Orleans from the west bank of the Mississippi, modern Algiers Point, done in 1726 by the surveyor Jean-Pierre de Lassus. Beyond the site of the town is the portage road from the Bayou Saint-Jean.

View of the camp at New Biloxi for John Law's concession on the Arkansas, drawn by Jean-Baptiste Michel Le Bouteux on December 10, 1720. Though nobody in Louisiana knew it, Law had just fallen from power.

The marriage of James III and Clementina Sobieska at Montefiascone in September, 1719. The picture, attributed to Agostino Masucci, was commissioned by King James after the Queen's death in 1735.

The Chevalier Roze leads a troop of one hundred convicts to clear the plague dead from the esplanade of the Tourette in Marseilles on September 16, 1720. By Michel Serre.

The Great Stables at Chantilly, built by the duc de Bourbon with his gains from investing in John Law's companies. They are unlikely monuments to Law's financial theories.

The Seine and Mississippi embrace while ships discharge merchandise from Louisiana. Fragment of Gianantonio Pellegrini's oil sketch for the allegorical ceiling of the shareholders' gallery at Law's bank in Paris.

Portion of the iron balustrade of the main staircase at the hôtel de Nevers, made probably by the master-ironworker Guillaume Cressart. The monogram JL is much simplified from that on the banknotes.

Coins, recognisably from the reign of Louis XV, spill from a cornucopia in the bottom right-hand corner of the balustrade section. The gilding is from the nineteenth century.

Gambling at the Palazzo dei Dandolo by Francesco Guardi. To the left of the door to the coffee shop, the bank-holder sits at a table, in patrician robes and wig, and unmasked.

The eastern end of St Mark's Square, by Canaletto. Law's last apartment was to the right of the vanished church of San Geminiano, behind the temporary stage on trestles.

Jean Le Blond by Rosalba Carriera. Le Blond, who succeeded his father as French consul at Venice, was a devoted friend to John Law and his children.

Portrait of a young girl holding a monkey, by Rosalba Carriera, in the Louvre in Paris. The girl is believed to be Mary Catherine Law, who sat for the artist on June 11, 1720, at ten years of age.

to the east of the modern Porter Avenue and the Biloxi Visitors Center. Though the slash pines were long ago blown to sticks, some of the evergreen oaks that Le Bouteux drew as saplings may survive. As an afterthought, Le Bouteux added himself, from the back, his long hair or wig tied with two ribbons.[11]

The colony's capital or headquarters was on the north-east shore of Biloxi Bay at the place first selected twenty years before by Iberville for Fort Maurepas, now the site of Ocean Springs, Mississippi. Against Bienville's wishes, the two local company directors had moved operations there from île Dauphine. The newly arrived engineers were not impressed.

There, surrounded by insanitary marsh, and poorly supplied with fresh water, were officers and men, convicts, deserters, salt smugglers, vagrants and the Salpêtrière women, "all mixed together" with recruits for the great concessions. They were immobilised for want of boats to take them up-country. Parts of the camp were in ruins after a sergeant named Louis Colet, known as Joly Coeur, lighting his pipe in bed while full of drink, threw down the brand, set fire to his pine-log cabin and, the wind getting up, to eleven others.[12]

Supplies were short and mortality high. According to a register of burials made later by the Luxemburgian Capuchin Father Raphael, vicar general of the Bishop of Quebec for the province, twelve persons were buried at the place in August, thirty in September, and thirty-four in December.[13] The engineers advised an immediate move to the open shore opposite Ship Island to the west of Law's camp at what became known as New Biloxi, where there was room for an earth-and-timber star fort, a hospital and quarters for both military and civilians.[14] At some point, a separate camp was made for the African slaves in the back bay.[15]

As for Bienville, he looked to the new arrivals not forty years of age but sixty. "Service in this country," Franquet wrote, "is evidently no present to the complexion [*ne tiennent point le teint frais*]."[16]

In Marseilles, the plague penetrated the new town and crept along the south shore of the harbour into the Rive-neuve. In the last ten days of August, the mortality climbed. By August 23, nearly a thousand persons were dying each day.[17] Rich and poor were tumbled into ditches dug fourteen feet deep beyond the walls. The rolling of the tumbrils, pulled first by beggars on fifteen livres a day and then by convicts pressed from the Arsenal, and the cries of the halberdiers going before them, filled people with terror. The streets were littered with contaminated cloths, bedding, furniture and bandages tossed from windows. Infants, their mothers or wet-nurses dead, were taken to an abandoned convent where they were fed on soup or goat's milk and died thirty or forty each day. Dogs roamed the lanes, gorging on the dead, and the night was punctuated by their howling.

The convicts, armed with hooks and ropes to drag out the bodies, pillaged the houses, or absconded through back doors.[18] They dropped like flies and were replaced by Turkish and Arab captives, who died in their turn. The tumbrils were constantly overturned or tangled in their harnesses. For want of anyone to work on them, the country had to be scoured for replacements. Alderman Moustier had himself to put the horses in the traces and lead the convicts to work, ensure that the bodies were not simply dumped in the road, and then at sunset stable the horses.[19] In the old town, around Saint-Jean, where the tumbrils could not penetrate, it was proposed to throw the bodies into the church crypts.

All but a few of the officers of the town, guards, health inspectors, butchers, bakers, masons and street sweepers were dead or had fled. There were no porters to bring grain from the barrier, no apothecaries or druggists, no notaries to take a will.

There was no linen or straw to make mattresses for the dying, no hay for the tumbril-horses, no muleteers to bring wood for the bakers' ovens, no carpenters to make stretchers and no shoes for the convicts for want of a cobbler.[20] Shops and churches were shuttered. No bell sounded.

New plague hospitals filled with a constantly changing population and the squares, quays and the cours were carpeted with dying men, women and children, shut out by their families, husband by wife, wife by husband, child by parents, gathered for shade under the trees or the awnings of closed shops, whimpering for water. Occasionally, a figure would stumble by, livid and delirious, before falling among the dead.[21]

The religious, stepping between the bodies, died like the convicts: by September 4, forty-two Capuchins, twenty-one Jesuits, twenty-two Augustinians and many more.[22] Others barricaded themselves into their convents, to the fury of Belsunce, who threatened them with the loss of their benefices. The bishop was everywhere, on foot, with or without attendants, comforting the sick and distributing his fortune in alms.[23] In the port, families crammed onto boats in the belief that the infection would not pass across the water, surrounded by the bloated corpses of dead dogs.[24] By September 6, up to thirty thousand had died and there were some 2,000 unburied bodies in the streets.

On September 4, the duc d'Orléans appointed Charles de Langeron, a rear admiral of the galleys, commandant of the city of Marseilles with martial-law powers. On the 12th, he arrived on horseback at the town hall and set up headquarters. Able to draw on resources outside the municipality, now reduced to a staff of seven, he had no compunction about commandeering men from the Arsenal and the countryside. He forced shopkeepers to open. Like all good officers, he made others brave.

There was one quarter, facing the sea to the west and known

as the Tourette, where everybody was dead, and the scalding esplanade between the fort of Saint-Jean and the old church of La Major was covered in more than one thousand corpses. Nicolas Roze, a former merchant of Alicante, volunteered to reconnoitre. In a stench that could not be borne longer than two minutes, he inspected two ancient subterranean bastions. On September 16, he led one hundred convicts each with his face masked by a handkerchief soaked in vinegar into the Tourette and in half an hour dragged the bodies into the bastions and covered them with quicklime and soil.[25] (There is a nineteenth-century bust to the Chevalier Roze in the place Fontaine Rouvière. There is no monument to the six hundred and twenty-one convicts who lost their lives during the Marseilles plague of 1720–22.)

Then came a ray of light. "On September 24," Pichatty de Croissante wrote in his Sunday French,

> . . . at the time when the misery and calamity are at their height; when everybody groans and sighs and dies as much in the countryside as in the town; and those who escape the fury fall prey to famine and despair more terrible yet and more cruel than even the plague itself; when the springs of charity that have flowed till now are altogether dried up and the sky seems to have turned to bronze and the earth to iron, as scripture has it [Deut. 28:23] and one wishes for nothing so much as to die, lo! from far away a helping hand reaches down on this unfortunate town.
>
> Mr Law, greater in his intellect and virtues than in his dignities or fortune, lets fall a succour worthy of his great charity, and remits to Messrs Aldermen 100,000 livres for distribution to the poor. A thousand blessings rise from every side. So worthy an act of mercy, and at a time of such extreme necessity, will be graven for all time in the hearts

of this poor people, as it will be in the book of life and of God, who is its origin and will be its recompense.[26]

The magistrates wrote to Law the next day, September 25, wishing that God would reward him "even in this world, for his great generosity".[27] That day, the cargo of the *Grand-Saint-Antoine* was burned on Jarre island, and the day after, the vessel, less her sails but still with her ballast of clinker, was towed to the Jarron creek to the west and burned. (She is visible at about forty-five feet of depth. Her anchor was brought to the surface in 1978.)[28] As the days and nights cooled, so the mortality fell and on October 20 Langeron ordered the Angélus to sound again.[29] On November 1, the feast of All Saints, Belsunce, barefoot among the blood and shit, carrying a cross and with a cord round his neck, led a procession of expiation to the Aix gate.[30]

The magistrates soon found that they could do nothing with Law's paper money. With the prospect of the notes ceasing to be legal tender, they could find nobody beyond the barrier to convert them into silver. The mint in Aix had ceased operations because of the plague, and that in Montpellier refused to cash them, as the aldermen informed Law on November 3.[31] With pockets of plague inland, the markets at the barrier broke down and Langeron and the aldermen proposed sending out ships for grain, but were constrained for want of silver money. "The plague seems to have abated," Pichatty wrote, "only to augment famine and misery."[32]

The aldermen pleaded with Law for silver. Law wrote back, saying that when he had sent the 100,000 livres, "I did all I could. Had it been in my power, I would have had you receive the money in specie [silver], but however sensible I am to the misfortune that overwhelms your town, I find myself unable to convert the bills."[33] Villars wrote that he had reserved some of the new 2½ per cent annuities for the conversion of the town's paper money, while recognising that was not quite what was needed.[34]

Throughout Europe and North America, payment was breaking down. With the re-opening of its stock-transfer books on August 22 by the English calendar, South Sea began to fall, and continued falling. On August 30/September 10, the directors tried to stabilise the price with the promise of a Christmas dividend of £30 per share and a minimum dividend of £50 per year for twelve years. Since it had no trading business, nobody believed that the company could sustain some £15 million a year in dividends. By September 16/27, South Sea could be had for £520 and by the end of the month sold for £290.

The Edinburgh merchant James Wauchope wrote to Alexander Shairp in Holland on September 13/24: "The tumbling of the stocks at London makes many a Cheild claw where he is not youkie [fellow scratch where he is not itching]."[35] "Gyllé" from Paris told Colonel Cornelius Kennedy in London: "Your stocks will in a little tyme be as contemtable as ours."[36]

Investors and merchants fled from paper securities, such as stocks and bills of exchange, and the Kingdom of Great Britain fell back on the metal currency it had outgrown fifty years earlier. Private people called in their debts. Eleanor, Lady Stair, wrote from Bath to Lord Londonderry in "the utmost pain" that the Duchess of Hamilton was demanding repayment of £4,200 by Monday, October 3, and "without your help I don't know which way to turn".[37] Brokers and goldsmith-bankers, unable to meet their mid-summer obligations to deliver South Sea at much higher prices, collapsed like ninepins.

Expert investors came to grief. Lord Londonderry, who had sold forward his shares to Mitford & Merttins at low prices ranging from 540 to 491, could not collect the proceeds when that firm could not pay. He had to go into the Alley himself and cry out the shares for what prices (in the low 200s) he could get. He wrote to Lord Stanhope "under all the concern in the world" that he had lost his sister a large sum of money.[38]

East India dropped with South Sea. On September 20/October 1, Middleton wrote to William Law, with that tact for which Scots bankers have ever been known: "I'm sorry your India Bargains had not a month longer to run, which would have saved a great part of that loss. It is now 230 & the other day under 200." (East India fell under the wager price of 180 in the second week of October.)[39] Middleton was not willing to deliver the East India shares to Londonderry and his partners until the Laws made up their account with him, amounting to about £130,000.[40] (Middleton's book-keeping, never of the most lucid, is now impossible to follow.) Yet their bills of exchange on bankers in Hamburg, Amsterdam and Genoa returned protested.

The Dutch boom was also subsiding. Wauchope in Edinburgh was £900 to the bad for his Dutch investments, and was in dire straits. "Your Rotterdam Insurance has but a sorry aspect," he told William Dundas, Scottish merchant in that town, on October 18/29. "We believe now too late [that] these [were] chimeras." By the 25th, shares in the Rotterdam company had fallen two-thirds from their peak. "They tell at 32 [132]," Wauchope wrote. "Good God whatt's that!"[41] The *junta* of ministers in Madrid rejected all the projects. One scheme they thought so scandalous that had the proposer been a Spanish subject, "His Majesty would have been within his rights to send him to the galleys."[42]

In London, the rising Norfolk politician Sir Robert Walpole and the Bank of England had between them the makings of a rescue for South Sea, for the unfortunate annuitants that had converted into its shares at high prices, and for the reputation of the ministry and court. They were selling dear, Walpole for the premiership that he was to hold for two decades and the Bank for the uncontested financial prominence it has guarded to this day. King George was still in Hanover and Parliament in recess.

For the Jacobites in Paris, the disorder in British credit was manna from heaven. Dillon was beside himself with excitement. At Windsor Castle, his letters to his master in Rome are still dimpled and smudged where post officers in the Italian states had doused them with vinegar against the plague. He drew up a scheme in French, dated October 2 by the English calendar and supposedly from British Jacobites, by which ships of the Company of the Indies would sail from Port Louis "ostensibly for their establishments" (in Louisiana) but carrying 8,000 foot, 2,000 horse and 20,000 muskets for a descent on the English West Country. A second fleet, from either Port Louis or Brest, would embark for Scotland "laying fire at both ends of the Kingdom".[43]

On the 13th, Law reported that the Regent had refused to read or even receive the memorial.[44] Nor was Law inclined to ask the duc d'Orléans for a safe-conduct for James to make his own way, without attendants, to Britain. Law, who had quite enough to do and was anxious about Dubois's agents, did what he could to discourage Dillon. "I'm very sorry to tell you," Dillon wrote to King James on the 21st, "that I find by Mr Arrington [Law] he has little or no hopes of being able to prevail on Seymour [duc d'Orléans] to act against present arrangements, so that if Rowley [King Philip of Spain] does not give a helping hand the most favourable and happiest occasion that ever was will be lost."[45]

In Madrid, the Duke of Ormonde was no more encouraging. Concerning Law's plan for a "union" between France and Spain, he pointed out to James that Philip was still sore at the French aggression of the previous winter. In addition, the marchese Annibale Scotti, the principal adviser to Queen Elizabeth Farnese, had told him nothing could be achieved with France unless the champion of the Hanoverian alliance, the abbé Dubois, were removed.[46] He said James would not be permitted to cross Spanish territory.

Philip was equipping a fleet to relieve his beleaguered possessions in North Africa, Ceuta and Mellilla, which James thought much better deployed in restoring him to his three kingdoms.[47] "Rowley's ingaging in the African stocks damps in a great measure expectations . . . on his assistance," Dillon conceded.[48] The Earl of Strafford wrote from England that James's adherents there were "so concerned in South Sea that it was impossible to get them to aid or [even] treat of your concerns".[49] That left only Law, whose position, Dillon saw, was precarious.

On September 15, Law had tried to re-establish his scheme with the bank accounts taking the place of the banknotes. He created a dual system of payments: one based on silver and the other on bank accounts and shares. The value of the bank accounts was cut to a quarter, but they could be converted into shares at 2,000 livres apiece, which carried the right to a dividend. He thus retained a sort of skeleton of his system, in which money could still be created against the assets and profits of a trading company. If his luck had abandoned him, his ingenuity had not.[50]

On October 10, Law brought forward the demonetisation of all the banknotes to November 1. The decree computed that some 700,327,460 livres in notes had been burned and another 820 millions brought in but not yet destroyed.[51] The notes were now changing hands at the hôtel de Soissons and elsewhere at about a quarter of their face value in silver. The rush to repay debts in cheap paper became a scramble. In the notarial records of the pays d'Auge in Normandy, studied by Jérôme Jambu, debt repayments in the second half of the month were three or four times those of the first fortnight.[52] The Neapolitan philosopher, Ferdinando Galiani, later compared this period to the semi-centennial debt-holidays or "jubilees" of ancient Israel.[53]

Protected by the Regent, and the duc de Bourbon and his mother,

Law was holding on. For all Lord Stanhope's advice, the duc d'Orléans was reluctant to restore the financial system of the old King's reign. As long as Law could still supply him with money, he would retain him. For example, he ordered Law to find 60,000 livres in silver to pay the wages of soldiers of the Champagne regiment, who were digging a canal alongside the river Loing to link the basins of the Loire and the Seine.[54] It was a pet project of his, "which on no account was to be retarded", was completed in good time and remained with his family till the execution of his great-grandson in 1793 during the Revolution.

On the 15th, Law survived an attempt in the Regency Council to strip the Company of the Indies of the collection of indirect taxes and the mints.[55] Dubois, who was building a dossier on Law's dealings with the Jacobites, was proceeding with caution. The harvest had been plentiful and, but for a crime wave in Paris blamed on "the public misery the banknotes have produced" (Buvat),[56] the country orderly. At some point, the Regent would need the Parlement back but it was not yet.

Law's enemies turned their spite on his family. It was said that Lady Katherine had sent Mary Catherine to court in a coach with two footmen outside and two outriders. With her was the ten-year-old Elisabeth-Sophie de Guise, of the ruling house of Lorraine, in the worse of the two seats, facing backwards.[57] (The court memoirists, such as the duc de Saint-Simon, do not mention such presumption.) Young William was nicknamed the *chevalier Systême* or Little Lord System, some said by the Regent himself. Rumours that William was illegitimate and that Seignior was alive at the time of his birth reached the journalist Jean Buvat that month.[58]

On October 23, dining at Law's for the first time in the best part of a year, Thomas Crawford lectured him on his own conduct and that of Lady Katherine. Crawford had heard of "bitter jocose things" said of Law by the Regent's "intimate favourites" without reproof from His Royal Highness. Law, who was as courteous as ever, said that with Great Britain in distress, he was the more inclined to offer the hand of friendship. He called the Jacobites "a parcel of fools", but would not do anything to injure his friends.[59]

Crawford's chief, Sir Robert Sutton, thought that "even with his wings clipped", Law was a "dangerous man" and a threat to British commerce. He was reluctant to tackle him head on.[60] Sutton's embassy had begun badly, for though reckoned a connoisseur he had not asked to view Elisabeth Charlotte's cabinet of coins and medals and she felt hurt and neglected.[61] He never achieved Stair's standing with either the Regent or Lord Stanhope, or the ubiquity of Thomas Crawford. Instead, he devoted some energy to destroying Law's industries in France, and shipping home the British (or Huguenot) artificers "debauch'd into the French service".

The fall in value of the banknotes, and thus of their wages, had caused many of Law's craftsmen to abscond. On October 19, Sutton wrote to London that the best workers had quit Gun Jones's iron foundry at Chaillot; there were just two or three skilled watchmakers at Versailles; the wool cloth and camlet works Law had established in Charles IX's hunting-lodge at Charleval was "deserted"; and, though the Harfleur steel and glass furnaces were operating, there were no markets in Paris for their products.[62] On the 30th, Sutton told Craggs in London that the horologists Henry and Richard Sully and William Blakey were willing to return to England if they were granted pardon and "freedom from molestation": that is, protection from the British creditors who had driven them abroad in the first place.[63] The next day, the workers at Chaillot were paid off, principally in banknotes on which, on conversion into silver, they lost 56 per cent.[64]

Law had one last throw. On October 24, he offered to guarantee the King of France a revenue of 140 million livres in silver for the year to November, 1721 for the expenses of his court, ministry and armed services. The rent the company paid for the right to collect the indirect taxes would rise from 52 million livres to 120 million, or 10 million livres a month beginning on November 1, and the company would pay an extra 20 million livres for the mint privilege as a "free gift" or *don gratuit* in four monthly payments.[65] Where was Law to find this money, and particularly the first 15 million livres due for November?

Nicolas Du Tot, the under-cashier at the bank, reported that the mints had some 52 millions in gold and silver at the end of August, but that had leaked away, paid out to influential people (*gens de faveur*) in return for their banknotes.[66] Law could hope, by his incessant manipulations of the currency, to profit from the various recoinages, but that would not meet his urgent need. While his twenty thousand shares had lost most of their value, he still had a fortune of some 11 million livres in property at cost and other assets that he proposed borrowing against for the sake of the company.[67] By an edict of the 27th, the directors received permission to raise 15 million livres "on their own security".[68]

He also turned on the architects of his success, the Mississippians. In language that might have been left over from the previous reign, the speculators in the company stock were accused of profiting at the expense of the state, sending the proceeds abroad or flaunting an "opulence odious to the public", buying diamonds and other superfluities, cornering markets in provisions and driving up the value of real estate. Rather than impose a tax on surplus profits, the King had resolved that all the original subscribers to the company's share issues must take their certificates to the company secretary to be stamped. Those who could not produce their certificates must buy them from the company for 13,500 livres apiece in banknotes.[69] They must then hold them, immobilised, for three years, collecting only the semi-annual dividends.

The stock market in the garden of the hôtel de Soissons was

ordered closed. On the 29th, guards were posted to clear the garden, driving the regulated trade back to the palais Mazarin and the unregulated to the Quincampoix, and inns around the rue Saint-Martin and elsewhere. Police later raided a café run by a certain Rossignol, in rue de l'Arbre-sec, to find some forty persons hawking paper in front of the entrance and inside, and the landlord, by his own account, powerless to prevent them.[70]

That same October 29, to prevent Mississippians taking their gains abroad, an edict banned any subject of the King from leaving France without a passport, on pain of losing his or her life, until January 1, 1721.[71] Sir Robert Sutton was doubtful that, with such tyrannical policies, Law would succeed. "If he can maintain himself long by *pillage outrez* [barefaced extortion], it will be a wonder of the world," he told Stanhope.[72]

Out at Pontoise, rumours reached the magistrates of rats leaving the sinking ship. It was said, correctly, that François-Matthieu Vernezobre, a senior officer of the company, had fled the country for Holland and, incorrectly, that the bank treasurer, Etienne Bourgeois, had left "[both] having made or rather stolen and pilfered so many millions".[73] (Vernezobre, a Huguenot, travelled to Berlin, where he prospered in business and built the rococo Prinz-Albrecht-Palais in Friedrichstadt.) Matthieu Marais reported that Domenico Angelini, Law's Italian secretary who had handled correspondence with the Durazzo and also Middleton, had retired to Rome, supposedly to bury his father.[74]

Louisiana would once again have to fend for herself. On November 4, Fanny Oglethorpe's husband, the marquis des Marches, wrote to Jean Gravé de La Mancelière, the former captain of the *Union*, who was going out to manage the Mézières-Marches concessions, recommending economy because it would be hard to send funds. "The times, as you see, are changing prodigiously," he wrote.[75]

On November 11, Sutton reported to London that he had provided Richard Sully with money to persuade the master craftsmen to leave Law's factories in France. Though passports were all but impossible to procure, Sully was "vers'd in the Trade, having made several Turns into England to bring away Workmen." Once the master craftsmen were gone, "the Fabricks [factories] will come to nothing in a very short time."[76] Two days later, Rigby was relieved of his command at Lorient.[77]

On the 17th, Law announced two measures to meet the payments to the King's treasury. The first made some changes to the terms of the loan to the directors, which had found no lenders. The second was a compulsory levy on all shareholders of the company of 150 livres a share, 100 livres in gold and 50 livres in paper, paying 4 per cent interest, to raise 22.5 million livres. While it was a forced loan, and those who did not pay up would lose their shares, it had its attractions. The loan would be reimbursed entirely in silver and gold and the banknotes, then at an 84 per cent discount to silver, would be paid at par.[78] The true rate of interest was 44 per cent, which is what bankrupts pay.

That day, November 17, the aldermen of Marseilles received a letter from Law, written on November 6. By hook or by crook, William Law had managed on October 8 to ship 20,000 gold louis to Amsterdam to provide letters of credit for Chavigny to pay the balance of Mlle de Valois's dowry to the Duke of Modena's Genoese creditors.[79] The cash sent earlier to Marseilles for the dowry could now be distributed to the poor.

In his letter to the aldermen, Law said that, with the Regent's approval, he had instructed Jean Taxil, the company representative in Marseilles, to transfer to the town 25,000 piastres and 1,600 marks or 800 pounds of silver in ingots.[80] The next day the money was sent in nineteen chests to Montpellier to be recoined. On the 20th, the town began equipping vessels to buy grain in the east for the coming winter.[81] Law was later held personally liable to the Company of the Indies for 275,184 livres, 17 sols and four deniers.[82]

The Jacobites now mobilised their fantastical imaginations to save their ally, and deployed their expertise in lost causes. Dillon prepared a memorial for Law to show the Regent that proposed a French alliance with Tsar Peter of Russia against Hanover and Austria. It would include the throne of Poland for the duc de Bourbon or, as Dillon put it to James, "a bait for his [Law's] chief friend". James thought that "a very distant" prospect. He himself redoubled his efforts to gain the cardinal's cap for Dubois. "I shall press it the more that that step may have influence over greater matters," he wrote to Paris on November 23.[83]

Ecclesiastical politics now impinged on John Law's fate. Pope Clement's anti-Jansenist Bull of 1713, known as *Unigenitus*, had damaged the French Church to the point of schism and would torment the country until mid-century. For all the efforts of Dubois and the Regent, the Cardinal Louis-Antoine de Noailles, Archbishop of Paris, and a number of colleagues objected to the language of the Bull. In the Parlement of Paris, the Jansenists allied with the defenders of Gallican rights, insisting that *Unigenitus* could not become the law of the land until it first became a law of the Church.

The duc d'Orléans resolved to put an end to an affair whose theological character did not much interest him and, as he is reported to have said of the bishops, "put a bridle on my donkeys".[84] On Monday, November 11, *lettres de cachet* were sent to Pontoise ordering the magistrates to remove themselves for the next term to Blois, 120 miles to the south. This super-exile would make even the routine administration of justice difficult and threatened the destruction of the court.

Under pressure, Cardinal de Noailles agreed on the 16th to publish pastoral instructions, showing how *Unigenitus* should be interpreted.[85] "No action in his life," he is said to have told the young King, "had cost him so much."[86] The Regent rescinded the order directing the Parlement to Blois and ordered the magistrates to assemble at Pontoise on November 25 to register the royal declaration and letters patent on the Bull. As the price of registration, they would be allowed to return with honour to Paris. For their part, they expected that Law would be banished, for the Regent had, as President Hénault put it, "to decide either for us or for Law".[87]

Worse was the looming deadline for the payments to the King's Treasury which Law could not meet. On November 27, at 10 a.m., the bank's under-cashier Du Tot was told to cease paying and receiving cash.[88] That day the leading painters of the French court, including Hyacinthe Rigaud (who had painted Law in 1719), Nicolas de Largillière and Louis de Boullogne II, came to the bank to view Pellegrini's almost completed ceiling.[89] It must have been a grim occasion.

On December 3, from across the rue Vivienne, Buvat spotted the arrival of the Regent, who spent two hours in the bank, closeted with Law and the directors.[90] The next day at Pontoise, the Parlement unanimously registered the King's declaration on *Unigenitus* "in conformity with the maxims of the Kingdom on the authority of the church".[91] Dillon wrote to King James: "We approach a decision of matters here. God send it be as wish'd to Ashburn's [Law's] advantage."[92]

On Monday, December 9, Law gave up. That evening, he waited on the duc d'Orléans and asked to be released from his service. As Law told Thomas Crawford a couple of days later, he asked permission to retire to Rome with the one-and-a-half million livres in hard cash he had brought into France. He proposed that his lands and estate be sold to cover his debts and his obligations to the King.

The Regent had at first demurred, saying Law had a family and children who would lack property. Nor did he wish him to leave the country. For all the loyalty and disinterested service that Law had shown, he, the Regent. would not be able to prevent a public murmur '"if he left the Kingdom before there was a clear picture of his private financial affairs". The duc d'Orléans added with a smile that Mr Law, who had governed and shaped the Kingdom of France for three years as he wished, would find it hard to settle in another European country. Mr Law should not go too far away for he could be sure of his friendship and protection against enemies. He then embraced Law tenderly.[93] Elisabeth Charlotte later heard (perhaps from her son) that Law said: "Sire, I have made great errors, because I am a human being, but you will find neither malice nor deceit in my conduct."[94] It was by now about nine in the evening.[95]

By noon the next day, Paris was full of rumour although it took another day, the roads being deep in mud, for the magistrates at Pontoise to hear the news. Sutton reported on the 11th that Law had been told to retire to his property at Guermantes, twenty miles to the east, "but remains at liberty".[96] On the 12th, Rosalba Carriera called at the hôtel Langlée for a jaunt she had planned with Lady Katherine to the Gobelins tapestry factory in the faubourg Saint-Marcel on the left bank. There she found the whole family had left for the opera at the Palais-Royal.[97] It was a revival of Jean-Baptiste Lully's musical tragedy *Thésée* (which has been revived again in recent years). The audience was flabbergasted by Law's audacity. "English impudence as usual," Matthieu Marais wrote in his journal. With the Law family was the duc de La Force, Law's one-time "head clerk".[98]

On the morning of Saturday, December 14, Father Lewis Inese or Innes of the Scots College at the Sorbonne, rue des Fossés-Saint-Victor, called at the bank. Back in October, Law had given him fifty shares in the Company of the Indies, with backdated dividends, to pay for the training of twelve priests and to help old and decrepit missioners.[99] Inese brought with him James III's letter of thanks.

"When he had read it over," Father Inese wrote to the King,

> . . . he said he could not but admire your Majesties goodness in takeing so much nottice of what little he had done; & added that he hopd yo was satisifed that it was not for want of goodwill that he did not your Majesty more essentiall service. He was going on with that discourse when people of quality came up to him & interrupted him, for there was a great crowd in the appartement. He seem'd not in the least dejected, but spoke to everybody in the same easy way he used, & in appearance, with the same chearfull countenance, which I found everybody admired. That same afternoon he went to Guermande.[100]

In the coach with him, Law took the Earl of Mar, who had been in Versailles and Paris since September, whether for his company or to show the town that he was under the protection of the Stuart court. That was with the permission of the duc d'Orléans.[101]

In the evening, at the abbey of Saint-Martin overlooking Pontoise, the magistrates of the Parlement of Paris sat down to a great supper for the marriage of the First President's daughter, Marie-Anne de Mesmes, to Guy de Durfort, duc de Lorges, There was cannon fire and fireworks and the town beneath the abbey windows was illuminated.

In the middle of supper, a visitor arrived with news that Law had left Paris and the Parlement would be summoned back to the capital on Monday. "We were overjoyed at the news," one of the judges remembered.[102] The orchestra played and Michel Richard de Lalande popped up amid the tables with his violin. At midnight, the magistrates processed in a body to church, and at 2 a.m. the bridal couple were bedded.[103]

Later that Sunday morning, Thomas Crawford drove out to Guermantes but was obliged (or so he said) to cool his heels at the village inn till "the late" Earl of Mar had returned to Paris on the Monday morning. As he told Secretary Craggs in an eight-page letter in French, his principal business was for Lord Londonderry but "curiosity" caused him to while away with Law that whole day and night. Guermantes still stands, as a place for business conferences. It requires no great imagination to place the two Scotsmen in the great salon or have them walk before the tall windows overlooking the drizzly park, so far from where each of them had begun.

Law blamed his disgrace on an alliance of the Regent's principal mistress, Marie-Madeleine, widowed marquise de Parabère, and her friend and his boon companion, Charles, comte de Nocé. He lamented he had never had an aptitude for intrigue, and never would have. Crawford noted that in speaking of the Regent, and of all the kind words the prince had said at their parting, "a look of sadness passed over his physiognomy." Law clung to the hope that the bank accounts might survive.[104]

In Paris, there were reports that Law would be sent to his estate at Effiat in the Auvergne. Eleanor de Mézières was alarmed for his life. "I fear he will come to a bad end [*je crien le surcs funeste qu'il auras*]," she wrote to King James that Monday. "It's a shame really that he did not once place limits on his boundless imagination for he has something great about him. He has perished for too grand a conception of himself."[105]

Dubois now made his move. Word spread of Law's correspondence with the Duke of Ormonde in Madrid and the court of Spain. There were rumours that an officer and detachment were on their way to Guermantes to escort Law to the fortress of Pierre Encise that stands on a crag above the two rivers in Lyons.

On Tuesday, Law wrote to the Regent, blithely employing the Hanoverian name for James III "the Pretender". "I learned today that I am accused of helping the Pretender and of being in contact with Spain. What I did was give succour to unfortunate people who did not have bread, among whom were such as had done me service in the past. The Duke of O[rmonde] saved my life." As for reconciling France and Spain, that was a policy approved by HRH. "Posterity will vindicate me," he wrote.[106]

Law also wrote to Crawford, asking him to call on Dubois and explain that he had helped the Jacobites only with money, which was, in its way, true.[107] Crawford did as he was asked and found the Archbishop of Cambrai in an excellent frame of mind. The Archbishop denied that he was Law's enemy but, on the contrary, he claimed he had dissuaded the duc d'Orléans from having Law arrested on December 14. Crawford did not believe him. Dubois added that "even if he [Law] had engagements with the Pretender they could not have been of great consequence."[108]

In the course of the day, Law heard from the duc de Bourbon that the Regent had promised him to let Law leave the country, and would issue passports. Law should find a safe place "for the indecision we see everywhere makes me tremble for you".[109] Brother William, Lady Katherine and Mary Catherine would remain in Paris, at least for the present, as also young William's governor or tutor, Miles Thornton.[110] Notary Ballin or one of his clerks ensconced himself at Guermantes to record Law's powers of attorney over his properties. On Wednesday, December 18, Law gave "Dame Catherine Knowles, his wife" the authority to sell furniture, plate, silver, horses, carriages and harness.[111]

The passport, signed by the King in the presence of the duc d'Orléans, arrived later that day. It permitted "Mr Dujardin", travelling with three persons, to leave the country without let or hindrance, but on the contrary to be furnished with any aid or assistance he might require.[112]

That evening, Law, young William, and one or more servants set off in coaches belonging to the duc de Bourbon or his mistress, the marquise de Prie.[113] They rolled through the mud by way of Saint-Denis and Chantilly. One of M. le Duc's gentlemen escorted them, and several of his hunt servants. The *Gazette d'Amsterdam*, in its report from Paris on December 23, said the post houses had orders to provide no relay horses to anybody else until Law had had an "eight-hour start".[114]

At Valenciennes, the last town before the border with the Austrian Netherlands, they were held up. Argenson's son, René-Louis, who was now Intendant of the generality, wanted some sport at Law's expense. Why was William's name not on the passport? How did he know that Law had not obtained the passport by subterfuge? He must send to Paris for HRH's orders. In the end, after two days, young Argenson let Law go, but not before relieving him of various papers and more than "two hundred pistoles in new-minted coin".[115] Law had with him a diamond "of inferior water" that young Argenson did not find.[116] The party carried on through Quiévrain and Mons but at the gate into Brussels, Law found his incognito was blown.

In Paris, on the 21st, Rosalba Carriera called at the bank. She was keen to see the ceiling on the first floor, painted seventy-five years before by Giovanni Francesco Romanelli for Cardinal Mazarin. Peeping into the gallery, she found the vault "covered from top to bottom with books of banknotes".[117] On the 24th, Lady Katherine sold to a certain Lafontaine ten coaches for the sum of 24,600 livres.

The sales deed has been soaked with water, and from the flaking paper only the odd word can still be read: "two-seater", "gilded", "upholstered in green velvet", traces of an existence otherwise scarcely believable.[118] Lady Katherine moved with Kate into furnished lodgings in the faubourg Saint-Germain. It was said that she did not intend to leave Paris until all her husband's debts were discharged.[119] With their departure, unpaid tradesmen and others stormed the hôtel Langlée and carted away the pictures and looking-glasses.[120] Law's destitution left his creditors abroad with no recourse. The same day, December 13, in London, Middleton shut up shop. Threatened with arrest, Abraham Mouchard in Amsterdam kept to his house.[121] Edward Crean in Madrid eventually took refuge in the British Embassy.[122]

On the last day of that year, a procession wound its way along the walls of Marseilles, led by Bishop Belsunce, and accompanied by soldiers with their heads uncovered and their weapons lowered. As they passed along the ramparts, Belsunce's steward looked down into the pits where "most of the dead were only half-covered, and one could see here a head, there arms and legs."[123]

That evening, in Charroux, a high village in the Bourbonnais, the parish priest of the church of Saint-Sulpice, François Dalouhe, completed his register of baptisms, marriages and funerals in duplicate for the year.

From the depths of France, after the last of the infants' burials, Father Dalouhe wrote a note for God and posterity on the year just ending. He spoke of the abundant harvest of fruit and grain, the plague at Marseilles and the fire that ravaged the city of Rennes, the reconciliation of the bishops on *Unigenitus*, the humiliation of the Parlement of Paris at Pontoise, the rise in price of provisions and the manipulations of the currency. He concluded: "An infinite number of private citizens were ruined by the banknotes and the operations of the system of Mr Lavv, who made the state his dupe."[124]

CHAPTER THIRTEEN

A Broken Dandy

M. le D. d'O a encore une foiblesse pour cet homme.
(The Duke of Orleans still has a weakness for that man.)

GUILLAUME DUBOIS[1]

Law's flight from Paris saved his life and rescued his name. Had he tried to take his fortune abroad, France and history would have called him a crook and forgotten him. Instead John Law set off, at the age of forty-nine, into a second exile.

With his incognito in pieces, Law did not linger in Brussels, leaving on Christmas Eve, 1720. As he told the duc de Bourbon, he expected "insult" from his enemies.[2] Rumours reached Paris that he had been stabbed to death at Brussels by servants of the comte de Horn, while Sir Robert Sutton believed the Regent, to preserve his secrets, planned "to do him a bad turn on the road".[3] Thomas Crawford, always better informed than his chief, reported that the duc d'Orléans was distressed and drinking.[4]

The party passed on bad roads through Louvain, Aachen or Aix-la-Chappelle and Cologne. At Bonn on December 29, Law was said to have had a meeting of several hours with the Prince-Elector, Joseph Clemens.[5] Travelling south through the German states, by January 10 they were at Augsburg, and then Munich, where

Law certainly did not call on Prince-Elector Maximilian II, and then Innsbruck on January 16.

In young William's papers at Maastricht in the Netherlands are passports in French and German, signed at Copenhagen on January 18 by King Frederick IV of Denmark and Norway, permitting Colonel Pierre/Peter de Ferry, commander of the fortress of Christiansand on the Norwegian side of the Skagerrak, and his son, Navy Lieutenant Laurence/Lorenz de Ferry to "make a voyage in Italy".[6] William, at fourteen, was young even for eighteenth-century navies.

The passports were probably procured by the roving Huguenot financier and sometime Scottish subject, Jean-Henri Huguetan, who as Count Gyldensten or Guldenstein was in King Frederick's service and was anxious to have Law work on his master's shattered finances.[7] Law may not have received the passports until he was in Italy. From Innsbruck, the Laws crossed the Brenner and on January 19 came to Venice with its unique topography, peculiar constitution and safety from prosecution. They gave their name as Gardiner.[8]

In 1721, the Most Serene Republic of Venice was a shadow. With the loss of Cyprus, the Morea and Crete, the Republic had ceased to be a Mediterranean power, but its commerce was still important and it was a resort for pleasure of all sorts, and the world capital of music and painting.

The Senate permitted libertinage, as the writer Giacomo Casanova put it in the next generation, as a sketch or caricature of the liberty that should have reigned.[9] The nobility were discouraged from consorting with foreigners. Citizens spied on one another for the Inquisitors of State of the Council of Ten, placing unsigned denunciations in the mouths of stone lions in the walls of the ducal palace and certain churches. Without the mask, an eastern institution adapted to Venetian purposes, social life would have been impossible.

At that time, neither Great Britain nor France had embassies at Venice. The Senate objected to Louis XIV appointing a Venetian nobleman, Cardinal Pietro Ottoboni, as Protector of France at the Holy See in Rome. Ambassadors were recalled. Representing France as chargé d'affaires was Nicolas de Frémont, who had instructions from Dubois to shun Law, but "discreetly" (*sans affectation*)[10] and also to find out if he had any money. Frémont followed the spirit rather than the letter of his instructions, refused to see Law or accept an invitation to dinner and did all that he could to undermine him. He put it about that Law had brought with him a jewel-box of diamonds worth 25–30 million livres.[11]

Frémont was a functionary but he had with him as consul and Italian secretary Jean Le Blond, who succeeded his father in 1718 and was succeeded by his son, so that his family occupied the post for more than a century. He was to be a friend to Law, and to young William and Mary Catherine, as later to Jean-Jacques Rousseau (never an easy or rewarding line of conduct). Le Blond knew everybody and was so self-effacing that he once waited on the Papal Nuncio and a visiting Roman princess at the Ambassador's table.[12] He later sent sonatas and cello strings to young Kate.[13] His reward is Rosalba Carriera's pastel of him in the Accademia picture galleries in Venice.

It was not until late 1723 that the Ottoboni affair subsided and Jacques-Vincent de Languet, comte de Gergy (1667–1734) arrived as French Ambassador. His public entry in 1726 is portrayed by the artist Antonio Canal, known as Canaletto. Gergy had little to do, all of it delicate, and maintained a household of thirty-six and, after his public entry, fifty persons, including six gondoliers and at least one resident spy for the Inquisitors of State, his *maestro di casa* or butler, Stefano La Platz.[14] Even so, the Venetians thought the comte de Gergy stingy.[15]

The British resident, Colonel Elizeus Burges (*c.*1670–1736) had known Law in London in the 1690s, where he lived a brawling life, killing two men in fights. Renowned for his drinking and swearing, Burges was an unlikely appointment as Governor of puritan Massachusetts in 1715, and gave up the commission for a pay-off from the colony's London agent of £1,000. That was what the eighteenth century called a "job".[16] In 1719, Burges was appointed resident at Venice. When the young Earl of March came to Venice in 1721, his mother, the Duchess of Richmond, begged him not to "keepe Mr. Burges company too much, for I hear he is a violent drinker which is that has killed all our English youths in Italy".[17] Burges was troubled by gout.

He was also a connoisseur of music and painting, There are at least two portraits of him. One is a caricature labelled "Mister Collonel" by the virtuoso Anton Maria Zanetti the Elder, who had joined the Pellegrini-Carriera party in Paris the previous summer and met Law.

The other is in a corner of a view by Canaletto of the Santa Chiara canal, now in the Cognacq-Jay Museum in Paris. Burges is standing in front of his residence about to board his gondola, the boatmen in livery, but is distracted by a pretty woman on the quay, and makes as if to follow her. Colonel Burges lived with a Spanish lady, Mrs Victoria Hernandez, to whom he left in his will 15,000 French livres.[18] He had a commission to collect a debt of £5,000 from Law.[19] He later told Frémont that "at heart, he did not care for Law" and would have had nothing to do with him but for orders from the Court in London.[20]

Burges's principal business, besides the usual maritime disputes, was to clear through customs duty-free a great volume of French wine and to deter British and Irish tourists from going on to Rome. In that city, there was no Hanoverian resident, and the Stuarts were profuse with passports, introductions to the leading Roman families, medical care, opera tickets, an Anglican chapel and, later, a Protestant burial ground. A Hanoverian spy reported to London about this time that Jacobite courtiers haunted "all the cafés in the piazza di Spagna, where the foreigners live . . . and make themselves agreeable in hundreds of different ways."[21]

The Jacobites had seen a revolution in their fortunes. In the early evening of December 31, 1720, at the Palazzo Muti in the Piazza dei Santi Apostoli, renamed the Palazzo del Re ("Palace of the King"), Clementina Sobieska gave birth to a son. The guns on the papal fortress of Castel Sant'Angelo sounded a salute. The boy was baptised an hour later Charles Edward Louis, the "Bonnie Prince Charlie" of Scottish history but to the palace under-servants and even his parents "Carluccio".

The birth of a Prince of Wales promised to preserve the Jacobite cause for another lifetime. Amid a blizzard of letters to the King of France, the Regent, Elisabeth Charlotte, the duc de Bourbon, the Tsar and the Emperor, James III found time on January 3 to write to John Law. "Neither the joy I have for the great blessing God have been pleased to send me," the King wrote in English, "nor the hurry of writing wch that occasions, can make me delay a moment letting you know how truly concerned I am at all that befalls you. No Change of Fortune shall ever alter those just sentiments I have for you. You show yourself superior to all the Variations of Courts & by that deserve to have the first rank in them."[22]

In telling the duc d'Orléans that he intended to go to Rome, Law probably meant no more than that he would not enter the service of a rival prince. "I have always hated work," he told the duc de Bourbon from the road. "I have returned to myself."[23] None the less, he may have thought of working with James III. There were rumours in Rome that Law's former secretary,

Domenico Angelini, had bought for him the Palazzo Orsini for 92,000 scudi (£22,500) and deposited 120,000 Spanish pistoles (£100,000) at the Vatican bank, the Banco di Santo Spirito.[24] (By way of comparison, Pope Clement paid a rent of 1,632 scudi or £400 per annum to house the Stuart court in the Palazzo del Re.)[25]

James was, as ever, short of money and since Mar's retirement had no Secretary of State. Yet despite the invitation in his letter of January 3, James III was interested less in Law in Rome than in Law in Paris. "'Tis thought Mr Law may chance to come here," he wrote to the Duke of Ormonde in Madrid on the 11th, "wch I should be very glad of, but I cannot but be truely concernd for his leaving the ministery [in France], for I shall never get a better friend than him in that country."[26] (As it turned out, Clement XI died that March but his successor, Innocent XIII named Dubois Cardinal in July. Under urging from Tencin, by then French chargé d'affaires at Rome and close to the Stuarts, the new cardinal and chief minister to the Regent renewed James's French pension in 1722.)

The morning after his arrival in Venice, January 20, Law called on Burges at Santa Chiara and, as Frémont reported, spent a long time shut up with him, while young William swung his heels outside.[27] Law explained that Rome would suit him best. So it very well might, said Burges, "if the Pretender did not happen to be resident there".

Burges warned Law that if he travelled to Rome, he would make himself "very suspect to the Ministry in England". He said that Law had always been taxed with Jacobitism, and the Ministry in London would conclude he had gone to offer his "counsel, services and means" to the enemy of the King their master. In short, he "would shut for ever the door to England". (That is what happened to Law's disciple in the next generation, Sir James Steuart of Goodtrees, inventor of the phrase "political economy", who visited Rome on his Grand Tour in the winter of 1739 and was won over by James III.)[28]

Burges was a rough customer and not above a little menace. Should Law travel to Rome, he would face "very disagreable consequences, and new perils".[29] He invited Law to dinner the next afternoon but one.

With the help of Giovanni Battista Santirota, a Venetian who made himself useful to foreigners, on January 30 Law rented a furnished house in the parish of Santo Stefano,[30] and gave every sign of seeing out Carnival, due to end on Ash Wednesday, February 26. Frémont said Santirota had been delegated by the Inquisitors to spy on Law but, if that was the case, his reports have not been preserved.[31] (In Venice, everybody thought everybody else was a police spy.)

Santirota may have felt Law was good for a loan but he was disappointed, and a couple of months later he mortgaged some valuable pictures that became the foundation of the Schulenburg collection.[32] Venice had had its share of merchant bankruptcies at the end of 1720.[33]

To Lord Londonderry, Law wrote on February 14, that "Mr Burgess my friend and old acquaintance thinks I should not continue my journey to Rome. The reasons he gives me, and which are conforme to my way of thinking, have determined me to put off that journey."[34] Law never saw Rome.

In Venice, there was no need, or even possibility, of a coach and team, and gondolas and other boats were subject to sumptuary limits. Law was living on half a Spanish pistole or nine or ten shillings sterling a day.[35] "I have no more ambition," he wrote to the abbé Tencin on February 22. Despite a touch of rheumatism in his legs, "I go every evening to the opera, and I very much like being alone without a valet or coach, going everywhere on foot without attracting any more notice than the most ordinary citizen." He preferred a private existence "with a moderate sufficiency" to "all the employments and honours the King of France could give me".[36]

He only wished that Kate were with him to enjoy the operas,

which included, at San Giovanni Grisostomo on or about February 11, the first night of Giuseppe Maria Orlandini's *Nerone* with the stars Faustina Bordoni (Ottavia) and Francesca Cuzzoni (Poppaea), battles, coronations and elephants.[37]

Law attended the open house given each night in San Simeone Grande to distinguished foreigners by the Imperial Ambassador, Count Johann Baptist von Colloredo, and his second wife, Antonia von Thurn und Valsassina.[38] Colloredo was as musical as Law and commissioned festival pieces from, among others, Antonio Vivaldi. One person Law did not see was Rosalba Carriera who returned that March to Venice and was displeased with him. Lady Katherine had paid for the family portraits, but Pellegrini was still waiting for much of his fee for the ceiling at the bank.[39] Her correspondents in Paris pressed her for gossip about Law, but she gave no answer.[40]

Law returned to the gaming table, but without his old skill or luck. For centuries, the Venetian Senate had attempted to suppress public gaming in the streets and the arcades of St Mark's Square, and in private clubs called *ridotti* or *casini*. Wishing to control and profit from something it could not abolish, the Senate in 1638 licensed a *Ridotto pubblico* for games of chance and rented for the purpose from the Dandolo family a house on the Calle Vallaresso, in the parish of San Moisè. Under precise regulations, only noblemen, unmasked and in full wig, stole and patrician robes, could hold the bank (though they sold shares to commoners).[41] Everybody else had to mask. This place with its mortuary decor appears in paintings of the mid-eighteenth century, the best of them Francesco Guardi's *Il Ridotto* in the Ca' Rezzonico. The principal room survives, much altered, within the Hotel Monaco-Grand Canal.

The ordinance of 1638 did not kill off the private *ridotti.* In an investigation in 1744 on behalf of the Council of Ten, the Inquisitors counted one hundred and eighteen private clubs, not all for gaming, the majority in San Moisè, but also in the neighbouring parish of San Geminiano.[42] (A dozen survive in the city and on the lagoon island of Murano, put to other uses.) Law's principal loss was to a nobleman named Vittorio Delfino, so he may have played like the punter in the Pulcinella mask and tricorn hat leaning on the banker's table on the left of Guardi's picture. As Casanova says, in the only wisdom in his writings, "The punter always loses [*Qui ponte doit perdre*]."[43]

Frémont reported to Dubois that Law had lost 4,000 or 5,000 sequins (£2,000–£2,500) at play, and had pawned the diamond with the banker Aurelio Rezzonico for 1,000 pistoles, a third of its value.[44] By some means or other, Frémont was reading Law's letters to Londonderry and others. On March 14, Law left for a tour of Lombardy, and Ravenna, where he tried to call in a debt from Cardinal Cornelio Bentivoglio, who as papal nuncio or ambassador in Paris had invested in Law's company.[45] He returned to Venice on the 23rd. Frémont reported that the death of Pope Clement (on March 19), and the resulting vacancy, had caused him to fear assassination and come hurrying back.[46]

"The richest citizen there has ever been" was broke.[47] Though he was receiving money from Lady Katherine, he was drawing bills on the marquis de Lassay, a large shareholder in the Company of the Indies and devoted friend of the dowager duchesse de Bourbon, who remained loyal to Law;[48] and on Chavigny, French minister in Genoa. He tried to borrow against some pictures Ippolito De Mari was holding for him in that city. He wrote to the duc d'Orléans, reminding him of their parting interview, and saying that he had no means to "subsist decently" let alone discharge his debts.[49]

The Regent of France had other matters to occupy him. With Law gone, there appeared to be no alternative to restoring the French national debt in the form of perpetual annuities and venal offices financed by private tax collectors. The new controller general of the finances, Félix Le Pelletier de La Houssaye, appointed on December 12, 1720 after years as a provincial Intendant, immediately recalled the Pâris brothers from their rustic exiles with a request from the Regent that they present themselves "as promptly as possible".[50]

Law's last efforts to raise money from shareholders had succeeded and the company met its obligations to the King for December. Yet, as Le Pelletier de La Houssaye told a meeting of the Company of the Indies on December 29, there were still the troops to be paid for the first ten days of January and the interest on the Town Hall annuities. The company must immediately advance fifteen million livres or give up its role in collecting taxes and operating the mints. The duc de Bourbon, "a little warm" as Thomas Crawford reported, tried to gain a few days' delay, but the tide was against him, and the company was left only with its overseas commerce.[51] According to the duc d'Antin, a substantial shareholder, "The Regent and the Controller General then retired, delighted to revert to the ancient form of finance."[52]

The Pâris brothers were in the capital by January 3, and set about clearing away the wreckage of Law's System. It was not an easy matter. If they converted all the liabilities of the System into debts of the Crown, they would exhaust the King's revenue with interest payments. If they loaded them onto the Company of the Indies, they would bankrupt it and leave France dependent on the Dutch and English long-haul trade for luxuries such as pepper, coffee, tea and porcelain. If they defaulted, they would injure many families who had, at the King's request, invested dowries and inheritances in Law's company shares.

Between those extremes, the four brothers chose a course that would spread the pain "in proportion with the capacities of the kingdom and the requirements of justice".[53] By an edict of January 26, all the securities created by John Law, from the company shares to the banknotes, bank accounts and annuities had to be submitted within two months to examination by special commissioners to receive a stamp or "Visa". They would then be converted into perpetual or life annuities, offices and coin on a sliding scale according to how respectably the securities had been acquired. The Regent made available just over 40 million livres a year to pay interest on the annuities to be created.

At the meeting of the Regency Council that Sunday, in the presence of the King, the Regent and the duc de Bourbon quarrelled as to who had let Law leave the country. The members of the Council vied with one another to make presents to the King of their company shares. The Regent offered his 4,000, M. le Duc 1,500, the comte de Toulouse 300 and the duc d'Antin 200. The prince de Conti proposed to renounce the duchy of Mercoeur in Auvergne that he had bought with his speculative gains. Such adult squabbling must have alarmed the boy King.[54]

The Visa would be minute and brutal, take eighteen months to complete, employ thousands of clerks and notaries and cost, according to Nicolas Du Tot, 9–10 million livres.[55] The commissioners reduced some two and a half billion livres in paper securities to a new national debt of 1.7 billion. Responding to grumbles that those speculators who had sold out before the crash were enjoying lives of ease and luxury, the Regent imposed the following year a windfall tax or "extraordinary capitation" on two hundred and seventy-four "Mississippians".

Those did not include any of the dukes and peers, which would have been scandalous, or any foreigners who might invoke diplomatic protection, except Arbuthnot and Cantillon who (one presumes) had become Frenchmen. Heading the list, with a penalty of 8 million livres, were Antoine Chaumont and his wife, Catherine Barré, said to be vulgarians. The total in penalties was 188 million livres but it is most unlikely that was recovered.[56] The Chaumonts were refractory, refusing to vacate their estate at

Yvry-sur-Seine for its new owner or provide keys to the store cupboards.

As for the Company of the Indies, it was at first made answerable for the banknotes. The shareholders, led by the duc de Bourbon, protested that the merger of bank and company had been forced on them by the Crown, and managed in the end (June 1725) to prevail but not before, on April 7, 1721, the company was placed under government administration and receivers were appointed to cast up its assets and liabilities.[57]

On April 21, Gérard Mellier, mayor of the city of Nantes, was appointed receiver of the company in Lorient. Arriving at the port on April 27, he found ships still not despatched after fourteen months swinging at anchor and oak gun carriages rotting for want of a £50 shed to keep out the rain. He was mobbed by hungry sailors and their wives clamouring for pay. The next day a flûte named the *Charente*, carrying German settlers for the Arkansas but unable to pass Cape Finisterre for disease and unseaworthiness, was wrecked on the Jument reef in the approaches.[58] On May 20, the Regent ordered that all the German families still in Lorient should be sent home with 20 livres per man, woman and child.[59]

Mellier spurned all offers of hospitality from Rigby's deputies and for six weeks barricaded himself in with the books of the former cashier, Gabriel Rodollet.

"Here is daylight robbery," he wrote to the former Intendant of Brittany, François-Antoine Ferrand, on May 19. "Erasures, items crossed-out, others inserted: one can make no sense of it. It is chaos."[60] He suspected Rigby had used company funds to speculate in the money market, booking the gains from foreknowledge of Law's devaluations and revaluations to a secret account. He confronted Rodollet who denounced Rigby. The following week, Rigby was arrested for corruption (*dilapidation*) in Paris and taken to the Bastille. (The Regent later permitted him to have his valet with him.)[61] Mellier found no malfeasance on Law's part. After six weeks in Lorient, he was convinced that the company John Law had created, properly managed, was a going concern.

A balance sheet, drawn up a year later, showed the company possessed seventy ocean-going vessels, not including lighters and brigantines, whether at sea, laid up at Lorient, or on the stocks or in dry dock in the French Channel ports. With merchandise, slaves and property in Barbary, Louisiana, Senegal, Saint-Domingue, China and the Indies, as well as cash and bills, the company had net assets of 46,108,745 livres 15 sols and 4 deniers not including some 12 million livres supposedly owed the company by John and William Law Sr.[62] That was net of all debts except the bank-notes and bank accounts of the defunct Banque royale.

It was a great achievement and the work of a single man, John Law of Lauriston, in just over three years of activity. Here was capital and to spare for a worldwide business,[63] but only after a more rigorous attention to expense than Law had ever applied.

The first casualty of the receivers' parsimony was Louisiana, which had cost the company some six million livres under Law and returned nothing.[64]

Through the first half of 1721, vessels continued to arrive, offloading African slaves and French and German settlers in numbers far beyond the resources of the colony. In a single week in March, 531 enslaved West Africans were landed at Biloxi.[65] On June 4, the *Portefaix* brought news that Law had left France which, as Bénard de La Harpe wrote, "distressed many people for fear that the establishment of Louisiana would not proceed with the same enthusiasm".[66] The traffic from France diminished. Unable to feed his private soldiers, Bienville sent them to live in the villages of the Biloxi and Pascagoulas.[67] None the less, in his brief time in power, Law had ensured the settlement would survive and preserve, within the modern United States of America, a distinct character.

In August, the *Solide*, the *Vierge de Grâce* and the *Amphitrite* sailed into Lorient after nearly two years away in the East Indies, bringing six hundred tons of pepper, silks, chintzes and muslins from Pondicherry and Bengal. The cargoes were auctioned at Nantes in December, yielding some six million livres. Half a dozen other vessels, despatched under Law in 1720 to Yemen, Mozambique, Surat and China returned in the course of 1722.[68] Those rewarding voyages caused the company, when it emerged from administration in 1723, to redirect its commerce away from wilderness Louisiana to the trading cities of Asia. The shares changed hands at about 1,000 livres apiece.

As for Law's own affairs, by a decree of January 9, the Regency Council appointed an extraordinary commission to examine and rule on all claims on Law's estate in France, as if he were already dead. That took the matter out of Lady Katherine's hands. This commission sat until the end of the old regime in 1790, and its records form the entire sub-series G/6 in the French National Archives. Already on January 18, Sir Robert Sutton reported to Stanhope that "it is to be feared that his creditors will recover only very little of their claims."[69]

Law insisted that he had left more than enough property in France to cover his debts in that country and, on the contrary, that the French state owed him money. "Besides the actions [company shares] & the estates I have in France," he wrote to Londonderry on April 10, "what I am in advance by the Kings order amounts to more than will satisfie my creditors and give me the same capital I brought with me to France, which is all I desire."[70] An inventory drawn up for him on New Year's Day of 1722 proposed that, even after the sale of his furniture at the hôtel Langlée, Guermantes and La Marche, his estates, library, bonds and offices were valued at the end of 1721 at cost (net of associated debts) at 10,418,882 livres.[71] His twenty thousand company shares were, because of the

Visa, impossible to value but might be worth as much as twice that.

The problem was that Law had made no distinction between his private affairs and those of the company and of the King. In that, he was not unique. The practice of eighteenth-century finance was for private men to advance money on their own credit and then recover it with interest from the straitened public purse. For example, Secretary Craggs paid for the repatriation of Law's artificers out of his own pocket rather than wait on the deliberate motions of the Lords of Treasury.[72]

Over and over, Law told his correspondents in France that he had paid for the building works on the company's headquarters, the palais Mazarin, and built vessels for the fleet at his own expense, and that he had always planned to turn over his property to the company. "I never regarded the great fortune I had as belonging to me, but to the state," he told the marquis de Lassay.[73] He also said that at the Regent's order, he had used company funds to pay subsidies to the Crown of Sweden and relieve the starving poor in Marseilles. What he did not say, but seems all too probable, is that he used company funds to meet the margin calls on his wagers against the English stocks. Middleton drew on the Law brothers' account or on the company account depending on which had funds. Had the wagers been successful, would Law have turned his gains over to the Company of the Indies?

Creditors paraded before the special commission: masons, master ironworkers, carpenters, suppliers of timber, gardeners, the under-librarian in the rue Vivienne, the guard or Swiss at the hôtel Langlée, and an apothecary-druggist of Les Halles, Jacques Morin, who said his business had suffered for having to wait on the Law family day and night. Their number included eleven lacemakers to whom William Law had given a credit of 263,896 Dutch guilders.[74] Men and women who had sold their estates for banknotes or shares, such as the financier Paulin Prondre at

Guermantes, convinced the commissioners of the Visa and the receivers that they had never been paid and took back their property.[75] People of influence picked off plums. Dubois bought the books that cost Law 250,000 livres for a fifth of the price while the abbé Bignon persuaded the Regent to detach from the company the hôtel Nevers to house the King's library (where it remains today).[76] Ill-repaying Law's generosity, Bignon and the duc d'Antin, superintendent of the King's Buildings, destroyed Pellegrini's ceiling, and filled the gallery with works of theology from floor to cornice.[77]

Law had written to Lady Katherine asking her to join him. She should travel by Strasbourg and Augsburg, avoid Munich, and go under an assumed name. "I want [miss] your company and to live as we used to before I engaged in publick business," Law wrote on April 19. She replied that she did not wish to come to Venice.[78] She either could not bear to return to the vagabond life they had known before Paris, and ruin Kate's marriage prospects, or was not free to leave. The *Nouveau Mercure* reported mother and daughter were living at the hôtel de Luynes, rue du Colombier (now rue Jacob) in the faubourg Saint-Germain, with one maid and one manservant.[79] They continued to receive kindness from the dowager duchesse de Bourbon.[80]

On May 7, the commander of the city guard, Jean Guillemin Duval, arrested William Law under *lettres de cachet* at the watch factory in Versailles and took him to the Bastille.[81] Crawford reported that William had left Paris and his furniture "lay in the house the most of it in Balles [crates] which they [police informers] interpreted as a sure mark of his design to run away". It is likely that William had paid Sully or Blakey to smuggle him out to England by the escape route used for the artificers, and been betrayed.

William's wife, Rebecca Dewes, called on Le Pelletier de La Houssaye who, as Crawford wrote on the 10th, "received her very civilly as most men would doe for she is very handsome". The controller general explained that the company had a claim on her husband of three million livres, which was also now the King's claim, and "information having been given against him of his intentions to leave the Kingdom, they were obliged to be diligent and carefull in secureing the King's payment." He would speak to the Regent that she be allowed to visit him.[82]

William was transferred to the ancient For-l'Evêque prison, on the quai de la Mégisserie, on the right bank of the Seine opposite the île de la Cité. He was later joined by Rigby (pursued for 4 million livres) and, according to the English gazettes, Gun Jones.[83] William could probably still afford to pay four livres a day to have his own cell with a fireplace, and dine with his gaolers.[84]

John Law protested that William had sent gold to the value of 3,468,694 livres and 16 sols to the company's agent in Holland, Abraham Mouchard, to reimburse Hamburg for the Swedish subsidy.[85] To no effect. Relations between the brothers, strained since Law's flight in December, broke down beyond repair.

By now, John Law was set on England. As he told the Earl of Ilay on May 16, he was keen to "to doe justice to Mr Middleton . . . and I should be nearer France, where my Effects are, to putt them in order."[86] Alas!, his champion at the court of St James's was no more. On February 4, during a vicious debate in the House of Lords on the South Sea scandal, the Earl of Stanhope suffered a brain haemorrhage and died the next day. (It was said he had been drinking all night before the debate at the Duke of Newcastle's.)[87] "So ended one of the best men we had," wrote John, Lord Carteret, who was himself capable.[88]

Two weeks later, Stanhope's colleague in the Southern Department, James Craggs the younger, to whom Law had written for permission to return, followed him to the grave. Sir Robert Walpole, since April First Lord of the Treasury and effective Prime

Minister, was intent on sweeping the broken glass of the South Sea scandal under the parliamentary carpet and had no wish to entertain a haggard Frenchified ghost of that era. Law wrote to Carteret, Craggs's successor at the Southern Department, who replied in general terms that Law had been pardoned by the King and had the right to live in his own country, but there were certain difficulties and he should wait until he heard "a more positive response". Carteret informed Dubois who said Law in England would be agreeable neither to himself nor to the Regent of France.[89]

Colonel Otway now hobbles back into view. After his interviews with Law in Paris in June 1720, Otway continued on his way to take up his post as governor of St Philip's Castle in Minorca, writing to Londonderry at Brussels and Frankfurt and receiving no reply. At Verona, he could not resist a side trip to Venice to see his old friend Burges. They made a night of it and Otway was poured into a gondola at 6 a.m.[90] His letters dissolve into scrawl.

Held up at Leghorn and Genoa by an adverse wind, he learned in January 1721 of Law's fall, and wrote that "I think his disgrace must be good for England."[91] He was scarcely arrived in Minorca when he heard of Stanhope's death, and immediately asked permission to return to England to attend Milady Lucy.

Leaving St Philip's to govern itself, he set off but during his quarantine at Genoa in May, he had word of William Law's arrest. "God help my poor thousand," he wrote.[92] With nothing to do but gather gossip, he wrote: "At Genoa, I find there it is generally thought both by his freinds and enimies (wch last are in great plenty there) that he is very rich in jewells, and my son brings me the same generall opinion from Rome where Mr Law & his affairs have been very much talkt on." While in Genoa, he received letters from both Burges and Law encouraging him to come to Venice, "more for yr sake," he told Londonderry, "than my own, for I cannot think my little affair [£1,000] in any great danger unless both brothers are utterly destroyed."[93] He set off on July 9. He was reunited with Colonel Burges and his letters turn to liquid.

It was in Venice that at last he received a reply from Londonderry, as did Law. As far as one can tell from Otway's smudges, Londonderry said Law should come to England, where he would be safe from violence and prosecution, would be granted his pardon and would be received by the King. Otway was to escort him on the road.

"I am heartily gladd," Otway wrote to Londonderry on July 18, "the Court and Justice are able to use him civilly, it would have been a downright madness I think to have discouraged his coming home. Burgess & I drink yr Lordsp's health twice every day." Law was beyond his understanding. "Your Lordsp knows I have a great love & esteem for Mr Law's person, & think him a very wise man, but how a wise man can leave his own & his children's fortune even whether they shall have bread, or want it [do without], to the justice of any man in the world is above my way of thinking."[94]

In the middle of July, Law suffered three days of fever. He also quarrelled with Ippolito De Mari.[95] (De Mari came to Venice in August and they were reconciled, the marchese even speaking up for Law to Frémont.)[96] "Life is not so pleasant," Law wrote to Lassay on July 11 "to be worth suffering long to preserve it."[97]

To recover his health and spirits away from the lagoon, and start him on the road back to England, Burges and Otway took him for a jaunt to Vicenza, where many Venetians kept country houses. There and in Verona they waited for the post to bring a letter from Secretary of State Carteret, confirming Londonderry's offer and safe conduct. There was nothing by the post of July 21, but there was one letter that further upset Law. Rebecca Dewes, William's wife, had arrived incognito in Venice. Law could do no more for her than to provide a speculative bill on Paris for 500 gold louis.[98]

It cannot have been easy for Law, hemmed in by the two old

soldiers, part bodyguards, part gaolers, and wearied by the endless drinking. "Mr Law was last night very much out of order [ill]", Otway wrote on the 26th, "& is so this morning. He had resolved to have gone directly for England if he had received a letter from Lord Cartwright [Carteret]. He had forgot my affair wch I do not wonder of in so grat hurry of affairs as he may have been in but he says I shall loose nothing. I love Mr Law very heartily & I am resolved not to leave him at least till he is better." He added in sorrow: "[Burges] does not drink quite so hard as he used to do."[99]

After a week, and with Law still not decided, Otway left for Innsbruck, promising to wait for Law there. There, hearing nothing from Law, after five days he continued northwards, fully expecting "to meet Lady Katherine & young Mr Law [that is, Mary Catherine Law] on the road who I had Mr Law's order to stopp. I have a letter from him to Her Ladyp desiring her to stay in Flanders Holland, or goe to England which she pleased but I hear nothing of her Ladyp." Writing from Utrecht on August 29, near the end of his odyssey, Otway wrote: "I heartily wish mr Law may be safe in England & do not at all wonder at the uncertainty he was under for a man of the strongest mind must be under very great agitation with his circumstances wch nobody can truly know but himselfe."[100] He never saw his thousand.

Otway's appearance in the idle society of Venice had set tongues wagging. While they were in Verona for the "change of air", Frémont seems to have written to the new Cardinal Dubois that Law intended to sacrifice French interests and "travel to that country [England] with Coll. Otway." Law had already written to the Regent about Frémont's lies (*mensonges*).[101] In a letter to Dubois from Venice on August 2, he mingled threat with blandishment. He said he did not wish to work, but might have no choice if the Regent did not give him means to satisfy his creditors. On the other hand, in England he might be "of some use" to an Anglo-French union.[102]

The Regent must have been upset, for Dubois exercised an about-face and on September 23 sent Frémont a reprimand. The poor man took refuge in the usual excuses of scolded diplomats, repeating back to the Cardinal his instructions, and pleading incapacity and excessive zeal for the King's service.[103] John Law was not finished yet.

He had offers of employment not only from Denmark but also from Tsar Peter of Russia, who in a personal letter invited him to set up a company (with his own funds) to trade with Iran and the Indies.[104] Law decided to set off for Copenhagen and there make up his mind whether to stay, or wheel right for St Petersburg or left for London.[105]

On August 24, he started out for Bologna.[106] Travelling under the name Wilmot, together with young William, he passed by unfrequented post roads as far as Hanover. There he was received by King George's adviser, Count Andreas Gottlieb von Bernstorff and learned that Carteret had spoken to the King who "appeared disposed to" receive him in his British and Irish territories.[107]

They skirted Hamburg, passed on the back road through Bremen, Elsfleth and Glückstadt in Holstein, where they were entertained for several days by the viceroy of Holstein, Count Carl von Ahlefeldt, and reached Copenhagen in the evening of October 7.[108] Law attended court the next day but Frederick IV was leaving to spend his birthday at his queen's estate at Vallø, and a private audience would have to wait. By now, Dubois's man in Hamburg, Jean-Baptiste Poussin, had picked up his trail.[109]

The sight on October 8, of twenty-one sail of the British Baltic Squadron off Drakoe (Dragør) – something our age can only imagine – decided John Law for England.

Admiral Sir John Norris, originally despatched to the Baltic in 1715 to protect British trade in Baltic timber and other naval stores from Swedish privateers, had like the British government been drawn into George I's Hanoverian politics to contain the power not only of Sweden but of Tsar Peter and the rising kingdom of Prussia.

Norris had plenipotentiary powers, and took Law and William on board his ninety-gun flagship, the second-rate *Sandwich*, on the sight of the original letter from Carteret and Law's word of honour that, if the King were displeased by his presence in England, he would do as the King commanded.[110] The fleet sailed from Helsingør on the 17th.[111] Norris, known as "foul-weather Jack" for his talent in attracting bad weather, duly rustled up a violent nor'wester, and the squadron was scattered, only reaching the rendezvous at the Shoe Beacon at the edge of Foulness Sand, at the mouth of the Thames Estuary, on the 19th by the English calendar. Norris appears to have landed despatches, including the names of his passengers. The next day they were at Blackstakes, in the mouth of the Medway on the Kent side. On the 21st, Law trod the streets of London for the first time in twenty-five years.[112]

Writing from Copenhagen, Lord Glenorchy, the British Ambassador, expressed a general belief: "I think 'tis very well he's in England, for if we don't think it proper to make use of him ourselves, at least we hinder him from serving other people."[113] Cardinal Dubois did not share that opinion, nor did his agent in London, the poet and dramatist Philippe Néricault Destouches.

Dubois had been frightened by Law's reception at Hanover. While as ever pleading his friendship to Law, he told Destouches on the 18th that he was "deeply anxious about anything that could alter our union with England". He said that people would assume that Law was there with the Regent's approval or by his order, or just as bad, against his wishes. Creditors might pester the Regent to allow them to pursue his former minister through the English courts.[114] In reality, Dubois feared Law would return to Paris and displace him. As he had told Crawford back in December, 1720,

"His Royal Highness still has a weakness for that man."[115] He instructed Destouches to watch Law, but to be very discreet (*fort circonspect*) in what he said about him.

On October 22, the morning after their arrival, according to one report, Admiral Norris brought Law to the King's morning reception or Levee at St James's Palace.[116] If that did happen, the visit was not repeated. (Lord Carteret, the Secretary of State, told Destouches that Norris was met on landing and given orders not to bring Law to court.)[117]

Law did call on Carteret, who was embarrassed but, as he told Destouches, could not refuse a visit from John Law or any man. Law said that he had not intended to offend the King or his ministers by his return, and if his presence caused the Regent of France unease he was ready to leave the country or "shut himself up in the depths of Scotland".[118] Carteret told Destouches the King and his British ministers had no part in the Hanover affair and were "extremely irritated" by Sir John Norris's despatch.[119]

The next day, October 23/November 3, in the evening, Destouches had a long meeting with Carteret in his office. It was a brilliant performance by the Englishman on shaky ground. While dismantling Dubois's sham arguments against Law's presence in London, he also spoke to the Cardinal's underlying fear that Britain might either employ Law or help him return to France.

It was only the next day that Destouches found out that, immediately after he left, Law had been shown in for another conference with Carteret and the Earl of Sunderland, the former First Lord of the Treasury, that lasted until 2 a.m.[120] Sunderland repeated to Destouches that ministers had no wish to employ Law which was, anyway, impracticable after what had happened in France. Destouches remained suspicious. He attended court and, not seeing Law, thought he might be holding private conferences with the King.[121]

Destouches also enclosed in his packet a letter from Law to the Regent, dated November 1, 1721. Since the letter is in the French foreign ministry archives, it seems Dubois never passed it to the duc d'Orléans. After listing his grievances, including the arrest of William and the detention (*retention*) of his wife and daughter, Law wrote: "More than the state to which I am reduced, it is the indifference Your Royal Highness has shown in my regard that wounds me."[122]

Londonderry found Law furnished rooms near him at Hanover Square, then being laid out and built. Carteret told Destouches Law was living "in a little house in a distant part of town".[123] (It is ten minutes' walk from Hanover Square to St James's Palace.) By the 25th, Law had regained his poise, for he appeared that evening with young William at the theatre in Drury Lane at a gala revival of Ben Jonson's *The Alchemist*, in the presence of the Prince and Princess of Wales.[124]

On the 28th, Law and Londonderry had a further audience with Carteret. Then, it being Saturday, Law drove into the country with Sir John Chardin, the son of a Huguenot jeweller and expert on Safavid Iran, to view Chardin's new estate at what is now Kempton racecourse. He observed an industrious people, well-nourished and -clothed, and a more even prosperity than in France. "One sees not magnificence but a general sufficiency," he told Lassay two days later. "There are no arbitrary impositions or contributions. Everybody knows what he has to pay and pays it." As for himself, he wrote: "To be in bad odour at Court is here no crime."[125]

Two days earlier, the Earl of Coningsby, an extreme Whig and Catholic-baiter, launched an attack on Law in the House of Lords. Coningsby had been useful to the Whigs as a sort of fighting dog against Harley and Prior and the Tory architects of the Utrecht treaties, but his unstable conduct both in the House and in his native Herefordshire had made him a liability and was soon to bring him to the Tower. (The poet Alexander Pope lampoons him in the *Epistle to Bathurst.*) He called Law "the author of England's misfortunes" in the South Sea speculation, who had renounced the Protestant religion. When the House began to laugh, he lost his temper and vowed he would hang Law before the end of the Parliamentary session. Carteret batted him away. At the sitting on November 9, Coningsby accused Law of "openly countenancing the Pretender's friends" and called him a "renegade assassin".[126] A Tory peer demanded an inquiry into Sir John Norris's instructions.

That was a godsend to Carteret. Law was now a party matter, that bareknuckle business of "Wigths" and "Torries" that bored and disgusted the French.

The Secretary of State told Destouches on November 12 that if they had wanted to expel Law, they now could not, but must support him.[127]

By slow roads, Law had won through to England and the protection of the English common law, his noble friends and the King. On November 28, he gave himself up at the gate of the King's Bench Prison in Borough High Street. He was taken to Westminster Hall. There, on his knees and attended by Lords Ilay and Londonderry, he pleaded his pardon before the judges of the Court of King's Bench.[128]

Yet his situation in London was neither comfortable nor dignified. Away from the courtesy of France and the languor of Venice, he was exposed to the party politics of Great Britain, an insubordinate public and a press that fawned or bit. Back on November 4, when Law and William attended Orlandini's opera *Arsace* at the Haymarket theatre, they were hissed.[129]

"Everybody here wonders", wrote Gyllé from Paris on November 27/ December 8 "what took Mr Law to London, especialy unless he was very sur of being well received at Court. I fancy he and his pal favourite Doctor [Jacobite code for Ilay] will make but a mean figur at Whytes", the gambling house at the foot of St James's Street (which, as White's Club further up the street, survives).[130] On December 6, Anne, Duchess of Richmond wrote from Goodwood to her son in Italy: "Who ever encouraged Mr Law to come to England does not acknowledge it, and he has been so indifferently used I believe he will make no long stay here."[131]

Law was often in the press. On December 9, the *London Journal* reported that he would stand for Parliament for Westminster, generally the most hotly contested seat in the House of Commons. That was something Law, as a Roman Catholic, could not do unless he abjured his religion a second time, which would demolish his standing in France. On the 23rd, the same gazette reported that he had escaped an attack while returning to Hanover Square, and for that reason had moved to St James's Street. "Mr Law has a numerous Levee to attend him," the *Journal* wrote on January 6, "among which are Variety of Projectors; and it seems that no less than 130 projects have been laid before him." One correspondent suggested he take over the South Sea Company, another that he colonise Madagascar.[132] He was pestered with requests for loans or charity.[133]

The bankrupt Danish court, through Count Gyldensten, continued to send flattering invitations. Count Philipp Josef von Rosenberg, a counsellor to the Habsburg emperor, who had read *Money and Trade* in the 1720 French edition, invited Law to set up a bank on land security in Serbia. To all those proposals, Law answered that he must wait on the Regent of France's pleasure and that he wished, above all things, for repose.

In Venice, Law had made or renewed acquaintance with the German soldier of fortune commanding the Venetian land forces, Count Matthias von der Schulenburg, who by tactical genius, nerve and luck had defended Corfu against the Ottoman Turks in 1716. Though nobody knew it at the time, that was the high tide of Ottoman power which was now ebbing towards its end in 1918.

The Venetian Senate voted Schulenburg a statue, which still stands at the gates of the castle he defended, beside the cricket pitch, and a pension that let him live in the Ca' Loredano on the Grand Canal and make a start on a picture collection that he was to transfer to Berlin. Schulenburg gave Law an introduction to his sister, Melusine, who was King George's principal mistress and had just been raised to the peerage of Great Britain as Duchess of Kendal.[134] Tall, skinny and unpopular, she was known as the Maypole. Sir Robert Walpole once said "her interest did everything; that she was, in effect as much Queen of England as ever any was."[135]

The following is conjecture. On January 8, a Monday, probably at the instance of the Duchess of Kendal, Law was presented to the King at the evening Drawing-Room, as it was known, at St James's Palace.[136] In the heat and crush, something happened, some snub or discourtesy, that plunged John Law into despair. Evidently, the problem did not arise with the King, "who appears to be well enough disposed towards me".[137] As it was the Paris Post Day, he wrote as usual to Lady Katherine, but broke off. "I'll finish the letter, for I grow angry," he wrote.[138]

Law attended Court, where the King spoke to him, as also the Prince and Princess of Wales (in English), but the sight of their daughters – Anne, Amelia and Caroline – brought Kate to mind. He wrote to Lady Katherine on the 20th: "The young Princesses are handsome, gentile, and weel fashioned. If my daughter was here I believe would be lyked by them."[139] Writing English again after so many years, Law reverts to the Scots dialect of his youth.

Law was searching for a good house to re-establish his credit. He was looking for the effect that he had achieved in The Hague in 1712 and Paris in 1714, but in incomparably worse circumstances.

Londonderry suggested Stanhope's old lodgings at the Cockpit in Whitehall, which his sister Lucy, dividing her time between Chevening and Bath, had no use for but did want money.

It was an old-fashioned place, which had once been part of Henry VIII's covered tennis court but was converted in the 1670s into lodgings for Charles II's bastard son, the Duke of Monmouth, and showed a 36-foot frontage on the extension of Whitehall known as The Street. (The pilastered first-floor rooms and a staircase survive within the nineteenth-century Treasury Buildings, and are used by the Cabinet Office.) In 1717, when he became in effect Prime Minister, Stanhope received a lease of thirty-one years in the name of his father-in-law, Thomas "Diamond" Pitt. He immediately spread next door and was granted a new lease in 1719 for a further thirty-one years. At the time, the house was still draped in mourning for the minister, with the Stanhope arms above the door, but all that would come down in February once a year had passed since his death.

King George had no objection to Law as a leasehold tenant. The problem was that Law had no money, and Londonderry was caught between his desire to settle his debtor and friend and the absolute need to act in his younger sister's interest.

The first proposal, made to Lucy at Bath on January 25, was that Law live there three months and then either buy the lease for £5,000 or rent the place, furnished, for £400 per annum.[140] Lucy, who was annoyed that the 75,000 livres raised from the sale of her jewels in Paris in 1720 had been swept into the Visa, was having nothing of that and wanted payment in advance.[141]

The mails between Bath and London were quicker then than today, and Londonderry came back with the proposal of £1,000 down, and the remaining £4,000 with interest in six months, and enlisted the support of Diamond Pitt. "You don't make any conveyance untill the whole is paid," Londonderry wrote on

February 1, "therefore on consulting my father, we think att all events you run no risque, and that tis adviseable for you to accept of it by all means." Lucy accepted on February 3, but insisted on agreement on the furniture before he moved in, "for that is so easeyly damaged."[142]

Londonderry, already owed a fortune by Law, was unwilling to lend the £1,000 and Law could not find it elsewhere.[143] A letter to Henrietta Howard, the mistress of the Prince of Wales and notorious for her good heart, may have been written at this time. It is dated only "Tuesday", that is the morning after a St James's Palace Drawing-Room, and is the most dejected of Law's letters to survive. It reveals he was receiving a half-yearly pension, probably administered by her friend and his chief, the Duke of Argyll. "Can you no prevaile one the Duke to help me some thing more than the half-year," he wrote to Mrs Howard, "or is there no body that could have good nature enough to lend me 1000 pds."

That John Law was trying to borrow from Mrs Howard, who was at that time not well off, shows how deep his fortunes had sunk. He was not proud of himself, for he continued: "I bege that if nothing of this can be done, that it may only be betwixt us two, as I take you as my real friend & I am very well assurd of it by the honour I had done me yesterday at Court by the King. Excuse this Dear Madam & only put your self in my place & know at the same time that you are the only friend I have"[144]

The letter brought nothing. On February 10, Londonderry wrote to his sister about her "house at the Cockpitt, but find Mr Law coulds [cools] on it, and I would not seem to press him."[145] Lucy was irritated to read about the negotiation in the press. She wrote on February 12: "In my opinion he was not in ernest about my house, only to serve a turn [as a tactic]."[146] (After Lucy's death, the house was sold in 1725 to the Duke of Dorset for £4,650, with £2,000 down.)[147]

In Edinburgh, both Whigs and Jacobites awaited Law. George Mackenzie, an Edinburgh physician with literary tastes, dedicated to him the third volume of his *Lives and Characters of the Most Eminent Writers of the Scots Nation* that appeared that spring. "It is not in the power of fortune," he wrote, "either to give or take away from the souls of great men, those bright and shining qualities they are endued with."[148]

Yet when the Duke of Argyll invited Law in February to accompany him north, Law did not stir and, as far as this author can tell, never saw his home city or estate at Lauriston again. He told Lady Katherine that he dared not travel more than a day's journey from London.[149] A Dr Mendez had a claim on him for £15,000 and was threatening to have him imprisoned. (In the stock ledgers of the Bank of England for 1720–25, there are fifteen persons called Mendez or Mendes, four of them Londoners and the others Dutch.)[150]

John Law fell into a torpor. When Vernezobre wrote from Berlin to explain or excuse his departure from France in 1720, Law said that at the time he had been displeased. "Now I am a private citizen, I wish you well," he wrote.[151]

He cared not at all for the Germans he had lured to the Arkansas. On March 15, in reply to an offer from the Neuchâtel wine merchant and colonial theorist, Jean-Pierre Purry, to send Swiss families to the settlement, he wrote: "As for my colony in Louisiana, I am not in a position to continue making the expenses necessary to maintain it, so do not hesitate to take the course that best suits your interests."[152] (Purry went out in the next decade to found the settlement of Purrysburg, on the lower Savannah River in South Carolina, which also failed.)

Soon after his arrival in the colony the April before, the Arkansas concession's director Elias Stutheus had died. His deputy, Jacques Levens, sent up a party of indentured workers (*engagés*) to the

Arkansas to begin clearing the ground. At Law's disgrace, the administrators of the Company of the Indies could find no person in France to take over the concession. They offered it to Levens but he refused, wishing to return to France, by way of Cap Français, a drink and a woman.[153] Bienville and the Superior Council of Louisiana took over Law's camp at Nouveau Biloxy, impounded his stores, distributed his workmen and appointed another Malouin, Bertrand Dufresne du Demaine, on a salary of 2,000 livres, to travel up to the Arkansas and allocate the land to the indentured workers already there.

Bénard de La Harpe, by now a capable backwoodsman, acted as his guide. Arriving on March 1, 1722 in the afternoon, they found "about forty-seven person of all sexes" including the commander, storeman, surgeon and apothecary. In addition, there was an officer and seventeen soldiers.

Their achievement in the eleven months they had been there consisted of "about a score of cabins badly laid out and three arpents [2½ acres] of cleared ground . . . .They were astonished to learn they were no longer bound [*n'appartiennent plus*] to Mr Law."[154]

Bienville decided to settle the German and Swiss farmers, who had survived shipwreck, disease, famine on the beaches, and a devastating hurricane, to feed the new capital at New Orleans.[155] Later that year, they were given land partly protected by a levee (embankment) on Bienville's concession in what is now the Garden District of New Orleans.[156] Most then migrated further upstream and the Louisiana parishes of St Charles and St John the Baptist were known as the "German Coasts" (that is, *côtes des Allemands*) until the United States went to war with Imperial Germany in 1917. The Germans' industry kept the settlement from starving.

By March 22, 1722, the Alley coffee houses were laying 10:1 against Law returning to France. "If that could get me out of my engagements," Law wrote, "I would be tempted to take it."[157] No doubt to save money, Law ceased to go to court. He was more afraid by the day that he would be imprisoned for debt. He wrote to Lady Katherine on April 11: "There is nothing I would stop at, rather than be reduced to that extremity."[158]

In reality, Law's fortunes were improving. The previous autumn, the Regent had accepted as his representatives or attorneys Jean-Louis de l'Etendard, marquis de Bully, and Philippe de Vendôme, the former Grand Prior of France of the Knights of Malta.[159] Bully, from a Norman family old at the time of William the Conqueror, had served in the wars and retired with his wounds to the governorship of Menin, a Vauban fortress in the Spanish Netherlands, which he proceeded to lose in 1706 to the Duke of Marlborough. Vendôme seems to have offered nothing but his prestige but Bully was conscientious. Arbuthnot, the Scots banker in Rouen, later said that he did more harm than good, not from ill will but from his "want of proper judgment in affairs of accounts".[160]

Law now had the help of Lady Katherine's nephew, William Knollys, titular Viscount Wallingford (b. October 15, 1694), a young officer who was devoted to his uncle and could travel to see Bully in Paris without fear of arrest. The dowager duchesse de Bourbon was pressing the Regent to allow Law the wherewithal to pay his foreign debts.[161]

The breakthrough came in June when Londonderry imposed on the other members of the East India syndicate a stand-still agreement. By an indenture dated the 29th of the month, Londonderry, the men to whom he had laid off the East India wagers (including his father, Diamond Pitt) and Middleton agreed to accept 3,000 shares in the Company of the Indies that Law had left in Crawford's custody in Paris as security for £96,000 in wagers and sub-wagers "which by agreement was not to affect Mr Law's person". The Dukes of Argyll and Chandos agreed to act as Law's bondsmen, with the right to recover sums due only from his "Estate beyond sea".[162]

While Law was taking the waters at Bath in September, Middleton wrote to Abraham Mouchard in Holland: "Had I taken any violent measures with him, it might have put it out of his power to do me justice. Several [other creditors] who had gone the length of taking out Writts of Arrestment against him have thought it best to suspend any further diligence . . . being informed his affairs in France are at last upon the point of being ended in such a manner that all the foreign debts shall be soon paid."[163]

At some point about that time, Lady Katherine also received protection. In an undated letter to the Regent, professionally spelled and signed "K. Law", which was found by the nineteenth-century French collector, Benjamin Fillon, and printed in the auction catalogue of his estate, she thanked the Regent for issuing a stay of proceedings.[164] Such stays, known as *arrêts de surséance*, were unpopular. At the Revolution, one of its principal theorists, the abbé Sieyès, listed them as among the most tyrannical privileges of the old nobility.[165] Jean Buvat reported in December that Louis XV had granted her a pension of 12,000 livres a year secured on the revenues of the mint.[166]

As if on cue, the marchese De Mari, as good a friend as any man could desire, sent over to England a consignment of pictures insured for 132,440 lire. They arrived in London on or about July 10, 1722, ostensibly in trust for young William.[167] Law sold six of the largest to King George for the sum of £4,000 (or the price of a large London house). George Vertue, a connoisseur and engraver, wrote in his *Notebooks* in 1723: "The King bought 6 large paintings of Mr Laws. Venus a dressing with her Nymphs of Guido, Andromeda of Guido, two other of Rubens & two besides, for all which he [the King] paid 4000 pounds. Many more paintings was brought over by Mr Laws."[168]

The pictures by the Bolognese artist Guido Reni, known in English as *The Toilette of Venus* (insured for 33,000 lire) and the somewhat smaller *Perseus and Andromeda* (5,000 lire) are still in London.[169] At first they hung in the Great Drawing Room at Kensington Palace. George Bickham, in a guide to the royal collections in 1755, wrote: "On each side of the door is a large Picture, painted by that great Master, Guido Reni: one of Venus, dressing by the Graces: the other is of Andromeda, chained to the Rock . . . These two Pictures were bought of the late Mr Laws by King George I at a large Price: There are great Beauties and Strength of Expression in them, best known to the Profound, and much admired by all."[170]

The pictures moved with the Royal Family to Buckingham House and then Windsor Castle, gathering wear and tear, and were given by King William IV in 1836 to the new National Gallery, being built in Trafalgar Square. They hung there for a while, and the American writer Herman Melville saw *Andromeda* and was not impressed by the sea-monster.[171]

Guido's stock declined. In 1861, the pictures were consigned to the basement and then sent to the provinces, *Andromeda* to Dublin and *Venus* to Edinburgh. *Andromeda* remained in Dublin long after Irish independence, and by 1957 was "in extremely poor state, with deep heavy cracking, numerous small losses, and very considerable repainting".[172] It was brought back to London in 1968 and remains in the basement at Trafalgar Square, a ruin of what it was; but amid the blisters and dirty varnish, in the beauty of Andromeda's stance, there is a trace of what captivated Law and his century.

Venus fared better, returning from Edinburgh in 1937, but is marked by horizontal cracks as if it had been a long time rolled up.

How did Law come by those pictures? *Venus*, a famous composition, was commissioned by the Duke of Mantua in 1622, and passed into the collection of King Charles I of Great Britain and Ireland. After the King's execution in 1649, a "Venus sitting to be dressed by the 3 Graces. Guido. bullones" was valued at £200, taken by a syndicate of his trade creditors in 1651 and sold to the Spanish ambassador.[173] The picture was then either bought by the De Mari, or given as a present to one of the Doges in the family, for both Pierre Crozat and the comte de Caylus (in 1715) saw it at the De Mari palace near the Piazza Banchi in Genoa.[174] By coincidence, a copy of it was hanging in the picture gallery at Guermantes when Law bought the estate.

This author believes that Law bought the pictures in 1719 or 1720 for the hôtel Langlée or the palais Mazarin but they were still in Genoa at the time he left France. By rights, they should have gone into the liquidation of his estate in France. It may have been these pictures that Law asked De Mari to sell to cover his Venetian gambling debts. If so, the marquis either ignored him or refused.

In the spring of 1723, the *London Journal* reported that Law was about "to dispose of a Second Collection of very fine Paintings, amongst which is a curious Piece of King Charles the First, valued at Fifteen Hundred Guineas."[175] That August, he was able to lend a former clerk at the bank, William Neilson, £750.[176] (Neilson set up a bleachworks beside the River North Esk at Roslin, south of Edinburgh.) William Law was now out of prison. With his credit largely restored, Middleton in September re-opened his shop in the Strand.

At some point, Law bought two leasehold houses in Shepherd or Sheppard Street, site until lately of the disorderly May Fair which gave the district its name, but now being developed. It was not the best address in town, but a distance better than Borough High Street.

Across the Channel, the regency was drawing to its end. On October 25, 1722, in the cathedral of Rheims where French Kings had been consecrated since the eleventh century, Louis XV received a new crown with John Law's "very perfect great diamond" mounted at the front.[177]

The ceremony, delayed a month to allow the champagne grapes to be picked, vindicated the Regent's love and care for the boy. Elisabeth Charlotte managed to attend on her swollen feet, but she was dying. Her sister Luise had sent her a map of the Palatinate. Confined to her room, Elisabeth Charlotte crisscrossed her homeland in her imagination: "I have already travelled from Heidelberg to Frankfurt, and from Mannheim to Frankenthal, and from there to Worms," she wrote.[178] She died at Saint-Cloud in the early morning of December 8, 1722.

In 1723, Dubois's health broke down. The odds in the Alley on Law returning began to shorten. Questioned in April by Sutton's successor as envoy in Paris, Sir Luke Schaub, Walpole wrote that "power might fall into worse hands" than those of a man "who has sundry ties to wish well to his native country". In short, "it is not our business to obstruct" John Law's return to France.[179]

That is precisely what Walpole set about doing. Ever insecure, he wanted to push aside Carteret, with his strong mind and fluent German, evict his man Schaub from Paris and bring the most important foreign embassy under the control of the Norfolk interest. Law, who had broken one British ambassador in Paris, could not be permitted to return to France, but he had influence over the "uncertain temper" of the duc d'Orléans and must be managed. In the correspondence that survives are traces of an unequal fight between one of the most capable politicians that ever lived and a wasted visionary.

On August 10, 1723, at Versailles where the King was now established, Cardinal Dubois died under surgery. Walpole and Lord Townshend, Secretary of State for the Northern Department and his brother-in-law, resolved to send to Paris Walpole's brother Horatio, usually called Horace, to spy out the new territory, undermine Schaub and through him Carteret, and also John Law.

In a letter to Townshend on October 12/23, Sir Robert wrote: "I have so ordered my brother's journey to Paris with him [Law], that he thinks Horace goes with his advice [on his advice]."[180] Horatio duly arrived in Paris, trawled the embassies, insinuated himself with the favourite Nocé (who hated Schaub and Law), and was received by the duc d'Orléans, now the King's first minister. In a long despatch to Townshend in Hanover on October 21/November 1, Horace wrote that far from Law being recalled, "the door appears to have been shut on him for all time."[181] That may not have been true on November 1, 1723, but it soon was.

On December 2, Philippe II, duc d'Orléans died of apoplexy at Versailles at the age of forty-nine. He was alone, but for the person the wits called his "usual confessor", the young Marie-Thérèse d'Haraucourt, duchesse de Fallary.[182]

He was succeeded as first minister by the duc de Bourbon, which raised Law's hopes. The Walpoles were having none of that. On the 16th, Horace wrote to his brother that "the insinuations that may be made to you by the friends of Mr Law . . . of . . . being capable to be useful to us at this time here, is no otherwise so, than as we think fit to make it to ourselves." None the less, they should show Law "all outward civilities".[183] Horace was appointed minister plenipotentiary at Paris the following year and, as far as this author can tell from his correspondence, never had the interests of Law, Lady Katherine or their creditors at heart. Middleton later complained: "But how to gett our Ambassador to recommend this with any Earnestness I am att a loss."[184] Law wrote at length at least twice to the duc de Bourbon but received no encouragement. M. le Duc did lift the cloud hanging over the company by releasing it from any liability for Law's banknotes.

In the course of 1724, whether to lie low or to save money, or both, Law spent several months in Ireland, possibly at a property of Lord Londonderry's. He was back in London on October 16.[185] The standstill agreement began to disintegrate.[186] Londonderry, unable to repair his own fortunes and responsible now for the Stanhopes as well as his own family, was thinking like his father before him of the West Indies. He would not be in London to keep the sub-wagerers off Law. (In 1728, Londonderry was appointed governor of the Leeward Islands.)

With reluctance, John Law decided to return to Venice but asked Sir Robert Walpole for "some sort of commission from his majesty to any prince or state, not to be made use of, but to be kept as a protection in case of necessity". On July 29, 1725, Walpole wrote to his brother-in-law Townshend in Law's favour.[187] On August 5, after laying a false scent with the London gazettes,[188] Law set off with young William and his nephew, Hugh Hamilton (son of sister Agnes), who was proving unemployable. With journey-money from Walpole, they travelled "with their own horses" under the name Hamilton.

At Aaachen/Aix on August 18, Law received the letter of credence signed on the 12th by King George at Herrenhausen, his country house outside Hanover. Addressed in Latin to Doge Alviso III Mocenigo of Venice, the King asked the Most Serene Republic to recognise "our faithful and dear John Law, Gent., in Italy or wherever our affairs at this time will take him . . . as authorised to expound our wishes to you."[189]

At the little spa town, Law whiled away the season waiting for the King's instructions for "though I can amuse myself here I would prefer to be at my duty."[190] He wrote again to Hanover, offering his services in Vienna (to encourage the Emperor to suspend the Austrian Indies company at Ostend), Denmark or Muscovy or in Venice, Genoa and Florence where he was well known. Receiving no answer, he said he was leaving for Berlin on an old blank escape (*passeport en blanc*) signed by the King of Prussia.[191]

That last brought an answer from the long-serving under-secretary, George Tilson, who had devilled for Stanhope on his visit to Paris in April, 1720, and toured the Quincampoix and the inn where Horn had stabbed his stockbroker. His letter of November 8, which is informal to the point of chummery, said Law should proceed "to the same place which you was first designed for". The Secretary of State was "in a perpetual hurry of business" and Law should wait for his instructions either at Cologne or some illegible "entertaining town".[192]

In a mood that can be well imagined, Law left Aachen, writing from Mannheim and Augsburg, and arrived in Munich on January 2, 1726. The next day he was summoned by the Elector Maximilian, who was in bed with rheumatism. He dismissed his chamberlain and asked Law for a loan. "He reckoned I was very rich," Law wrote to London. He explained that all his property was tied up in France. Maximilian died a month later.

John Law spent almost a year in Munich and the countryside nearby. Visiting statesmen called on the becalmed celebrity, including Count Ludwig von Sinzendorf, the Austrian chancellor whom he had known at Utrecht in 1713. The Landgrave of Hesse-Kassel proposed he visit his court where he would introduce him to his son, King Frederick of Sweden. (Since the Swedes had killed their last foreign financial adviser, Baron Görtz, the offer was not hard to refuse.)

Ercole Tomasso, marchese di Cortanze, invited him to Turin. When Cortanze grumbled that luxury and Victor Amadeus were bankrupting the Savoyard nobility, Law reassured him with a modern sentiment. "The more that real property [*bien fonds*] is dispersed in a state, the more powerful that state will be," he said.*

* The rich hoard proportionally more of their income than the poor. For a while in the twentieth century, economists thought this "marginal propensity to save" might hold clues to the workings of the economy.

Law reported all those interviews to Sir Robert Walpole and his ministry, but appears to have had no reply.[193]

There is a glimpse of Lady Katherine. As Londonderry prepared to sail to Antigua, he needed to tie up some loose ends, including a "Miss Stanhope", who was surely a love child of the great minister.[194] He deputed Lady Katherine to look out a convent in France. That April, she found a place with a garden, "nuely established, in a very good aire & cleane", 1,200 livres a year without fire, laundry, linen or candles, which "had not the aire of a monostry & therfor think it more agreabl". Best of all, the mother superior would permit Miss Stanhope to have a gentlewoman with her, and "they ashure me that they will not mention in the least to her of her religion nor thers." She herself would wait on Miss Stanhope "as often as my tender health will allow me".[195]

At Munich, Law decided to sell the larger of the two houses in Shepherd Street, about which Middleton was his usual discouraging self. "There's so many houses in that Quarter of the Town to be sold," he wrote on July 26, 1726, "it's not very probable there will be any offers soon."[196] In November, 1726, he told Law that the Court of Common Pleas had given judgment against him over £1,000 and £100 in interest, from which there was no appeal.[197]

Law may have delayed his departure from Munich so as to accompany the Dowager Electress of Bavaria, Therese Kunigunde, aunt of Clementina Sobieska, who wished to spend her widowhood in Venice to the excitement of the Venetians.[198] As it turned out, she decided first to bid farewell to her son, the Elector Clemens August at his court in Bonn in the Rhineland, leaving in the middle of November. A day or two after her, Law set off for Venice, like Lord Byron a century on, "a nameless sort of person,/(A broken Dandy lately on my travels)".[199]

CHAPTER FOURTEEN

Facing Nothing

Itt is so cold I scarse feell my pen.

KATHERINE KNOWLES[1]

John Law arrived in Venice in pieces, exhausted by his winter crossing of the Alps.[2]

Ambassador Gergy, who claimed to have lost 100,000 livres in salary during the year of the System, none the less invited Law to dinner on December 8, 1726, "in good company, everybody curious to see him".[3] Gergy and others were astonished how Law had aged under the strain of the last six years. Asked about his plans, Law told the ambassador that he had been persuaded that the air of Venice was "an excellent remedy for a species of asthma which torments him".[4] It is hard to imagine a worse place for an asthmatic.

Law settled with the two young men in a house most probably in the Calle Larga, in the parish of Santi Apostoli, an old church in the district of Cannaregio to the east of the Grand Canal.[5] The *abate* or abbé Antonio Conti, a poet and natural scientist who had just returned after thirteen years in Paris and London, told his correspondents in Paris that Law kept company only with gamblers. By April, 1727, Conti wrote that Law had won at the tables 2,000 sequins (£900), had taken a villa on the Brenta canal, where many Venetians had summer places, and expected Lady Katherine at the end of May. "He is much talked about, and watched closely, but everybody avoids him like the plague," he wrote.[6]

Law continued to seek a settlement of his debts in France. A document survives from the summer of 1727 in his son's papers at Maastricht in Holland, offering a scheme for settling some 19 million livres demanded from him by the Company of the Indies. It begins: "For six and a half years, Mr Law has suffered for his service to the state."[7] He had Middleton send £100 to his brother William in Paris who was said to be "reduced to very great straits".[8] Neither Law appears to have taken any part in the founding that year in Edinburgh of the Royal Bank of Scotland, with the Earl of Ilay as its first governor.

During the winter season of 1727–8, Law was back at the gaming tables. Asked by the comtesse de Caylus in Paris for news of Law, Conti reported him playing from "morning to night". He listed two wagers offered by Law that have entered, in various guises, the museum of gaming. It sounds as if Law was holding his own bank.

"He is always cheerful when he plays," Conti wrote,

> . . . and every day he proposes some new bet. He has offered to give 10,000 sequins to anyone who throws six sixes at dice, but if it does not come up the punter must pay him one sequin. Mr Nicole will tell you if this is large-scale usury. He has found nobody to take it up. He has offered also to give 1,000 sequins to anyone who wins twelve bets in a row at faro on the same condition of one sequin per loss. This time, he has found people stupid enough to be snared.[9]

*

Madame will not have needed the mathematician François Nicole (1683–1758) to tell her the odds were to Law's advantage. The probability of six sixes with a single throw of six dice is one in 46,656. In probability, Law would win 46,655 sequins before he had to pay out 10,000 sequins. The odds of twelve wins in succession at faro is one in 4,096. In probability, Law would win 4,095 sequins before he had to pay out 1,000. Conti added that Law and William "lived entirely on milk".

In Paris, Lady Katherine had a suitor for Mary Catherine, who was rising eighteen. For some time, Lady Katherine had been friendly with Anne-Marguerite Blondel, wife of the Habsburg minister in Paris, Marcus, baron de Fonseca. Fonseca had been in Paris in the time that Law made the rain and the fine weather and stood in for Pentenrieder as chargé d'affaires throughout the 1720s.[10] He was about to be appointed treasurer general of the Austrian Netherlands at Brussels. His eldest son was besotted with Kate.

Montesquieu wrote that the baron was the son of a Jew and wondered why, with so many subjects in his dominions, the Emperor should need to employ at Paris a Jew.[11] Lady Katherine could not afford such prejudices. Mary Catherine was a precociously gifted musician and pretty as a picture but she was illegitimate, while her dowry of 50,000 livres a year that Law had bought in July, 1720 had been cut almost to nothing by the Visa of 1721.[12]

John Law, who no doubt remembered that the distinguished Jews of Amsterdam had backed him in 1712, was satisfied with the match. With his health deteriorating, he surely wanted Kate settled in life and William to have the support of a rising family. On March 26, 1728, which was Good Friday, Law gave power of attorney to the marquis de Bully, together with "Milady Katharine Knolles", to negotiate the match, sign the marriage contract, represent him at the celebrations and, fantastically, recover for Mary Catherine the capital and arrears on her 50,000-livre annuity.

In the document, witnessed by Consul Le Blond, Law left a blank for the young man's first name; this author has been unable to supply it.[13]

That spring and summer of 1728 brought visitors. James III, who was living at Bologna to save money, arrived in Venice incognito on May 4 for a week to attend the feast of Ascension, where each year the Doge in the golden state barge, the *bucintoro*, led out a procession of boats to celebrate the Republic's "marriage" with the sea. According to Consul Neil Brown, James was lodged by the papal Nuncio, Cardinal Gaetano Stampa, at a public house under the name "Count Boussi".[14] Burges, who returned to Venice for a second tour of duty in the midst of the festival, lodged a protest with the Venetian executive on the 10th at "the Pretender's" reception.[15] Burges was now on Londonderry's payroll, with orders to watch Law,[16] but Law had ceased to trust him.[17]

Did James III and John Law meet at last? "Everybody must have known I was here," James told Clementina Sobieska on the 8th, "as one does not mask in the morning any more than at church." Also, Consul Brown reported James was attended everywhere by five gentlemen, six servants and six Bolognese "bravos" as a sort of guard.[18] At the opera, James called on Clementina's aunt, the Dowager Electress of Bavaria, Therese Kunigunde, with whom Law was acquainted.[19] If the two men did meet, there is no trace in either the Stuart correspondence at Windsor Castle or young William's papers in Maastricht.

The same month, two young Frenchmen turned up in the cafés in St Mark's Square, telling everybody that they were owed money by William and, if they were not paid, they would kill either him or his father.[20] They claimed to be brothers by the name of Berdin de Longueville and had an introduction to Gergy. The Venetians encouraged them.[21]

According to Law's account, written in the summer, one of the young men as a boy in The Hague in 1713 had played with William, while his father, a Huguenot refugee named Berdin, worked on the house in the Nieuwe Uitlegging. In 1720, after Law's appointment as controller general, young Berdin came to Paris and attached himself to William, who gave him fine clothes and jewels and more than 40,000 livres in silver and paper to buy the little estate of Longueville, south-east of Paris. On another occasion, William gave him 24,000 livres.[22] William's governor, Miles Thornton, became alarmed at Berdin's demands and informed Lady Katherine, who banned Berdin from the house.

After the Laws' flight from Paris, Berdin accosted Thornton and said William had made certain promises to his sister, which included an income of 4,000 livres a year. Thornton said he should be ashamed of himself. Young William was a diffident boy, and the episode reeks of blackmail.[23]

In Venice, Gergy was inclined to help them, but after interviewing Thornton, who had rejoined William, the Ambassador was persuaded that their "pretensions had no good foundation". Deputed by a nobleman and collector of antiquities, Antonio Nani di San Trovaso, Anton Maria Zanetti tried to persuade Law to give the young men their journey-money back to France, and "not reduce them to despair". Law appears to have refused.[24] (The case is hard to judge because Berdin's successors have tampered with William's papers in Maastricht.)[25]

On August 16, the French philosopher, Charles-Louis de Secondat, baron de Montesquieu, arrived in Venice in a bad mood. He was annoyed by his gondoliers who took him to every whore's jetty.[26] He found only Gergy of the foreign ministers entertained visitors, and that with a minimum of expense. "This is a town that preserves nothing but its name," he wrote to James III's brother, James, Duke of Berwick. "No more armed strength, commerce, wealth or laws, only debauchery which they call liberty."[27]

On the 28th, the abate Conti took him to see John Law. The meeting did not go well. In his *Lettres persanes* (*Persian Letters*) of 1721, Montesquieu had made fun of Law and his ideas and Law did not appreciate ridicule. Montesquieu found him argumentative (*captieux*) "and besides in love more with his ideas than his money".[28]

In his most substantial work *De l'esprit des loix* (*The Spirit of the Laws*), published in 1748, Montesquieu blamed the Scotsman for destroying the intermediate social classes that restrain a monarchy from despotism.

"Mr Law," he wrote, "ignorant alike of the republican and monarchical constitutions, was one of the greatest promoters of despotism that one had seen in Europe up to that point . . . In his chimerical reimbursements [of annuities and offices], he dissolved the monarchy and seemed on the point of liquidating the constitution itself."[29] Here Montesquieu speaks in his robes and mortarboard as a president of the Parlement of Bordeaux. Law's idea that a state might be funded not by hereditary creditors and sinecurists but by investors at risk did not interest him.

To discharge his debts in London, Law that midsummer sent to Middleton a shipment of six chests of pictures, together with a valuation and inventory. Conti said in April that he had spent on pictures at least 3,000 ducats (£1,350).[30] The bill of lading arrived in London on August 13/24 but the vessel bearing the chests was held up in quarantine, and they were not opened until December.[31] Law was in for disappointment. Middleton, who admitted "I'm pretty much unacquainted with things of this nature," showed them to two dealers, one of them Isaac Franks, who was part of the East India wager syndicate.

Middleton wrote on December 31, 1728 that the unnamed dealer said that "none of them will do for him" and "he desired to tell you that thers an Zonetti (or some such name) a sort of picture Broker who he is informed is sometimes about you & of whom he would have you beware for he once imposed much upon him in that way."[32] The pictures would scarcely cover duty and freight of about £125.

Anton Maria Zanetti the Elder was a connoisseur of painting and drawing, a pioneering printmaker and expert on antique gems who had dealt in France with Pierre Crozat, and in England with the Duke of Devonshire and the Earl of Pembroke. Law was fortunate to have his advice. Law was also acquainted with such leading collectors of 1720s Venice as Schulenburg, Consul Joseph Smith (who acted as his post box) and the Grassi family.[33] Middleton was out of his depth but, alas!, Franks and the other gentleman were well within theirs. Burges also later said that Law bought badly, but he was not in Venice while Law assembled the collection, and anyway disliked him.[34]

No doubt, Law did not take the same care as Schulenburg, who employed Venetian artists to authenticate his purchases,[35] but like the German he had a relatively free hand in Venice before the tourists arrived in numbers. During his first posting in the early 1720s, Burges said there were seldom more than "eight or ten of His Majesty's subjects in a winter", but now there were thirty "so much is the Humour of Travelling increased since that time".[36] When a nun in Milan eloped with an Englishman and took refuge in Venice, Conti complained: "These gentlemen are not satisfied with carrying off our medals and statues and enticing away our musicians and painters. They begrudge us even our nuns."[37]

The British interest in Venice had much to do with the success of the Italian operas staged in London since 1720 by Georg Friedrich Händel or Handel. On June 6, 1727, at a performance at the King's Theatre, Haymarket of Giovanni Bononcini's *Astianatte*, in the presence of the Princess of Wales, the rival supporters of

Faustina Bordoni and Francesca Cuzzoni fought in the pit and the season had to be cancelled.[38]

Faustina, "the tenth muse", was booked by the San Cassiano theatre in Venice for the 1728–9 season, and some of her British fans intended to follow her. Not to be outdone the Grimani family, owners of San Giovanni Grisostomo, enticed the star castrato, the 23-year-old Carlo Broschi known as Farinelli, for a fee rumoured to be 1500 sequins (£675).[39] At his first appearance in St Mark's Square, Farinelli was attended by three hundred persons.[40] The English did not know much about music, but they liked a match. Among the English and Scottish young gentlemen to travel to Venice that winter were James, 5th Duke of Hamilton (who flirted with the Jacobites), Sir John Buckworth and Edward and Robert Coke of Holkham in Norfolk.[41]

At the beginning of the autumn season,[42] Law took an apartment in the Procuratie Vecchie, the long building that still stands mostly intact on the north side of St Mark's Square. Law's apartment was at the north-western end of the square, beside the church of San Geminiano which was demolished by Napoleon Bonaparte. Built in the sixteenth century for the Procurators or vestry of St Mark's, the building had long been abandoned by those officials but its rooms were in demand during the opera and Carnival season as *ridotti* or retreats: bolt-holes for those not wishing to take a night gondola home, love-nests, places for men and women to mask, answer a call of nature or make repairs to their toilette, clubs and gambling dens. This author's conjecture is that Law established in the apartment a faro bank.[43] (By now, Hugh Hamilton had left Venice.)

John Law began to win and win and win. By January 5, 1729, Conti reported that Law had won "at roulette and faro" 25,000 sequins or more than £11,000. "We are insane to play with him, but we are reluctant to abandon our folly despite the losses we suffer," he wrote.[44] Lady Katherine wrote from Paris on the 20th that she was "glade you meet suxess in your play".[45]

That winter was cold all over Europe: the coldest, people said, since the hard winter of Malplaquet in 1709.[46] In the first week of December, Lady Katherine set out for Versailles to see Cardinal André-Hercule de Fleury, who had replaced the duc de Bourbon as Louis XV's chief minister, but was kept waiting and then sent away till after the Christmas holidays. "I was so disdord [disordered] with lying out of my bed which I have not done since I saw you & with the cold that I was not able to wright," she told Law on December 7.[47]

Then came the blow. "I am prepaird to have a civill reception [from Fleury] but that is all, being I heare under hand [unofficially] the orders are giving [given] to the Commissaris to pay the creditors with what they have in ther hands & for the rest to leave as a debt due to the Company . . . soe that we shall be left vis a vis de rien [facing nothing]."

This is the first of three unsigned letters from Lady Katherine to Law that survive that bitter winter. They are intimate but not improper. The woman who wrote them is affectionate, faithful and brave and not at all the haughty dame of Voltaire and the duc de Saint-Simon. That she had forgotten how to write English is no very dark spot on her character.

Lady Katherine tried to soften the blow.

> You have a greatt deall of fermety [firmness] or I woud not wright this. I shall endeavouer to follow yr exampels but finde I am inferiore to you in every thing. If I can but keep my health to deliver you yr daughter I belive you will be contendted with the care I have had of her in cultivating the tallents that god has giving her. She presents her duty to

you, & pray both our loves to my son. Itt is so colde, that I scarse feell my pen. We wish you both a happy nue yeare, wich is the sincerest wish as perhaps you have recued [received] & I am sure you dont doubt ofe.[48]

She wrote again on the 17th. The marquis de Bully was at Versailles, but had been unable to speak to Fleury. She herself had gone to Ambassador Walpole that he might beg for her "an audience particular of the Card[inal] for me that [I] may have a little time to spake to hime, allone." Finally, in the new year, she received an appointment and set off for Versailles but "in the violent cold weather we was obliged to ly in a cabarett [inn] 2 nights."

Fleury was the opposite of forthcoming. "He told me our affairs would soon be ended," she wrote on January 20. "I asked him how, for that I was told that [it] was ordered to leave us nothing upon which he maed noe anser but in a nother occasion told me the wholl statte [state] was of the same oppinion one yr account." She did not press the matter, fearing she was unprepared. Fleury did ask her to present a memoir and to name commissioners to act for her.

"To what regards me . . . it is as cold as in the hard winter, we can't go out, besids I have loast a coach hors whoe drapit dead in the stable." Rebecca Dewes, William's wife, was having a difficult pregnancy in the rue Saint-Jacques on the other side of the river.

I am sorry I cant goe to se her, heare is fears any coaches can stirr it [cause premature birth]. 'Tis a quiet as the country. If it [the freeze] laste any time longer we shall keep our beds for thers noe keeping our selves warm upe, tho with great fiers which ruins me at this tim [I cannot afford]. [Word missing] is frozed by my bed.

My party is taken [I have played my hand], & hope

notwithstanding all they can doe to make us unhappy I may hope for yr esteem & aprobation for what lys in my power to doe & that we may meett in good health which is the chiefest blessing. I thank god Kitty [Mary Catherine] has [is] well, & is a heroing in all theis difficultys, adieu. I cant say more for I dont feell my pen tho in my bed.[49]

It was snowing too in Venice[50] but that did not bring down the opera fever. Farinelli made his Venetian debut at San Giovanni Grisostomo to "maximum applause" in Leonardo Leo's *Catone in Utica* ("Cato in Utica") on December 26, while Faustina "gained immortal honour" in Geminiano Giacomelli's *Gianguir* ("Jahangir") at San Cassiano on the night following.[51]

"Here people are so obsessed with Farinello," Conti wrote on December 30, "that if the Turks sailed into the Gulf [of Venice] we would let them land rather than miss two minor arias."[52] Farinelli was alleged to have forty vocal chords "and passes from one to another by imperceptibles shades," or so the connoisseurs told Conti.[53] Handel was in town to book singers for the winter in London, and called three times on the celebrity, but the young man refused to see him in private or return his visits.[54] The copyists were overloaded with demands for the music and turned away customers.[55]

"The lady's strength [support] lies chiefly among the foreigners, especially the English and French," Burges wrote to London on February 11, "but the Eunuch has almost all the Italiens of his side, a powerful band; and esteem'd by much the best judges of musick."[56] The next night, Law and William almost certainly attended the first performance of Nicola Porpora's music for Pietro Metastasio's *Semiramide riconosciuta* ("Semiramis Recognised") at San Giovanni Grisostomo, with Farinelli singing the part of the Egyptian prince.

On February 23, at the apartment in the Procuratie Vecchie, John Law came down with a cold which spread to his chest as pneumonia.[57] Burges reported the symptoms as "a shivering cold fit which lasted him five or six hours, & that was succeeded by a violent hot one, which has never intermitted".[58] As he shook in his bed the next day, Fat Thursday, and all Venice gathered beneath his window to watch two men on cardboard steeds fight with swords and pistols on a high-wire struck between the bell-tower of St Mark's and the loggia of the Doge's Palace, an immense piece of the Campanile fell in the high winds and embedded itself in the pavement.[59]

William and Le Blond engaged the most distinguished physician in Venice, Pietro Antonio Michelotti (?1673–1740), and four colleagues from the University of Padua to attend the sick man.[60] Excellency Michelotti, a member of the Royal Society of London and, like his patient, of the Académie royale des sciences in Paris, had a European reputation for his theories of the purely mechanical character of illness. His treatment of Law, which began on February 27 and continued until March 19, was traditional. It consisted of purges and costly oriental drugs administered in "spirit of wine" or pure alcohol. His assistants emptied the pharmacies of Venice of white poppy, eastern daisy, myrrh, hyssop, oximel, julep of terebinth, camphor, bezoar of both goat and porcupine and something called "Spanish badger" (*melis hispanicus*).[61]

The Carnival was over but, as Conti once told his French correspondents, "we pass without the least effort from the excess of folly to the most profound sobriety. We are as moved by a Jesuit sermon as by an aria."[62] In the cafés and arcades of St Mark's Square below, Farinelli and Faustina were out and John Law was in. Would he stay true to the Roman Catholic faith, or revert, as the English and Scottish colony was boasting, to the religion of his fathers? With Lent approaching, it made an edifying bet. For

Gergy and Burges, the one acting for the King of France and the other for Lord Londonderry, it was time for Law to confess his sins and reveal, "with death at the end of his bed", whether he had spirited millions out of France.[63]

Ambassador Gergy climbed up to the sick room on Shrove Tuesday, March 1, and chided Law "for in all his stay here not having made one single act of Catholicity". In some discomfort, Law revealed the existence of the Credence Letter from the late King George I, though he said he had never made use of it. (Presumably, he would have embarrassed the British government had he attended Roman Catholic service.) Law said that he had instructed his son, as soon as he was no more, to travel to France and "throw himself at the feet of His Majesty" Louis XV.[64]

Colonel Burges called the next day, Ash Wednesday, March 2. The patient was "very sensible of the danger he was in, and, as he told me, very desirous to die; believing his death would be of greater service to his family at this juncture than any other". Law told Burges of the commissioners Lady Katherine had mentioned in her letter of January 20 "and he thinks they will be more inclined to do him justice in France, when they shall know how poor he dies."[65] After Burges took his leave, Gergy returned with a Jesuit father.

The Jesuit was Father Dionigi Origo, one of the star Lenten preachers of Venice. He had been recommended by the Papal Nuncio, Cardinal Stampa. Father Origo seems to have had a worldly side, for he later gave Casanova this advice as to how to take revenge on an enemy without effort: smother him or her in praise, such that it becomes nauseating to others, and there is a reaction of dispraise.[66]

Father Origo took Law's confession and a little later, Father Lorenzo Bianchi, parish priest at San Geminiano, administered the last rites.

On the morning of Friday, March 4, Ambassador Gergy returned and urged Law to write a will. Law refused, saying that it was quite redundant (*inutile*), since all his property was in France and in the hands of his creditors. That, excepting the houses in Shepherd Street and some cash with Middleton, a large number of pictures and his gambling money, was true. Gergy persisted, saying that a will in the ordinary form was "always an authentic proof of the religion in which a man passed away".[67] Exhausted, Law agreed and that afternoon wrote a page and asked Le Blond to inform Gergy that it was done. At the same time, fearing he would not live out the day, he called for Father Origo.

Law's "will" or what he calls his "manifesto", which was copied on the 5th but not notarised, is printed and translated as Appendix IV. In it, Law declares that he possessed "no funds or capitals of any sort outside the Kingdom of France". Father Origo appears to have supplied the Latin phrase *in puncto mortis* and such pulpit eloquences as "the hazards of Fortune at play" or "God before whom only the truth has lustre" that have no counterpart in Law's surviving writings, any more than does the name of God. One passage sounds like Law: "Play . . . was besides never an inclination of mine but merely forced on me by those financial straits which left me insufficient money to support myself and my family in a respectable condition, as is well known."[68] On the Sunday, there was such a gale of wind that nobody dared go outside, gondolas foundered in the canals, and a lady of quality and her maid were rescued from the water.[69]

The wagers were no doubt paid. On the 10th, the abate Conti wrote to his French correspondents: "His confession was edifying in the extreme, and he has promised to make great acts of charity if he recovers. The English here are enraged that he will not die a Protestant and that the abjuration he made in France has been sincere."[70]

The Papal Nuncio was moved to eloquence. Demetrio della Frattina, a Udinese nobleman and poet,[71] who eked out his living by passing intelligence to the Inquisitors of State on the doings of the Imperial and Spanish ambassadors, the Papal Nuncio and the Receiver of Malta, or what he called "foreign reports" (*notizie forastiere*), wrote to the Council of Ten: "Law's continued illness inspired Mgr Nuncio to make a long, edifiying and erudite discourse: first on his conversion to the church, and then on his good fortune to die in the bosom of the Catholic religion in this dominion."

Count Giuseppe di Bolagno, the Habsburg Ambassador, concurred and added "that nowhere else in Italy, not even in Rome, were there such examples of devotion as in Venice."[72] In reality, Law was interested not in the fate of his soul but in the succession of his property, which he still dreamed of being restored, to Lady Katherine and his children. Because she was not his wedded wife, his brother William or his creditors might claim the inheritance (and did). Lady Katherine's meeting with Cardinal Fleury had kindled the cold ashes of his hopes. The world thought that Law was concealing a great secret, which in their imagination was gold, securities and jewels, but it was only the hope that some day, perhaps far in the future, the King of France would do justice to his family and recognise his service.

Having put Gergy and Burges off the scent, Law had decided on a legal form known as a "*donatio inter vivos sed causa mortis*", or gift between living persons but in expectation of death, where he would pass to Lady Katherine not so much his property as his expectations. Young William sought a written opinion from two Venetian lawyers on seven questions, including whether "the brother of the donor" or other creditors could have claims in law on a donation made in Venice to a beneficiary abroad. (This document confirms that William had not followed his father into the Roman Catholic Church.)[73] The true question, which was not legal in character, was how they could keep the donation secret in a city populated by chatterboxes and police spies.

From then on, when the comte de Gergy called, young William or Le Blond told him that Law was sleeping. On the 12th, William wrote to the marchese De Mari, offering some hope.[74] In fact, Gergy heard from the doctors that day that they did not believe Law could live.[75] The fever never left him, and though some nights were better than others, the doctors concluded his lung was ulcerated and "he cannot survive without a species of miracle."[76] Gergy asked Paris for permission to seal the house in event of death.

On the 19th, a Saturday, the notary Carlo Gabrieli, one Don Lorenzo Reali and Le Blond witnessed the donation "at the residence of the Most Excellent John Law above the square of St Mark in the Parish of St Geminian". By its terms, Law donated "all and severally the goods, securities, capitals, rents, moveables, cash, chattels, gold, silver, gems, loans, accounts, shares and everything else without exception that the aforementioned Excellency Law should possess at the time of his death . . . to Milady Catterina Knowels sister of the Earl of Banbury, the said lady at present residing in Paris at her house in rue Louis-le-Grand, near the palais d'Antin."[77] That night Michelotti ended treatment.[78]

Law lingered on for two days, lucid until the last quarter of an hour and, as young William told his mother on the 26th, doing "everything he could think on in order to facilitat our affaires". His last wishes were that Lady Katherine remain in France until William should arrive and "he was mighty desyrous my sister was married with the Baron de Fonsseca's sone."[79]

John Law died on Monday, March 21, 1729. His death certificate, issued by Father Bianchi at the church of San Geminiano, gave cause of death as *mal di petto* or chest ailment.[80] He was buried two days later in the sacristy of San Geminiano.[81]

*

"He died with great calmness and constancy," Colonel Burges wrote to London on the 25th, "& is spoke of here with much esteem."[82] On the 26th, the comte de Gergy wrote to Louis XV, describing Law's last hours and making a handsome plea for him. "At the end, he begged me to place before the throne of justice of Your Majesty the interests of his family."[83] He also invited young William to come and live with him, which William declined.

Gergy wrote the same day to the King's foreign secretary, Germain Louis Chauvelin, saying that he had come to believe Law really was a pauper. He wrote: "I never saw a man so intoxicated as he was by his accursed System, and that in such a way that it is probable that, at the commencement of his operations, he came to believe his projects infallible and so gave no thought to his own affairs. Then, when he saw things go awry, he dared not put anything aside, either because it was too late, or because he feared to destroy entirely his diminishing credit."[84]

Before sealing the letter, Gergy either learned about the donation and his suspicions returned in a rush, or wished to add a private note that could be detached. He remembered how, after his visit on March 4, young William and Le Blond had not admitted him to the sick man. He summoned and interrogated Notary Gabrieli and Father Origo, then added a long postscript to the minister: "I feel I cannot hide from you that there is something in the conduct of the late Mr Law, and since then of Mr Le Blond, consul of France, and of Mr Law his son, which is not straightforward and could give rise to more than a little suspicion."[85]

Elsewhere in town, there were doubts about the sincerity of Law's conversion. Della Frattina reported a conversation on the 25th at the house of the Imperial Ambassador, Count Bolagno. A Neapolitan named Don Vicenzo said that, after Gergy's visit, Law had consoled himself with the thought that "Catholicity would not only save his soul but preserve for his lady (?) his property in

France, and so he suddenly decided to make a show of conversion, and called with unwonted urgency for Father Origo, whom up to then he had avoided like the plague," Frattina went on to the Papal Nuncio, and told him the story. "He said nothing," Frattina wrote in his confidential report to the Inquisitors on the 27th, "but by his silence showed he held an opinion more unfavourable than favourable of the deceased."[86]

Paris advised Gergy against placing seals on the house, or indeed making any sort of display. Instead, he was to ask Le Blond to note anything relating to "the King's business" but not to bully him to betray any confidences of the dead man "as a friend [*comme amy*]".[87] Chauvelin had heard that Law had composed memoirs relating to his time in France, and he wanted those and any "letters of the late duc d'Orléans and his ministers".[88] His tone became more urgent: "What is absolutely indispensable is that the papers of the deceased which the Consul has in his possession reach me as soon as possible."[89] In fact, William and Le Blond had already brought in some of Law's papers, on Wednesday, March 30. Those did not include King George's Letter of Credence which was returned to Burges along with eight letters from the British ministers, and private papers which, in the way of such things, also included material from 1719 and 1720 that Chauvelin might have wished to have had.[90]

The papers given in, weighing a hundred pounds, Gergy sent in thirteen packets, wrapped in red waxed cloth and sealed with his arms, to Louis-Augustin Blondel, chargé d'affaires in Turin, to be despatched each with a separate courier to Lyons.[91] Among them were three quarto books of Law's outletters, copied by young William and Hamilton, covering the period from his disgrace in December, 1720 to the last months of his stay in Munich in September, 1726. Those Gergy looked over.

Of the three volumes, only the first, from December, 1720 to

May, 1722, has been seen by this author. The other two volumes, and most likely the other material, have vanished. On April 16, Louis XV replied to Gergy from Versailles through the Secretary of State of his household, the comte de Maurepas: "I had imagined he would have left a rich inheritance, but the circumstances that you describe make me recognise the opposite."[92]

Amidst the fantasies about his father's estate, William discharged two pitiful legacies. John Law left his housekeeper in Shepherd Street, Mrs Gibbs, £50, or two years' wages, and the furniture of the two houses (if she could hold the door against his creditors).[93] William also sent a note of 300 pistoles to his uncle William in France. He had difficulty in finding bills for Paris on his own credit.[94]

William wrote to inform Middleton, who replied with the minimum of condolence. "It's a fate we must all submitt to," he wrote on April 3/14, and added: "I shall be extreamly oblig'd if you'll be so kind to favour me with a line and lett me know so far as you think it proper if your father has made a will and to whom I should apply for reliefe in the mony oweing me."[95]

On or just before April 11, a stone was placed on the tomb. In addition to a bas relief, the grey stone slab carried this Latin epitaph:

IOANNES LAW

WILIELMI FILIVS

EDIMBVRGI SCOTORVM SVMMO LOCO NATVS

REGII ERARY IN GALLIA PRAEFECTVS

OBIIT VENETIIS ANNO SALVTIS

MDCCXXIX

AETATIS VERO

LVIII

("John Law, son of William, born to the highest estate in Edinburgh in Scotland, superintendent of the royal treasury in France, died at Venice in the year of grace 1729 at the true age of fifty-eight.")[96] William or Le Blond cavilled at the mason's invoice, which was reduced on arbitration from 150 to 110 lire.[97]

The grave became a resort for Scottish tourists. Lady Grisel Baillie, wife of old Baillie of Jerviswood, advised her grandsons in 1740 to visit San Geminiano as "Mr Law that made such a figur in France in the Messasipie year your country man is buried there."[98]

In 1807, after the fall of the Venetian Republic to Napoleon, the church of San Geminiano was demolished to make way for a palace for the French viceroy across the western end of St Mark's Square. It is known as the Ala Napoleonica. Brother William Law's grandson, Jacques-Alexandre Law (1768–1828), comte de Lauriston, who had risen like a rocket in Napoleon's service and was military governor of Venice, ensured that his great-uncle's remains were removed two hundred yards to the west to the church of San Moisè. An inscription was cut into the pavement just inside the west door of that church, and can still be seen.

During his last winter in Venice, John Law sent seven cases of pictures to London, which Isaac Franks was content to leave at the Customs House till he should receive the bill of lading.[99] A much larger collection was destined not for London and his British creditors but for Amsterdam, for it was to guarantee the future of Lady Katherine and his children.

The inventory, which is signed by Le Blond, beggars belief. Among the 485 items were works by Mantegna, Raphael, Michelangelo, Leonardo, Titian, Moroni, Poussin, Rubens, Van Dyck and other famous names, some of them *finitissime* or "done to the highest standard". In addition, there were marbles and furniture and, for Mary Catherine, a cello made by the Amati family of Cremona and a violin by Jacob Stainer of Innsbruck, and arias from the operas of the past three seasons by Tomaso Albinoni, Antonio Vivaldi, Leo and Porpora as well as much other music.[100] Burges wrote to Londonderry that Law "was horribly imposed on in every bargain he made", for he "advised with nobody", and above all not with Colonel Elizeus Burges. (The letter never reached Londonderry, who died at St Kitts on September 12.)[101]

A painter named Piccini packed up the pictures and musical instruments into eighty-one cases, charging 440 lire for paper and packing and 550 lire for his trouble, which bill William settled on June 7.[102] He left the crates in the care of Consul Le Blond. He paid his father's account with Burges for postage.[103] Provided with a passport for himself and two servants, signed by Consul Neil Brown, William set off on August 6 to see his mother and sister for the first time in nine years.[104]

No doubt for fear of arrest, William did not go to Paris. Instead, the family was reunited at Brussels some time before August 31, 1729, for on that day young Fonseca wrote to William: "I would more sensibly share your joy at seeing Madame your mother and Mademoiselle your sister had not the excessive pain of watching them depart hence robbed me of every other sensation."[105]

The family took lodgings in Brussels in the aristocratic district of Sablon, rue de la Grosse-Tour (modern rue du Grand Cerf), in the parish of Notre-Dame-de-la-Chapelle.[106] Their furniture, books, musical instruments and linen from Paris were sent by barge and boat to Antwerp, where they were stored by the sheriff of the city, requiring a trip later by William to pick up nightgowns and winter petticoats for his mother.[107]

They lived in some style, with a carriage and eight servants, at a rate William computed at over 18,000 livres a year.[108] In the autumn, Le Blond wrote from Venice to say that he was shipping the pictures on a Dutch vessel to Amsterdam. William travelled to

Amsterdam where, on December 10, 1729, he swore before the Town Clerk Joan Thierry the Younger an oath that he would be "a good and faithful freeman [*poorter*] of this town". Th. P. M. Huijs, the expert on the Law papers in Maastricht, believes that William took the freeman's oath to make it easier to deal with the Venetian shipment.[109] In Paris, his uncle, William Law Sr, was demanding that the produce from the sales of his brother's property in France should pass to his children, as legitimate heirs.[110]

In the new year, the Baron de Fonseca came to Brussels.[111] Whatever happened at the interview, the marriage scheme collapsed. In September 1730, Lady Katherine was ill and the family travelled to Aachen or Aix, staying at an inn run by the Bouget family, known as Zum roten Löwen (The Red Lion) or Maison Bouget, Komphausbadstraße 11–13, which was the principal resort and assembly for those taking the waters of the town. (King Frederick IV of Denmark had lived there with his court in 1724.) There William received word from Le Blond in Venice that the vessel with the pictures had been wrecked and many of the pictures ruined.

The ship had limped back to Venice at the end of August. To float her off the reef or sands when she struck, the crew had thrown the crates into the sea, and though many were recovered, the pictures on wood and leather were damaged and certain marble tables "are probably still at the bottom of the sea". Among the pictures declared to the insurers as lost or irreparable were a *Crucifixion* and *Miracle of St Benedict* by Andrea Mantegna, *Madonna and Child* by Gentile Bellini and *Portrait of a Man* by Giorgione.[112]

"The pastels are all spoiled beyond repair," Le Blond wrote on September 8. Those included portraits of Law and William done by Rosalba Carriera.[113] Not a person to bear grudges,[114] Rosalba offered to redo them and succeeded to the extent, Le Blond later wrote, "that you would not know that they had been an instant in the sea. Truly, as regards her profession, nothing is beyond that girl."[115] Alas!, though her portrait of John Law survived in at least one version into the nineteenth century, the attribution is now lost.[116] In other words, the picture may survive but it is not possible to identify the sitter as Law.

Lady Katherine's nerve, hitherto strong, now began to flicker. John Ker, a Scotsman on the edge of the Earl of Mar's circle, had seen her at Antwerp and Liège and taken a shine to her. (He was possibly John Ker of Kersland, who had "died" in the King's Bench Prison in 1726, a career step sometimes necessary in the eighteenth century.)

He wrote early in the new year of 1731: "Your Ladyship is apt to give way to melancholy and that forms darker still and darker ideas which destroy your quiet, impair your health and afflicts your children. You do the best you can (and no body can do better). Let that comfort you, and rouse up your courage to encounter what cannot be avoided."[117]

That year they moved to Munich for Mary Catherine's musical education, travelling with thirteen trunks that included one for flutes, one for violins, one for printed music and one each for clean and dirty laundry.[118] Good Le Blond sent from Venice cello strings and two sonatas for the cello, "specially written by Mr Aliprandi".[119] Bernardo Aliprandi, till that summer a teacher of music at the orphanage known as the Ospedale dei Mendicanti in Venice, appears in the records of the Bavarian court as a chamber musician from October 1 that year and probably took Kate on as a pupil.

Thus they rattled about the Low Countries and Germany, drawing on their French life annuities and making work for notaries and consuls. Le Blond sent bulletins on Piccini's interminable negotiations with the insurers of the damaged cargo. The Earl of

Mar, his son Thomas and daughter Frances settled in Aix in the autumn of 1731, and it is likely that the two families visited each other. (Mar died in May, 1732.)[120]

It is young William's misfortune before history that his jottings survive. His papers are scattered with notes to himself to do this and read that, lists, invoices, accounts, address books and court directories, many started and then allowed to lapse. He seems to have had difficulty applying himself.

In the course of 1732, he resolved to follow a military career. Jonkheer Douwe Sirtema van Grovestins (1710–1778), a young Frisian officer in the service of Prince William of Orange-Nassau, wrote from camp to William at the Bougets in September, 1732 that a company or captaincy in his regiment would soon be vacant and suggested William buy it.[121] He offered to speak to the Prince on William's behalf.

Whether out of diffidence or economy, or both, William elected to serve in Grovestins' squadron as a cornet, the lowest commissioned rank, or what we now call a second lieutenant. The regiment was quartered at Maastricht, a fortified frontier town about twenty-five miles from Aix in the Dutch Netherlands.

The family moved there in the spring of 1733, renting a house from the Van Slijpe family opposite the main court of law at 8–10 Bouillonstraat, which house survives as a department of Maastricht University.[122] William became a freeman of the town on March 30, and was commissioned an officer at the end of May.[123]

The pleasant young man and his beautiful mother and sister must have been an addition to the society of the little town. Count von Schlippenbach, John Law's old acquaintance from Genoa and now a lieutenant-colonel of dragoons, was stationed there and welcomed them. As for Baron Grovestins, who was aide-de-camp to Prince William, he had his eye on Kate but took care also to pay court to Lady Katherine. "Dammit, tell them I love them both," he wrote that August.[124] His gallantries, a world away from young Fonseca's heartache, cannot have been much more welcome to William.

The cloud on the horizon was a man named Pierre Douvry or Douvrij who had either taken over the Berdins' claim on William or was working with them. He had had dealings with the Laws in Paris in 1720[125] and pursued the family to Maastricht, for it was at this time William commissioned from Venice the notarised witness statements over the Berdins' threats against his life in 1728.[126] Nothing more is heard of the wrecked shipment of pictures, which remains the family's great mystery. William had little time to defend himself or his family. In the new year, he contracted smallpox and on February 4, 1734, at the age of about twenty-eight, he died. He is buried in the Sint Janskerk.[127]

On the 17th, an inventory was made of the property in the Bouillonstraat and Mary Catherine, who had reached her legal majority, petitioned the States General to be served sole heiress. Douvry and the other creditors intervened, inaugurating nine years of litigation before the High Court of Brabant and the appeal courts. Eventually, the High Court ruled that William's furniture must be sold for his creditors but his papers should be sealed and deposited with the Clerk of the Court.[128] Without intending it, the Berdins and Douvry ensured that John Law's story could be told.

With Lady Katherine now of little help to her, Mary Catherine needed support. Her cousin William Knollys, Lord Wallingford, MP for Banbury in Oxfordshire, stepped forward and on July 4, 1734, they were married. At forty, he was much older than his bride, but he was by all accounts both capable and kind. They moved to London.

Lady Katherine did not accompany her daughter to England. Voltaire, who was in Brussels for long periods between the summer of 1739 and 1742, while the husband of his beloved Emilie de

Châtelet pursued a lawsuit, claims to have seen her in that city and drew a moral on the mutability of human fortune: "I saw [Law's] widow at Brussels, as humbled as she had been proud and triumphant at Paris. Such revolutions are not the least useful of history's objects."[129] Since Voltaire and the Châtelets were living in the rue de la Grosse-Tour in the Sablon,[130] where the Laws had certainly taken a house in 1729 and probably later, he may truly have seen her. (Voltaire does not claim to have seen Lady Katherine in Paris and surely did not.)

With Douvry threatening to contest Mary Catherine's inheritance in the English courts, it was necessary to question Lady Katherine on William's precise birth-date.[131] (If William was a minor in 1720, as he almost certainly was, he was not capable of making the Berdins or anybody else financial promises.) In Mary Catherine's surviving papers in Winchester, Lady Katherine appears as someone remote and not lightly to be disturbed. The last reference to her alive is in a lawyer's letter of July 9, 1743.[132] There is also a letter to her in French, dated "July 31st" and probably from that year, which speaks of some document that must at all costs be kept secret.[133]

Some authors say that Lady Katherine Knowles died destitute in a beguinage or community of lay women in Liège or Brussels, but there is no trace of her in the burial records of either place or in the papers of the religious houses later brought to England.

One piece of evidence places her at Aachen at the Bougets. On July 29, 1750, her brother Banbury's bastard son, Charles Knowles, whom Lady Katherine and Lord Wallingford had befriended and sent to sea, married a "Miss Bugit".[134] She was Maria Magdalena Bouget, who was born at Aix in 1733. That might be coincidence. More likely is that Rear-Admiral Knowles met his bride while on a visit to his old aunt and benefactress.

*

A British historian once wrote that had the Mississippi and South Sea projects not collapsed in 1720, the new techniques for making textiles, chemicals and ironwork known as the Industrial Revolution might have occurred "forty or fifty years" earlier. He imagined the British and French fighting in North America and India with machine guns and Dr Samuel Johnson travelling to Edinburgh by steam train.[135] It is a vivid fancy but, in truth, capital is just one contributor to innovation and not the most important. It took the genius of James Watt in the 1760s to remedy the inefficiencies of the steam engine that had defeated men such as Gun Jones in the 1720s.

Better said is that Law left in France a suspicion of paper money and banking that handicapped her in her rivalry with Great Britain; or, to be precise, neutralised some of her advantages in extent, population and public administration. The Battle of Plassey was won in Exchange Alley and the Heights of Abraham fell to the clerks of the Bank of England.

For the remainder of the century, loan contracts in France were often written with a clause that the sum could be repaid only in current gold and silver and not, as a constitution in Caen of 1751 put it, "in bills of whatever kind or species they might be".[136] The French, as the Jacobite political economist Sir James Steuart wrote in 1767, returned "to the old system of rents [annuities] upon the town-house of Paris; and of coming at money in the best way they could".[137]

French Louisiana survived Law's downfall. Yet as the colony grew, so French and native Americans came into conflict. Bienville's recall in 1725, and the death the same year of Tattooed Serpent, the advocate of the French alliance among the Natchez, were ill omens.

To cut costs, the directors reduced the military garrison from sixteen to eight companies (of, at best, fifty officers and men each). On November 29, 1729, provoked by demands on their lands for tobacco cultivation at Fort Rosalie, the Natchez attacked the French settlements and killed some two hundred and thirty French and Canadian men. Two years later, the Company of the Indies ceded its monopoly to the French Crown so as to concentrate on India and China. (In 1803, Napoleon Bonaparte sold the territory amounting to over 800,000 square miles to the United States of Thomas Jefferson for 60 million livres – $11.25 million, £2.5 million.)

The Stanhope-Dubois peace lasted until 1740 when Europe, North America and India were engulfed in conflict over the Habsburg succession. The Earl of Stair came out of his Ayrshire retirement in 1743 to rescue a British and Hanoverian army menaced by his old friend the duc de Noailles at Dettingen, east of Frankfurt. Little Carluccio, now Prince Charles Edward Stuart, landed with French assistance in western Scotland in 1745, defeated a Hanoverian army at Prestonpans, near Edinburgh, and marched as far as Derby in England, before all hope of his father's restoration vanished in defeat at Culloden, near Inverness, the next year.

Worn out by sorrow and good works, Clementina had died and James III followed her to the grave in 1766. Charles had no legitimate issue while his brother, Henry, Duke of York, preferred the rich benefices of a cardinal of the Church to the vanished prospect of restoration. The Stuart correspondence, with its sidelights on John Law's starring hour in Paris, was bought by George IV while Prince Regent, transported from Italy in two consignments in 1810 and 1817, and lodged at Windsor Castle.

The War of Austrian Succession (1740–8) and the Seven Years War (1756–63) strained the French system of finance. For want of naval superiority, the Company of the Indies was at the mercy of the British fleet in the approaches to Lorient, Canada, Senegal and India. The leading French thinkers, such as the abbé André Morellet and P. S. du Pont de Nemours, reinforced by Hume and

Smith who both lived in Paris in the 1760s, argued that monopoly companies were noxious both to commerce and the state and trade was best left open to competition. Voltaire dismissed European India as "shop clerks bickering over muslin and chintzes".[138] In 1770, the Company of the Indies suspended operations.

The summoning of the Estates General in 1789, which the duc d'Orléans with John Law's help had been able to avoid, set in train a revolution which demolished the old regime and cost Louis XVI his head.

As nephews of the revered founder, William and Rebecca's two sons were early destined for the Company of the Indies.[139] Presented to the directors by Lassay's son on behalf of the old duchesse de Bourbon, between them the largest shareholders, the brothers were engaged for India in 1741.[140] The duchess insisted that the boys should start at the very bottom: "the better," as she said about the older brother, Jean, "to learn what he needs to know".[141]

Jean, born in Paris at the height of Mississippi fever in 1719, went out as a clerk or writer, but was promoted to head the French trading post or factory at Kasim Bazar, across the river from Murshidabad in Bengal, buying raw silk, and then at Patna.

At the outbreak of the Seven Years War, the British captured the French settlements in Bengal. Jean escaped in April 1757 up the Ganges with a force of 180 Europeans and some sepoys or Muslim militiamen, fighting at every bend in the river, and also gathering materials for an Indo-Persian dictionary.

Known to the Mogul historians as موسی لاس (Musa Laas, "Monsieur Lasse"),[142] Jean became commander of artillery to the embattled Mogul emperor Shah Alam II, until they were defeated by the British near Patna in January, 1761.

Jean, who seems to have known English, was much liked by

the British officers. Paroled, he returned to France and wrote an account of his adventures for the then controller general, Henri Bertin, which was published from a manuscript in the British Library early in the twentieth century.[143] He returned in 1765 as Governor General of French India on a salary (soon reduced) of 50,000 livres per year. The district in the town of Pondicherry called Lawspet is named after him. By then William Law Sr had died, and by the terms of Jean Campbell's entail, Jean was master of Lauriston Castle on the Firth of Forth. Sir Walter Scott's father, Walter Scott, WS, handled his business in Scotland.

The younger brother, Jacques-François Law, chevalier de Lauriston, born in 1724, went out as a clerk but found civilian life did not suit him. Beginning as an ensign, he fought at all the chief engagements of the Carnatic Wars, and took a sabre wound in the defence of Madras in 1746. In 1749, at the battle of Ambur, an arrow passed through his left shoulder. Directing the siege of Tanjore from the trenches, he was hit in the left eye by a pistol shot which passed on to smash his jaw.

The next year, at Gingee Fort, supposedly impregnable, he detonated a mine at the main gate and was the first to enter the fortress. In 1752, he was admitted a knight of the Order of St Louis, but his cross and citation went down with the *Prince* when she caught fire and sank off the coast of Brazil. Later that year, he was forced to surrender his force besieging Trichinopoly.

In 1758, at the siege of the British Fort St David, his left foot was riddled with canister shot but he managed to carry the north-western redoubt. The following year, a grenade threatened to take away the sight of his remaining eye. With the fall of Pondicherry to Robert Clive in 1761, Jacques lost his property, including three houses and a garden. He had already sold his plate and his wife's jewels to pay his men. Sent a prisoner to England, he was robbed of his baggage at Plymouth.

On his way back from France in 1766 to take command of the French forces in India for his brother, Major General the chevalier Law died at île de France (Mauritius), at the age of forty-two.[144]

The brothers married the cousins Jeanne and Marie Carvalho, daughters of the Portuguese brothers Alexandre and François Carvalho, merchants who partnered company officers trading on their own account in cargoes from Chandernagor and Madras to the Philippines.[145] At her marriage to Jacques, at the church of Notre-Dame-des-Anges at Pondicherry on February 22, 1751, Marie (b.1731) brought with her a dowry of 30,000 rupees (£3,000)[146] and Jeanne, married at Chandernagor four years later (September 13, 1755), at least that sum.[147]

The second son of Jean Law and Jaan Begum to survive childhood, Jacques-Alexandre-Bernard, was born at Pondicherry in 1768. He was sent at sixteen to the Ecole Militaire in Paris, where he became friend to a brother-cadet, the Corsican Napoleon Bonaparte. After his service in Venice, where he supervised the reburial of his great-uncle's remains, Jacques-Alexandre commanded one hundred pieces of cannon at Wagram, near Vienna, in 1809 and destroyed an Austrian army. (That action is commemorated each year at the French army artillery college at Draguignan.) He was French Ambassador to Moscow at the time of Napoleon's invasion in 1812 and it was his mission to General Mikhail Kutuzov after the Battle of Borodino (at least in Tolstoy's *War and Peace*) that convinced the Russian commander that the French were licked.

After Napoleon was exiled to Elba, Jacques-Alexandre made his peace with the restored Bourbon monarchy and was granted the marquisate of Lauriston and the title of Marshal of France. His name was inscribed on the eastern pillar of the Arc de Triomphe in Paris. His descendants and those of his siblings serve France to this day: "one of very few of French noblesse of pure Scottish descent," as the Victorian genealogist Sir Bernard Burke once wrote, "still resident and flourishing in France".[148]

Viscountess Wallingford, *née* Law, made an exotic figure in the London society of the eighteenth century. She was described in 1737 as "extremely pretty and in the French dress".[149] Though she spoke English it was some years before Kate learned to write in that language.

In the years after 1737, she was a friend of Margaret, Duchess of Portland, and a member of a circle of high-minded women known as the Bluestockings. She is mentioned as being often at one of the Duchess's country houses, Bulstrode Park in Buckinghamshire. She was known as "Wall".

Mary Catherine remained true to her talent. Elizabeth Robinson (later Montagu), the "Queen of the Blues", writing to the Duchess in 1739 as if from ancient Hades, said she had there told Eurydice "there was one Lady Wallingford in the other world who could sing and play like her own Orpheus."[150] The following June Mary Catherine contracted a mild bout of smallpox and while she was laid up at her house in Grosvenor Street, up "two pairs of stairs", her husband died of quinsy or "a cramp in his throat".[151]

She outlived him by fifty years. Once the greatest heiress in Europe, Mary Catherine transforms into a character such as existed at the beginning of this author's lifetime: a kind old lady, living alone in Marylebone, beset by dogs, illnesses and the smell of beer from the brewery next door, sending her country nieces old-fashioned books in French and chivvying her nephew and heir Thomas to get on.

Her lawyers wore out Douvry but Kate was not so well off that she did not think it prudent, in 1759, to petition King George II for a pension.[152] She does not appear to have succeeded. In 1782, she sold at Christie's saleroom a group of pictures that probably included the portrait done of her in the autumn of 1720 by Rosalba Carriera. All that remains in the county records in Winchester is a label, of a type that used to be sold at the door of Cologne Cathedral and invoking the aid of the Three Kings, which Rosalba pasted on the back of her pictures to protect them from mischief in shipping.[153] The Louvre believes that one of its pastels by Rosalba, called *Young Girl Holding a Monkey*, may be of Kate.[154]

On October 14, 1790, Mary Catherine Law, dowager Viscountess Wallingford, died at her house in London at the age of eighty.[155] She is buried in the crypt of the Grosvenor Chapel in South Audley Street, Mayfair. With her death, the direct posterity of John Law of Lauriston, secretary to the King of France and controller general of His Majesty's finances, comes to an end.

APPENDIX I

John Law's trial for murder, Old Bailey, London, April 18, 1694[1]

John Lawe, of St. Giles's in the Fields Gent. was Arraigned upon an Indictment of Murther, for killing one Edward Wilson Gent. commonly called Beaux Wilson, a Person, which by the common Report of Fame, kept a Coach and six Horses, maintained his Family in great Splendor and Grandeur, being full of money, no one complaining of his being their Debtor; yet from whence, or by what hand he had the Effects which caused him to appear in so great an Equipage, is hard to be determined. The manner of Fact was thus: There was some difference hapned to arise between Mr. Lawe and the Deceased, concerning a Woman, one Mrs. Lawrence, who was acquainted with Mr. Lawe; upon which, on the 9th of April instant, they met in Bloomsbury-Square, and there fought a Duel, in which Mr. Wilson was killed. It was made appear also, that they had met several times before, but had not opportunity to fight. Besides, that there were several Letters sent by Mr. Lawe, or given to Mr. Wilson by him; which Letters were very full of Invectives, and Cautions to Mr. Wilson to beware, for there was a design of Evil against him; and there was two Letters sent by Mr. Wilson, one to Mr. Lawe, and the other to Mrs. Lawrence.

Mr. Wilson's man, one Mr. Smith, swore that Mr. Lawe came to his Master's house a little before the Fact was done, and drank a Pint of Sack in the Parlor; after which, he heard his Master say, That he was much surprized with somewhat that Mr. Lawe had told him. One Captain Wightman, a person of good Reputation, gave account of the whole matter, and said, That he was a familiar Friend of Mr. Wilsons, and was with him and Mr. Lawe at the Fountain Tavern in the Strand, and after they had staid a little while there, Mr. Lawe went away, after which Mr. Wilson and Captain Wightman took Coach, and were drove towards Bloomsbury; whereupon Mr. Wilson stept out of the Coach into the Square, where Mr. Lawe met him; and before they came near together, Mr. Wilson drew his Sword, and stood upon his Guard. Upon which, Mr. Lawe immediately drew his Sword, and they both pass'd together, making but one pass, by which Mr. Wilson received a mortal Wound upon the lower part of the Stomach, of the depth of two Inches, of which he instantly died. This was the Sum of the Evidence for the King. The Letters were read in Court, which were full of Aggravations on both parts, without any Name subscribed to them. There were other Witnesses that saw the Duel fought, who all agreed in their Depositions, that they drew their Swords and pass'd at each other, and presently Mr. Wilson was killed. Mr. Lawe in his defence, declared, That Mr. Wilson and he had been together several times before the Duel was fought and never no Quarrel was betwixt them, till they met at the Fountain Tavern, which was occasioned about the Letters; and that his meeting with Mr. Wilson in Bloomsbury was meerly an accidental thing, Mr. Wilson drawing his Sword upon him first, upon which he was forced to stand in his own defence. That the misfortune did arise only from a sudden heat of Passion, and not from any Propense Malice. The Court acquainted the Jury, That if they found that Mr. Lawe and Mr. Wilson did make an Agreement to fight, though Wilson drew first, and Mr. Lawe killed him, he was (by the construction of the law) guilty of murder: For if two men suddenly quarrel, and one kill the other, this would be but Manslaughter; but this case seemed to be otherwise, for this was a continual Quarrel, carried on betwixt them for some time before, therefore must be accounted a malicious Quarrel, and a design of murder in the person that killed the other; likewise that it was so in all Cases. The Tryal lasted long and the Prisoner had persons of good Quality, who gave a fair account of his Life in general, and that he was not given to Quarrelling, nor a person of an ill Behaviour. The Jury having considered of a Verdict very seriously, they found that Mr. Lawe was guilty of Murder.

The Proceedings of the King and Queens Commissions on the Peace, and Oyer and Terminer, and Gaol-Delivery of Newgate, held for the City of London and the County of Middlesex, at Justice-Hall, in the Old Bayly. On Wednesday, Thursday and Friday, being the 18th, 19th and 20th days of April, 1694. And in the Sixth Year of Their Majesties Reign.

APPENDIX II

Lady Katherine Knowles's marriage allegation[2]

27 July, 1695

On which day personally appeared George Seignior of the parish of St. Andrew Holborne London Gent. aged about 24 yeares and a batchelor and alleaged that he intendeth to marry with the Honoble the Lady Katherine Knowles maiden aged about 22 yeares whose parents are dead and she at her owne disposeing and that he Knoweth of noe lawfull lett or impediment by reason of any p[ast] contract consanguinity affinity or otherwise to hinder the said intended marriage and of the truth hereof he made Oath, and prayd Licence to be married in the parish Church of St. Clements Danes in the County of Midd or [blank]

Geo: Seignior
Jurat coram me*
C. Hedges

* "Swears in my presence"

APPENDIX III

John Law's Estates in France[3]

Date of Purchase	Name	Price (in livres)	Money Owing*
1718			
April 30	La Marche	80,000	
June 30	Tancarville	650,000	363,250
1719			
August 26	Toucy	130,000	81,250
October 2	Valençay	200,000	208,860
October 18	La Rivière	900,000	112,783
October 24	La Mare du Parc	85,000	
November 11	Roissy	1,000,000	
November 17?	Tournelle	80,000	88,833
December 12	Orcher	420,000	213,000
December 12	Brian	48,000	
1720			
January 6	Charleval	400,000	
?	Saint-Ouen/Villers		18,560
January 20	Berville	200,000	
March 12	La Fontaine Romé	150,000	

* With interest accumulated to October 1, 1720.

Date of Purchase	Name	Price (in livres)	Money Owing
March 28	Gerponville	860,000	25,000
April 20	Effiat	2,300,000	326,000
April 23	Guermantes	600,000	620,525
April 24	Serville	100,000	112,525
June 28	Yville	300,000	
November 10	Two Auvergne properties	130,000	66,300
	TOTAL	8,633,000	
	Less money owing		2,236, 886
	NET VALUE AT COST	6,396,114	

The Tancarville purchase was annulled on September 9, 1720.

APPENDIX IV

John Law's Will, March 5, 1729[4]

A dì 5 Marzo 1729 in Venetia
Dichiaro Io sottoscritto Giovanni Law figlio Guglielmo qualmente non ho' mai avuto, ne di presente in attrocco avere Fondi, ne Capitali di alcuna sorte fuori del Regno di Francia, ne mai avuto pensiere di fare stabilimento ne stati stranieri; anziche quando sortii dalla Francia ero debitore à miei Corrispondenti di somme considerabili, delle quali S. A.za R.e. il fu Sig. duca d'Orleans di gloriosa memoria ne fecce pagare buona parte. Onde che convenne appigliarmi di novo à tentativi della Fortuna nel Gioco, che non fú per altro di mia inclinatione ma solo necessitato dá quelle distrettezze che non amonettevano il conveniente mio mantenimento e della mia Famiglia corrispondente al Grado sostenuto, com'è notorio. Ciòche di presente manifesto parerà strano per rapporto alle Cose andate, et alli impieghi avuti, mà protesto avanti di dio, là dove altro che verità non splende, esser tale quella de miei Casi, e così in puncto mortis ho voluto dichiarire acciòche anche al Mondo tutto possi constare il vero delle mie Vicende à fine siano riflesse, e compatite.

. . . . *Law*

This fifth day of March, 1729, at Venice, I, the undersigned John Law, son of William, do declare how I have never possessed, nor do I at present possess any funds or capitals of any sort outside the Kingdom of France, nor have I thought of settling in any foreign state; for when I left France I owed considerable sums to my correspondents, to a good part of which His Royal Highness the late Duke of Orleans of glorious memory saw to the payment. Thus I was obliged to apply myself anew to the hazards of Fortune at play, which besides was never an inclination of mine but merely forced on me by those financial straits which left me insufficient money to support myself and my family in a respectable condition, as is well known. The present manifesto will appear strange in relation to things past and tasks undertaken, but I declare before God, before whom only the truth has lustre, that such was the case with me and so, in the article of death, I have desired to make this declaration so that the whole world too may ascertain the truth of my circumstances, and reflect on them, and have sympathy.

NOTES

ABBREVIATIONS

AAE: Archives des affaires étrangères, Paris
ADG: Archivio Durazzo-Giustiniani, Genoa
AMM: Archives municipales de Marseille
AMN: Archives municipales de Nantes
AN: Archives nationales, Paris
Arsenal: Bibliothèque de l'Arsenal, Paris
AStG: Archivio di Stato di Genova
AStT: Archivio di Stato di Torino
AStV: Archivio di Stato di Venezia
BL: British Library, London
BnF: Bibliothèque nationale de France, Paris
Coutts & Co.: Coutts & Co., London
CSP: *Calendar of State Papers*
FR ANOM: Archives nationales d'outre-mer, Aix-en-Provence
HALSH: Hertford Archives and Local Studies, Hertford
HALSW: Hampshire Archives and Local Studies, Winchester
HMC: Historical Manuscripts Commission
HMC, *Calendar of the Stuart Papers*: HMC, *Calendar of the Stuart Papers at Windsor Castle*, London
HNOC: The Historic New Orleans Collection, New Orleans
KHLC: Kent History and Library Centre, Maidstone
Lambeth Palace: Lambeth Palace Library, London
LMA: London Metropolitan Archives
Méjanes: Bibliothèque Méjanes, Aix-en-Provence,
NA: National Archives, London
NLS: National Library of Scotland, Edinburgh
NRS: National Records of Scotland, Edinburgh
NS: New Style (dates)
OBP: *Old Bailey Proceedings*, London
OS: Old Style (dates)
RHC Limburg: Regionaal Historisch Centrum Limburg, Maastricht
SA: Stadsarchief Amsterdam
Stafford RO: Staffordshire Record Office

CHAPTER ONE: LOTTERIES AND OTHER GAMES

1. NRS, *Old Parish Registers: Births* 685/1/70 195. The date of registration is either birth or baptism, more usually baptism. The baptism probably took place in St Eloi's Chapel in the North Transept, which the Edinburgh Incorporation of Goldsmiths shared with the Incorporation of Hammermen, comprising armourers, smiths and cutlers.

2. Henry Paton, ed., *Register of Interments in the Greyfriars Burying-Ground, Edinburgh, 1658–1700*, Edinburgh, 1902, p. 376. Jonet, b. September 9, 1677 and d. before July 25, 1683 is not listed in the burial register.
3. Sir George Mackenzie of Rosehaugh, *Memoirs of the Affairs of Scotland from the Restoration of King Charles II*, Edinburgh, 1821, p. 223.
4. In 1691, Jean was recorded as living in a four-hearth set of rooms in a land or tenement house belonging to Baillie Thomas Robertson, who owned several "statelie buildings" along the east side of the Close. *A list of Hearths in the Old Church Paroch of Edinburgh 1691*, NRS E69/16/2/64.
5. NRS 685/1/70 195. This "Mr John Law" graduated from Glasgow University MA in 1624. He received relief from Parliament of £100 out of vacant stipends in 1661. NRS PA6/16, July 12, 1661. A less likely candidate is the Mr John Law who was minister at Campsie (b.1622) and was also turned out.
6. NRS, PA2/19, f. 7v. "The Act anent the furnesing of Necessaris for Ministratioune of the Sacraments". William Green, *The Acts of the Parliaments of Scotland, 1424–1707*, Edinburgh, 1908, p. 78.
7. NRS GD1/482/1, Edinburgh Goldsmiths' Minutes, B158.
8. NRS GD1/482/1, Edinburgh Goldsmiths' Minutes, A274.
9. John A. Fairley, *Lauriston Castle: The Estate and its Owners*, Edinburgh and London, 1925, p. 91.
10. NRS 685/1/440/59.
11. Paton, *Register of Interments*, p. 377.
12. "Arret du conseil d'etat qui maintient etc." March 12, 1735, RHC Limburg, Brabantse Hooggerecht, nr 205. Appears as "St Calchbert".
13. Edinburgh Commissary Court, Wills and Testaments, NRS CC8/8/86, pp. 708–20.
14. *History of the Art of Printing in Scotland*, Edinburgh, 1713, p. 13.
15. Fairley, *Lauriston Castle*, pp. 80–1.
16. NRS GD1/482/1, Edinburgh Goldsmiths' Minutes, B197.
17. Fairley, *Lauriston Castle*, p. 91.
18. Thomas Burns, *Old Scottish Communion Plate*, Edinburgh, 1892, p. 556.
19. John Law, *Money and Trade Considered*, Edinburgh, 1705, p. 54.
20. Fairley, *Lauriston Castle*, p. 96.
21. James Donaldson (attr.), *Money encreased and Credit Raisd*, Edinburgh, 1705, NRS PA7/19, no. 176.
22. Law, *Money and Trade*, p. 54.
23. NRS RH15/57/17, inventory no. 9.
24. Extract Contract of May 26, 1681, registered in the Burgh Court Books of Edinburgh, March 15, 1708. NRS GD/1/51/40.
25. Robert Chambers, *Notices of the Most Remarkable Fires in Edinburgh*, Edinburgh, 1824, pp. 11ff.
26. Robert Law, *Memorialls, or the Memorable Things that Fell Out Within This Island of Brittain from 1638 to 1684*, Edinburgh, 1818, p. 174.
27. Law, *Memorialls*, p. 170.
28. William Steven, *The History of the High School of Edinburgh*, Edinburgh, 1849, Appendix, p. 209.
29. NRS GD1/482/1, Edinburgh Goldsmiths' Minutes, B242, f. 126.
30. Fairley, *Lauriston Castle*, pp. 140ff.

31. John Philip Wood, *The Antient and Modern State of the Parish of Cramond*, Edinburgh, 1794, pp. 95–7.
32. NRS GD44/43/1.
33. Innes to James III, April 9, 1720, Stuart Papers at Windsor Castle, Vol. 46, f. 50.
34. Edinburgh Commissary Court, Wills and Testaments, NRS CC8/8/77, pp. 532–8. Fairley, *Lauriston Castle*, pp. 99–113.
35. Fairley, *Lauriston Castle*, p. 116.
36. *Dr Trotter* contra *Agnes Campbell &c*, March, 1682, and *Agnes Campbell* contra *Robert Sandilands &c*, January 10, 1682 in Sir Roger Hog of Harcarse, *Decisions of the Court of Session from 1681 to 1691*, Edinburgh, 1757, pp. 84 and 190.
37. *Hislops* contra *Agnes Campbell and Robert Currie*, NRS CS157/66A.
38. NRS GD1/51/41.
39. Robert Innes, merchant of Leith, for the sum of £219 Scots. She released him six weeks later. John A. Fairley, "The Old Tolbooth: Extracts from the Original Records", November 26, 1684 (Warding) and January 7, 1685 (Relief) in *The Book of the Old Edinburgh Club*, Vol. 9 (1916), p. 116 and Vol. 11 (1922), pp. 21–2.
40. NRS GD3/1/11/34/ 23 and 24.
41. "Summa of the Haill" in "Inventar of the bonds and tickets given up by Jeane Campbell in her curatrix for John Law sone of the umqle Wm Law Goldsmith", NRS RH15/57/17.
42. *Life of James Wodrow, A. M.*, Edinburgh and London, 1828, pp. 69–70.
43. NRS 685/1/440 248. *A History of the Society of Writers to Her Majesty's Signet*, Edinburgh, 1890, p. 92.
44. Papers of George Cessford, Writer in Edinburgh, NRS RH15/57/17.
45. NRS RH15/57/17.
46. "On the Fashionable Amusements and Entertainments in Edinburgh in the Last Century", *Archaeologica Scotica*, 1792, Vol. 1, p. 503.
47. John Philip Wood, *Memoirs of the Life of John Law of Lauriston*, Edinburgh, 1824, p. 4.
48. NRS Warrant GD 90/2/58.
49. Charles-Louis de Secondat, baron de Montesquieu, *Voyages*, Bordeaux, 1894, Vol. 1, p. 62.
50. NRS RH15/57/17.
51. NRS RD 4/65, p. 944.
52. NRS GD109/2871; Fairley, *Lauriston Castle*, p. 106.
53. Jean's rents from Lauriston were assessed for the Poll Tax of 1694 at between £500 and £1,000 Scots. At the time, she was living in Edinburgh with Robert, Hugh and Lilias and a servant, Jonet Henderson. *Pole Money Booke of the Olde Kirke Parish of Edinburgh*, March, 1694, NRS E70/4/5/9. In 1708, the Lauriston rents were valued for the Land Tax at £566/13/4 Scots. *Valuation of the Shireffdome of Edinburgh*, November 7, 1708. NRS E106/22/2/10.
54. NRS GD45/16/3013.
55. "Discharge and Ratification be John Law to his tutors and curatrix", April 16, 1692, Register of Deeds, Second Series, Dalrymple's Office, NRS RD 2/74, pp. 779–83.
56. May 28, 1679. NRS GD1/482/1, Edinburgh Goldsmiths' Minutes, B238, f.125v.
57. "A Rate on the Inhabitants of Spurr Alley and the Exchange Wards within the parish of St Martin in the ffields in the county of Middx", June 20, 1692, LMA, Westminster Rate Books.

CHAPTER TWO: A MONEY BUSINESS

1. (Epigraph) Liselotte von der Pfalz, *Briefe an Johanna Sophie von Schaumburg-Lippe*, ed. Jürgen Voss, St Ingbert, 2009, p. 40.
2. "A Speach in the Starre-Chamber, June 20, 1616" in C. H. McIlwain, *The Political Works of James I*, Cambridge, Mass., 1918, p. 343.
3. *The Diary of Samuel Pepys*, July 29, 1667.
4. Thomas Shadwell, *The Volunteers, or the Stock-Jobbers*, Act IV, scene i.
5. G. A. Aitken, *The Life of Richard Steele*, London, 1889, Vol. 1, pp. 62–4. "I . . . will not suppose you have wholly forgot me." Steele to Law, August 12, 1719 in J. Nichols, ed., *The Epistolary Correspondence of Sir Richard Steele*, London, 1809, Vol. 2, p. 521. Steele wanted Law and his brother William to invest in his patent tank for transporting live fish or "fish-pool".
6. Daniel Defoe, *An Essay upon Projects*, London, 1697, pp. 171–2.
7. Ibid., p. xii.
8. J. H. Thomas, *Thomas Neale, a Seventeenth-century Projector*, unpublished PhD thesis, University of Southampton, 1979, p. 111.
9. Matthew Prior to Charles Montagu, Paris, August 30, 1698 in Prior Papers, *Calendar of the Manuscripts of the Marquis of Bath*, HMC, London, 1908, Vol. iii, p. 259.
10. *London Gazette*, August 31, 1693.
11. Pepys to Newton, London, November 22, 1693 in H. W. Turnbull, *The Correspondence of Isaac Newton*, New York, 1961, Vol. 3, p. 293.
12. J. Houghton, *A Collection for Improvement of Husbandry and Trade*, July 13, 1694.
13. *Journal of the House of Commons*, London, 1802, Vol. 10, January 12, 1692.
14. "An Act for Granting to theire Majesties severall Rates and Duties upon Tunnage of Shipps", *Statutes of the Realm*, Vol. 6 (1605–94), ed. John Raithby, n.p., 1819, Chapter 20.
15. "Mémoire sur les banques", in Paul Harsin, ed., *Oeuvres complètes de John Law*, Paris/Louvain, 1934, Vol. 2, p. 15.
16 "London in 1689–90 by the Rev. R. Kirk", *Transactions of the London and Middlesex Archaeological Society*, New Series, Vol. 6 (1929), p. 489.
17. *A Summary View of the . . . Scots Corporation in London*, London, 1738, p. 8.
18. Ibid., p. 19.
19. "Will of William Stonehewer, Merchant in St. Catherine's Coleman of London", July 11, 1698, NA, PROB 11/446/407.
20. John A. Fairley, *Lauriston Castle: The Estate and its Owners*, Edinburgh and London, 1925, p. 119.
21. "Inventar of the wryts concerning the debt deue by Charles E. of Marr to John Lawe", NRS, GD45/16/3013.
22. "The names of the Prisoners on the Pressyard the 9 Aprile 1694", NA C110/71. Law is described among "Prisoners come in since" the list was struck, so he may have spent his first night or nights among the common prisoners.
23. Batty Langley, *An Accurate Description of Newgate*, London, 1724, p. 55.
24. Even when the upper rooms in the Press-Yard were sleeping three to a bed, the Parlor might be unoccupied. It was a privileged place, like the first-class cabin on a long-haul flight.
25. Greenwich Hospital News Letters 4, No. 38, April 10, 1694 in W. J. Hardy, ed., *CSP Domestic: William and Mary, 1695 Addenda 1689–1695*, London, 1908, p. 252.

26. John Evelyn, *The Diary of John Evelyn*, April 22, 1694.
27. Lapthorne to Richard Coffin, April 14, 1694, Devon Archives and Local Studies Service, Exeter, Z19/40/5. Lapthorne reported that Wilson had been "some years since an Ensign in Ireland or Flanders" (for which there is no other evidence) but had been living four years in London "at the rate of 4000 l. p. An to the great wonder of all the towne."
28. *Diary of Mary, Countess, Cowper*, London, 1864, entry for November 30, 1714.
29. *The Spectator*, No. 91, June 14, 1711.
30. Copied in "Mr Law Pardon", December 13 [1717], BL Eg Ch 7524.
31. Ibid.
32. Mrs Lawrence may have been Law's hostess or landlady. Evelyn reported talk that Law kept a mistress in her house which caused Wilson to oblige one of his sisters, who was lodging there, to move out. The lady of the house, thinking that "a disparagement to it, and losing by it, instigated Laws to this duel". *Diary*, April 22, 1694.
33. John Strype, *A Survey of the Cities of London and Westminster*, London, 1720, Book 4, Chapter 7.
34. *The Proceedings of the King and Queens Commissions on the Peace, and Oyer and Terminer, and Gaol-Delivery of Newgate, held for the City of London and the County of Middlesex, at Justice-Hall, in the Old Bayly. On Wednesday, Thursday and Friday, being the 18th, 19th and 20th days of April, 1694. And in the Sixth Year of Their Majesties Reign*. BL 555.l. 2. (154).
35. Wightman's will and probate inventory is at NA PROB 31/7/583.
36. "Mr Gray", *The Memoirs, Life and Character of the Great Mr Law*, London, 1721, p. 7.
37. Charles Dalton, *English Army Lists, 1661–1714*, London, 1898, Vol. 3, p. 137, n. 18 and Vol. 4, p. 123; Gen. Sir F. W. Hamilton, *The Origin and History of the First or Grenadier Guards*, London, 1874, Vol. 1, pp. 381–90; "State of the Army in England" BL Add Ms 17918.
38. The judge is not named in the Old Bailey Sessions Papers. He was from among Ashurst, Holt, Pervell, Jeffryes, Stampe and Lovell. BL Eg Ch 7524.
39. James Johnston (attr.), *Papers Concerning the Case of John Law*, NA SP 35/18/118.
40. John Evelyn, *Diary*, April 22, 1694.
41. *OBP Online*, June 29, 1692, Trial of Nath. Williams (t16920629-26); October 12, 1692, Charles Nourse (t16921012-14); October 12,1692, Henry Tankard (t16921012-20); January 14, 1698, Anthony Robinson (t16980114-52).
42. On April 3, Drury Wake, a suspect in a recent robbery, was recognised and pursued into the fields behind Montagu House by "a great Rabble". *OBP Online*, May 24, 1694, Trial of Drury Wake (t16940524-26).
43. "The humble Petition of John Law of the Kingdom of Scotland, Gent." in *Petitions to the Queen 1704–1708*, Harley Papers, BL Add Ms 70040, f. 30.
44. William Cowper, *A Report at Large of the Case of the Appeals brought by Wilson* vs. *Law Pasche 6th Gul & Mar BR*, HALSH, DE/P/F96, f. 46.
45. *CSP Dom W and M, 1694–5*, p. 108.
46. NA PROB 11/697/158.
47. Katherine Windham to William Windham ii, November 20, 1728, Norfolk Record Office, Norwich, WKC 7/21, 404x1.
48. Thomas Carthew, *Report of Cases Adjudged in the Court of King's Bench from the*

Third Year of King James the Second to the Twelfth Year of King William the Third, London, 1728.

49. Cowper, *Report at Large*, HALSH DE/P/F96.
50. "The humble Petition", BL Add Ms 70040, f. 30.
51. Cowper, *Report at Large*, HALSH DE/P/l6, f. 46.
52. "The names of the Prisoners on the Pressyard the 7 May, 1694", NA C110/71, has against Law's name "to K. B. 9th".
53. *Journal of the House of Commons*, Vol. 12, May 4, 1699.
54. Ibid.
55. *An act for revesting in the Crown the power of appointing the Marshal of the Marshalsea of the Court of King's Bench*. Public Act 27 Geo ii cap. 17 at Parliamentary Archives HL/PO/PU/1/1754.27G2, n. 47.
56. *Journal of the House of Commons*, Vol. 10, November 11, 1690.
57. Ibid., December 20, 1690.
58. Ibid., December 18, 1690.
59. Ibid., December 23, 1690.
60. NA SP 35/18/118.
61. Cowper, *Report at Large*, HALSH DE/P/F96, f. 48.
62. Dated "31e mai" without the year. NRS GD406/1/7749.
63. Cowper, *Report at Large*, HALSH DE/P/F96 f. 49; Carthew, *Report*, Vol. 3, pp. 332–5; Greenwich Hospital News Letters, *CSP Dom Wm iii, Addenda 1689–1695*, p. 262.
64. Narcissus Luttrell, *A Brief Historical Relation of State Affairs from September 1678 to April 1714*, Oxford, 1857, Vol. 3, p. 338.
65. Sir Harris Nicolas, *A Treatise on the Law of Adulterine Bastardy*, London, 1836, p. 404.
66. Luttrell, *Brief Relation*, January 14, 1696/7, Vol. 4, p. 169; G. E. Cokayne, *The Complete Peerage*, London, 1910, Vol. 1, p. 405.
67. *OBP*, December 7, 1692, s16921207–1; Luttrell, *Brief Relation*, Vol. 2, p. 637.
68. In her marriage allegation of July 27, 1695, Lady Katherine is described as "aged about 22 years". Lambeth Palace, London FM/1/15.
69. NA SP 35/18/118.
70. Cowper, *Report at Large*, HALSH, DE/P/F96, f. 49.
71. Cowper, *Report at Large*, HALSH, DE/P/F96, f. 50; Carthew, *Report*, Vol. 3, p. 335.
72. Cowper, *Report at Large*, HALSH, DE/P/F96, f. 50; Luttrell, *Brief Relation*, Vol. 3, p. 400.
73. Luttrell, *Brief Relation*, Vol. 3, p. 398.
74. Ibid., p. 401.
75. A letter from Selkirk, dated April 24, 1694, is written from London and he was still in London, waiting for a convoy to Flanders, on July 24. NRS GD406/1/7631 and 7149. He presumably returned from campaign with the King.
76. NA SP 35/18/118.
77. John Gray, ed., *Memoirs of Sir John Clerk of Penicuik*, Edinburgh, 1892, p. 80.
78. Dillon to King James, May 17, 1720, Royal Archives, Windsor Castle, Stuart Papers, Vol. 47, f. 28.
79. Law to Regent, December 17, 1720 in Law's outletter book, Méjanes, MS 614 (355), f. 14.
80. Cowper, *Report at Large*, HALSH, DE/P/F96, f. 50.

81. Carthew, *Report*, Vol. 3, p. 335.
82. NA SP 35/18, f. 118.
83. *London Gazette*, January 3–7, 1694, i.e. 1695.
84. *Journal of the House of Commons*, Vol. 11, April 15, 1697; Vol. 12, February 8, 1699.
85. *An Act for the more effectual Relief of Creditors in Cases of Escapes*, 8 & 9 William III c.27, Art. 4.
86. *The Spectator*, No. 9, March 10, 1710 (i.e. 1711).
87. Law to Londonderry, n.d. [June, 1721], Méjanes, MS 614 (355), f. 76.

CHAPTER THREE: GIBBERISH LANGUAGE

1. (Epigraph) Charles-Louis de Secondat, baron de Montesquieu, *Pensées*, Bibliothèque municipale de Bordeaux, Ms 1866, Vol. 2, f. 38v.
2. John Evelyn, *Diary*, ad loc.
3. Hans Vogel and Marjan Smits, eds., *"Een oorlogsman van dezen tijd": De autobiographie van Casimir graaf von Schlippenbach*, Amsterdam, 2007, p. 67.
4. Vernon to Prior, London, August 10, 1694, in Prior Papers, HMC, *Calendar of the Manuscripts of the Marquis of Bath*, London, 1904, Vol. 3, p. 31.
5. *CSP, Dom W and M, 1694–5*, ed. W. J. Hardy, London, 1906, p. 76.
6. *Warrants and Passes: Nottingham and Shrewsbury*, NA, London, SP44/344.
7. Law to Abraham Mouchard, October 16, 1724, NA C108/417/4.
8. *A Report at Large of ye Case of ye Appeals brought by Wilson vs. Law Pasche 6th Gul & Mar BR*, HALSH, DE/P/F96, f. 50.
9. Acts of June 26, 1695 and July 17, 1695, NRS, PA2/36, ff. 28–31 and 168–71.
10. Order of November 13, 1696 in John Hill Burton, *The Darien Papers*, Edinburgh, 1849, p. 39.
11. NRS, GD1/482/1, Edinburgh Goldsmiths' Minutes, C345, f. 225.
12. *Journal of the Court of Directors of the African and Indian Company*, 30 June, 1699, Royal Bank of Scotland Archive, Edinburgh, D/1/2.
13. NRS GD1/482/1, Edinburgh Goldsmiths' Minutes, C381, f. 232.
14. Widdrington to Coke, November 23, 1697, in HMC, *The Manuscripts of the Earl Cowper, KG*, London, 1888, Vol. 2, p. 370.
15. Du Hautchamp (attrib.), *Histoire du système des finances sous la minorité de Louis XV*, The Hague, 1739.
16. Ibid., Vol. 1, pp. 69–70.
17. The marquis de Dangeau mentions faro for the first time on November 20, 1709. On February 21, 1710, faro was among various games of chance banned in Paris. *Journal du marquis de Dangeau*, Paris, 1854, Vol. 13, pp. 65 and 105.
18. E. J. F. Barbier, *Journal historique et anecdotique*, ed. A. de La Villegille, Paris, 1849, Vol. 2, p. 291.
19. AAE, Mémoires et documents, Affaires intérieures, 1701, 1093, f. 117, printed in A. Beljame, "La prononciation du nom de Jean Law le financier" in *Etudes romanes dédiées à Gaston Paris*, Paris, 1891, p. 492, n.4.
20. M. de Beaufort, *Recueil concernant le tribunal de nosseigneurs les maréchaux de France*, Paris, 1784, Vol. 1.
21. Marriage Allegation, July 27, 1695, Lambeth Palace, FM/1/15.
22. H. A. C. Sturgess, *Register of Admissions to the Honourable Society of the Middle Temple*, London, 1949, Vol. 1, p. 225.

23. NA, PROB/11/387/170.
24. Ibid., *The diary of Robert Hooke, M.A., M.D., F.R.S., 1672–1680*, ed. M. W. Robinson and W. Adams, London, 1935, p. 182. Entry for September 22, 1675.
25. NA PROB/11/387/170.
26. Court of Chancery, *Davenant vs. Seignior*, May 7, 1703, NA C5/235/19.
27. T. E. Harwood, *Windsor Old and New*, 1929, pp. 304ff.
28. Court of Chancery, *Seignior v Brownlow et al.*, October 22, 1696, NA C6/307/24; *Brownlow v Seignior*, December 16, 1696, NA C6/387/48; *Seignior v. Trinder*, 1694, NA C5/111/50; *Trinder v Seignior*, April 7, 1696, NA C6/493/52.
29. Lady Katherine Knowles by George Middleton v Earl of Nottingham, February 10, 1714/15, NA C11/5/36.
30. Seignior appears again in an answer to Davenant's Bill of Complaint over the wager in 1702 (NA C5/235/19) and as a subsidiary defendant in Lady Katherine's lawsuit of 1715 (NA C11/5/360). Neither is proof of his being alive.
31. A novelist would have Law hiding out in the "liberties" of Whitefriars, which abutted the Inns of Court to the east and retained until 1697 ancient rights of immunity from arrest and where the law feared to tread. The place was known as Alsatia, and supplied the Inns with what were known as Affidavit-Men, who would swear to anything (*A New Canting Dictionary*, London, 1725, under *Alsatia*). In *The Fortunes of Nigel* (1822), Sir Walter Scott has his Scots hero Nigel Olifaunt take refuge there in the reign of James I/VI.
32. "Mr Gray", *Memoirs, Life and Character of the great Mr Law*, London, 1721, p. 11.
33. Another passport, valid for two months, was issued that day to the Huguenot banker Jean-Henri Huguetan, who later sought to employ Law in Denmark. AAE,Mémoires et documents, Affaires intérieures, 1702 (mai–août) 1100, f. 211v.
34. Haags Gemeentearchief, oud archief, 1055, f. 14.
35. List in *Guide de la Haye*, The Hague, 1705, pp. 78ff.
36. Jean Pierre Ricard, *Le négoce d'Amsterdam*, Amsterdam, 1722, pp. 52 and 55.
37. John A. Fairley, *Lauriston Castle: The Estate and its Owners*, Edinburgh and London, 1925, pp. 125–6.
38. NRS, GD1/482/1, Edinburgh Goldsmiths' Minutes, C381.
39. NRS CC8/8/84, f. 232.
40. "The humble Petition of John Law of the Kingdom of Scotland, Gent" in *Petitions to the Queen 1704–1708*, Harley Papers, BL Add Ms 70040.
41. NRS PA2/38 ff. 178–80.
42. Daniel Defoe, *The History of the Union of Great Britain*, Edinburgh, 1709, p. 83.
43. "The Humble Petition of Several Owners . . . of the Ship Worcester", *Petitions to the Queen, 1704–1708*, Harley Papers, BL Add Ms 70040, f. 225.
44. T. B. Howell, ed., *A Complete Collection of State Trials*, London, 1816, Vol. 14, col. 1212.
45. Defoe, *History of the Union*, p. 86.
46. *An Act for the Effectual Securing the Kingdom of England*, iii and iv Anne, c.7 (1705).
47. Law states that he was in Scotland at the time the Bank of Scotland stopped payment. Paul Harsin, ed., *Oeuvres complètes de John Law*, Paris/Louvain, 1934, Vol. 2, pp. 35–6.
48. *State Trials*, Vol. 14, col. 1281.
49. Duncan Forbes to the House of Commons, 1736, in *State Trials*, Vol. 14, col. 1311.
50. Secretary Johnston to Jerviswood, London, April 9, 1705, in *Correspondence of Baillie of Jerviswood*, Edinburgh, 1842, p. 70.

51. *Journal of the House of Commons*, Vol. 11, November 25, 1696.
52. John Law, *Money and Trade*, Edinburgh, 1705, p. 82.
53. "Sur l'établissement d'une banque en France", Bibliothèque Mazarine, Paris, Ms 2342/5.
54. Halifax to Stair, February 14, 1715 in John Murray Graham, *Annals and Correspondence of the Viscount and the First and Second Earls of Stair*, Edinburgh and London, 1875, Vol. 1, p. 264.
55. Law to Philipp Joseph, Count von Ursin Rosenberg, London, March 16, 1722 in Law's outletter book, Méjanes, Ms 614 (355), f. 194.
56. Law, *Money and Trade*, p. 100.
57. *Ethica Nicomachea*, 1133a, 19–31.
58. Law, *Money and Trade*, p. 65.
59. Ibid., p. 100.
60. Ibid., pp. 59–60.
61. Ibid., p. 97.
62. Ibid., p. 98.
63. Ibid., p. 98.
64. Ibid., pp. 84–6.
65. Ilay to Bute, October 19, 1716. HMC, *Fifth Report, Part 1*, London, 1876, Vol. 1, p. 618.
66. Greg to Harley, June 9, 1705, Harley Papers, HMC, *Manuscripts of the Duke of Portland*, London, 1897, Vol. 4, p. 195.
67. Ibid., Vol. 4, p. 194.
68. Greg to Harley, June 9, 1705 and June 11, 1705, HMC, *Portland Manuscripts*, Vol. 4, pp. 195–6.
69. *Petitions to the Queen 1704–1708*, BL Add Ms 70040.
70. Greg to Harley, June 9, 1705, HMC, *Portland Manuscripts*, Vol 4, p. 195.
71. NRS PA7/19, No. 176.
72. Sir David Hume of Crossrigg, *A Diary of the Proceedings in the Parliament of Scotland*, Edinburgh, 1828, p. 164; NRS PA3/7 lists six articles.
73. NRS GD220/5/800.
74. Greg to Harley, July 14, 1705, HMC, *Portland Manuscripts*, Vol. 4, p. 207.
75. Gilbert Burnet, *History of My Own Time*, London, 1725, Vol. 3, p. 1098.
76. Secretary Johnston to Jerviswood, London, July 13, 1705, in *Correspondence of Baillie of Jerviswood*, p. 115.
77. Mar to Countess of Mar at Alloa, Monday, July 16, 1705, NRS GD124/15/231.
78. An unsigned report to Harley of July 17, 1705 said that the detachment of horse guards came into view and the seconds were "glad of this Handle to save the honour of their Principals". BL Add Ms 28055, f. 248.
79. Mar to Lady Mar, July 16, 1705, NRS GD124/15/231
80. NRS PA7/19, No. 175.
81. NRS PA2/39, f. 14.

CHAPTER FOUR: PLUM MAN

1. (Epigraph) Law to Townshend, Aix-la-Chapelle, October 24, 1725. NA, SP81/91.
2. In a contract to sell wine from his mother's vines at Savignac to the *négociants* Ayma and Pujols on January 6, 1709, the Bordeaux lawyer Joseph de Labat de

Savignac specified "le tout sans billets de monnaie". Caroline le Mao, *Chronique du Bordelais au crépuscule du Grand Siècle: le Mémorial de Savignac*, Bordeaux, 2004, p. 57.

3. *Doop-, trouw- en begraafboeken 's Gravenhage*, Haags Gemeentearchief, 0377-01. William was described as "scarcely fifteen years old" in 1720, and twenty-seven years old in 1733. RHC Limburg, Burgerboek van de Brabantse Hoogschout, Vol. 7, p. 234; and Brabants Hooggerecht, no. 5955, "Antwoord voor den Heer Milord, exhibitum 6 september 1734". Both quoted in Th. Huijs, *Inventaire des archives de John Law et de William Law.1715–1734*, Maastricht, 1978, p. 23, n. 20.
4. Charles Montagu, Lord Halifax, who had been Chancellor of the Exchequer at the time of the founding of the Bank of England, reported that he "had the honour to know Mr Law a little at the Hague". Halifax to Stair, February 14/25, 1714/5 in John Murray Graham, *Annals of Stair*, Edinburgh and London, 1875, Vol. 1, p. 264. Halifax was sent by Queen Anne in April 1706 to Hanover to invest the prince who later became King George II with the Order of the Garter. Halifax spent the last week of April and the first week of May at The Hague on his way out, and about two weeks there on his return in June.
5. "Par rapport a l'Italie j'y a passee six annees de ma vie." Law to Townshend, Aix-en-Chapelle, October 24, 1725, NA SP81/91.
6. Nationaal Archief, The Hague, Staten-Generaal, inv. nr 7759 (January–April, 1734), Requesten Maastricht, quoted in Huijs, *Inventaire*, p. 23, n. 21.
7. AN, G/7/1629 printed in Paul Harsin, *Etude critique sur la bibliographie des oeuvres de Law*, Liège and Paris, 1928, pp. 5–6.
8. Reading "Monsieur de Torcy" for Harsin's "Monsieur de Gorcy".
9. *Mémoire pour prouver qu'une nouvelle espèce de monnaie peut être établie meilleure que l'or et l'argent*, Arsenal, Ms-6113, f. 49ff.
10. NRS, *Old Parish Registers: Deaths* 685/1/860 70 127. "Brae face [hillside] before Halls Tomb". Sir John Hall of Dunglass was Lord Provost of Edinburgh, d. 1695.
11. *Valuation of the Shireff dome of Edinburgh*, November 7, 1708, NRS E106/22/2/10.
12. "Defences for John Law of Lauristoun against the Earl of Rutherglen", June 24, 1713, NRS GD18/1676.
13. To the Countess of Mar, Genoa, August 28, 1718 in Lord Wharncliffe, ed., *The Letters and Works of Lady Mary Wortley Montagu*, London, 1861, Vol. 1, pp. 385–7.
14. Francisco Gómez de Quevedo, "Poderoso Caballero es Don Dinero".
15. AStG, Archivio segreto, 1025/43. Giovanni Assereto, *Un gioco così utile ai pubblicci introiti: il lotto di Genova dal XVI al XVIII secolo*, Rome, 2013, p. 57.
16. AStG, AS 61/1616, April 12, April 25 and July 24, 1710.
17. "Monseignr Law never answer'd my last letter to him." Chandos to Drummond, January 11, 1719 (i.e. 1720), NRS, GD24/1/487.
18. Law to Townshend, Aix-en-Chapelle, October 24, 1725. NA SP81/91.
19. "Mémoire sur les banques", in Paul Harsin, ed., *Oeuvres complètes de John Law*, Paris/Louvain, 1934, Vol. 2, p. 16.
20. Giuseppe Felloni, *Amministrazione ed etica nella Casa di San Giorgio (1407–1805): Lo statuto del 1568*, Florence, 2014, pp. 3–33.
21. *Mémoire sur les Monnoyes*, BL, Add Ms 18965, ff. 33–4.
22. Coutts & Co., Letter Book No. 4, February 25, 1708 (i.e. 1709) to June 22, 1710.
23. *Journal de ma Vie, Tome premier, contenant mon Origine, mon Education, mes campagnes Depuis l'an 1696 jusqu'à la paix d'Utrecht*, Nationaal Archief, The Hague,

This work had been translated into Dutch by Hans Vogel and Marjan Smits and published as *"Een oorlogsman van dezen tijd en beminnar der sexe"*: *De autobiografie van Casimir graaf von Schlippenbach (1682–1755)*, Amsterdam, 2007.

24. *Journal de ma Vie*, Vol. 1, f. 48.
25. Ibid., f. 51.
26. John Chetwynd to Brydges, Alexandria, May 9, 1709, Staffordshire RO, D649/15; also J. Chetwynd to Furnese, Alexandria, May 9, 1709, KHLC, U1590/C9/22.
27. William Chetwynd to Stanhope, May 22, 1709, KHLC, U1590/C9/23.
28. AStG, Banco di San Giorgio, Banco 2o, Moneta Corrente, 10942, C2 1709, f. 372.
29. After Stanhope's death, on June 23, 1721, the duc d'Orléans told the British envoy, Sir Luke Schaub, "how dear to him was the memory of the late Milord", KHLC, U1590/C12/3.
30. *Mr Stanhope's Answer to the Report of the Commissioners Sent into Spain*, London, 1714, p. 39, KHLC, U1590/Z82.
31. Law to Londonderry, June 27, 1721 in Law's outletter book, Méjanes, Ms 614 (355), f. 80.
32. AStG, Banco di San Giorgio, Banco 2o, Moneta Corrente, 10944, C1 1710, f. 786; Banco 10, Moneta Corrente, 10445, C1 1710, f. 455.
33. Stanhope to Sir John Norris, December 2, 1710, BL Add Ms 35838, f. 368.
34. *Mr Stanhope's Answer*.
35. AStG, Banco di San Giorgio, Banco 2o, Moneta Corrente, 10950, C2 1711, f. 282.
36. W. Blackley, ed., *The Diplomatic Correspondence of the Right Hon. Richard Hill*, London, 1845, Vol. 2, p. 811.
37. Law to Victor Amadeus, Paris, August 16, 1715, printed in A. D. Perrero, "Law e Vittorio Amedeo II di Savoia", *Curiosità e ricerche di storia subalpina*, Turin, 1874, Vol. 1, p. 42.
38. Elisabeth Charlotte, duchesse d'Orléans to Caroline, Princess of Wales, November 10, 1720, in H. F. Helmolt, *Elisabeth Charlottens Briefe an Karolin von Wales*, Annaberg, 1909, p. 368. November 10, 1719 is a more likely date.
39. Luigi Einaudi, *La finanza sabauda all'aprirsi del secolo XVIII*, Turin, 1908, pp. 281 and 287.
40. Reproduced in Giuseppe Prato, "Un capitolo della vita di Giovanni Law", *Memorie della reale accademia delle scienze di Torino (1913–1914)*, Turin, 1914, p. 13.
41. Printed in Perrero, "Law e Vittorio Amedeo", pp. 31–3.
42. AStT, Ufficio generale delle Finanze, Lotterie, tontina e banco di deposito, Mazzo 1, printed in Antoin Murphy, "John Law's Proposal for a Bank of Turin (1912)", Institut des Sciences Mathématiques et Economiques Appliquées, Paris, *Economies et Sociétés*, Vol. 15 (May, 1991), p. 24.
43. AStG, Banco di San Giorgio, Banco 2o, Moneta Corrente, 10951, 1711, ad loc.
44. That day, the De Mari brothers witnessed a document giving power of attorney over Law's Genoese affairs to Consul Henshaw. AStG, Banca di San Giorgio, Mandati, 7552, 1709–1712, ad loc. Accordingly, the next withdrawal in the daybook, on January 8, 1712 for 20,000 lire, is signed by Henshaw. AStG, Banco di San Giorgio, Banco 2o, Moneta Corrente, 10951, 1711, ad loc.
45. Perrero, "Law e Vittorio Amedeo", pp. 37–8.
46. Ibid., p. 38.
47. AStG, Banco di San Giorgio, Banco 2o, Moneta Corrente, 10952, C1 1712, f. 227.
48. Entry of March 8, 1712 (i.e. 1713), Coutts & Co., Ledger A, f. 314.

49. See note 70 below.
50. Haags Gemeentearchief, Transportakten reg. 396, f. 145v. Ibid., 0372-01 Notarieel archief, 3.132 (Gijsbert Cretser), Nr 695 (1718), p. 308. Both quoted in Huijs, *Inventaire*, p. 24.
51. Gijsbert Cretser, *Beschryvinge van 's Gravenhage*, Amsterdam, 1711, p. 57.
52. *Gazette d'Amsterdam*, December 13, 1712.
53. SA, Archief van de Wisselbank, 5077-197 "142" 2e deel (August 1712–February 1713), p. 1383. He is credited with a balance of fl257 17s. 8d. on August 5. The previous volume is defective. Entry of January 20, 1712 (i.e. 1713), Coutts & Co., Ledger I, f. 201.
54. NA PROB 11/530/170, Will of John Campbell of St Martin in the Fields, Middlesex, November 6, 1712; NA PROB 32/57/96, Deceased John Campbell, Inventory, June 4, 1713.
55. Jan de Vries and Ad van der Woude, *The First Modern Economy*, Cambridge, 1997, p. 119.
56. Heinsius to Buys, April 6, 1711, printed in J. Veenendahl Jr et al., eds, *Briefwisseling van Anthonie Heinsius, 1702–1720*, The Hague, 1976–2001, Vol. 11 (1710–1711), p. 708.
57. *Gazette d'Amsterdam*, July 29 and August 9, 1712.
58. Heinsius to van der Dussen, October 26, 1712, in *Briefwisseling van Heinsius*, Vol. 14 (1712–1713), p. 164. "The lottery of the States General is not above half full, neither will it fill in haste if at all." Drummond to Harley, October 25, 1712, printed in HMC, *The Manuscripts of His Grace the Duke of Portland*, London, 1899, Vol. 5, p. 234.
59. *Gazette d'Amsterdam*, July 29, 1712.
60. Ibid., December 6, 1712.
61. Card index at dutchjewry.org/P.I.G./image/00012201.jpg
62. Law to William Chetwynd at Genoa, presently at Turin, February 9, 1713, Stafford RO D649/8/11.
63. Law to William Chetywnd at Genoa, January 24, 1713 Stafford RO D469/8/11.
64. Law to John Chetwynd at Turin, March 21, 1713, Stafford RO D649/8/11.
65. SA, Archief van de Wisselbank, 5077-199 "143" 2e deel (February–August 1713), p. 1280.
66. SA, Archief van de Notarissen ter Standplaats Amsterdam, 5075N174 (Dirk van der Groe), nr 4225, p. 28, January 6, 1713.
67. Ibid.
68. SA, Notarissen, 5075–174 (Van der Groe), nr 4225, p. 125, January 21, 1713.
69. SA, Notarissen, 5075–241 (Pieter Schabaalje), nr 6073, n.p., May 21, 1713. This is a receipt signed by Law for the ticket 16141 "en op welk Lot in de eerste Classe getrocken is een prijs Van vijff en twintig duijzent gulden".
70. Law to William Chetwynd at Genoa, February 3, 1713, Stafford RO D649/8/11.
71. SA, Notarissen, 5075–238 (Joan Hoekebak), nr 5924, n.p., July 7, 1712.
72. Drummond to Harley, May 8, 1713, HMC *Portland Manuscripts*, Vol. 5, p. 287.
73. Nicolaas Struyck, *Uytreekening der kanssen in het speelen: door de arithmetica en algebra, beneevens een verhandeling van looteryen en interest*, Amsterdam, 1716, p. 15.
74. Ibid., p. 90.
75. SA, Wisselbank, 5077–198, "143" 1e deel (1713), Nr 1280.
76. The loan from van Aferen was discharged on Law's order by "Sr [Sinjeur or Senhor] Ab. Barugh Henriques" on July 5. Note in margin of SA, Notarissen,

5075–174 (Van der Groe), Nr 4225, p. 28, January 6, 1713. It seems Henriques bought Law's house in the Nieuwe Uitleg as he is registered for the property tax of 1732–3 at the only dwelling in that part of the street (Verponding-nummer 1960) not owned by Jacob van Dijk. Nationaal Archief, Financie van Holland, 1579–1806, inv. nr 549, f. 126.

77. "Origine des Biens de M. Law", May 10, 1724. RHC Limburg, Papieren Law, inv. nr 74.
78. Destouches to Dubois, November 10, 1721, AAE, 8CP/338.
79. Law to Lady Katherine Knowles, Venice, n.d. [February, 1721], Méjanes, Ms 614 (355), f. 35.
80. Coutts & Co., Ledger A, ff. 420 and 422. Middleton to Law, February 22, March 22 and April 29, 1714, Coutts & Co., Letter Book No. 8, pp. 11, 17, 30.
81. Autograph memoir by John Law, Venice, 1728. RHC Limburg, Papieren Law, inv. nr 130.

CHAPTER FIVE: LAW AND COMPANY

1. (Epigraph) Law to Count Rosenberg, London, May 15, 1722, in Law's outletter book, Méjanes, Ms 614 (355), f. 217.
2. *Mémoires de Saint-Simon*, ed. A. M. de Boislisle, Paris, 1879–1931, Vol. 12, p. 87.
3. "Etat des despence que Monsieur Lasse a fait dans la maison de Madame la duchesse de Granmons, Novembre 10, 1717" and "Etat des augmentations fait dans la Maison de Madame la Duchesse de gramont, ou demeure Monsieur Law, outre les Bureau." RHC Limburg, Papieren Law, inv. nr 65. Law in 1720 lodged the duc de Mazarin at the hôtel de Gramont as part of the contract to buy the palais Mazarin for the use of the Company of the Indies.
4. Law to Desmaretz, Paris, December 24, 1713 and January 11, 1714, AN, G/7/1629. Printed in Paul Harsin, *Etude critique sur la bibliographie des Oeuvres de Law*, Paris and Liège, 1928, pp. 11–12.
5. Same to same, AN G/7/1629, in Harsin, *Etude critique*, p. 12.
6. Ibid.
7. Argenson said Torcy had written on November 16, 1708, asking him to find a "professional gambler named Mr Law suspected of bad intentions towards the King's service" but the police had been unable to find him. Law was probably then in Genoa. AAE, Correspondance Politique, 262 (Angleterre), ff. 286–7.
8. Middleton to Law, March 22, 1713/14, Coutts & Co., Letter Book No. 8, p. 17.
9. Lady Katherine Knowles by George Middleton v. Earl of Nottingham, February 10, 1714/15, NA C11/5/36. The Marquess of Halifax had died in 1700 and his estate was handled by his father-in-law, the Earl of Nottingham.
10. Middleton to Law, March 22, 1715/16, Coutts & Co., Letter Book No. 9, p. 162. Middleton advised Law to retain William Abdy, a lawyer with a substantial foreign and Jacobite business, to handle the case. "If some gratuity were promis'd him quarterly it would be of more effect than being at the charge of some person to follow thate affair." Middleton to Law, October 19, 1715, Coutts & Co., Letter Book No. 9, p. 103.
11. NRS, GD220/5/380. The date of September 29, 1712 in the *Third Report of the Royal Commission on Historical Manuscripts*, London, 1872, p. 378, is incorrect.
12. *The Life of John, Earl of Stair*, London, 1748, p. 257.

13. Treasury Warrants, April 17, 1718 in *Calendar of Treasury Books*, Vol. 32 (1718), ed. William A. Shaw and F. H. Slingsby, London 1962.
14. John Murray Graham, *Annals and Correspondence of the Viscount and the First and Second Earls of Stair*, Edinburgh and London, 1875, Vol. 1, p. 391.
15. In Copenhagen, Lords Marchmont (1716–21) and Glenorchy (1721–30) were successive envoys to the Danish court. Col. James Haldane of Gleneagles served in Russia (1716–17), George Mackenzie in Poland (1710–14) and Alexander Cunningham at Venice (1715–19).
16. Crawford to Col. Pitt, November 15, 1717, NA C108/417/1.
17. Stair to Stanhope, Paris, February 12, 1715, *Annals of Stair*, Vol. 1, p. 265.
18. Halifax to Stair, London, February 14/25, 1715, *Annals of Stair*, Vol. 1, p. 264.
19. Stanhope to Stair, London, April 30/May 11, 1715, *Annals of Stair*, Vol. 1, p. 267. As the letter is in French, "him" probably refers to "Your Lordship", that is, Stair.
20. Law to Desmaretz, May 9, 1715, AN G/7/597, printed in A. M. de Boislisle, *Correspondance des contrôleurs généraux des finances*, Paris, 1897, Vol. 3, p. 695.
21. "Mémoire sur les banques", BnF, Ms français 7768, printed in Paul Harsin, *Oeuvres complètes de John Law*, Paris/Louvain, 1934, Vol. 2, p. 18.
22. Stair to Montrose, Paris, May 20 (or 28), 1715 in NRS, GD220/5/488.
23. Ibid.
24. Stair to Montrose, Paris, June 16, 1715, NRS GD220/5/488.
25. "Mémoire sur les banques", Harsin, *Oeuvres de Law*, Vol. 2, p. 29.
26. Ibid., p. 25.
27. Law to Desmaretz, July 31, 1715, Harsin, *Oeuvres de Law*, Vol. 2, p. 64.
28. "Extracts from Lord Stair's Journal at Paris in 1715 and 1716", Philip, Earl of Hardwicke, *Miscellaneous State Papers from 1501 to 1726*, London, 1778, Vol. 2, p. 535.
29. Stair to Stanhope, Paris, February 12, 1715, *Annals of Stair*, Vol. 1, p. 265.
30. *Histoire de ma vie*, Paris, 2013, p. 707.
31. Law to Victor Amadeus, Paris, August 16, 1715, printed in A. D. Perrero, "Law e Vittorio Amedeo II di Savoia", *Curiosità e ricerche di storia subalpina*, Turin, 1874, Vol. 1, pp. 42–3.
32. Stair to Montrose, Paris, September 1, 1715, NRS GD220/5/488.
33. Donaudi to Victor Amadeus, Paris, September 6, 1715, in Perrero, "Law e Vittorio Amedeo", p. 45.
34. Ibid., p. 47.
35. *Mémoires de Saint-Simon*, ed. Boislisle, Vol. 26, p. 286.
36. Tony Sauvel, "Saint-Simon et les appartements du Régent", *Revue d'histoire littéraire de la France*, Vol. 62, No. 2 (April–June, 1962), pp. 189–97.
37. Elisabeth Charlotte to Johanna von Schaumburg-Lippe, June 7, 1718. Liselotte von der Pfalz, *Briefe an Johanna Sophie von Schaumburg-Lippe*, ed. Jürgen Voss, St Ingbert, 2003, p. 49.
38. Elisabeth Charlotte to Raugräfin Amalie, August 22, 1698 in W. L. Holland, ed., *Briefe der Herzogin Elisabeth Charlotte von Orléans*, Stuttgart/Tübingen, 1867–1881, Vol. 1, p. 113; Elisabeth Charlotte to Electress Sophia of Hanover, December 10, 1712 in E. Bodemann, ed., *Aus den Briefen der Herzogin Elisabeth Charlotte von Orléans an die Kurfürstin Sophie von Hannover*, Hanover, 1891, Vol .2, p. 323.
39. Elisabeth Charlotte to Raugräfin Luise, September 24, 1715 in Holland, ed., *Briefe*, Vol. 2, p. 635.

40. "Délibérations du conseil des finances, tome 1 (1715–1716)", BnF Ms français 6930, f. 1, printed in Herbert Lüthy, *La banque protestante en France*, Paris, 1959, Vol. 1, p. 278.
41. Regent to comte de Luc, November 11, 1716, AN KK 1323, f. 67, printed in *Mémoires de Saint-Simon*, ed. Boislisle, Vol. 29, p. 550.
42. The sources for this passage are BnF Ms français 7740 and those assembled by François Velde in *Government Equity and Money: John Law's System in 1720 France*, Chicago, 2003, p. 8, Table 2, "The debt in France 1700–1726".
43. "Idée générale du nouveau Système des finances", AN K884 (No. 4). Attributed to Law or his ghostwriter and dated to early 1720 by Harsin, *Oeuvres de Law*, Vol. 3, p. 81.
44. "Délibérations du conseil des finances, tome 1 (1715–1716)", BnF Ms français 6930, f. 46ff, printed in Emile Levasseur, *Recherches historiques sur le système de Law*, Paris, 1854, pp. 39–43. *Journal du marquis de Dangeau*, Paris 1854–60. Vol. 16, p. 220.
45. Law to duc de Bourbon, August 25, 1724, printed in Harsin, *Oeuvres de Law*, Vol. 3, p. 245.
46. Law to Victor Amadeus, Paris, December 7, 1715, printed in Perrero, "Law e Vittorio Amedeo", p. 52.
47. Pierre-Edouard Lermontey, *Histoire de la régence et de la minorité de Louis XV*, Paris, 1832, Vol. 1.
48. *Edit du Roy portant Etablissement d'une Chambre de Justice, donné à Paris au mois de Mars 1716*, Paris, 1716, p. 4.
49. Ibid.
50. *Arrest de la Chambre de Justice Rendu contre Jean-François Gruet, Huissier à Cheval au Chastelet de Paris, du 7 Decembre, 1716*, Paris, 1716.
51. Erik Goldner, "Corruption on Trial: Money, Power and Punishment in France's *Chambre de Justice* of 1716", *Crime, Histoire & Sociétés*, Vol. 17, No. 1 (2013), pp. 5–28.
52. Law to duc de Bourbon, August 25, 1724, printed in Harsin, *Oeuvres de Law*, Vol. 3, p. 251. "La chambre de justice et le visa du papier, enrichirent bien des fripons qu'on a eu intention de punir." Law to Bully, February 26, 1722, Méjanes, Ms 614 (355), f. 174.
53. Beauvoir to Elizabeth Beauvoir, Paris, March 27, 1716, Lambeth Palace, Ms 1556, f. 21.
54. By January, 1718, the yield had increased to 95 million livres. AN G7 1837 quoted in Jean Villain "Naissance de la chambre de justice", *Revue d'histoire moderne et contemporaine*, Vol. 35 (1988), p. 576.
55. "Je n'aurois pas même pensé à faire une seconde proposition, s'il [le prince] ne m'eut pressé de la faire." Law to duc de Bourbon, August 25, 1724, printed in Harsin, *Oeuvres de Law*, Vol. 3, p. 245.
56. *Registres des procès-verbaux des séances du Conseil de Régence, X Finances II (1715–1717)*, BnF Ms français 23672, f. 54v, printed in *Mémoires de Saint-Simon*, ed. Boislisle, Vol. 30, p. 92.
57. *Lettres patentes du Roy, portant privilege au Sieur Lavv & sa Compagnie d'establir une Banque generale. Données à Paris le 2 mai 1716*, Paris, 1716.
58. *Lettres patentes du Roy, contenant Reglement pour la Banque generale, accordée au Sieur Law, & à sa Compagnie. Données à Paris le 20 mai 1716*, Paris, 1716.

59. AN X/1a/ 8715, f. 266v, printed in *Mémoires de Saint-Simon*, ed. Boislisle, Vol. 30, p. 93.
60. *Gazette d'Amsterdam*, June 19, 1716.
61. Claude Pâris de La Montagne, *Discours à ses enfans pour les instruire de sa conduite*, 1729, AN KK 1005D, p. 121.
62. *Gazette de la Régence*, June 19, 1716, Koninklijke Bibliotheek, The Hague, KB:75 D4–5. Printed by E. de Barthélemy, ed., Paris, 1887.
63. Baron de Vigan, ed., *Mémoires du président Hénault*, Paris, 1855, p. 4.
64. *Gazette de la Régence*, July 17, 1716.
65. Ibid., September 18, 1716.
66. Crawford to Col. Pitt, September 16, 1716, NA C108/418/17.
67. *Journal du marquis de Dangeau*, Paris, 1854–60, Vol. 16, pp. 488–9.
68. BnF Ms français 6908–47, Vols 31 and 32, printed in Levasseur, *Recherches historiques*, pp. 49–52.
69. "Les billets de Lasse étoient bons." Crawford to Craggs, June 3, 1719, NA SP 78/164, f. 105.
70. There are two specimens in the Law papers in the RHC Limburg, one in the museum in Poitiers and at least one in the trade.
71. Law to Marcello Durazzo, January 12, 1717, ADG, Carteggi, Lettere in arrivo, 136.
72. Marcello Durazzo to Vercassoni, March 20, 1717, ADG, Carteggi, Copialettere in partenza, 214.
73. Law to Marcello Durazzo, April 10, April 13 and April 27, 1717, ADG, Carteggi, Lettere in arrivo, 136.
74. Law to to Jacques Philippe and Joseph Maria Durazzo, December 25, 1717, ADG, Carteggi, Lettere in arrivo, 137. Vercassoni disappeared from Rome, without informing his wife or children, "for fear of imprisonment". Fratelli Durazzo to Law, February 22, 1718, ADG, Carteggi, Copialettere in partenza, 215.
75. NRS GD205/37/7; Coutts & Co., Letter Book No. 10, July 1716, p. 6.
76. Receipts for Law's advances to French envoys in Turin, London, Madrid and The Hague are in RHC Limburg, Papieren Law, inv. nr 6.
77. Elisabeth Charlotte to Johanna von Schaumburg-Lippe, December 7, 1717, *Briefe an Johanna*, p. 11.
78. On August 30, the Regent wrote to Dubois: "Le plus grand service qu'il [Dubois] pouvoit me rendre et celuy qui me contente le plus estoit de désabuser le Roy de la Grande Bretagne des mauvaises impressions qu'on lui avoit données contre moy et d'avoir par là ouvert le chemin à une amitié réciproque." The letter is in Stanhope's papers, KHLC, U1590/0145/24,
79. Receipt by Dubois for 10,000 florins (guilders) from Mme Testas at Amsterdam, January 8, 1717, RHC Limburg, Papieren Law, inv. nr 6, f. 116. The Testas were Huguenot bankers originally from Bordeaux.
80. Dubois in Hanover to Regent, November 4, 1716, AAE, 8 CP 278, printed in Charles Aubertin, "Un diplomate au xviiie siècle: l'abbé Dubois d'après les archives du ministère des affaires étrangères", *Revue des deux mondes*, May, 1872, p. 161.
81. Dubois in Hanover to Regent, October 30, 1716, AAE, 8 CP 277, printed in Aubertin, *Un diplomate*, p. 156. Stanhope's modern biographer, Basil Williams, in a slip of the pen, writes £3,000. *Stanhope: A Study in Eighteenth-Century War and Diplomacy*, Oxford, 1932, p. 223.

82. Dubois in Hanover to Regent, October 30, 1716, AAE, 8 CP 277, printed in Aubertin, *Un diplomate*, p. 156.
83. Aubertin, *Un diplomate*, p. 157.
84. Receipt signed by Baron de parry [Erik Sparre of Sundby], October 18, 1716, in RHC Limburg, Papieren Law, inv. nrs 24 and 25.
85. Elisabeth Charlotte to Princess of Wales, various dates, in H. F. Helmolt, *Elisabeth Charlottens Briefe an Karoline von Wales*, Annaberg, 1909, pp. 338–40.
86. Elisabeth Charlotte to Princess of Wales, April 16, 1716, in Helmolt, *Elisabeth Charlottens Briefe*, p. 355.
87. *Mémoires de Saint-Simon*, ed. Boislisle, Vol. 31, pp. 353ff.
88. Josiah Child to Thomas Papillon, October 22, 1698, printed in H. Yule, ed., *The Diary of William Hedges*, London, 1889, Vol. 3, p. xxxv.
89. Thomas Pitt at Bergen, Norway, July 29, 1710, "for his son Robert in case of death", BL, Add Ms 59485, ff. 44–5, printed in Yule, *Diary*, p. cxxxviii.
90. BL Add Ms 22852, printed in Yule, *Diary*, p. cxxvi.
91. Cope's pocket-book is at NA C104/197. His will of 1710 is at NA PROB 5/541A.
92. Robert Pitt to Thomas Pitt, January 10, 1706 (i.e. 1707), HMC, *The Manuscripts of J. B. Fortescue, Esq., Preserved at Dropmore*, London, 1892, Vol. 1, p. 25.
93. Thomas Pitt to Robert Pitt and Evance, February 5, 1704 [i.e. 1705], BL Add Ms 22848, printed in Yule, *Diary*, p. cxxix.
94. Thomas Pitt to Alvaro da Fonseca, September 12, 1707, BL Add Ms 22850, printed in Yule, *Diary*, p. cxxxi.
95. *Gazette d'Amsterdam*, 1714, no. 88, November 2, 1714.
96. Thomas Pitt to Col. Thomas Pitt, April 13/24, 1717, NA C108/419/13 printed in Larry Neal, *"I am not Master of Events"*, New Haven, 2012, p. 47.
97. *Mémoires de Saint-Simon*, ed. Boislisle, Vol. 31, pp. 354–5.
98. BnF Ms français 23669, printed in *Mémoires de Saint-Simon*, ed. Boislisle, Vol. 31, p. 436.
99. "Estat de tous ce que je reconnois dans La Maison à Maestricht appartenant à Madame et à Mademoiselle le 17 fevrier 1734", HALSW, 21M69/3/3.

CHAPTER SIX: THE ISLAND OF MISSISSIPPI

1. [Epigraph] Antoine-Simon Le Page du Pratz, *Histoire de la Louisiane*, Paris, 1758, Vol. 1, p. 203.
2. *Récit des voyages et des découvertes du R. Père Jacques Marquette*, Albany, NY, 1855, pp. 1–92.
3. *Procés-verbal de la prise de possession de la Louisiane*, FR ANOM C13C3, f. 28. Online at http://www.louisiane.culture.fr/fr/ow_zoom/ow_caom_108_loupe.htm
4. Francis Parkman, *La Salle and the Discovery of the Great West*, Boston, 1869, Chapter XX.
5. "Mémoire de M. Argoud, du 10 décembre 1697" in Pierre Margry, ed., *Découvertes et établissements des Français dans l'ouest et dans le sud de l'Amérique septentrionale (1614–1754)*, Paris, 1881, Vol. 4, pp. 19ff.
6. "Iberville au Ministre de la Marine, 18 juin 1698" in Margry, *Découvertes*, Vol. 4, pp. 51ff. Also undated letter, "Le sr Dibivuille propoze" in HNOC, acc. 99-110-L.
7. "Journal de Lemoyne d'Iberville, décembre 1698–3 mai 1699" in Margry, *Découvertes*, Vol. 4, pp. 164–5.

8. "Journal du chevalier d'Iberville, dans son second voyage au Mississippi, décembre 1699–1700" in Margry, *Découvertes*, Vol. 4, p.399.
9. C. J. Franquet de Chaville, "Relation du voyage de la Louisiane pendant les années 1720, 1721, 1722, 1723 et 1724", ed. E.G. Musset, *Journal de la Société des Américanistes*, Vol. 4 (1902), No. 1, p. 117.
10. Le Page de Pratz, *Histoire de la Louisiane*, Vol. 1, p. 169.
11. Ibid.
12. Margry, *Découvertes*, Vol. 4, p. 395.
13. Jean Delanglez, "Cadillac's Last Years", *Mid-America*, Vol. 33 (1951), p. 22.
14. Diron d'Artaguiette to Minister, September 8, 1712, FR ANOM C13A2 in Mathé Allain, "L'immigration française en Louisiane, 1718–1721", *Revue d'histoire de l'Amérique française*, Vol. 28 (1975), p. 559.
15. *Lettres patentes du Roy qui permettent au sieur Crozat Secretaire du Roy, de faire seul le Commerce etc.*, Paris, 1712. BnF, F-21068 (47).
16. "Un amas de la lie du Canada, gens de sac et de corde." Cadillac to Pontchartrain, October 26, 1713, FR ANOM C13A3 printed in D. Rowland, ed., *Mississippi Provincial Archives: French Dominion*, Jackson, Miss. (1929) Vol. 2, p. 167.
17. AAE, Mémoires et documents, Amérique, Vol. 1, ff. 177–9. This is an anonymous document that Giraud attributes to Crozat "with certainty". Marcel Giraud, *Histoire de la Louisiane française*, Paris, 1966, Vol. 3, pp. 4–5.
18. *Mémoire à SAR*, May, 1717, AAE, Mémoires et documents, France 1220, printed in *Mémoires de Saint-Simon*, ed. A. M. de Boislisle, Paris, 1879–1931, Vol. 31, p. 278.
19. *Lettres patentes en forme d'edit, Portant Etablissement d'une Compagnie de Commerce, sous le nom de Compagnie d'Occident, Paris*, 1717, BnF F-21078. Also *Arrest du conseil d'estat du Roy qui nomme les commissaires pour passer les Contractes de Rentes de la Compagnie d'Occident du 24 Septembre 1717*, Paris, 1717 in HNOC, Williams Research Center, MSS 268, folder 28, 2000-105-L.
20. Law immediately bought 13,000 pounds of beaver pelts, which were shipped from Quebec on the royal frigates, the *Victoire* and *Astrée*, in November, 1717. Chartier de Lotbinière, *Etat des Ballots de Castor . . . que j'ay chargé pour le compte de Monsieur Law*, Quebec, October 28, 1717, FR ANOM COL C11A 37, f. 365.
21. AN U360 printed in *Mémoires de Saint-Simon*, ed. Boislisle, Vol. 32, pp. 398–9.
22. *Gazette d'Amsterdam*, September 17, 1717.
23. *Mémoires de Saint-Simon*, ed. Boislisle, Vol. 32, p. 106.
24. Fanny Oglethorpe to Mar, Monday night 12 o'clock [i.e. September 6, 1717], HMC, *Calendar of the Stuart Papers*, London, 1912, Vol. 5, p. 17.
25. *Arrest du conseil d'estat du Roy qui nomme les directeurs de la Compagnie d'Occident du 12. Septembre 1717*, Paris, 1720.
26. AAE, Mémoires et documents, Amérique, Vol 1, f. 138; Giraud, *La Louisiane*, Vol. 3, p. 32.
27. Law to duc de Bourbon, August 25, 1724, printed in Paul Harsin, ed., *Oeuvres complètes de John Law*, Paris/Louvain, 1934, Vol. 3, p. 246.
28. RHC Limburg, Papieren Law, inv. nr 64.
29. AAE, Mémoires et documents, Amérique, Vol. 1, ff. 324–35, printed in Paul Harsin, "La création de la compagnie d'Occident", *Revue d'histoire économique et sociale*, Vol. 34, No.1 (1956), pp. 38–42.
30. *Gazette d'Amsterdam*, December 24, 1717.
31. AN, Minutier Central, Répertoire de l'étude Ballin, 1718 (Et. XLVIII).

32. F.-D.Camusat, *Histoire critique des journaux*, Amsterdam, 1734, Vol. 2, p. 230.
33. "Nouvelle relation de la Louisianne", *Le Nouveau Mercure*, September, 1717, pp. 139–40.
34. Ibid., p. 130.
35. On November 15, 1717, Crawford wrote to Pitt to say he had drawn on him for £500 to cover a loan from Law for a "project . . . of stockjobbing in this country". He planned to buy over 20,000 livres in *billets d'état* for the rise. The idea was surely suggested by Law. NA, London, C108/417/1.
36. Arsenal, Paris, Archives de la Bastille, Registre d'écrou 12479, f. 31 in Delanglez, "Cadillac's Last Years", p. 29.
37. "Nouvelle Relation", p. 133.
38. Arsenal, Bastille 10631, f. 37 in Delanglez, "Cadillac", p. 29.
39. Emile Raunié, *Chansonnier historique du xviiie siècle*, Paris, 1880, Vol. 2, p. 244.
40. Giraud, *La Louisiane*, Vol. 3, p. 92.
41. Ibid. pp. 108–9.
42. "J'ai fait les batimens a mes frais." Law to Lassay, June 14, 1721 in Law's outletter book, Méjanes, Ms 614 (355), f. 74.
43. Chartier de Lotbinière, *Etat de la Recette des Castors . . . faite par Monsieur Law . . . et des lettres de change qui ont este tirees sur ledite sieur Law*, Quebec, November 7, 1717, FR ANOM COL C11A 37, f. 356.
44. "Extrait des délibérations . . . faites par les directeurs de la Cie d'Occident", Service historique de la Défense, GR A 2592 f150; Giraud, *La Louisiane*, Vol. 3, p. 317.
45. J.-B. Bénard de La Harpe, *Journal historique de l'établissement des Français à la Louisiane*, New Orleans and Paris, 1831, p. 142.
46. FR ANOM DPPC G1 465, Dossier Le Moyne de Bienville; Giraud, *La Louisiane*, Vol. 3, p. 322.
47. AAE, 8 CP/302, ff. 86–7.
48. *Journal du marquis de Dangeau*, November 25, 1717, Paris, 1854, Vol. 17, p. 201; Amelot to Gualterio, November 29, 1717, BL, Add Ms 20365, f. 263; letters from Paris of November 26 and November 29 in the issues of the *Gazette d'Amsterdam* of December 7 and December 14, 1717.
49. Letter from Paris of December 6 in *Gazette d'Amsterdam* of December 14, 1717.
50. Crawford to Addison, December 8, 1717, NA SP 78/161, f. 161.
51. Fanny Oglethorpe to Mar, December 14, 1717, HMC, *Calendar of the Stuart Papers*, Vol. 5, p. 276.
52. AAE, 8 CP/303.
53. *Gazette d'Amsterdam*, December 17, 1717.
54. AN U361, quoted in *Mémoires de Saint-Simon*, ed. Boislisle, Vol. 33, p. 359.
55. *Gazette de la Régence*, January 9, 1718, Koninklijke Bibliotheek, The Hague, KB:75 D4-5, printed by E. de Barthélemy, ed., Paris, 1887.
56. Giraud, *La Louisiane*, Vol. 3, pp. 45–6, 94. In the eighteenth century, it cost roughly 200 livres per ton to rig, man and victual a merchantman
57. Marc Cheynet de Beaupré, *Joseph Pâris-Duverney: Les sentiers du pouvoir (1684–1720)*, Paris, 2012, p. 655.
58. Claude Pâris de La Montagne, *Discours à ses enfans pour les instruire sur sa conduite*, 1729, AN KK//1005/D,p.122. Instructions to Voyer are dated December 10, 1717, FR ANOM COL B42, f. 185.

59. Regent's order of June 23, 1719, in RHC Limburg, Papieren Law, inv. nr 7.
60. Law to duc de Bourbon, August 25, 1724, printed in Harsin, ed., *Oeuvres de Law*, Vol. 3, p. 246. Law also controlled another 2.9m livres in shares, probably for others, according to the shareholders' list in AAE, Mémoires et documents, Amérique, Vol. 1, ff. 324–35, printed in Harsin, "La création de la compagnie d'Occident", pp. 38–42.
61. Hop to Heinsius, March 10, 1719 in A. J. Veenendaal, Jr, *De Briefwisseling van Anthonie Heinsius, 1702–1720*, The Hague, 1976–2001 , Vol. 19, p. 130. His estimates are accurate.
62. "Waarom de rijzing van de actie te minder is te verwonderen." Hop to Heinsius, June 23, 1719, in Veenendaal, ed., *Briefwisseling van Heinsius*, Vol, 19, p. 263.
63. Receipt of January 6, 1718, RHC Limburg, Papieren Law, inv. nr 19.
64. RHC Limburg, Papieren Law, inv. nr 6, f. 117.
65. Destouches to Dubois, November 4, 1721, AAE, 8/CP/338, f. 95.
66. Law to Londonderry, June 27 1721 in Law's outletter book, Méjanes, Ms 614 (355), f. 80.
67. "Mr Law's Pardon", BL, Eg Ch 7524.
68. Law to Ilay, Venice, August 15, 1721, Méjanes, Ms 614 (355), f. 92.
69. Dubois to Made Lass, December 30, 1717, AAE 8 CP/303, f. 284.
70. Dubois to Made Law, January 3, 1718, AAE 8CP/314, f. 15.
71. RHC Limburg, Papieren Law, inv. nr 6, f. 118.

CHAPTER SEVEN: THE BED OF JUSTICE

1. [Epigraph] Law to duc de Bourbon, n.p, n.d. [Aachen or Cologne, December 1720], in Law's outletter book, Méjanes, Ms 614 (355), f. 19.
2. Dillon to Crescit (Mar), July 14, 1717, HMC, *Calendar of the Stuart Papers*, 1910, Vol. 4, p. 451.
3. On January 19, 1719, Law issued bills to cover Mar's purchases of silver knives and gold watches from the London jeweller, Garrard. Stuart Papers at Windsor Castle, Vol. 42, f. 23.
4. Mar to Law, April 25, 1717 in HMC, *Calendar of the Stuart Papers*, Vol. 4, pp. 211–12.
5. Same to same, February 18, 1718, HMC, *Calendar of the Stuart Papers*, London, 1912, Vol. 5, p. 493.
6. Hamilton to Mar, January 3, 1718, HMC, *Calendar of the Stuart Papers*, Vol. 5, p. 354.
7. HMC, *Calendar of the Stuart Papers*, Vol, 5, p, 494.
8. Mar to Dillon, February 18, 1718, HMC, *Calendar of the Stuart Papers*, Vol. 5, p. 492.
9. John J. Hurt, *Louis XIV and the Parlements*, Manchester, 2002, p. 103.
10. Sigismond Ropartz, *La famille Descartes en Bretagne, 1586–1762*, Saint-Brieuc, 1876, pp. 165, 206–9.
11. *An Inquiry into the Nature and Causes of the Wealth of Nations*, II.iii.12.
12. *Etat General des Biens Immeubles & des Dettes actives & passives de Mr Lavv au Premier Janvier 1722*, RHC Limburg, Papieren Law, inv. nr 68.
13. Stair to Stanhope, January 23, 1718, KHLC, U1590/0145/24.
14. *Minutes du Parlement*, AN, X/Ib/8899, printed in *Mémoires de Saint-Simon*, ed. A. M. de Boislisle, Paris, 1879–1931, Vol. 33, p. 326.
15. Nancré to Dubois, January 17, 1718, AAE, 8CP/304, f. 15.

16. *Mémoires de Saint-Simon*, ed. Boislisle, Vol. 33, pp.28–9.
17. Ibid., p. 29; Jules Flammermont, *Remontrances du Parlement de Paris au XVIIIe siècle*, Paris, 1888, Vol. 1, pp. 58ff.
18. Stair to Stanhope, January 23, 1718, KHLC, U1590/0145/24.
19. *Mémoires de Saint-Simon*, ed. Boislisle, Vol. 30, p. 282.
20. [Bernard Le Bovier de Fontenelle], "Eloge de M. d'Argenson", *Histoire de l'Académie royale des Sciences, Année 1721*, Paris, 1723, p. 103.
21. *Mémoires de Saint-Simon*, ed. Boislisle, Vol. 33, p, 114,
22. AN, Minutier Central, Répertoire de l'étude Ballin, 1718 (Et. XLVIII), AN MC/RE/XLVIII/1.
23. *Mémoires de Saint-Simon*. ed. Boislisle, Vol. 33, p. 58.
24. *Journal du marquis de Dangeau*, Paris, 1854, Vol. 17, p. 254, February 28, 1718.
25. Gualterio Papers, BL Add Ms 20365, f. 285.
26. *Gazette de la Régence*, January 9, 1718, Koninklijke Bibliotheek, The Hague, KB: 75 D4–5. Printed by E. de Barthélemy, ed., Paris, 1887.
27. *Journal du voyage de la Louisiane fait par le sr Bernard de Laharpe et les decouvertes qu'il a fait dans le party de l'ouest de cette colonie*, BnF, Ms français 8989, f. 1v.
28. Marcel Giraud, *Histoire de la Louisiane française*, Paris, 1966, Vol. 3, pp. 158–9.
29. Nathan Bailey's *An Universal Etymological English Dictionary*, London, 1721 has: "*To sell a* BEAR [*among Stock-jobbers*] to sell what one hath not."
30. *Gazette d'Amsterdam*, May 31, 1718.
31. The trades were with the Geneva banker Gédéon Mallet (May 5, 100 shares); Isaac Martin & Co. (May 6, 200 shares); Sauvage (May 14, 100 shares); and Thomas Crawford, secretary of the British Embassy (May 17, 40 shares). André-E. Sayous, "L'affaire de Law et les Genevois", *Revue d'histoire suisse*, Vol. 17 (1937), p. 321; RHC Limburg, Papieren Law, inv. nr 29, p. 36; *Commissions extraordinaires du Conseil: Law (Jean)*, Minutes des jugements, Judgment of June 25, 1722, AN V/7/254; ibid.
32. The house is described in the 1722 notice of sale in a collection of contemporary printed papers in NLS labelled *Pièces particulières à Law*, NLS Ry.iii.a.7 (10); *Etat General des Biens de M. Lavv*, RHC Limburg, Papieren Law inv. nr 68; Dangeau, *Journal*, Vol. 12, p. 84, February 24, 1708; Vol. 17, p. 296, April 23, 1718.
33. Achille Deville, *Histoire du château et des sires de Tancarville*, Rouen, 1834, p. 316; *Journal de Dangeau*, Vol. 17, p. 350, July 31, 1718.
34. AN MC/RE/XLVIII/1.
35. In the tower of the parish church of Thuret, near Effiat in Auvergne, the largest of three bells bears the inscription that, at its "baptism" or dedication in 1720, "Jean Law chevalier comte de Tancarville etc" had stood godfather. Law may have paid for the bell but there is no other evidence that he attended its baptism in person. Bernard Craplet and Pierre-François Aleil, *Les cloches du Puy-de-Dôme*, Clermont-Ferrand, 1995.
36. Excluding Tancarville, where the vendor annulled the sale contract. *Etat des Acquisitions faites par Mr Law*, October 1, 1720, RHC Limburg, Papieren Law, inv. nr 155.
37. AN MC/RE/XLVIII/1; Germain Brice, *Nouvelle description de la ville de Paris*, Paris, 1725, Vol. 1, p. 415.
38. Germain Brice, *Description nouvelle de la ville de Paris*, Paris, 1706, Vol. 1, p. 268. There is a plan of the house in *Terrier du Roy pour la ville de Paris*, 1700, Vol. 4, ff.

129v and 148r, AN Q/1/*/1099/6. It is marked on Jaillot's map of 1713, No. 65 in the key, labelled "Mr de Montargis". Delagrive's map of 1728 misplaces the rue Lyonne.

39. AN MC/RE/XLVIII/1.
40. *Edit du Roy Pour la Fabrication de nouvelles Especes d'Or & d'Argent, avec faculté de porter à la Monnoye Deux Cinquièmes en sus de billets de l'Estat*, Paris, May 1718.
41. Coutts & Co., Letter Book No. 12, pp. 57 and 62.
42. Jérôme Jambu, *Tant d'or que d'argent: la monnaie en Basse Normandie*, Rennes, 2013, p. 397.
43. Edmond Barbier, *Chronique de la Régence*, Paris, 1857, Vol. 1, pp. 8–9.
44. Dangeau, *Journal*, Vol. 17, p. 311, May 18, 1718.
45. Flammermont, *Remontrances*, Vol. 1, p. 77,
46. Ibid., Vol. 1, p. 86.
47. Stair to Stanhope, October, 1717, AAE 8 CP/301, f. 243.
48. Marqués de la Mina, *Memorias militares sobre la guerra de Cerdeña y Sicilia*, Vol. 1, pp. 62ff, Biblioteca Nacional de España, Madrid, MSS 5590. Online at http://bdh.bne.es/bnesearch/detalle/bdh0000015437.
49. Byng to William Stanhope, the *Barfleur* off the coasts of Spain, June 20, 1718. Printed in Basil Williams, *Stanhope*, Oxford, 1932, Appendix C, pp. 451–2.
50. Ibid., p. 452.
51. J. L. Cranmer-Byng, *Pattee Byng's Journal 1718–1720*, London, 1950, p. 20.
52. Dangeau, *Journal*, Vol. 17, p. 322, June 28, 1718.
53. Rigby to Mar, July 16, 1718, HMC, *Calendar of the Stuart Papers*, Vol. 7, p. 49.
54. Elisabeth Charlotte to Johanna von Schaumburg-Lippe, July 20, 1718. Liselotte von der Pfalz, *Briefe an Johanna Sophie von Schaumburg-Lippe*, ed. Jürgen Voss, St Ingbert, 2003, p. 54.
55. Dangeau, *Journal*, Vol. 17, p. 345, July 20, 1718.
56. John Murray Graham, *Annals of Stair*, Edinburgh and London, 1875, Vol. 2, p. 77.
57. Stair to Stanhope, July 26, 1718, KHLC, U1590/0145/24.
58. Flammermont, *Remontrances*, Vol. 1, p. 106.
59. Edmond Barbier, *Chronique de la Régence*, Vol. 1, p. 10.
60. Dangeau, *Journal*, Vol. 17, p. 359, August 17, 1718.
61. Ibid. p. 342, July 15, 1718.
62. François Calandrini, *Private Memoirs Concerning the Family*, Vol. 1, Archives Edmond Pictet, Geneva, quoted in Herbert Lüthy, *La Banque Protestante en France*, Paris, 1959, p. 358; chevalier de Piossens, *Mémoires de la Régence*, The Hague, 1730, Vol. 2, pp.110–11.
63. *Mémoires de Saint-Simon*, ed. Boislisle, Vol.35, p. 30.
64. Ibid., Vol. 35, p. 42; Vol. 38, p. 75.
65. Ibid., Vol. 35, p. 21.
66. Ibid., Vol. 35, p. 140.
67. Ibid., Vol. 35, p. 184.
68. Ibid., Vol. 35, p. 185.
69. Ibid., Vol. 35, p. 198.
70. Ibid., Vol. 35, p. 210.
71. Flammermont, *Remontrances*, Vol. 1, p. 111. There are several other accounts of the ceremony, including *Mémoires de Saint-Simon*, ed. Boislisle, Vol. 35, pp. 210–37, which includes a seating plan.

72. Lüthy, *Banque Protestante*, p. 310.
73. *Mémoires de Saint-Simon*, ed. Boislisle, Vol. 35, p. 267.
74. Elisabeth Charlotte to Johanna von Schaumburg-Lippe, August 30, 1718, *Briefe an Johanna*, p. 57. Supplying "Angst" or "Furcht" after "setzt mich in Todtes".
75. *Pattee Byng's Journal*, p. 28.
76. Dangeau, *Journal*, Vol. 17, p. 375, August 30, 1718.
77. *Pattee Byng's Journal*, p. 31.
78. To conte di Rocca, September 5, 1718, E. Bourgeois, ed., *Lettres intimes de J. M. Alberoni*, Paris, 1892, p. 601.
79. Same to same, September 12, 1718, ibid, p. 602.
80. Elisabeth Charlotte to the Raugräfin Luise, September 22, 1718 in W. L. Holland, ed., *Briefe der Herzogin Elisabeth Charlotte*, Stuttgart/Tübingen, 1867–1881, Vol. 3, p. 386.
81. Elisabeth Charlotte to Johanna von Schaumburg-Lippe, September 20, 1718, *Briefe an Johanna*, p. 59.
82. *Le Nouveau Mercure*, September 1718, p. 214.
83. La Harpe, *Journal du voyage*, ff. 2, 3.
84. Ibid., f. 3.
85. Ibid., f. 3v.
86. Archives de Morbihan, Vannes, EN 3909, Minutes Kersal, February 17, 1719 quoted in Giraud, *Histoire de la Louisiane*, Vol. 3, p. 175.
87. Marquis des Marches to Gravé de La Mancelière, November 4, 1720, HNOC, Williams Research Center, 2008.0077. The 30,000 livres was to buy some twenty slaves at Saint-Domingue. By the time Gravé arrived at Cap-Français on the *Vénus* on May 22, 1721, Law had left France and the local directors refused to make available the funds. Directors to Morin at Cap-Français, April 12, 1720 with endorsements at Cap-Français (June 5, 1721) and Biloxi (July 24, 1721). Kuntz Collection, Tulane University, New Orleans, 600-1-36.
88. AN O/1/57, f. 196v, November 20, 1713; Fénelon to P. Le Tellier, September 24, 1713 in Jean Orcibal, ed., *Correspondance de Fénelon: Les dernières années*, Geneva, 1999, p. 232; Dangeau, *Journal*, Vol. 15, p. 360, February 16, 1715.
89. Fanny Oglethorpe to Mar, July 8, 1716, HMC, *Calendar of the Stuart Papers*, Vol. 2, pp. 264–5.
90. Beauvoir to Elisabeth Beauvoir, Paris, November 3, 1716, Lambeth Palace, Ms 1556, f. 120; *Gazette d'Amsterdam*, October 1, 1717.
91. November 19, 1718. Minutes et Répertoire de l'étude Michel Martin (Et XLVI), AN/MC/ET/LXVI/370, July 31, 1719 and August 23, 1719, printed in Antoin Murphy, "Richard Cantillon – Banker and Economist", *Journal of Libertarian Studies*, Vol. 7, No. 2 (1985), pp. 201–2.
92. Dangeau, *Journal*, Vol. 18, pp. 15–16, March 12, 1719. In French sources, Gage is known as "Guech" or "Guej".
93. "Thomas Marwood's Diary (1699–1703)" in *Catholic Record Society: Miscellanea VI, Bedingfield Papers, &c*, Edinburgh, 1909.
94. "This nineteen years past", Gage to Powis, July 7, 1736, National Library of Wales, Aberystwyth, PC 2153 printed in Martin Murphy, "Maria's Dreams", *Montgomeryshire Collections*, Vol. 85 (1997), pp. 98–9.
95. Minutes et répertoire de l'étude Nicolas I de Savigny (Et XLIV), AN/MC/ET/XLIV/ 276, October 26, 1722, quoted in A. Murphy, *Richard Cantillon: Entrepreneur*

and Economist, Oxford, 1986, pp.101–2.

96. Regent to Bignon, March 15, 1716 in *Procès-verbaux de l'Académie royale des Sciences*, March 21, 1716, Vol. 35, f. 99.
97. *Procès-verbaux de l'Académie royale des Sciences*, May 20, 1716, Vol. 35, f. 157.
98. Ibid., June 13, 1716, f. 186.
99. *Règle artificielle du temps . . . par Mr Henry Sully, nouvelle édition corrigée . . . par M. Julien le Roy*, Paris, 1737, p. 389.
100. Pierre Narbonne, *Journal des règnes de Louis XIV et Louis XV*, Paris, 1866, p. 54. Narbonne was first a bailiff then commissioner of police for Versailles.
101. Contract of *rente fieff ale* of 300 livres per annum with mayor and aldermen of Harfleur, *Pièces particulières à Law*, NLS Ry.iii.a.7 (14); *Etat General*, RHC Limburg, Papieren Law, inv. nr 68.
102. William Blakey, Jr, *L'art de faire les ressorts de montres*, Amsterdam, 1780, p. viii.
103. January 17, 1719. *Le Nouveau Mercure*, January 1719, pp. 141–5.
104. "Minute Book, H. M. Commission for Rebuilding St Paul's Cathedral (From February 20, 1685/6 to June 25, 1724)", *Wren Society*, Vol. 16 (1939), p. 109. The railings were cast at the Gott foundry in Sussex.
105. "Building Account, June 24, 1714" in ibid., p. 165.
106. *Fact against Scandal; to which is added an Appendix relating to Mr. Jones*, London, 1713, pp. 63–73.
107. Ruth Rhynas Brown, "Notes from the Board of Ordnance Papers, 1705–1720", *Wealden Iron*, Second Series, No. 19 (1999), p. 42.
108. *Flying Post*, October 9, 1718 OS.
109. "Journal, November 1718: Journal Book V" in K. H. Ledward, ed., *Journals of the Board of Trade and Plantations*, London, 1925, Vol. 4 (November 1718–December 1722). Sully appears here as "Sally".
110. *An Act to Prevent the Inconveniencies arising from Seducing Artificers in the Manufactures of Great Britain into Foreign Parts*, 5 Geo. 1 c. 27 (1719); *Journal of the House of Lords*, Volume 21 (1718–1721), April 14, 1719.
111. To Anne Thistlethwayte, Paris, October 16, 1718 OS, *The Letters and Works of Lady Mary Wortley Montagu*, ed. Lord Wharncliffe, London, 1861, Vol, 1, p. 398.
112. Gordon to Drummond, Paris, November 10, 1718, NRS, GD24/3/271.
113. A. B. Gent [Daniel Defoe], *Curious and Diverting Journies thro' Great Britain*, London, 1734, p. 103.
114. "On dit que milord Stairs a eu quelque part à cette découverte." *Gazette de la Régence*, December 26, 1718.
115. *Mémoires de Madame de Staal, Écrits par elle-même*, London [i.e. Paris], 1755, Vol. 2, p. 74.
116. *Mémoires de Saint-Simon*, ed. Boislisle, Vol. 36, p. 47.
117. Le Blanc to La Billarderie, October 4, 1719 in F. Ravaisson, ed., *Archives de la Bastille*, Paris, 1882, Vol. 13, p. 273.
118. *Gazette de la Régence*, December 12, 1718.
119. Louis-Antoine de Pardaillan de Gondrin, duc d'Antin, *Mémoires de la Régence*, Vols 4 and 5 (1718), BnF Ms NAF 23933 and 23934.
120. *Déclaration du Roy pour convertir la Banque générale en Banque royale*, Paris, December 4, 1718.
121. Law to duc de Bourbon, August 25, 1724, printed in Harsin, *Oeuvres de Law*, Vol. 3, p. 246.

122. *Commissions extraordinaires du Conseil: Law (Jean)*, AN V7/254, quoted in C.-F. Lévy, *Capitalistes et Pouvoir au Siècle des Lumieres*, Paris, 1981, Vol. 3, p. 48.
123. *Arrest du Conseil d'État du Roy, Concernant la Banque Royale. Du 27 Décembre 1718*, Article IV.
124. "Vente, faite par la Compagnie du Sénégal à celle d'Occident, 15 décembre 1718", reproduced in A. Delcourt, *La France et les établissements français au Sénégal entre 1713 et 1763*, Dakar, 1952, p.380.
125. AN MC/RE/XLVIII/1; Giraud, *Histoire de la Louisiane*, Vol. 3, p. 49 has January 16.

CHAPTER EIGHT: MILLS OF PAPER

1. [Epigraph] *Œdipe*, Act II, sc. iii.
2. *Relation de l'entrée de son excellence milord comte de Stair*, Paris, 1719.
3. *Post-Boy*, January 31–February 3, 1718/19.
4. "That of My Lord Portland is even eclips'd quite." Crawford to Tickell, February 8, 1719, NA SP 78/163, f. 53.
5. William Beauvoir to Elizabeth Brown, February 8, 1719, Lambeth Palace, Ms 1558, f.44.
6. "Les carosses" in *Relation de l'entrée*, p. 4.
7. Crawford to Lawson, July 16, 1717, HMC, *Calendar of the Stuart Papers*, London, 1907, Vol. 4, p. 457.
8. William Beauvoir to Elizabeth Brown, October 7, 1718, Lambeth Palace, Ms 1558, f. 21.
9. *Ordonnance du Roÿ portant declaration de Guerre contre l'Espagne, du 9. janvier 1719*, Paris, 1719.
10. Fanny Oglethorpe to Mar, February 13, 1719 and February 17, 1719, Stuart Papers at Windsor Castle, Vol. 42, ff. 35 and 42.
11. Stair to Craggs, February 11, 1719, NA SP 78/163, f. 56. Dangeau says they were harnessed for eight. *Journal du marquis de Dangeau*, Paris, 1854, Vol. 17, p. 475, February 10, 1719.
12. "Je parloy au Roy en Anglois." Stair to Craggs, February 11, 1719, NA SP 78/163, f. 57. The translation into French is at f. 59.
13. Hop to Heinsius, February 27, 1719, A. J. Veenendaal, Jr, *De Briefwisseling van Anthonie Heinsius, 1702–1720*, The Hague, 1976–2001, Vol. 19, p. 112. Stair's circular letters signed by the Ambassadors of Austria, Portugal, Sardinia and Holland are in NA SP 78/163, ff. 140ff.
14. "Extremement en colère". Stair to Craggs, March 8, 1719, NA SP 78/163, f. 163.
15. *Mémoires de Saint-Simon*, ed., A. M. de Boislisle, Paris, 1879–1931, Vol. 36, p. 125. Amelot to Gualterio, March 6, 1719, BL, Add Ms 20365, f. 364.
16. *Gazette de la Régence*, November 23, 1718, Koninklijke Bibliotheek, The Hague, KB:75 D4-5. Printed by E. de Barthélemy, ed., Paris, 1887.
17. Stair to Craggs, April 2, 1719, NA SP 78/163, f. 264.
18. Hop to Heinsius, February 3, 1719, *Briefwisseling van Heinsius*, Vol. 19, p. 94; Beauvoir to Elizabeth Brown, March 4, 1719 Lambeth Palace, Ms 1558, f. 51.
19. Graham, *Annals of Stair*, Vol. 2, p. 102.
20. Dubois to Craggs, May 5, 1719, NA SP 78/163, f. 362.
21. Stair to Craggs, April 29, 1719, NA SP 78/163, f. 337.
22. Hop to Heinsius, May 5, 1719, *Briefwisseling van Heinsius*, Vol. 19, pp. 206–7.

23. Stair to Stanhope, March 6, 1718, KHLC, U1590/0145/24.
24. Craggs to Stair, October 30, 1718, Graham, *Annals of Stair*, Vol. 2, p. 60.
25. "I believe the true reason is he's lost all his money at cards, and has not wherewithal to finish furnishing his house nor make the figure that is fit." Fanny Oglethorpe to Mar, September 6, 1717, HMC, *Calendar of the Stuart Papers*, London, 1912, Vol. 5, p. 17.
26. Graham, *Annals of Stair*, Vol. 2, p, 98.
27. Warrant signed April 7, 1719. Joseph Redington, ed., *Calendar of Treasury Papers 1714–1719*, London, 1883, Vol. 5, pp. 493–506.
28. Tonyn to Polwarth, The Hague, October 5, 1720, HMC, *Report on the Manuscripts of Lord Polwarth*, London, 1916, Vol. 2, p. 631.
29. Andrew Henderson, *The Life of John, Earl of Stair, by an Impartial Hand*, London, 1748, p. 215.
30. J.-B. Bénard de La Harpe, *Journal historique de l'établissement des Français à la Louisiane*, New Orleans, 1831, p. 47.
31. Ibid., pp. 147–8; Marcel Giraud, *Histoire de la Louisiane française*, Paris, 1966, Vol. 3, p. 300.
32. La Harpe, *Journal historique*, p. 159; J. Dumont de Montigny, *Mémoires historiques sur la Louisiane*, Paris, 1753, Vol. 2, p. 16.
33. Crawford to Craggs, June 3, 1719, NA SP 78/164, f. 404; [Nicolas] Du Tot, *Histoire du système de John Law (1716–1720)*, ed. Antoin Murphy, Paris, 2000, p. 84; *Journal de Dangeau*, Vol. 18, p. 22.
34. Crawford to Craggs, June 3, 1719, NA SP 78/164, f. 404. This leaf has become detached from Crawford's June 3 letter and is bound later in the volume. The correct pagination of the letter is: ff. 104–5, 403–4, 402v, 402r, 106–7.
35. Mellier to Ferrand, May 24, 1721, AMN, HH 209, printed in Gaston Martin, *Nantes et la compagnie des Indes, 1664–1769*, Paris, n.d., p. 54.
36. Wager with Conflans, possibly Alexandre-Philippe, first gentleman of the bedchamber to the duc d'Orléans, March 15, 1719, RHC Limburg, Papieren Law, inv. nr 30.
37. Crawford to Craggs, August 2, 1719, NA SP 78/164, f. 413.
38. Law to Marcello Durazzo, May 11, 1717, ADG, Carteggi, Lettere in arrivo, 136.
39. *Journal de Dangeau*, Vol. 18, pp.51–2, May 23, 1719.
40. AN, Minutier Central, Répertoire de l'étude Ballin, 1719 (Et. XLVIII), AN MC/RE/XLVIII/1; RHC Limburg, Papieren Law, inv. nr 68; "Documents pour servir à l'histoire de la Bibliothèque impériale", *Le Cabinet historique*, Paris, 1857, Vol. 3, pp. 136–7.
41. Crawford to Craggs, June 3, 1719, NA SP 78/164, f. 402.
42. Law to duc de Bourbon, August 25, 1724, printed in Paul Harsin ed., *Oeuvres complètes de John Law*, Paris/Louvain, 1934, Vol. 3, p. 247.
43. Ibid., p. 248.
44. Hop to Heinsius, May 12, 1719, *Briefwisseling van Heinsius*, Vol. 19, p. 214.
45. In his meeting with Montesquieu in Venice in August, 1728, Law listed these associates as: the ducs de Bourbon and de La Force, the maréchal d'Estrées, and the marquis de Nangis and de Lassay. Albert de Montesquieu, ed., *Voyages de Montesquieu*, Paris, 1894, Vol. 1, p. 60.
46. *Edit du Roy Portant Reünion des Compagnies des Indes Orientales & de la Chine, à la Compagnie d'Occident. Donné à Paris au mois de May 1719*. Law, in his 1724 letter to

the duc de Bourbon, says the edict was passed on the "Sunday" [May 21].

47. Law to duc de Bourbon, August 25, 1724, printed in Harsin, ed., *Oeuvres de Law*, Vol. 3, p. 248.
48. Ibid., pp. 248–9.
49. *Journal de Dangeau*, Vol. 18, p. 52.
50. Law spoke to him "two days agoe". Crawford to Craggs, June 3, 1719, NA SP 78/164, f. 106. In the despatch, he says the shares were at 125 per cent, that is, 625 livres.
51. Crawford to Craggs, June 3, 1719, NA SP 78/164, f. 104.
52. Same to same, July 22, 1719, ibid., f. 367.
53. Same to same, June 3, 1719, ibid., f. 106.
54. Philippe Haudrère, *La Compagnie française des Indes au XVIIIe siècle*, Paris, 2005, Vol. 1, p. 49.
55. Regent to Bourgeois, treasurer of the Banque royale, June 23, 1719, RHC Limburg, Papieren Law, inv. nr 7.
56. "Hondertenvijftig pr.cto" of the original issue price of 500 livres. Hop to Heinsius, June 23, 1719, *Briefwisseling van Heinsius*, Vol. 19, p. 263.
57. Navy Council to Clairambault, June 28, 1719, quoted in Giraud, *Histoire de la Louisiane française*, Vol. 3, p. 122.
58. John Charnock, *Biographia Navalis*, London, 1795, Vol. 3, p. 51.
59. British Museum, BM 1950.0520.144.
60. *Flying-Post*, December 17–20, 1698.
61. Jennings to Dartmouth, November 30, 1711, NA SP 42/68, f. 72.
62. Rigby to Mar, September 7, 1718, HMC, *Calendar of the Stuart Papers*, Vol. 7, p. 255.
63. Abel Boyer, *The Political State of Great Britain*, Vol. 17 (January–June, 1719), p. 411.
64. Stair to Stanhope, May 27 and May 28, 1719, NA SP 78/164, ff. 40–51.
65. Mellier to Receivers, May 12, 1721 and Mellier to Ferrand, May 14, 1721, AMN, HH 209, quoted in Gaston Martin, *Nantes et la compagnie des Indes*, Paris, n.d., p. 54.
66. RHC Limburg, Papieren Law, inv. nr 32.
67. Law to duc de Bourbon, October 15, printed in Harsin, ed., *Oeuvres de Law*, Vol. 3, p. 263.
68. Engagement, AN MC/ET/XCV/70, November 28, 1720; Commission de Jean Law à Louis Elias Stutheus et Jacques Levense, AN MC/XLVIII/35, January 28, 1720.
69. Morris S. Arnold, *Colonial Arkansas*, Fayetteville, 1991, pp. 5ff.
70. William Poidebard, ed., *Correspondance littéraire et anecdotique entre Monsieur de Saint-Fonds et le Président Dugas*, Lyons, 1890, pp. 107–8.
71. *Mémoires de Saint-Simon*, ed. Boislisle, Vol. 36, pp. 265–6.
72. Hop to Heinsius, July 21, 1719, *Briefwisseling van Heinsius*, Vol. 19, p. 285; Crawford to Craggs, July 22, 1719, NA SP 78/164, f. 367.
73. Besides the Bank of England, seven banks in Scotland, Northern Ireland and the Channel Islands issue banknotes.
74. Law gave that number to Crawford at their meeting in June. Crawford to Craggs, July 22, 1719, NA SP 78/164, f. 367.
75. These quotations should be taken as approximate. The sources are: for July 29, Chevalier de Piossens, *Mémoires de la Régence*, The Hague, 1730, Vol. 2, p. 322; for July 31, Hop to Heinsius, July 31, 1719, *Briefwisseling van Heinsius*, Vol. 19, p. 289; for August 2 and 3, Crawford to Craggs, August 2, 1719, NA SP 78/164, f. 413 and [Du

Tot] *Histoire du systême*, p. 113; for August 4, Hop to Heinsius, August 4, 1719, *Briefwisseling van Heinsius*, Vol. 19, p. 291.

76. Hop to Heinsius, August 4, 1719, *Briefwisseling van Heinsius*, Vol. 19, p. 291.
77. Same to same, October 30, 1719, ibid., p. 355.
78. Caumartin de Saint-Ange to the marquise de Balleroy, August 11, 1719, E. de Barthélemy, ed., *Les correspondants de la marquise de Balleroy*, Paris, 1883, Vol. 2, pp. 68–9.
79. François Courtin, who was given the abbey of Mont-Saint-Quentin at the age of nineteen, was a poet and Epicurean described by Voltaire as "big, fat, round, short and lazy". The Cumaean Sybil wrote her prophecies on oak leaves in a windy cave. She guides Aeneas down to the Underworld in *Aeneid*, Book VI.
80. *Œuvres complètes de Voltaire: Correspondance*, Vol. 33, ed. Louis Moland, Paris, 1880, p. 53. The letter is undated. As there is no mention of the refunding of the King's debt, it was surely written in August.
81. "Ce système éclaira les esprits, comme les guerres civiles aiguisent les courages." *Précis du Siècle de Louis XV*, Chapter 2.
82. Stair to Craggs, August 20, 1719 in Philip, Earl of Hardwicke, *Miscellaneous State Papers from 1501 to 1726*, London, 1778, Vol. 2, p. 584.
83. *Histoire de France, Vol. 17: La Régence*, p. 1.
84. *Régistres des procès-verbaux des séances du Conseil de Régence, XI Finances III (1717–1719)*, BnF Ms français 23672, f. 54v.
85. *Arrest du conseil d'estat du Roy par lequel Sa Majesté casse et annulle . . . le Bail des Fermes Générales fait à Aymard Lambert. Du 27 Aoust 1719.*
86. Hop to Heinsius, August 28, 1719, *Briefwisseling van Heinsius*, Vol. 19, p. 314.
87. Caumartin de Boissy to Mme de Balleroy, September 1, 1719, *Les correspondants de la marquise de Balleroy*, Vol. 2, pp. 71–3.
88. *Arrest du conseil d'estat du Roy qui ordonne le remboursement de toutes les Rentes perpetuelles. Du 31 Aoust 1719.*
89. *Variations exactes de tous les effets en papier qui ont eu sur la place de Paris, à commencer au mois d'aoust 1719 jusques au dernier mars 1721, par le sr Giraudeau, neveu, négociant à Paris, 1724.* The three copies, which have been studied by Antoin Murphy and François Velde of the Chicago Federal Reserve, are Arsenal ms. 4061, BnF Ms français 14092 and Bibliothèque de Mazarine ms 2820. Many surviving banknotes from 1719 and 1720 are signed "Giraudeau" on behalf of the bank's inspector, Jean-Baptiste Fenellon.
90. Stair to Craggs, September 1, 1719, *Hardwicke Papers*, Vol. 2, p. 589.
91. Stair to Londonderry, March 18, 1720 and April 29, 1720; Stair to Vandergrift, April 29, 1720, NA C108/418/17.
92. Durazzo brothers to Law, September 19, 1719, ADG, Carteggi, Copialettere in partenza, 216.
93. In 1717, Thomas Pitt married Lady Frances Ridgeway, one of the heiresses of the Earl of Londonderry, and was created Baron of Londonderry in the Irish peerage in 1719.
94. Stair to Stanhope, September 8, 1719, NA SP 78/165, f. 139.
95. James III to Mézières, June 20, 1717, HMC, *Calendar of the Stuart Papers*, London, 1907, Vol. 4, p. 369.
96. Ilay to Mrs Howard, n.d. (September or October, 1719) BL Add Ms 22628, ff. 47–9.

97. Same to same, Paris, January 16, 1720, ibid. Belhaven arrived in Paris on December 5. Crawford to Stanyan, December 6, 1719, NA SP 78/165, f. 499.
98. That is conjecture. Elisabeth Charlotte did not keep her inletters.
99. Crawford to Londonderry, October 12 and 19, 1718, NA C108/417/1 in Larry Neal, *"I am Not Master of Events"*, New Haven, 2012, p. 70.
100. Londonderry to de Kater, August 13, 1719, NA C108/418 in Neal, *"I am Not Master"*, p. 74.
101. A record of the bargain (BL Add Ms 36152, f. 203) gives the twelve-month term of the contract as the "25th of August 1720". That is probably an English or Old Style date, and the wager took place on the equivalent date a year earlier by the French or New Style calendar, September 6, 1719.
102. Prof. Larry Neal, the expert on the Londonderry Papers in London, believes the dinner was at the British Embassy and Stair, not for the first or last time, was telling less than the truth. *"I am Not Master"*, p. 52.
103. BL Add Ms 36152, f. 203.
104. Stair to Craggs, September 9, 1719, *Hardwicke Papers*, Vol. 2, p. 593.
105. Stair to Stanhope, private, October 20, 1719, NA SP78/165 ff. 341ff. Also Crawford to Tickell, September 30, 1719, ibid., f. 226. As to Cato the Elder, "In one thing, he was even more savage, adding to his vote on any subject whatsoever, 'In my opinion, Carthage should cease to exist.'" Plutarch, *Life of Cato the Elder*.
106. *The Weekly Packet*, September 5/16, 1719. "Paris, Sept. 22 NS: 'Tis said Mr Law hath laid a wager with the Chevalier Pitt that English South Sea will fall next January." *Post-Boy*, September 22–4, 1719.
107. Craggs to Stair, September 24/October 5, 1719 in Graham, *Annals of Stair*, Vol. 2, p. 404.

CHAPTER NINE: ATLAS IN THE QUINCAMPOIX

1. [Epigraph] Alphonse, comte Fortia de Piles, *Quelques réflexions d'un homme du monde sur . . . le jeu et le duel*, Paris, 1812, p. 83.
2. Charles Le Gac, a director of the company in Louisiana, gives the date as September 14. Glenn Conrad, ed., *Immigration and War: From the Memoir of Charles Le Gac*, Lafayette, La., 1970, p. 35.
3. J. Dumont de Montigny, *Regards sur le monde atlantique, 1715–1747*, Quebec, 2008, p. 107.
4. *Rôles des passagers embarqués sur les vaisseaux de la compagnie des Indes . . . depuis le premier juillet 1719*, FR ANOM, G/1/464 no. 22.
5. Royal decrees of November 10, 1718; January 8, 1719; and March 12, 1719.
6. Arsenal, Archives de la Bastille, 10660, Bicestre, Dossier Girard, f. 110v.
7. "Les plus part gens inutiles et à charge." *Mémoire des services du sr. de Bienville, commandant general de la Loüisianne*, Bienville to [Navy Council], n.d. [after 1724], FR ANOM E 277, Dossier Le Moyne de Bienville, f. 12v.
8. Arsenal, Archives de la Bastille, 10659, Salpêtrière, Dossier Fontaine, f. 26ff.
9. *Journal du marquis de Dangeau*, Paris, 1854, Vol. 18, p. 117, September 1, 1719. Jean Buvat, *Journal de la Régence*, ed. E. Campardon, Paris, 1865, Vol. 1, p. 434, has Law promising a million.
10. J. Dumont de Montigny, *Mémoires historiques sur la Louisiane*, Paris, 1753, Vol. 2, pp. 29–31.

11. Letter signed by Mlle Pataclin, September 23, 1718, Arsenal, Archives de la Bastille, 10659, ff. 29–30.
12. Marcel Giraud, *Histoire de la Louisiane française*, Paris, 1966, Vol. 3, p. 265.
13. *Arrest du Conseil d'Estat du Roy qui permet à la compagnie des Indes de faire pour Cinquante Millions de Nouvelles Actions du treize Septembre 1719*.
14. None of these notes has turned up. The evidence for them includes *Arrest du conseil d'estat du Roy qui ordonne qu'il sera fabriqué pour cent vingt millions de livres de billets de la Banque, de dix mille livres chacun. Du 12 Septembre 1719*; and Hop to Heinsius, September 18, 1719, A. J. Veenendaal Jr, ed., *De Briefwisseling van Anthonie Heinsius, 1702–1720*, The Hague, 1976–2001, Vol. 19, p. 334.
15. Crawford to Tickell, September 23, 1719, NA SP 78/165, f. 214. It is not clear if Law had yet moved to the hôtel Langlée or was still living in the place Vendôme. In a notarial minute of September 6, 1719, Law is still listed as "demeurant place de Louis le grand paroisse Saint Roch". RHC Limburg, Papieren Law, inv. nr 19. He had moved house by October 10, 1719.
16. *Journal de Dangeau*, Vol. 18, p. 136, October 10, 1719. Dangeau reports that Law by now "is established in his new house".
17. "Will: Law is gone to paris with all his family & will have some great bussiness there." John Drummond to William Drummond, London, September 9/20, 1719, NRS, GD24/3/436.
18. Their son Jean, who later headed the Company of the Indies in India, was born in Paris on October 15, 1719 and baptised at the church of Saint-Roch on November 3, 1719. In the baptismal certificate, William and Rebecca were described as living "place loüis le grand". "Extrait des Registres de la Paroisse S. Roch à Paris", copy of June 6, 1781, FR ANOM E 264, Dossier Jean Law de Lauriston, f. 46.
19. Crawford to Tickell, September 30, 1719, NA SP 78/165, f. 225.
20. *Arrest du conseil d'estat du Roy qui accepte les Offres de la Compagnie des Indes de prester à Sa Majesté au lieu de la Somme de Douze cens millions . . . celle de Quinze cens millions. Du 12 Octobre 1719*. To that must be added the original loan of one hundred millions by the Company of the West.
21. Margaret Panmure to William Law, September 9, 1719, NRS GD 45/14/381. The date is wrong since Lady Panmure refers to "28th September last". She probably intended to write "October 9". The Panmure estates were auctioned on October 9/20, 1719, and sold for £60,400 to the London carpetbaggers, the York Buildings Company. The attorney acting for Lady Panmure failed to produce a "caution" or financial guarantee for her bid of £60,300.
22. Hop to Heinsius, August 28, 1719, *Briefwisseling van Heinsius*, Vol. 19, p. 314.
23. Elisabeth Charlotte to Princess of Wales, October 4, 1719, H. F. Helmolt, *Elisabeth Charlottens Briefe an Karoline von Wales*, Annaberg, 1909, p. 367.
24. Same to same, October 24, 1719, ibid., p. 368.
25. Elisabeth Charlotte to the Raugräfin Luise, October 7, 1719, W. L. Holland, ed., *Briefe der Herzogin Elisabeth Charlotte von Orléans*, Stuttgart/Tübingen, 1867–1881, Vol. 4, p. 265.
26. Elisabeth Charlotte to Johanna von Schaumburg-Lippe, June 7, 1718. Liselotte von der Pfalz, *Briefe an Johanna Sophie von Schaumburg-Lippe*, ed. Jürgen Voss, St Ingbert, 2003, p. 50.
27. *Journal de Dangeau*, Vol. 18, pp. 164–5, November 25, 1719.
28. *Elisabeth Charlottens Briefe*, ed. Helmolt, p. 368.

29. *Journal de Dangeau*, Vol. 18, p. 189, December 24, 1719.
30. Dugas to Saint-Fonds, October 22, 1719, quoting a letter from Cheinet, in William Poidebard, ed., *Correspondance littéraire et anecdotique entre Monsieur de Saint-Fonds et le Président Dugas*, Lyons, 1890, p. 131.
31. *Ordonnance du Roy du vingt-sixième Octobre 1719 etc.*, AN, Actes royaux, O/1/63, f. 302v.
32. Hop to Heinsius, September 4, 1719, *Briefwisseling van Heinsius*, Vol. 19, p. 322.
33. Prior to Bolingbroke, October 17, 1712, *Letters and Correspondence of Lord Visc. Bolingbroke*, London, 1798, Vol. 3, p. 143.
34. Peterborough to Mme de Ferriol, 8/19 February, 1721, *Lettres historiques de Bolingbroke*, Paris, 1808, Vol. 3, p. 70.
35. "Elle le fit gorger par Law." *Mémoires de Saint-Simon*, ed. A. M. de Boislisle, Paris, 1879–1931, Vol. 37, p. 9.
36. Of Matthew Prior, Lord Bolingbroke wrote that "we hear much of a certain eloped nun, who has supplanted the nut-brown maid." Bolingbroke to Hanmer, n.d. (January, 1713) in *Bolingbroke Correspondence*, Vol. 3, p. 274. The nut-brown maid appeared in Prior's best-selling ballad of 1708, *Henry and Emma.*
37. Act of November 28, 1719, Archives départmentales de l'Isère, Grenoble, 2-E461, printed in A. Prudhomme, *Notes pour servir à l'histoire de Mme de Tencin*, Grenoble, 1906, pp. 18–23.
38. Hop to Heinsius, December 15, 1719, *Briefwisseling van Heinsius*, Vol. 19, p. 381. London *Evening Post*, December 5–8, 1719.
39. William Law was not present at the baptism on November 3, 1719. Rebecca and the godparents, Capt. John or Jean Murphy and Dame Winifrid Clarke, made "declaration of the Catholic religion or signed". Murphy was described as a ship-of-the-line captain. Dame Winifrid was the wife of the Jacobite medallist at Saint-Germain, Norbert Roettiers, who in 1716 had made punches for a new English and Scottish coinage in expectation that the Jacobite uprising would succeed. FR ANOM E 264, Dossier Jean Law de Lauriston, f. 46.
40. The chevalier de Piossens says Law gave Saint-Roch 100,000 crowns or 500,000 livres. *Mémoires de la Régence*, The Hague, 1730, Vol. 2, p. 360.
41. Law to duc de Bourbon, August 25, 1724, printed in Paul Harsin, ed., *Oeuvres complètes de John Law*, Paris/Louvain, 1934, Vol. 3, pp. 250–1.
42. *Arrest du Conseil d'Estat du Roy qui . . . supprime des Droits Establis sur les Suifs etc. du 19 Septembre 1719*. Law's argument was this. In agreeing to lower its interest on its first loan of 100 million livres from 4 per cent to 3 per cent, the Company had given the King a windfall of one million livres per year. He could therefore afford to forgo the 1,063,000 livres per annum provided by the oil, fat and fish taxes.
43. "Droits Esteints & Supprimez depuis la Régence" in *Etat général des dettes de l'Etat à la mort du feu Roy Louis XIV*, Paris, 1720, pp. 17 and 20.
44. James III to Mar, October 15, 1719, Stuart Papers at Windsor Castle, Vol. 45, f. 51.
45. James III to Dicconson, July 9, 1719, ibid., Vol. 44, f. 13.
46. James III to Law, September 24, 1719, ibid., Vol. 45, f. 3.
47. "Many of our countrey men [are now] worth 5 to 10 [thousand pounds] who had little or nothing but were on the spot and Mr Law lent them mony." John Drummond to William Drummond, December 5, 1719, NRS GD24/3/436.
48. Minute de notaire, Palais-Royal, September 6, 1719, RHC Limburg, Papieren Law, inv. nr 19.

49. *Journal de Dangeau*, Vol. 18, p. 120, September 8, 1719.
50. RHC Limburg, Papieren Law, inv. nr 19.
51. *Contrat de mariage de Madame la Princesse de Modene, avec les Estats & Esimations y annexez*, February 11, 1720, printed in N. Du Rousseaud de La Combe, *Arrêts et Règlements notables du Parlement de Paris*, Paris, 1743, pp. 189–95. In addition, the bride received jewels valued at 498,000 livres.
52. Acts of November 29, 1762 and June 20, 1763, AN, Minutier Central, Minutes de l'étude Baron (Et. XXXV), AN MC/ET/XXXV/ 732 and 734, quoted in Philippe Haudrère, *La compagnie française des Indes*, Paris, 2005, Vol. 1, p. 120.
53. In a balance sheet struck during its period of public administration, the Company listed the following debtors for "deliveries of lead and tin" to a value of 205,728 livres and 18 sols: His Majesty (91,588 livres), M. le Duc [de Bourbon] (42,065 livres), Mr. J. Law (32,639/17/-), HRH the Regent (18,177/15/-), HRH Mme l'abesse de Chelle (12,734/9/-), the Prince Charles (8,523/17/-). Those sums are listed with other doubtful or hopeless assets "that will be added to Capital as and when they are recovered". It is not clear if the metals were delivered, or whether it was purely a financial operation. *Tableau général de la Compagnie des Indes au 15 Avril 1722*, BnF, Ms français 8973.
54. *Mémoires de Saint-Simon*, ed. Boislisle, Vol. 33, p. 95.
55. Ibid., Vol. 36, pp. 209–10.
56. Ibid.
57. Armand Baschet, *Le duc de Saint-Simon, son cabinet et l'historique de ses manuscrits*, Paris, 1874, pp. 176–7.
58. *Départements de messieurs les Directeurs de la Compagnie des Indes* and *Journal du Travail de messieurs les Directeurs de la Compagnie des Indes, pour l'Année qui commencera le premier Octobre 1719*, Paris, 1719. Of the two versions of the *Journal*, one is dated September 18 and the other October 13.
59. *Arrest du Conseil d'Estat du Roy pour fair cesser les Fonctions des Receveurs Généraux des Finances. 12 octobre 1719*, Paris, 1719; Crawford to Craggs, November 7, 1719, NA SP78/165, f. 426.
60. Hop to Heinsius, October 20, 1719, *Briefwisseling van Heinsius*, Vol .19, p. 350.
61. *Post-Boy*, November 19–21, 1719 OS, quoting the *Amsterdamse Courant* of November 23, 1719 NS. His first step was to buy, on October 24, the small estate of La Mare or Marre du Parc on the left bank from the Carel sisters and their husbands for 85,000 livres. RHC Limburg, Papieren Law, inv. nr 68; *Pièces particulières à Law*, NLS, Ry.iii.a.7 (10).
62. Law, in March, 1720, gave Arbuthnot power-of-attorney to collect revenues and feudal dues on his properties in Normandy. Procuration, March 20, 1720, AN, Minutier Central, Minutes de l'étude Ballin, 1720 (Et. XLVIII), AN MC/ET/XLVIII/37.
63. RHC Limburg, Papieren Law, inv. nr 68; *Pièces particulières à Law*, NLS Ry.iii.a.7 (7). *Commissions extraordinaires du Conseil: Law (Jean)*, Minutes des jugements, AN V/7/254, Judgment of February 6, 1721.
64. Dulin's plan (BnF, Département des Estampes, Grande pièce, VIIIe Arrondissement) is reproduced in Christiane Lorgues, "L'ancien hôtel de la monnaie de Paris", *Revue numismatique*, 6th Series, Vol. 10 (1968), p. 164; *Post-Boy*, November 19–21, 1719 OS, quoting the *Amsterdamse Courant* of November 23, 1719 NS.

65. Saint-Fonds to Dugas, October 22, 1719, Poidebard, ed., *Correspondance entre Monsieur de Saint-Fonds et le Président Dugas*, pp. 128–9.
66. AN, Minutier Central, Répertoire de l'étude Ballin, 1719 (Et. XLVIII), AN MC/RE/XLVIII/1. The vendor was Louis Colbert, comte de Lignières, a younger son of the great minister, Jean-Baptiste Colbert. The price was 300,000 livres, of which 175,000 livres was paid. *Pièces particulières à Law*, NLS Ry.iii.a.7 (1).
67. Law to duc de Bourbon, August 25, 1724, printed in Harsin, ed., *Oeuvres de Law*, Vol. 3, p. 251.
68. "Vous jugez qu'il ne s'accommodera pas des dedans gothiques qui y sont." Caumartin de Boissy to Mme de Balleroy, March 9, 1719, E. de Barthélemy, ed., *Les correspondants de la marquise de Balleroy*, Vol. 2, p. 35.
69. AN O/1/63, ff. 253–4v.
70. Jean Buvat, a scribe at the Royal Library and memoirist, says Law paid 180,000 livres plus a 20,000-livre sweetener or *pot-de-vin*. E. Campardon, ed., *Journal de la Régence*, Paris, 1865, Vol. 1, p. 467. Law's inventory of 1722 gives an acquisition cost of 250,000 livres. *Etat General des Biens, Immeubles & des Dettes actives & passives de Mr Lavv au Premier Janvier 1722*, RHC Limburg, Papieren Law, inv. nr 68.
71. *Bibliotheca Duboisiana, ou Catalogue de la Bibliothèque . . . Recueillie ci-devant par Monsieur l'abbé Bignon*, The Hague, 1725.
72. Law to duc de Bourbon, Venice, June 1, 1721, in Law's outletter book, Méjanes, Ms 614 (355), f. 70; Declaration by Pellegrini, May 6, 1729, AStV, Notarile, Atti, Carlo Gabrieli, 7130.
73. Pierre Crozat to Rosalba Carriera, Paris, November 25, 1719, in Bernardina Sani, ed., *Rosalba Carriera: Lettere, diari, frammenti*, Florence, 1985, Vol. 1, p. 360; same to same, December 22, 1719, ibid., Vol. 1, p. 362.
74. The coins are clearly of the early Regency. Jean Duplessy, *Les monnaies françaises royales*, Paris, 1999, Vol. 2, pp. 331ff. The monogram is less elaborate than that on the engraved banknotes, where it was designed to hinder counterfeiting.
75. The balustrade is mentioned in a survey done on behalf of the duc d'Antin, superintendent of the King's buildings, on August 10, 1725. "Le Grand Escalier . . . une belle rampe de fer garnie et ornée de bronze." BnF, Département des Estampes, Hc. 12e, pièce 2, quoted in Peter Hughes, *The Wallace Collection: Catalogue of Furniture, III*, London, 1996, p. 1189. The gilding is from the nineteenth century. Designed for a single side of the three flights at the hôtel de Nevers, the balustrade was altered to run both sides of the double flight at Hertford House. *Commissions extraordinaires du Conseil: Law (Jean)*, Minutes des jugements, Judgment in favour of Guillaume Cressart, March 27, 1721, AN V/7/254.
76. RHC Limburg, Papieren Law, inv. nr 68; *Pièces particulières à Law*, NLS Ry.iii.a.7 (7). Law's property is the vacant lot marked in the square L6 of Delagrive's map of 1728.
77. Stair to Londonderry, November 4, 1719, NA C108/418/17. Stair later tried and failed to remit £15,600 by bills on Holland. Stair to Vandergrift, April 29, 1720, ibid.
78. Stair to Stanhope, November 7, 1719, NA SP 78/165, f. 429.
79. "An account of what Sums Mr Pulteney has drawn for", June 12, 1720, NA SP 78/166, f. 237.
80. "Anecdotes and other Miscellaneous Pieces Left by the Rt. Hon. Arthur Onslow"

in HMC, *The Manuscripts of the Earl of Buckinghamshire etc.*, London, 1895, p. 465.

81. John Drummond to William Drummond, London, October 7/18, 1719, NRS, GD24/3/436. Drummond intended to set off for Paris the next day, but does not appear to have reached Paris until the beginning of November as the shares were at 1,300 per cent (6,500 livres) on his arrival. Same to same, December 5, 1719, ibid.
82. *Post-Boy*, November 24–6, 1719 OS.
83. Report from Paris of November 22 in the *Daily Courant*, November 18/29, 1719 OS.
84. Crawford to Stanyan, November 22, 1719, NA SP 78/165, f. 456. In theory, there was no Sunday trading in the Quincampoix.
85. Hop to Heinsius, November 27, 1719, *Briefwisseling van Heinsius*, Vol. 19, p. 369.
86. *Post-Boy*, November 21–4, 1719 OS.
87. [Nicolas] Du Tot, *Histoire du système de John Law (1716–1720)*, ed. Antoin Murphy, Paris, 2000, p. 140; and elsewhere.
88. Chandos to Drummond, December 3/14, 1719, NRS GD24/1/487.
89. Archives de Chantilly, 1B9, quoted in Christophe Levadoux, "L'organisation socio-économique des écuries de Chantilly", *In Situ*, Vol. 12 (2009), p. 5.
90. Dillon to James III, September 23, 1720, Stuart Papers at Windsor Castle, Vol. 49, f. 9.
91. James III to Dillon, September 24, 1719, ibid., Vol. 45, f. 2.
92. James III to Sobieski, September 24, 1719, ibid., Vol. 45, f. 1.
93. Mar to James III, October 19, 1719, ibid., Vol. 45, f. 52.
94. Sobieski to James III, November 3, 1719, ibid., Vol 45, f.81. There is a hint in the Radziwiłł papers in Minsk that Pelucki was speculating in the Compagnie des Indes on behalf of Prince James's younger brother, Konstanty, in Breslau/Wrocław. "I am curious to know whether it is true, and certain, that His Lordship Peluki has brought a great advantage to the Most Glorious Lord, having risked his money on the Indies fleet, as was written here from Wrocław. That is to say, if Mr. Peluki earned as much as he did, he could pay our obligations." Janicki to Wierusz Kowalski, Złoczów/Zolochiv, March 5, 1720, NIAB, Minsk, F. 695, op. 1, nr 385, k. 29.
95. Dicconson to James III, November 13, 1719, ibid., Vol. 45, f. 90.
96. James III to Dicconson, December 4, 1719, ibid., Vol. 45, f. 104.
97. James III to Dicconson, December 11, 1719, ibid., Vol. 45, f. 111.
98. Dicconson to James III, January 15, 1720, ibid., Vol 45, f.138. There is no mention of the annuity in the pensions listed by the Queen in her testament, done at Rome on April 20, 1713 and February 23, 1714. Adrien Bonvallet, *Le château des Bordes et ses seignieurs*, Nevers, 1869, pp. 150–61.
99. Same to same, April 1, 1720, ibid., Vol. 46, f. 34.
100. James III to Dicconson, February 5, 1720, ibid., Vol. 46, f. 9.
101. Dicconson to James III, April 1, 1720, ibid., Vol., 46, f. 34.
102. Same to same, January 15, 1720, ibid., Vol., 45, ff.138–9.
103. "A list of gratifications given by Mr Law", ibid., Vol. 281, f. 166. The total is 124,050 livres. The list is in Dicconson's handwriting but has found its way into the volume for 1747.
104. Dixon [Dillon] to James III, December 19, 1719, ibid., Vol. 45, f. 115.
105. Dillon to James III, January 16, 1720, ibid., Vol. 45, f. 141.

106. Same to same, January 16, 1720, ibid., Vol. 45, f. 141.
107. Crawford to Craggs, November 29, 1719, NA SP 78/165, ff. 483–4.
108. "Thursday and Friday last." Pulteney to Craggs, December 5, 1719, NA SP 78/166, f. 38.
109. *Procès-verbaux de l'Académie royale des Sciences*, December 2, 1719, Vol. 38, f. 292.
110. Minutes et répertoires du notaire Jean Moet (Et CXIX), décembre 1719, AN MC/ET/XCIX/170; *Journal de Dangeau*, Vol. 18, p. 167.
111. BL, Add Ms 20365, f. 423.
112. Hop to Heinsius, December 4, 1719, *Briefwisseling van Heinsius*, Vol. 19, p. 374.
113. [?Hamilton] to Mar, December 17, 1719, Stuart Papers at Windsor Castle, Vol. 45, f. 120. *The Orphan Reviv'd* of Dec 12–19, 1719 OS reported the supposed assassination plot from French newsletters of December 20 NS.
114. Saint-Simon relates how the postmistress at Nonancourt near his estate at La Ferté-Vidame, Suzanne L'Hospital or Delacour, foiled Stair's assassins. *Mémoires de Saint-Simon*, ed. Boislisle, Vol. 29, pp. 274–83. Mme Delacour's deposition is printed in Pierre-Edouard Lermontey, *Histoire de la régence*, Paris, 1832, Vol. 2, pp. 384–7.
115. Act V, sc. iv. The Code Duello, agreed at the Clonmel Assizes in 1777 and followed on both sides of the Atlantic, deals specifically with the "Lie direct".
116. Stair to Craggs, December 11, 1719 in Philip, Earl of Hardwicke, *Miscellaneous State Papers from 1501 to 1726*, London, 1778, Vol. 2, p. 600.
117. Stair to Craggs, January 6, 1720, NA SP 78/165, f. 578f; Hop to Heinsius, December 15, 1719, *Briefwisseling van Heinsius*, Vol. 19, p. 381.
118. Stair to Craggs, December 20, 1719, NA SP 78/165, f. 537; Stair to Stanhope, December 27, 1719, ibid., f. 553.
119. "Si Monsr Law n'a pas le Courage de Cœur . . ." Stair to Craggs, December 23, 1719, NA SP 78/165, f. 543; Stair to Stanhope, December 27, 1719, ibid. f. 553.
120. Dubois to Stanhope, December 18, 1719, KHLC, U1590/0145/10.
121. Stanhope to Dubois, December 18/29, 1719, ibid.
122. Crawford to Tickell, December 16, 1719, NA SP 78/165, f. 526.
123. Stair to Craggs, December 23, 1719, NA SP 78/165, f. 543.
124. Three hundred livres per quintal [hundredweight] of Spanish snuff, 150 livres for Brazilian leaf, 75 livres for Virginia. *Arrest du conseil d'estat du Roy qui revoque . . . le privilège exclusif de la vente du tabac accordé à Jean Ladmiral . . . du 29 Décembre 1719*, Paris, 1719.
125. Hop to Heinsius, January 1, 1720, *Briefwisseling van Heinsius*, Vol. 19, p. 392.
126. Du Tot, *Histoire du systême de John Law*, p. 168.
127. Saint-Fonds to Dugas, January 5, 1720, Poidebard, ed., *Correspondance entre Monsieur de Saint-Fonds et le Président Dugas*, p. 140.
128. Faligny to Mme de Balleroy, January 3, 1720, *Les correspondants de la marquise de Balleroy*, Vol. 2, p. 98.

CHAPTER TEN: THE GOLDEN FLEECE

1. [Epigraph] Chandos to Drummond, April 13/24, 1720, NRS, GD24/1/487, f. 33.
2. *Mémoires de Saint-Simon*, ed. A. M. de Boislisle, Paris, 1879–1931, Vol. 37, p. 128.
3. AN G/7/1903.
4. Saint-Fonds (?) to Dugas (?), January 6, 1720, William Poidebard, ed.,

Correspondance littéraire et anecdotique entre Monsieur de Saint Fonds et le Président Dugas, Lyons, 1890, p. 144. The editor ascribes this letter to Dugas, but he was not in Paris at that time.

5. Hop to Heinsius, January 2, 1720 in A. J. Veenendaal Jr, ed., *De Briefwisseling van Anthonie Heinsius, 1702–1720*, The Hague, 1976–2001, Vol. 19, p. 398.
6. Law's invitation of January 10 to Stanhope to dine with him, in a secretary's hand but dictated by Law, is in Stanhope's papers in Maidstone. KHLC, U1590/0145/10.
7. Hop to Heinsius, January 15, 1720, *Briefwisseling van Heinsius*, p. 400.
8. John Murray Graham, *Annals of Stair*, Edinburgh and London, 1875, Vol. 2, pp. 412–13.
9. *Journal du marquis de Dangeau*, Paris, 1854, Vol. 18, p. 204, January 10, 1720. Stair's request for recall is in Stair to Craggs, February 20, 1720, NA SP78/167, f. 111.
10. Stair to Craggs, February 14, 1720, in Philip, Earl of Hardwicke, *Miscellaneous State Papers from 1501 to 1726*, London, 1778, Vol. 2, p. 604.
11. *Journal de Dangeau*, Vol. 18, p. 225, February 3, 1720; ibid., p. 229, February 7, 1720; *Gazette d'Amsterdam*, February 9, 1720. *Le Nouveau Mercure*, in its issue of February, 1720, p. 184, says William did dance in a troupe of gypsies [*Bohemiens*] on February 24. That is probably incorrect.
12. Hop to Heinsius, February 12, 1720, *Briefwisseling van Heinsius*, Vol. 19, p. 416. "Presque tous tombés malade de la rougeole." Amelot to Gualterio, February 12, 1720, BL Add Ms 20366, f. 9.
13. Caumartin de Boissy to Mme de Balleroy, February 21, 1720, E. Barthélemy, ed., *Les correspondants de la marquise de Balleroy*, Paris, 1883, Vol. 2, p. 128.
14. Saint-Fonds (?) to Dugas (?), January 12, 1720, Poidebard, ed., *Correspondance entre Monsieur de Saint Fonds et le Président Dugas*, p. 144.
15. Mary, Duchess of Perth to Alexander, Duke of Gordon, January 9, 1720, NRS, GD44/43/9.
16. "Les maris y sont d'avance." Faligny to Mme de Balleroy, January 3, 1720, Barthélemy, ed., *Les correspondants de la marquise de Balleroy*, Vol. 2, p. 98.
17. The King was paying an average of 4.5 per cent on his old obligations, whereas the shares at 10,000 livres cost just 2 per cent in dividend payments.
18. [Nicolas] Du Tot, *Histoire du systême de John Law (1716–1720)*, ed. Antoin Murphy, Paris, 2000, pp. 170–1.
19. Coutts & Co., Letter Book No. 14, December 30, 1719 to February 13, 1720 [i.e. 1721].
20. Crawford to Tickell, September 30, 1719, NA, SP78/165, f. 226.
21. AN MAR/4JJ/111, Journal de bord, quoted in Philippe Haudrère, *La Compagnie française des Indes au XVIIIe siècle*, Paris, 2005, Vol. 1, p. 345.
22. Twelve ocean-going company vessels were condemned as unseaworthy in the 1720s, against nine in the 1730s, and seven in the war years of the 1740s, chiefly at the îles de France and Bourbon (Mauritius and Réunion). Haudrère, *La Compagnie française des Indes*, Vol. 1, p. 478.
23. "Pour ménager les peuples du Royaume." Law to duc de Bourbon, October 15, 1724, in Paul Harsin, ed., *Oeuvres complètes de John Law*, Paris/Louvain, 1934, Vol. 3, p. 263.
24. Charles-Louis de Secondat, baron de Montesquieu, *Voyages*, Bordeaux, 1894–6, Vol. 1, p. 60.
25. Gardane to Navy Council, September 15, 1718, AAE, Correspondance Politique

(Perse), Vol 5, ff. 174–8. Navy Council to Law, October 16, 1720, ibid., f.313.

26. "Notte de la cargaison du vaisseau *l'Indien* de Saint-Malo remise par le sr Gravé au Bender le 25 mars 1720", ibid., f. 269.
27. At a meeting at Qazvin on September 12, 1720, Padéry showed the prime minister, Fath Ali Khan Daghestani, drawings of the ships "sur du papier que Monsieur de Law mavoit chargé". Fath Ali Khan promised to show them to the Shah. Padéry to Navy Council, October 31, 1720, ibid., ff. 324–9.
28. FR ANOM COL C2 72, ff. 45–6; A. Martineau, *Les origines de Mahé en Malabar*, Paris, 1917, p. 24.
29. Session of November 18, 1720, *Procès-verbaux des délibérations du Conseil Souverain de la Compagnie des Indes*, Pondicherry, 1911–14, Vol. 1, pp. 266–8.
30. Only the *Neptune* returned home, reaching Lorient in January, 1723.
31. Miguel Artola, *La Hacienda del Antiguo Regímen*, Madrid, 1982, p. 285.
32. Santiago Aquerreta "Reforma fiscal: la renta de lanas en el reinado de Felipe V", in González Enciso, ed., *El negocio de la lana en España (1650–1830)*, Pamplona, 2001, p. 122.
33. Ormonde to Crean et Compagnie, March 27, 1719, W. K. Dickson, ed., *The Jacobite Attempt of 1719*, Edinburgh, 1895, p. 98.
34. While a prisoner of war in Valladolid, Stanhope drew on Arthur & Crean for more than £30,000 to keep his captive army alive. Stanhope to Arther & Crean, March 21, 1711, KHLC, U1590/0141/18. Straggling officers in Madrid were instructed to call at Crean's house to be clothed and fed. Arther & Crean to Stanhope, December 17, 1710, KHLC, U1590/0140/1.
35. Sutton to Stanhope, January 7/18, 1721, NA SP78/170, f. 23.
36. *Por Don Simón de la Cancela . . . con Don Eduardo Crean, y Compañia, sobre la paga de 42,206 pesos y medio*, n.p., n.d. [Madrid, 1724], Biblioteca de la Universidad de Sevilla, A113/147 (6), f. 3v. Sir Robert Sutton gives a figure of 60,000 pieces-of-eight. Sutton to Stanhope, January 7/18, 1721, NA SP78/170, f. 23.
37. Dillon to James III, May 17, 1720, Stuart Papers at Windsor Castle, Vol. 47, f. 28.
38. P. G. M. Dickson, *The Financial Revolution in England*, New York, 1967, p. 70.
39. Victoria Gardner Sorsby, *British Trade with Spanish America under the Asiento, 1713–1740*, unpublished PhD thesis, University College London, 1975.
40. *The Speech of the Right Honourable John Aislabie, Esq; Upon his Defence made in the House of Lords . . . on Wednesday the 19th of July, 1721*, London, 1721, p. 14.
41. *A Collection of Several Pieces of Mr. John Toland*, London, 1726, Vol. 1, pp. 406–7. The editor says that the *Secret History* is not by Toland but was "found among his MSS, and is enlarged and corrected throughout with his own hand". John Toland was an original and prolific Irish pamphleteer on political and religious questions.
42. Adam Smith, *Lectures on Jurisprudence*, ed. R. L. Meek et al., Oxford, 1978, p. 519.
43. Thomas Brodrick to Lord Middleton, January 24, 1720 in W. Coxe, ed., *Memoirs of . . . Sir Robert Walpole*, London, 1798, Vol. 2, p. 182.
44. *Journal of the House of Commons*, London, 1802, Vol. 19, February 16, 1720 [i.e. 1721], pp. 425–6.
45. The author refers to the Banque royale buying company shares but not to Stair's recall.
46. Daniel Defoe (attrib.), *The Chimera; or the French Way of Paying National Debts Laid Open*, London, 1720, pp. 5–6.
47. Pulteney to Craggs, December 24, 1719, NA SP78/166. f. 94; same to same,

January 3, 1720, ibid., f. 97; same to same, February 22, 1720, ibid., f. 156.

48. Chandos to Drummond, February 8, 1719 [i.e. February 8/19, 1720], NRS GD24/1/487, f. 23.
49. Middleton to William Law, February 1, 1719 [i.e. February 1/12, 1720], Coutts & Co., Letter Book No. 14, pp. 47–8.
50. Same to same, February 4, 1719 [i.e. February 4/15, 1720], ibid., pp. 50–1.
51. Middleton to William Law, March 3, 1719 [i.e. March 3/14, 1720], Coutts & Co., Letter Book No. 14, p. 88.
52. Same to same, February 1, 1719 [i.e. February 1/12, 1720], ibid.
53. Same to same, February 15, 1719 [i.e. February 15/26, 1720] ibid.
54. AAE, Correspondance Politique (Genève). Vol. 34, f. 126, printed in André-E. Sayous, "L'affaire de Law et les Genevois", *Revue d'histoire suisse*, Vol. 17 (1937), p. 335.
55. An act of engagement of August 22, 1721 is in AN/MC/ET/X/353. Reproduced in Agnès Paul, "Les auteurs du théâtre de la foire à Paris au XVIIIe siècle", *Bibliothèque de l'école des chartes*, Vol. 141 (1983), pp. 328–9.
56. *Le theatre de la foire, ou L'opera comique*, Paris, 1724, Vol. 4, pp. 95ff.
57. "Le jeu était considérable cette année, à cause de la quantité de billets de banque." Edmond Barbier, *Chronique de la Régence*, Paris, 1857, Vol. 1, p.32, March 1720.
58. Pye to Strafford, February 6, 1720, BL Add Ms 31140, f. 18.
59. Reeve to James III, n.d. [September, 1716], HMC, *Calendar of the Stuart Papers*, London, 1907, Vol. 4, p. 87.
60. Mar to Mary of Modena, October 1, 1716, HMC, *Calendar of the Stuart Papers*, Vol. 3, p. 4.
61. Pye to Strafford, February 16, 1720, BL Add Ms 31140, f. 27; same to same, February 23, 1720, ibid., p. 31.
62. Pye to Anne, Countess of Strafford, February 13, 1720, BL Add Ms 31140, f. 24.
63. Pye to Hamilton, February 10, 1720, BL Add Ms 31140, f. 20.
64. Pye to Strafford, February 23, 1720, BL Add Ms 31140, f. 31.
65. Elisabeth Charlotte to the Raugräfin Luise, March 7, 1720, C. Künzel, ed., *Die Briefe von Liselotte von der Pfalz*, Ebenhausen, 1912, p. 424.
66. Strafford to Pye, February 18/29, 1720, ibid., f. 26; Pye to Strafford, February 23, 1720, ibid., f. 31.
67. Du Tot, *Histoire du systême de John Law*, p. 193.
68. Pulteney to Crags, January 27. 1720, NA SP 78/166, f. 116.
69. Caumartin de Boissy to Mme de Balleroy, January 28, 1720, E. Barthélemy, ed., *Les correspondants de la marquise de Balleroy*, Vol. 2, p. 109.
70. *Déclaration du Roy portant Deffenses de porter des Diamans, donnée à Paris le 4 Fevrier*, 1720; William Beauvoir to Elizabeth Brown, February 7, 1720, Lambeth Palace Archives, Ms 1558, f. 112.
71. Louis Sergent, "Le procès des épiciers contre le duc de La Force", *Bulletin de la Société de l'histoire de la pharmacie*, Vol. 14 (1926), No. 49, pp. 211–14.
72. *Déclaration du Roy portant Réglement pour la fabrique & le poids des Ouvrages & Vaisselles d'Or & d'Argent du 18 fevrier 1720.*
73. *Arrest du conseil d'etat du Roy qui fixe à Cinq cens livres les sommes que chaque personne & communauté ecclésiastique etc. du 27 fevrier 1720.*
74. Du Tot, *Histoire du systême de John Law*, p. 191.
75. Hop to Heinsius, March 1, 1720, *Briefwisseling van Heinsius*, Vol. 19, p. 424. The

quarrel erupted "a fortnight ago": that is, about February 15. Hop wrote to the States General, which on March 5 asked the States of Holland to take measures to ensure such offensive terms did not appear in the gazettes. W. P. Sautijn Kluit, "De Haarlemsche Courant", *Jaarboek van de Maatschappij der Nederlandse Letterkunde te Leiden*, Leiden, 1873, p. 32.

76. The lawyer Mathieu Marais reported on June 10 that [Antoine-Urbain] Coustelier, the publisher of the letters, fearing prosecution by the Parlement de Paris, had shown the court Law's orders and manuscript comments on the letters. M.de Lescure, ed., *Journal et mémoires de Mathieu Marais*, Paris, 1863, Vol. 1, p. 284.
77. "Lettre écrite à M. *** sur le nouveau Systême des Finances", *Le Nouveau Mercure*, February, 1720, p. 55.
78. Ibid., p. 58.
79. Scholars such as Voltaire and President Dugas had used the word about Law's reforms, but facetiously.
80. *Le Nouveau Mercure*, February, 1720, p. 54.
81. Saint-Fonds to Dugas, February 19, 1720, Poidebard, ed., *Correspondance entre Monsieur de Saint-Fonds et le Président Dugas*, p. 147.
82. AN, Minutier Central, Minutes de l'étude Ballin, 1720 (Et. XLVIII), AN MC/ET/XLVIII/36. The sale price was one million livres and various properties.
83. Hop to Heinsius, February 23, 1720, *Briefwisseling van Heinsius*, Vol. 19, p. 421; Pulteney to Craggs, February 22, 1720, NA SP78/166, f. 157.
84. Chandos to Drummond, February 18, 1719 [i.e. February 18/29, 1720], NRS GD24/1/487, ff. 25–6.
85. Du Tot, *Histoire du systême de John Law*, p. 225. Dangeau on March 1 said that the price had gone as low as 8,100 livres. *Journal de Dangeau*, Vol. 18, p. 244, March 1, 1720.
86. *Arrest du conseil d'état du Roy concernant les Billets du Banque . . . du 5 Mars 1720.*
87. *Déclaration du Roy Pour Abolir l'Usage des Especes d'Or . . . Donné à Paris le 11 Mars 1720.*
88. AN AD+ 758, no. 26.
89. E. Campardon, ed., *Journal de la Régence (1715–1723) par Jean Buvat*, Paris, 1865, Vol. 2, p. 51.
90. Elisabeth Charlotte to Johanna von Schaumburg-Lippe, March 19, 1720. Liselotte von der Pfalz, *Briefe an Johanna Sophie von Schaumburg-Lippe*, ed. Jürgen Voss, St Ingbert, 2003, p. 74.
91. Drummond to Chandos, March 13,1720, NRS GD24/1/487, f. 26.
92. Buvat, *Journal de la Régence*, Vol. 2, p. 59.
93. *Mémoires de Saint-Simon*, ed. Boislisle, Vol. 37, p. 225.
94. *Jugement de mort par délibération du conseil et jugement dernier du comte de Horn et de Laurent de Mille, du mardi saint 26 mars 1720*, Registre du greffe criminel du Châtelet de Paris (Jean-Jacques Brussel, greffier). Printed in Buvat, *Journal de la Régence*, Vol. 2, pp. 503–10.
95. *Mémoires de Saint-Simon*, ed. Boislisle, Vol. 37, p.229.
96. Hop to Heinsius, March 29, 1720, *Briefwisseling van Heinsius*, Vol. 19, p. 440.
97. *Journal de Dangeau*, Vol. 18, p. 256, March 24, 1720.
98. Elisabeth Charlotte to Friedrich von Harling, March 31, 1720, C. Künzel, ed., *Die Briefe von Liselotte von der Pfalz*, Ebenhausen, 1912, pp. 425–26; Elisabeth Charlotte to the Raugräfin Luise, the same day, ibid. pp. 426–7.

99. Hop to Heinsius, November 29 [i.e. March 29], 1720, *Briefwisseling van Heinsius*, Vol. 19, p. 440.
100. "Gyllé" in Paris to Col. Cornelius Kennedy, London, March 27, 1720, NRS GD27/6/19.
101. Stanhope to St Saphorin in Vienna, April 1, 1720, NA SP78/167, f. 242. Stair's bank project is in Stair to Stanhope, April 12, 1720, ibid., ff. 271–3. Stanhope left Paris on April 8.
102. Dubois to Law, March 24, 1720, AAE, Correspondance Politique (Gènes), Vol. 73, f. 96.
103. On March 14, he bet 30,000 livres with the maréchal d'Estrées that the exchange rate would be 50 English pence per crown by the end of the year. *Commissions extraordinaires du Conseil: Law (Jean)*, Minutes des jugements, AN V/7/254, Judgment of March 13, 1721.
104. "Letters to Lucy Countess Stanhope & Papers relating to her Jewels", KHLC U1590 C12/3.
105. "II Lettre où l'on traite du Credit & de son usage", *Lettres sur le nouveau systême des finances,* Paris, 1720, p. 5. This author was unable to find a March 1720 number of the *Nouveau Mercure.*
106. Ibid., p. 6.
107. Ibid., p. 9.
108. Ibid., p.12.
109. Ibid., p. 15.
110. Hop to Heinsius, November 29 [i.e. March 29], 1720, *Briefwisseling van Heinsius*, Vol. 19, p. 441.
111. Chandos to Drummond, March 12, 1719 [i.e. March 12/23, 1720], NRS GD24/1/487, f. 27.
112. Katherine Windham to Ashe Windham, April 4, 1720, Norfolk Record Office, Norwich, WKC7/21, 404X1.
113. *Applebee's Weekly Journal*, April 16/27, 1720.
114. Jules Flammermont, *Remontrances du Parlement de Paris au XVIIIe siècle*, Paris, 1888, Vol. 1, pp. 126–39.
115. Ibid., p. 137. "Mr Law has said that the interest of mony shall, in a year, be reduced from 2 to 1 per cent; this looks like spinning the thread too fine." Pulteney to Craggs, May 10, 1720, NA SP 78/166, f. 210.
116. Flammermont, *Remontrances*, Vol. 1, p. 131.
117. Included in Pulteney to Craggs, May 17, 1720, NA SP 78/166, f. 219.
118. Arsenal, Archives de la Bastille, 10707, Dossier Massy or Massis, f. 60v. Dangeau, *Journal*, Vol. 18, p. 274, says that the campaign began on April 24.
119. Hop to Heinsius, May 3, 1720, *Briefwisseling van Heinsius*, Vol. 19, p. 455; Buvat, *Journal de la Régence*, Vol. 2, p. 78.
120. Arsenal, Archives de la Bastille, 10702, Dossier Faucheau, f. 28; ibid., 10713, Dossier Parizet, f. 117; ibid., 10704, Dossier Soeurs Janet, f. 55; ibid., 10697, Dossier La Vallée, f. 216.
121. Ibid., 10697, f. 229.
122. Archives départementales de Loiret, Orléans, Police criminelle, B1979, paraphrased in J. Doinel and C. Bloch, *Inventaire Sommaire des archives départementales de Loiret*, Orléans, 1900, Vol. 3, p. 41.
123. "Recueil De Lisle", AN U363, quoted in A.-P. Herlaut, "Les enlèvements

d'enfants à Paris en 1720 et en 1750", *Revue historique*, Vol. 139 (January–April 1922), p. 46.

124. *Ordonnance du Roy du trois May 1720 concernant ce qui doit estre observé en arrestant les mendians et vagabons.*
125. *Arrest du Conseil d'Estat du Roy qui ordonne qu'il ne sera plus envoyé de vagabonds . . . à la Loüisianne . . . du 9 may 1720*. In 1729, the directors complained that the transported people "risk everything to escape the misery in which they find themselves, fomenting local trouble or causing unrest among the natives, or making their way to the English in Carolina where they pass intelligence very harmful to the security or at least the good order" of the colony. Directors to Maurepas, March 31,1729, FR ANOM COL C2 22, ff. 63–4, quoted in Haudrère, *La Compagnie française des Indes*, Vol. 1, p. 111.
126. Some 450 West Africans arrived with the *Aurore* and the *Grand-duc-du- Maine* in June, 1719. The *Rubis* and the *Hercule* landed a further 120 slaves in July, 1720.
127. J.-B. Le Moyne de Bienville, *Mémoire sur la Louisiane* (1725), ff. 120v–121r, quoted in Marcel Giraud, *Histoire de la Louisiane française*, Paris, 1966, Vol. 3, p. 347; "Memoire des services du sr. de Bienville, commandant general de la Loüisianne", Bienville to [Navy Council], n.d [after 1724], FR ANOM E 277, Dossier Le Moyne de Bienville, f. 13r. Bienville is attributed thirty-three African and seven native American slaves in the censuses of 1721.
128. "III Lettre où l'on traite encore des Constitutions etc.", *Lettres sur le nouveau systême des finances*, Paris, 1720; *Le Nouveau Mercure*, May 1720, pp. 28–69.
129. *Le Nouveau Mercure*, May, 1720, p. 56.
130. Ibid., pp. 68–9.
131. Ibid., p. 63.
132. *Journal de Dangeau*, Vol. 18, p. 290, May 19, 1720.
133. *Arrest du Conseil d'Estat du Roy, concernant les Actions de la Compagnie des Indes . . . du 21 may 1720*, Paris, 1720, HNOC, Williams Research Center, 2010.0158.4; also, Du Tot, *Histoire du systême de John Law*, pp. 239ff.
134. Du Tot, *Histoire du systême de John Law*, p. 236.
135. Chandos to Drummond, May 19/30, 1720, NRS GD24/1/487. F. 39. Also, Wauchope in Edinburgh to Whyteford in Paris, June 2/13, 1720, NRS GD377/399.
136. Buvat, *Journal de la Régence*, Vol. 2, p. 93.
137. *Journal de Dangeau*, Vol. 18, p. 292, May 23, 1720.
138. A printed quarto letter by Law under the title *Lettre au sujet de l'arrest du conseil d'Etat du 22 mai 1720* is at BnF, Clairambault 522. An English translation is included in the volume *The Present State of the French Revenues*, London, 1720, pp. 105–10.
139. On May 28, at the notary of Moyaux, near Caen, the widow Marguerite Leblond attempted to buy back a piece of land with four 100-livre notes at face value while Olivier de Montargis, the vendor, would accept the notes only at 80 livres each "in conformity with the King's declaration of the 21st of this month". Archives départementales de Calvados, Etude Moyaux, 8E4905, printed in Jérôme Jambu, "Le système de Law dans les campagnes: l'exemple du Pays d'Auge", *Annales de Normandie*, Vol. 50 (2000), No. 2, pp. 316–17.
140. *Mémoires de Saint-Simon*, ed. Boislisle, Vol. 37, p. 314.
141. Buvat, *Journal de la Régence*, Vol. 2, pp. 93–4.
142. Hop to Heinsius, May 31, 1720, *Briefwisseling van Heinsius*, Vol. 19, p. 471.

143. Pulteney to Craggs, May 24, 1720, NA SP 78/116, f. 224; same to same, private letter, same day, ibid., f. 226; Pulteney to Stanhope, same day, ibid., f. 227.
144. *Journal de Dangeau*, Vol. 18, p. 293, May 25, 1720.
145. The Paris banker Pierre Nolasque Couvez or Couvay, to whom the bill was endorsed, protested on the grounds that the bill specified payment in silver which had become illegal in France. *Por Don Simón*, f. 4.
146. Barbier, *Chronique de la Régence*, Vol. 1, p. 35; *Journal de Dangeau*, Vol. 18, p. 294, May 27, 1720.
147. *Voyages de Montesquieu*, Vol. 1, p. 61.
148. "Mémoires du duc d'Antin", *Mélanges publiés par la société des bibliophiles français*, Paris, 1822, p. 138.
149. Louis Antoine de Pardaillan de Gondrin, duc d'Antin, *Mémoires de la Régence*, BnF NAF 23929-23937, Vol. 7, printed in E. Faure, *La banqueroute de Law*, Paris, 1977, p. 441.
150. *Journal de Dangeau*, Vol. 18, pp. 294–5, May 27, 1720; AN U363.
151. *Arrest du Conseil d'Estat du Roy, qui revoque celui du 21 may . . . du vingt-septiéme May 1720.*
152. *Voyages de Montesquieu*, Vol. 1, p. 61.
153. Hop to Heinsius, May 3, 1720 (incorrect for June 3, 1720), *Briefwisseling van Heinsius*, Vol. 19, p. 456.
154. Barbier, *Chronique de la Régence*, Vol. 1, p. 38; Buvat, *Journal de la Régence*, BnF Ms français 10383, f. 250 quoted in E. Levasseur, *Recherches historiques sur le système de Law*, Paris, 1854, p. 247.
155. *Inventaire general des Effets estans dans la caise du Sr. Law pour composer et remplir la somme de 952,144,027 livres 12 sols 8 deniers par luy recüe suivant son Registre et ses billets delivrez dont il est comptable . . . ce 29 May 1720*. RHC Limburg, Papieren Law, inv. nr 9.
156. René-Louis Voyer de Paulmy, marquis d'Argenson, *Mémoires et journal inédit*, Paris, 1857, Vol. 1, p. 164.
157. Claude Pâris de La Montagne, *Discours à ses enfans pour les instruire sur sa conduite*, 1729, AN KK//1005/D, p. 129.
158. *Voyages de Montesquieu*, Vol. 1, p. 62.
159. *Journal et mémoires de Matthieu Marais*, Vol. 1, p. 269.
160. *Journal de Dangeau*, Vol. 18, p. 296, May 31, 1720.
161. *Voyages de Montesquieu*, Vol. 1, p. 62.
162. *Journal de Dangeau*, Vol. 18, p. 297, June 1, 1720.
163. "Giugno 10. Poi andata alla Banca, e veduta la stessa, ed il Modello." G. Vianelli, ed., *Diario degli anni MDCCXX e MDCCXXI scritto di propria mano in Parigi da Rosalba Carriera*, Venice, 1793, pp. 15–16.
164. A. M. Zanetti il Giovane, *Della pittura veneziana*, Venice, 1771, p. 446n.
165. [Comte de Caylus], "Vie de François Le Moyne" in F. B. Lépicié, *Vies des premiers peintres du Roi*, Paris, 1752, Vol. 2, p. 89; Germain Brice, *Description de la ville de Paris*, Paris, 1752, Vol. 1, p. 363.
166. [Comte de Caylus], "Vie de François Le Moyne" in Lépicié, ed., *Vies des premiers peintres du Roi*, Vol. 2, p. 89; *Procès-verbaux de l'Académie royale de peinture et sculpture*, ed. A. de Montaiglon, Paris, 1885, Vol. 6, p. 123.
167. "Projet d'un Plafond qui devoit estre executé dans la grande Gallerie de la Banque à Paris, inventé et peint par François le Moyne et gravé par Nic. Char. Sylvestre",

Paris, n.d. [*c.*1721];[Comte de Caylus], "Vie de François Le Moyne" in Lépicié, ed., *Vies des premiers peintres du Roi*, Vol. 2, p. 94.

168. "Description de la peinture de la galerie de la Banque Royale" in ibid., pp. 124 and 126–7.

CHAPTER ELEVEN: 888

1. [Epigraph] "Gyllé" to Col. Cornelius Kennedy, September 25, 1721, NRS, GD27/6/19.
2. Parish registers quoted in R. Carrière, M. Courdurié and F. Rebuffat, *Marseille ville morte: La peste de 1720*, Gémenos, 2008, pp. 41–2.
3. "Divers abus qui se commettent dans les Infirmeries de Marseille déclarés par des personnes qui y ont été jusques aujourd'hui employées pendant plusieurs années" quoted in Carrière et al., *Marseille ville morte*, pp. 163–4.
4. Villars to Lebret, July 28, 1720, in marquis de Vogüé, ed., *Mémoires du maréchal de Villars*, Paris, 1904, Vol. 6, p. 85.
5. Charles Carrière, "Le commerce de Marseille et le Système de Law", *Actes du 78e congrès national des sociétés savantes, Toulouse 1953*, Paris, 1954, p. 79; Law to Chamber of Commerce, Marseille, March 29, 1720, ibid., p. 78.
6. Grégoire to the Chamber of Commerce, June 14, 1719, quoted in C. Carrière, "Le commerce de Marseille", p. 74.
7. Text in V.-L. Bourilly, "Le contrebande des toiles peintes au Provence au XVIIIe siècle", *Annales du Midi*, Vol. 26 (1914), p. 55.
8. R. Carrière et al., *Marseille ville morte*, p. 164.
9. Ibid., p. 180.
10. N. N. Pichatty de Croissante, *Journal abrégé de ce qui s'est passé en la ville de Marseille depuis qu'elle est affligée de la contagion*, Paris, 1721, p. 2. A modern project to reconstruct pathogen genomes from teeth in one of the Marseilles plague pits argues that the 1720–22 plague was a survivor of the disease, known as the Black Death, that entered Europe in the fourteenth century. K. I. Bos et al., "Eighteenth-century *Yersinia pestis* genomes", *eLife* 2016; 5:e12994.
11. Ibid., pp. 2–3.
12. Ibid., pp. 4–5.
13. J.-B. Bertrand, *Relation historique de la peste de Marseille en 1720*, Cologne, 1721, pp. 50–1.
14. Ibid., p. 491.
15. Augustin Fabre, *Histoire des hôpitaux et des institutions de bienfaisance à Marseille*, Marseilles, 1854, Vol. 1, p. 347.
16. AMM, CE, p. 150, quoted in P. Gaffarel and marquis de Duranty, *La peste de 1720 à Marseille & en France*, Paris, 1911, p. 30. Pichatty de Croissante, *Journal abrégé*, pp. 10–11, says the aldermen that day wrote to "health inspectors in all the ports of Europe".
17. Pichatty de Croissante, *Journal abrégé*, p. 11. R. Carrière et al., *Marseille ville morte*, pp. 44–5.
18. Villars to Aldermen of Marseilles, July 22, 1720, *Mémoires de Villars*, Vol. 6, p. 84.
19. Pichatty de Croissante, *Journal abrégé*, p. 12.
20. Ibid., p. 13.

21. The insurers refused to pay. B. M. Émerigon, *Traité des assurances et des contrats à la grosse*, Marseilles, 1783. Vol. 2, pp. 54–5.
22. *Arrêt du Parlement du 31 Juillet* 1720, AMM FF292, Registre de peste.
23. Pichatty de Croissante, *Journal abrégé*, p.23.
24. Pulteney to Craggs, June 11, 1720, NA SP78/166, f. 234.
25. Constitution, June 25, 1720, AN, Minutier Central, Actes de l'étude Ballin, 1720 (Et. XLVIII), AN MC/ET/XLVIII/40.
26. The constitutions, and a receipt signed by Jacques Deshayes, cashier of the Company of the Indies and dated July 31, 1720, are at RHC Limburg, Brabants Hooggerecht, nr 205.
27. Dicconson to James III, June 10, 1720, Stuart Papers at Windsor Castle, Vol. 47, f. 69. By 1727, according to rough notes on the King's income made by Sir William Ellis, the annuity was just 12,000 livres. In other words, the rate of interest was just 2 per cent or the capital had been halved. Of that, for reasons that are illegible, James III was receiving just 8,860 livres and 10 sols. Ibid., Vol. 112, f. 163.
28. On June 6. [Nicolas] Du Tot, *Histoire du systême de John Law (1716–1720)*, ed. Antoin Murphy, Paris, 2000, p. 269.
29. Hop to Heinsius, June 7, 1720, in A. J.Veenendaal Jr, ed., *De Briefwisseling van Anthonie Heinsius*, 1702–1720, The Hague, 1976–2001, Vol. 19, p. 474.
30. Du Tot, *Histoire du systême de John Law*, p. 278.
31. Ibid., pp. 269 and 275.
32. Desgranges to Dubois, Genoa, June 4, 1720, *Cérémonies à l'occasion du mariage de Mlle Charlotte-Aglaé d'Orléans et de François-Marie d'Este*, Centre de recherche du château de Versailles, Ms F 822, f. 112.
33. Regent to Princess of Modena, n.d. [June, 1720], quoted in E. de Barthélemy, *Les filles du Régent*, Paris, 1854, Vol. 1, p. 411.
34. Chavigny to Dubois, July 30, 1720, January 14, 1721, AAE, Correspondance Politique (Gênes), Vol. 73, f. 291; same to same, August 12, 1720, ibid., f. 303; same to same, September 4, 1720, ibid., f. 335.
35. Dicconson to James III, July 2, 1720, Stuart Papers at Windsor Castle, Vol. 48, f. 11.
36. Pulteney to Delefaye, July 9, 1720, NA SP78/166, f. 26.
37. "18 [giugno] Dimandai alla puttella Law cambio di bullettini". G. Vianelli, ed., *Diario degli anni MDCXX e MDCXXI scritto di propria mano in Parigi da Rosalba Carriera*, Venice, 1793, p. 19.
38. Hop to Heinsius, June 10, 1720, *Briefwisseling van Heinsius*, Vol. 19, p. 474.
39. [Bernard le Bovier de Fontenelle], "Eloge de M. d'Argenson", *Histoire de l'Académie royale des Sciences, Année 1721*, Paris, 1723, p. 107.
40. *Mémoires de Saint-Simon*, ed. A. M. de Boislisle, Paris, 1879–1931, Vol. 37, p. 338.
41. Balleroy to Mme de Balleroy, July 3, 1720, E. Barthélemy, ed., *Les correspondants de la marquise de Balleroy*, Paris, 1883, Vol. 2, p. 179.
42. "Mr O" to Strafford, July 13, 1720, BL Add Ms 31140, ff. 56–7.
43. Dillon to James III, June 15, 1720, Stuart Papers at Windsor Castle, Vol. 47, f. 84.
44. Same to same, July 2, 1720, ibid., Vol. 48, f. 12.
45. Dillon to Ormonde, July 2, 1720, ibid., f. 13.
46. In May, Dillon was authorised to offer William Law the "title of a Scotch Earl . . . As to 888 there is no proposing such to him at present. In case he should be thought fitt hereafter, what you formerly mentioned will not suffice." Dillon to

James III, May 17, 1720, Stuart Papers at Windsor Castle, Vol. 47, f. 28.

47. James III to Ormonde, ibid., Vol. 48, ff. 77. The date is given as "July, 1720".
48. RHC Limburg, Papieren Law, inv. nr 3. With it is a similar letter to Lady Katherine Knowles from another petitioner.
49. Edmond Barbier, *Chronique de la Régence*, Paris, 1857, Vol. 1, p. 47.
50. Ibid.
51. Hop to Heinsius, Ju1y 19, 1720, *Briefwisseling van Heinsius*, Vol. 19, p. 491.
52. Report of Commissioner J.-F. Letrouy Deslandes, July 10, 1720, AN Y10974, printed in E. Faure, *La banqueroute de Law*, Paris, 1977, pp. 657–8.
53. E. Campardon, ed., *Journal de la Régence (1715–1723) par Jean Buvat*, Paris, 1865, Vol. 2, pp. 106–7.
54. Pulteney to Craggs, July 19, 1720, NA SP 78/166, f. 266.
55. Hop to Heinsius, Ju1y 22, 1720, *Briefwisseling van Heinsius*, Vol. 19, p. 491.
56. *Gazette d'Amsterdam*, July 19, 1720; Letters from Paris of July 18 in ibid., July 26, 1720.
57. Registre du greffier Delisle, AN U 363.
58. Elisabeth Charlotte to the Raugräfin Luise, July 18, 1720, W. L. Holland, ed., *Briefe der Herzogin Elisabeth Charlotte von Orléans*, Stuttgart/Tübingen, 1867–1881, Vol. 5, pp. 199–201.
59. Dillon to James III, July 23, 1720, Stuart Papers at Windsor Castle, Vol. 48, f. 57.
60. Pulteney to Craggs, July 25, 1720, NA SP 78/166, f. 271.
61. *Ordonnance du Roy, portant défenses de s'attrouper, du 17. juillet* 1720, AN O/1/64, f. 205.
62. "La Banque promet d'étouffer a veüe le Porteur du present billet." Pulteney to Craggs, August 27, 1720, NA SP 78/166, f. 317.
63. Boislisle, ed., *Mémoires de Saint-Simon*, Vol. 37, pp. 359ff.
64. Hop to Heinsius, July 22, 1720, *Briefwisseling van Heinsius*, Vol. 19, p. 491.
65. Jean Gilbert Delisle, *Journal du Parlement séant à Pontoise depuis le 21 juillet* 1720, AN U 747, printed in Isabelle Storez Brancourt, *Le journal d'un greffier du Parlement au xviiie*, halshs-00187579, p. 4, f. 2.
66. Ibid., p. 23, f. 11v.
67. Ibid., p. 7, f. 3v.
68. Ibid., p. 12, f. 6v. Entry for July 28, 1720.
69. *Diary of Mary, Countess Cowper, Lady of the Bedchamber to the Princess of Wales, 1714-1720*, London, 1864, p. 142.
70. The source for this is an unsigned newsletter in French dated May 30/June 10, 1720 in the Strafford Papers, BL Add Ms 31140, f. 48. Since May 29 was a Sunday, this exchange is more likely to have taken place on May 28, which was the King's birthday.
71. *Lady Cowper's Diary*, p. 172, entry for May 31/June 11, 1720. Lady Cowper writes, in error, "King" for "Regent".
72. *A Compleat History of the Late Septennial Parliament*, London, 1722, p. 51.
73. *An Act for better securing certain Powers and Privileges, intended to be granted by His Majesty by Two Charters, for Assurance . . . and for restraining several extravagant and unwarrantable Practices therein mentioned*, 6 Geo. I, c. 18.
74. Chandos to Drummond, August 20/31, 1720; same to same, June 12/23, 1720, NRS GD24/1/487, ff. 43 and 45.
75. Middleton to William Law, April 25/May 6, 1720, Coutts & Co., Letter Book No.

14, pp. 163–6; same to same, April 28/May 9, 1720, ibid., p. 170; same to same, May 2/13, 1720, ibid., p. 173

76. Same to same, August 8/19, 1720, ibid., pp. 327–9; same to same , September 8/19, 1720, ibid., p. 369.
77. Same to same, May 5/16, 1720, ibid., p. 177.
78. Same to same, May 23/ June 3, 1720, ibid., p. 194.
79. Same to same, June 23/July 4, 1720, ibid., pp. 238–9.
80. In the case of his sister Lady Stanhope's shares, Londonderry sold at 491 when the market price was 850. Londonderry to Stanhope, October 12, 1720, KHLC, U1590/C9/16.
81. Prior to Harley, July 2/13, 1720, HMC, *Calendar of the Manuscripts of the Marquis of Bath, Preserved at Longleat, Wiltshire*, London, 1908, Vol. 3, p. 483.
82. Stefano Condorelli, *The 1719–1720 stock euphoria: a pan-European perspective*, Working Paper, December 2015, mpra.ub.uni-muenchen.de/68652/
83. William Stanhope to Craggs, July 22, 1720, NA SP 94/89; W. Stanhope to Lord Stanhope, July 29, 1720, ibid. W. Stanhope to Craggs, October 21, 1720, NA SP 94/90; same to same, October 28, 1720, ibid.
84. Crean to Londonderry, Madrid, August 26, 1720, NA C108/418/17.
85. Law to duc de Bourbon, August 25, 1724, printed in Paul Harsin, ed., *Oeuvres complètes de John Law*, Paris/Louvain, 1934, Vol. 3, p. 255. Tabarqa, given as a fief to the Lomellini family of Genoa in the sixteenth century, was sublet on May 7, 1719 to a syndicate including Giacomo Filippo Durazzo.
86. Oscar Gelderblom and Joost Jonker, *Mirroring Different Follies: The Character of the 1720 Bubble in the Dutch Republic*, Working Paper, Utrecht, October, 2009, p. 9.
87. Jean-Pierre Ricard, *Le négoce d'Amsterdam*, Amsterdam, 1722, p. 401.
88. "Weder-antwoord van de Heer A.Z. aan de Heer N.N.", *Het groote tafereel der dwaasheid*, [Amsterdam?], 1720. The pagination of this title varies.
89. Wauchope to Shairp, July 14/25, 1720, NRS GD377/399; Wauchope to William Dundas, July 23/August 3, 1720, ibid.
90. John Gordon to Duke of Gordon, August 2, 1720 NS, NRS GD44/43/9.
91. Wauchope to Dundas, August 16/27, 1720, NRS GD377/399; Wauchope to Shairp, August 13/24, 1720, ibid.
92. Middleton to William Law, August 22, 1720, Coutts & Co. Letter Book No. 14, pp. 335–7.
93. "Lock & Herring vs. Ridgeway Pitt et al.", House of Lords, January 1735, BL Add Ms 36152, f. 203.
94. Warrant Books, January 17 and 18, 1715, *Calendar of Treasury Books*, Vol. 29 (1714–1715), ed. W. A. Shaw and F. A. Slingsby, London, 1957.
95. Dangeau reports him home by July 25. *Journal du marquis de Dangeau*, Paris, 1854, Vol. 18, p. 327.
96. Otway to Londonderry, July 20, 1720 [OS], NA C 108/417/5. Same to same, July 23, 1720, ibid. (Otway is assumed still to be using English calendar dates).
97. The transaction was notarised by Paul Ballin on August 5 and August 30, AN MC/RE/XLVIII/1. The vendor was Michel Chamillart, or rather the trustees for his grandchildren. Guillaume Tartel, "Au Roy et nos seigneurs les commissaires deputez . . . pour la discussion des biens du Sieur Jean Lavv", Paris, 1721, *Pièces particulières à Law*, NLS Ry.iii.a.7 (2). Tartel, the receiver appointed for Law's estate, estimated that the lots were worth no more than 200,000 livres.

98. Dillon to James III, July 30, 1720, Stuart Papers at Windsor Castle, Vol. 48, f. 73.
99. John Law, "Mémoire sur les banques", in Harsin, ed., *Oeuvres de Law*, Vol. 2, p. 29.
100. Buvat, *Journal de la Régence*, Vol. 2, pp. 117–18.
101. "Plan de la Bourse de Paris", reproduced in C. Piton, *Histoire de Paris: Le Quartier des Halles*, Paris, 1891, pp. 122–3.
102. The diary entry is for August 25, which was a Sunday. *Diario*, p. 33.
103. Pulteney to Craggs, August 3, 1720, NA SP 78/166, f. 291; "een zeer groote huur", Hop to Heinsius, June 24, 1720, *Briefwisseling van Heinsius*, Vol. 19, p. 482.
104. *Journal de Dangeau*, Vol. 18, p. 332, August 3, 1720.
105. Louis Antoine de Pardaillan de Gondrin, duc d'Antin, *Mémoires de la Régence*, BnF, NAF 23935, f. 125.
106. Elisabeth Charlotte to Princess of Wales, August 13, 1720, H. F. Helmolt, *Elisabeth Charlottens Briefe an Karoline von Wales*, Annaberg, 1909, p. 375; same to same, August 16, 1720, ibid.
107. Law to Tencin, Venice, February 22, 1721, in Law's outletter book, Méjanes, Ms 614 (355), f. 32. Dangeau (*Journal*, Vol. 18, pp. 334–5) says the Regent drove out to Saint-Cloud on Sunday, August 11 and returned the following afternoon.
108. *Arrest du Conseil d'Estat du roy concernant le cours des billets de banque*, Paris, août 1720.
109. Pulteney to Craggs, August 15, 1720, NA SP 78/166, f. 307.
110. Montesquieu, *Lettres persanes*, 1721; Rica to —, Letter CXXXII.
111. Jérôme Jambu, *Tant d'or que d'argent: la monnaie en Basse Normandie*, Rennes, 2013, p. 413.
112. Gilbert Larguier, "L'église, le crédit et les effets du système de Law en Roussillon au xviiie siècle", in G.Larguier, *Découvrir l'histoire de Roussillon*, Perpignan, 2010, pp. 349–64.
113. Montrose to Stair, May 29, 1720, OS in John Murray Graham, *Annals of Stair*, Edinburgh and London, 1875, Vol. 2, p. 423.
114. Destouches to Dubois, Hanover, September 8, 1720, printed in Philip Henry, Earl Stanhope (under the name Lord Mahon), *History of England from the Peace of Utrecht to the Peace of Aix-la-Chapelle*, London, 1837, Vol. 2, Appendix, pp. 51–2.
115. Delisle, *Journal du Parlement séant à Pontoise*, p. 36, f. 17, August 27, 1720.
116. Ibid., p. 29, f. 14v, August 20, 1720.
117. Ibid., p. 20, f. 10, August 6, 1720.
118. Ibid., p. 58, f. 28v, September 8, 1720.

CHAPTER TWELVE: FALL FROM GRACE

1. [Epigraph] BnF, Ms français 7768, f. 205. This is a memoir from 1717 or 1718 that proposes the conversion of the Banque générale into a "universal Royal bank". The style is not Law's but he surely supplied the argument.
2. J. Dumont de Montigny, *Regards sur le monde atlantique, 1715–1747*, Quebec, 2008, p. 121. The inspector was possibly Didier de Saint-Martin, later governor of île Bourbon (Réunion).
3. "Armements effectués par la Compagnie de mai 1719 à la fin de décembre 1720: iv Louisiane", Philippe Haudrère, *La Compagnie française des Indes*, Paris, 2005,

Vol. 2, p. 847; Marcel Giraud, *Histoire de la Louisiane française*, Paris, 1966, Vol. 3, p. 225.

4. Their original instructions of November 8, 1719 were to fortify Pensacola, but that was now to be returned to Spain. "Instruction pour MM. Le Blond de La Tour . . . ." in Pierre Margry, ed., *Découvertes et établissements des Français dans l'ouest et dans le sud de l'Amérique septentrionale (1614–1754)*, Paris, 1883, Vol. 5, pp. 610ff.
5. Charles-Joseph Franquet de Chaville, "Relation du voyage de la Louisiane", ed. G. Musset, *Journal de la Societé des Américanistes de Paris*, 1902, Vol. 4, No. 1, p. 103.
6. Mellier to Ferrand, May 24, 1721, AMN, HH209 in Gaston Martin, *Nantes et la Compagnie des Indes*, Paris, n.d, p. 46.
7. Elisabeth Charlotte to the Raugräfin Luise, May 30, 1720, C. Künzel, ed., *Die Briefe von Liselotte von der Pfalz*, Ebehausen, 1912, pp. 427–8. The *Nouveau Mercure* reported in its May issue (p. 171) that some 589 men, women and children arrived at Toul on the 26th.
8. Giraud, *Histoire de la Louisiane française*, Vol. 3, p. 280.
9. Report of Du Vergier, May 25, 1721 in Service historique de la Défense, Paris, GR A 2592, f. 128 quoted in Giraud, *Histoire de la Louisiane française*, Vol. 3, p. 282.
10. Franquet de Chaville, "Relation du voyage," p. 111.
11. *Veuë du camp de la concession de Monseigneur Law au nouveau Biloxy, coste de la Louisianne, dessignee par Jean baptiste Michel le Bouteux le dixieme Decembre 1720. De l'ordre de Mr. Elias Stuteus directeur general*, Newberry Library, Chicago, Ayer MS Map 30 Sheet 77.
12. J. Dumont de Montigny, *Regards sur le monde atlantique*, pp. 139–40. Jolicoeur is a character in Dancourt's comedy, *La femme d'intrigues*, which was first performed in 1710.
13. *Registre de ceux qui sont morts au vieux fort de Biloxi pendant l'administration de M. Damien depuis le 8 aoust 1720, venu avec la lettre de M. delachaise du* [illegible] *1727*. FR ANOM COL G1 412, ff. 1–3.
14. Leblond de La Tour to the Directors, Vieux Biloxy, January 8, 1721, FR ANOM COL C13A6 f121; "Minutes of the Council of Commerce of Lousiana", December 20, 1720, translated in D. Rowland and A. G. Sanders, *Mississippi Provincial Archives*, Jackson, Miss., 1932, Vol. 3, pp. 298–301.
15. It is marked on a plan by Leblond de La Tour, dated April 23, 1723. BnF Cartes et Plans, GE SH 18 Pf 138 bis.
16. Franquet de Chaville, "Relation du voyage", p. 116.
17. N. N. Pichatty de Croissante, *Journal abrégé de ce qui s'est passé en la ville de Marseille depuis qu'elle est affligée de la contagion*, Paris, 1721, p. 62.
18. Ibid., p. 49.
19. Ibid., p. 51.
20. Ibid., pp. 58 and 71.
21. Ibid., pp. 78ff.
22. Ibid., p. 92.
23. T. Bérengier, ed., "Journal du sieur Goujon, maître d'hôtel de mgr de Belsunce durant la peste de Marseille, 1720–1722", *Revue des questions historiques*, Vol. 24 (July, 1878), p. 569.
24. Pichatty de Croissante, *Journal abrégé*, pp. 78 and 120.
25. Ibid., pp. 120–1.

26. Ibid., pp. 131–2. That paragraph, so favourable to Law, is dropped from the 1721 printed text, but is in manuscript copies of Pichatty's journal (for example, occitanica.eu/omeka/items/show/2174, f. 135) and the edition of 1794 (Marseille, An II, p. 50).
27. AMM, BB268, quoted in P. Gaffarel and marquis de Duranty, *La peste de 1720 à Marseille & en France*, Paris, 1911, p. 245.
28. Michel Goury, "L'épave présumée du *Grand Saint Antoine*", *Provence historique*, Vol. 47 (1997), No. 189, pp. 449–67.
29. Pichatty de Croissante, *Journal abrégé*, p. 148.
30. Ibid., p. 153.
31. AMM, BB268, quoted in J. T. Takeda, *Between Crown and Commerce*, Baltimore, Md. 2011, p. 152.
32. Pichatty de Croissante, *Journal abrégé*, p. 150.
33. Law to the Marseilles Aldermen, [November, 1720], quoted in R. Carrière, M. Courdurié and F. Rebuffat, *Marseille ville morte: La peste de 1720*, Gémenos, 2008, p. 210.
34. Villars to Aldermen, November 4, 1720 in marquis de Vogüé, ed., *Mémoires du maréchal de Villars*, Paris, 1904, Vol. 6, pp. 96–7.
35. Wauchope to Shairp, September 13/24, 1720, NRS, GD377/399.
36. "Gyllé" to Cornelius Kennedy, September 3/14, 1720, NRS GD27/6/19.
37. E. Stair to "My Lord" [Londonderry], September 30/October 11 [1720], NA C108/417/12.
38. Londonderry to Stanhope, October 12/23, 1720, KHLC, U1590/C9/16.
39. Middleton to William Law, September 8/19, 1720, Coutts & Co., Letter Book No. 14, p. 361.
40. Same to same, September 8/19, 1720, Coutts & Co., Letter Book No. 14.
41. Wauchope to Dundas, October 18/29, 1720; same to same, October 25/November 6, 1720, NRS GD377/399.
42. W. Stanhope to Lord Stanhope, Escurial, July 29, 1720, NA SP 94/89.
43. Memorial enclosed in Dillon to James III, October 7, 1720, Stuart Papers at Windsor Castle, Vol. 49, f. 36.
44. Same to same, October 14, 1720, ibid., Vol. 49, f. 55.
45. Same to same, October 20, 1720, ibid., Vol. 49, f. 76.
46. Ormonde to James III, October 14, 1720, ibid., Vol. 49, f. 51.
47. James questioned why "so great an armement as is now fitting out in Spain be thrown away on some airy project when the 3rd part of it might effectually do my business & indeed the King of Spain's also". James III to Ormonde, November 11, 1720, ibid., Vol. 50, f. 4.
48. Dillon to James III, December 2, 1720, Stuart Papers at Windsor Castle, Vol. 50, f. 67.
49. Strafford to James III, October 20/31, 1720, ibid., Vol. 49, f. 74.
50. *Arrest du Conseil d'Estat du Roy, portant Reglement pour les billets de banque, et les actions de la Compagnie des Indes. Du 15 Septembre 1720.*
51. *Arrest du Conseil d'Estat du Roy, portant suppression des billets de banque au premier novembre prochain. Du 10 octobre 1720*. Paris, 1720.
52. Jérôme Jambu, "Le système de Law dans les campagnes: l'exemple du Pays d'Auge", *Annales de Normandie*, Vol. 50 (2000), no. 2, p. 312.
53. F. Galiani, *Della moneta*, ed. F. Nicolini, Bari, 1915, Book 4, Chapter 4; p. 276.

54. The order is dated September 19, 1720. RHC Limburg, Papieren Law, inv. nr 16.
55. Sutton to Stanhope, October 19, 1720, NA SP78/169, f. 39.
56. E. Campardon, ed., *Journal de la Régence (1715–1723) par Jean Buvat*, Paris, 1865, Vol. 2, p. 173, October, 1720.
57. Pulteney to Craggs, July 25, 1720 NA SP 78/166, f. 270.
58. Buvat, *Journal de la Régence*, Vol. 2, p. 175, October, 1720.
59. Crawford to Craggs, October 23, 24 and 29, 1720, NA SP 78/169, f. 65.
60. Sutton to Craggs, October 19, 1720, ibid., f. 39ff.
61. Elisabeth Charlotte to the Raugräfin Luise, May 9, August 24 and September 19, 1720, W. L. Holland, ed., *Briefe der Herzogin Elisabeth Charlotte von Orléans*, Stuttgart/Tübingen, 1867–1881, Vol. 5, pp. 141, 254 and 283.
62. Sutton to Delafaye, October 19, 1720, NA SP 78/169, ff. 57ff.
63. Sutton to Craggs, October 30, 1720, ibid., f. 87.
64. *Mémoire signifié pour les Entrepreneurs de la Fonderie de Chaillot, Demandeurs, contre le Sieur Lavv*, Paris, 1728.
65. *Arrest du Conseil d'Estat du Roy, Portant qu'il ne sera plus reçeû de Billets de Banque dans les Hôtels des Monnoyes. Du 24 octobre 1720*, Paris, 1720.
66. [Nicolas] Du Tot, *Histoire du systême de John Law (1716–1720)*, ed. Antoin Murphy, Paris, 2000, pp. 309, 323 and 383.
67. The sums are: 11,988,940 livres in property at cost, plus 3,770,100 livres in other assets, less 4,985,113 livres in liabilities and purchase money still to pay. *Etat des acquisitions faites par Mr Law et de ce qui est par luy deue, tant par les dites acquisitions que par obligations et billets au premier Octobre 1720*, RHC Limburg, Papieren Law, inv. nr 155.
68. *Arrest du Conseil d'Estat du Roy, qui permet aux Directeurs de la Compagnie des Indes d'emprunter sur les Billets solidaires la somme de Quinze millions . . . Du 27 Octobre 1720.*
69. *Arrest du Conseil d'Estat du Roy, concernant les Actions de la Compagnie des Indes. Du 24 Octobre 1720.*
70. *Registres du greffe de la police du Chastelet de Paris*, November 8, 1720, printed in Du Hautchamp (attrib.), *Histoire du systême des finances sous la minorité de Louis XV*, The Hague, 1739, Vol. 6, p. 227.
71. *Ordonnance du Roy, portant Deffenses sous peine de la Vie . . . de sortir du Royaume jusqu'au premier de Janvier prochain, sans passeport ou permission. Du 29 Octobre, 1720.*
72. Sutton to Stanhope, November 9, 1720, NA SP 78/169, f. 134.
73. Jean Gilbert Delisle, *Journal du Parlement séant à Pontoise depuis le 21 juillet 1720*, AN U 747, printed in Isabelle Storez Brancourt, *Le journal d'un greffier du Parlement au xviiie*, halshs-00187579, p. 83. Entry for October 31, 1720.
74. M. de Lescure, ed., *Journal et mémoires de Matthieu Marais*, Paris, 1863, Vol. 1, p. 475. October 29, 1720.
75. Marches to Gravé de la Masselière, November 4, 1720, Williams Research Center, New Orleans, 2008.0077.
76. Sutton to Craggs, November 11, 1720, NA SP 78/169, ff. 145ff.
77. AMN, HH 209, in Philippe Haudrère, "L'origine du personnel de direction générale de la Compagnie française des Indes, 1719–1794", *Revue française d'histoire d'outre-mer*, Vol. 67 (1980), No. 248, p. 360.

78. *Arrest du Conseil d'Estat du Roy, qui permet aux Directeurs de la Compagnie des Indes d'emprunter des Actionnaires de la dite Compagnie la somme de vingt-deux millions cinq-cens mille livres . . . Du 17 Novembre* 1720. For the exchange rate of banknotes into silver, Dillon to James III, November 12, 1720, Stuart Papers at Windsor Castle, Vol. 50, f. 18.
79. RHC Limburg, Papieren Law, inv. nr 37. Chavigny to Dubois, October 21, 1720, AAE, Correspondance Politique (Gênes), Vol. 73, f. 376; same to same, November 11, 1720, f. 399v.
80. Pichatty de Croissante, *Journal abrégé*, p. 162. R. Carrière, M. Courdurié and F. Rebuffat, *Marseille ville morte: La peste de* 1720, Gémenos, 2008, p. 208.
81. Pichatty de Croissante, *Journal abrégé*, p. 163.
82. Law to duc de Bourbon, October 5, 1724 in Paul Harsin, ed., *Oeuvres complètes de John Law*, Paris/Louvain, 1934, Vol. 3, p. 265.
83. Dixwell [Dillon] to James III, November 4, 1720, enclosing memoir "A monsieur Law", Stuart Papers at Windsor Castle, Vol. 49, ff. 107–8; James III to Dixon, December 2, 1720, Vol. 50, f. 62; same to same, November 23, 1720, ibid., f. 43.
84. *Journal de Marais*, Vol. 1, p. 267.
85. *Mandement de Son Eminence Monseigneur le Cardinal de Noailles . . . pour l'acceptation & la publication de la Constitution Unigenitus*, Paris, 1720.
86. Letter from Paris of November 15, 1720, *Nouvelles ecclésiastiques*, Utrecht, 1720, p. 42.
87. *Mémoires du Président Hénault: Nouvelle édition*, Geneva, 1971, p. 339.
88. Du Tot, *Histoire du systême de John Law*, p. 370.
89. G. Vianelli, ed., *Diario degli anni MDCXX e MDCXXI scritto di propria mano in Parigi da Rosalba Carriera*, Venice, 1793, p. 58. The date for the diary entry is "26., 27".
90. Buvat, *Journal de la Régence*, Vol. 2, p. 192.
91. Delisle, *Journal du Parlement séant à Pontoise*, pp. 111–12.
92. Dixwell [Dillon] to James III, December 9, 1720, Stuart Papers at Windsor Castle, Vol. 50, f. 85.
93. Crawford to Craggs, December 21, 1720, NA SP78/169, ff. 321ff.
94. Elisabeth Charlotte to Princess of Wales, December 27, 1720, H. F. Helmolt, ed., *Elisabeth Charlottens Briefe an Karoline von Wales*, Annaberg, 1909, p. 377. In a letter to the duc de Bourbon from Venice in January, 1721, Law wrote: "Je suis homme, et je puis me tromper, mais mes intentions étoient droits." Law's outletter book, Méjanes, Ms 614 (355), f. 25.
95. Sutton to Craggs, December 11, 1720, NA SP78/169, f. 311.
96. Ibid.
97. Rosalba Carriera, *Diario*, p. 63.
98. *Journal de Marais*, Vol. 2, p. 18.
99. Innes to James III, October 28, 1720, Stuart Papers at Windsor Castle, Vol. 49, f. 101.
100. Same to same, December 16, 1720, ibid., Vol. 50, f. 102.
101. Crawford to Craggs, December 21, 1720, NA SP78/169, f. 323.
102. Baron de Vigan, ed., *Mémoires du président Hénault*, Paris, 1855, p. 398.
103. Delisle, *Journal du Parlement séant à Pontoise*, pp. 120–1.
104. Crawford to Craggs, December 21, 1720, NA SP78/169, ff. 321–4.

105. Mme de Mézières to James III, December 16, 1720, Stuart Papers at Windsor Castle, Vol. 50, f. 99a; Amelot to Gualterio, December 16, 1720, BL Add Ms 20366, f. 80.
106. Law to Regent, December 17, 1720 in Law's outletter book, Méjanes, 614 (355), f. 14.
107. Law to Crawford, n.p., n.d, enclosed in Crawford to Craggs, December 21, 1720, NA SP78/169, f. 325.
108. Crawford to Craggs, December 21, 1720, NA SP78/169, f. 323.
109. Duc de Bourbon to Law, December 17, 1720, Archives d'Argenson, Bibliothèque universitaire de Poitiers, quoted in Antoin Murphy, *John Law, économiste et homme d'état*, Brussels, 2007, p. 400; Law to duc de Bourbon, December 17, 1720, Méjanes, Ms 614 (355), f. 15. Elisabeth Charlotte said, improbably, that the Duke came in person, in a coach belonging to Mme de Prie, and servants in grey livery "else the mob would have mistreated him". Elisabeth Charlotte to Princess of Wales, December 17, 1720, Helmolt, ed., *Elisabeth Charlottens Briefe*, p. 376.
110. On December 17, young William gave power of attorney to Thornton, which suggests that he remained. AN Minutier Central, Minutes de l'étude Ballin, 1720 (Et. XLVIII), AN MC/ET/XLVIII/44.
111. Ibid. RHC Limburg, Papieren Law, inv. nr 181.
112. RHC Limburg, Papieren Law, inv. nr 66 (3). An "s" on the end of "Dujardin" has been rubbed out.
113. Law wrote to thank Mme de Prie and asked Lady Katherine to do the same. Sutton reported the coaches bore the royal arms of France. Sutton to Craggs, December 28, 1720, NA SP78/169, f. 344.
114. *Gazette d'Amsterdam*, December 31, 1720.
115. Law to duc de Bourbon, Brussels, 1720, Méjanes, Ms 614 (355) f. 17; same to same, n.p., n.d, ibid., f. 19; [duc de Bourbon] to [Lady Katherine Knowles], n.p., n.d. [Paris, December, 1720], RHC Limburg, Papieren Law, inv. nr 19; Marquis d'Argenson, ed., *Mémoires et journal inédit du marquis d'Argenson*, Paris, 1857, Vol. 1, p. 164.
116. Law to duc de Bourbon, August 25, 1724, in Harsin, ed., *Oeuvres de Law*, Vol. 3, p. 253.
117. *Diario*, p. 66. She writes in error "Romanino".
118. AN MC/ET/XLVIII/44.
119. Elisabeth Charlotte to Princess of Wales, December 27, 1720, Helmolt, ed., *Elisabeth Charlottens Briefe*, p. 377.
120. *Commissions extraordinaires du Conseil: Law (Jean)*, Minutes des jugements, Judgment in the case of the duc de Mazarin, March 27, 1721, AN V/7/254.
121. Mouchard to Londonderry, November 19, 1721, NA C108/417/4.
122. *Por Don Simón de la Cancela . . . con Don Eduardo Crean, y Compañia, sobre la paga de 42,206 pesos y medio*, n.p., n.d. [Madrid, 1724], Biblioteca de la Universidad de Sevilla, A113/147 (6), f. 6v.
123. T. Bérengier, ed., "Journal du sieur Goujon", p. 576.
124. "Registre des mariages batemes et enterremens faits en cette paroisse en mil sept cent vingt", Archives departementales de la Vienne, Registres paroissiaux, Charroux, Saint-Sulpice, E Depot 61 GG7, p. 108; and "Registre de lannee mil sept cent vingt", ibid. 9 E 73/1.

CHAPTER THIRTEEN: A BROKEN DANDY

1. [Epigraph] Crawford to Craggs, December 21, 1720, NA, SP78/169, f. 323.
2. Law to duc de Bourbon, December 17, 1720, Méjanes, MSS 614 (355), f. 15.
3. Pye to Strafford, December 24, 1720, BL Add Ms 31140, f. 98; Sutton to Craggs, December 21, 1720, NA SP78/169, f. 329.
4. Crawford to Craggs, January 2, 1721, NA SP78/170, f. 3.
5. Hetzler to Strafford, December 30, 1720, BL Add Ms 31140, f. 101.
6. RHC Limburg, Papieren Law, inv. nr 66.
7. Law to "conte de Guldenstein", April 18, 1721, Méjanes, Ms 614 (355), ff. 49–50. "Act of Naturalisation of John Henry Huguetan", March 25, 1707, NRS, PA6/36, f. 89.
8. Burges to Craggs, January 24, 1721, NA SP99/62.
9. Giacomo Casanova, *Histoire de ma vie*, Paris, 2013, p. 505.
10. Frémont to Dubois, October 11, 1721, AAE, 138CP/174, f. 348.
11. Law to Regent, June 21, 1721, printed in A. M. de Boislisle, ed., *Mémoires de Saint-Simon*, Paris, 1879–1931, Vol. 38, p. 406.
12. Antonio Caimo to Inquisitori, August 27, 1736, printed in Giovanni Comisso, *Agenti segreti veneziani nel '700*, Milan, 1945, pp. 20ff.
13. Le Blond to William Law Jr, June 29 and July 13, 1731, RHC Limburg, Papieren Law, inv. nr 80.
14. *Recueil des instructions données aux ambassadeurs et ministres de France: XXVI Venise*, Paris, 1958, p. xv, n.10; AStV, Inquisitori di Stato (Riferte dei Confidenti), La Platz, b. 625.
15. Conti to Mme de Caylus, January 23, 1728, printed in Antonio Conti, *Lettere da Venezia a madame la comtesse de Caylus (1727–1729)*, Venice, 2003, p. 177.
16. *Diary of Mary, Countess Cowper, Lady of the Bedchamber to the Princess of Wales, 1714–1720*, London, 1864, p. 47. Entry for February 17, 1715. Albert Matthews, "Colonel Elizeus Burges", *Transactions of the Colonial Society of Massachusetts*, Vol. 14 (1911–1913), Boston, 1913, pp. 360ff.
17. Duchess of Richmond to Earl of March, December 6/17, 1721, printed in Earl of March, *A Duke and His Friends*, London, 1911, Vol. 1, p. 53.
18. Will of August 15, 1736, NA PROB 11/680.
19. Burges to Molesworth, April 26, 1721, HMC, *Report on Manuscripts in Various Collections*, London, 1913, Vol. 8, p. 306.
20. Frémont to Dubois, March 29, 1721, AAE 138CP/174, f. 121.
21. "John Walton" (Baron Philipp von Stosch) to Carteret, December 1, 1722, NA SP 85/14, f. 181, quoted in Edward Corp, *The Stuarts in Italy 1719–1766: A Court in Permanent Exile*, Cambridge, 2011, p. 125.
22. James III to 888 [Law], January 3, 1721, Stuart Papers at Windsor Castle, Vol 51, f. 16.
23. Law to duc de Bourbon, n.p, n.d. [Aachen or Cologne, December 1720], Méjanes, Ms 614 (355), f. 19.
24. Poerson to Antin, January 21, 1721 in A. de Montaiglon and J. Guiffrey, *Correspondance des directeurs de l'Académie de France à Rome*, Paris, 1898, Vol. 6, p. 13; Gualterio to [unknown], January 21, 1721, in E. Griselle, *Documents d'Histoire*, Vol. 1 (1910), p. 558.
25. Archivio Segreto Vaticano, Palazzo Apostolico, Computisteria, Vol. 5044,

pp. 15–70, quoted in Edward Corp, *The Stuarts in Italy, 1719–1766*, Cambridge, 2011, p. 44, n. 21.

26. James III to Ormonde, January 11, 1721, Stuart Papers at Windsor Castle, Vol. 51, f. 38.
27. Frémont to Dubois, February 1, 1721, AAE 138CP/174, f. 59.
28. Edgar to Steuart, January 14, 1720, Stuart Papers at Windsor Castle, Vol. 219, f. 155, quoted in A. S. Skinner, ed., *Sir James Steuart: An Inquiry into the Principles of Political Œconomy*, Edinburgh and London, 1966, p. xxvi, n. 26.
29. Carteret interview with Destouches of October 23/November 3, 1721, in Destouches to Dubois, November 4, 1721, AAE 8CP/338, ff. 96–7.
30. Law is reported as living in the parish in an act of May 24, 1721. AStV, Notai di Venezia, Atti, Carlo Gabrieli, busta 7114, ff. 242v–243r.
31. Frémont to Dubois, February 1, 1721, AAE 138CP/174, f. 59; "Inquisitori di Stato: Lettere e riferte dei confidenti (1601–1797)", manuscript index, AStV 199 Ex. 137–9.
32. Niedersächsisches Staatsarchiv, Hanover, 82 Abt. III Nr. 33, reproduced in Alice Binion, *La Galleria scomparsa del maresciallo von der Schulenburg*, Milan, 1990, after p. 129.
33. Frémont to Dubois, January 18, 1721 AAE 138CP/174.
34. Méjanes, Ms 614 (355), f. 29.
35. Law to Lady Katherine Knowles, April 19, 1721, ibid., f. 55.
36. Law to Tencin, February 22, 1721, ibid., f. 32.
37. Law to Mlle Law, February 15, 1721, ibid., f. 29; Edward Wright, *Some Observations Made in Travelling Through France, Italy &c. in the Years 1720, 1721, and 1722*, London, 1730, Vol. 1, p. 84.
38. Law to Lady Katherine Knowles, April 19, 1721, Méjanes, Ms 614 (355), f. 55; Frémont to Dubois, February 1, 1721, AAE 138CP/174, f. 59.
39. Law said he had given Pellegrini £1,000 sterling and 9,000 livres. He proposed that the Company of the Indies pay a further £1,000 to discharge him. Law to duc de Bourbon, June 1, 1721, Méjanes, Ms 614 (355), f. 70.
40. Pierre Crozat to Rosalba Carriera, June 7, 1721, in Bernardina Sani, ed., *Rosalba Carriera: Lettere, diari, frammenti*, Florence, 1985, Vol. 1, p. 395.
41. Casanova, *Histoire de ma vie*, pp. 677, 1,050 and 1,060.
42. "Casini di giuoco e conversazione", AStV, Inquisitori di Stato, b. 914. This item has been catalogued by Alberto Fiorin, "Ritrovi da gioco: i casini" in A. Fiori, *Fanti e denari*, Venice, 1989, p. 204, n. 8.
43. Casanova, *Histoire de ma vie*, p. 1050.
44. Frémont to Dubois, March 15, 1721 AAE 138CP/174, f. 103.
45. Law to Dubois, August 21, 1721, Méjanes, Ms 614 (355), f. 95.
46. Frémont to Dubois, March 29, 1721, ibid. f. 122.
47. The phrase is from Law's letter to the marquis de Lassay, June 14, 1721, Méjanes, Ms 614 (355), f. 71.
48. Lassay's widow owned 1,237 shares in 1763. Discharge, 5–6 May 1763, AN MC Et. XXXV/374, quoted in Philippe Haudrère, *La Compagnie française des Indes au XVIIIe siècle (1719–1795)*, Paris, 2005, Vol. 1, p. 121.
49. Law to Regent, March 1, 1721, Méjanes, Ms 614 (355), f. 38.
50. Claude Pâris de La Montagne, *Discours à ses enfans pour les instruire sur sa conduite*, 1729, AN, KK//1005/D, p. 135.

51. Crawford to Craggs, December 29, 1720, NA SP 78/170, ff. 1–2. Crawford says the payment was 3 million livres beyond what was promised, the duc d'Antin 3.5 million livres. Louis Antoine de Pardaillan de Gondrin, duc d'Antin, *Mémoires de la Régence*, BnF, NAF 23935, f. 192.
52. Antin, *Mémoires*, ibid., f. 193.
53. AN M/1025 (II) and AN K/885, quoted in Philippe Haudrère, *La Compagnie française des Indes*, Paris, 2005, Vol. 1, p. 75.
54. The accounts by Saint-Simon, who was present, and Buvat are similar. *Mémoires de Saint-Simon*, ed. A. M. de Boislisle, Paris, 1879–1931, Vol. 38, pp. 82–97; E. Campardon, ed., *Journal de la Régence (1715–1723) par Jean Buvat*, Paris, 1865, Vol. 2, pp. 197–202.
55. *Réflexions politiques sur les finances et le commerce*, The Hague, 1738, Vol. 1, p. 330n.
56. *Arrest du conseil du Roy, qui ordonne qu'il sera fait une Imposition, à titre de supplément de Capitation Extraordinaire . . . du 29 juillet 1722*; Barthélemy Marmont du Hautchamp (attrib.), *Histoire générale et particulière du Visa fait en France*, The Hague, 1743, Vol. 2, pp. 153ff; Jean Villain, "Le rôle de la capitation extraordinaire de 1722" and "Le recouvrement de la capitation extraordinaire de 1722", *Revue historique de droit français et étranger*, Vol. 31 (1954), pp. 108–116, and Vol. 37 (1960), pp. 263–307.
57. *Arrest du Conseil d'Estat du Roy qui commet Messieurs Trudaine, Fagon, Ferrand & de Machault pour dresser Procès-verbal & inventaire des registres, papiers & effets de ladite Compagnie & Banque y jointe du 7 Avril 1721.*
58. AMN, HH 206, quoted in Haudrère, *La Compagnie française des Indes*, Vol. 2, p. 861; J. Dumont de Montigny, *Regards sur le monde atlantique, 1715–1747*, Quebec, 2008, p. 128.
59. FR ANOM COL G1 465.
60. Mellier to Ferrand, May 19, 1721, AMN, HH 208, quoted in Gaston Martin, *Nantes et la Compagnie des Indes*, Paris, n.d., p. 56.
61. He was admitted on May 22, 1721. Machault to Argenson, May 18, 1722 in F. Ravaisson, ed., *Archives de la Bastille: Documents inédits*, Paris, 1882, Vol. 13, pp. 331–2.
62. *Tableau général de la Compagnie des Indes au 15 Avril 1722*, BnF Ms français, 8973. The balance sheet lists thirty-four vessels at Lorient, nine under construction or undergoing repairs, and forty-one at sea. The total must be adjusted to exclude two ships belonging to the King, the *Découverte*, which had been confiscated by the Spanish authorities in Peru, the *Joseph Royal* and the *Diligent* condemned as unseaworthy there, and likewise the *Saint-Louis* in Louisiana, four ships that are counted twice, and the hulks the *Saint-Guillaume*, *Président*, *Fortune* and the "old" *Apollon* (launched in 1683). The weakness in the balance sheet was a lack of cash and invoices due for immediate payment. Three-quarters of the company's capital was at sea or in distant ports.
63. The English East India did not own its ships, or publish a balance sheet at this time.
64. *Arrest du Conseil du 11 avril 1721*, quoted in Marcel Giraud, *Histoire de la Louisiane française*, Paris, 1966, Vol. 4, pp. 312 and 331.
65. There were 533 African slaves counted in the census of New Orleans of November 24, 1721; and 241 at Mobile, the Fort des Alibamons on the Alabama River, and île Dauphine on June 28, 1721, FR ANOM DPPC G1/464. Those figures do not include

the slaves still at Biloxi. The company balance sheet of April, 1722 states that 1,753 African slaves had arrived by then in Louisiana.

66. J.-B. Bénard de La Harpe, *Journal historique de l'établissement des Français à la Louisiane*, New Orleans, 1831, p. 251.
67. J. Dumont de Montigny, *Regards sur le monde atlantique, 1715–1747*, Quebec, 2008, p. 142.
68. Dernis, *Recueil ou collection des titres . . . concernant la Compagnie des Indes Orientales*, Paris, 1755, Vol. 3, pp. 412–15, 497–502, 505–11; Haudrère, *La Compagnie française des Indes*, Vol. 1, p. 86.
69. Sutton to Stanhope, January 18, 1721, NA SP 78/170, f. 13.
70. Law to Londonderry, April 10, 1721, Méjanes, Ms (355), f. 43.
71. *Etat general des Biens Immeubles & des Dettes actives & passives de Mr. Lavv au Premier Janvier, 1722*, RHC Limburg, Papieren Law, inv. nr 68.
72. Craggs to Sutton, January 5, 1721, NA SP 78/170, f. 11.
73. Law to Lassay, June 14, 1721, Méjanes, Ms 614 (355), f. 75.
74. *Commissions extraordinaires du Conseil: Law (Jean)*, Minutes des jugements (1721), AN V/7/254.
75. Law to Bully, February 26, 1722, Méjanes, Ms 614 (355), ff. 173–4.
76. *Arrêt du Conseil d'Etat du 14 septembre, 1721*. The *lettres patentes* were registered in the Parlement on May 16, 1724.
77. Jacques-François Blondel, *Architecture françoise*, Paris, 1752–1756, Vol. 3, p. 74. The gallery is marked "B" on the plan of the first floor after p. 80.
78. Law to Lady Katherine Knowles. April 19, 1721, Méjanes, Ms 614 (355), ff. 52–5; same to same, May 10, 1721, ibid., f. 59.
79. *Le Nouveau Mercure*, May 1721, p. 139.
80. Law to duchesse de Bourbon, January 2/13, 1721, Méjanes, Ms 614 (355), f. 132.
81. The order is dated May 7 in the Bastille archives. Arsenal, Archives de la Bastille, 10732, f. 150. *Le Nouveau Mercure*, May 1721, p. 138 also says May 7. Crawford says "Thursday last" or May 8 in Crawford to Tickell, May 10, 1721, NA SP 78/170, f. 102.
82. Crawford to Tickell, May 10, 1721, NA SP 78/170, f. 102.
83. Rigby was released in May, 1723 and died the following September, without having made up his account. Conseil du Roi, Arrêt du 18 octobre, 1723, AN E//2050, ff. 574–7. Jones died at Toledo in 1727, broken-hearted when the city suspended his contract to provide a water supply. *London Daily Journal*, October 27, 1727.
84. *Arrest de la cour de parlement du 18 juin 1717 portant règlement général pour les prisons etc.*, Paris, 1717.
85. Law to duc de Bourbon, October 15, 1724 in Paul Harsin, ed., *Oeuvres complètes de John Law*, Paris/Louvain, 1934, Vol. 3, p. 274.
86. Law to Ilay, May 16, 1721, Méjanes, Ms 614 (355), f. 62.
87. Harley to Oxford, February 18, 1720 [i.e.1721], HMC, *Report on the Manuscripts of the Duke of Portland*, London, 1899, Vol. 5, p. 616.
88. Carteret to Polwarth, February 7, 1720 [i.e. 1721], HMC, *Report on the Manuscripts of Lord Polwarth*, London, 1911, Vol. 3, p. 40.
89. Destouches to Dubois, October 24/November 4, 1721, AAE 8CP/338, f. 97.
90. Otway to Londonderry, Venice, November 10/21, 1720, NA C108/417/5.
91. Same to same, Leghorn, January 10/21, 1721, ibid.
92. Same to same, Genoa, May 16/27, 1721, ibid.
93. Same to same, Leghorn, June 28/ July 9, 1721, ibid.

94. Same to same, Venice, July 7/18, 1721, ibid.
95. Law to De Mari, July 12, 1721, Méjanes, Ms 614 (355), f. 87. At the height of the boom in the shares, Law had paid for a consignment of pictures from De Mari with twenty shares in the Company of the Indies. Doria to De Mari, December 30, 1719, Archivio Doria di Genova, registro 745 (copialettere), quoted in Giuseppe Felloni, *Gli investimenti finanziari genovesi in Europa tra il seicento e la restaurazione*, Milan, 1971, p. 243.
96. Frémont to Dubois, September 13, 1721 AAE 138CP/174, f. 320.
97. Law to Lassay, July 11, 1721, Méjanes, Ms 614 (355), f. 86.
98. Law to Fonspertius, Venice, n.d. [August 1721], ibid., f. 96; Law to Bully, March 19, 1722, ibid., f. 195.
99. Otway to Londonderry, Venice, July 15/26, 1721, NA C108/417/5.
100. Same to same, Utrecht, August 18/29, 1721, ibid.
101. Law to Regent, June 21, 1721 in Boislisle, ed., *Mémoires de Saint-Simon*, Vol. 38, p. 406.
102. Law to Dubois, August 2, 1721, Méjanes, Ms 614 (355), f. 90.
103. Dubois to Frémont, September 23, 1721, AAE 138CP/174, f. 314; Frémont to Dubois, October 11, 1721, ibid., f. 348.
104. Law to Fich, November 10/21, 1721, Méjanes, Ms 614 (355), ff. 98–9; Law to Tsar Peter of Russia, November 10/21, 1721, ibid., f. 100; Law to Fich, January 23/ February 3, 1722, ibid., f. 101.
105. Law's memorial for Townshend of October 24, 1725, NA SP81/91.
106. Burges to Southern Department, August 29 and September 12, 1721, NA SP 99/62, ff. 620 and 622; Frémont to Dubois, September 13, 1721 AAE 138CP/174, f. 32.
107. Law to Nieubourg, Hagenberg, September 20, 1721, Méjanes, Ms 614 (355), ff. 103–5.
108. Tigh to Tilson, October 7, 1721, NA SP 75/45.
109. Poussin to Dubois, October 13, 1721, AAE CP (Hambourg) 49, f. 82. Back in January, Dubois had instructed Poussin to see if Law had funds in Hamburg, but "discreetly [*sans affectation*]". Poussin found nothing. Dubois to Poussin, January 17, 1721, ibid., f. 12; ibid., f. 82.
110. Glenorchy to Townshend, October 14, 1721, NA SP75/45.
111. Tigh to Tilson, October 18, 1721, NA SP 75/45; Norris to Burchett, October 19, 1721 OS, NA ADM 1/3.
112. *Whitehall Evening Post*, October 24, 1721; *Applebee's Original Weekly Journal* of October 28, 1721 says "yesterday sev'nnight".
113. Glenorchy to Polwarth, October 21/November 1, 1721, HMC, *Report on the Manuscripts of Lord Polwarth*, London, 1931 Vol. 3, p. 72.
114. Dubois to Destouches, October 18/29, 1721, AAE 8CP/338, f. 52.
115. Crawford to Craggs, December 21, 1720, NA, SP78/169, f. 323.
116. *London Journal*, October 28, 1721.
117. Destouches to Dubois, October 24/November 4, 1721, AAE 8CP/338, f. 97v. Destouches uses Gregorian or New Style dates for his correspondence.
118. Ibid., f. 98v.
119. Same to same, October 19/30, 1721, ibid., f. 74.
120. Same to same, October 26/November 6, 1721, ibid., f. 105.
121. Ibid., f. 108.
122. Law to Regent, November 1, 1721, AAE 8CP/338 f87; Méjanes, Ms 614 (355), f. 119.

123. Destouches to Dubois, October 24/November 4, 1721, AAE 8CP/338, f. 98.
124. *Whitehall Evening Post*, October 26, 1721.
125. Law to Lassay, October 30, 1721, Méjanes, Ms (355), ff. 113–18.
126. *The History and Proceedings of the House of Lords*, London, 1742, Vol. 3, p. 186; Destouches to Dubois, November 9/20, 1721, AAE 8CP/338, f. 155.
127. Same to same, November 13/24, 1721, ibid., f. 165.
128. *London Journal*, December 2, 1721.
129. Ibid., November 11, 1721.
130. "Gyllé" to Col. Cornelius Kennedy, Paris, December 8 [1721], NRS GD27/6/19.
131. March, *A Duke and his Friends*, p. 54.
132. Law to Foreman, n.d. [February 19, 1722] Méjanes, Aix-en-Provence, Ms 614 (355), f. 167.
133. Law to Bully, March 19, 1722, ibid., f. 195.
134. Law to Schulenburg, November 7/18, 1721, Méjanes, Ms 614 (355), f. 122.
135. *Diary of Mary, Countess Cowper*, p. 132. Entry for April 13, 1720.
136. Monday was one of the evenings for the Drawing-Room. Lady Mary Wortley Montagu to Alexander Pope, June 17 [1717], *The Letters and Works of Lady Mary Wortley Montagu*, ed. Lord Wharncliffe, London, 1861, Vol. 1, p. 332.
137. Law to Rank, January 8/19, 1722. Méjanes, Ms (355), f. 146.
138. Law to Lady Katherine Knowles, January 8/19, 1722, ibid.
139. Same to same, n.d. [January 20/31, 1722], ibid., f. 151.
140. Londonderry to Lucy, Lady Stanhope, January 25, 1721 [i.e. 1722], KHLC U1590/C12/2.
141. "Letters to Lucy Countess Stanhope & Papers relating to her Jewels", KHLC, U1590/C12/3; Lady Stanhope to Londonderry, Bath, January 27, 1721 [i.e. 1722], NA C108/417/12.
142. Same to same, Bath, February 3, 1721 [i.e. 1722], NA C108/417/12.
143. According to a later lawsuit, Law transferred to Londonderry at this time £6,000 of a debt of £14,000 owed him by Edward Rolt, Tory MP for Grantham. "Appeals in the House of Lords", January, 1735, BL Add Ms 36152, ff. 203–4.
144. Law to Henrietta Howard, "Tuesday", BL Add Ms 22628.
145. Londonderry to Lady Stanhope, February 10, 1721 [i.e. 1722), KHLC, U1590/C12/2.
146. Lady Stanhope to Londonderry, February 12, 1721 [i.e. 1722], NA C108/417/12.
147. "The Accts of the late Countesse Stanhope and Thos Pitt Esqr as Admrs of the late Earle Stanhope", KHLC, U1590/E206/1.
148. George Mackenzie, MS, *Lives and Characters of the Most Eminent Writers of the Scots Nation*, Edinburgh, 1722, Vol. 3, n.p.
149. Law to Lady Katherine Knowles, n.d. [between February 26 and March 5, 1722], Méjanes, Ms 614 (355), f. 175.
150. P. G. M. Dickson, *The Financial Revolution in England*, London, 1967, p. 314.
151. Law to Vernezobre, February 19, 1722, Méjanes, Ms 614 (355), f. 168.
152. Law to Purry, March 15, 1722, Méjanes, Ms 614 (355), f. 192; *Réflexions sur une nouvelle proposition que fait le Sr J.-P. Purry . . . pour l'établissement d'une nouvelle colonie française dans la Louisiane*, AN M//1027, quoted in Giraud, *Histoire de la Louisiane française*, Vol. 3, pp. 151–2.
153. Levens to Gravé de La Mancelière, Fort Louis [Nouveau Biloxi], January 23, 1722, Kuntz Collection, Tulane University, New Orleans, 600.1.60.

154. *Journal du voyage de la Louisiane fait par le sr Bernard de Laharpe et les decouvertes qu'il a fait dans le party de l'ouest de cette colonie*, BnF Ms français 8989, ff. 69–70; Morris S. Arnold, *Colonial Arkansas: 1686–1804*, Fayetteville, 1991, p. 12. On February 18, 1723, Bernard Diron d'Artaguiette counted at the concession fourteen European men and one woman, and six African slaves. FR ANOM COL G1 465.
155. The company attempted to claim from Law 450,000 livres for the "nourishment" of the German families. RHC Limburg, Papieren Law, inv. nr 162.
156. *Procés Verbal de la Concession de M. de Bienville au dessus de la nouvelle Orléans*, November 25, 1737, FR ANOM COL E277, Dossier Le Moyne de Bienville, ff. 20r–22r. Bienville's property consisted by then of 213 arpents in river frontage and 40 arpents in depth, or about eleven square miles, stretching from the modern Felicity Street to opposite Nine-Mile Point.
157. Law to Lassay, n.d. [March 22 or 23, 1722], Méjanes, Ms 614 (355), f. 198.
158. Law to Lady Katherine Knowles, April 11, 1722, ibid., f. 209.
159. Law sent his power of attorney from London on November 9/20, 1721. Same to same, November 9, 1721, ibid., f. 123.
160. Middleton to Law, June 15, 1727, Coutts & Co., Letter Book No. 17.
161. "M[e] la Duchese me charge de vous mander qu'un des grands plaisirs qu'elle puisse avoir sera quand on vous contentera." [Lassay] to [Law], n.d. [1722], RHC Limburg, Papieren Law, inv. nr 75. A reference to the visit to Paris of "md Wallingford" dates this letter to early 1722.
162. NA C108/422/10, printed in Larry Neal, *"I Am Not Master of Events"*, Newhaven and London, 2012, p. 111. "Appeals in the House of Lords", January, 1735, BL Add Ms 36152, ff. 203–4.
163. Middleton to Mouchard, September 18, 1722, Coutts & Co., Letter Book No. 15.
164. Printed in Boislisle, ed. *Mémoires de Saint-Simon*, Vol. 38, p. 407.
165. E. J. Sieyès, *Qu'est-ce que le Tiers-État?*, [Paris], 1789, p. 78.
166. Buvat, *Journal de la Régence*, Vol. 2, p. 427. Entry for December 12, 1722. The *Gazette d'Amsterdam* (January 23, 1722) gave a figure of twice that.
167. RHC Limburg, Papieren Law, inv. nr 160.
168. "Vertue Notebooks III", *The Volume of the Walpole Society*, Vol. 22 (1933–1934), p. 19.
169. In the consignment inventory, they are listed as: "Quadro del Guidoreno rappresentante una venere con 3. altre figure al naturale e due putti" and "un'Andromeda legata ad un scoglio". Three Rubens are listed: a Nativity (18,500 lire), an equestrian portrait (7,000 lire) and a Venus and Neptune (4,000 lire). RHC Limburg, Papieren Law, inv. nr 160.
170. George Bickham, *Deliciae Britannicae: or the Curiosities of Kensington, Hampton Court and Windsor Castle*, London, 1755, p. 18.
171. *Moby Dick; or, The Whale*, Chapter 55, "Of the Monstrous Pictures of Whales".
172. Derek Mahon, "Note on No. 87", May, 1957, National Gallery Archive, London, NG87.
173. "A true Inventorye of Severall Pictures now remayneinge in Somersett House . . . appraised the . . . Septembr, 1649, that Came from white hall and St James", Corsham MS, f. 22, No. 285, printed in O. Millar. "The Inventories and Valuations of the King's Goods 1649–1651", *The Volume of the Walpole Society*, Vol. 43 (1970), p. 316.

174. Crozat to Duke of Devonshire, February 10, 1723, Chatsworth Archive, CS1/170.5; Comte de Caylus, *Voyage d'Italie 1714–1715*, ed. A.-A. Pons, Paris, 1914, p. 338.
175. *London Journal*, April 13, 1723.
176. RHC Limburg, Papieren Law, inv. nr 72.
177. *Le Mercure*, issue of November, 1722, p. 218.
178. Elisabeth Charlotte to the Raugräfin Luise, October 1, 1722, W. L. Holland, ed., *Briefe der Herzogin Elisabeth Charlotte von Orléans*, Stuttgart/Tübingen, 1867–1881, Vol. 6, p. 470.
179. Robert Walpole to Schaub, April 19, 1723, printed in William Coxe, *Memoirs of the Life and Administration of Sir Robert Walpole*, London, 1798, Vol. 2, p. 252.
180. Robert Walpole to Townshend, October 12, 1723, printed in ibid., p. 274.
181. Horatio Walpole to Townshend, November 1, 1723, printed in comte de Baillon, *Lord Walpole à la cour de France*, Paris, 1867, p. 55.
182. With his usual professionalism, Crawford interviewed the distraught duchess. Crawford to Carteret, December 6, 1723 in Philip, Earl of Hardwicke, *Miscellaneous State Papers from 1501 to 1726*, London, 1778, Vol. 2, pp. 626–7.
183. William Coxe, *Memoirs of Horatio, Lord Walpole*, London, 1808 (2nd edn), Vol. 1, p. 114.
184. Middleton to Law at Venice, February 25, 1726 [i.e. 1727], Coutts & Co., Letter Book No. 16.
185. [Law] to [Abraham Mouchard], October 16, 1724, NA C108/417/4.
186. In instructions to Burges, undated but from the spring of 1728, Londonderry said that he should refute the "insinuations they [the East India syndicate] are giving out, viz. that Mr L.'s going from hence was a contrivance of his and mine, to avoid his giving an answer to their bill". NAC108/421/4.
187. Walpole to Townshend, July 29, 1725, printed in Coxe, *Life of Robert Walpole*, Vol 2, p. 453. Law to [Townshend], July 27, 1725, NA SP 81/91.
188. On August 7, the *British Journal* reported Law had taken "a fine house near Hanover Square where he lives in great Request and Splendor".
189. NA SP 104/210.
190. Law to [Townshend?], Aachen, August 18/29, 1725, NA SP 81/91.
191. Law to [Townshend?], Aachen, October 24, 1725, ibid.
192. Tilson to Law, October 28/November 8, 1725, HALSW, 21M69/3/6.
193. Law's letters to the ministry in London of December 31, 1725; January 9, 1726; April 15, 1726; April 17, 1726; May 15, 1726, NA SP 81/91. The meeting with Cortanze occurred at Augsburg, where his coach had broken down and needed three days to repair.
194. Stanhope's legitimate daughters were each known as "Lady N. Stanhope".
195. Lady Katherine Knowles to Londonderry, April 27, 1726, NA C108/418/17.
196. Middleton to Law at Munich, July 26, 1726, Coutts & Co., Letter Book No. 16.
197. Same to same at Munich, November 26, 1726, Coutts & Co., Letter Book No. 16.
198. The Irish impresario Owen McSwiny on November 8 told the Duke of Richmond from Venice that the Duchess Dowager had taken Colloredo's house and was expected for Carnival "with a great train . . . in company with Myn Heer. Two Millions of Gold Ducats". T. D. Llewellyn, ed., *Owen McSwiny's Letters*, Venice, 2009, p. 258. Gergy reported she had sent fourteen wagons of baggage from Augsburg. Gergy to Paris, November 24, 1726, AAE 138 CP/180, f. 394.
199. *Beppo*, Canto 52.

CHAPTER FOURTEEN: FACING NOTHING

1. [Epigraph] [Lady Katherine Knowles] to [John Law], December 7 [1728], RHC Limburg, Papieren Law, inv. nr 166.
2. Middleton to Law, January 6, 1726 [i.e. 1727], Coutts & Co., Letter Book No. 16.
3. Gergy to Paris, AAE, 138 CP/180, f. 423.
4. Gergy to Louis XV, December 14, 1726, ibid., f. 426.
5. This is the address given for William by Le Blond in a Certificate of Life for the purposes of his life annuity on July 23, 1729. RHC Limburg, Papieren Law, inv. nr 93.
6. Conti to Mme de Caylus, February 27, 1727, Antonio Conti, *Lettere da Venezia a madame la comtesse de Caylus, 1727–1729*, ed. Sylvie Mamy, Venice, 2003, p. 127; same to same, April 15, 1727, ibid., p. 137.
7. *Memoire sur le compte de Monsieur Law avec la Compagnie des Indes*, RHC Limburg, Papieren Law, inv. nr 162.
8. Middleton to Law, August 25, 1727, Coutts & Co., Letter Book No. 17.
9. Conti to Mme de Caylus, April 2, 1728, Conti, *Lettere da Venezia*, p. 191.
10. Pentenrieder presented him to the King and the Regent on March 11, 1720. Hop to Heinsius, March 15, 1720, in A. J. Veenendaal Jr, ed., *De Briefwisseling van Anthonie Heinsius, 1702–1720*, The Hague, 1976–2001, Vol. 19, p. 434.
11. Albert de Montesquieu, ed., *Voyages de Montesquieu*, Paris, 1894, Vol. 1, pp. 28–9.
12. By 1731, young William was receiving on his life annuity just 6,250 livres a year, a reduction of ⅞ on his original annual payment of 50,000 livres. Presumably, Kate was treated in the same way. Alexander to William Law Jr, July 9, 1731, RHC Limburg, Papieren Law, inv. nr 180.
13. "Par ces presentes je soussigné Jean Law . . .", Venice, March 26, 1728, RHC Limburg, Brabants Hooggerecht, nr 205.
14. Brown to Newcastle, May 7, 1728, NA, SP 99/63, f. 57.
15. Burges to Newcastle, May 14, 1728, ibid., f. 59.
16. Londonderry's Instructions to Col. Burges, London, n.d. [1728], NA C108/421/4.
17. "I am sorry mr de Bully sent you the pacquet by the colonel burges seeing it makes you uneasey." [Lady Katherine Knowles] to "Monsieur Hamilton" [John Law], January 20 [1729], RHC Limburg, Papieren Law, inv. nr 166.
18. Brown to Newcastle, May 7, 1728, NA SP 99/63, f. 57; Conti to Mme de Caylus, May 15, 1728, *Lettere da Venezia*, p. 199.
19. James III to Clementina Sobieska, May 8, 1728, Stuart Papers at Windsor Castle, Vol. 115, f. 167. The operas that Ascension season were Giovanni Porta's *Nel perdono la vendetta* (San Moisè) and Antonio Pollarolo's *Nerina* (San Samuele). Conti found them "detestable".
20. "Li quali diceranno . . . nelle Botteghe di Caffè a S. Marco che . . . si sodisferanno sopra la vita di d:o Sig: Giovanni Laus, o di suo Figlio." Witness statement, signed by Pietro Vasserot and Giacomo Martin before Notary Giovanni Domenico Redolfi, September 28, 1733, RHC Limburg, Papieren Law, inv. nr 142. The Vasserots and Martins were Huguenot families active in finance in Geneva and elsewhere.
21. Conti to Mme de Caylus, May 19, 1728, Conti, *Lettere da Venezia*, pp. 200–1.
22. In a receipt dated May 17, 1720, Berdin acknowledged he had received 24,000 livres from Douvry on young William's account. RHC Limburg, Papieren Law, inv. nr 132.

23. Unsigned and undated letter to William Law, RHC Limburg, Papieren Law, inv. nr 141.
24. "Etant en hollande l'annee 1713 . . .", autograph affidavit by John Law, n.d. [summer/autumn, 1728]. RHC Limburg, Papieren Law, inv. nr 130.
25. Veugen to Beelen, June 21, 1743, HALSW, IM44/9/5.
26. Montesquieu to Waldegrave, August 18, 1728, F. Gébelin, ed., *Correspondance de Montesquieu*, Bordeaux, 1914, Vol. 1, p. 238. He later came to recognise that only the gallant women of Venice could extract money from a tight-fisted nobility and mobilise it for commerce and industry. *De l'esprit des loix*, Book VII, Chapter III.
27. Montesquieu to Berwick, September 15, 1728, *Correspondance*, Vol. 1, pp. 246–7.
28. The interview is printed in A. de Montesquieu, ed., *Voyages de Montesquieu*, Vol 1, pp. 59–64.
29. *De l'esprit des loix*, Book II, Chapter IV.
30. Conti to Mme de Caylus, April 2, 1728, Conti, *Lettere da Venezia*, p. 191.
31. Middleton to Law, August 27, 1728; October 20, 1728; and December 31, 1728, Coutts & Co., Letter Book No. 17.
32. Same to same, December 31, 1728, ibid., p.299.
33. In William Law's papers in Maastricht there is an inventory of "Quadri di Casa Gravi", RHC Limburg, Papieren Law, inv. nr 172. Linda Borean reads the name as "Grassi", a rising merchant family of Chioggia who bought a patent of nobility in 1718. L. Borean, "Nuovi elementi e considerazioni sulla collezione di John Law" in Michel Hochmann, *Venise et Paris, 1500–1700: la peinture vénitienne de la Renaissance et sa réception en France*, Geneva, 2010, p. 451.
34. Burges to Londonderry, n.d. [September/October 1729] NA C108/415/4.
35. Alice Binion, *La Galleria scomparsa del maresciallo von der Schulenburg*, Milan, 1990, p. 213.
36. Burges to Newcastle, January 20, 1730, NA SP99/63, f. 123.
37. Conti to Mme de Caylus, September 3, 1727, Conti, *Lettere da Venezia*, p. 161.
38. *Whitehall Evening Post*, June 6–8, 1727.
39. Conti to Mme de Caylus, August 4, 1728, Conti, *Lettere da Venezia*, p. 213.
40. Same to same, December 4, 1728, ibid., p.226.
41. McSwiny to the Duke of Richmond, March 30, 1729, T. D. Llewellyn, ed., *Owen McSwiny's Letters*, Venice, 2009, pp. 318–20.
42. Law's death certificate from the parish of San Geminiano of March 29, 1729 describes him as having lived in the parish for six months [*habitante in contrada mesi 6*]. RHC Limburg, Papieren Law, inv. nr 168.
43. The *curia* of St Mark's, which blocked the opening of a municipal casino in the Palazzo dei Dandolo in the 1930s, was more easygoing in the eighteenth century. An undated document in the library of the Museo Correr lists the members of a patrician club that met in the Procuratia. *Nomi de N.N.H.H, e Nobil Donne Associati del Casino Nuovo in Procuratia*, Biblioteca del Museo Correr, Cod. Cic. 3383/4, reproduced in A. Fiorin, *Fanti e denari*, Venice, 1989, p. 115. Montesquieu in 1728 (*Voyages*, Vol. 1, p. 33) says such *cazins* could be hired for two sols a day, which sounds much too little.
44. Conti to Mme de Caylus, January 5, 1729, Conti, *Lettere da Venezia*, p. 231. The French is "On est bien fou de jouer . . ."
45. [Lady Katherine Knowles] to "Monsieur Hamilton" [John Law], January 20 [1729], RHC Limburg, Papieren Law, inv. nr 166.

46. C. Easton, *Les hivers dans l'Europe occidentale*, Leiden, 1928, p. 126.
47. Unless Lady Katherine managed to slip out of Paris to Aix in 1725, they last saw each other in December, 1720.
48. [Lady Katherine Knowles] to [John Law], December 7 [1728], RHC Limburg, Papieren Law, inv. nr 166.
49. [Lady Katherine Knowles] to "Monsieur Hamilton" [John Law], January 20 [1729], RHC Limburg, Papieren Law, inv. nr 166.
50. "La neige et le froid . . . a été extrême ces jours passées." Conti to Mme de Caylus, January 26, 1729, Conti, *Lettere da Venezia*, p. 232.
51. *Diario ordinario*, Rome, January 12, 1729, p. 5; McSwiny to the Duke of Richmond, March 30, 1729, T. D. Llewellyn, ed., *Owen McSwiny's Letters*, p. 322; A. M. Zanetti the Elder to Gabburi, January 11, 1728 [i.e. 1729], G. Bottari, *Raccolta di lettere sulla pittura, &c*, Rome, 1757, Vol. 2, Letter LXXV, pp. 151–3. The performance dates are from Eleanor Selfridge-Field, *A New Chronology of Venetian Opera, 1660–1760*, Stanford, 2007.
52. Conti to Mme de Caylus, December 30, 1728, Conti, *Lettere da Venezia*, p. 230.
53. Same to same, February 8, 1729, ibid., p. 235.
54. McSwiny to the Duke of Richmond, March 30, 1729, T. D. Llewellyn, ed., *Owen McSwiny's Letters*, p. 320; Burges to Newcastle, January 20, 1730, NA SP 99/63, f. 123.
55. Conti to Mme de Caylus, March 10, 1729, Conti, *Lettere da Venezia*, p. 238.
56. Burges to Delafaye, February 11, 1729, NA SP 99/63, f. 85.
57. Gergy to Chauvelin, March 5, 1729, AAE 138CP/183, f. 6.
58. Burges to Newcastle, March 4, 1729, NA SP 99/63, f. 91.
59. Conti to Mme de Caylus, n.d., Conti, *Lettere da Venezia*, p. 238.
60. Invoice in RHC Limburg, Papieren Law, inv. nr 171; also *Coppia tratta dal Libro de' morti della Parochiale, & Collegiata Chiesa di San Geminiano per mè Don Lorenzo Bianchi in detta Chiesa. 3 agosto* 1729, ibid., nr 168.
61. The invoice total is 772.14 Venetian lire. William paid 672 French livres, ibid., nr 171.
62. Conti to Mme de Caylus, February 27, 1727, Conti, *Lettere da Venezia*, p. 126.
63. The phrase is Gergy's. Gergy to Chauvelin, March 5, 1729, AAE 138CP/183, f. 60.
64. Ibid.
65. Burges to Newcastle, March 4, 1729, NA SP 99/63, f. 91.
66. Giacomo Casanova, *Histoire de ma vie*, Paris, 2013, p. 1226.
67. Gergy to Chauvelin, March 5, 1729, AAE 138CP/183, f. 60.
68. *A dì 5 Marzo 1729 in Venezia, Dichiaro io sottoscritto Giovanni Lauu* . . . RHC Limburg, Papieren Law, inv. nr 167.
69. Conti to Mme de Caylus, March 10, 1729, Conti, *Lettere da Venezia*, p. 239.
70. Ibid.
71. G. Valentinelli, *Bibliografia del Friuli*, Venice, 1861, pp. 57–62.
72. Della Frattina to the Inquisitors of State, March 19, 1729, AStV, Inquisitori di Stato, Riferte dei Confidenti Fer-Fra, busta 597.
73. *Nel primo quesito si ricerca se il Donatario* . . . Undated legal opinion by Baldissera Vio, Venetian Advocate, and Alessandro Torighello, junior. RHC Limburg, Papieren Law, inv. nr 76. It is not clear if the opinion was given before or after Law's death.
74. De Mari's reply of March 19 says William's letter "mi apporta la sodisfazione di

sentire il vro Sig. Padre ben si indisposto, ma non già nel stato di grave infermità . . . e spero che a quest' hora si troverà ristabilito in Salute." De Mari to William Law Jr, March 19, 1729, RHC Limburg, Papieren Law, inv. nr 76.

75. Gergy to Chauvelin, March 12, 1729, AAE 138CP/183, f. 70.
76. Same to same, March 19, 1729, ibid., f. 79.
77. AStV Notarile, Atti, Gabrieli, 7130, c. 29. Other copies are at AAE 138 CP/183 and RHC Limburg, Papieren Law, inv. nr 169.
78. The last item on the doctors' invoice appears to have been administered at the sixth hour on the 19th. If Michelotti is using Venetian time (*ore venete*) where the day began a half-hour after sunset, then treatment stopped around 1 a.m. on the 19th by modern reckoning. RHC Limburg, Papieren Law, inv. nr 171.
79. William Law to Lady Katherine Knowles, March 26, 1729, ibid., inv. nr 170.
80. *Coppia tratta dal Libro de' morti della Parochiale, & Collegiata Chiesa di San Geminiano per mè Don Lorenzo Bianchi in detta Chiesa. 3 agosto 1729*, RHC Limburg, Papieren Law, inv. nr 168.
81. *Gazette d'Amsterdam*, April 8, 1729.
82. Burges to Newcastle, March 25, 1729 NA SP 99/63, f. 95.
83. Gergy to Louis XV, March 26, 1729, AAE 138CP/183, f. 89.
84. Gergy to Chauvelin, March 26, 1729, ibid., f. 90.
85. Ibid., Postscript.
86. Della Frattina to the Inquisitors of State, March 27, 1729, AStV, Inquisitori di Stato, busta 597. The text has *al Sig:e* which may refer to young William or be an error for *alla Sig:a* meaning Lady Katherine. Della Frattina reports the meeting as taking place "Venerdi giorno dei 25 su le 21 ore". If that is OV, the meeting took place at about 4 p.m. on Friday, March 25.
87. Chauvelin to Gergy, March 29, 1729, AAE 138CP/183, ff. 71–2.
88. Same to same, April 5, 1729, ibid., f. 85.
89. Same to same, April 18, 1729, ibid., f. 93.
90. Gergy to Chauvelin, April 2, 1729, ibid., f. 93; Burges to Newcastle, April 22, 1729, NA SP 99/63, f. 99.
91. Gergy to Chauvelin, June 4, 1729, AAE 138 CP/183.
92. Maurepas to Gergy, April 16, 1729, AAE 138 CP/183, f. 96.
93. William Law to Mrs Gibbes, March 25, 1729, RHC Limburg, Papieren Law, inv. nr 170.
94. William Law Jr to William Law Sr, n.d. [March/April, 1729], ibid.
95. Middleton to William Law Jr, April 3/14, 1729, Coutts & Co., Letter Book No. 17.
96. E. A. Cicogna, *Delle inscrizioni Veneziane*, Venice, 1834, Vol. 4, pp. 111–13.
97. Invoice from Antonio Breda, stonecutter of Calle dei Orbi, Santa Maria Formosa, of April 11, 1729 of 150 lire reduced on the audit of the *perito publico* Paolo Tremignon to 110 lire, which received by Breda, August 1729. RHC Limburg, Papieren Law. inv. nr 171.
98. "Memorandums for Earl Hadinton and Mr Baillie in their Travelling", Oxford, March 10, 1740. Robert Scott-Moncrieff, ed., *The Household Book of Lady Grisell Baillie, 1692–1733*, Edinburgh, 1911, p. 398.
99. Middleton to William Law Jr, March 14, 1728 [i.e. March 14/25, 1729], Coutts & Co., Letter Book No. 17; William Law Jr to Middleton, March 25, 1729, RHC Limburg, Papieren Law, inv. nr 170.
100. *Quadri contenuti nella Cassa no: 10 --*, Inventory signed by Le Blond, August 6,

1729, RHC Limburg, Papieren Law, inv. nr 77. Further inventories are ibid., nrs 78 and 79. At least one picture was sent by the marchese De Mari from Genoa. De Mari to William Law Jr, March 19, 1729, ibid., nr 7.

101. Burges to Londonderry, October 21, 1729, NA C108/415/4.
102. RHC Limburg, Papieren Law, inv. nr 105. Linda Borean has identified this man as Valentino Piccini, listed as a member of the *fraglia degli pittori veneziani* or guild of painters in Venice, between 1726 and 1733. Borean, "Nuovi elementi", pp. 452–3.
103. RHC Limburg, Papieren Law, inv. nr 100.
104. Ibid., inv. nr 174.
105. Fonseca to William Law Jr., August 31, 1729, ibid., inv. nr 82.
106. Act of Notary Albert Joseph Planchon, September 19, 1729, ibid., inv. nr 93.
107. *Note de ce qui est chez M. le Conte Baillet Margrave d'Anvers*, ibid., inv. nr 145.
108. William proposed in December that they move to Amsterdam, where they might live on 12,282 French livres a year, a reduction of "one in three". William Law to Lady Katherine Knowles, draft letter of December 12, 1729, ibid., inv. nr 175.
109. *Poorter Eed, Guillaume Law van 's Gravenhage*, December 10, 1729, ibid., inv. nr 94.
110. *Au Roy et a nosseigneurs les commissaires generaux du Conseil deputez par Sa Majesté pour la discussion des biens du feu Sieur Jean Law*, Paris, 1730, ibid., inv. nr 81.
111. Baron de Fonseca to William Law Jr, January 9, 1730, ibid., inv. nr 82.
112. *[P]oliza delli quadri che mancano che non li hanno potuto recuperare*, ibid., inv. nr 80.
113. Le Blond to William Law, September 8, 1730, inv. ibid. nr 80. It is not clear whether these were the portraits done by Rosalba in Paris in 1720, or whether they were done later in Venice.
114. They were on speaking terms before July 4, 1729, because Rosalba and her sister Angela wrote that day to their mother complaining of not having had a line from her, while "they had sent their news by Mr Zanetti [Anton Maria Jr] & Mr Las [William Law Jr]". Bernardina Sani, ed., *Rosalba Carriera: Lettere, diari, frammenti*, Florence, 1985, Vol. 1, p. 498. According to a power of attorney notarised by Carlo Gabrieli on May 23, 1732, Pellegrini received a further payment of 14,000 livres from the French treasury. Quoted in Alessandro Bettagno, *Antonio Pellegrini*, Venice, 1998, p. 19.
115. Le Blond to William Law Jr, September 19, 1732, RHC Limburg, Papieren Law, inv. nr 80.
116. One version, owned by Sir Robert Walpole's son Horace, hung at his house in Twickenham, Strawberry Hill, and is just visible in a watercolour in the Victoria & Albert Museum by Thomas Sandby, Paul Sandby and Edward Edwards, *The Gallery at Strawberry Hill* (1781). The Law portrait vanished at the sale of the collection in 1842 (May 18, Lot 73).
117. Ker to Lady Katherine Knowles, January 15, 1731, RHC Limburg, Papieren Law, nr 179.
118. Ibid., inv. nr 99.
119. Le Blond to William Law Jr, July 13, 1731, ibid. inv. nr 80.
120. Lady Frances Erskine to Lady Mar, December 22, 1731, NRS, GD124/15/1396; Miscellaneous accounts of the deceased Earl of Mar at Aix-la-Chapelle, September 1731–July 1732, NRS GD124/61/61.
121. Grovestins to William Law Jr, September 20, 1732, ibid., nr 119.
122. The address is from William's Certificate of Life before Notary Johan Guichard

of August 1, 1733 quoted in Th. P. M. Huijs, *Inventaire des archives de John Law et de William Law, 1715–1734*, Maastricht, 1978, p. 27, n. 45.

123. *Burgerboek van de burgemeesters*, Vol. 5, p. 355, quoted in Huijs, *Inventaire*, p. 238; RHC Limburg, Papieren Law, inv. nr 120.
124. Grovestins to William Law Jr, August 31, 1733, ibid., inv. nr 119.
125. It was Douvry who paid the 24,000 livres to Berdin in 1720 on William's order (even though he was a minor). RHC Limburg, Papieren Law, inv. nrs 132 and 141. Another transaction between the two, concerning 173,510 livres in banknotes, is dated December 18, 1720 at Guermantes, but is a scrap of paper, unwitnessed and not notarised. ibid., nr 137.
126. See note 20.
127. *Begrafenisregister St Janskerk*, reg. 116, f. 62v, quoted in Huijs, *Inventaire*, p. 28, n. 51.
128. Brabantse Hooggerecht, January 18, 1743 and March 8, 1743, quoted in Huijs, *Inventaire*, p. 20, n. 8.
129. Voltaire, *Précis du siècle de Louis XV*, Paris, 1768, Vol. 1, Chapter 2.
130. Voltaire dates letters of June 5 and June 27, 1740 to the printer Johannes van Duren in The Hague from the rue de la Grosse-Tour. M. Beuchot, *Oeuvres de Voltaire*, Paris, 1881, Vol. 54, pp. 119 and 143.
131. R. Knight to [Wallingford], July 4, 1739, HALSW IM44/9/1. The writer is almost certainly Robert Knight, the disgraced cashier of the South Sea Company, who lived as a fugitive in Paris until he was pardoned in 1742.
132. Sharpe to Lord North, July 9, 1743, HALSW 1M44/9/6.
133. Unknown to unknown, July 31 [1743], HALSW 1M 44/9/10.
134. "Biographical Memoir of Admiral Sir Charles Knowles, Bart.", *The Naval Chronicle*, Vol. 1 (1799), p. 118.
135. John Carswell, *The South Sea Bubble*, London, 1960, p. 272.
136. Archives départementales du Calvados, Caen, 8E/3090, Jérôme Jambu, *Tant d'or que d'argent: La monnaie en Basse Normandie*, Rennes, 2013, p. 417.
137. Sir James Steuart, *An Inquiry into the Principles of Political Oeconomy*, iv.ii.xxxii: Andrew S. Skinner, ed., Vol. 2, pp. 556–7.
138. *Fragments sur l'Inde*, Paris, 1773, pp. 80–1.
139. "Neveu d'un Ministre que la Compe regarde comme son fondateur et dont la mémoire lui sera toujours pretieuse . . ." Unsigned company memoir, n.d. [1760]. FR ANOM COL E264, Dossier Law de Lauriston, no. 94.
140. Law de Lauriston, "Etat des services du sr. Law de Lauriston", Paris, September 27, 1780, ibid., no. 105.
141. Directors to the Superior Council of Pondicherry, November 25, 1741, printed in A. Martineau, *Correspondance du conseil supérieur de Pondichéry*, Paris, 1920–30, Vol. 3, p. 475.
142. Gholam Ali Khan, *Shah Alam Nama*, ed. A. A. M. Suhrawardy and A. M. K. Shirazi, Calcutta, 1914, p. 153.
143. Jean Law de Lauriston, *Mémoire sur quelques affaires de l'Empire mogol*, ed. Alfred Martineau, Paris, 1913.
144. "Etat des services du chevalier Law, mort en 1766", Marie Carvalho de Law to the Controller General of Finances, n.d. [?1776], FR ANOM COL E264, Dossier chevalier Law, no folio number.

145. A. Martineau, *Dupleix et l'Inde française*, Paris 1920 (Vol. 1: 1722–1741) and 1923 (Vol. 2: 1742–1749). Especially, Vol. 1, p. 304 and Vol. 2, p. 418.
146. A. Martineau, *Résumé des actes de l'état-civil de Pondichéry*, Pondicherry, 1919–1920, Vol. 2 (1736–1760), pp. 148–9; Gnanou Diagou, ed., *Arrêts du conseil supérieur de Pondichéry*, Paris and Pondicherry, 1937, Vol. 2 (1765–1774), pp. 184–5. Decision of February 26, 1770.
147. At his death, Alexandre Carvalho left an estate net of debts of 76,891 rupees (£7,700). E. Gaudart, *Catalogue de quelques documents des archives de Pondichéry*, Pondicherry, 1931, pp. 155–6.
148. Bernard Burke, "The Laws of Lauriston", *Vicissitudes of Families*, London, 1869, Vol. 2, p. 159; "Notice historique et généalogique sur la maison Law de Lauriston", *Annuaire de la noblesse de France*, Vol. 20 (1863), pp. 261–70; ibid., Vol. 21 (1864), pp. 222–4.
149. Duchess of Portland to Elizabeth Robinson, November 21, 1737, printed in Emily J. Climenson, *Elizabeth Montagu, the Queen of the Blue-Stockings, her Correspondence from 1720 to 1761*, London, 1906, Vol. 1, p. 22.
150. Elizabeth Robinson to Duchess of Portland, n.d. [1739], printed in Matthew Montagu, ed., *The Letters of Mrs Elizabeth Montagu*, London, 1809, Vol. 1, pp. 69–70.
151. Elizabeth Robinson to Mrs Robinson, n.d. [1740], Climenson, *Queen of the Blue-Stockings*, Vol. 1, p. 48; Elizabeth Robinson to Sarah Robinson, n.d. [1740], Montagu, *Letters of Mrs Montagu*, Vol. 1, p. 131.
152. HALSW, 21M69/4/3 and 4.
153. HALSW 1M44/11/6.
154. Geneviève Monnier, *Inventaire des collections publiques françaises: Pastels XVIIe et XVIIIe siècles*, Paris, 1972, no. 37.
155. Thomas Knollys to Margaret Ellis, October 15, 1790, HALSW 1M44/12/3.

APPENDICES

1. BL, 555.l. 2. (154).
2. Lambeth Palace, F/M/1/15.
3. *Etat des acquisitions faites par Mr Lavv et de ce qui est par lui deue Tant sur les dites acquisitions que par Obligations et Billets au premier Octobre 1720*, RHC Limburg, Papieren Law, inv. nr 155; *Etat General des Biens Immeubles & des Dettes actives & passives de Mr Lavv au Premier Janvier 1722*, ibid., inv. nr 168; Répertoire et minutes de l'étude Ballin, 1718 (Et. XLVIII), AN, Minutier central, AN MC/RE/XLVIII/1; *Pièces particulières à Law*, NLS, Ry.iii.a.7; Achille Deville, *Histoire du château et des sires de Tancarville*, Rouen, 1834, pp. 316–19; Adrien Mentienne, *Le fief de la Grange Batelière*, Paris, 1910, p. 40; John Philip Wood, *Memoirs of the Life of John Law of Lauriston*, Edinburgh, 1824, pp. 159–60.
4. RHC Limburg, Papieren Law, inv. nr 167.

ACKNOWLEDGMENTS

I would like to thank Her Majesty the Queen for her gracious permission to quote from the Stuart Papers at Windsor Castle.

In Edinburgh, I wish to thank the staffs of the National Record of Scotland and the National Library of Scotland and Lyn Crawford and Sally Cholewa, archivists at the Royal Bank of Scotland. Diane Baptie kindly helped me with difficult passages in Scottish Secretary Hand. I am grateful to the Marquess of Bute for his permission to reproduce the portrait of Lord Stair at Dumfries House, Ayrshire. Paul Walker took the photograph.

In London, I am indebted to the staffs of the National Archives; the British Library; Hilary Davies of the City of Westminster Archives Centre; the staff of the Lambeth Palace Library, especially Paul Upton; and Sarah Radford of the St Paul's Cathedral Architectural Archive. Above all, I must thank Tracey Earl and her staff at the archive of Coutts & Co. for their patience with me over several long visits.

In the English counties, I received help and hospitality at the Staffordshire Record Office, Stafford; the Hertfordshire Archives and Local Studies, Hertford; the Norfolk Record Office, Norwich; the Kent History and Library Centre, Maidstone; and the Hampshire Archives and Local Studies, Winchester. James Ward kindly sent materials from the Devon Archives and Local Studies Service in Exeter. I must thank the Duke of Devonshire and his archivist, James Towe, for permitting me to read some letters in the Devonshire Archives at Chatsworth. The Taylorian Institution in Oxford made available a complete run of the *Gazette d'Amsterdam* for John Law's lifetime.

In assembling John Law's artistic posterity, I am grateful to Nicola

Normanby, former trustee of the National Gallery, and Letizia Treves, curator of Italian and Spanish painting there; Helen Jacobsen of the Wallace Collection, London; and Andreas Henning and Sabine Schumann at the Staatliche Kunstsammlungen Dresden. I have profited from Linda Borean's work on Law as a collector of pictures. In the matter of Law and music, I have blazed for more expert writers the first stage of the trail.

I am deeply grateful to Sister Mary Magdalene, archivist of the Canonesses of the Holy Sepulchre, for searching through the surviving records of the English religious communities in what is now Belgium for traces of Lady Katherine.

I have profited from conversation or correspondence with Philip Mansel, David Crackanthorpe, Constantine Normanby, Toby Tweedsmuir, Anne Somerset, Jonathan Moyne, Berthold Over, Jérôme Jambu, Stefano Condarelli, Hamish Riley-Smith and Antonella Barzazi. The book has been improved by my editors, Dominique Tweedsmuir and Paul Engles, my proofreader, Anthony Hippisley, my publisher, Christopher MacLehose, and my agent of thirty-five years, Caroline Dawnay. Bill Donohoe drew the maps and Rich Carr sorted and laid out the photographs. Susan Tricklebank compiled the index.

In the Netherlands, I must thank Eveline Lambrechtsen of the Stadsarchief Amsterdam; Jan van Wandelen of the Haags Gemeentearchief; and the whole staff of the Regionaal Historisch Centrum Limburg in Maastricht and, most particularly, Jacques van Rensch. Judith Nagel in Norwich helped me with troublesome passages in the Hop–Heinsius correspondence. In Germany, Stefan Wild and Gerlind Wülker-Wild in Bonn provided the same service for Elisabeth Charlotte's letters. Richard Kornicki in London and Wojtek Matusiak in Warsaw translated for me from Polish.

In France, I would wish to thank the staffs of the Archives nationales; the Archives des affaires étrangères; the Bibliothèque nationale de France (all in Paris); and the Archives nationales d'outre-mer and the Bibliothèque Méjanes in Aix-en-Provence. Jean-Christophe

Clamagirand of Roger-Viollet was helpful in providing photographs of works of art in Paris and Rennes. I have relied on three modern works of French scholarship: Philippe Haudrère's *La Compagnie française des Indes au XVIIIe siècle*; Commandant Alain Demerliac's *Nomenclature des navires français de 1715 à 1774: La marine de Louis XV*; and the section, *Armements pour la longue course* on the website *Mémoire des hommes* of the Service historique de la Défense.

In the United States, I must thank Emerson Hunton of the Newberry Library, Chicago; Rebecca Smith of the Williams Research Center, New Orleans; and Jane Shambra of the Local History & Genealogy Department, Biloxi Public Library. Raymond H. Bellande kindly showed me the site of Vieux Biloxy at Ocean Springs, Miss. and Edmond Boudreaux reconstructed for me Nouveau Biloxy. Mr Boudreaux also gave me his multi-sheet enlargement of the Le Bouteux drawing, which permits a minute analysis of Law's camp. Mc Wixon showed me the LaPointe-Krebs House at Pascagoula, Miss., which he is stabilising for posterity. I have learned much from the work of François Velde of the Federal Reserve Bank of Chicago.

In Italy, I am grateful to the staff of the Archivio di Stato di Venezia. In Genoa, where John Law was happiest, I must thank the marchesi di Cattaneo Adorno and their archivist at the Archivio Durazzo-Giustiniani, Maddalena Giordano; my friend Giampiero Buzelli, formerly of the Archivio di Stato di Genova, and his wife Caterina; Francesco Tripodi of the Archivio di Stato; and Giuseppe Felloni and his kind and learned wife, Valeria Polonio.

Professor Felloni died before I could show this book to him. My debt to that famous scholar remains undischarged.

James Buchan
Alby, Norfolk

INDEX

PICTURE CREDITS

1: National Library of Scotland, Edinburgh.

2, 3, 4, 20: **Getty Images** and Karol Kozlowski (2); Hulton Archive (3); Olaf Protze (4); Stephen Sacks, Lonely Planet Images (20).

5, 6, 10, 18, 19, 24, 25, 26, 27: **Bridgeman Art Library** and De Agostini Picture Library (5); Prado, Madrid, Spain (6); Deutsches Historisches Museum, Berlin, Germany (10); National Galleries of Scotland, Edinburgh (18); De Agostini Picture Library / G. Dagli Orti (19); De Agostini Picture Library / A. Dagli Orti (24, 26); Royal Collection Trust, Her Majesty Queen Elizabeth II, 2018 / Bridgeman Images (25); Musée du Louvre, Paris France (27).

7: Paul Walker, The Bute Collection at Mount Stuart.

8, 11: Musée Carnavalet, Paris, Agence Roger-Viollet.

9: bpk-Blidagentur, Staatliche Kunstsammlungen Dresden.

12: Alain Amet, Musée de Bretagne, Rennes.

13: Regionaal Historisch Centrum Limburg, Maastricht.

14, 17: Edward E.Ayer Collection, Newberry Library, Chicago.

15: Bibliothèque nationale de France, Paris.

16: Archives nationales d'outre-mer, Aix-en-Provence.

21: Musée des Beaux-Arts de la ville de Paris, Agence Roger-Viollet.

22, 23: Wallace Collection, London.

JAMES BUCHAN is a novelist and historian, whose books have won many prizes and have been translated into more than a dozen languages. *John Law: A Scottish Adventurer of the Eighteenth Century* is his third work on the Scottish Enlightenment. The others are the classic *Capital of the Mind: How Edinburgh Changed the World* (2003) and *Adam Smith and the Pursuit of Perfect Liberty* (2006). He is a fellow of the Royal Society of Literature. He lives on a farm in Norfolk.